◇ HANDBOOK OF ◇
TODAY'S RELIGIONS

OTHER JOSH McDOWELL BOOKS

Evidence That Demands a Verdict
More Evidence That Demands a Verdict
Guide to Understanding Your Bible
The Resurrection Factor
Prophecy: Fact or Fiction?

with John Gilchrist:

The Islam Debate

with Bart Larson:

Jesus: A Biblical Defense of His Deity

with David Stoop:

Resurrection Factor Growth Guide

with Dale Bellis:

Evidence Growth Guide I: Uniqueness of Christianity
Evidence Growth Guide II: Uniqueness of the Bible
Evidence Growth Guide III: Trustworthiness of the Bible

with Don Stewart:

Answers to Tough Questions Skeptics Ask About Christianity
Reasons Skeptics Should Consider Christianity
Understanding the Cults
Understanding the Occult
Understanding Non-Christian Religions
Understanding Secular Religions
Family Handbook of Christian Knowledge—The Bible
Family Handbook of Christian Knowledge—The World

by Joe Musser:

Josh: The Excitement of the Unexpected

Josh McDowell & Don Stewart

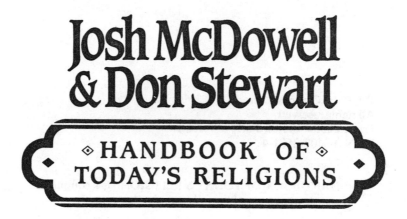

◈ HANDBOOK OF ◈
TODAY'S RELIGIONS

THOMAS NELSON PUBLISHERS
Nashville • Atlanta • London • Vancouver

© 1983 by Campus Crusade for Christ, Inc.
All rights reserved
Printed in the United States of America
ISBN 0-8407-3501-4

HANDBOOK OF TODAY'S RELIGIONS is a compilation
of the following books:

Understanding the Cults © 1982
Library of Congress Catalog Card 81-81850
ISBN 0-86605-090-6

Understanding the Occult © 1982
Library of Congress Catalog Card 81-86544
ISBN 0-86605-091-4

Understanding Non-Christian Religions © 1982
Library of Congress Catalog Card 81-86543
ISBN 0-86605-092-2

Understanding Secular Religions © 1982
Library of Congress Catalog Card 82-74300
ISBN 0-86605-093-0

Unless otherwise indicated, Scripture quotations are from *The New American Standard Bible,* © The Lockman Foundation 1960, 1962, 1963, 1968, 1971, 1972, 1975, 1977, and are used by permission.

10 11 12 13   00 99 98

"Beloved, believe not every spirit, but try the spirits whether they are of God, because many false prophets are gone out into the world" (1 John 4:1 KJV).

Table of Contents

Introduction

Why This Book

Over the years the authors have had many requests to write a book on the various alternatives to Christianity—the cults, non-Christian religions, secular religions, and the occult. This volume contains the series of works dealing with these subjects.

Frequently we are challenged by people of other religious beliefs when we affirm the uniqueness and finality of the Christian faith. They argue that Christianity is compatible with other religions and cults and that we should not stress the uniqueness of Jesus Christ as being the only way a person can know the true and living God. This book demonstrates that Christianity is *not* compatible with cults, the occult, non-Christian religions, or secular religions.

It should also be pointed out that it is not Christianity that has attacked those other religions, but rather, the other religions have attacked Christianity. The result is that orthodox Christianity has had to go on the defensive, presenting its truth to combat the deviations perpetrated as historic Christian doctrine.

The Scope of Our Study

This volume is intended to be a general reference work for those who are interested in knowing what various groups believe and why those beliefs are not compatible with biblical Christianity. It is not intended to be an exhaustive treatise on any one group or a comprehensive guide to all alternatives to Christianity. Rather, we have confined ourselves to deal with specific groups with which we have had the most contact. We believe that the movements we have chosen to discuss are representative of those alternatives. However, because we haven't dealt with a particular group doesn't mean we advocate its beliefs.

Whole libraries are built to the honor of religion, as we have defined it. For instance one could read a different book each day for several years on Marxism alone. There are those, both within and without the camp of biblical Christianity, who have spent their entire careers studying and commenting upon such subjects. We do not pretend that we have such expertise; rather, we cite those scholars who are recognized generally as authorities. It has been necessary for us to limit ourselves to evaluating the central beliefs of each chosen group, spending little time dealing with its history, organization, methods, or secondary beliefs, unless specifically related to their doctrines in a fashion that thus warrants consideration.

Our goal in presenting this volume to the Christian public is to provide the Christian with enough background in the subjects under discussion so that he can understand the basic tenets of each system. We have chosen to present, therefore, summaries of the teachings of the various religions. Following the background, we have given ways to think about the subjects from biblical and rational perspectives. We are more concerned with principles than with details, with general biblical responses than with meticulous critiques. This book has enough information to give the reader a Christian perspective on each subject which has been addressed.

Our desire is for this work also to serve as a springboard for further study. We have prepared extensive annotated bibliographies to give the reader further help if he wishes to know more about any one group.

If we give Christians a biblical perspective on non-Christian religions, or enable Christians to think in a rational and biblical manner as they respond to the challenges of those religions, we will consider our task successfully accomplished.

The Proper Attitude

We live in a society where a person has the freedom to follow the religious belief of his or her choice. We have no quarrel with this. However, when individuals or groups publicly claim they are now God's true work here upon the earth and orthodox Christianity, which has existed throughout the centuries, is now wrong, we feel we must answer such challenges. They have the freedom to say it, but as Christians we have the responsibility to answer them.

The Bible commands us to "be ready always to give an answer to every man that asketh you a reason of the hope that is in you with meekness and fear" (1 Peter 3:15 KJV). This work is that answer to those who have attacked historic Christianity and placed their own beliefs above it. We are not attacking these groups; we are merely answering their accusations. An example of the type of accusations we are answering can be found in the writings of The Church of Jesus Christ of the Latter-day Saints, better known as the Mormons.

> Every intelligent person under the heavens that does not, when informed, acknowledge that Joseph Smith, Jr., is a prophet of God, is in darkness and is opposed to us and to Jesus and His kingdom on the earth (*Journal of Discourses* 8:223).
>
> What does the Christian world know about God? Nothing;...Why, so far as the things of God are concerned, they are the veriest fools; they know neither God nor the things of God (*Journal of Discourses* 13:225).

We cannot allow these types of accusations to pass. They must be answered. However, in answering the charges made by the cults and other non-Christian groups, we desire to do so without resorting to name-calling or sarcasm. It is possible to disagree with a person's beliefs and yet love the person holding those beliefs. What we oppose is the teachings of these groups, not the people in the groups nor their right to believe whatever they want. We speak out because the Bible commands us to "earnestly contend for the faith which has been once and for all delivered" (Jude 3).

Finally, the apostle Paul has exhorted us to "prove all things; hold fast that which is good" (1 Thessalonians 5:21 KJV). That is what this book is all about.

What Is Religion?

There are more than four billion people living in the world today, most of whom are associated with one or another of the world's major religions. Although most people have some sort of religious affiliation, they are woefully ignorant as to the basic beliefs of their own religion. Not only do most people have a shallow understanding of their own faith, but most have very little knowledge of any of the other world religions.

With the advance of modern technology, the world has shrunk to the point that we would do well to know and understand what our neighbors believe. This book is an effort to fill this information gap by giving the reader a working knowledge of the great religions of the world. No attempt has been made to treat each religion in an exhaustive manner, but rather to present each one's basic beliefs and key concepts.

We have evaluated each religion briefly in light of the beliefs and teachings of Christianity. An extensive treatment of Christian belief and truth can be found in the lengthy section on Christian doctrine in Part I of this book, "Understanding the Cults." Annotated reading lists included in this volume will guide you in further study.

Religion Defined

The term religion has many definitions. None is agreed upon by everyone, but certain common aspects and implications of religion can be observed. We define religion as that aspect of one's experience in which he attempts to live harmoniously with the power or powers he believes are controlling the world.

John B. Noss relates some of the implications of religious belief:

> All religions imply in one way or another that man does not, and cannot, stand alone, that he is vitally related with and even dependent on powers in nature and society external to himself. Dimly or clearly, he knows that he is not an independent center of force capable of standing apart from the world.... Religions, as a general rule, relate men closely with the power or powers at work in nature and society.... Most men, from primitives in the jungle to members of societies far advanced in technology and intercultural relationships, do not think that men are all that matters (John B. Noss, *Man's Religions*, New York: MacMillan Company, 1969, p. 2).

The derivation of the word *religion* suggests several possible readings, as Herbert Stroup reveals:

> The English word "religion" derives from the Latin *religio*. Even so, there is no clear agreement as to the meaning of the word. Servius and others, for example, held that it came from the root "lig", which means "to bind." Religion in this sense would signify a relationship—the binding relationship between man and God. Yet Cicero believed that the word was derived from the root "leg", which means "to take up, gather, count, or observe." The meaning here suggests the observation of the signs of divine communication. In later times, both meanings were accepted by Augustine, for example, and today there seems to be little if any question regarding the propriety of either derivation (Herbert Stroup, *Four Religions of Asia*, New York: Harper & Row, 1968, p. 6).

Even secular religions, though they have no belief in God or the supernatural, and involve no form of worship or liturgy, still are more or less unified comprehensive world views which seek to explain the "why" of existence. Because they have their own "creeds," "scriptures," "clergy," and closely knit groups, they may properly be labeled *religions*.

Religion Is Universal

Religion is a universal phenomenon. Wherever man lives he is found giving some recognition to a power or powers beyond himself. Joseph Gaer comments appropriately:

> As far as we can determine, religion has existed in every society, from the most primitive to the most culturally advanced. The more keys modern science finds with which to open the locked doors of the past, and the more we learn about the early days of man on earth, the more evidence there is that all these societies in the past had one thing in common—some form of religion.
>
> Some of these early men were more advanced than others. And while some progressed continually in an upward trend, others remained stationary after reaching a certain stage of development. Still others retrogressed. Yet all of these early men, whatever their rate of development or whatever their differences, left behind unmistakable signs that they had each practiced a religion of their own (Joseph Gaer, *What the Great Religions Believe*, New York: Dodd, Mead, and Company, 1963, p. 16).

Religion is not only universal, it is also one of the features separating man from the animal world. "Religion is one of the things which distinguishes man from the other animals. Apes and dolphins, as far as we know, have no religions, but no group of human beings has ever been discovered which did not have religious beliefs" (Richard Cavendish, *The Great Religions*, New York: Arco Publishing, Inc., 1980, p. 2).

Religion Meets Needs

The function of religion has an indispensable aspect in all human life. It is those higher beliefs or ultimate concerns which keep us all going. Robert E. Hume comments on the function of religion:

> Religion gives to a person what he can obtain from no other source—a confidence in the outcome of life's struggles through a personal connection with the superior Power or powers in the world. Every religion does many things

for the religious individual and also usually for society. For example, it assists in providing the individual with added power and satisfaction; it helps him to bear the troubles of life uncomplainingly; it offers a solution of the problem of evil; it improves the quality of this present life; it offers the hope of a better life in the future; it outlines an ideal society; it sets a working plan of salvation.

The distinguishing function of religion, in contrast with that of philosophy or ethics, or any of the idealizing or cultural activities, is to give to a human being the supreme satisfaction of his life through a vital relationship with what he recognizes as the superhuman Power, or powers, in the world (Robert E. Hume, *The World's Living Religions*, New York: Charles Scribner's Sons, rev. ed., 1959, pp. 3, 4).

The Practice of Religion

The practice of religion is as varied as the religions themselves. Marcus Bach writes:

Religion means different things to different men. To the primitive it means offering his animal sacrifices, and to the aborigine it means mutilating his body. It may be expressed in baptismal ceremonies for the dead and in spiritual exercises for the living. It is man attempting to prove the mystery of life and probing the riddle that death is but the lighted passage to another world.

Religion is the priest at his altar and the minister in his pulpit. It is the neophyte first learning the concepts of his faith and the penitent in his confession. It is a cross, a book, a candle, a hope, a song. It is work and play and even ceremonies for war and peace (Marcus Bach, *Major Religions of the World*, Nashville: Abingdon Press, 1977, p. 12).

All Religions Are Not the Same

A common misconception is that all religions are basically saying the same thing or that all religious "paths" eventually reach the same summit—God.

An advocate of this view, Bhagavan Das, writes the following in the introduction to one of his books:

Throughout history men have followed the religious faith of their own culture, and the majority have accepted their own faith as the only embodiment of truth. Yet in every religion there have been wise men holding the candle of light by which wisdom can be seen. This book shows how false are the barriers which have been erected between the different religions. The author has compiled passages from the scriptures of the world's eleven major living religions to show the similarity of their principles. Excerpts from the holy writings of the Christians, Jews, Hindus, Buddhists, Muslims, as well as other religions of India, Persia, China and Japan—all translated into English—have been arranged in parallel form to illustrate their unity. The author demonstrates how each great religion is another statement of the same timeless truths (Bhagavan Das, *The Essential Unity of All Religions*, Wheaton, IL: The Theosophical Publishing House, 1966).

Das goes on to advocate that this universal religion must be taught to all mankind:

The Universal Religion—That in which there may be Universal Agreement. We have heard of the Three R's long enough. This fourth R, of genuine Universal

Religion, is more important than them all, and ought to be added to them everywhere, in every school and college (*Ibid.*, p. 54).

It simply is not true that all religions are basically the same. Although similar teachings do occur in more than one religion, the differences between them are as marked as night and day. Richard Cavendish illustrates the point in this manner:

> For example, the attitudes of the major religions to salvation and the purpose of life are quite different. In Judaism, Christianity and Islam, salvation means the survival of the individual personality in a happy existence in heaven after death. In Hinduism and Buddhism, on the other hand, salvation may mean the opposite, not the survival but the obliteration of the individual personality.
>
> Christianity believes in a divine Saviour, who came into the world to rescue man, but Judaism and Islam strongly disapprove of this belief as a gross breach of monotheism, the belief in a single god. Christianity, Judaism and Islam all agree, however, that human beings live only once on the earth and so have only one chance to make sure of a happy afterlife.
>
> Life on earth is therefore a profoundly serious affair and it is essential to get it right. But in Hinduism and Buddhism human beings live over and over again on the earth, born and reborn again indefinitely, and there is literally all the time in the world to get things right. It is hardly surprising, consequently, that Hinduism and Buddhism are far more tolerant than Judaism, Christianity and Islam (Richard Cavendish, *op. cit.*, p. 8).

We especially would like to thank Robert and Gretchen Passantino for their advice, which was actively solicited on all four volumes comprising this book and, particularly, for their considerable help with the chapters on Marxism and atheism. We also would like to thank our publishers for their close cooperation in this project.

Part I

Understanding the Cults

What Is a Cult?

A cult is a perversion, a distortion of biblical Christianity and/or a rejection of the historic teachings of the Christian church. The Apostle Paul warned there would be false Christs and a false gospel that would attempt to deceive the true church and the world.

> For if one comes and preaches another Jesus whom we have not preached, or you receive a different spirit which you have not received, or a different gospel which you have not accepted, you bear this beautifully. . .for such men are false apostles, deceitful workers, disguising themselves as apostles of Christ and no wonder for even Satan disguises himself as an angel of light. Therefore it is not surprising if his servants also disguise themselves as servants of righteousness; whose end shall be according to their deeds (2 Corinthians 11: 13-15 NASB).

Walter Martin gives us a good definition of a cult when he says:

> A cult, then, is a group of people polarized around someone's interpretation of the Bible and is characterized by major deviations from orthodox Christianity relative to the cardinal doctrines of the Christian faith, particularly the fact that God became man in Jesus Christ (Walter Martin, *The Rise of the Cults*, p. 12).

Why Do Cults Prosper?

We live in a day in which the cults show rapid growth. For example:

> The Mormon Church has grown from 30 members in 1830 to more than 4,000,000 as of April, 1978, and its growth rate is a religious phenomenon. In 1900 the church numbered 268,331; in 1910, 393,437; in 1920, 526,032; in 1930, 672,488; in 1940, 862,664; in 1950, 1,111,314; in 1960, 1,693,180; in 1962, 1,965,786; in 1964, over 2,000,000 members, and in 1976 their projection for the year 2000 was for more than 8,000,000 members (Walter Martin, *The Maze of Mormonism*, p. 16).

We believe there are several basic reasons people join cults and why they prosper.

The Cults Provide Answers

A major reason the cults are flourishing is that in an unsure world they provide authoritative answers to man's basic questions: *Who am I? Why am I here? Where am I going?*

Max Gunther, the writer, describes the plight of a young woman, common to many in our generation. "I thought I wanted to become a nurse but I wasn't sure. I thought Christianity meant a lot to me but I wasn't sure of that either. I guess I was kind of desperately looking for somebody who had firm yes-and-no answers, somebody who was sure about things and could make me sure" (*Today's Health*, February, 1976, p. 16).

Unfortunately, this young lady eventually joined a cult which willingly supplied her with answers. She put it this way, "I kept going back and asking them questions and they always knew the answers—I mean, really knew them." Thus the cults offer certainty and easy answers to those who are unsatisfied with the present state of their lives.

The Cults Meet Human Needs

Cults also flourish because they appeal to man's basic human need. All of us need to be loved, to feel needed, to sense our lives have direction and meaning. Individuals who experience an identity crisis or have emotional problems are particularly susceptible to cults. During such difficult moments, many cults give the unsuspecting a feeling of acceptance and direction.

Furthermore, within all of us there is a basic desire to know and serve God. The cults take advantage of this and offer ready-made, but ultimately unsatisfying, solutions. Most cults tell their followers what to believe, how to behave and what to think, and emphasize dependence upon the group or leader for their emotional stability. The Passantinos give an example of this:

> A person does not usually join a cult because he has done an exhaustive analysis of world religions and has decided that a particular cult presents the best theology available. Instead, a person usually joins a cult because he has problems that he is having trouble solving, and the cult promises to solve these problems. Often these problems are emotional.
>
> We talked to a young man who had just left the army, hadn't been discharged a week, and had already joined the Children of God (the Family of Love) and had given them 100 dollars. He said that he was lonely, wanted to serve God, and didn't know where to go or what to do. The Family of Love seized on his loneliness, smothered him with love and attention, and almost secured his permanent allegiance.
>
> Fortunately his mother called us and we talked to him, and within an hour he saw how wrong the cult was and decided not to join. We urged him to join a good small Bible study and to become involved in a strong church. Without a good Christian foundation and close relationships with other Christians, he would still be a candidate for the cults (Robert and Gretchen Passantino, *Answers to the Cultist at Your Door*, Harvest House, Eugene, Oregon, 1981, pp. 22, 23).

The Cults Make a Favorable Impression

The cults prosper because Christians have sometimes failed to be a vital influence in the world. Pierre Berton astutely noted:

The virus that has been weakening the church for more than a generation is not the virus of anti-religious passion but the very lack of it. . . .The Church to its opponents has become as a straw man, scarcely worth a bullet. . . .Most ministers are scarcely distinguishable by their words, opinions, actions, or way of life from the nominal Christians and non-Christians who form the whole of the community (Pierre Berton, *The Comfortable Pew*, Philadelphia: J. B. Lippincott, 1965, pp. 15-16).

If the church fails to carefully and seriously provide spiritual warmth and a true exposition of the Word of God, those with spiritual needs will find other avenues of fulfillment. Many cults prey on ignorance, and try to impress the uninformed with pseudo-scholarship.

An example is The Way International's leader, Victor Paul Wierwille, who quotes profusely from Hebrew and Greek sources in an attempt to give the impression of scholarship.

Representatives of Jehovah's Witnesses who go door to door give a similar impression of great learning. To combat this, the believer must know what he believes and why he believes it and thus be able to expose the cult's teachings.

Many people involved in the cults were raised in Christian churches but were untaught in basic Christian doctrine, making them prey for the cultists. Chris Elkins, a former Unification Church "Moonie" member, points this out:

> In most cults, a majority of the members left a mainline, denominational church. Perhaps in the church's attempt to explain why its members are leaving and joining cults, brainwashing is seen as an easy out.
>
> My contention is that brainwashing is really not the issue. In most cases we would be hard-pressed to isolate any element in the methodology of a cult that is not present in some form in mainstream churches. For Christians, the main issue with cults should be theology.
>
> Many of us accepted Christ at an early age. We had a child's understanding of Jesus, the Bible and salvation.
>
> That is okay for children and new Christians. But many of us older Christians are still babies spiritually. We have not learned to feed ourselves, much less anyone else (*Christian Life*, August 1980).

CHAPTER TWO

The Characteristics of Cults

E xtensive travel throughout the United States and abroad, has made us aware of certain features that characterize the cults. These include:

New Truth

Many cults promote the false idea that God has revealed something special to them. This is usually truth that has never before been revealed and supersedes and contradicts all previous revelations. Sun Myung Moon's claim is that the mission of Christ was left unfinished and the world is now ready for the completion of Christ's work on earth.

The Unification Church teaches that the Rev. Moon is bringing truth previously unrevealed. Moon has said, "We are the only people who truly understand the heart of Jesus, the anguish of Jesus, and the hope of Jesus" (Rev. Moon, *The Way of the World*, Holy Spirit Ass'n for the Unification of World Christianity, Vol. VIII, No. 4, April, 1976).

The Mormon Church teaches that Christianity was in apostasy for some 18 centuries until God revealed new "truth" to Joseph Smith, Jr., restoring the true gospel that had been lost. Today the Mormon church has its living prophets who receive divine revelation from God, continually bringing new "truth" to the world.

These and other cults justify their existence by claiming they have something more than just the Bible and its "inadequate message."

The cults have no objective, independent way to test their teachings and practices. It's almost as though they feel just a firm assertion of their own exclusivity is sufficient proof of their anointing by God. However, as members of the universal Christian church, we can and should test all of our teachings and practices objectively and independently by God's infallible Word, the Bible, and history.

New Interpretations of Scripture

Some cults make no claim to new truth or extra-biblical revelation, but believe they alone have the key to interpreting the mysteries in the Bible. The Scriptures are their only acknowledged source of authority, but they are interpreted unreasonably and in a way different from that

of orthodox Christianity. They testify that the historic beliefs and interpretations of Scripture are based upon a misunderstanding of the Bible
or were pagan in origin. An example of this is found in the writings of
Herbert W. Armstrong:

> . . . I found that the popular church teachings and practices were not based
> on the Bible. They had originated . . . in paganism. The amazing, unbelievable
> TRUTH was, the sources of these popular beliefs and practices of professing
> Christianity was quite largely, paganism and human reasoning and custom,
> not the Bible! (Herbert W. Armstrong, *The Autobiography of Herbert W. Arm-
> strong*, Pasadena: Ambassador College Press, 1967, p. 298, 294).

The Bible is then reinterpreted, usually out of context, to justify the
peculiar doctrines of the cult. Without an objective and reasonable way
to understand what the Bible teaches, the cult member is at the mercy
of the theological whims of the cult leader.

A Non-biblical Source of Authority

Some cults have sacred writings or a source of authority that supersedes
the Bible. The Mormon Church says, "We believe the Bible to be the Word
of God in so far as it is translated correctly. . ." (*Articles of Faith of the
Church of Jesus Christ of Latter-day Saints*, Article 8). Although this
sounds like the Mormons trust the Bible, they, in fact, believe it has been
changed and corrupted. Listen to what the Mormon apostle Talmage has
said:

> There will be, there can be no absolutely reliable translation of these or other
> Scriptures unless it is effected through the gift of translation, as one of the
> endowments of the Holy Ghost. . . Let the Bible then be read reverently and
> with prayerful care, the reader ever seeking the light of the Spirit that he may
> discern between the truth and the errors of men (James E. Talmage, *The Ar-
> ticles of Faith*, Salt Lake City: Deseret News Press, 1968, p. 237).

Such a statement opens the door for their additional sacred books, i.e.,
The Book of Mormon, *The Pearl of Great Price* and *Doctrines and
Covenants*, as greater authoritative sources. Thus, the Bible is *not* truly
their final source of authority.

In Christian Science, the Bible is characterized as being mistaken and
corrupt and inferior to the writings of Mary Baker Eddy.

The Unification Church believes the Bible to be incomplete, while Rev.
Moon's *Divine Principle* is the true authoritative source.

Other groups such as The Way International and the Worldwide Church
of God claim the Bible to be their final authority when in actuality their
authority is the Bible as interpreted by the cult leader. Regardless of
whether the Bible is superseded by other works or reinterpreted by a cult
leader, a sure mark of a cult is that the final authority on spiritual matters rests on something other than the plain teaching of Holy Scripture.

Another Jesus

One characteristic that is found in all cults is false teaching about the
person of Jesus Christ in the light of historical biblical Christianity. The
Apostle Paul warned about following after "another Jesus" (2 Corinthians

11:4) who is not the same Jesus who is revealed in Scripture. The "Jesus" of the cults is always someone less than the Bible's eternal God who became flesh, lived here on earth, and died for our sins.

The Bible makes it clear that Jesus was God in human flesh, second person of the Holy Trinity, who lived a sinless life on earth and died as a sacrifice for the sins of the world. Three days after His crucifixion, Jesus rose bodily from the dead. Fifty days afterward He ascended into heaven, where He now sits at the right hand of the Father, interceding on behalf of believers. He will, one day, return bodily to planet earth and judge the living and the dead while setting up His eternal Kingdom.

The Jesus of the cults is not the Jesus of the Bible.

According to the theology of the Jehovah's Witnesses, Jesus did not exist as God from all eternity but was rather the first creation of Jehovah God. Before coming to earth, He was Michael the Archangel, the head of all the angels. He is not God.

The Mormon Church does not accept the unique deity of Jesus Christ. He is, to them, one of many gods, the "first-born spirit child," spiritually conceived by a sexual union between the heavenly Father and a heavenly mother. He was also the spirit-brother of Lucifer in His preexistent state. His incarnation was accomplished by the physical union of the heavenly Father and the human Mary.

No matter what the particular beliefs of any cult may be, the one common denominator they all possess is a denial of the biblical teaching on the deity of Jesus Christ.

Rejection of Orthodox Christianity

Characteristic of many cultic groups is a frontal attack on orthodox Christianity. They argue that the church has departed from the true faith. Helena P. Blavatsky, founder of Theosophy, had this to say of orthodox Christianity:

> The name has been used in a manner so intolerant and dogmatic, especially in our day, that Christianity is now the religion of arrogance, par excellence, a stepping-stone for ambition, a sinecure for wealth, shame, and power; a convenient screen for hypocrisy (H. P. Blavatsky, *Studies in Occultism*, Theosophical University Press, n.d., p. 138).

Joseph Smith, Jr., the founder of Mormonism, said he was given this assessment of the Christian Church when he inquired of the Lord as to which church to join:

> . . .I was answered that I must join none of them, for they were all wrong; and the personage who addressed me said that all their creeds were an abomination in His sight; that those professors were all corrupt; that "they draw near to Me with their lips, but their hearts are far from Me, they teach for doctrines the commandments of men, having a form of godliness, but they deny the power thereof" (Joseph Smith, Jr., *The Pearl of Great Price*, 2:18-19).

Double-Talk

A feature of some cultic groups is that they say one thing publicly but internally believe something totally different. Many organizations call themselves Christians when in fact they deny the fundamentals of the faith.

The Mormon Church is an example of this kind of double-talk. The first article of faith in the Church of Jesus Christ of Latter-day Saints reads, "We believe. . . in His Son, Jesus Christ." This gives the impression Mormons are Christians since they believe in Jesus Christ. However, when we understand the semantics of what they mean by Jesus Christ, we discover they are far removed from orthodox Christianity. Nevertheless, the impression the Mormon Church gives from their advertising is that they are another denomination or sect of Christianity. One, therefore, must be on the alert for organizations that advertise themselves as "Christians" but whose internal teachings disagree with Scripture.

Non-biblical Teaching on the Nature of God (Trinity)

Another characteristic of all non-Christian cults is either an inadequate view or outright denial of the Holy Trinity. The biblical doctrine of the Trinity, one God in three Persons, is usually attacked as being pagan or satanic in origin.

The Jehovah's Witnesses are an example of this. They say, "There is no authority in the Word of God for the doctrine of the trinity of the Godhead" (Charles Russell, *Studies in the Scriptures*, V, Brooklyn: International Bible Students, 1912, p. 54). "The plain truth is that this is another of Satan's attempts to keep the God-fearing person from learning the truth of Jehovah and His Son Christ Jesus" (*Let God Be True*, Brooklyn: Watchtower Bible and Tract Society, 1946, p. 93).

The Way International takes a similar position. "Long before the founding of Christianity, the idea of a triune god or a god-in-three-persons was a common belief in ancient religions. Although many of these religions had many minor deities, they distinctly acknowledged that there was one supreme god who consisted of three persons or essences. The Babylonians used an equilateral triangle to represent this three-in-one god, now the symbol of the modern three-in-one believers" (*Jesus Christ Is Not God*, Victor Paul Wierville, New Knoxville, Ohio: American Christian Press, 1975, p. 11).

Cults, therefore, are marked by their deviation on the doctrine of the Trinity and the nature of God.

Changing Theology

Cult doctrines are continually in a state of flux and have no sure foundation on which to anchor their hope. Adherents of a particular cult will learn a doctrine only to find that doctrine later changed or contradicted by further revelation. Most cults will deny this, with the possible exception of the Unification Church. Recently they admitted their theology was in a state of flux.

The Jehovah's Witnesses, for example, used to believe vaccinations were sinful. Anyone who allowed himself to be vaccinated would lose his good standing in the organization. Today this is no longer taught.

Christianity Today, in an article interviewing William Cetnar (a former high official in the Jehovah's Witnesses), says:

> The controversial ban on receiving blood transfusions will probably be lifted after Franz's death, [Frederick Franz, 87, is the president of the Jehovah's Witnesses] Cetnar thinks.
>
> A new date for the end of the world (JWs have previously predicted Christ's return seven times) is likely to be announced, possibly 1988.
>
> By sheer mathematical necessity, some change will have to be made in the JW doctrine that Christ will return before an elect 144,000 Witnesses have died. The 144,000 places were filled by those living in 1914 and few remain alive today. But Christ is supposed to return before the entire generation has died (*Christianity Today*, Nov. 20, 1981, p. 70).

The Mormon Church is equally guilty of changing doctrine. The most famous is its belief and practice, later prohibited, of polygamy.

Strong Leadership

Cults are usually characterized by central leader figures who consider themselves messengers of God with unique access to the Almighty. Since the leader has such a special relationship with God, he can dictate the theology and behavior of the cult. Consequently, he exercises enormous influence over the group. This is true, for example, in the Unification Church, The Way International and the Worldwide Church of God.

This strong leadership leads the cult follower into total dependence upon the cult for belief, behavior and lifestyle. When this falls into the hands of a particularly corrupt leader, the results can be tragic, as with Jim Jones and the People's Temple tragedy. The more dramatic the claims of a cult leader, the more the possibility of a tragic conclusion.

Salvation by Works

One teaching that is totally absent from all the cults is the gospel of the grace of God. No one is taught in the cults that he can be saved from eternal damnation by simply placing his faith in Jesus Christ. It is always belief in Jesus Christ and "do this" or "follow that." All cults attach something to the doctrine of salvation by grace through faith. It might be baptism, obedience to the laws and ordinances of the gospel, or something else, but it is never taught that faith in Christ alone will save anyone.

Herbert W. Armstrong, founder and leader of the Worldwide Church of God, exemplifies this:

> Salvation, then, is a process! But how the God of this world would blind your eyes to that! He tries to deceive you into thinking all there is to it is just "accepting Christ" with "no works"—and presto-chango, you are pronounced "saved." But the Bible reveals that none is yet saved (Herbert W. Armstrong, *Why Were You Born?* p.11).

False Prophecy

Another feature of the cults is they often promulgate false prophecy. Cult leaders, who believe they have been divinely called by God, have made bold predictions of future events, supposedly revealed by the inspiration of God. Unfortunately, for the cult leaders, these predictions of future events do not come to pass. The one who prophesied is exposed as a false prophet.

Writing in 1967, Herbert W. Armstrong, (leader of the Worldwide Church of God), said, "Now other prophecies reveal we are to soon have (probably in about four years) such drought and famine, that disease epidemics will follow, taking millions of lives. . . . Well, we have been getting foretastes of them! That condition is coming! And I do not mean in 400 years—nor in 40 years—but in the very next four or five!" (Herbert W. Armstrong, *The United States and British Commonwealth in Prophecy.* Pasadena: Ambassador College Press, 1967, p. 184).

The Jehovah's Witnesses have a well-established record of making false prophecies. This pattern was established by their founder and first president, Charles T. Russell, who conclusively prophesied the end of the world for 1914. Judge for yourself (1 John 4:1).

The Founder Speaks

1. "ALL PRESENT GOVERNMENTS WILL BE OVERTHROWN AND DISSOLVED" IN 1914.— *The Time Is At Hand*, pp. 98-99 (1889)
2. 1914—"THE FARTHEST LIMIT OF THE RULE OF IMPERFECT MAN."— *The Time Is At Hand*, p. 77 (1906 ed)*
3. "THE RE-ESTABLISHMENT OF ISRAEL IN THE LAND OF PALESTINE."— *Thy Kingdom Come*, p. 244, EARTHLY JERUSALEM TO BE RESTORED TO DIVINE FAVOR. — *The Time Is At Hand*, p.77
4. "THE FULL ESTABLISHMENT OF THE KINGDOM OF GOD *IN THE EARTH* AT A.D. 1914."— *Thy Kingdom Come*, p. 126 (1891)* "ON THE RUINS OF PRESENT INSTITUTIONS."— *The Time Is At Hand*, p. 77 (1912 ed)*
5. CHRIST WAS SPIRITUALLY PRESENT IN 1874. — *Thy Kingdom Come*, pp. 127-129, "AND WILL BE PRESENT AS EARTH'S NEW RULER" IN 1914.— *The Time Is At Hand*, p. 77
6. "BEFORE THE END OF A.D. 1914, THE LAST MEMBER OF THE 'BODY OF CHRIST' WILL BE GLORIFIED WITH THE HEAD."— *The Time Is At Hand*, p. 77, (1906 ed)*

> * The Watchtower Society in later editions made changes in what Russell stated here in an attempt to cover up his erroneous predictions.

Conclusion

While not every group that possesses these characteristics can be labeled a cult, beware of a group that embraces some of these features. The sure mark of a cult is what it does with the person of Jesus Christ. All cults ultimately deny the fact that Jesus Christ is God the Son, second Person of the Holy Trinity, and mankind's only hope.

CHAPTER THREE

The Beliefs of Orthodox Christianity

For the last two thousand years, the Christian Church has held certain beliefs to be vital to one's faith. While there is some doctrinal disagreement within the three branches of Christendom—Roman Catholic, Eastern Orthodox and Protestant—there is a general agreement among them as to the essentials of the faith. Whatever disagreement the church may have among its branches, it is insignificant compared to the heretical non-Christian beliefs of the cults. We offer this section as a yardstick to compare the errant beliefs of the cults.

The Doctrine of Authority

When it comes to the matter of final authority there is agreement among the major branches of Christianity with regard to the divine inspiration of the Old and New Testaments. However, the Roman Catholic and Eastern Orthodox branches of the church go somewhat beyond the Bible as to their source of authority.

Roman Catholic The historic Roman Catholic Church accepts the 66 books of the Old and New Testaments as the inspired Word of God. They also accept the Apocrypha as being inspired of God. Further, they consider church tradition just as authoritative as the Scriptures. (In a previous work, we have dealt with reasons why we do not accept the Apocrypha as sacred Scripture—*Answers*, Here's Life Publishers, 1980, pp. 36-38.)

Eastern Orthodox The historic Eastern Orthodox church also accepts the 66 books of the Old and New Testaments as God's inspired revelation. To this they add their church tradition as equally authoritative.

Protestant The historic Protestant church holds that Scripture alone is the final authority on all matters of faith and practice. The Lutheran formula of Concord put it this way: "We believe, confess, and teach that the only rule and norm, according to which all dogmas and doctrines ought to be esteemed and judged, is no other whatever than the prophetic and apostolic writings both of the Old and of the New Testaments."

Scripture itself testifies that it is complete in what it reveals and the standard and final authority on all matters of doctrine, faith and practice. "All Scripture is inspired by God and profitable for teaching, for reproof, for correction, for training in righteousness" (2 Timothy 3:16 NASB).

"But know this first of all, that no prophecy of Scripture is a matter of one's own interpretation, for no prophecy was ever made by an act of human will. But men moved by the Holy Spirit spoke from God" (2 Peter 1:20, 21 NASB).

"You shall not add to the word which I am commanding you, nor take away from it, that you may keep the commandments of the Lord your God which I command you" (Deuteronomy 4:2 NASB).

"I testify to everyone who hears the words of the prophecy of this book: if anyone adds to them, God shall add to him the plagues which are written in this book; and if anyone takes away from the words of the book of this prophecy, God shall take away his part from the tree of life and from the holy city, which are written in this book" (Revelation 22:18, 19 NASB).

The Doctrine of God

The Doctrine of God is the same in all three branches of Christianity. The Westminster Shorter Catechism (Question 6) reads, "There are three persons in the Godhead: the Father, the Son, and the Holy Ghost; and these three are one God, the same in substance, equal in power and glory."

The Athanasian Creed elaborates on the doctrine of the Trinity:
. . .we worship one God in Trinity, and Trinity in Unity; Neither confounding the Persons, nor dividing the Substance [Essence]. For there is one Person of the Father, another of the Son, and another of the Holy Ghost. But the Godhead of the Father, of the Son, and of the Holy Ghost is all one, the Glory equal, the Majesty co-eternal. Such as the Father is, such is the Son, and such is the Holy Ghost. The Father uncreate, the Son uncreate, and the Holy Ghost uncreate. . .The Father eternal, the Son eternal, and the Holy Ghost eternal. And yet they are not three eternals, but one eternal. . .So the Father is God, the Son is God, and the Holy Ghost is God. And yet they are not three Gods, but one God. . .the Unity in Trinity and the Trinity in Unity is to be worshipped.

In a previous work, *Answers to Tough Questions*, (Here's Life Publishers, 1980), we explained in a simple way the biblical doctrine of the Trinity. We are reprinting it here as an attempt to clarify what Orthodox Christianity believes regarding the nature of God.

One of the most misunderstood ideas in the Bible concerns the teaching about the Trinity. Although Christians say that they believe in one God, they are constantly accused of polytheism (worshipping at least three gods).

The Scriptures do *not* teach that there are three Gods; neither do they teach that God wears three different masks while acting out the drama of history. What the Bible does teach is stated in the doctrine of the Trinity as: there is *one* God who has revealed Himself in three persons, the Father, the Son and the Holy Spirit, and these three persons are the one God.

Although this is difficult to comprehend, it is nevertheless what the Bible tells us, and is the closest the finite mind can come to explaining the infinite mystery of the infinite God, when considering the biblical statements about God's being.

The Bible teaches that there is one God and only one God: "Hear, O Israel! The Lord is our God, the Lord is one!" (Deuteronomy 6:4 NASB). "There is one God" (1 Timothy 2:5 KJV). "Thus says the Lord, the King of Israel and his Redeemer, the Lord of hosts: 'I am the first and I am the last, and there is no God besides Me'" (Isaiah 44:6 NASB).

However, even though God is one in His essential being or nature, He is also three persons. "Let us make man in our image" (Genesis 1:26 KJV). "God said, Behold, the man has become like one of us" (Genesis 3:22 RSV).

God's plural personality is alluded to here, for He could not be talking to angels in these instances, because angels could not and did not help God create. The Bible teaches that Jesus Christ, not the angels, created all things (John 1:3; Colossians 1:15; Hebrews 1:2).

In addition to speaking of God as one, and alluding to a plurality of God's personality, the Scriptures are quite specific as to naming God in terms of three persons. There is a person whom the Bible calls the Father, and the Father is designated as God the Father (Galatians 1:1).

The Bible talks about a person named Jesus, or the Son, or the Word, also called God. "The Word was God..." (John 1:1 KJV). Jesus was "also calling God His own Father, making Himself equal with God" (John 5:18 NASB).

There is a third person mentioned in the Scriptures called the Holy Spirit, and this person—different from the Father and the Son—is also called God ("Ananias, why has Satan filled your heart to lie to the Holy Spirit?...You have not lied to men, but to God," Acts 5:3,4 RSV).

The facts of the biblical teaching are these: There is one God. This one God has a plural personality. This one God is called the Father, the Son, the Holy Spirit, all distinct personalities, all designated God. We are therefore led to the conclusion that the Father, Son and Holy Spirit are one God, the doctrine of the Trinity.

Dr. John Warwick Montgomery offers this analogy to help us understand this doctrine better:

"The doctrine of the Trinity is not 'irrational'; what *is* irrational is to suppress the biblical evidence for Trinity in favor of unity, or the evidence for unity in favor of Trinity.

"Our data must take precedence over our models—or, stating it better, our models must sensitively reflect the full range of data.

"A close analogy to the theologian's procedure here lies in the work of the theoretical physicist: Subatomic light entities are found, on examination, to possess wave properties (W), particle properties (P), and quantum properties (h).

"Though these characteristics are in many respects incompatible (particles don't diffract, while waves do, etc.), physicists 'explain' or 'model' an electron as PWh. They have to do this in order to give proper weight to all the relevant data.

"Likewise the theologian who speaks of God as 'three in one.' Neither the scientist nor the theologian expects you to get a 'picture' by way of his model; the purpose of the model is to help you take into account *all* of the facts, instead of perverting reality through super-imposing an apparent 'consistency' on it.

"The choice is clear: either the Trinity or a 'God' who is only a pale imitation of the Lord of biblical and confessional Christianity" (*How Do We Know There is a God*, pp. 14, 15).

The Person of Jesus Christ

Two thousand years ago, Jesus asked His disciples the ultimate question: "Who do you say that I am?" (Matthew 16:15). Central to the Christian faith is the identity of its founder, Jesus Christ, and it is of monumental importance to have a proper view of who He is.

Jesus Was Human

The Christian Church has always affirmed that, although He was supernaturally conceived by the Holy Spirit, God in human flesh, Jesus Christ was also fully man. The teaching of the Scriptures is clear with regard to His humanity.

- He grew intellectually and physically.
  "Jesus kept increasing in wisdom and stature, and in favor with God and man" (Luke 2:52 KJV).
- He desired food.
  "And after He had fasted forty days and forty nights, He then became hungry" (Matthew 4:2 NASB).
- He became tired.
  ". . . Jesus therefore, being wearied from his journey. . ." (John 4:6 NASB).
- He needed sleep.
  "And behold, there arose a great storm in the sea, so that the boat was covered with the waves; but He Himself was asleep" (Matthew 8:24 NASB).
- He cried.
  "Jesus wept" (John 11:35).
- He died.
  ". . . but coming to Jesus, when they saw He was already dead, they did not break His legs." (John 11:33 NASB).

Therefore, it is made plain by Scripture that Jesus was genuinely human. He possessed all the attributes of humanity.

Jesus Was God

Jesus of Nazareth was a man but He was more than just a man. He was God in human flesh. While the Scriptures clearly teach He was a man, they likewise make it clear that he was God.

Jesus Made Divine Claims

There are many references by Jesus and His disciples concerning who He was.

- "In the beginning was the Word and the Word was with God and the Word was God" (John 1:1).
- "Jesus said to him, . . . He who has seen me has seen the Father" (John 14:9).
- "For this cause therefore the Jews were seeking all the more to kill Him, because He not only was breaking the Sabbath, but also was

calling God His own Father, making Himself equal with God" (John 5:18 NASB).

- "Looking for the blessed hope and the appearing of the glory of our Great God and Saviour, Christ Jesus" (Titus 2:13 NASB).
- "From now on I am telling you before it comes to pass so that when it does occur, you may believe that I am He" (John 13:19 NASB).

Jesus Exercised Divine Works

Jesus' friends and enemies were constantly amazed at the works He performed. In John 10, Jesus claims, "I and the Father are one." Then when the Jews again attempted to stone Him, "Jesus answered them, 'I showed you many good works from the Father; for which of them are you stoning Me?' The Jews answered Him, 'For a good work we do not stone You, but for blasphemy; and because You, being a man, make Yourself out to be God'" (John 10: 30-33 NASB).

Some of the works attributed to Christ as well as to God are:

1. Christ created all things (John 1:3, Colossians 1:6, Hebrews 1:10).
2. Christ upholds all things (Colossians 1:17, Hebrews 1:3).
3. Christ directs and guides the course of history (1 Corinthians 10:1-11).
4. Christ forgives sin (Mark 2:5-12, Colossians 3:13).
5. Christ bestows eternal life (John 10:28, 1 John 5:10).
6. Christ will raise the dead at the resurrection (John 11:25, John 5:21, 28, 29).
7. Christ will be the judge of all men in final judgment (John 5:22, 27, Matthew 25:31-46, 2 Corinthians 5:10).

One of these works drew an especially strong reaction from Jesus' critics, the religious leaders. This is number four: Christ forgives sin. Mark 2:5-12 reads:

"And Jesus seeing their faith said to the paralytic, 'My son, your sins are forgiven.'

But there were some of the scribes sitting there and reasoning in their hearts, 'Why does this man speak that way? He is blaspheming; who can forgive sins but God alone?'

And immediately Jesus, perceiving in His spirit that they were reasoning that way within themselves, said to them, 'Why are you reasoning about these things in your hearts? Which is easier, to say to the paralytic, "Your sins are forgiven;" or to say, "Arise, and take up your pallet and walk"? But in order that you may know that the Son of Man has authority on earth to forgive sins'— He said to the paralytic, 'I say to you, rise, take up your pallet and go home.'

And he rose and immediately took up the pallet and went out in the sight of all; so that they were all amazed and were glorifying God, saying, 'We have never seen anything like this.'"

Now, it's true that I can forgive the sins you commit against me, but that doesn't prove I'm God. So why does the fact that Christ forgives sin help prove He's God? Only God can forgive sins committed against Himself. Yet Christ claimed to forgive sins committed against God. Thus, by forgiving the paralytic his sins, Jesus makes one of His boldest claims to deity.

There are many other references to Jesus making divine claims which establish without a doubt that He believed Himself to be God.

Jesus Possessed Divine Attributes

By Demonstration

Jesus not only claimed to be God; He also demonstrated that He had the ability to do things that only God could do.

- Jesus exercised authority over nature.

"And on that day, when evening had come, He said to them, 'Let us go over to the other side.'

And leaving the multitude, they took Him along with them, just as He was, in the boat; and other boats were with Him.

And there arose a fierce gale of wind, and the waves were breaking over the boat so much that the boat was already filling up.

And He Himself was in the stern, asleep on the cushion; and they awoke Him and said to Him, 'Teacher, do You not care that we are perishing?'

And being aroused, He rebuked the wind and said to the sea, 'Hush, be still.' And the wind died down and it became perfectly calm. And He said to them, 'Why are you so timid? How is it that you have no faith?'

And they became very much afraid and said to one another, 'Who then is this, that even the wind and the sea obey Him?'" (Mark 4:35-41 NASB).

- Jesus reported events which occurred when He was far away from the scene.

"Jesus saw Nathanael coming to Him, and said of him, 'Behold an Israelite indeed, in whom is no guile!'

Nathanael said to Him, 'How do You know me?' Jesus answered and said to him, 'Before Philip called you, when you were under the fig tree, I saw you.'

Nathanael answered Him, 'Rabbi, You are the Son of God; You are the King of Israel.'

Jesus answered and said to him, 'Because I said to you that I saw you under the fig tree, do you believe? You shall see greater things than these'" (John 1: 47-50).

- Jesus knew the very thoughts of people.
"But He knew what they were thinking..." (Luke 6:8 NASB).

- Jesus had authority over life and death.
"And it came about soon afterwards, that He went to a city called Nain; and His disciples were going along with Him, accompanied by a large multitude.

Now as He approached the gate of the city, behold a dead man was being carried out, the only son of his mother, and she was a widow; and a sizable crowd from the city was with her.

And when the Lord saw her, He felt compassion for her, and said to her, 'Do not weep.'

And He came up and touched the coffin; and the bearers came to a halt. And He said, 'Young man, I say to you, arise!'

And the dead man sat up, and began to speak. And Jesus gave him back to his mother.

And fear gripped them all, and they began glorifying God, saying, 'A great prophet has arisen among us!' and, 'God has visited His people!'

And this report concerning Him went out all over Judea, and in all the surrounding district" (Luke 7: 11-17 NASB).

By Association

Not only did Christ demonstrate the ability to do the things only God could do, but the attributes which were attributed to God were also attributed to Jesus Christ. These attributes are found both in the Old Testament prophecies attributed to the Messiah, the Christ, and in the New Testament as direct references to Jesus. Old Testament prophecies which refer to Jesus Christ and His attributes can be examined in Chapter 9, in *Evidence That Demands a Verdict*. Here the direct New Testament references will be considered.

The customary division of the attributes of God into metaphysical and moral is assumed here.

As regards metaphysical attributes we may affirm firstly that God is self-existent; secondly that He is immense (or infinite). In regard to immensity or infinity He is eternal, unchangeable, omnipresent, omnipotent, perfect, incomprehensible, omniscient.

As regards moral attributes God is holy, true, loving, righteous, faithful and merciful. In these respects man differs from the ideal of manhood in the sense that He is the Author of these qualities. They are un-derived in Him. It will not be deemed necessary here to go beyond mere proof that all these attributes of God existed in Him. If the metaphysical attributes of God exist in Christ, then the moral attributes are un-derived and infinite in degree. Emphasis therefore will be laid on the metaphysical attributes.

Jesus' several statements of His oneness with the Father bear upon this subject, especially John 16:15, "All things whatsoever the Father hath are mine." This is a marvelous claim. This explains why in the previous verse (John 16:14) He could say that the work of the Holy Spirit is to glorify Christ: "He shall glorify me for he shall take of mine and shall declare it unto you." Beyond Christ there is nothing to know about the character of God (John 14:9).

- Christ possesses the metaphysical attributes of God. These attributes involve what might be called the essence of God. (The following is not an exhaustive list.)

1. *Self-existence.*

   Christ has the quality that He is not dependent on anyone or anything for His existence, and all other life is dependent on Him. John 1:4 reads, "In Him was life." Jesus states in John 14:6, "I am the life." He does not say "I have" but "I am." There is no life from amoeba to archangel apart from Christ. These verses must be explained against the background of the name Jehovah (Yahweh) as explained in Exodus 3:13-15 and 6:2-9 (also see Colossians 1:15-23).

2. *Eternal*

   When used of created things this adjective means without end. As used of God, of course, it means without beginning or end. Some clear evidence is found in 1 John 5:11, 20 —"And the witness is this, that God has given us eternal life, and this life is in His Son."

   "And we know that the Son of God has come, and has given us understanding, in order that we might know Him who is true, and we are in Him who is true, in His Son Jesus Christ. This is the true God and eternal life."

   Also see John 8:35, 1 John 1:2, Micah 5:2 and Isaiah 8:6.

3. *All-knowing.*

   This attribute, also known as omniscience, is the quality of having all knowledge. Biblical evidence for omniscience attributed to Christ is found in three areas.

   First is the opinion of the disciples. "Now we know that You know all things, and have no need for anyone to question You; by this we believe that You came from God" (John 16:30 NASB). Also compare John 21:17.

   Second, the testimony of Scripture. "But there are some of you who do not believe. For Jesus knew from the beginning who they were who did not believe, and who it was that would betray Him" (John 6:64 NASB). Also see John 2:23-25.

   Third, from examples in Scripture. "But Jesus, aware of their reasonings, answered and said to them, "Why are you reasoning in your hearts?" (Luke 5:22 NASB) Also see John 4:16-19, John 21:6 and Matthew 17:24-27.

   Often people refer to Matthew 24:36 as an exception, to illustrate that Christ was not all-knowing. However, many scholars, including Augustine, understand the word "know" here to mean "to make known or declare." This is a proper meaning of the text. Thus Jesus is stating that it is not among his instructions from the Father to make this known at this time (Shedd, *Dogmatic Theology II*, 276).

4. *All-powerful.*

   This means God can do anything not forbidden by His divine nature. For example, God cannot sin, for He is holy and righteous. Allowing for this exception, God can do anything (Mark 10:27). Another name for this attribute is omnipotence.

Christ claimed equality with God in this area. "Jesus therefore answered and was saying to them, 'Truly, truly, I say to you, the Son can do nothing of Himself, unless it is something He sees the Father doing; for whatever the Father does, these things the Son also does in like manner'" (John 5:19 NASB).

Jesus is called the Almighty. "I am the Alpha and the Omega," says the Lord God, "who is and who was and who is to come, the Almighty" (Revelation 1:8 NASB). Compare this with Revelation 1:17, 18; 22:12, 13 and Isaiah 41:4.

5. *Present everywhere.*
This is commonly called omnipresence. This means God is everywhere, there is no place where He is not present. What is important here is to note this does not mean God is everything. Rather, He is everywhere. God is separate from His creation. ". . . teaching them to observe all that I commanded you; and lo, I am with you always, even to the end of the age" (Matthew 28:20 NASV).

- Christ possesses the moral attributes of God. These are attributes which deal with the character of God. Again, this list is not complete.

1. *Holy.*
This means that God is pure, He cannot sin, and is unspoiled by evil or sin either by act or nature. Christ also possesses this attribute. "And the angel answered and said to her, 'The Holy Spirit will come upon you, and the power of the Most High will overshadow you; and for that reason the holy offspring shall be called the Son of God'" (Luke 1:35 NASV).

2. *Truth.*
Truth is the quality of being consistent with your words and actions and having those words and actions correspond to the real world. Thus it means you never lie. Christ's claims were strong here. He not only claimed to know the truth, He claimed He was the truth. The truth can never lie.

"Jesus said to him, 'I am the way, and the truth, and the life; no one comes to the Father, but through Me'" (John 14:6 NASV). "And to the angel of the church in Philadelphia write: 'He who is holy, who is true, who has the key of David, who opens and no one will shut, and who shuts and no one opens, says this. . .'" (Revelation 3:7 NASV).

3. *Love.*
This means that love, unconditional in its nature, is an attribute of God. Here again bold statements are made with regard to Christ's love. "For God so loved the world, that He gave His only begotten Son, that whoever believes in Him should not perish, but have eternal life" (John 3:16 NASV).

"A new commandment I give to you, that you love one another, even as I have loved you, that you also love one another. By this all men will know that you are My disciples, if you have love for one another" (John 13:34,35 NASV).

4. *Righteous.*

God is a righteous or just God. Righteousness means a standard. God's standard of love, justice, holiness is what He expects of us. Only God's righteous standard is acceptable to Him. If God is righteous and God can only accept righteous people before Him, yet He alone can be perfectly righteous, but Christ was accepted as our righteousness, as a perfect substitute. . .

"Much more then, having now been justified by His blood, we shall be saved from the wrath of God through Him" (Romans 5:9 NASV).

"For if by the transgression of the one, death reigned through the one, much more those who receive the abundance of grace and of the gift of righteousness will reign in life through the One, Jesus Christ.

"So then as through one transgression there resulted condemnation to all men; even so through one act of righteousness there resulted justification of life to all men.

"For as through the one man's disobedience the many were made sinners, even so through the obedience of the One the many will be made righteous.

"And the Law came in that the transgression might increase; but where sin increased, grace abounded all the more, that, as sin reigned in death, even so grace might reign through righteousness to eternal life through Jesus Christ our Lord" (Romans 5:1 7-21 NASV).

"My little children, I am writing these things to you that you may not sin. And if anyone sins, we have an Advocate with the Father, Jesus Christ the righteous" (1 John 2:1 NASV).

". . .in the future there is laid up for me the crown of righteousness, which the Lord, the righteous Judge, will award to me on that day; and not only to me, but also to all who have loved his appearing" (2 Timothy 4:8 NASV).—Then Christ's righteous sacrifice demonstrates His deity by His acceptance by God.

Now, concerning the moral attributes, some say, "I love unconditionally" or "I tell the truth, but that doesn't make me God." So why does it make Christ God? This question is answered by understanding two concepts, one having to do with God's nature, the other with our nature.

God's attributes are qualities that are all true of God and do not exist in isolation. In other words God's justice exists with God's love. One does not exclude the other. Thus, the attributes which represent the character of God are affected by those qualities which are true of His essence.

So if God is love and God is infinite (another attribute not touched on here) then God's love is infinite. This is in contrast to man. Man may love, but his love is not infinite.

Second, man's basic nature is sinful and has the tendency to continue to sin. Thus although man may act righteously at times, on his own, or may love unconditionally, ultimately he is bounded by and infected with his sin nature which results in disobedience to God's standard.

Jesus Received Worship as God

Jesus allowed Himself to be worshipped, something that is reserved for God alone.

- "You shall fear only the Lord your God; and you shall worship Him, and swear by His name" (Deuteronomy 6:13 NASB).
- "Then Jesus said to Him, 'Begone, Satan! For it is written, you shall worship the Lord your God, and serve Him only'" (Matthew 4:10 NASB).
- "Where is He who has been born King of the Jews? For we saw His star in the East, and have come to worship Him...And they came into the house and saw the child with Mary His mother; and they fell down and worshipped Him" (Matthew 2:2,11 NASB).
- "And behold, Jesus met them and greeted them. And they came up and took hold of His feet and worshipped Him" (Matthew 28:9)
- "And when they saw Him, they worshipped Him" (Matthew 28:17)
- "And he said, 'Lord, I believe.' And he worshipped Him" (John 9:38).

James Bjornstad, director of the Institute for Contemporary Christianity, makes an important observation:

To worship any other God, whether angel, man or manmade image is idolatry. In Colossians 2 we are warned, "Let no one keep defrauding you of your prize by delighting in...the worship of the angels" (Colossians 2:18).

We are not to worship angels and this is consistently demonstrated throughout the Bible. In Revelation 19:10 an angel (see 18:1) refuses worship from John. In Revelation 22:8,9, an angel refuses John's worship a second time, saying, "Do not do that...worship God."

Furthermore, Romans 1 explains that fools "exchanged the glory of the incorruptible God for an image in the form of corruptible man" (Romans 1:23). Obviously, we are not to worship man either. This, too, is consistently demonstrated throughout the Bible. In Acts 10:25,26, Peter refuses worship from Cornelius. In Acts 14:11-15, Paul and Barnabas refuse worship at Lystra.

From this evidence we can conclude that neither angels nor men are to be worshiped. Yet Jesus is worshiped, as we shall see, because He is God. He is not an angel or mere man. He is God, and God alone is to be worshiped. (James Bjornstad, *Counterfeits At Your Door*, G/L Publications, 1979, pp. 21, 22.)

Jesus Is God Yahweh

Attributes ascribed to Yahweh in the Old Testament are also used in reference to Jesus in the New Testament, demonstrating that Jesus is Yahweh.

"THERE IS ONE GOD" 1 Corinthians 8:6

GOD IS...	YAHWEH IS JESUS	....JESUS IS
Genesis 1:1		John 1:1-3
Job 33:4	CREATOR	Colossians 1:12-17
Isaiah 40:28		Hebrews 1:8-12
Isaiah 41:4	FIRST	Revelation 1:17
Isaiah 44:6	&	Revelation 2:8
Isaiah 48:12	LAST	Revelation 22:13
Exodus 3:13,14		John 8:24,58
Deuteronomy 32:39	I AM	John 13:19
Isaiah 43:10	(EGO EIMI)	John 18:5
Genesis 18:25		2 Timothy 4:1
Psalm 96:13	JUDGE	2 Corinthians 5:10
Joel 3:12		Romans 14:10-12
Psalm 47		Matthew 2:1-6
Isaiah 44:6-8	KING	John 19:21
Jeremiah 10:10		1 Timothy 6:13-16
Psalm 27:1		John 1:9
Isaiah 60:20	LIGHT	John 8:12
Psalm 106:21		John 4:42
Isaiah 43:3,11	SAVIOUR	Acts 4:10-12
Isaiah 45:21-23		1 John 4:14
Psalm 23		John 10:11
Psalm 100:3	SHEPHERD	Hebrews 13:20
Isaiah 40:11		1 Peter 5:4

(Ibid. p.89)

The teaching on the person of Jesus Christ from the Scripture is very clear. He was fully God and at the same time fully man. Any deviation from this position is not only unscriptural, it is also heretical. Those who attempt to make Jesus something less than God cannot go to the Bible for their justification. Therefore, if one takes the Bible seriously, one must conclude that Jesus of Nazareth was God in human flesh.

For further material and sources see *More Than a Carpenter*, chapter 1 and *Evidence That Demands a Verdict*, chapter 6.

The Doctrine of the Church

The Westminster Confession of Faith contains a statement about the church that is accepted by all branches of Christendom.

> The catholic or universal Church, which is invisible, consists of the whole number of the elect, that have been, are, or shall be gathered into one, under Christ the head thereof, and is the spouse, the body, the fullness of Him that filleth all in all. The visible Church, which is also catholic or universal under the gospel (not confined to one nation, as before under the law), consists of all those, throughout the world, that profess the true religion, and of their

children, and is the kingdom of the Lord Jesus Christ, the house and family of God, out of which there is no ordinary possibility of salvation.

The true church is made up of all those individuals who have put their trust in Christ as their Savior. It is not merely the attending of church or having a name on the membership list that makes on a member of Christ's true church. Only the transforming work of the Holy Spirit in the heart of the repentant sinner qualifies one for membership in the true body of Christ.

The Atonement

Within all branches of Christianity there is agreement that the deity of Christ was a perfect satisfaction to God as just and substitutionary punishment for the sins of the world:

> Therefore as in Adam we had fallen under sin, the curse, and death, so we are delivered from sin, the curse, and death in Jesus Christ. His voluntary suffering and death on the cross for us, being of infinite value and merit, as the death of one sinless, God and man in one person, is both a perfect satisfaction to the justice of God, which had condemned us for sin to death, and a fund of infinite merit, which has obtained him the right, without prejudice to justice, to give us sinners pardon of our sins, and grace to have victory over sin and death (The longer catechism of the Eastern Orthodox Church, answer to question 208).

Doctrine of Salvation

The doctrine of salvation is linked with the atoning death of Christ on the cross. While all major branches of Christianity agree that Christ's death was satisfactory to God as a sacrifice for the world's sins, there is a disagreement on how that sacrifice is appropriated. We believe the Bible teaches that salvation is by grace, a free gift of God to all those who believe in Christ. Those who receive Christ by faith have their sins forgiven and become children of God, a new creation in Christ Jesus:

> "For by grace you have been saved through faith; and that not of yourselves, it is the gift of God; not as a result of works, that no one should boast" (Ephesians 2:8, 9 NASB).
> "He saved us, not on the basis of deeds which we have done in righteousness but according to His mercy, by the washing of regeneration and renewing by the Holy Spirit" (Titus 3:5 NASB).
> "But as many as received Him, to them He gave the right to become children of God, even to those who believe in His name" (John 1:12 NASB).
> "In Him we have redemption through His blood, the forgiveness of our trespasses, according to the riches of His grace" (Ephesians 1:7 NASB).
> "Therefore if any man is in Christ, he is a new creature; the old things are passed away; behold, new things have come" (2 Corinthians 5:17 NASB). (2 Corinthians 5:17 NASB).

Since salvation is a free gift from God, no one can add anything to the completed work of Christ to receive it. It is received by faith and faith alone.

The Doctrine of Man

The Doctrine of Man is succinctly expressed in the Westminster Shorter Catechism, that "God created man, male and female, after his own image, in knowledge, righteousness, and holiness, with dominion over the creatures."

Francis Schaeffer, contemporary Christian philosopher, elaborates on what it means for modern man to be created in the image of God:

> What is it that differentiates Adam and Eve from the rest of creation? We find the answer in Genesis 1:26: "And God said, Let us make man in our image. . ." What differentiates Adam and Eve from the rest of creation is that they were created in the *image of God*. For twentieth-century man this phrase, *the image of God*, is as important as anything in Scripture, because men today can no longer answer this crucial question, "Who am I?" In his own naturalistic theories, with the uniformity of cause and effect in a closed system, with an evolutionary concept of a mechanical, chance parade from the atom to man, man has lost his unique identity. As he looks out upon the world, as he faces the machine, he cannot tell himself from what he faces. He cannot distinguish himself from other things.
>
> Quite in contrast, a Christian does not have this problem. He knows who he is. If anything is a gift of God, this is it—knowing who you are. As a Christian, I know my differentiation. I can look at the most complicated machine that men have made so far or ever will make and realize that, though the machine may do some things that I cannot do, I am different from it. If I see a machine that is stronger than I am, it doesn't matter. If it can lift a house, I am not disturbed. If it can run faster than I can, its speed doesn't threaten me. If I am faced with a giant computer which can never be beaten when it plays checkers—even when I realize that never in history will I or any man be able to beat it—I am not crushed. Others may be overwhelmed intellectually and psychologically by the fact that a man can make a machine that can beat him at his own games, but not the Christian" (Francis Schaeffer, *Genesis in Space and Time*, InterVarsity Press, 1972, pp. 46-47).

The Deity of the Holy Spirit

Central to the Christian faith is the teaching that the Holy Spirit is personal and is God, the third person of the Holy Trinity. The doctrine that the Holy Spirit is a person is clearly taught in Scripture. Notice the following examples of personal attributes displayed by the Holy Spirit. He can be grieved (Ephesians 4:30), resisted (Acts 7:51) and lied to (Acts 5:3). Moreover, the Holy Spirit can speak (Acts 21:11), think (Acts 15:28) and teach (Luke 12:12). Thus, the Holy Spirit is personal.

Furthermore, the Holy Spirit is spoken of in the Bible as a divine person. The Holy Spirit has the attributes of God, for He is all-powerful (Luke 1:35-37), eternal (Hebrews 9:14), and all-knowing (1 Corinthians 2:10,11). The Scriptures teach that lying to the Holy Spirit is lying to God (Acts 5:3,4).

The Holy Spirit also was involved in divine works, including creation (Genesis 1:2, Job 33:4), the new birth (John 3:5), the resurrection of Christ (Romans 8:11) and the inspiration of the Bible (2 Peter 1:20,21). Finally, to blaspheme against the Holy Spirit is an unforgivable sin (Matthew 12:31,32). The conclusion is that the Holy Spirit is God, the third person of the Holy Trinity.

Conclusion

As Bible-believing Christians, we know that God is personal, eternal and triune. However, the cults each deny one or more of the essential Bible doctrines we have discussed. Beware of any group or individual that changes essential doctrines. The Bible's teachings cannot be exploited at the whim of any group or individual. It contains "the faith once for all delivered to the saints" (Jude 3) and one who changes its divine pronouncements acts like those condemned in 2 Peter 3:16: "The untaught and unstable distort, as they do also the rest of the Scriptures, to their own destruction."

CHAPTER FOUR

Hare Krishna

History

The origin of the Hare Krishnas (International Society for Krishna Consciousness or ISKCON) dates back to the fifteenth century A.D., when Chaitanya Mahaprabhu developed The Doctrines of Krishnaism from the Hindu sect of Vishnuism.

Simply stated, Vishnuism believed Vishnu, the Supreme God, manifested himself at one time as Krishna. Chaitanya Mahaprabhu taught the reverse: Krishna was the chief God who had revealed himself at one time as Vishnu. The doctrinal system of Krishnaism is Hinduistic and while worshiping Krishna, acknowledges universal monism. This system believes every individual must go through a series of successive lives (reincarnation) to rid himself of the debt of his actions (karma).

Krishnaism was one of the early attempts to make philosophical Hinduism appealing to the masses. While pure Hinduism's god is impersonal and unknowable, Krishnaism (and other sects) personalize god and promote worship of and interaction with the personalized aspects of god, such as Krishna.

In 1965 Krishnaism came to America by means of Abhay Charan De Bhaktivedanta Swami Prabhupada, an aged Indian exponent of the worship of Krishna. He founded ISKCON and remained its leader until his death in 1977. Presently, ISKCON is ruled by two different groups, one group of eleven men rule over spiritual matters, while a board of directors heads the administrative matters. This wealthy organization presently has about 10,000 members in America. Part of ISKCON's wealth comes from soliciting funds and distributing its lavishly illustrated literature including the *Bhagavad-Gita: As It Is* and its periodical *Back to Godhead.*

ISKCON's beliefs are those of Hinduism and are wholly incompatible with Christianity. This can be observed by a comparison between the statements of ISKCON on matters of belief with those of the Bible.

God

The Bible speaks of God as the infinite-personal creator of the universe. He is eternally a separate entity from His creation. He existed before His creation came into being. The Scripture says, "In the beginning God created the heavens and the earth" (Genesis 1:1), showing God was there before His creation existed.

ISKCON practices monotheism. However it assumes traditional Hinduistic monism (essential pantheism). To them they are all one. "In the beginning of the creation, there was only the Supreme Personality Narayana. There was no Brahma, no Siva, no fire, no moon, no stars in the sky, no sun. There was only Krishna, who creates all and enjoys all.

"All the lists of the incarnations of Godhead are either plenary expansions or parts of the plenary expansions of the Lord, but Lord Sri Krsna (alternate spelling of Krishna) is the original Personality of Godhead Himself," Srimad Bhagavatam 1:3:28 (Bhaktivedanta Book Trust, n.d.).

Jesus Christ

According to Scripture, Jesus Christ is God Almighty who became a man in order to die for the sins of the world. He has been God from all eternity. "In the beginning was the Word and the Word was with God and the Word was God" (John 1:1).

ISKCON denies this by making Christ no more than Krishna's son. "Jesus is the son, and Krsna is the Father, and Jesus is Krsna's son" (*Jesus Loves Krsna*, Los Angeles Bhaktivedanta Book Trust, n.d., p. 26).

Salvation

The Bible teaches that all of us have sinned against a holy God and are therefore in need of a Savior: "For all have sinned and come short of the glory of God" (Romans 3:23); "For the wages of sin is death but the gift of God is eternal life through Jesus Christ our Lord" (Romans 6:23).

This is not so in the teachings of ISKCON. According to ISKCON, salvation must be earned by performing a series of works.

To get rid of the ignorance, one must practice disciplinary devotion by chanting the name of God, hearing and singing his praises, meditating upon the divine play and deeds of KRSNA, and engaging in the rites and ceremonies of worship. One must also repeat the name of God to the count of beads (Abhay Charan de Bhaktivedanta Swami Prabhupada, *Bhagavad-Gita As It Is* p. 326).

Self-denial and sacrifice are crucial for salvation in ISKCON. Note the following quotation,

> All these performers who know the meaning of sacrifice become cleansed of sinful reactions, and, having tasted the nectar of the remnants of such sacrifices, they go to the supreme eternal atmosphere (ibid p. 81).

The Passantinos have done extensive research in the area of the cults, and they offer pertinent comments regarding salvation in ISKCON:

> Salvation in Hare Krishna is thoroughly entwined with the Hindu concept of karma, or retributive justice. This teaching, which requires belief in reincarnation and/or transmigration of the soul, says that one's deeds, good and bad, are measured and judged either for or against him. Only when his good

deeds have "atoned" for his bad deeds (and he is thus cleansed of this evil world) can he realize his oneness with Krishna and cease his cycles of rebirth.

The idea of karma and reincarnation is anti-biblical. Is it just or reasonable for a man to suffer in this life or be required to atone for sins in this life that he committed in a previous life that he doesn't even remember? How can suffering for an unknown sin reform the sinner and mature him to the point where he no longer performs that sin? Such so-called justice is cruel and absolutely opposed to the God of the Bible (Robert and Gretchen Passantino, op. cit., p. 150).

Conclusion

Since ISKCON has a different God, a different Jesus, and a different way of salvation from what the Bible reveals, it is impossible for there to be any compatibility between the two. They differ on all crucial issues. A person must choose between Krishna and Jesus Christ; no harmony can exist between the sect of Hare Krishna and Christianity.

Hare Krishna Terms

ISKCON—Acronym for the official name for the Hare Krishna movement: The International Society for Krishna Consciousness.

Prabhupada, A. C. Bhaktivedanta—Late founder and spiritual head of ISKCON, a religious philosophy of self-denial where the devotees stress asceticism to attain God-consciousness. Born in India in 1896, he came to America in 1965 with the message of Krishna. He was considered by his devotees as Krishna's representative on earth.

Back to Godhead—The best-known of the Hare Krishna (ISKCON) publications.

Bhakti Yoga—The type of yoga, or exercise to spirituality, practiced by Hare Krishnas.

Karma—The Hindu idea of one's accumulated debts (bad deeds). Karma must be paid for during an individual's succession of lives (reincarnation).

Karmis—The Hare Krishna term for non-members, who are said to be captives of their own bad karma.

Laksmi—The Hare Krishna term for money. Also the name of one of the Hindu god Krishna's consorts. (Also Lakshma.)

Mantra—The Hindu prayer chant, specialized for each Hindu sect, including the Hare Krishnas.

Nirvana—The Hindu concept of heaven or bliss.

Paramatma—The Hare Krishna term for the Holy Spirit.

Sankirtana—The mantra, or religious chant in the Hare Krishna movement. Chanting of the Sankirtana "brings one ever closer to God-consciousness." This term is now used loosely to refer to any income-producing activity.

CHAPTER FIVE

Jehovah's Witnesses

History

O fficially known as the Watchtower Bible and Tract Society, the Jehovah's Witnesses are a product of the life work of Charles Taze Russell, born February 16, 1852, near Pittsburgh, Pennsylvania. In 1870, while still in his teens and without formal theological education, Russell organized a Bible class whose members eventually made him "pastor."

In 1879 he founded the magazine *Zion's Watchtower* in which he published his own unique interpretation of the Bible, and in 1886, the first volume of seven books (six written by Russell) entitled *The Millennial Dawn* was published (later retitled *Studies in the Scriptures*).

By the time of his death in 1916, "Pastor" Russell, according to the Watchtower, traveled more than a million miles, gave more than thirty thousand sermons, and wrote books totalling over fifty thousand pages (*Qualified to be Ministers*, Anon., 1955, p. 310).

Joseph F. Rutherford

A few months after the death of Charles Taze Russell, the society's legal counselor, Joseph Franklin Rutherford, became the second President of the Watchtower Society. It was under his leadership that the name "Jehovah's Witnesses" was adopted. Rutherford not only moved the Society's headquarters to Brooklyn, he also moved toward "theocratic" control with the power to make all policy decisions.

Nathan Knorr

Rutherford died in 1942 and was succeeded by Nathan H. Knorr. It was during Knorr's presidency that the society increased from 115,000 to over two million members. In 1961, under Knorr's leadership, the society produced its own English translation of the Bible entitled *The New World Translation of Holy Scriptures*.

When Knorr died in 1977, Frederick W. Franz became the new president of the Watchtower and is currently conducting business in Knorr's manner. Franz was the spokesman for the translation committee of the

New World Translation.

Claims of the Jehovah's Witnesses

Today, worldwide, the Jehovah's Witnesses number over two million. The members are zealous and sincere and claim to accept the Bible as their only authority. However, their theology denies every cardinal belief of historic Christianity including the Trinity, the divinity of Jesus Christ, His bodily resurrection, salvation by grace through faith, and eternal punishment of the wicked.

"Pastor" Russell, not known for his humility, made the following statement, "Be it known that no other system of theology even claims, or has ever attempted to harmonize in itself every statement of the Bible, yet nothing short of this can we claim" (Charles Taze Russell *Studies in the Scriptures*, 1:348). The Watchtower has this to say about itself:

> It is God's sole collective channel for the flow of Biblical truth to men on earth (*The Watchtower*, July 15, 1960, p. 439).
>
> The Watchtower Bible and Tract Society is the greatest corporation in the world, because from the time of its organization until now the Lord has used it as His channel through which to make known the glad tidings (*The Watchtower*, 1917, p. 22, quoted in *Studies in the Scriptures*, p. 144).
>
> F.W. Franz, president of the Watchtower, relaying how their interpretations come from God, stated, "They are passed to the Holy Spirit who invisibly communicates with Jehovah's Witnesses and the Publicity Department" (*Soottish Daily Express*, November 24, 1954)

We conclude from these statements that the Watchtower believes itself to be *the* organization that speaks for God in today's world. Note the following statement by "Pastor" Russell:

> If the six volumes of "Scripture Studies" are practically the Bible, topically arranged with Bible proof texts given, we might not improperly name the volumes "the Bible in an arranged form," that is to say, they are not mere comments on the Bible, but they are practically the Bible itself. Furthermore, not only do we find that people cannot see the divine plan in studying the Bible by itself, but we see, also, that if anyone lays the *Scripture Studies* aside, even after he has used them, after he has become familiar with them, after he has read them for ten years—if he then lays them aside and ignores them and goes to the Bible alone, though he has understood his Bible for ten years, our experience shows that within two years he goes into darkness. On the other hand, if he had merely read the *Scripture Studies* with their references and had not read a page of the Bible as such, he would be in the light at the end of two years, because he would have the light of the Scriptures (Charles Taze Russell, *The Watchtower*, September 15, 1910, p. 298).

Source of Authority

There are no "articles of faith" or authoritative doctrinal statements issued by the Watchtower. Their theological views are found in their various publications, including *The Watchtower* and *Awake*. The doctrine that proceeds from these works is considered authoritative.

They contend their ultimate source of authority is the Bible:

To let God be found true means to let God have the say as to what is the truth that sets men free. It means to accept His Word, the Bible, as the truth. Hence, in this book, our appeal is to the Bible for the truth. Our obligation is to back up what is said herein by quotations from the Bible for proof of truthfulness and reliability (*Let God Be True*, 1946, p. 9).

Although the Watchtower contends that the Scriptures are their final authority, we find they constantly misuse the Scriptures to establish their own peculiar beliefs. This is accomplished chiefly by quoting texts out of context while omitting other passages relevant to the subject. For all practical purposes their publications take precedence over the Scriptures.

Trinity

The Watchtower makes it clear they do not believe in the doctrine of the Trinity. "The trinity doctrine was not conceived by Jesus or the early Christians" (*Let God Be True*, 1952, p. 111). "The plain truth is that this is another of Satan's attempts to keep the God-fearing person from learning the truth of Jehovah and His Son Christ Jesus" (*Let God Be True*, p. 93).

In Watchtower theology neither Jesus Christ nor the Holy Spirit is God.

Jesus Christ

In the theological system of the Jehovah's Witnesses, Jesus Christ is not God in human flesh, but rather a created being.

"Jesus, the Christ, a created individual, is the second greatest personage of the Universe. Jehovah God and Jesus together constitute the superior authorities" (*Make Sure of All Things*, p. 207).

... "He was a god, but not the Almighty God, who is Jehovah" (*Let God Be True*, p. 33).

"If Jesus were God, then during Jesus' death God was dead in the grave" (*Let God Be True*, 1946, p. 91).

"The truth of the matter is that the word is Christ Jesus, who did have a beginning" (*Let God Be True*, p. 88).

The denial of the deity of Christ is nothing new in the history of the Church. It is a revival of the ancient heresy known as Arianism (named after the fourth century A.D. heretic Arius.) Arianism teaches that the Son was of a substance different than the Father and was, in fact, created).

To the Jehovah's Witnesses, Jesus is not equal to Jehovah God. He was rather, Michael the Archangel in his preexistent state, having a brother named Lucifer who rebelled against God while he (known then as Michael) remained obedient (see J. Rutherford, *The Kingdom Is At Hand*, p. 49).

During his earthly existence Michael was transformed into a man:

"The life of the Son of God was transferred from his glorious position with God his Father in Heaven to the embryo of a human" (*Let God Be True*, p. 36).

Upon His resurrection He went back to His former state as an invisible spirit, no longer having a body, according to Jehovah's Witnesses' theology.

The Jehovah's Witnesses, in an attempt to demonstrate that Jesus Christ is not Jehovah God, appeal to the Bible to substantiate their beliefs. However, it is the Bible that contradicts their theology, revealing it to be both unbiblical and non-Christian.

John 14:28

One favorite passage used by Jehovah's Witnesses to prove Christ is less than God is John 14:28: "My Father is greater than I." This verse refers to the voluntary subordination of Jesus during His earthly life when He willingly placed Himself in submission to the Father. It says nothing about His nature, only His temporary rank on earth. Thus, the "greater than" refers to His position rather than His person.

Revelation 3:14

One of the crucial phrases the Watchtower Society uses to support its doctrine of the creation of Christ is the latter part of Revelation 3:14, ". . .the beginning (αρχη) of the creation of God." It is used in their extended work on *"The Word" Who is He? According to John* to set forth that the Lord was a product of the creative activity of God. "Plainly it means the first one or original one of God's ways to be created." (*"The Word" Who is He? According to John* [Brooklyn: Watchtower Bible and Tract Society, 1962], p. 47.)

The Watchtower, which proclaims the authentic doctrinal views of the Watchtower Bible and Tract Society, states with reference to Revelation 3:14:

> This is true because his firstborn Son was the first of God's creations. Then with him as His active agent God went on to create everything else that has been brought into existence. He was the "beginning of the creation of God," not that he was the author of creation, but that he was the first one whom God made and whom God made without the co-operation of anyone else. ("Resurrection to a New World," *The Watchtower,* 68:99, April 1, 1947.)

Grammatically, there are two ways in which to understand this phrase: ". . .the beginning of the creation of God." It might be interpreted passively of Christ as the "beginning of the creation of God," as the first and most excellent creature of God's hands, or, it might declare of Christ, "that He was the active source, author, and in this sense, *'beginning'* and beginner of all creation; as in the words of the Creed, 'by whom all things were made.'" (Trench, *Seven Churches,* pp. 256-57.)

Although both meanings are possible if merely considered as entities, but with reference to the many statements of Scripture concerning Christ's deity, the latter is imperatively demanded. The Catholic Church rejected the former interpretation because it would "place this passage in contradiction with every passage in Scripture which claims divine attributes..." (*Ibid.,* p. 257.)

The *New World Translation of the Christian Greek Scriptures* is in error at this point by rendering this portion of the verse, ". . .the beginning of the creation by God." The genitive case means, "of God" and not, "by God."

Bruce Metzger points out if the passage were to teach that Christ was created "by God" it would have required the preposition "hupo" rather than "tou theou" which means "of God" (*Theology Today*, Bruce Metzger, 1953, pp. 79-80).

One need go no farther than these seven church letters referred to above by Trench. All the titles given to Christ by Himself are either divine or consistent with His divinity.

Several expressions of Paul to the Colossians are prototypes of certain phrases of John in Revelation. Paul wrote an epistle to the Laodiceans (Colossians 4:16) and gave directions for the Colossian epistle to be read in the church of Laodicea. The message inscribed by St. John to the Laodicean Church continues the theme commenced by St. Paul to the Colossians. It is highly probable that John was acquainted with Paul's epistle and was aware of the Laodicean problem. Lightfoot's remarks here are pertinent to this discussion:

> Thus, while St. Paul finds it necessary to enforce the truth that Christ is the image of the invisible God, that in Him all the divine fullness dwells, that He existed before all things, that through Him all things were created and in Him all things are sustained, that He is the primary source (αρχη) and has the pre-eminence in all things; so in almost identical language St. John, speaking in the person of our Lord, declares that He is the Amen, the faithful and true witness, the primary source (αρχη) of the creation of God.
>
> Some lingering shreds of the old heresy, we may suppose, still hung about these Churches, and instead of "holding fast the Head" they were even yet prone to substitute intermediate agencies, angelic mediators, as links in the chain which should bind man to God. They still failed to realize the majesty and significance, the completeness, of the Person of Christ. (Lightfoot, *Colossians*, pp. 41-42.)

Wordsworth corroborates the above statement of Lightfoot's that ". . . there may be some reference to the false teaching of those at Laodicea who substituted *Angels* as *Creators* and *Mediators* in the place of Christ." (Chr. Wordsworth, *The New Testament of our Lord and Saviour Jesus Christ, in the Original Greek*, p. 180.)

A few years before John's letter, Laodicea had been laid waste by an earthquake. After this catastrophe she was rebuilt better than her former splendor. She boasted that she did it herself, without the assistance of the Roman emperor (Lightfoot, *Colossians*, p. 43.). In Revelation 3:17, 18, John condemned this pride of wealth. Christ gave Himself this name in the Epistle, so that they would rely on Him for their salvation and not look for any good thing except from Him (Revelation 3:18).

The Laodiceans were probably familiar with this term, "beginning of the creation of God," as meaning the originating source through whom God works. Revelation 1:18; 2:8; 3:21; and 5:15 are passages that make it clear this concept in Colossians 1:15-18; John 1:3; and Hebrews 1:2 was well known to the Laodiceans. Christ is presented as the unqualified medium of the whole creation.

The Lord, in the other passages of Revelation, refers to Himself as not only the "Beginning," but the "End." (See also: Revelation 1:8; 21:6; 22:13;

compare with 1:17; 2:8; Isaiah 41:4; 44:6; 48:12). Christ is the end to which all creation tends. Christ is also called the "Amen," and the "faithful and true Witness," in Revelation 3:14. The Amen seems to refer to Isaiah 65:16 where the "God of Amen," was translated in the LXX (The Septuagint) as, the God of truth. . . ."

"The Amen" signifies the truth of His promises and "the true witness" points to the validity of His revelations of heaven, earthly things, and the purpose and nature of God (See also: John 1:3; 3:11, 12; 8:28, 29; 10:28; 14:9). Revelation 3:14 introduces a strong antithesis as a condemnation for the unfaithful and immature condition of the Church of Laodicea.

John refers to Christ as the beginning in the active sense: "the living beginning," the "first cause of creation." (Arndt and Gingrich, *A Greek-English Lexicon of the New Testament*, pp. 456-457). It signifies the causal relation of Christ to the creation of God.

A. T. Robertson, the Greek grammarian had this to say: "Not the first of creatures as the Arians held and Unitarians do now, but the originating source of creation through whom God works" (*Word Pictures in the New Testament*, Vol. VI, p. 321).

αρχη, as the "source of creation," not only coincides with the historical and etymological use of the word, but also the context and scriptural teaching about Christ. The Watchtower Society, in its strict adherence to this verse in order to verify a created beginning for Christ, not only disregards a thorough exegesis of αρχη but also ignores the overall biblical teaching.

Proverbs 8:22

The interpretation of Proverbs 8:22 has raised a greater controversy than almost any other passage in the Old Testament (F. C. Burney, "Christ as the APXH of Creation," *Journal of Theological Studies*, 27:160, 1926). This is a verse the Jehovah's Witnesses (along with Arians of every age) appeal to most frequently to confirm their view that Jesus Christ was a created Being (Bruce M. Metzger, "The Jehovah's Witnesses and Jesus Christ," *Theology Today*, 15:80, April, 1953). Their own Bible, *The New World Translation of the Hebrew Scriptures* (*New World Translation of the Holy Scriptures* [Brooklyn: Watchtower Bible and Tract Society, 1963].) purportedly rendered from the original languages by the New World Bible translation committee, translates Proverbs 8:22 as follows:

Jehovah himself produced me as the beginning of his way, the earliest of his achievements of long ago.

A footnote makes reference to the meaning "to create." (*Ibid.*, p. 1945.)

Their teaching on Christ being a created being with reference to Proverbs 8:22 permeates many of their publications. *The Watchtower*, the authoritative voice of the society (Also known as: *Millennial Dawn. Watchtower Bible and Tract Society. The People's Pulpit Association. The International Bible Student's Association*, etc.) states:

What then was his first creation? a son—his first son... Wise Sayings for the Modern Day *Watchtower*, 78:659 November 1 1957.) This created son

of God... (*Ibid.*, p. 660.)
   ...before he created his wise son... (*Ibid.*, p. 662.)

In their book, *What Has Religion Done for Mankind?*, it reads:

In the proverbs of wisdom, he speaks of himself as wisdom and calls attention to his being a creation of the eternal heavenly Father. (*What Has Religion Done for Mankind?* [Brooklyn: Watchtower Bible and Tract Society, Inc., 1951], p. 37.)

"The Word": Who Is He? According to John mentions that Proverbs 8:22,

does not mean Beginner, Origin, or Originator. Plainly, it means the first one or original one of God's ways to be created. (*"The Word": Who is He? According to John* [Brooklyn: Watchtower Bible and Tract Society, Inc., 1962], p. 47.)

There is no doubt that the Witnesses teach from this Old Testament verse the creation of Christ.

The pivotal point of the controversy centers on the Hebrew word *ganah*. The basic meaning of the word here should be understood as "beget," or "create," not to "produce" as translated by the Watchtower. The lexicons, the biblical usage, substantives derived from the root word, extra-biblical literature, the cognate languages, the early versions and the context of the Bible, all support the biblical usage and not the Watchtower.

The context is the critical stage in the exegesis of the passage. The decision whether Π λ means "to create," or "to beget," ultimately must be based upon the meanings of the verbs descriptive of the production of wisdom in the immediate context of Proverbs 8:22-25.

In Proverbs 8:23, "set up" means "I was woven" (prenatal growth of the embryo) and verses 24, 25 means "I was brought forth with travail" (birth). The conclusion is obvious that the verb "set up" in verse 22 is "beget me" (act of procreation). The above discussion of Proverbs 8:22-25 is summed up adequately by Kidner when he said that, "the passage as a whole may be meant to bring to mind a 'royal' birth." (Derek Kidner, *The Proverbs*, p. 8).

Colossians 1:15

Jesus is called the "firstborn" of all creation in Colossians 1:15. The Watchtower takes this to mean "first created." However, the passage itself states that Christ is the Creator of all things (vs. 16, 17), not a created being. The title firstborn refers to His preeminent position, not that he is Jehovah's "first creation."

The meaning of "firstborn" in Colossians 1:15 is perhaps impossible, or at least difficult, to understand without an accurate understanding of its Old Testament implications. The Hebrew term specifies the firstborn of human beings as well as animals (Exodus 11:5). A word from the same root denotes firstfruits (Exodus 23:16). This rendering "firstfruits," may mean the "first ripe" or "choicest" of the fruit.

Firstborn was a term applied in the Mosaic Law concerning the specific rights and obligations of the first male child of a family (Louis Hartman,

Encyclopedic Dictionary of The Bible [New York: McGraw-Hill Book Co., Inc., 1963], p. 777). The firstborn of the father had the right of primogeniture: he acquired a special blessing (Genesis 27); he became heir of a double share of the father's wealth (Deuteronomy 21:17); he replaced his father as head of the family and, therefore, possessed authority over the younger brothers and sisters (Genesis 27:29-40; 49:8; *Ibid.*, p. 778). Primogeniture involved representation of the father in the civil as well as religious capacity.

The firstborn was believed to possess a specific precedence in holiness since through him flowed the common blood of the tribe (Genesis 49:3; Deuteronomy 21:17). (I. Benzinger, "Family and Marriage Relations, Hebrew," *The New Schaff-Herzog Encyclopedia of Religious Knowledge* [New York: Funk and Wagnalls Company, 1908], IV, 277). This importance attached to the firstborn was believed to indicate a priesthood relating to the eldest sons of the families. (John McClintock and James Strong, "First-born," *Cyclopedia of Biblical, Theological and Ecclesiastical Literature* [New York: Harper and Brothers, 1873], III, 571.) This eminence was inferred from the particular claim of Yahweh to all the firstborn (Exodus 22:29). (Benzinger, *ibid.*).

Casanowicz, writing in *The Jewish Encyclopedia*, notes that the prerogatives of the firstborn consisted of: (1) a kind of *potestad* over the family; (2) a double share of inheritance; (3) the right of the priesthood; (4) God's promises to the patriarchs were considered as attached to the line of the firstborn (I. M. Casanowicz, "Primogeniture," *The Jewish Encyclopedia* [New York: Funk and Wagnalls Company, 1905], X, 198).

From the apparent regulations in the rabbinical law, Casanowicz concludes that ". . . the prerogative of primogeniture was not conceived as an inalienable right inherent in the firstborn, but rather as a gift by the law . . ." (*Ibid.*) Wine adds that the use of the term is not a reverence to birth but to position of favor. (W. B. Wine, *Epistles to the Philippians and Colossians* [London: Oliphant Limited, 1955], p. 135.)

After Reuben had forfeited his right of primogeniture, his priority in time was not passed on to Judah; but the dominion belonging to it was transferred to Judah and the double portion to Joseph (1 Chronicles 5:2).

This conclusion is also evident in the case of Esau and Jacob (Genesis 25:23-33). Jacob purchased the birthright from Esau, but he could not purchase Esau's priority in time. Another case in which the birthright was transferred is in the case of the Levites in Numbers 3:9:

> By destroying the firstborn of Egypt and sparing those of Israel, YHWH acquired an especial ownership over the latter. But as it was not feasible to select the firstborn of the entire nation and thus disturb the family organization, the Levites were substituted for them (Casanowicz, *op. cit.*, p. 199).

It is apparent that to receive this supremacy one did not have to be born first. Rees concludes in *The International Standard Bible Encyclopedia* that

> the laws and customs of all nations show that to be "firstborn" means, not only priority in time, but a certain superiority in privilege and authority (T.

Rees, "First-Begotten," *The International Standard Bible Encyclopedia* [Grand Rapids: Wm. B. Eerdmans Publishing Company, 1960], II, 1113).

Firstborn is also rendered metaphorically in the Old Testament (Francis Brown, S. R. Driver, and Charles Briggs, *A Hebrew and English Lexicon of the Old Testament* [Oxford: Clarendon Press, 1955], p. 114). The term was used figuratively in Job 18:13, "the firstborn of death . . .". "The firstborn son," notes Fausset, "held the chief place (Genesis 49:3); so here *the chiefest (most deadly) disease* that death has ever engendered" (Robert Jamieson, A. Fausset, and David Brown, *A Commentary Critical, Experimental and Practical on the Old and New Testaments* [Grand Rapids: Wm. B. Eerdmans Publishing Co., 1961], III, 44). Another use parallel to the above is Isaiah 14:30, "and the firstborn of the poor shall feed. . ." This denotes the poorest of the poor, the ". . . most abject poor" (*Ibid.*, p. 612).

It is also applied in the Old Testament to Israel as the firstborn of God (Exodus 4:22; Jeremiah 31:9), implying Israel as ". . . the prerogative race" J. B. Lightfoot, *Saint Paul's Epistles to the Colossians and to Philemon* [Grand Rapids: Zondervan Publishing House, 1961], p. 146). This paved the way for the later Messianic reference to "firstborn" as "the ideal representative of the race" (Thomas K. Abbott, *Epistles to the Ephesians and to the Colossians* [The International Critical Commentary. Grand Rapids: Wm. B. Eerdmans Publishing Company, 1957], p. 210).

Abbott indicates from the writings of Rabbi Nathan in *Shemoth Rabba*, on the interpretation of Psalms 89:27 (Psalms 89:28 in the LXX), that this term "seems to have been a recognized title of the Messiah (see Hebrews 1:6) (*Ibid*).

The title firstborn had been used so much as a title of sovereignty that God Himself is called "Firstborn of the world," by R. Bechai on the Pentateuch. (Lightfoot, *Colossians*, p. 47).

It may be ascertained from the above evidence that the use of "firstborn" in the Old Testament to mean "priority of birth" or "in time" has been overshadowed by and sometimes even lost in the idea of "supremacy" or "preeminence." This meaning may be distinctly seen in Genesis 49:3 where Jacob said of Reuben, "Thou art my firstborn, my might, and the beginning of my strength, the excellency of dignity, and the excellency of power." The dominating thought here is not primogeniture, but dignity, honor, strength and sovereignty.

It is used in Romans 8:29 to denote one who ". . . is chief, or who is highly distinguished and preeminent" (Albert Barnes, *Notes on the New Testament: Explanatory and Practical* [London: Blackie and Sons, 1851], VII, 246). Arndt and Gingrich use it figuratively "of Christ, as the firstborn of a new humanity which is to be glorified, as its exalted Lord is glorified. . ." (William F. Arndt and F. Wilbur Gingrich, *A Greek-English Lexicon of the New Testament and Other Early Christian Literature* [Chicago: The University of Chicago Press; Cambridge: at The University Press, 1960], p. 734). He is their chief and most excellent ruler.

The Messiah is preeminently the "Firstborn" (Ps. 89:28); and Israel was God's firstborn (Exodus 19:6); a "kingdom of priests" to God (Revelation 1:6); and therefore, the believer becomes part of God's "church of the firstborn" in Hebrews 12:23 (Jamieson, Fausset, and Brown, *op. cit.*, VI, 576). Radford writes that it is

> a description of the communion of the saints, living and departed, all alike eldest sons in a family where there is historical succession from generation to generation of the faithful, but no priority of spiritual status as between generations or within any generation (Lewis B. Radford, *The Epistles to the Colossians and the Epistle to Philemon* [London: Mouthen and Co., LTD, 1931], p. 168).

Pink would say the title, "Church of the Firstborn," is synonymous with the "...appointed heirs of all things..." (Hebrews 1:2) (Pink, *op cit.*, p. 53).

In Hebrews 1:6 we have a clear example of Christ's superiority, excellency and dignity, where the writer to the Hebrews tells us that God referred to Christ as His firstborn. And because Christ is superior to angels, they shall do obeisance to Him: "...And let all the angels of God worship him."

In Revelation 1:5 and Colossians 1:8, Christ is referred to as the "firstborn from the dead." It is obvious that the literal sense of the word cannot be used here. Also it cannot be used as the first to be raised from the dead. It can only mean preeminence or sovereignty, in that Christ was the first to be raised from the dead by His own power and to be exalted to immortality (John Gill, *An Exposition of the New Testament, both Doctrinal and Practical* [London: George Keith, 1876], IV, 382.), as the context in both cases corroborates. He is the "one to whom the bodies of His saints shall be conformed—see Philippians 3:21" (Pink, *loc. cit*). Both of these verses will be discussed in more detail.

In all these uses the employment of "firstborn" belongs to the Lord Jesus Christ, both as to the superiority of His nature, of His office and of His glory.

Church fathers gave strict attention to the fact that the Apostle Paul wrote πρωτοτοκος (first-born) and not πρωτοκτιοτι (first-created).

It is evident that there is a great contrast between the ideas of "birth" and "creation." They are not equivalent terms. Christ was "born" and the universe was "created." Meyer writes that the term πρωτοτκος is chosen, because...

> in the comparison as to time of origin, it points to the peculiar *nature* of the origination in the case of *Christ*, namely, that He was not *created* by God, like the other beings in whom this is implied in the designation *ktisis*, but *born*, having come forth homogeneous from the nature of God. (H. A. W. Meyer, *Critical and Exegetical Handbook to the Epistles to the Philippians and Colossians and to Philemon* [New York: Funk and Wagnalls Publishers, 1885], p. 226.)

C. S. Lewis gives one of the best explanations of the difference between the concepts of begetting and creating:

> One of the creeds says that Christ is the Son of God "begotten, not created";

and it adds "begotten by His Father before all worlds." Will you please get it quite clear that this has nothing to do with the fact that when Christ was born as a man on earth, that man was the son of a virgin? We are now thinking about something that happened before Nature was created at all, before time began. What does it mean?

Jesus Christ, the "firstborn," is before all creation in time, but not a part of creation.

The above discussion illustrates that the concept of priority is significant in the interpretation of "firstborn." But it is used in a secondary sense as will be seen below.

Lordship over (sovereignty). This meaning in the Old Testament often overshadowed and sometimes excludes the root meaning of priority in time. Moulton has determined that...

> when the Jew thought of a firstborn son his emphasis was not so much on the date of his birth as on his priority in the family and the privileges that were his by right. Paul's thought may be partly that Jesus is before us in time, but probably much more on the fact that He is supreme in rank above all the created world (Harold M. Moulton, *Colossians, Philippians, and Ephesians* [Epworth Preacher's Commentaries. London: The Epworth Press, 1963], p. 16).

God's firstborn is, "the natural ruler, the acknowledged head, of God's household." (Lightfoot, *Colossians,* p. 147.) The right of the firstborn is closely related to Messiah over all the created world. The phrase in Psalms 89:27, "...I will make him my firstborn," is explained by the addition of the "higher than the kings of the earth," speaking of Messianic sovereignty. This reference to the meaning of sovereignty so predominated references to the Messiah that here "firstborn of all creation" would mean "Sovereign Lord over all creation by virtue of primogeniture" *(Ibid.,* p. 146).

The phrase, "...whom he hath appointed heir of all things..." in Hebrews 1:2, definitely relates to the "...I will make him my firstborn..." in Psalm 89:27. The latter phrase of Hebrews 1:2, "by whom also he made the worlds," is an epitome of Colossians 1:15-17. The meaning of supremacy so dominated the title in some of its uses that it was, as seen above, even used as a title of God Himself.

The Jehovah's Witnesses, in trying to establish Christ as a created being, render the "firstborn of all creation" in 1:15 as a partitive genitive (the whole of which it is part). In doing this they ignore the Old and New Testament usage of the term. This view is grammatically permissible; however, "this interpretation is exegetically and historically impossible; for verses 16, 17 emphatically distinguish between 'him' and the 'all things' of creation" (L. J. Baggott, *A New Approach to Colossians* [London: A. R. Mowbray and Co., Limited, 1961], p. 58).

The Witnesses try to substantiate their doctrine of Christ being one of the creation by a deliberate insertion of a word for which there is no basis in the Greek text. A clear example occurs here in *The New World Translation of the Christian Greek Scriptures,* Colossians 1:16, 17, which is pertinent to this discussion.

...because by means of him all [other] things were created in the heavens and upon the earth, the things visible and the things invisible, no matter whether they are thrones or lordships or governments or authorities. All [other] things have been created through him and for him. Also, he is before all [other] things and by means of him all other things were made to exist...

The word "other" has been inserted all the way through the passage unjustly. There is no equivalent word in the Greek text and no reputable translation includes it (Ray C. Stedman, "The New World Translation of the Christian Greek Scriptures," *Our Hope,* 50:32, July, 1953). When it is considered that the Jehovah's Witnesses assume Jesus Christ to be a created being, it is easy to understand why they insert "other." The Greek solely states, "He is before all things and by him all things hold together," which is interpreted logically by Stedman to plainly teach "...that Christ is the Creator of everything that has existence, material or immaterial, and therefore He cannot Himself be a creature" (*Ibid*).

However, when the word "other" is unwarrantably interjected four times, it alters the thought to imply that Christ was the author of all created things, with the exception of one, Himself, who the Watchtower Society says was created. A footnote in the *New World Translation* reads, "All other: as at Luke 13:2, 4 and elsewhere" (*New World Translation of the Holy Scriptures* [Brooklyn: Watchtower Bible and Tract Society, 1963] p. 3385).

The reference here to Luke 13:2, 4 corresponds to the Lord's question about the Galileans whom Pilate had killed, and the 18 men who were slain by the falling tower of Siloam. He asks, "Do you suppose that these Galileans were greater sinners than all *other* Galileans..." and, "Or do you suppose that those 18...were worse culprits than all [the other— NWT] men who live in Jerusalem?" (*New American Standard Bible New Testament* [La Habra: The Foundation Press for the Lockman Foundation, 1963], p. 125).

Stedman, in his article, "The New World Translation of the Christian Greek Scriptures," set forth clearly the reason for the inclusion of "other" here and its exclusion in Colossians 1:15-18:

Now here, though the original has no word for "other," it is plainly implied in the context, for, of course, these dead men were being put in contrast with all their fellow-citizens. However, there is no such implication in Colossians 1:15-17 *unless one presupposes that Christ Himself was nothing but a creature.* But no translator has the right thus to presuppose on a doctrinal issue. If the text were simply rendered as it is, leaving out the inserted word "other," it would agree exactly with other New Testament passages that declare plainly that the Lord Jesus Christ is Creator of everything that has been created (Hebrews 1:10; John 1:3).

Again it is evident that the translators have taken special care to make the text say what they suppose it ought to say rather than to let it speak plainly for itself (Stedman, *op. cit.,* p. 33).

Hebrews 2:10, not Luke 13, is the true parallel of Colossians 1:16, 17. It speaks so distinctly of Christ's creating all things that the New World committee did not dare to insert "other," in the text: ". . .for whose sake all things are and through whom all things are. . ." (Hebrews 2:10). (New World Translation, *op. cit.*, p. 3432).

It was decided by Baggott that "the idea of the Son of God being *part of* creation was entirely foreign to Paul's mind (see 2:9; I Corinthians 8:6; Philippians 2:6-8), and also the thought of his day (Baggott, *loc. cit.*). The partitive genitive in which πρωτοτοκος would be as one of the class referred to, "creation," is usually expressed in the plural number, but the Apostle does not here use the plural (John Eadie, *Commentary on the Epistle of Paul to the Colossians* [Grand Rapids: Zondervan Publishing House, 1957], p. 49).

The use of sovereign as the primary meaning of "firstborn" in Colossians 1:15 also has its confirmation in Paul's aggressive denunciation of the Colossian heresy.

Thus, in a brief but concise passage of Scripture, Paul makes plain to his readers that Jesus Christ existed before creation and therefore is sovereign over creation. This passage does not teach or even support the Witnesses' doctrine that Jesus Christ was the first created being.

Paul used language that was understood in the Colossians' nomenclature. He purposely chose "firstborn."

We describe Christ in relation to all creation because it best characterizes the dignity, preeminence and sovereignty that belongs to Him as Lord of all. Therefore, in light of the historical, literal and metaphorical meanings of πρωτοτοκος, the Jehovah's Witnesses are unscriptural in the application of it to Christ as created.

Jesus Christ, as taught in Colossians 1:15-18, is prior to, distinct from and sovereign over the universe.

Holy Spirit

According to the Watchtower Society the Holy Spirit is not part of the Godhead. Both the personality and the deity of the Holy Spirit [defined as "the invisible active force of Almighty God which moves His servants to do His will" (*Let God Be True*, p. 108)] are denied. The personality of the Holy Spirit is consistently rejected throughout the New World Translation by not capitalizing the term "spirit" when referring to the Holy Spirit.

To promulgate this error they mistranslate such passages as Ephesians 4:30 ("also, do not be grieving God's holy spirit, with which you have been sealed for a day of releasing by ransom"), and John 14:26 ("But the helper, the holy spirit which the Father will send in my name, that one will teach you all things and bring back to your minds all the things I told you").

However, both of these verses teach the personality of the Holy Spirit. How can one grieve something impersonal? Or how can an "impersonal force" teach all things? Competent translations substitute "with which" in Ephesians 4:30 with "by whom" and have "whom the Father will send" and "he will teach you" in John 14:26 rather than the impersonal holy spirit of the Watchtower.

Salvation

In Watchtower theology, salvation is not regarded as a free gift from God based upon Jesus Christ's work on the cross. Rather, their literature stresses a salvation by works. Russell wrote, "They must be recovered from blindness as well as from death, that they, each for himself, may have a full chance to prove, by obedience or disobedience, their worthiness of life eternal" (Charles Taze Russell, *Studies in the Scriptures,* Vol. 1, p. 158).

Elsewhere they state: "All who by reason of faith in Jehovah God and in Christ Jesus dedicate themselves to do God's will and then faithfully carry out their dedication will be rewarded with everlasting life..." (*Let God Be True*, p. 298).

The Bible teaches we are saved by grace through faith alone. Man's good works can never contribute to his salvation. "For by grace you have been saved through faith; and that not of yourselves, it is the gift of God; not as a result of works, that no one should boast" (Ephesians 2:8, 9 NASB). "He saved us, not on the basis of deeds which we have done in righteousness, but according to His mercy" (Titus 3:5 NASB).

Everlasting Punishment

The Watchtower denies the existence of hell as a place of everlasting punishment for the wicked. They argue, "The doctrine of a burning hell where the wicked are tortured eternally after death cannot be true mainly for four reasons: (1) It is wholly unscriptural; (2) it is unreasonable; (3) it is contrary to God's love; and (4) it is repugnant to justice" (*Let God Be True*, p. 9).

In response to this we contend that the doctrine is absolutely scriptural: "...when the Lord Jesus shall be revealed from Heaven with His mighty angels in flaming fire, dealing out retribution to those who do not know God and to those who do not obey the gospel of our Lord Jesus. And these will pay the penalty of eternal destruction, away from the presence of the Lord and from the glory of His power" (2 Thessalonians 1:7-9).

Matthew 25:46 speaks of eternal punishment and eternal life in the same context. Eternal punishment lasts as long as eternal life: "And these will go away into eternal punishment, but the righteous into eternal life."

The doctrine of everlasting punishment is neither contrary to God's love nor justice, as the Watchtower claims. Jesus Christ has taken the sins of the world upon Himself and offers everlasting life to all who will receive the free gift of God. If people reject His offer then they must suffer the penalty for their own sins.

False Prophecies

"When Jesus said He would come again He did not mean He would return in the flesh visible to men on earth. He has given up that earthly life as a ransom and therefore, can not take such life back again...The good news today is that Christ Jesus has come again, that God's Kingdom by Him has been set up and is now ruling in heaven . . . all the evidence shows that Jesus took up His Kingdom power and began his reign from Heaven in the year 1914" (Pamphlet, "This Good News of the Kingdom", pp. 19, 21).

The idea that the second coming of Christ took place in 1914 is important to Watchtower theology. That was the time, they say, that God's kingdom was fully set up in heaven. However, this was not always their teaching. Before 1914, the Watchtower was predicting that God's Kingdom was to be set up on *earth* (not in heaven) in 1914!

"'The times of the Gentiles' extend to 1914. And the Heavenly Kingdom will not have full sway till then, but as a 'stone' the Kingdom of God is set up 'in the days of these Kings' and by consummating them it becomes a universal Kingdom—a 'great mountain and fills the whole earth'" (*Watchtower Reprints*, Vol. I, March, 1880, p. 82).

Charles Taze Russell also stated that the world would see "the full establishment of the Kingdom of God in the earth at A.D. 1914, the terminus of the times of the Gentiles" (C. T. Russell, *Thy Kingdom Come*, 1891, p. 126).

The prophecies made by Russell and the Watchtower concerning 1914 totally failed because the Kingdom of God was not established upon the earth. Today, as already observed, the Watchtower teaches that Christ returned invisibly in 1914 and set up His Kingdom only in Heaven. However, this idea clearly opposes the scriptural teaching of the visible bodily return of Christ: "Ye men of Galilee, why stand ye gazing up into heaven? This same Jesus which is taken up from you into heaven, shall so come in like manner as ye have seen Him go into Heaven" (Acts 1:11).

Jesus warned against such false teaching about His return: "Wherefore if they shall say unto you, Behold, he is in the desert; go not forth: Behold, he is in the secret chambers; believe it not. For as the lightning cometh out of the East, and shineth even unto the West; so shall the coming of the Son of Man be" (Matthew 24:26, 27). The Scriptures also state: "Behold, he cometh with the clouds; and every eye shall see Him . . ." (Revelation 1:7).

The Watchtower is guilty of false prophecy (Deuteronomy 18:21, 22) in wrongly predicting the date 1914 to be the return of Christ. They are also wrong in asserting His coming is secret and invisible because the Scriptures teach completely to the contrary (Revelation 1:7).

The New World Translation

In 1961, the Watchtower Bible and Tract Society published the *New World Translation of the Holy Scriptures*. The rationale for this new translation was given when the New Testament was published in 1950:

> But honesty compels us to remark that, while each of them (other translations) has its points of merit, they have fallen victim to the power of human traditionalism in varying degrees, consequently, religious traditions, hoary with age, have been taken for granted and gone unchallenged and

uninvestigated. These have been interwoven into the translations to color the thought. In support of a preferred religious view, an inconsistency and unreasonableness have been insinuated into the teachings of the inspired writings.

The Son of God taught that the traditions of creed-bound men made the commandments and teachings of God of no power and effect. The endeavor of the New World Bible Translation committee has been to avoid this snare of religious traditionalism. (Foreword to *New World Translation of the Christian Greek Scriptures*, 1961).

The translators of the New World Translation have not achieved their goal. Their work is a highly biased attempt to justify some of their non-biblical doctrines. In terms of scholarship, the New World Translation leaves much to be desired. The following examples will make the point clear.

John 1:1

One of the readings of the New World Translation that has caused considerable outrage among Greek scholars is its totally unsupportable rendering of the last clause of John 1:1, "The word was a god." This translation makes Jesus Christ less than God, relegating Him to the position of a "created being" in accordance with Watchtower theology. There is no basis whatsoever for this rendering, although the Watchtower would have people believe the contrary.

"...How are we to understand John 1:1, 2 of which there are differing translations? Many translations read: 'And the Word was with God, and the Word was God.' Others read: 'And the Word (The Logos) was divine." Another: 'and the Word was God.' Others 'And the Word was a god.' Since we have examined so much of what John wrote about Jesus who was the Word made flesh we are now in a position to determine which of those several translations is correct. It means our salvation" (*The Word Who Is He? According to John*, p. 52).

This is a misleading statement because it gives the impression that other translations agree with their rendering when the opposite is true. There are *no* reputable authorities or translations that support the reading, "The Word was a god."

The only other translation quoted in this Watchtower publication that reads the same way is *The New Testament in an Improved Version upon the Basis of Archbishop Newcome's New Translation: with a Corrected Text*, printed in London in 1808. Such an antiquated and obscure translation done by a Unitarian cannot be considered reputable.

Grammatical Explanation of John 1:1 The grammatical explanation given by the Watchtower for its translation of John 1:1 is unsatisfactory. They contend that when *theos* (the Greek word for God) appears in John 1:1 it appears twice, once with the definite article (the) and once without. When it appears without the definite article (in the last clause of John 1:1) they feel justified in translating it, "And the Word was a god..."

"Careful translators recognize that the articular construction of the noun [with the definite article] points to an identity, a personality, whereas an anarthrous construction (without the definite article) points to a quality about someone" (Appendix to the *Kingdom Interlinear Translation of the Greek Scriptures*, Watchtower Bible and Tract Society, p. 1158).

Not only is the above statement incorrect, it is also inconsistently applied throughout the Watchtower's own translation. In the first 18 verses of John's gospel, the word for God—*theos*—appears six times without the definite article (vs. 1, 6, 12, 13, and twice in 18). Yet, it is rendered God (referring to Jehovah) in each instance except for the last clause of verse one when it refers to Jesus!

If the Watchtower's translations were consistent, verse six should read, "There arose a man that was sent forth as a representative of a god." Moreover, verse 12 should read "to become a god's children," etc. Why only in verse one do they refuse to translate *theos* as God (meaning Jehovah)?

We conclude that there is no basis for translating John 1:1, "The Word was a god" as in the *New World Translation*. It is a biased rendering that cannot be justified grammatically.

They do not want to acknowledge what is clearly taught in verse one: Jesus Christ is God. Also, it should be observed that the absence of the definite article does *not* indicate someone other than the true God. The entry on *theos* in the authoritative *Arndt and Gingrich Greek Lexicon* states *theos* is used "quite predominately of the true God, sometimes with, sometimes without, the article" (William F. Arndt and F. Wilbur Gingrich, *Greek-English Lexicon of the New Testament*, 1957, p. 357).

(Further information on the Greek construction and translation of John 1:1 has been presented by many other writers in complete form. See the recommended reading list for works that deal extensively with Jehovah's Witnesses. Suffice it to say, the Watchtower mistranslation of John 1:1 is not supported by any contextual grammatical study.)

Even without going to the Greek grammar of John 1:1, we can see that the Watchtower translation of John 1:1 goes against the clear teachings of the Bible. In both the Old and New Testaments we are taught that there is only one true God (Isaiah 43:10; John 17:3; 1 Corinthians 8:4-6, etc.). All other "gods" are false gods. Those who would acknowledge any god as true except for Jehovah God are guilty of breaking the first commandment: "You shall have no other gods before me" (Exodus 20:3).

By translating the last part of John 1:1 as, "The Word was a god," the Watchtower has declared its belief in polytheism, or the belief in more than one god. According to the whole testimony of the Bible, the Word (Jesus Christ) of John 1:1 must be either the only true God, Jehovah, or a false god. The Bible knows only one true God, Jehovah.

Jehovah's Witnesses will not call Jesus Christ a false god. Neither will they call him Jehovah, the one true God. By calling Jesus Christ "a god" in John 1:1, they have acknowledged their own polytheism, which is contrary to the Bible, the Word of God.

John 8:58

In the eighth chapter of the gospel of John, Jesus is asked by the religious leaders, "Whom do you make yourself out to be?" (verse 58). His answer is a direct reference to Exodus 3:14 where God identifies Himself from the burning bush to Moses by the designation, "I Am." The Jews, realizing that Jesus claimed to be God, attempted to stone Him for blashemy (verse 59).

The *New World Translation* mistranslates this verse by making it read, "Before Abraham came into existence I have been." The footnote to John 8:58 in the 1950 edition is enlightening: "I have been—'ego eimi' after the aorist infinitive clause and hence properly rendered in the perfect indefinite tense. It is not the same as 'Ho ohn' meaning 'The Being' or 'the I AM' at Exodus 3:14 LXX" (*New World Translation*, 1950, p. 312).

This is not any "perfect indefinite tense." The Watchtower then changed the note to read "the perfect tense," dropping the word *indefinite* (see *The Kingdom Interlinear Translation of the Greek Scriptures*, 1969). However, this is also incorrect since the verb *eimi* is in the present tense, indicative mood, and hence should properly be translated, "I Am." Moreover, the context of John 8:58 (8:42 – 9:12), the verb "to be" occurs 22 times in the indicative mood and the *New World Translation* correctly renders 21 out of 22. The only incorrect rendering is in John 8:58. Why?

Furthermore, the footnote is deliberately misleading. The Septuagint (abbreviated as LXX), the Greek translation of the Hebrew Old Testament, translated the name of God in Exodus 3:14 with the Greek *Ego Eimi ho ohn* (I am The Being). The Watchtower's note obscures the correlation between the two passages by failing to cite *ego eimi* as part of the Septuagint translation. Their note reads, "It is not the same as *oh ohn*, meaning 'the being' or 'The I Am' at Exodus 3:14, LXX."

While the Hebrew text repeats the same form of the "to be" verb in Exodus 3:14, customary Greek usage makes it more natural for the Grek translation of Exodus 3:14 to first express the term as *ego eimi* (I am) and then a different variation of the same term *ho ohn* (the Being),. In conclusion, the Watchtower has blatantly misrepresented the Greek argument for Christ's deity from John 8:58. Jesus Christ is clearly identifying Himself as the *Ego eimi (ho ohn)* of Exodus 3:14

Dr. A. T. Robertson, one of the greatest Greek scholars who ever lived, after translating *"ego eimi"* as "I AM," had this to say about John 8:58: "Undoubtedly here Jesus claims eternal existence with the absolute phrase used of God" (*Word Pictures in the New Testament*, Vol. V, pp. 158-159).

The Watchtower betrays itself in its own *Kingdom Interlinear Translation* which contains a literal English translation beneath the Greek text as well as the New World Translation reading. In John 8:58 under the Greek *ego eimi*, *The Kingdom Interlinear* rightly translates it, "I am", but *New World Translation* changes it to, "I have been." This inconsistency is striking.

There is no sufficient basis for the translation, "I have been," in John 8:58. This is another example of the scholarly shortcomings of the Watchtower. It obscures the fact that Jesus Christ is Jehovah God.

Colossians 1

In Colossians one, the Apostle Paul stresses the Lordship and deity of Jesus Christ by emphasizing that He is the creator of all things: "For by Him all things were created" (1:16). However, the *New World Translation*, with absolutely no legitimate justification, adds the word "other" in this verse and five other places in chapter one in an attempt to make Jesus a created being:

Vs. 16, Because by means of Him all [other] things were created in the Heavens and upon the earth (NWT).

Vs. 16, All [other] things have been created through Him and for Him (NWT).

Vs. 17, Also, He is before all [other] things and by means of Him all [other] things were made to exist (NWT).

Vs. 20, And through Him to reconcile again to Himself all [other] things (NWT).

There is no basis for adding the world "other" to the texts listed above. On the contrary, to do so destroys the natural context of the passages and improperly implies that Jesus Christ is Himself a creature. Since Jehovah God alone created all things (Isaiah 44:24; Hebrew 3:4), and Colossians calls Jesus Christ the creator, we can justifiably assume that Jesus Christ is Jehovah God.

We conclude, *The New World Translation* is not a work of competent scholarship, but rather an attempt to promulgate the doctrines of the Watchtower. The foreword of the New World Translation states, "It is a very responsible thing to translate the Holy Scriptures from their original languages." We agree wholheartedly and we wish the Watchtower had lived up to this high principle.

Conclusion

A close examination of the Watchtower has demonstrated that it is not what it claims to be: the "sole collective channel for the flow of biblical truth." It is guilty of false prophecy, anti-biblical theology, and misrepresentation of the truth.

We heartily recommend to Jehovah's Witnesses that they act on the following instruction from the Watchtower: "We need to examine, not only what we personally believe, but also what is taught by any religious organization with which we may be associated. Are its teachings in full harmony with God's Word, or are they based on the traditions of men? If we are lovers of the Truth, there is nothing to fear from such an examination" (*The Truth That Leads to Eternal Life*, 1968, p. 13).

Such an examination will show the shortcomings of the man-made Watchtower and the all-sufficient perfection of Jesus Christ, our "great God and Saviour" (Titus 2:13).

Jehovah's Witnesses Terms

Annihilation — According to Jehovah's Witnesses, unbelievers will not receive eternal punishment but rather will be annihilated, or cease to exist.

Arius — A heretic who lived in the fourth century A.D. arguments the fact that Jesus Christ was eternal God. His arguments against the deity of Christ have been repeated by such groups as Jehovah's Witnesses and the Unitarians.

Christadelphians — Cult founded in 1848 by John Thomas. It teaches among other unbiblical doctrines that Jesus Christ is not God and that the Holy Spirit is only a power, a forerunner of Jehovah's Witnesses.

Franz, Frederick W. — Fourth and current president of the Watchtower Bible and Society.

Little Flock — Another designation for the 144,000 Jehovah's Witnesses who live in heaven after their death. All other Jehovah's Witnesses are barred from heaven and live instead on Paradise Earth.

Michael the Archangel — According to the Watchtower, Jehovah's first creation, the archangel who later became the man Jesus.

Nathan Knorr — Third president of the Watchtower Bible and Tract Society. During his leadership (1942-1977) the Society increased from 115,000 to over two million members.

New World Translation of the Holy Scriptures — The official translation of the Bible by the Jehovah's Witnesses, characterized by their own biased interpretations.

Russell, Charles Taze — The founder of what is the present-day Jehovah's Witness (Watchtower Bible and Tract Society). Russell wrote voluminously including the six-volume work, *Studies in the Scriptures*, where he expounded his aberrational doctrines.

Rutherford, Judge J. F. — Second president of the Watchtower Bible and Tract Society. Gave group the name Jehovah's Witnesses in 1931. Rutherford centralized the authority of the Witnesses during his reign to its present-day headquarters in Brooklyn, New York.

Studies in the Scriptures — Seven-volume work, six of which were written by Charles Taze Russell, founder of Jehovah's Witnesses, that expounds the basic teachings of the Jehovah's Witnesses.

The Awake — Watchtower periodical designed to evangelize the public.

The Harp of God — A book by Judge Joseph Rutherford, second president of Jehovah's Witnesses, explaining Watchtower theology.

The Truth That Leads to Everlasting Life — Watchtower study book designed to introduce one to the Watchtower teachings

The Watchtower — One of the official publications of the Jehovah's Witnesses.

CHAPTER SIX

Mormonism

"B ut even though we, or an angel from heaven, should preach to you a gospel contrary to that which we have preached to you, let him be accursed" (Galatians 1:8 NASB).

History

The founder of Mormonism, or The Church of Jesus Christ of Latter-day Saints, Joseph Smith, Jr., was born on December 23, 1805 in Sharon, Vermont. Smith was the fourth of ten children of Joseph and Lucy Mack Smith. In 1817 the family moved to Palmyra, New York (near present-day Rochester).

Most of the members of the Smith family soon joined the Presbyterian church, but young Joseph remained undecided. His argument was that all the strife and tension among the various denominations made him question which denomination was right. It was this conflict that set the stage for Joseph's alleged first vision.

The First Vision

In 1820 Joseph allegedly received a vision that became the basis for the founding of the Mormon Church. According to Mormon history, the background of Joseph's first vision was a revival that broke out in the spring of 1820, in Palmyra, New York:

> Indeed, the whole district of the country seemed affected by it, and great multitudes united themselves to the different religious parties, which created no small stir and division amongst the people, some crying, "Lo, here!" and others, "Lo, there!" Some were contending for the Methodist faith, some for the Presbyterian and some for the Baptist (Joseph Smith, *The Pearl of Great Price*, 2:5).

This led to Joseph's inquiry of the Lord as to which of these denominations was right. Smith reported the incident as follows:

> My object in going to inquire of the Lord was to know which of all the sects was right, that I might know which to join. No sooner, therefore, did I get possession of myself, so as to be able to speak, than I asked the personages who stood above me in the light, which of all the sects was right—and which I should join.

I was answered that I must join none of them, for they were all wrong; and the personage who addressed me said that all their creeds were an abomination in His sight; that those professors were all corrupt; that: "they draw near to me with their lips, but their hearts are far from me, they teach for doctrines the commandments of men, having a form of godliness, but they deny the power thereof" (Joseph Smith, *The Pearl of Great Price*, 2:18, 19).

The Second Vision

Joseph then recounts a second vision he had on September 21, 1823, in which he claims:

...a personage appeared at my bedside, standing in the air, for his feet did not touch the floor.... Not only was his robe exceedingly white, but his whole person was glorious beyond description.... [He] said unto me that he was a messenger sent from the presence of God to me, and that his name was Moroni; that God had a work for me to do; and that my name should be had for good and evil among all nations, kindreds, and tongues, or that it should be both good and evil spoken of among all people. He said there was a book deposited, written upon gold plates, giving an account of the former inhabitants of this continent, and the source from whence they sprang. He also said that the fullness of the everlasting Gospel was contained in it, as delivered by the Savior to the ancient inhabitants; Also, that there were two stones in silver bows—and these stones, fastened to a breastplate, constituted what is called the Urim and Thummim—deposited with the plates; and the possession and use of these stones were what constituted "seers" in ancient or former times; and that God had prepared them for the purpose of translating the book.... While he was conversing with me about the plates, the vision was opened to my mind that I could see the place where the plates were deposited, and that so clearly and distinctly that I knew the place when I visited it.... Convenient to the village of Manchester, Ontario County, New York, stands a hill of considerable size, and the most elevated of any in the neighborhood. On the west side of this hill, not far from the top, under a stone of considerable size, lay the plates, deposited in a stone box.... I looked in, and there indeed did I behold the plates, the Urim and Thummim, and the breastplate, as stated by the messenger.... I made an attempt to take them out, but was forbidden by the messenger, and was again informed that the time for bringing them forth had not yet arrived, neither would it, until four years from that time; but he told me that I should come to that place precisely in one year from that time, and that he would there meet with me, and that I should continue to do so until the time should come for obtaining the plates.... on the twenty-second day of September, one thousand eight hundred and twenty-seven, having gone as usual at the end of another year to the place where they were deposited, the same heavenly messenger delivered them up to me with this charge: that I should be responsible for them; that if I should let them go carelessly, or through any neglect of mine, I should be cut off; but that if I would use all my endeavors to preserve them, until he, the messenger, should call for them, they should be protected (*The Pearl of Great Price*, Joseph Smith, 2:50-54).

Obeying the Heavenly Messenger

Joseph then moved to his father-in-law's house in Harmony, Pennsylvania where, with supposedly divine help, he began to copy the characters off the plates and translate them. The publication of the translation of the plates was financed by a New York farmer named Martin Harris who was told by Smith that the writing on the plates was "reformed Egyptian." The translation was finally completed and placed on sale on March 26, 1830.

A little over a week later, on April 6, 1830, at Fayette, New York, "the church of Christ" was officially organized with six members. The name was eventually changed to the Church of Jesus Christ of Latter-day Saints. The number of members increased rapidly and a group of them moved to Kirtland, Ohio (near present-day Cleveland). It was here that Joseph supervised the first printing of the divine revelations he had received.

First known as the *Book of Commandments*, the work has undergone significant and numerous changes and now constitutes one of the Mormon sacred works, retitled *Doctrine and Covenants*. Smith also worked on a revision ("divinely aided") of the King James Version of the Bible.

Although the Mormon church began to grow in numbers while expanding westward, it was not without persecution. Battles were fought between Mormons and their non-Mormon counterparts in Far West, Missouri, a town founded by the Mormons. Here Smith was imprisoned along with some other Mormon leaders.

After escaping, he and his followers moved to Illinois to a town Smith named Nauvoo, where he organized a small army and gave himself the title of Lieutenant-General. During this time, the Mormons were busily constructing a temple and evangelizing the populace.

When a local paper, the *Nauvoo Expositor*, began publishing anti-Mormon material, Smith ordered the press destroyed and every copy of the paper burned. This act led to Smith's arrest and imprisonment. Released and then rearrested, Smith was taken to jail in Carthage, Illinois along with his brother Hyrum.

On June 27, 1844, a mob of about 200 people, their faces blackened to avoid recognition, stormed the jail and shot and killed Joseph and Hyrum Smith. Joseph did not die without a fight. According to the church's own account he shot several of the mob members with a gun he had (see *History of the Church*, 6:617-18). The Mormons, however, considered Joseph Smith a martyr for the cause.

Brigham Young

After the death of Joseph Smith the leadership went to Brigham Young, the President of the Twelve Apostles, who convinced the great majority of Mormons that he was their rightful successor.

Young led the group westward in a journey which saw many hardships including Indian attacks, exposure and internal strife. On July 24, 1847, they arrived at Salt Lake Valley in Utah which became the headquarters of the Mormon church. By the time of Young's death in 1877, the members numbered approximately 150,000. Today, the church has over four million members worldwide.

The Claims of Mormonism

The Mormons claim they are the restoration of the true church established by Jesus Christ. It is not Protestant or Catholic, but claims, rather, to be the only true church. "If it had not been for Joseph Smith and the restoration, there would be no salvation outside the Church of Jesus Christ of Latter-Day Saints" (Bruce R. McConkie, *Mormon Doctrine*, p. 670).

"No salvation without accepting Joseph Smith...If Joseph Smith was verily a prophet, and if he told the truth...then this knowledge is of the most vital importance to the entire world. No man can reject that testimony without incurring the most dreadful consequences, for he can not enter the Kingdom of God" (Joseph Fielding Smith, *Doctrines of Salvation*, pp. 189-190).

The claims of Joseph Smith and his followers are clear. The Church of Jesus Christ of Latter-Day Saints claims it is God's true church on earth while all the others are wrong. Commenting on Joseph Smith's first vision, Dr. Walter Martin puts the matter into perspective:

> With one "Special Revelation" the Mormon Church expects its intended converts to accept the totally unsupported testimony of a fifteen-year-old boy that nobody ever preached Jesus Christ's gospel from the close of the Apostolic age until the "Restoration" through Joseph Smith, Jr., beginning in 1820! We are asked to believe that the Church Fathers for the first five centuries did not proclaim the true gospel—that Origen, Justin, Iraneaus, Jerome, Eusebius, Athanasius, Chrysostom, and then later Thomas Aquinas, Huss, Luther, Calvin, Zwingli, Tyndale, Wycliffe, Knox, Wesley, Whitefield, and a vast army of faithful servants of Jesus Christ all failed where Joseph Smith Jr., was to succeed!
>
> With one dogmatic assertion, Joseph pronounced everybody wrong, all Christian theology an abomination, and all professing Christians corrupt—all in the name of God! How strange for this to be presented as restored Christianity, when Jesus Christ specifically promised that "the gates of Hell" would not prevail against the church (Matthew 16:18)! In Mormonism we find God contradicting this statement in a vision to Joseph Smith Jr., some 18 centuries later! (*The Maze of Mormonism*, 1978, p. 31).

The Mormons make the claim that they are the "restored church of Jesus Christ" but the facts totally discount their claim.

Sources of Authority

The Mormon Church has four accepted sacred works: the Bible, the *Book of Mormon, Doctrine and Covenants,* and *The Pearl of Great Price.* The present prophet's words are also a source of authority.

The Bible

The Mormon articles of faith read, "We believe the Bible to be the Word of God in so far as it is translated correctly..." (*Articles of Faith of the Church of Jesus Christ of Latter-Day Saints*, Article 8). The Book of Mormon claims that a correct translation of the Bible is impossible since the Catholic Church has taken away from the word of God "...many parts which are plain and most precious; and also many covenants of the Lord have they taken away. And all this have they taken away. And all this have they done that they might pervert the right ways of the Lord" (1 Nephi 13:26b, 27).

Orson Pratt, an early apostle of the Mormon Church, put it this way,

"Who knows that even one verse of the Bible has escaped pollution, so as to convey the same sense now that it did in the original?" (*Orson Pratt's Works*, 1891, p. 218).

Thus the Mormons put more trust in the other three sacred books, which have escaped pollution, than they do in the Bible. This opens the door for the Mormons to add their new non-biblical teachings by claiming they were doctrines deliberately removed by the Catholic Church. The claim that the Scriptures have been changed and corrupted throughout the centuries is totally false (see *Answers*, Here's Life Publishers, 1980, pp. 4-6).

The Book of Mormon

The *Book of Mormon* is also considered inspired: "We also believe the Book of Mormon to be the Word of God" (*Articles of Faith*, Section Eight). The *Book of Mormon* is supposedly an account of the original inhabitants of America to whom Christ appeared after His resurrection.

Doctrine and Covenants

Doctrine and Covenants is a record of 138 revelations revealing some of Mormonism's distinctive doctrines such as baptism for the dead and celestial marriage.

The Pearl of Great Price

The *Pearl of Great Price* contains the *Book of Moses*, which is roughly equivalent to the first six chapters of Genesis, and *The Book of Abraham*, a translation of an Egyptian Papyrus that later proved to be fraudulent. It also contains an extract from Joseph Smith's translation of the Bible; extracts from the *History of Joseph Smith*, which is his autobiography; and the *Articles of Faith*.

The Living Prophets

The living prophet also occupies an important part in present-day Mormonism. Ezra Taft Benson, who at the time of this writing is President of the Council of the Twelve Apostles, said in a speech on February 26, 1980, at Brigham Young University, that the living prophet (head of the church) is "more vital to us than the standard works." This echoed what was given to the ward teachers (similar to Christian Education adult teachers) in 1945.

> Any Latter-day Saint who denounces or opposes, whether actively or otherwise, any plan or doctrine advocated by the prophets, seers, and revelators of the Church is cultivating the spirit of apostasy...Lucifer...wins a great victory when he can get members of the Church to speak against their leaders and to do their own thinking...
>
> "When our leaders speak, the thinking has been done. When they propose a plan—it is God's plan. When they point the way, there is no other which is safe. When they give directions, it should mark the end of the controversy (*Improvement Era*, June 1945, p. 354).

The Bible Says

The Bible contradicts the Mormon reliance on multiple contradictory revelations. While the Mormon scriptures contradict each other and the Bible, the Bible never contradicts itself and the God of the Bible never contradicts Himself. Hebrews 1:1-3 tells us what the source of our knowledge of God comes from:

> God, after He spoke long ago to the fathers in the prophets in many portions and in many ways, in these last days has spoken to us in His Son, whom He appointed heir of all things, through whom also He made the world. And He is the radiance of His glory and the exact representation of His nature, and upholds all things by the word of His power. When He had made purification of sins, He sat down at the right hand of the Majesty on high...

Any message that purports to be from God must agree with the message already brought by Jesus Christ in fulfillment of the Old Testament (Luke 24:27). Eternal life comes from the works and gift of Jesus Christ, not from Joseph Smith, Brigham Young, or any other false Mormon prophet (John 20:31). Proverbs 30:5, 6 warns those who try to add to God's Word, saying, "Every word of God is tested; He is a shield to those who take refuge in Him. Do not add to His words lest He reprove you, and you be proved a liar."

The Mormon Doctrine of God

"We believe in God, the Eternal Father, and His Son Jesus Christ, and in the Holy Ghost" (Joseph Smith, *The Pearl of Great Price*, Articles of Faith, p. 59).

The above statement leaves the impression that Mormons believe the biblical doctrine of the Holy Trinity—namely, there is one God who manifests himself in three persons, the Father, the Son, and the Holy Spirit, and these three persons are the one God. However, nothing could be further from the truth.

The Mormon doctrine of God is contradictory to what the Bible teaches. The Mormons believe in many gods and teach that God himself was once a man. Moreover, Mormon males have the possibility of attaining godhood. Joseph Smith made this clear in *The King Follett Discourse:*

> I am going to inquire after God: for I want you all to know him and be familiar with him...I will go back to the beginning before the world was, to show you what kind of a being God is.
>
> God was once as we are now, and is an exalted man, and sits enthroned in yonder heavens...I say, if you were to see him today, you would see him like a man in a form like yourselves in all the person, image, and very form of a man.
>
> I am going to tell you how God came to be God. We have imagined and supposed that God was God from all eternity. I will refute that idea and take away the veil so that you may see.
>
> It is the first principle of the gospel to know for certainty the character of God and to know that we may converse with him as one man with another, and that he was once a man like us; yea, that God himself, the father of us all, dwelt on an earth, the same as Jesus Christ did.
>
> Here then, is eternal life—to know the only wise and true God; and you

have got to learn how to be Gods yourselves, and to be kings and priests to God, the same as all Gods have done before you (Joseph Smith Jr., *King Follett Discourse*, pp. 8-10).

Other statements by Smith and Young reveal further the Mormon concept of God:

In the beginning, the head of the Gods called a council of the Gods; and they came together and concocted a plan to create and populate the world and people it (Joseph Smith, *Journal of Discourses*, 6:5).

The Father has a body of flesh and bones as tangible as man's (Joseph Smith, *Doctrine and Covenants*, 130:22).

Lorenzo Snow repeated Joseph Smith's words about the Mormon idea of God,

As Man is, God was,
   As God, is, Man may become.
(Joseph Smith, *King Follett Discourse*, p. 9, note by Lorenzo Smith).

The Mormon writer Milton Hunter came to the obvious conclusion:

Mormon prophets have continuously taught the sublime truth that God the Eternal Father was once a mortal man who passed through a school earth similar to that through which we are passing. He became God—an exalted being (Milton R. Hunter, *The Gospel Through the Ages*, p. 104).

Smith's teaching on the nature of God not only contradicts the Bible, it also contradicts the Book of Mormon!

And Zeezrom said unto him: 'Thou sayest that there is a true and living God?' And Amulek said: 'Yea, there is a true and living God.' Now Zeezrom said: 'Is there more than one God?' And he answered, 'No!' (Alma 11:26-29).

See also Alma 11:21, 22; 2 Nephi 11:7; 2 Nephi 31:21; 3 Nephi 11:27, 36; Mosiah 15:1-5, Mosiah 16:15.

The Bible repeatedly affirms that there is only one true God. Isaiah 43:10 emphatically declares, "You are My witnesses, declares the Lord, and My servant whom I have chosen, in order that you may know and believe Me, and understand that I am He. Before Me there was no God formed, and there will be none after Me."

In the New Testament we are assured that though there are false gods and idols worshipped by men, they are worthless. ". . .we know there is no such thing as an idol in the world, and that there is no God but one" (1 Corinthians 8:4).

Jesus Christ

The Mormon Church teaches that Jesus Christ was a preexistent spirit like the rest of us. Even though we are all literally brothers and sisters of Jesus, He is set apart from the rest of us by being the firstborn of God's spirit-children. "And now, verily I say unto you, I was in the beginning with the Father, and am the Firstborn; and all those who are begotten through me are partakers of the glory of the same, and are the church of the Firstborn. Ye were also in the beginning with the Father" (*Doctrine and Covenants* 93:21-23).

In Mormonism Jesus is not the unique Son of God:

> His humanity is to be recognized as real and ordinary—whatever happened to Him may happen to any one of us. The Divinity of Jesus and the Divinity of all other noble and stately souls, in so far as they, too, have been influenced by a spark of Deity—can be recognized as manifestations of the Divine (Elder B. H. Roberts citing Sir Oliver Lodge in Joseph Smith, *King Follett Discourse*, p. 11 note).

Man

According to Mormonism, man is a preexistent soul who takes his body at birth in this world.

> Man is a spirit clothed with a tabernacle. The intelligent part of which was never created or made, but existed eternally—man was also in the beginning with God (Joseph Fielding Smith, *Progess of Man*).
>
> Speaking of man, John Widtsoe said, "He existed before he came to earth: He was with God 'in the beginning.' Man's destiny is divine. Man is an eternal being. He also is 'everlasting to everlasting'" (*Varieties of American Religion*, p. 132).

Contrary to Mormon theology, Jesus Christ is the unique Son of God. John 1:14 declares that He "became flesh, and dwelt among us, and we beheld His glory, glory as of the only begotten from the Father, full of grace and truth." Jesus Christ reflected the power of God while on earth that no other man could ever achieve: "He is the image of the invisible God, the firstborn of all creation" (Colossians 1:15). To think that we can one day be God like Jesus Christ and the Father is blasphemous. There is an eternal chasm between the Creator and the created. The Bible soundly condemns those who would think otherwise:

> Professing to be wise, they became fools, and exchanged the glory of the incorruptible God for an image in the form of corruptible man and of birds and four-footed animals and crawling creatures. Therefore God gave them over in the lusts of their hearts to impurity, that their bodies might be dishonored among them. For they exchanged the truth of God for a lie, and worshipped and served the creature rather than the Creator, who is blessed forever. Amen (Romans 1:22-25).

Salvation

Articles 2 and 3 of the *Mormon Articles of Faith* spell out their doctrine of salvation:

> No. 2: "We believe that men shall be punished for their own sins and not for Adam's transgression."
>
> No. 3: "We believe that through the atonement of Christ, all mankind may be saved, by obedience to the laws and ordinances of the Gospel."

James Talmage in his work *Articles of Faith* explains what this means:

> The extent of the Atonement is universal, applying alike to all descendants of Adam. Even the unbeliever, the heathen and the child who dies before reaching the years of discretion all are redeemed by the Saviour's self-sacrifice from the individual consequences of the fall. . .of the saved not all will be exalted to the higher glories. No one can be admitted to any order of glory, in short, no soul can be saved until Justice has been satisfied for violated law. . .In the

kingdom of God there are numerous levels of gradations provided for those who are worthy of them (James Talmage, *Articles of Faith*, pp. 85, 91).

Thus in Mormonism there is a general salvation for all mankind and an individual salvation for each person. There is, to the Mormon, no such thing as hell or everlasting punishment. Everyone will eventually go to one of the three levels of glory: the celestial kingdom which is reserved for the Melchizedek priesthood members who will become gods; the terrestrial kingdom, for those who failed the requirements of exaltation; and lastly, the telestial kingdom, for those who have no testimony of Christ.

> I want you to tell them and tell all the great men of the earth, that the Latter-day Saints are to be their redeemer...Believe in God, believe in Jesus, and believe in Joseph his prophet, and Brigham his successor, and I add, If you will believe in your hearts and confess with your mouth Jesus is the Christ, that Joseph was a prophet, and that Brigham is his successor, you shall be saved in the kingdom of God...
>
> No man or woman in this dispensation will ever enter into the Celestial Kingdom of God without the consent of Joseph Smith...every man and woman must have the certificate of Joseph Smith, Junior, as a passport to their entrance into the mansions where God and Christ are—I can not go there without his consent...He reigns there as supreme, a being in his sphere, capacity, calling, as God does in Heaven (Brigham Young, *Journal of Discourses*, 6:229, 7:289).

Salvation according to the Bible is a free gift from Jesus Christ our Lord. Ephesians 2:8-10 declares, "For by grace you have been saved through faith; and that not of yourselves, it is the gift of God; not as a result of works, that no one should boast. For we are His workmanship, created in Christ Jesus for good works, which God prepared beforehand, that we should walk in them."

When the people asked Jesus, "What shall we do, that we may work the works of God?" (John 6:28), Jesus replied, "This is the work of God, that you believe in Him whom He has sent" (v. 29). There is no way to earn salvation. One's good works are testimony to the accomplished fact of one's salvation, purchased not by works, but by the blood of Jesus Christ. We are saved through Christ's sacrifice on the cross for our sins, not because of anything we can do ourselves. Hebrews 7:27 says that when Jesus offered Himself for man's sin it was "once for all."

Changes in the Book of Mormon

The *Book of Mormon* according to Joseph Smith, Jr., is "the most correct of any book on earth" (Joseph Smith, Jr., *History of the Church*, 4:461). However, this "most" correct book has, from the 1830 edition to the modern edition, undergone some 3,000 changes.

> And after having received the record of the Nephites, yea even my servant Joseph Smith, Jr., might have power to translate through the mercy of God, by the power of God, the Book of Mormon (*Doctrine and Covenants*, Section 1, verse 29).
>
> And gave him (Joseph Smith, Jr.) power from on high, by the means which were before prepared, to translate the Book of Mormon (*Doctrine and Covenants*, Section 20, verse 8).

The two quotations from the *Doctrine and Covenants*, according to Mormon belief, are revelations given through Joseph Smith, Jr., from the Lord, and they confirm the authenticity and genuineness of the *Book of Mormon*. The first quotation is from a revelation dated November 1, 1831, well over a year after the *Book of Mormon* was published in early 1830.

The revelations claim the *Book of Mormon* was translated by the power of God, that Joseph Smith was a servant used of God to translate the *Book of Mormon* using means that God had prepared for translating and that well over a year after its publication, the Lord affirmed the authenticity of the *Book of Mormon*. Yet a comparison of the latest edition with the first edition (the 1830 edition that was supposed to be translated by the power of God) will show the more than 3,000 changes.

Original (1830) Edition	Modern Version
. . . King Benjamin had a gift from God, whereby he could interpret such engravings. . . (p.200).	. . . King Mosiah had a gift from God, whereby he could interpret such engravings (p.176, v.28).
. . . Behold the virgin which thou seest, is the Mother of God (p. 25).	. . . Behold the virgin whom thou seest is the mother of the Son of God. . . (1 Nephi 11:18).
. . . that the Lamb of God is the eternal Father and the Saviour of the world. . . (p.32).	. . . that the lamb of God is the Son of the Eternal Father . . . (1 Nephi 13:40).

The Book of Mormon and Archaeology

Mormon scholars can be frustrated and embarrassed understandably when they realize that after all the years of work by Mormon and other archaeologists:

1. No *Book of Mormon* cities have been located.
2. No *Book of Mormon* names have been found in New World inscriptions.
3. No genuine inscriptions have been found in Hebrew in America.
4. No genuine inscriptions have been found in America in Egyptian or anything similar to Egyptian, which could correspond to Joseph Smith's "reformed Egyptian."
5. No ancient copies of *Book of Mormon* scriptures have been found.
6. No ancient inscriptions of any kind in America, which indicate that the ancient inhabitants had Hebrew or Christian beliefs, have been found.
7. No mention of *Book of Mormon* persons, nations, or places have been found.
8. No artifact of any kind, which demonstrates the *Book of Mormon* is true, has been found.
9. Rather than finding supportive evidence, Mormon scholars have been forced to retreat from traditional interpretations of *Book of Mormon* statements (Hal Hougey, *Archaeology and the Book of Mormon*, p. 12).

Dr. Gleason Archer has done an excellent job in listing a few of the anachronisms and historical inaccuracies in the Mormon scriptures (*A Survey of Old Testament Introduction,* pp. 501-504):

In 1 Nephi 2:5-8, it is stated that the river Laman emptied into the Red Sea. Yet neither in historic nor prehistoric times has there been any river *in Arabia* at all that emptied into the Red Sea. Apart from an ancient canal which once connected the Nile with the coast of the Gulf of Suez, and certain wadis which showed occasional rainfall in ancient times, there were no streams of any kind emptying into the Red Sea on the western shore above the southern border of Egypt.

Second Nephi states that only the family of Lehi, Ishmael, and Zoram were left in Jerusalem in 600 B.C. to migrate to the New World. These totaled fifteen persons, plus three or four girls, or no more than twenty in all. Yet in less than thirty years, according to 2 Nephi 5:28, they had multiplied so startlingly that they divided up into two nations (2 Nephi 5:5-6, 21). Indeed, after arriving in America in 589 B.C., they are stated to have built a temple like Solomon's.

Now Solomon's temple required 153,000 workers and 30,000 overseers (1 Ki. 5:13, 15; 6:1, 38; 9:20,21; 2 Ch 2:2, 17,18) in seven and a half years. It is difficult to see how a few dozen unskilled workers (most of whom must have been children) could have duplicated this feat even in the nineteen years they allegedly did the work. Nor is it clear how all kinds of iron, copper, brass, silver, and gold could have been found in great abundance (2 Nephi 5:15) for the erection of this structure back in the sixth-century B.C. America.

According to Alma 7:10, Jesus was to be born at Jerusalem (rather than in Bethlehem, as recorded in Lk. 2:4 and predicted in Mic. 5:2).

Helamen 14:20, 27 states that darkness covered the whole earth for three *days* at the time of Christ's death (rather than three hours, as recorded in Mt. 27:45 and Mk. 15:33), or beyond Easter morning, which would have made it impossible for the woman at the tomb to tell whether the stone had been rolled away from its mouth.

Alma 46:15 indicates that believers were called "Christians" back in 73 B.C. rather than at Antioch, as Acts 11:26 informs us. It is difficult to imagine how anyone could have been labeled Christian so many decades before Christ was even born.

Helaman 12:25,26, allegedly written in 6 B.C., quotes John 5:29 as a prior written source, introducing it by the words, "We read." It is difficult to see how a quotation could be cited from a written source not composed until eight or nine decades after 6 B.C.

Quite numerous are the instances in which the Mormon scriptures, said to have been in the possession of the Nephites back in 600 B.C., quote from or allude to passages or episodes found only in exilic or postexilic books of the Old Testament. Several examples follow.

1. First Nephi 22:15 states: "For behold, saith the prophet, the time cometh speedily that Satan shall have no more power over the hearts of the children of men; for the day soon cometh that all the proud and they who do wickedly shall be as stubble; and the day cometh that they must be burned." Compare this with Malachi 4:1 (ca. 435 B.C.): "For, behold, the day cometh, that shall burn as an oven; and all the proud, yea, and all that do wickedly, shall be stubble: and the day that cometh shall burn them up, saith the Lord of hosts, that it shall leave them neither root nor branch."

2. Second Nephi 26:9: "But the Son of righteousness shall appear unto them; and he shall heal them, and they shall have peace with him, until three generations shall have passed away." Compare this with Malachi 4:2: "But unto you

that fear my name shall the Sun of righteousness arise with healing in his wings; and ye shall go forth and grow up as calves of the stall." Note the confusion between *Son* and *Sun*, which could only have originated from their similar sound in the English language.

3. Third Nephi 28:21-22: "And thrice they were cast into a furnace and received no harm. And twice they were cast into a den of wild beasts; and behold they did play with the beasts as a child with a suckling lamb, and received no harm." Compare this with Daniel 3 and 6 where such adventures befell Shadrach, Meshach and Abednego, along with Daniel himself. It is difficult to understand how these Mormon believers could have had experiences just like those related in the book of Daniel, which was not even composed until several decades after their alleged departure for the New World in 589 B.C. (Daniel could have found written form only after the fall of Babylon to the Persians in 539 B.C., since it contains at least fifteen Persian loanwords.)

4. Alma 10:2 states that Aminadi "interpreted the writing which was upon the wall of the temple, which was written by the finger of God." Surely this is a reminiscence of Daniel's feat in reading the divine handwriting upon the wall of Belshazzar's banquet hall in 539 B.C.

Even more remarkable is the abundance of parallels or word-for-word quotations from the *New* Testament which are found in the Book of Mormon, which was allegedly in the possession of the Nephites back in 600 B.C. Jerald and Sandra Tanner (*The Case Against Mormonism*, Vol. 2, Salt Lake City, 1967, pp. 87-102) have listed no less than 400 clear examples out of a much larger number that could be adduced; and these serve to establish beyond all question that the author of the Book of Mormon was actually well acquainted with the New Testament, and specifically in the KJV of 1611. A few examples follow:

1. 1 Nephi 4:13: "That one man could perish than that a nation should. . .perish in unbelief." Compare this with John 11:50: "That one man should die for the people, and that the whole nation perish not."

2. 1 Nephi 10:8: "Whose shoe's latchet I am not worthy to unloose." Compare this with John 1:27: "Whose shoe's latchet I am not worthy to unloose."

3. 1 Nephi 10:9: "In Bethabara beyond Jordan. . .he should baptize." Compare this with John 1:28: "In Bethabara beyond Jordan, where John was baptizing."

4. 1 Nephi 11:22: "The love of God, which sheddeth itself abroad in the hearts of the children of men." Compare this with Romans 5:5: "The love of God is shed abroad in our hearts by the Holy Ghost."

5. 1 Nephi 11:27: "The Holy Ghost come down out of heaven and abide upon him in the form of a dove." Compare this with Luke 3:22: "The Holy Ghost descended in bodily shape like a dove upon him."

6. 1 Nephi 14:11: "The whore of all the earth, and she sat upon many waters; and she had dominion over all the earth, among all nations, kindreds, tongues, and people." Compare this with Revelation 17:1, 15: "The great whore sitteth upon many waters. . .The waters which thou sawest, where the whore sitteth, are peoples, and multitudes, and nations, and tongues."

Most interesting is the recently exposed fraud of the so-called Book of Abraham, part of the Mormon scripture known as *The Pearl of Great Price*. This was assertedly translated from an ancient Egyptian papyrus found in the mummy wrappings of certain mummies which had been acquired by a certain Michael H. Chandler.

In 1835 Joseph Smith became very much interested in these papyrus leaves, which he first saw in Kirtland, Ohio, on July 3, and arranged for the purchase of both mummies and manuscripts. Believing he had divinely received the gift of interpreting ancient Egyptian, he was delighted to find that one of the rolls contained the writings of Abraham himself, whose signature he had personally inscribed in the Egyptian language.

In 1842, Smith published his translation under the title, "The Book of Abraham" in *Times and Seasons*. He even included three drawings of the pictures or vignettes appearing in the manuscript, and interpreted the meaning of these illustrations: Abraham sitting upon the throne of Pharaoh, the serpent with walking legs who tempted Eve in Eden.

For many years this collection of papyri was lost, but somehow they (or else a duplicate set of them from ancient times) were presented to the Mormon Church by the Metropolitan Art Museum of New York City on November 27, 1967. This made the translation skill of Joseph Smith susceptible of objective verification.

The unhappy result was that earlier negative verdicts of scholars like Theodule Devaria of the Louvre, and Samuel A. B. Mercer of Western Theological Seminary, and James H. Breasted of the University of Chicago, and W. F. Flinders Petrie of London University (who had all been shown Smith's facsimiles) were clearly upheld by a multitude of present-day Egyptologists.

Their finding was that not a single word of Joseph Smith's alleged translation bore any resemblance to the contents of this document. It turned out to be a late, even Ptolemaic, copy in hieratic script of the Sensen Papyrus, which belongs to the same genre as the Egyptian Book of the Dead.

As John A. Wilson, professor of Egyptology at the University of Chicago, described it in a published letter written on March 16, 1966, it contains vignettes familiar from the Book of the Dead. The first illustration shows the god of embalming named Anubis preparing the body of the deceased for burial, with the soul hovering over his head in the form of a bird, and the canopic jars containing the dead man's inwards set beneath his bier.

The third picture shows the deceased led into the presence of Osiris, the infernal deity who judged the souls of the dead. (This is what Smith had identified as Abraham sitting on Pharaoh's throne!). Figure 2 was a round disc made of cloth and jesso and customarily placed as a pillow under the head of a corpse in the Late Egyptian period.

The accompanying text, as can be ascertained from other copies of this not uncommon document, deals with magical spells intended to open the mouth of the deceased and to prepare him for his audience before Osiris in the judgment hall of the dead (as set forth in detail in chap. 125 of the Book of the Dead, the Egyptian title of which is *P-r m h-r-w,* or, "The Going Forth by Day"). Needless to say, the completely mistaken concept of Joseph Smith as to his competence in ancient Egyptian is now clearly demonstrated to be beyond debate.

False Prophecies

The Mormon religion contains false prophecies. 2 Nephi 10:7, speaking of the Jews, predicts, ". . .When the day cometh that they shall believe in me, that I am Christ, then have I covenanted with their fathers that they shall be restored in the flesh, upon the earth, unto the lands of their inheritance." The Jews are today back in their land, but do not believe that Jesus is the Christ. The prophecy is false.

Building the Temple in Zion

Joseph claimed that the Lord told him the Latter-day Saints would build a temple in Zion (Jackson County, Missouri) during his generation. Zion would never be removed from its place. ". . .This generation shall not all pass away until an house shall be built unto the Lord. . .upon the consecrated spot as I have appointed" (*Doctrine and Covenants*, 84:5, 31, September 1832).

"Surely Zion is the city of our God, and surely Zion can not fall, neither be moved out of place, for God is there, and the hand of the Lord is there. . ." (*Doctrine and Covenants*, 97:19, August 1833).

These two prophecies failed since a temple was never built at the "appointed" place. Moreover, two weeks *before* Joseph gave the prophecy that Zion would not be "moved out of her place" the Mormons were unceremoniously run out of Zion. Their printing presses were destroyed, and some of their leaders were tarred and feathered! Joseph was in Kirtland, Ohio at that time and thus was ignorant of the situation in Jackson County, Missouri, when he uttered his prophecy. Later on that year Smith prophesied a return to Zion!

> Zion shall not be moved out of her place, notwithstanding her children are scattered. They that remain and are pure in heart, shall return and come to their inheritances, they and their children, with songs of everlasting joy, to build up the waste places of Zion—And all these things that the prophets might be fulfilled.
>
> And, behold, there is none other place appointed than that which I have appointed; neither shall there be any other placed appointed than that which I have appointed for the work of the gathering of my saints—Until the day cometh when there is found no more room for them; and then I have other places which I will appoint unto them, and they shall be called stakes, for the curtains or the strength of Zion (*Doctrine and Covenants* 101:17-21, 1833).

This is yet another false prophecy. It has been about 150 years since this "revelation" was given and a temple still has not been built on that site. Joseph said, "There is none other place appointed" and that it would be built during "his generation." He has failed all requirements of being a true prophet.

The God of the Bible never prophesies falsely. What He declares always comes to pass. Deuteronomy 13:1-4 and 18:18-22 gives us the two best tests of a self-proclaimed prophet. Deuteronomy 13 warns that a prophet, even if his prophecies come true, must lead you to believe in Jehovah God, the God of the Bible, or he is a false prophet. One who leads you to follow false gods is a false prophet and was to be stoned to death under the Old Testament theocracy.

Deuteronomy 18 warns that a prophet must be right about his prophecies every single time, or he is not a true prophet of God. The Mormon prophets fail the biblical tests of a prophet from God. Their prophecies are not from the Lord, and "the prophet has spoken presumptuously; you shall not be afraid of him" (v. 22).

Conclusion

When all the evidence is considered, the Mormon claim to be the restoration of Jesus Christ's church falls to the ground. We have taken up the challenge of Brigham Young who said, "Take up the Bible, compare the religion of the Latter-day Saints with it, and see if it will stand the test" (*Journal of Discourses*, Volume 16, p. 46, 1873).

Orson Pratt echoed the same sentiment, "Convince us of our errors of Doctrine, if we have any, by reason, by logical arguments, or by the Word of God and we will ever be grateful for the information and you will ever have the pleasing reflections that you have been instruments in the hands of God of redeeming your fellow beings" (*The Seer*, p. 15).

Our conclusion is that when Mormonism is weighed in the balances it is found wanting.

Mormonism Terms

Aaronic Priesthood—One of the two Mormon priesthoods into which Mormon leadership is divided. Includes the Presiding Bishopric, priests, teachers and deacons.

Adam—God—Said to be the God of this earth. Taught by second president, Brigham Young, now denied by LDS church.

Apostles—In Mormonism there are twelve apostles in the Melchizedek Priesthood, who are subordinate to the President of the Mormon Church.

Atonement—Jesus' atonement is not sufficient to cleanse all sins. Some sins must be atoned for by the individual. Early LDS teachings said one's own blood was to be spilt for such atonement.

Baptism for the Dead—Since LDS believes baptism is necessary for salvation, even the dead must be baptized by proxy, performed by living relatives.

Book of Abraham—Part of the Mormon sacred work *The Pearl of Great Price*, which contains the Mormon teachings that the black race is cursed.

Book of Mormon—One of the four sacred books of the Mormons containing a supposed history of the former inhabitants of America. It was supposedly translated from the golden plates.

Celestial Heaven—The highest of the three heavens in Mormon teaching.

Cumorah—The hill near Palmyra, New York where Joseph Smith, Jr. allegedly found the golden plates from which he translated the *Book of Mormon*.

Doctrine and Covenants—One of the four sacred books of the Mormons containing many revelations given allegedly by God to Joseph Smith, Jr.

High Priests—In Mormonism, the fourth level of the Melchizedek Priesthood. Consists of the Mormon stake presidents.

Lamanites—According to the *Book of Mormon*, the ancestors of the American Indian and their spiritual activities.

Living Prophets—In Mormonism, the current president of the Mormon church supposedly has the ability to receive divine revelations and is considered a "living prophet." His revelations are considered superior to all past revelations.

Lucifer—According to Mormonism, the spirit-brother of Jesus. In Mormon theology Lucifer is the second-born creature of God after Jesus.

Manuscript Found—A novel (1812-1814) by Solomon Spaulding which many believe was later plagiarized by Joseph Smith to form the *Book of Mormon*.

Melchizedek Priesthood—The most important of the two Mormon priesthoods consisting of the presidency, apostles, patriarch, high priest, seventies, and elders.

Moroni—The angel who supposedly revealed the location of the golden plates to Joseph Smith, Jr. Smith translated them into the *Book of Mormon*.

Nephites—One of the groups of people who, according to the *Book of Mormon*, came to America from the Middle East.

Patriarch—The nominal head of Mormon hierachy. It is an honorific title intially given to the father of the prophet.

Pearl of Great Price—One of the four sacred books of the Mormons containing, among other things, the *Book of Abraham* which teaches that the black race is cursed.

Presiding Bishopric—In Mormonism, the first division of the Aaronic Priesthood designated. The bishopric administers the local congregations, called wards.

Smith, Joseph Jr. (1805-1844)—Founder of the Church of Jesus Christ of Latter-day Saints (Mormon). Supposedly received a vision from God the Father informing him of certain golden plates which gave an account of the former inhabitants of America. Smith translated these plates which became the *Book of Mormon*.

Telestial Kingdom—Lowest division of glory (heaven) in Mormonism, reserved for those having no belief in Christ or the gospel.

Terrestrial Kingdom—a secondary degree of glory (heaven) reserved for those who, though honorable, failed to comply with the requirements of exaltation to Godhood.

Young, Brigham—Second president and successor to Joseph Smith, Jr., founder of the Church of Jesus Christ of Latter-day Saints (Mormon). Led the Mormons westward to Salt Lake City, Utah, where church is still headquartered.

CHAPTER SEVEN

Transcendental Meditation

The founder of TM, Mahesh Prasad Warma, later known as Maharishi Mahesh Yogi, was born in India around 1910. After graduating from Allahabad University in 1942 with a degree in physics, Mahesh became the disciple of the Indian religious leader Guru Dev. It was Guru Dev who instructed Maharishi to devise a meditation technique from the Vedas (part of the Hindu scripture).

The Maharishi (as he is referred to) was devoted to fulfilling the plan of Guru Dev in bringing his teachings to the world. In 1958 Maharishi founded the Spiritual Regeneration Movement in India. He came to America the following year and set up his organization while spreading the gospel of Guru Dev. Today, several million people in the United States and around the world have been taught the Maharishi's meditation techniques, said to be nonreligious, although thoroughly Hindu.

The Claims of TM

How would you like to have your health improved, your self-image and productivity increased, and your intelligence and creativity heightened without stress or tension?

According to its advertisements, these are some of the ways TM will benefit individuals. Allegedly all this can be done within any religious or nonreligious system since TM supposedly has no religious basis. Moreover, TM has developed some very admirable goals to accomplish this in the lives of people by setting up nationwide centers.

Under a World Plan, 350 teaching centers of the Science of Creative Intelligence have been founded in the largest cities throughout the United States and the world. In fact, resolutions drawn up by the Maharishi and promoting TM have been adopted by legislatures throughout the country.

TM can appeal to all segments of society, including the famous (such as the Beatles in the mid-60's), the counter-culture, the business community and the intelligentsia. Stanford law professor John Kaplan testifies, "I use it the way I'd use a product of our technology to overcome nervous tension. It's a non-chemical tranquilizer with no unpleasant side effects" (*Time Magazine*, October 30, 1975).

TM, however, is not a neutral discipline that can be practiced without harm to the individual. In actuality, TM is a Hindu meditation technique that attempts to unite the meditator with Brahman, the Hindu concept of God.

The Religious Nature of TM

Despite claims to the contrary, TM is religious in nature. The following is a translation of the Puja, the initiation ceremony read in Sanskrit by the TM instructor.

PUJA

Whether pure or impure, whether purity or impurity is permeating everywhere, whoever opens himself to the expanded vision of unbounded awareness gains inner and outer purity.

Invocation

To Lord Narayana, to lotus-born Brahma the Creator, to Vashishta, to Shakti, and to his son, Parashar, to Vyasa, to Shukadava, to the great Gaudapada, to Govinda, ruler among yogies, to his disciple, Shri Trotika and Varttika-Kara, to others, to the tradition of our masters I bow down. To the abode of the wisdom of the Shrutis, Smritis and Puranas, to the abode of kindness, to the personified glory of the Lord, to Shankara, emancipator of the Lord, I bow down. To Sharkaracharya, the redeemer, hailed as Krishna and Badarayana, to the commentator of the Brahma Sutras, I bow down again and again. At whose door the whole galaxy of gods pray for perfection day and night, adorned with immeasurable glory, perceptor of the whole world, having bowed down to him, we gain fulfillment. Skilled in dispelling the cloud of ignorance of the people, the gentle emancipator, Bramananda Saraswati—the supreme teacher, full of brilliance, him I bring to my awareness.

Offering

Offering the invocation to the lotus feet of Shri Guru Dev, I bow down.
Offering a seat to the lotus feet of Shri Guru Dev, I bow down.
Offering an ablution to the lotus feet of Shri Guru Dev, I bow down.
Offering a cloth to the lotus feet of Shri Guru Dev, I bow down.
Offering sandalpaste to the lotus feet of Shri Guru Dev, I bow down.
Offering rice to the lotus feet of Shri Guru Dev, I bow down.
Offering a flower to the lotus feet of Shri Guru Dev, I bow down.
Offering incense to the lotus feet of Shri Guru Dev, I bow down.
Offering light to the lotus feet of Shri Guru Dev, I bow down.
Offering water to the lotus feet of Shri Guru Dev, I bow down.
Offering fruits to the lotus feet of Shri Guru Dev, I bow down.
Offering water to the lotus feet of Shri Guru Dev, I bow down.
Offering betel leaf to the lotus feet of Shri Guru Dev, I bow down.
Offering coconut to the lotus feet of Shri Guru Dev, I bow down.
Offering camphor light.
   White as camphor, kindness incarnate, the essence of creation, garlanded with Brahman, ever dwelling in the lotus of my heart, the creative impulse

of cosmic life, to that in the form of Guru Dev, I bow down.

Offering camphor light to the lotus feet of Shri Guru Dev, I bow down.

Offering water to the lotus feet of Shri Guru Dev, I bow down.

Offering a handful of flowers.

Guru in the glory of Brahma, guru in the glory of Vishnu, guru in the glory of the great Lord Shiva, guru in the glory of personified transcendental fullness of Brahman, to him Shri Guru Dev, adorned with glory, I bow down. The unbounded, like the endless canopy of the sky, by whom the moving and unmoving universe is pervaded, by whom the sign of That has been revealed, to him to Shri Guru Dev, I bow down. Guru Dev, Shri Brahmananda, bliss of the absolute, transcendental joy, the self-sufficient, the embodiment of pure knowledge which is beyond and above the universe like the sky, the goal of "thou art That" and other such expressions which unfold eternal truth, the one, the eternal, the pure, the immovable, to the very being of that which is the witness of all intellects, whose status transcends thought, the transcendent along with the three gunas, the teacher of the truth of the Absolute, to Shri Guru Dev, I bow down. To him by whom the blinding darkness of ignorance has been removed by applying the balm of knowledge; the eye of knowledge has been opened by him and therefore to him, to Shri Guru Dev, I bow down. Offering a handful of flowers to the lotus feet of Shri Guru Dev, I bow down. (*An English Translation of TM's Initiatory Puja*, Berkeley, Calif.: Spiritual Counterfeits Project, n.d.)

From the translation of the Puja, the religious nature of TM can clearly be seen. In 1977, a New Jersey federal court barred the teaching of TM in the schools of that state, the presiding judge concluding, "The teaching of SCI/TM and the Puja are religious in nature; no other inference is permissible or reasonable. . . although defendants have submitted well over 1500 pages of briefs, affidavits and deposition testimony in opposing plaintiffs' motion for summary judgment, defendants have failed to raise the slightest doubt as to the facts or as to the religious nature of the teaching of the Science of Creative Intelligence and the Puja. The teachings of SCI/TM courses in New Jersey violates the establishment clause of the First Amendment, and its teaching must be enjoined" (United States District Court, District of New Jersey, Civil Action No. 76-341). Therefore the claim of the Maharishi and his followers as to the non-religious basis of TM has no basis in fact.

Is It Harmless?

"The TM program has no adverse side effects and can promote what pills cannot—natural psychological growth" (Harold Bloomfield, meditator and psychiatrist, *Discovering Inner Energy and Overcoming Stress*, p. 149).

There are, however, some authorities that would disagree with Bloomfield's statement.

That the dangers of meditation are considerable among the immature appear to be overlooked by these (TM) enthusiasts who regard meditation as a universal panacea (Una Kroll, M.D., *London Times*, June 30, 1973).

There are risks in cultivating altered states of consciousness. One of these risks. . .may be a permanent alienation from ordinary human attachments (Elsa First, child psychotherapist, *Frontiers of Consciousness*, p. 65, John White, ed.).

As a person enters or is in an ASC (altered state of consciousness), he often experiences fear of losing his grip on reality, and losing his self-control (Arnold M. Ludwig, *Altered States of Consciousness*, p. 16, Charles Tart, ed.).

The Maharishi

Many of the statements made by the Maharishi concerning the Science of Creative Intelligence and the Age of Enlightenment are disturbing:

There has not been and there will not be a place for the unfit. The fit will lead, and if the unfit are not coming along, there is no place for them. In the place where light dominates there is no place for darkness. In the age of Enlightenment there is no place for ignorant people. the ignorant will be made enlightened by a few orderly, enlightened people moving around. Nature will not allow ignorance to prevail. It just can't. Nonexistence of the unfit has been the law of nature (Maharishi, *Inauguration of the Dawn of the Age of Enlightenment*, MIU Press, p. 47).

The Science of Creative Intelligence structures all knowledge in the awareness of everyone and thereby makes everyone infallible (ibid., p. 49).

It is only childish and ridiculous to base one's life on the level of thinking. Thinking can never be a profound basis of living. Being is the natural basis. . .thinking, on the other hand, is only imaginary (Maharishi, *Transcendental Meditation*, p.99).

It is disturbing to think that Maharishi would eliminate opposers and that thinking is useless! The Bible says that judgment belongs only to the Lord Jesus Christ (John 5:22, 27) and that one should examine and test all things by God's Word (1 John 4:1).

The Religious Beliefs of TM

We have already observed that TM is religious in nature, based upon Hinduism, consequently their theology is in direct contrast to Christianity.

God

The Maharishi's view of God reflects a denial of the infinite-personal God revealed in Scripture. He writes, "God is found in two phases of reality: as a supreme being of absolute, eternal nature and as a personal God at the highest level of phenomenal creation" (*Science of Being and Art of Living*, Maharishi Mahesh Yogi, Rev. Ed. 1967, p. 271).

This "supreme being" is identified with nature: "Everything in creation is the manifestation of the unmanifested absolute impersonal being, the omnipresent God" (Maharishi Mahesh Yogi, *Transcendental Meditation*, p. 266). "This impersonal God is that being which dwells in the heart of everyone" (ibid, p. 269).

Man is also identified with God: "Each individual is, in his true nature, the impersonal God" (Maharishi Mahesh Yogi, *Science of Being and Art of Living*, Rev. Ed. 1967, p. 276). This same God is controlling evolution:

"God, the supreme almighty being, in whose person the process of evolution finds its fulfillment, is on the top level of creation" (Maharishi Mahesh Yogi, *Transcendental Meditation*, p. 270). "He (God) maintains the entire field of evolution and the different lives of innumerable beings in the whole cosmos" (ibid, p. 271).

Maharishi's view of God and man is not in accord with the Bible. Scripture teaches that God is infinite while man is finite. Man can never become God or attain Godhood for he is part of God's creation. Man is the creature. God is the creator. Although man is part of God's creation, he is not to be identified with God. God, the creator, is a being separate from His creation. God is by nature eternal, whereas God's creation is temporal (it came into being at a particular time). Man, the finite, will never become God, the infinite.

Jesus Christ

The Maharishi does not have much to say about Jesus but when he does, he contradicts the Bible.

> Due to not understanding the life of Christ and not understanding the message of Christ, I don't think Christ ever suffered or Christ could suffer...It's a pity that Christ is talked of in terms of suffering...Those who count upon the suffering, it is a wrong interpretation of the life of Christ and the message of Christ...How could suffering be associated with the One who has been all joy, all bliss, who claims all that? It's only the misunderstanding of the life of Christ (Maharishi Mahesh Yogi, *Meditations of Maharishi Mahesh Yogi*, pp. 123-124).

It is the Maharishi who misunderstands the purpose of Christ's coming, which was to die for the sins of the world. "The next day he saw Jesus coming to him, and said, Behold, the Lamb of God who takes away the sin of the world!" (John 1:29 NASB), and "Just as the Son of man did not come to be served, but to serve, and to give His life a ransom for many" (Matthew 20:28 NASB). Jesus Christ, contrary to the teaching of the Maharishi, suffered on the cross for our sins so we might receive forgiveness from God for our sins. His suffering was real.

Conclusion

Transcendental Meditation (The Science of Creative Intelligence), though claiming to be a method of relaxation and personal growth without harmful side effects, can be a danger to the individual both emotionally and spiritually. Although some degree of success in relaxation can be achieved by practicing TM, the dangers far outweigh the benefits. There is a Christian alternative to TM and that consists of meditation on God's Word, the only source of real peace. No one said it better than the psalmist:

> Blessed is the man that walketh not in the counsel of the ungodly, nor standeth in the way of sinners, nor sitteth in the seat of the scornful. But his delight is in the law of the LORD; and in his law doth he meditate day and night. And he shall be like a tree planted by the rivers of water, that bringeth forth his fruit in his season; his leaf also shall not wither; and whatsoever he doeth

shall prosper. The ungodly are not so: but are like chaff which the wind driveth away. Therefore the ungodly shall not stand in the judgment, nor sinners in the congregation of the righteous. For the LORD knoweth the way of the righteous: but the way of the ungodly shall perish (Psalm 1:1-6).

Transcendental Meditation Terms

Transcendental Meditation—Hindu religious sect founded by Maharishi Mahesh Yogi under the guise of the supposedly nonreligious Science of Creative Intelligence. Promises to expand one's awareness and creativity.

American Foundation for the Science of Creative Intelligence—One branch of TM organization.

Brahmins—The Hindu priestly class.

Guru Dev—The late Hindu Swami (religious master) who was the teacher of Maharishi Mahesh Yogi, the founder of TM. Dev is addressed as deity in the TM initiation ceremony.

International Meditation Society—One branch of TM organization.

Maharishi Mahesh Yogi—The founder of Transcendental Meditation (TM).

Mantra—In Hinduism, a sacred word which embodies through some specific supernatural and spiritual power. Also used as the meditative words in TM.

Prana—In TM, it is the internal force within God by which He creates.

Puja—In TM, a written portion of the initiation ceremony read in Sanskrit by the instructor. It is a collection of prayers to Hindu deities.

Sanatana dharma—A Hindu term, referring to Hinduism as the eternal system, the one true religion.

Students International Meditation Society—One branch of TM organization.

TM—Abbreviation for Transcendental Meditation.

Vedas—The collection of Hindu sacred scriptures.

Yoga—According to Hinduism, an exercise (physical, mental, or spiritual) designed to aid in one's progress to God-realization.

CHAPTER EIGHT

Theosophy

History

Theosophy literally means "wisdom of God." The modern Theosophical movement was founded in 1875 by Helena P. Blavatsky. The wisdom of God, according to Theosophists, is to be found in all religions: "What we desire to prove is, that underlying every once popular religion was the same ancient wisdom-doctrine, one and identical, professed and practiced by the initiates of every country who alone were aware of its existence and importance. To ascertain its origin and the precise way in which it was matured is now beyond human possibility" (A. P. Sinnett, *The Purpose of Theosophy*, Boston, 1888, p. 25).

Since there is truth in all religions, a Theosophist may pursue any religion he desires. This, however, did not stop Mrs. Blavatsky from detesting organized Christianity: "The name has been used in a manner so intolerant and dogmatic, especially in our day, that Christianity is now the religion of arrogance, par excellence, a stepping-stone for ambition, a sinecure for wealth, sham, and power; a convenient screen for hypocrisy" (H. P. Blavatsky, *Studies in Occultism*, Theosophical University Press, n.d., p. 138).

Source of Authority

There are no sacred books in Theosophy. Revelation comes from "adepts," who are "beings perfected spiritually, intellectually, and physically, the flower of human and all evolution" (*The Theosophical Movement*, p. 112). Mrs. Blavatsky was the first individual in Theosophy who received messages from these adepts and passed them on to the world.

The Teachings of Theosophy

A few sample quotations from Theosophical writings demonstrate their non-Christian character.

God

"We reject the idea of a personal...God" (H. P. Blavatsky, *Key to Theosophy*, Point Loma, California, Aryan Theosophical Press, 1913).

"We believe in a universal divine principle, the root of all, from which all proceeds, and within which all shall be absorbed at the end of the great cycle of being" (ibid., p. 63).

The rejection of a personal God is a rejection of the God of the Bible, the infinite-personal creator. Theosophy has no room for a God who has created man in His personal image: "Then God said, let us make man in Our image to Our likeness..." (Genesis 1:26 NASB).

Man

Theosophists teach that man consists of seven parts: 1. The body; 2. Vitality; 3. Astral body; 4. Animal soul; 5. Human soul; 6. Spiritual soul; and 7. Spirit. "Man is also equated with God, "...for you are God, and you will only what God wills; but you must dig deep down into yourself to find the God within you and listen to His voice which is your voice" (Krishnamurti, *At the Feet of the Master*, p. 10).

Man is evolving individually and corporately. Salvation is achieved when man's seventh stage is attained involving progressing from one body to another based upon his own self-effort. This is similar to the eastern doctrine of the law of Karma.

There is nothing in Scripture to suggest that man has a seven-part constitution. Rather he consists of body, soul and spirit, "Now may the God of peace Himself sanctify you entirely; and may your spirit and soul and body be preserved complete, without blame at the coming of our Lord Jesus Christ" (1 Thessalonians 5:23 NASB).

Jesus Christ

"...for Christ———the true esoteric saviour———is no man but the DIVINE PRINCIPLE in every human being" (H. P. Blavatsky, *Studies in Occultism*, Theosophical University Press, n.d., p. 134).

Mrs. Blavatsky, sounding like Christian Science, attempts to separate Christ from the person Jesus. However, Christ is merely his title, meaning "anointed one" or "messiah," designating the office Jesus held. There is no justification for making any distinction between Jesus and "The Christ." Furthermore, making Christ a principle rather than a true man is a denial of the whole purpose of His coming: "And the word became flesh and dwelt amongst us" (John 1:14 KJV).

Reincarnation

"No one is to blame except ourselves for our birth conditions, our character, our opportunities, our abilities, for all these things are due to the working out of forces we have set going either in this life or in former lives..." (Irving S. Cooper, *Theosophy Simplified*, p. 55).

The idea of reincarnation, that people must go through a series of lives to atone for their sins, is a denial of the work of Christ accomplished on the cross. Salvation has been made complete by Christ's sacrifice. There is nothing any of us can do to add or subtract from it. Consequently, there is no need for a series of births to accomplish what Christ has already completed.

The Afterlife

There is no heaven or hell as such in Theosophy. The Theosophist can reach a state of "nirvana" in which the individual is absorbed by the impersonal world, losing all personal consciousness.

The Bible teaches that there is an existence after death for everyone. Those who have put their trust in Jesus Christ will forever reside in God's presence while those who reject Christ will spend eternity apart from him. John's gospel makes this plain: "He who believes in the Son has eternal life; but he who does not obey the Son shall not see Life, but the wrath of God abides on him" (John 3:36 NASB).

The Bible

"I confined myself to the Hindu Scriptures, and in all cases I stated that I regarded these scriptures and the Hindu religion as the origin of all scriptures and all religions" (Annie Besant, *The Daily Chronicle*, April 9, 1894).

This statement totally denies the basic premise of the Christian faith, namely, that God has given the world a unique revelation concerning who He is and who we are (Hebrews 1:1-3). The Bible cannot be God's inspired word if its origin is found in Hinduism.

Conclusion

When Theosophy beliefs are examined, we discover the whole Theosophical system is contrary to Christianity. There is, therefore, no possibility of reconciliation between the two, since the followers of Theosophy extol Buddhist and Brahmanic theories, and Christians follow Jesus Christ alone.

Theosophy Terms

Theosophy—Literally means "wisdom of God." Theosophy is a cult founded by Helena Blavatsky in 1875 and which attempts to expound on the wisdom of God found in all religions. Occultic practices are used within the group.

Adept—In Theosophy, a being from the spirit world who communicates revelations. Also known as Bodhisattva or Mahatma.

Animal Soul—The fourth principle of human nature, according to Theosophy. The majority of people alive today are at this level.

Atlantean—According to Theosophy, it is the second of three levels thus far reached in human evolution.

Besant, Annie—British woman who was a highly influential leader in Theosophy as a successor to founder Helena Blavatsky. In 1906 she publicly announced to the world the coming of the Messiah, Krishnamurti, whom she reared as a child. Krishnamurti later renounced his role.

Blavatsky, Helena Petrovna—(1831-1891). Founder of Theosophy. Incorporated occultic and eastern beliefs and practices together.

Devachan—The Theosophist's heaven.

Devas—Persons who, according to Theosophy, have been freed from their bodily prisons and are now in the world of the mind.

H.P.B.—Common designation in Theosophy for founder Helena P. Blavatsky.

Koot Hoomi—In Theosophy, one of the adepts who gave revelations to founder Madame Blavatsky.

Krishnamurti—Supposed Messiah figure in Theosophy who later renounced his role.

Leadbeater, C. W. Along with Annie Besant, succeeded Helena Blavatsky in directing the Theosophical movement.

Mahatma—In Theosophy, an adept, a being from the spirit world who communicates through spiritually receptive living persons.

CHAPTER NINE

EST

History

B ut don't get me wrong, I don't think the world needs EST; I don't think the world needs anything; the world already is and that's perfect."
"If nobody needs it then why do you do it?"
"I do it because I do it because that's what I do."
(Adam Smith, *"Powers of Mind, Part II: The EST Experience,"* New York, September 29, 1975, p. 284).

This statement is from an interview with former used car salesman John Paul Rosenberg, now known as Werner Erhard, founder and director of EST (Erhard Seminars Training) one of the fastest-growing movements in America. Thousands of people, including prominent public figures, have given glowing testimonies of the transforming effects of EST.

Dr. Herbert Hansher, psychology professor at Temple University, has called EST "one of the most powerful therapeutic experiences yet devised" (Adelaid Bry, EST: *60 Hours that Transform Your Life*, New York: Avon, 1976, p. 200). Singer/Songwriter John Denver has said of his EST encounters, "It's the single most important experience of my life" (*Newsweek*, December 20, 1976).

Although not primarily religious in nature, EST denies the basic beliefs of the historic Christian faith, yet claims compatibility with Jesus Christ and Christianity. It is for this reason we treat EST with the non-Christian cults.

By way of background, Erhard (or Rosenberg) traveled the religious merry-go-round of Scientology, Zen Buddhism, yoga, hypnosis, Silva Mind Control and a host of other religious movements before presenting the world with EST in 1971 ("Werner Erhard—An Interview with the Source of EST" Part 1, *The New Age Journal*, No. 7, Sept. 15, 1975, pp. 18-20).

What is EST?

EST consists of 60 hours of intensive training, usually on two successive weekends, where the initiate attempts to reach the goal of EST: "getting it." It is, however, never clear exactly what one gets, for Erhard's system is a unique combination of Zen Buddhism, Scientology, and Vendanta

Hinduism, coupled with the power of positive thinking.

Erhard has said, "We want nothing short of a total transformation — an alteration of substance, not a change of form" (Werner Erhard, *What's So*, Jan. 1975). This alteration or transformation is accomplished during the training sessions by attempting to change the individual's concept of who he is. Once a person's belief system is shredded, the person becomes vulnerable to accepting the ESTian world view.

The Philosophy of EST

Erhard's world view of life is perfect, with no difference between right and wrong. "Life is always perfect just the way it is. When you realize that, then no matter how strongly it may appear to be otherwise, you know that whatever is happening right now will turn out all right. Knowing this, you are in a position to begin mastering life" (Werner Erhard, *What's So*, January 1975). "Wrong is actually a version of right. If you are always wrong you are right" (Adelaide Bry, op. cit., p. 192).

Accordingly, there is no objective truth, no absolutes except the absolute of "whatever is, is right." With this viewpoint one could argue that anyone has the right to do whatever he wishes, including killing six million Jews, because he is perfect. Such a world view opens the door to frightening possibilities.

At the heart of the ESTian world view is the assumption that God is man and man is God, and that each individual must come to understand he is his own God. John Denver illustrated this assumption in his statement, "I can do anything. One of these days, I'll be so complete I won't be human, I'll be a god" (*Newsweek*, Dec. 20, 1976).

Erhard's seminars attempt to enlighten the uninitiated to this truth. As one EST trainer told his trainees, "It ought to be perfectly clear to everyone that you are all (expletive deleted) and I'm God. Only an (expletive deleted) would argue with God" (Luke Rhinehart, *The Book of EST*, New York: Holt Rhinehart and Winston, 1976, p. 47).

Seeing that all of us are God, we are now provided with justification to do whatever we please, since as God we are answerable to no one.

God

If indeed we ourselves are God, the need to look to a supreme being for salvation is gone, and the God of the Bible is unnecessary. Erhard has stated, "For instance, I believe that the belief in God is the greatest barrier to God in this universe — the single greatest barrier. I would prefer someone who is ignorant to someone who believes in God because the belief in God is a total barrier, almost a total barrier to the experience of God" (Werner Erhard, *East-West Journal*, September 1974).

The Bible reveals not only that man is not God, but that he can never become God. God is by nature infinite (unlimited) whereas man is finite (limited). God is the creator and man is the creature. We are dependent on Him for our very existence.

> The God who made the world and all things in it, since He is Lord of Heaven and earth, does not dwell in temples made with hands; neither is He served

by human hands, as though he needed anything since He Himself gives to all life and breath and all things (Acts 17:24, 25 NASB).

Jesus Christ

Jesus supposedly was saying the same sort of thing as Erhard. Consequently in EST there is no need to give Jesus Christ any special adoration.

> ...the church totally misinterpreted what Jesus said. He kept telling over and over that everybody was like He was: perfect. He was experiencing life, like Werner. He knew He was the total source, living moment to moment, and was spontaneous.
>
> Jesus is just another guru who happens to be popular here in Western Civilization. I can't go into a church and praise Jesus. But I really got where he is coming from. He wants to let everybody know "I'm you." So my whole point of view about religion has totally altered (Adelaid Bry, op. cit., p. 182).

It is difficult to understand how anyone who reads the Bible could believe Jesus said everyone was perfect. The truth is that Jesus said: "...for unless you believe that I am He, you shall die in your sins" (John 8:24 NASB). "For from within, out of the heart of men, proceed the evil thoughts, fornications, thefts, murders, adulteries, deeds of coveting and wickedness, as well as deceit, sensuality, envy, slander, pride and foolishness. All these evil things proceed from within and defile the man" (Mark 7:21-23).

Furthermore, as uniquely God in human flesh, Jesus deserves our worship, "...at the name of Jesus, every knee should bow, of those who are in heaven, and on earth, and under the earth, and that every tongue should confess that Jesus Christ is Lord to the glory of God the Father" (Philippians 2:10, 11).

Conclusion

The entire EST system centers around the self-centered individual rather than the biblical God. In EST, God is non-existent. Any religious or psychologically-manipulating system that leads people away from the true and living God is functioning as antichrist and should be avoided.

The experience EST offers is a pseudo-answer to man's deepest need. Only a personal relationship with Jesus Christ can truly satisfy the longing of the human heart. Jesus said, "If therefore the Son shall make you free you shall be free indeed" (John 8:36 NASB).

EST Terms

The Centers Network—New legal name for EST.

EST—Designation for Erhard Seminars Training, advertised as non-religious self-help training sessions designed to bring participants to fulfillment. Teaches that you are your own God, and that everything you experience (even bad things like assault) is a product of your own divine creative will.

Erhard, Werner—Founder of Erhard Seminars Training (EST). Born John Paul Rosenberg, Erhard experimented with a variety of groups including

Silva Mind Control, Zen, and Scientology before forming his own self-help cult, EST.

Games—EST's name for the external world and its events. EST declares that the world of games is illusory. The only reality exists in the individual's mind.

Trainers—EST staff persons who conduct and teach the EST seminars.

Truth Process—One segment of EST's seminar.

CHAPTER TEN

Children of God

T he founder of the original Children of God, now known as the Family of Love, is David Brandt Berg, born in Oakland, California, February 18, 1919. David Berg's parents were Virginia Brandt Berg, a prominent evangelist, and Mr. Berg, a minister with the Christian and Missionary Alliance. Eventually Mr. Berg's ministry was overshadowed by his wife's ministry, and he became part of her evangelistic team.

David Berg became a pastor with the Christian and Missionary Alliance Church sometime in the late 1940's. His first pastorate was in Arizona in 1949. However, a year later, in 1950, he left after a falling-out with the leadership of the church. This experience left him with great bitterness and permanent contempt for organized religion. His belief that God had a special destiny and mission for him developed shortly after this. In one publication, Berg recounted one of his early revelations:

> One of the first prophecies we ever received regarding my personal ministry was "I have made thee a sharp-toothed threshing instrument which shall beat the mountains as chaff and rip with violence the pillows from under the arms of them which sit at ease in Zion!" (Moses David, *The Disciple Revolution*, London: The Children of God, 1975, pp. 7, 8).

In 1968, with his wife Jane and their four children, Berg moved to Huntington Beach, California. It was here that Berg developed a small following of people, basically from the counter-culture. In 1969, Berg became convinced that a great earthquake was imminent and California would slide into the Pacific Ocean. He and about 50 followers left California for Arizona where their disruption of church services and condemnation of organized churches resulted in their being asked to leave.

The group, now numbering 75, wandered across the United States and Canada, staging demonstrations along the way. It was during this time they adopted the name, "Children of God, and Berg took the name of Moses David, or "Mo." All converts take Bible names as a symbol of their "new birth."

In 1970, the group was allowed to use the facilities in Texas and California owned by T.V. evangelist Fred Jordan. Within the next one and a half years the group grew to 250. However, a disagreement arose between Jordan and the group at one of his properties and they were banished from all his properties. The Children of God then divided into small groups of fewer than 12 people and scattered across the country.

The Children of God, who now call themselves the Family of Love, boast about 7,000 members (including children) in approximately 80 countries. Since 1972, Berg has permanently resided in Europe where he oversees his group and writes his letters.

Source of Authority

There is no question as to who is the authority in the Children of God. It is David Berg, a man who considers himself to be a prophet for this generation. Members of the Children of God can receive God's truth only through "Father" Moses David:

> The structure (of the Children of God organization)...like a tree, with Jesus as its Root and Foundation Stump, your Prophet and King (David Berg as its chief administrator, with the sap of God's Word as its life's blood). (Moses David, *The New Leadership Revolution*, London: The Children of God, 1975, p. 2).

He communicates to his disciples by means of MO letters, which are considered authoritative: "Do you want to know what the real avant-garde of this movement is? It's the MO letters! That's what is leading us all! All the general on the battlefield does is carry out the orders that come from higher up, from the Lord through MO!" (Faith David, *Pioneering, Popularity, and Persecution*, London: Children of God Trust, Oct. 25, 1973, DO #20, p. 5).

His "MO" letters are to be taken at face value:

> We have heard of quite a few instances where leaders have changed the meaning of my letters by their actions or verbal interpretations. My letters mean exactly what they say, literally, and they don't need explaining away, spiritualizing or reinterpreting by anyone (Moses David, *Reorganization, Nationalization, Revolution!*, Rome: Children of God, Jan., 1978, DO #650).

The Beliefs of the Children of God

There has never been a statement of belief issued by the Children of God, so their views on theology must be gleaned from the vague and contradictory writings of Berg. Since it is difficult to systematize their beliefs about God, we will cite some of Berg's statements to give you a sample of their erratic nature:

> "Well, if they believe in the virgin birth then they have got to believe in the divinity of Jesus, that He was partly God, even though according to some of their advocates they claim they don't. See they're contradicting their own Bible, because if He was virgin-born then He was the Son of God!
> "Even so God createth what He willeth"—In other words He, Jesus, was a creation of God. Oh, this is exactly according to the Scriptures! Can you think

of a verse on it? What does God's Word say about Jesus? It says that He was "the beginning of the creation of God!" (Rev. 3:14).

Now you know the Catholics and some are so strong on the so-called Trinity, but I don't even believe in the Trinity. You can't find that word in the Bible, so why should I believe it? But I believe in the Father and I believe in the Son, Jesus, and I believe in the Holy Ghost.

If you want to call it Trinity, all right, but I don't believe in it in some ways, the way some overemphasize and stress it, you know. You would think that Jesus just always was, just like God, but in a sense He was not until He was made man, although He was in the beginning and He was a part of God. But God's Word also says that He was the beginning of the creation of God—you know where that's found? I recall it's in Revelation in the first two or three chapters there" (Moses David, *Islam*, [Ch. 1], Rome Children of God, May 18, 1975, Dfo, No. 631, p. 14).

Revolution

The Children of God is a revolutionary organization, emphasizing "forsaking all" for Jesus. This includes giving up of all material possessions to the group and the forsaking of their allegiance to families. Originally, Berg's message was one of dropping out of the corrupt system and joining God's system, the Children of God. Recently, however, he has emphasized that his followers should use the system for their own end, rather than totally dropping out. The following is a sample of what Berg has said about "the system"·

You, my dear parents, are the greatest rebels against God and his ways—not us, and unto you will be the greater condemnation; for how can we rebel against a God whom we know not, whose ways you never showed us, and you denied Him. You heard His Word, but heeded it not. You were shown His Ways, but followed them not...

To hell with your devilish system. May God damn your unbelieving hearts. It were better that a millstone be hung around your neck and you be cast into the midst of the sea than to have caused one of these little ones to stumble. You were the real rebels, my dear parents, and the worst of all time. God is going to destroy you and save us, as we rebel against your wickedness, deny your ungodliness, break your unscriptural traditions and destroy your idolatrous System in the name of God almighty (Moses David, *The Revolutionary Rules*, London, Children of God, March 1972, GP No. S-RV, p. 1).

Sex

The writings of Berg are filled with references and allusions to unbiblical sex. Over the years his preoccupation with sex has become more and more noticeable in his writings. The sexual practices of the Children of God were exposed in an interview in *Christianity Today,* February 18, 1977, when Joseph Hopkins questioned two former members and leaders of the Children of God, Jack Wasson and David Jacks:

Hopkins: What about sex in the COG? There have been rumors of immorality and hanky-panky in the higher echelons. Are they true?
Jacks: Extramarital relationships, definitely. Berg cites Abraham, Solomon, David, and so on, as examples for his having concubines. The top leaders have

sexual affairs with girls in the group. But the disciples are practically eunuchs for a year or so until they get married in the COG.

Wasson: This fooling around with sex goes way back. Married couples were encouraged as a group to participate in "skinny-dipping"—swimming in the nude. It was considered unrevolutionary not to participate. And COG members will do almost anything to avoid being called unrevolutionary. It was also policy for all married couples to attend evening "leadership training" sessions at the TSC (Texas Soul Clinic) Ranch in west Texas in the early days of the COG. These sessions would be led by David Berg, and no matter what subject they started out about, they always ended up on the subject of sex, with David Berg frequently leading the couples into a mass love-making session while he looked on. Then this doctrine came up that was taught only among the top leadership: "all things common," based on Acts 2:44. They applied the "all things" even to wives and husbands. The wife-and-husband-swapping was not explicitly condoned in a MO letter, but it was allowed and participated in by the top leadership.

Conclusion

Over the years the Children of God have strayed further and further away from the truth of the Gospel. Many misguided individuals, including some Christians, have joined this cult only to be misled by their false and unbiblical teachings. David Berg is not who he claims to be, God's prophet for this generation. Rather, he is a false prophet—"the blind leading the blind." Anyone who truly desires to serve God should not join this cult. They are indeed *not* the Children of God.

Children of God (Family of Love) Terms

Children of God (Family of Love)—Small cult founded by David "Moses" Berg in Southern California in 1968. Emphasizes forsaking all, including family, to follow Jesus.

Berg, David Brandt—Former fulltime worker with the Christian and Missionary Alliance Church. Berg was asked to leave his church and soon thereafter founded the Children of God in Huntington Beach, California. He took the designation Moses and considers himself a modern-day prophet.

COG—Designation for the Children of God cult.

Family of Love—Current name of the Children of God cult.

Father David—Pseudonym for David Berg, founder of the Children of God cult.

Flirty Fishing (Ffing)—Term used by the Children of God cult referring to the use of sex to entice people to join or contribute to their cult.

King David—Pseudonym for David Berg, founder of the Children of God cult.

Litnessing—Term used by the Children of God referring to the passing out of literature in exchange for donations.

MO Letters—Letters written by David "Moses" Berg, leader of the Children of God, to his followers. These letters are considered by the

Children of God members as scripture on the same level of inspiration as both the Old and New Testaments.

Moses David—Pseudonym for David Berg, founder of the Children of God cult.

The New Nation News—Periodical published by the Children of God cult.

CHAPTER ELEVEN

The Unification Church "Moonies"

T he founder and leader of the Unification Church is Sun Myung Moon who was born in Korea on January 6, 1920. His family converted to Christianity when he was ten and became members of the Presbyterian Church.

The Vision

At age 16 young Moon experienced a vision while in prayer on a Korean mountainside. Moon claims that Jesus Christ appeared to him in the vision admonishing him to carry out the task that Christ had failed to complete. Jesus supposedly told Moon that he was the only one who could do it. Finally, after much repeated asking by Jesus, Moon accepted the challenge.

Moon spent the next few years of his life preparing for the great spiritual battle ahead. The years between his "conversion" experience and his coming to America are shrouded in much controversy. For documentation on those intervening years we would recommend *The Moon is Not the Son* by James Bjornstad, Minneapolis: Dimension Books/Bethany House Press, 1976.

Moon Comes to America

After achieving success with his new religion in the Far East, especially South Korea, Moon came to America at the end of 1971 and his cult began to flourish. Today they claim some two million members worldwide.

The Claims of Sun Myung Moon

Sun Myung Moon has made it clear that he believes himself to be the Messiah for this age.

> With the fulness of time, God has sent his messenger to resolve the fundamental questions of life and the universe. His name is Sun Myung Moon. For many decades, he wandered in a vast spiritual world in search of ultimate truth. On this path he endured suffering unimagined by anyone in human history. . . He fought alone against myriads of satanic forces in both the spiritual and physical worlds, and finally triumphed over them all. In this way, he came in contact

with many saints in paradise and with Jesus, and thus brought into Light all the heavenly secrets through his communion with God (Sun Myung Moon, *Divine Principle*, p. 16).

Moon has also said, "No heroes in the past, no saints or holy men in the past, like Jesus or Confucius, have excelled us" (Sun Myung Moon, "Our Shame," translated by Won Pok Choi, from *Master Speaks*, March 11, 1973, p. 3).

Even though Moon's doctrines are opposed to Christianity, he claims that it was Jesus who revealed them to him. "You may again want to ask me, 'With what authority do you weigh these things?' I spoke with Jesus Christ in the spirit world. And I spoke also with John the Baptist. This is my authority. If you cannot at this time determine that my words are the truth, you will surely discover that they are in the course of time. These are hidden truths presented to you as a new revelation. You have heard me speak the Bible. If you believe the Bible, you must believe what I am saying" (Rev. Moon, *Christianity in Crisis*, p. 98).

And, like all cult leaders, Moon claims exclusive knowledge. "We are the only people who truly understand the heart of Jesus, and the hope of Jesus" (Rev. Moon, *The Way of the World*, p. 20).

Source of Authority

In the Unification Church the writings and teachings of Moon take precedence over the Bible, "It may be displeasing to religious believers, especially to Christians, to learn that a new expression of truth must appear. They believe that the Bible, which they now have, is perfect and absolute in itself" (*Divine Principle*, 2nd ed., 1973, p. 9).

Moon further stated, "... The New Testament Words of Jesus and the Holy Spirit will lose their light ... to 'lose their light' means that the period of their mission has elapsed with the coming of the new age" (*Divine Principle*, p. 118). The basic work containing the supposed revelation given to Moon is entitled the *Divine Principle*.

The Divine Principle

For the members of the Unification Church, the *Divine Principle* is the ultimate authoritative work, superseding even the Bible. The *Divine Principle* is known as the completed testament because it supposedly contains the present truth for this age which heretofore had never been revealed.

The assertions of Moon are at complete odds with the Bible. The Scriptures testify that the Word of God is eternal: "The grass withers, the flower fades, but the Word of God stands forever" (Isaiah 40:8 NASB). Jesus said, "Heaven and earth shall pass away, but my Words shall not pass away" (Matthew 24:35). The idea that the words of Jesus will somehow lose their light is totally foreign to the teaching of the Bible.

Moreover, the Bible records the strongest condemnation for those who would add to what the Scriptures have revealed, "You shall not add to the Word which I am commanding you, nor take away from it. That you may keep the commandments of the Lord your God which I command you" (Deuteronomy 4:2 NASB). "I testify to everyone who hears the words of the prophecy of this book; if anyone adds to them, God shall add to him the plagues which are written in this book" (Revelation 22:18 NASB).

Furthermore, the Scriptures make it plain that the faith has been "once for all delivered to the saints" (Jude 3). Any so-called revelation that contradicts that which was previously revealed is guilty of adding to the Word of God and should be discarded. The *Divine Principle* is in this category.

Unification Doctrine

Basic to Moon's world view is the concept of dualism. All of existence is dual: Father God and Mother God; Male and Female; Light and Dark; Yin and Yang; Spirit and Flesh. Each part of existence has its dual aspect. Moon's God (with dual male/female aspects) always acts in a dual manner with his dual creation.

The Fall of Man

According to the *Divine Principle*, until now no one has correctly understood the Genesis account of the fall of man. The *Divine Principle* teaches there were two falls, one physical and one spiritual. Moreover, both falls were sexual in nature. Eve supposedly had an illicit sexual relationship with Lucifer causing the spiritual fall. Afterward, her sexual relationship with spiritually immature Adam resulted in the physical fall.

The *Divine Principle* justifies this by saying, "It is the nature of man to conceal an area of transgression. They covered their sexual parts, clearly indicating that they were ashamed of the sexual areas of their bodies because they had committed sin through them" (*Divine Principle*, p. 72).

Since there was a dual aspect of the fall there also needs to be a dual aspect of redemption, necessitating both physical and spiritual salvation.

The Coming of Christ

When Jesus Christ came to earth, He was supposed to redeem mankind both physically and spiritually, but He failed in His mission: "Jesus failed in His Christly mission. His death on the cross was not an essential part of God's plan for redeeming sinful man" (*Divine Principle*, pp. 142, 143).

The ministry of Christ, however, was not a total failure for He did accomplish a "spiritual" salvation at the cross of Calvary, but He failed in achieving a "physical salvation" for mankind (*Divine Principle*, p. 151).

John the Baptist

Moon believes the major reason for Jesus' crucifixion was John the Baptist's failure. John was supposed to clear the way for Jesus to come to the people of his day but failed because he lost faith. This caused the people to abandon Jesus and eventually resulted in His death. The crucifixion was not something God desired because the work of Christ was unfinished. It is here where Sun Myung Moon picks up where Jesus left off. Moon is supposedly the "third Adam," the one who is called to redeem mankind physically.

Jesus Christ

Moon has a non-biblical view of the person of Jesus Christ by denying the unique deity of Jesus Christ.

"Jesus is the man of this value. However great his value may be, he cannot assume any value greater than that of a man..." (Rev. Moon, *Divine Principle*, p. 255).

"It is plain that Jesus is not God Himself" (Rev. Moon, *Divine Principle*, p. 258).

"But after his crucifixion, Christianity made Jesus into God. This is why a gap between God and man has never been bridged. Jesus is a man in whom God is incarnate, but he is not God Himself" (Rev. Moon, *Christianity in Crisis*, pp. 12, 13).

Moon tells his followers that they can not only equal Jesus, they can also excel Him.

"You can compare yourself with Jesus Christ, and feel you can be greater than Jesus Himself" (Sun Myung Moon, "The Way" translated by Won Pok Choi, from the *Master Speaks*, June 30, 1974, p. 4).

Jesus, according to Moon, was a failure: "Abraham was the father of faith, Moses was a man of faith, Jesus was the Son of man, trying to carry out his mission at the cost of his life. But they are, in a way, failures" (Sun Myung Moon, "Victory or Defeat," translated by Won Pok Choi, from *Master Speaks*, March 31, 1973, p. 1).

Speaking of the work of Christ, the writer to the Hebrews said, "For by one offering He has perfected for all time those who are sanctified" (Hebrews 10:14). The Scriptures testify that the work of Christ on the cross is complete, sufficient to secure the salvation of the individual. Jesus accomplished all that was necessary for the full salvation of mankind. He was not a failure.

The Death of Christ

The Bible plainly states that Jesus Christ came to this earth for the specific purpose of dying for the sins of the world, "Just as the Son of Man did not come to be served, but to serve, and to give His life a ransom for many" (Matthew 20:28).

Rev. Moon, however, teaches to the contrary: "We, therefore, must realize that Jesus did not come to die on the cross" (Rev. Moon, *Divine Principle*, p. 178).

The Scriptures teach "that God was in Christ reconciling the world to Himself" (II Corinthians 5:19). But Moon declares, "...the physical body of Jesus was invaded by Satan through the cross" (Rev. Moon, *Divine Principle*, p. 438).

Moon also thinks that the death of Christ was a victory for Satan: "Satan thus attained what he had intended through the 4,000-year course of history, by crucifying Jesus, with the exercise of his maximum power" (Rev. Moon, *Divine Principle*, p. 435).

He also teaches Christ's death was without effect: "It is equally true that the cross has been unable to establish the Kingdom of Heaven on Earth by removing our original sin" (Rev. Moon, *Divine Principle*, p. 178).

Moon, the Messiah?

As previously noted, Moon believes himself to be the person to finish the task left uncompleted by Jesus. The failure of Jesus leaves the way open for Moon. The *Divine Principle* states that the Messiah, the Lord of the Second Advent, must be born physically on earth to accomplish man's physical salvation. While neither the *Divine Principle* nor Moon publicly declare that he is the Messiah, the inference is strongly given that Moon is indeed the Lord of the Second Advent.

To his followers there appears to be no question about it; Moon is the Messiah. He is reportedly worshipped by his followers and given the designation "Father." Moon has stated, "God is now throwing Christianity away and is now establishing a new religion, and this new religion is the Unification Church" (*Time Magazine*, September 30, 1974).

The Bible portrays two comings of the Messiah. The first coming was fulfilled when Jesus of Nazareth was born to the virgin Mary. "Now after Jesus was born in Bethlehem of Judea in the days of Herod the King, behold, Magi, from the east arrived in Jerusalem, saying, 'Where is He who has been born King of the Jews?'" (Matthew 2:1, 2 NASB).

The Bible speaks over and over again of the second coming of Christ which will be a visible, bodily, return from Heaven.". . Men of Galilee, why do you stand looking into the sky? This Jesus, who has been taken up from you into heaven, will come in just the same way as you have watched Him go into heaven" (Acts 1:11 NASB). "Behold, He is coming with the clouds, and every eye will see Him. . ." (Revelation 1:7 NASB).

There is no biblical teaching that the Messiah will be born physically a second time to accomplish any physical salvation. Jesus accomplished both physical and spiritual salvation at His first coming by His work on the cross. He is the only Savior. There is no need for another Messiah. "And there is salvation in no one else; for there is no other name under heaven that has been given among men, by which we must be saved" (Acts 4:12 NASB). Another Messiah is both unbiblical and unnecessary.

Conclusion

Although the Unification Church makes astounding claims for itself, the facts speak otherwise. The teaching of the *Divine Principle* is at odds with the Bible at all of its central points and therefore cannot be a completion of God's revelation. Moon has no messianic credentials and must be considered as a false prophet, of which Jesus warned us: "Beware of false prophets, who come to you in sheep's clothing, but inwardly are ravenous wolves. You will know them by their fruits" (Matthew 7:15, 16 NASB).

Unification Church Terms

Unification Church — Eastern cult founded by Korean Sun Myung Moon. Claims to have the complete truth of God which has just now been revealed to this present age through Moon. Considers its leader, Rev. Moon, the Messiah who is completing the salvation work unfinished by Jesus Christ.

Collegiate Association for the Research of Principles (CARP)—Front organization for the Unification Church, used to recruit members and funds from college areas.

Holy Spirit Association for the Unification of World Christianity—The complete name of the Unification Church.

Lord of the Second Advent—Title of the second Messiah, said to be Sun Myung Moon, who comes to complete the unfinished salvation work of Jesus Christ.

Master Speaks—Tapes and transcriptions of Moon's messages to his followers.

Moon, Sun Myung—Founder of the Unification Church. Born in Korea in 1920. Moon claims to have had a vision of Christ in 1936 in which he was told that he must finish the work which Christ began. His followers believe him to be the Messiah, the Lord of the Second Advent.

Moonies—Nickname (which they do not appreciate) for followers of Rev. Sun Myung Moon and the Unification Church.

New Hope Singers International—Singing publicity front organization for the Unification Church.

The Divine Principle—According to the Unification Church, the Divine Principle book is the completed testament, superseding the Bible, containing the present spiritual truth for this age which heretofore had not been revealed. Its author is the cult's founder and leader, Sun Myung Moon.

True Father and True Mother—Titles of Moon and his wife, ascribed to them by their followers in the Unification Church.

CHAPTER TWELVE

The Way International

History

The Way International, headquartered in New Knoxville, Ohio, was founded by Victor Paul Wierwille, a former Evangelical and Reformed minister. Wierwille was a pastor for some 16 years in northwestern Ohio when he resigned his pastorate and began teaching his own unique cult of Christianity. Disillusioned with orthodox biblical interpretation, he disposed of his library of some 3,000 volumes and began his own personal study of the Bible.

This culminated in his work, *Power for Abundant Living* (commonly seen on bumper stickers as PFAL), and around 1958, The Way International began. Membership today in The Way International can only be estimated since no official figures are released. The best estimates put it at about 50,000 active members

Claims of The Way International

Victor Paul Wierwille claims he had a so-called encounter with God:

> God spoke to me audibly, just like I'm talking to you now. He said he would teach me the word as it had not been known since the first century, if I would teach it to others (Elena S. Whiteside, *The Way: Living in Love*, New Knoxville, Ohio: American Christian Press, p. 178).

The inference from this is clear. God spoke to Wierwille and told him that *no one* since the first century has been teaching the Bible accurately but now if he (Wierwille) would teach it to others, God would reveal to him the way it should be taught. The logical conclusion to this claim is that anyone who teaches or who has taught contrary to Wierwille is teaching something wrong.

The Way Magazine states, "The so-called Christian Church today is built essentially on man-made doctrine, tradition, confusion, bondage trips, and contradiction to the word as it was originally God-breathed" (*The Way Magazine*, September-October 1974, p. 7).

The Way International believes Victor Paul Wierwille has the only true interpretation of the Scriptures, and is the only one who can lead fellow Bible students out of the confusion in which traditional Christianity has engulfed them. This exclusive claim to inspiration is a characteristic of cults.

What is The Way International?

In a pamphlet entitled "This is the Way," the following explanation is given:

> The Way International is a biblical research and teaching organization concerned with setting before men and women of all ages the inherent accuracy of the word of God (the Bible) so that everyone who so desires may know the power of God in his life. The Way is not a church, nor is it a denomination or a religious sect of any sort (*This is the Way*, New Knoxville, Ohio: The Way International, n.d.).

Contrary to its lofty claims, The Way International is a non-Christian cult, characterized by the twisting and perverting of Holy Scripture by its founder, Victor Paul Wierwille.

Source of Authority

Although The Way strongly asserts that the Bible is its only recognized source of authority, in actuality it is the peculiar interpretation of the Bible by Wierwille that is its yardstick for truth. For all intents and purposes, The Way International has a second source of authority in forming its beliefs: Wierwille's writings and teachings.

According to Wierwille and The Way International, the Bible does not teach that Jesus Christ is God. In 1975, Wierwille wrote a book titled *Jesus Christ Is Not God*, in which he stated, "If Jesus Christ is God and not the Son of God, we have not yet been redeemed" (p. 6).

In another work he had this to say, "God is eternal whereas Jesus was born. . . Jesus Christ's existence began when he was conceived by God's creating the soul-life of Jesus in Mary. God created, brought into existence, this life in an ovum in Mary's womb" (Victor Paul Wierwille, *The Word's Way*, Vol. 3, pp. 26, 37).

Wierwille further states: "Those who teach that Jesus Christ is God and God is Jesus Christ will never stand approved in 'rightly dividing' God's word, for there is only one God, and 'Thou shalt have no other gods'."

"The Bible clearly teaches that Jesus Christ was a man conceived by the Holy Spirit, God, whose life was without blemish and without spot, a lamb from the flock, thereby being the perfect sacrifice. Thus he became our redeemer" (Victor Paul Wierwille, *Jesus Christ is Not God*, p. 79).

> "If the Bible had taught that there is a Christian trinity, I would have happily accepted it. (Victor Paul Wierwille, ibid., p. 3).

Wierwille's view of the Bible is different from the historic view of the Church. He says, ". . .The records in the gospels are addressed at times to Israel and at other times to the Gentiles, but never to the Church of God. One of the greatest errors in the translations of the Bible was placing the four gospels in the New Testament. The gospels logically belong in the Old Testament" (Victor Paul Wierwille, *Power for Abundant Living*,

New Knoxville, Ohio: American Christian Press, 1980, p.5).

However, the rearrangement of the four gospels is not the only manipulating that Wierwille does with the Bible. As the Passantinos point out,

". . .Wierwille claims that he properly interprets the Bible and preserves the meaning of the text, confident that it is God's infallible Word. But in practice, he manipulates texts, adds words to them in brackets, and, if all else fails, claims that the original meaning was "lost" by the Apostate Church and that God has given it especially to him to reveal to the world. Such practices effectively make the Bible little more than a tool in Wierwille's work to build his own system (Robert and Gretchen Passantino, *Answers to the Cultist at Your Door*, Eugene Oregon: Harvest House Publishers, 1981 p. 166).

Danny Frigulti, who has done an extensive study and exposé of The Way, points out a few of the areas of Wierwille's poor research:

Wierwille: "Tertullian (early third century; the first person to use the word trinity of the Father, Son and Holy Spirit)".
The truth: Tertullian (160-220) was not the first person to use the word "Trinity". Theophilus (116-168-181) used the word "Trinity" in this writing. "In like manner also the three days which were before the luminaries, are types of the Trinity, of God, and His Word, and His wisdom."
Wierwille: "The Greek Christian Justin Martyr who wrote in the middle of the second century *never* quoted in the name of the Father, and of the Son, and of the Holy Ghost."
The truth: "For, in the name of God, the Father and the Lord of the universe, and of our Savior Jesus Christ, and of the Holy Spirit, they then receive the washing with water." These are the words of Justin Martyr.
Wierwille: "The Nicene Creed embraced the Son as co-equal with God. Two hundred eighteen of the 220 bishops signed this creed."
The truth: Approximately 318 bishops were present at the Council of Nicea, along with 1500 other bishops, elders and deacons.
Wierwille: "Thus the usage of God in Hebrews 1:8 shows Jesus Christ in an exalted position; he is, however, not God the Creator."
The truth: Chapter six shows that Jesus is God the Creator.
Wierwille: "The man worshipped him according to verse 38, not because he was God the Creator, but because he was a religious man superior to himself."
The truth: Jesus receives this worship, and the Greek word for worship in this verse (John 9:38) is the same that is given to God alone. Therefore, Jesus is God.
Wierwille: "He was not the alpha as God is the Alpha and Omega."
The truth: Jesus in Revelation 1:8, 11 and 22:13 declares that *He is* the Alpha and Omega. Therefore, He is from beginning to end.

To substantiate his claim that Christ is not God, Wierwille contends that the deity of Christ (as expressed in the Trinity) is not part of Christian teaching or writing in the first three centuries after Christ (Victor Paul Wierwille, *Jesus Christ is Not God*, p. 12). This dogmatic statement only reveals the shallowness of Wierwille's scholarship.

Ignatius, (A.D. 50-115), an early Church Father and disciple of the Apostle John, *clearly* writes of Christ's deity. Irenaeus (A.D. 115-190), another Church Father, makes clear reference in *Against Heresies* X. 1 when he calls Christ Jesus Lord and God. The apologist Tertullian (A.D. 160-220)

calls Christ the God of God. Also Hippolytus, Origen and Lucian of Antioch, all clearly refer to Christ as the one God.

One of the strongest arguments for deity is worship. The very word worship connotes divinity. Wierwille himself states," There has always been one sin which God did not and will not tolerate and that is worshipping any god other than God the Creator."

Here Wierwille is in agreement with Scripture, "Worship the Lord your God and serve Him only." The Old Testament reference is Deuteronomy 6:10 and Exodus 20:2-6. What is found in the New Testament is that Jesus Christ clearly receives worship, and approves of homage paid to him.

In Matt. 14:22-33, Christ clearly accepts the disciples' worship, after the storm. The blind man in John 9 worships Christ. The triumphal entry in the gospels is one of the clearest examples of Christ receiving worship, yet is often overlooked. God the Father commands us to worship the son in Hebrews 1:6. In all these passages the same word for worship is used.

The Trinity

Wierwille, like many other cultists, holds a unitarian view of God (that God is one person, not three). Consequently, he rejects the doctrine of the Trinity. "Long before the founding of Christianity the idea of a triune god or a god-in-three-persons was a common belief in ancient religions. Although many of these religions had many minor deities, they distinctly acknowledge that there was one supreme God who consisted of three persons or essences. The Babylonians used an equilateral triangle to represent this three-in-one-god, now the symbol of the modern three-in-one believers." Although the charge that the Trinity is pagan in origin is frequently brought up by cultists, it has no basis in fact. Any so-called parallel between the Trinity and pagan views of the nature of God do not exist. Any comparison will reveal the vast difference between the two.

"Trinitarian dogma degrades God from his elevated unparalleled position, besides it leaves man unredeemed."

The problem with Wierwille's position is that he misunderstands the doctrine of the Holy Trinity. Simply stated, there is one God and this one God is three distinct persons, the Father, the Son, and the Holy Spirit, and these three persons are equal to the one God. We do not believe in three gods but rather one God who is three persons. It is the clear teaching of Scripture and the historic belief of the Christian Church.

The Scriptures teach there is only one God, "For there is one God, and one mediator also between God and men, the man Christ Jesus" (1 Timothy 2:5 NASB). The Scriptures also teach that there is a person called the Father who is designated God, "Paul, an apostle (not sent from men, nor through the agency of man, but through Jesus Christ, and God the Father, who raised him from the dead" (Galatians 1:1 NASB).

The Bible speaks of a second person, called the Son, who is personally different from the Father but who is also called God: "In the beginning was the Word and the Word was with God and the Word was God . . . and the Word became flesh, and dwelt among us" (John 1:1, 14 NASB). "For this cause therefore the Jews were seeking all the more to kill Him, because He not only was breaking the Sabbath, but also was calling God His own Father, making Himself equal with God" (John 5:18 NASB).

Moreover the Bible talks about a third person who is distinct from both the Father and the Son who is also called God. "But Peter said, 'Ananias, why has Satan filled your heart to lie to the Holy Spirit...you have not lied to men, but to God'" (Acts 5:3, 4 NASB).

Thus the Father is called God, the Son is also referred to as God and the Holy Spirit is called God. The Bible clearly teaches that only one God exists. Therefore, the Father, the Son and the Holy Spirit are equal to the one God. This is the biblical doctrine of the Trinity.

Additional support for the Trinity comes from the choice of words in the Old Testament. In the famous Jewish *Shema* of Deuteronomy 6:4, the backbone of historic Judaic teaching, it reads, "Hear, O Israel! The Lord is our God, the Lord is one."

The passage says, "God is one." But what does this mean? The word for "one" here is *echod*, the exact same word used for "one" in Genesis 1:5 where it reads, "The evening and the morning were the first day." Also the same as the word "one" in Genesis 2:24, "They shall become one flesh."

All of these usages refer to a plurality. There is light and darkness in the one day. There is husband and wife in one flesh. "Here *echod* is used to show oneness in a compound sense."

The power of this argument is driven home by Hebrews where there is a word for perfect unity or oneness. The word is *yachid*. It is often translated as "only." The word can be found in Genesis 22:2, Judges 11:34 and Jeremiah 6:26.

Virgin Birth

Wierwille also denies that Jesus of Nazareth was virgin born.

If it said a virgin shall bring forth a son your Bible would fall to pieces. It says plainly that Mary was a virgin only at the time of conception, not at Jesus' birth; the theory of virgin birth has been a theological assumption and erroneous teaching. The Bible said in verse 20 that God told Joseph, "Take unto thee thy wife" when Joseph took her unto himself he lived with her as a husband lives with a wife. She was a virgin when she conceived by God, but when Joseph took her unto himself she was no longer a virgin. The divine conception made Mary no longer a virgin (*The Way Magazine*, Dec. 1970, p. 6).

His contention is refuted by Matthew: "Behold, the virgin shall be with child, and shall bear a son, and they shall call his name Immanuel which translated means, 'God with us'. And Joseph arose from his sleep, and did as the angel of the Lord commanded him, and took her as his wife, and kept her a virgin until she gave birth to a son; and he called His name Jesus" (Matthew 1:23-25 NASB).

Salvation

Wierwille believes salvation is manifest not only by believing in Christ but also by speaking in tongues.

...the only visible and audible proof that a man has been born again and filled with the gift from the Holy Spirit is *always* that he speaks in a tongue or tongues (Victor Paul Wierwille, *Receiving the Holy Spirit Today,* p. 148).

Thus, according to Wierwille, there must be a verbal confession of faith in Christ followed by the proof of speaking in tongues. However, the Scriptures attest that simple belief in Jesus Christ is sufficient for salvation. "He that believeth on the Son hath everlasting life" (John 3:36).

Wierwille also teaches the unbiblical doctrine that salvation includes physical wholeness in this life. "When we have salvation, we have wholeness, even physical wholeness, if we simply accept it" (Victor Paul Wierwille, *The New Dynamic Church,* Studies in Abundant Living, Vol. #2, p. 31). The Bible teaches that we will have physical wholeness but only at the resurrection of the dead. "So also is the resurrection of the dead. It is sown a perishable body, it is raised an imperishable body" (1 Corinthians 15:42 NASB).

The Way's doctrine of salvation is unscriptural in its advocating the visible sign of speaking in tongues. Salvation is a free gift from God given to all those who put their faith in Christ. There is never any hint in Scripture that it is authenticated by speaking in tongues. Furthermore, the basis of The Way's doctrine of salvation is an erroneous view of the person of Jesus Christ.

Wierwille also teaches a sinless perfection doctrine that says after a person is converted his spirit can never sin: ". . .Do we sin in the spirit? No, but in body and soul we fall" (Victor Paul Wierwille, *Power for Abundant Living,* p. 313).

But the apostle John said, speaking to the believer, "If we say we have no sin, we are deceiving ourselves, and the truth is not in us. . . .If we say that we have not sinned, we make Him a liar, and His word is not in us" (1 John 1:8, 10 NASB). Until the believer is changed from corruptible to incorruptible he will keep on sinning.

Holy Spirit vs. holy spirit

According to biblical teaching, the Holy Spirit is one of the Godhead, the third person of the Holy Trinity. According to Victor Paul Wierwille, there is Holy Spirit (which is the same as God the Father) and holy spirit, uncapitalized (which is God's gift to man). Wierwille has said, "The giver is God the Spirit. His gift is spirit. Failure to recognize the difference between the giver and His gift has caused no end of confusion in the Holy Spirit field of study" (Victor Paul Wierwille, *Receiving the Holy Spirit Today,* p. 3).

However, it is Wierwille who is confused on the subject for the Scriptures do not make the distinction he claims. In Matthew 28:19 (NASB) Jesus exhorts believers to baptize "in the name of the Father and the Son and the Holy Spirit." This demonstrates that the Father and the Holy Spirit are two distinct persons, not one and the same.

Another example of the distinction between the Father and the Holy Spirit can be found in the account in Luke of the baptism of Jesus. "Now it came about when all the people were baptized, that Jesus also was baptized, and while He was praying, heaven was opened and the Holy Spirit descended upon Him in bodily form like a dove, and a voice came out of heaven. 'Thou art my beloved son, in Thee I am well pleased'" (Luke 3:21, 22 NASB).

Wierwille's identification of the Father with the Holy Spirit is incorrect and his uncapitalizing holy spirit on certain occasions in order to demonstrate a difference between the gift and the giver is arbitrary and cannot be justified.

Abundant Life

The following is taken from a poster that can be seen on numerous college campuses announcing the Power for Abundant Living Course that The Way International uses to induct one into its teachings and practices:

You Can Have Power For Abundant Living

Abundant living means you can be SET FREE from all fear; doubt and bondage; DELIVERED from poverty, sickness and poor health; OVERFLOWING with life, vitality and zest; RESCUED from condemnation and self-contempt; CURED of drugs and sex abuse. You can RESTORE your broken marriage; ENJOY a happy united family, where there is no generation gap.

If you have power for abundant living you can GAIN self-respect; enjoy SATISFYING work with more than ADEQUATE income. You can OVERCOME depression, discouragement and disappointment and have LOVE, JOY AND REAL PEACE. There can always be a POSITIVE outlook on life, day after day, with no let down. There can be a new PURPOSE in your life. If you have the more abundant life.

You Can Have Whatever You Want!

Every problem you ever had can be overcome when you are fully and accurately instructed.

The claims are monumental: deliverance from doubt, poverty, sickness, overflowing with vitality, having a happy satisfied life; who would not want this?

The Deity of Jesus Christ

The central issue of Christianity as related to the cults is the divinity of Jesus Christ. Many teachings of the cults are similar to orthodox Christianity, but concerning the deity of Christ they never agree. No cult regards Christ as God come in the flesh.

The deity is considered here as a separate issue from the closely related teaching of the Trinity. The reason for this is due to the many critical implications if Jesus is not actually God's Son. Christ promises freedom, forgiveness, eternal life, all of which He makes dependent on His identity as God.

If a comparison is made between the attributes and titles attributed to God and those attributed to Christ, one is left with no choice but to conclude that Jesus is God. This is only one of many avenues of proof, but it is overwhelming in its impact.

Attributes of God	the Father	and the Son
1. from everlasting	Psalm 90:2	Micah 5:2
2. first and last	Isiah 44:6	Revelation 1:17
3. fills all	Jeremiah 23:24	Ephesians 4:10
4. does not change	Malachi 3:6	Hebrews 13:8
5. is the Almighty	Exodus 6:3	Revelation 1:8
6. God of truth	Deuteronomy 32:4	John 14:6
7. creates all things	Isaiah 44:24	Colossians 1:16
8. King of Kings	1 Timothy 6:15	Revelation 19:16
9. everlasting dominion	Psalm 145:13	Daniel 7:14
10. final Judge	Romans 14:10	2 Corinthians 5:10
11. name is above all	Psalm 83:18	Philippians 2:9
12. reward is with Him	Isaiah 40:10	Revelation 22:12
13. perfect love	1 John 4:8	John 15:9
14. the light	1 John 1:5	John 1:5-9; 8:12
15. our hope	Psalm 39:7	Titus 2:13
16. takes away death	Isaiah 25:8	2 Timothy 1:10
17. every knee bows	Isaiah 45:23	Philippians 2:10
18. blots out sin	Isaiah 43:25	1 John 1:7
19. forgives sin	Exodus 34:7	Mark 2:5
20. calms sea	Psalm 107:29	Matthew 8:26
21. prepares heavenly city	Hebrews 11:16	John 14:2
22. glorify His name	Isaiah 24:15	2 Thessalonians 1:12
23. glory forever	Galatians 1:4, 5	2 Peter 3:18

Conclusion

Victor Paul Wierwille's claim that he is teaching the Scriptures as they had not been known since the first century is a distortion of the facts. Wierwille's teachings are authoritarian and are at odds with Holy Scripture. The teachings deny basic Christian beliefs, such as the doctrine of Jesus Christ, the virgin birth, the Holy Spirit, the Trinity and salvation. The inescapable conclusion is that The Way International is a non-Christian cult and must be treated as such

The Way International Terms

The Way International—Contemporary American cult founded by Victor Paul Wierwille with headquarters in New Knoxville, Ohio. Denies the deity of Christ, personality and deity of the Holy Spirit. The Way also teaches a salvation by works. They sell a Power for Abundant Living course advertising the ability to solve life's problems by following their system.

The American Christian Press—The publishing arm of The Way International cult.

Lamsa, George—Aramaic teacher for The Way International cult. He erroneously taught that the New Testament was originally written in Aramaic instead of Greek.

Power for Abundant Living—Title of The Way International introductory course designed to induct one into the teachings and practices of the cult.

The Rock of Ages Annual convention of The Way International cult, held in New Knoxville, Ohio.

Wierwille, Victor Paul—Former minister in the Evangelical and Reformed Church who became dissatisfied with the way the church interpreted the Bible. Throwing away his entire theological library of over 3,000 volumes, he began his own study of the Bible. Claiming to have heard an audible voice from God informing him that he (Wierwille) would now teach the Bible like it had not been taught since the first century, Wierwille proceeded to found the cult called The Way International.

WOW Ambassadors—Volunteer missionaries of The Way International. WOW stands for "The Word Over the World."

CHAPTER THIRTEEN

The Worldwide Church of God "Armstrongism"

History

The founder of the Worldwide Church of God is Herbert W. Armstrong, born on July 31, 1892 in Des Moines, Iowa. As a young man, Armstrong worked in the advertising business and showed little interest in spiritual things. In a dispute with his wife over the issue of keeping the seventh-day Sabbath, Armstrong began an intensive personal study of the Bible. This resulted in his agreeing with his wife on observing the Saturday Sabbath. Further Bible study convinced Armstrong that much of what he had been taught in traditional churches was wrong.

> ...I found that the popular church teachings and practices were not based on the Bible. They had originated, as research in history had revealed, in paganism. Numerous Bible prophecies foretold it; the amazing unbelievable truth was, the SOURCE of these popular beliefs and practices of professing Christianity, was quite largely paganism, and human reasoning and custom, NOT the Bible! (Herbert W. Armstrong, *The Autobiography of Herbert W. Armstrong*, Pasadena: Ambassador College Press, 1967, pp. 298, 299).

According to Armstrong, the Worldwide Church of God began in January, 1934 when the "Sardis" era of the church ended and the "Philadelphia" era began (a reference to the seven churches listed in Revelation two and three that some see as a prefiguring of eras of church history). Armstrong put it this way:

> ...back in 1934...Jesus Christ (Rev. 3:8) was opening the gigantic mass media DOOR of radio and the printing press for the proclamation of His same original GOSPEL to all the world! (Ibid., p. 503).

Armstrong at this time began his radio braodcast and the publishing of the magazine *The Plain Truth*. Since its inception, the Worldwide Church of God has experienced significant growth reaching into millions of homes through the distribution of its magazine and the World Tomorrow radio broadcast.

Garner Ted Armstrong

An important figure in the Worldwide Church of God was Herbert W. Armstrong's fourth child, Garner Ted. Rejecting his father's religion,

Garner Ted wanted to be a television or movie star but certain crises in his life led him to study the Bible and then concur with his father's teachings.

Garner Ted became the national broadcaster of the Worldwide Church of God, the Vice-Chancellor of Ambassador College in Pasadena, California, and the Vice-President of the Worldwide Church of God. However, in 1972, Garner Ted fell out of favor with his father and for a short period was relieved of his responsibilities. A few months later, his responsibilities were restored.

More recently however, Garner Ted was expelled from his father's church. Not to be outdone, Garner Ted formed his own offshoot, the Church of God International, headquartered in Tyler, Texas. The reason for his dismissal was a charge of alleged immoral conduct.

The Claims of Armstrong

Herbert W. Armstrong makes no small claim for his work in the Worldwide Church of God. ". . . A.D. 69, the apostles and the church fled to Pella from Jerusalem according to Jesus' warning (Matthew 24:15, 16). That was the END of the organized proclaiming of Christ's gospel by His church to the world!. . . For eighteen and one-half centuries, all worldwide organized proclaiming of Christ's gospel was stamped out. . ." (Ibid., pp. 502, 503).

> I'm going to give you the frank and straightforward answer. You have a right to know all about this great work of God, and about me. First, let me say— this may sound incredible, but it's true—Jesus Christ foretold this very work—it is, itself the fulfillment of his prophecy (Matthew 24:14 and Mark 13:10).
>
> Astounding as it may seem, there is no other work on earth proclaiming to the whole world this very same gospel that Jesus taught and proclaimed!
>
> And listen again! Read this twice! Realize this, incredible though it may seem—no other work on earth is proclaiming this true gospel of Christ to the whole world as Jesus foretold in Matthew 24:14 and Mark 13:10! This is the most important activity on earth today! (Herbert W. Armstrong, Personal letter to Robert Sumner, November 27, 1958, cited by Walter Martin, *The Rise of The Cults*, Santa Ana, California: Vision House Publishers, Revised ed. 1977, pp. 35, 36).

Armstrong believes his work of restoring the lost gospel is preparatory to the second coming of Christ: "For eighteen and one-half centuries that gospel was not preached. The world was deceived into accepting a false gospel. Today Christ has raised up his work and once again allotted two nineteen-year time cycles for proclaiming His same gospel, preparatory to His second coming." He also states:

> "No man ever spoke like this man," reported the officers of the Pharisees regarding Jesus. The multitudes were astonished at his doctrine.
>
> It is the same today, the same living Christ through The World Tomorrow broadcast, The Plain Truth Magazine, and this work proclaims in mighty power around the world the same gospel preached by Peter, Paul and all the original apostles. . . The World Tomorrow and The Plain Truth are Christ's instruments which he is powerfully using. Yes, His message is shocking today. Once again

it is the voice in the wilderness of religious confusion (*The Inside Story of The World Tomorrow Broadcast*, pp. 2, 7).

The Worldwide Church of God considers Herbert W. Armstrong as the man God chose to bring the truth to this present age: "Jesus chose Paul, who was highly educated for spreading the gospel to the Gentiles. He later raised up Peter Waldo, a successful businessman, to keep his truth alive during the middle ages. In these last days WHEN THE GOSPEL MUST GO AROUND THE WORLD, Jesus chose a man amply trained in the advertising and business fields to shoulder the mission—Herbert W. Armstrong; (Herman Hoeh, *A True History of the Church*, p. 28).

The lines are clearly drawn. If you do not believe the message of Herbert W. Armstrong and the Worldwide Church of God then you do not believe the true message of Christ to this age.

God

Like the Mormons, Armstrong believes in a plurality of personal gods, based upon the Hebrew word for God, "Elohim."

"And as I have explained previously, God is not a single person, but the Hebrew word for God portrays God as a FAMILY of persons" (Herbert W. Armstrong, "What is the True Gospel?," *Tomorrow's World*, January, 1970, p. 7). "Elohim is a uniplural or collective noun, such as "church" or "family" or "kingdom." In other words, Elohim stands for a single class composed of TWO or MORE individuals. Elohim, then, is the "God Kingdom" or "God Family" (Herbert W. Armstrong, ed. *Ambassador College Correspondence Course*, 1972, Lesson 8, p. 5).

The Trinity

There is no biblical Trinity in Armstrong's theology. Presently the Godhead is limited to the Father and the Son but in the future more persons will be added to the Godhead. "God is a family—not a trinity. God's family will not be limited to an intractably closed circle of three...God's family is open" (B. McDowell, "Is the Holy Spirit a Person?," *Tomorrow's World*, September 1970, p. 31).

Armstrong feels that the doctrine of the Trinity is the result of the teaching of false prophets: ". . . the theologians and 'higher critics' have blindly accepted the heretical and false doctrine introduced by pagan false prophets who crept in, that the Holy Spirit is a third person—the heresy of the 'trinity.' This limits God to 'three persons.'" (Herbert W. Armstrong, *Just What Do You Mean—Born Again*, p. 19).

The accusations leveled by Armstrong against the doctrine of the Trinity are unfounded. Rather than being the invention of false prophets and heretics, the doctrine of the Trinity is the clear teaching of Scripture on the nature of God. Simply stated, the Bible teaches there exists one God who is three separate persons: the Father, the Son, and the Holy Spirit, and these three persons are the one God. There is no teaching whatever in Scripture that suggests God is a family.

The Holy Spirit

Herbert W. Armstrong and his followers reject the personality and deity of the Holy Spirit. ". . . the Holy Spirit is not a person but the power God the Father uses—much as a man uses electricity" (B. McDowell, op. cit., p. 32). "God's spirit is His mind, His power, His very essence, but it is not a distinct person as is the Father or Christ" (David John Hill, "Why is God the Father Called a Father?" *Tomorrow's World*, September 1970, p. 28.) "God's spirit, which is not a person, but the power of God. . ." (G. Geis, "The God Family: Open or Closed?," *Tomorrow's World*, September 1970, p. 30).

The views of Armstrongism concerning the Holy Spirit fly right into the face of true biblical teaching. The Bible clearly portrays the Holy Spirit as being deity, having a separate personality from both the Father and the Son.

This can be observed in Acts 5:3, 4 (NASB), where the Holy Spirit is spoken of as God, "But Peter said, 'Ananias, why has Satan filled your heart to lie to the Holy Spirit. . . You have not lied to men but to God.'"

Man

The final destiny of man is to become God: "You are setting out on a training to become creator—to become God!" (Herbert W. Armstrong, *Why Were You Born*, op. cit., p. 22). ". . .we develop spiritually ready to be finally BORN OF GOD—by a resurrection, or instantaneous conversion from mortal to immortal, from human to divine. . ." (David Hill and Robert Kuhn, "Why Does God Hide Himself?," *Tomorrow's World*, 1969, p. 34).

"The PURPOSE OF LIFE is that in us God is really recreating His own kind—reproducing Himself after His own kind—for we are, upon real conversion, actually begotten as sons (yet unborn) of God. . .we grow spiritually more and more like God, until, at the time of the resurrection we shall be instantaneously changed from mortal to immortal—we shall be born of God—WE SHALL THEN BE GOD!" (David John Hill, op. cit., p. 27).

The idea that man will some day be God can be found nowhere in the Bible. God is God by nature. He was, is and always will be God. Man cannot attain Godhood for he is finite, limited by his nature. There is no other God neither will there be any other God: "'You are my witnesses,' declares the Lord, 'and my servant whom I have chosen, in order that you may know and believe me and understand that I am He. Before Me there was no God formed, and there will be none after me'"(Isaiah 43:10 NASB).

Salvation by Works

As is the case with all non-Christian cults, Armstrongism teaches that salvation is achieved by the individual's self-effort rather than relying only on God's grace.

"Salvation, then is a process! But how the God of this world would blind your eyes to that!!! He tries to deceive you into thinking all there is to it is just 'accepting Christ' with 'no works'—and presto-change, you are pronounced 'saved.' But the Bible reveals that none is yet 'saved'" (Herbert W. Armstrong, *Why Were You Born?*, p. 11).

According to the Worldwide Church of God, salvation is a process beginning in this life and culminating in the resurrection. Salvation consists of repentance, faith and water baptism. No one is saved in this life. The doctrine of "simply" coming to Christ for salvation is rejected by Armstrong in the strongest of terms.

People have been taught, falsely, that "Christ completed the plan of salvation on the cross"—when actually it was only begun there. The popular denominations have taught "just believe, that's all there is to it; believe on the Lord Jesus Christ, and you are that instant saved!" That teaching is false! And because of deception, because the true gospel of Jesus Christ has been blotted out, lo these 1900 years by the preaching of a false gospel about the person of Christ— and often a false Christ at that—millions today worship Christ—and all in vain! (Herbert W. Armstrong, *All About Water Baptism*, p. 1).

According to Armstrong, a person must be baptized in order to be saved "...God commands water baptism; and for one who is able to either defy the command and refuse, or neglect...certainly would be an act of disobedience which would impose the PENALTY of sin, and cause loss of salvation" (Ibid., p. 19).

Moreover, the Saturday Sabbath needs to be observed to attain salvation: "Thus did God reveal which day is HIS SABBATH, and also that it DOES MAKE LIFE-AND-DEATH DIFFERENCE—for to break God's Holy Sabbath is SIN, and the penalty is eternal DEATH" (Herbert W. Armstrong, *Which Day is the Christian Sabbath?*, Pasadena: Ambassador College Press, 1971, p. 35).

Contrary to Armstrong's statements, the Scriptures teach that salvation is a free gift from God. The Scriptures further declare that salvation cannot be earned by doing any work, whether it be water baptism or the keeping of the Sabbath. Salvation comes as a result of a person simply placing his faith in Jesus Christ:

"For by grace you have been saved through faith; and that not of yourselves, it is the gift of God; not as a result of works, that no one should boast" (Ephesians 2:8, 9 NASB). "He saved us, not on the basis of deeds which we have done in righteousness, but according to His mercy, by the washing of regeneration and renewing by the Holy Spirit" (Titus 3:5 NASB).

Salvation, therefore, is totally a work of God. Man can add nothing to what Christ has already done when He died in our place on the cross.

Eternal Judgment

Armstrong rejects any idea of eternal punishment for the wicked. "The wages of sin is death" (Romans 6:23) and the death, which is the absence of life, is for ALL ETERNITY. It is eternal punishment by remaining DEAD for all eternity   not remaining alive and being tortured in a fictitious, burning hell-fire!" (Herbert W. Armstrong, *"Immortality,"* p. 7).

The fires of hell spoken of in the Bible will eventually burn themselves out, he says: "They (the fires in the valley of Hinnon) were never quenched or put out by anyone! The flames merely died out when they had nothing more to consume. Even so, it will be with the Gehenna fire. It will be unquenched — but it will finally burn itself out" (Herbert W. Armstrong, ed., *Ambassador College Correspondence Course,* Lesson 6, p. 14).

The idea that hell will eventually burn itself out is not scriptural: "And these will go away into eternal punishment, but the righteous into eternal life" (Matthew 25:46). If there is no eternal punishment, then certainly there is no eternal life for this verse uses the same word to describe both. Jesus said the fire is unquenchable, "And if your eye causes you to stumble, cast it out; it is better for you to enter the Kingdom of God with one eye, than having two eyes to be cast into hell, where the *worm does not die, and the fire is not quenched*" (Mark 9:47, 48 NASB, italics ours).

The Sabbath

Armstrong believes observing Sunday as the day of worship is the Mark of the Beast: "Sunday observance — this is the Mark of the Beast. . . If in your forehead and your hand, you shall be tormented by God's plagues without mercy, yes, you!" (Herbert W. Armstrong, *The Mark of the Beast,* Pasadena: Ambassador College Press, 1957, pp. 10, 11).

Since there are other cultic groups which teach a similar doctrine about the Sabbath, we feel it necessary to demonstrate that it was the policy of the New Testament believers and the early church to observe Sunday rather than Saturday as their day of worship.

The teaching that the day of worship was changed from Saturday to Sunday during the reign of the Roman Emperor Constantine (c. A.D. 325) does not fit the facts. The fact that the early church believed the Hebrew Sabbath was not binding on the Christian is demonstrated by the following quotations:

At the beginning of the second century, Ignatius, bishop of Antioch, wrote to the Magnesians:

> "Be not deceived with strange doctrines, nor with old fables. For if we still live according to the Jewish law, we acknowledge that we have not received grace"; and then goes on to categorize his readers as "those who were brought up in the ancient order of things" but who "have come to the possession of a new hope, no longer observing the Sabbath" (*The Ante-Nicene Fathers,* Vol. 1 pp. 62, 63).

During the middle of the second century, Justin Martyr explained why Christians did not keep the law of Moses and the Sabbath observance in *The Ante-Nicene Fathers,* Vol. I, pp. 199, 200, 204, 207; and *Dialogue with Trypho.*

The same is true with Cerenalus, Bishop of Lyons at the end of the second century (*Against Heresies,* Book IV, chap. 16). Also Clement of Alexandria (*The Stromata*) and Tertullian (*On Idolatry,* chap. 14 and *An Answer to the Jew,* chap. 2), testify of the early Christians' attitude concerning Sabbath observance. It was basically a Jewish institution.

The New Birth

Armstrong and his followers have a peculiar view regarding the new birth. They believe an individual is not born of God until the resurrection. Rather, he is only "begotten" (like pregnant) of God at his conversion: "When we are converted, our sins forgiven, we receive the Holy Spirit, we are then BEGOTTEN of God—not yet BORN of God...Even as Christ was BORN AGAIN, born of God by his resurrection, even so WE—the brethren—shall be BORN AGAIN as sons of God, through the RESURRECTION of the dead..." (Herbert W. Armstrong, "Was Jesus Christ Born Again?" in *The Plain Truth*, February 1963, p. 40).

Until now Christ is the only person who has been born again. The rest of the believers must await a future resurrection to experience the new birth.

Armstrongism is incorrect in this assertion. A person becomes born again the moment he trusts Christ. The Apostle Peter, while speaking to believers, said, "For you *have been* born again not of seed which is perishable but imperishable, that is, through the living and abiding word of God" (I Peter 1:23 NASB, italics ours). Either St. Peter is correct or Armstrong is correct. They cannot both be true at the same time. Again, Armstrong's teachings are contradictory to Scripture.

False Prophecy

Armstrongism teaches that in A.D. 70 the true believers were scattered after completing two 19-year cycles of ministry to the world (A.D. 31 to A.D. 69). The church, at this time, departed from the faith. As God allowed the true believers in the first century to complete their two cycles of ministry, He also has decided to again allow the genuine believers to complete two more 19-year cycles.

The work began in 1934 and should have ended in 1972. Anticipating this, Herbert W. Armstrong made predictions concerning the United States and Great Britain as the year 1972 approached. In 1967 he wrote, "...we are to have soon (probably in about four years) such drought, and famine, that disease epidemics will follow, taking millions of lives...that condition is coming! And I do not mean in 400 years—nor in 40 years—but in the very next FOUR or FIVE" (Herbert W. Armstrong, *The United States and British Commonwealth in Prophecy*, p. 184).

Armstrong wrote concerning a great drought that was to strike the United States: "...it will strike sooner than 1975—probably between 1965 and 1972! This will be the very beginning as Jesus said, of the Great Tribulation" (Herbert W. Armstrong, *1975 in Prophecy*, Pasadena: Ambassador College Press, 1952, p. 10).

Interestingly enough, Armstrong has disqualified himself as a prophet, "Emphatically I am NOT a prophet, in the sense of one to whom God speaks specially and directly, revealing personally a future event to happen or new truth, or new and special instruction direct from God—separate from, and apart from what is contained in the Bible" (Herbert W. Armstrong, "Personal from Herbert W. Armstrong," *Tomorrow's World,*

February, 1972, p. 1).

Even though Armstrong denies that he has been given a prophetic office, he nevertheless claims for himself to be God's messenger for this day and age, preaching the one true gospel. His false predictions demonstrate that he is not a true prophet of God and his claim as to being God's messenger is also untrue.

The Bible has harsh words to say for those who prophesy falsely, "But the prophet who shall speak a word presumptuously in My name which I have not commanded him to speak...that prophet shall die" (Deuteronomy 18:20 NASB). The Scriptures indicate that to prophesy falsely in the name of the Lord is a serious offense.

Conclusion

"And there is only ONE CHURCH on earth today which understands and is proclaiming that exact order of events, doing the WORK of God in preaching His message to the world as a last witness" (Roderick Meredity, "The True Church—Where Is It?, *The Plain Truth*, March 1963, p. 44).

The two 19-year cycles have come and gone (1934-1972), Armstrong's work continues and Christ has not appeared again as He was supposed to appear. Further, there have been no great catastrophes to hit the United States and Great Britain as Armstrong predicted. These facts totally undermine the claim of Armstrong and his followers that the Worldwide Church of God is God's true church today.

Furthermore, the totally unbiblical doctrines about God being a family, salvation by works, the new birth not taking place until the resurrection, along with their other teachings, signify them to be a non-Christian cult that should be avoided.

The Worldwide Church of God Terms

The Worldwide Church of God (formerly the Radio Church of God)— Founded in 1934 by Herbert W. Armstrong, it teaches a mixture of British-Israelism, Seventh-day Adventism, Jehovah's Witnesses, and Armstrong's own unique interpretations about salvation and the nature of God.

Ambassador College—Liberal arts and religious college of the Worldwide Church of God.

Anglo-Israelism (British Israelism)—Identifies the ten tribes of Israel, which were supposedly lost, with the Anglo-Saxon nations. These nations, particularly the U.S. and Great Britain, and the events affecting them, are seen as being the fulfillment of all Bible prophecy concerning Israel. This doctrine is taught by Herbert W. Armstrong and his Worldwide Church of God.

Armstrong, Garner Ted—Son of Herbert W. Armstrong and former broadcaster for the Worldwide Church of God before his dismissal from the cult. Presently leads the Church of God International, a similar cult headquartered in Tyler, Texas.

Armstrong, Herbert W.—Born in Des Moines, Iowa in 1892. In 1934, he founded the Radio Church of God, now known as the Worldwide Church of God, an American-based cult.

Radio Church of God—Former name of the Worldwide Church of God.

The Plain Truth—Magazine of the Worldwide Church of God cult.

The World Tomorrow—Radio and television show of the Worldwide Church of God.

Tomorrow's World—Former magazine of the Worldwide Church of God.

CHAPTER FOURTEEN

Christian Science

History

The founder of Christian Science was Mary Ann Morse Baker Glover Patterson Eddy, born in Bow, New Hampshire in 1821, to Mark and Abigail Baker. Her parents were members of the Congregationalist church which upheld a strict doctrine of predestination that unsettled young Mary.

"The doctrine of unconditional election or predestination, greatly troubled me: for I was unwilling to be saved, if my brothers and sisters were to be numbered among those who were doomed to perpetual banishment from God" (Mary Baker Eddy, *Retrospection and Introspection,* 13:5-9). Her life later became characterized by the rejection of doctrines that are central to the Christian faith.

Christian Science Discovered

In 1866, while still married to Daniel Patterson, she discovered the principle of Christian Science after a serious fall allegedly brought her near death. Her account of the severity of the injuries was contradicted by the attending physician. Nevertheless, the principles "discovered" during this time were to be the basis of Christian Science. In 1875, her work *Science and Health* was published with the additional *Key to the Scriptures* added in 1883. For this work she claimed divine revelation.

"I should blush to write of *Science and Health with Key to the Scriptures* as I have, were it of human origin and I apart from God its author, but as I was only a scribe echoing the harmonies of Heaven in divine metaphysics, I cannot be super-modest of the Christian Science Textbook" (*Christian Science Journal,* Jan. 1901).

In 1879 in Charlestown, Massachusetts, the Church of Christ Scientist was organized and was then changed in 1892 to the First Church of Christ Scientist. The Church Manual was published in 1895 establishing the procedures of governing the church.

The Death of Mrs. Eddy

Although she taught that death is "an illusion, the life of life" (*Science and Health,* 584:9), Mrs. Eddy passed away December 3, 1910. Today there is a self-perpetuating board of directors which governs the church. There is no way to get an accurate number of Christian Scientists today since the Church Manual says, "Christian Scientists shall not report for publication the number of the members of the Mother Church, nor that of the branch churches" (Article VIII, p. 48). Observers estimate worldwide membership at 420,000.

The Claims of Christian Science

Christian Science, like many other cults, claims further revelation that goes "beyond the Bible"—that is to say, new divine truth previously unrevealed.

On page 107, in her work *Science and Health*, Mrs. Eddy quotes the Apostle Paul:

"But I certify you, brethren, that the Gospel which was preached of me is not after man. For I neither received it of man, neither was I taught it, but by the revelation of Jesus Christ."

She follows the quotation with this claim:

"In the year 1866, I discovered the Christ Science or divine laws of Life, Truth, and Love and named my discovery Christian Science. God has been graciously preparing me during many years for the reception of this final revelation of the absolute divine Principle of scientific mental healing" (*Science and Health*, 107:1-6).

She goes on, "Whence came to me this heavenly conviction. . .When apparently near the confines of mortal existence, standing already within the shadow of the death-valley, I learned these truths in divine Science" (*Science and Health*, 108:1, 19-21).

She concludes:

"I won my way to absolute conclusions through divine revelation, reason, and demonstration. The Revelation of Truth in the understanding came to me gradually and apparently through Divine Power" (*Science and Health*, 109:20-23).

Mrs. Eddy's claims are clear: The revelation she received while near death was divine. She also claims exclusive truth: "Is there more than one school of Christian Science?. . .There can, therefore, be but one method in its teaching" (*Science and Health*, 112:3-5). Needless to say the one method is her method.

The Christian Science Church Manual states their purpose as "to commemorate the word and works of our master, which should reinstate primitive Christianity and its lost element of healing" (*The Christian Science Church Manual*, 89th ed., p. 17).

The following paragraph reveals Mrs. Eddy's monumental claims.

"Late in the nineteenth century I demonstrated the divine rules of Christian Science. They were submitted to the broadest practical test, and everywhere, when honestly applied under circumstances where demonstration was humanly possible, this science showed that truth had lost none of its divine and healing efficacy, even though centuries had passed away since Jesus practiced these rules on the hills of Judaea and in the valleys of Galilee" (*Science and Health*, 147:6-13).

Therefore, Christian Science claims to have restored the lost element in Christianity, namely healing, that when applied, demonstrates itself to work. Moreover, this knowledge of divine healing claims to have been revealed to Mrs. Eddy who is sharing this "exclusive truth" with the world. Thus, Christian Science claims to go further than the orthodox churches by reinstating that which was missing.

Source of Authority

Mrs. Eddy claimed that she derived her teachings from the Bible, which she considered her final authority. However, in practice, and as we have just seen above, she also claimed that her revelations were better and "higher" than the Bible. Where the Bible contradicted her beliefs, she felt free to dismiss its authority.

"The Bible has been my only authority. I have no other guide in 'The straight and narrow way' of Truth" (*Science and Health*, 126:29-31).

Although she claimed that the Bible was her guide, her view of Scripture was something less than desirable: "The material record of the Bible,...is no more important to our well-being than the history of Europe and America" (Mary Baker Eddy, *Miscellaneous Writings*, 1833-1896, p. 170:19-21).

"The decisions by vote of Church Councils as to what should and should not be considered Holy Writ; the manifest mistakes in the ancient versions; the thirty thousand different readings in the Old Testament, and the three hundred thousand in the New,—these facts show how a mortal and material sense stole into the divine record, with its own hue darkening to some extent the inspired pages" (*Science and Health*, 139:15-22).

Mrs. Eddy also assumes there are two different contradictory creation accounts in Genesis, "The Science of the first record proves the falsity of the second. If one is true, the other is false, for they are antagonistic" (*Science and Health*, 522:3-5). (For a thorough refutation of the so-called two-creation account theory, see our *Answers to Tough Questions*, pp. 170-196.)

In actuality, she does not obtain her teachings from the Bible even though the claim is made that "as adherents of Truth, we take the inspired Word of the Bible as our sufficient guide to eternal life" (*Science and Health*, 497: 3-4).

The fact is, the teachings of Christian Science are in direct contradiction to the Bible. The real authority in Christian Science is not the Bible, but the writings of Mrs. Eddy. She has this to say about her own work, *Science and Health*:

"...It is the voice of Truth to this age" (*Science and Health*, 456:27, 28).

"...The revealed Truth uncontaminated by human hypothesis" (*Science and Health*, 457:1-2).

"No human pen nor tongue taught me the Science contained in this book, SCIENCE AND HEALTH; and neither tongue nor pen can overthrow it" (*Science and Health*, 110· 16-19).

Christian Science does what so many of the cults do; it has a second authority which supersedes the Bible as the final authority in solving doctrinal matters. The writings of Mrs. Eddy constitute the final word as far as Christian Scientists are concerned, with the Bible relegated to a secondary status, although she paid lip service homage to the Bible.

Phineas Quimby

In a sermon delivered in June of 1890, Mrs. Eddy again made the claim to divine revelation: "Christian Science is irrevocable—unpierced by bold conjecture's sharp point, by bald philosophy, or by man's inventions. It is divinely true, and every hour in time and in eternity will witness more steadfastly to its practical truth" (Mary Baker Eddy, *Seven Messages to the Mother Church*, pp. 20-21). There is strong evidence to the contrary; that Mrs. Eddy's "divine revelation" is not original to her, but is a plagiarism of Phineas Quimby's writings and ideas.

Phineas Quimby was a self-professed healer who applied hypnosis and the power of suggestion in affecting his cures. He called his word, "The science of the Christ" and "Christian Science." Mrs. Eddy became an enthusiastic follower of Quimby in 1862 after her back injury was healed by him. She wrote letters to the Portland (Maine) Evening Courier praising Quimby and comparing him to Jesus Christ.

Upon his death she eulogized Quimby in a poem, titling it, "Lines on the Death of Dr. P. P. Quimby, who healed with the truth that Christ taught in contradistinction to all Isms." Eventually she attempted to separate any connection between herself and Quimby when charges of borrowing his ideas surfaced. However, the facts are otherwise.

In 1921, Horatio Dresser published *The Quimby Manuscripts*, which when compared with Mrs. Eddy's writings, revealed many parallels leading some to comment, ". . .as far as thought is concerned, *Science and Health* is practically all Quimby" (Ernest Sutherland Bates and John V. Dittermore, *Mary Baker Eddy: The Truth and The Tradition*, 1932, p. 156).

(For a thorough documentation of the Borrowing of Quimby's ideas we recommend Georgine Milmine, 1971, *The Life of Mary Baker G. Eddy*, Grand Rapids: Baker Book House reprint of a 1909 work, pp. 56-104).

Mrs. Eddy received the principles of Christian Science from some place other than the God of the Bible. Since her teachings contradict the teachings of God as revealed in the Bible, they are thereby condemned by the Bible and she is therefore a false teacher.

The Theology of Christian Science

Even though Christian Science claims to be a restatement of primitive, pure Christianity, it denies everything that is considered sacred to God's Word.

God

Mrs. Eddy defined God as, "The great I Am; the all-knowing, all-seeing, all acting, all-wise, all-loving, and eternal; Principle; Mind; Soul: Spirit;

Life; Truth; Love; all Substance; Intelligence (*Science and Health*, 587:5-8).

Elsewhere she calls God "Divine Principle, Life, Truth, Love, Soul, Spirit, Mind" (ibid., 115:13-14).

Mrs. Eddy claimed that the God she revealed through Christian Science was not pantheistic. (Pantheism is the belief that God is all of existent reality, including the material world. Hinduism, because it identifies God with the creation, is pantheistic.) In denying a pantheistic God Mrs. Eddy said:

> At this period of enlightenment, a declaration from the pulpit that Christian Science is Pantheism is anomalous to those who know whereof they speak— who know that Christian Science is science, and therefore, is neither hypothetical nor dogmatical, but demonstrable, and looms above the mists of Pantheism higher than Ararat above the deluge (*Seven Messages to the Mother Church*, Mary Baker Eddy, 1907, p. 10).

However, when Mrs. Eddy described her God, she clearly identified him with the creation. Her God actually is pantheistic. She said, "God is a divine Whole, and All, an all-pervading intelligence and love, a divine, infinite principle" (Mary Baker Eddy, *Miscellaneous Writings*, p. 16:21, 22).

The God of the Bible, on the other hand is infinite (Psalm 139:7-16), yet personal (Isaiah 45:20-25). He is the Creator, but He is not the creation (Isaiah 44:24). The God of the Bible and the God of Christian Science are not the same. The Apostle Paul declared the true God:

> The God who made the world and all things in it, since He is Lord of heaven and earth, does not dwell in temples made with hands; neither is He served by human hands, as though He needed anything, since He Himself gives to all life and breath and all things. . .(Acts 17:24, 25).

Jesus Christ

The Christian Science view of the person of Christ is wholly unbiblical: "Christ is the ideal truth that comes to heal sickness and sin through Christian Science, and attributes all power to God. Jesus is the name of the man who, more than all other men, has presented Christ, the true idea of God. . .Jesus is the human man, and Christ is the divine idea; hence the duality of Jesus the Christ" (*Science and Health*, 473:9-16).

Mrs. Eddy attempts to make a distinction between "Jesus" and "the Christ" as if they were two separate entities. This distinction is not possible for Jesus Christ is one person. Jesus is His name meaning "Yahweh is Salvation," Christ, His title, meaning "The Anointed One." The attempted distinction that Christian Scientists make between the two shows a complete lack of understanding of the Scriptures, such as Luke 2:11, 1 John 2:22, and 1 John 5:1.

Since Jesus and Christ are two different entities in Christian Science, the doctrine that Jesus Christ is God is rejected, ". . .the Christian believes that Christ is God. . . Jesus Christ is not God. . ." (*Science and Health*, 361:1, 2, 12).

In direct contradiction to the above statement, the Bible clearly teaches the docrine of the Holy Trinity. We do not believe in polytheism, or more than one God. We believe that in the nature of the one true God (Isaiah

43:10), there exists three eternal and distinct persons (Luke 3:22): the Father (2 Peter 1:17); the Word or Son (John 1:1, 14); and the Holy Spirit (Acts 5:3, 4). These three persons are the one God (Matthew 28:19).

Salvation

Concerning salvation, Mrs. Eddy said: "Life, Truth, and Love understood and demonstrated as supreme over all; sin, sickness and death destroyed" (*Science and Health*, p. 593:20-22). Since to the Christian Scientist there is no such thing as sin, salvation in the biblical sense is totally unnecessary. The teachings concerning salvation in Mrs. Eddy's writings are both ambiguous and inconsistent. She stated over and over again that sin is just an illusion (*Miscellaneous Writings*, 27:11-12, *Science and Health*, 71:2, 287:22, 23, 480:23, 24, etc.).

On the other hand, she states as quoted above, that salvation is "...sin, sickness and death destroyed." If sin is only an illusion, having no real existence, how can it be destroyed? Putting it another way, do you destroy something that does not exist? Since there is no harmonious teaching in Christian Science concerning salvation, it is difficult to evaluate it objectively. Nevertheless, the Christian Science view is a far cry from the Bible that teaches the reality of sin (Romans 3:23) and the need for a Savior (Acts 4:12).

Evil

In Christian Science there exists no evil: "Here also is found the path of the basal statement, the cardinal point in Christian Science, that matter and evil (including all inharmony, sin, disease, death) are unreal" (*Miscellaneous Writings*, 27:9-12). According to Christian Science, "Christ came to destroy the belief of sin" (*Science and Health*, 473:6, 7). It is further emphasized "...evil is but an illusion, and it has no real basis. Evil is a false belief, God is not its author" (*Science and Health*, 480:23, 24).

Since evil is an illusion, the idea of the death of Christ on the cross for our sins is unnecessary:

> The material blood of Jesus was no more efficacious to cleanse from sin when it was shed upon "the accursed tree" than when it was flowing in his veins as he went daily about his Father's business (*Science and Health*, 25:6-8).

In distinction, the Bible teaches that evil is real (1 John 5:19) and that we would be without salvation if Jesus Christ had not died on the cross for our sins (Hebrews 9:22). As Christians we can rejoice in the good news that Jesus Christ "gave himself for our sins, that He might deliver us out of this present evil age, according to the will of our God and Father, to whom be the glory forevermore. Amen" (Galatians 1:4, 5).

Christian Science and Healing

"Our Master...practiced Christian healing...but left no definite rule for demonstrating this Principle of healing and preventing disease. This rule remained to be discovered by Christian Science" (*Science and Health*, 147:24-29).

In a section entitled "Fruitage" in *Science and Health* the following claim is made:

> "Thousands of letters could be presented in testimony of the healing efficacy of Christian Science and particularly concerning the vast number of people who have been reformed and healed through the perusal or study of this book" (*Science and Health*, p. 600).

Followed by this claim are approximately 100 pages of testimonials of healing of every conceivable disease by those who have embraced the principles of Christian Science. The obvious question arises: Can Christian Science heal? While many of the healings in Christian Science can be explained without appealing to the miraculous, there are some accounts of seemingly true healings.

If this be the case, then it would be an example of the "signs and false wonders" the Apostle Paul spoke about (2 Thessalonians 2:9). Satan is the great counterfeiter and his attempt to duplicate the works of God and the miracle of healing is no exception. We all want to be healthy, but not at the cost of abandoning Christ.

Conclusion

Christian Science is neither Christian nor scientific because every important doctrine of historic Christianity is rejected by Christian Science. The claim of divine revelation by Mrs. Eddy is contradicted by the facts that clearly attest she does not represent the God of the Bible. Although she speaks in the name of Jesus, her teachings conflict with His in every respect.

Fortunately, Jesus warned us ahead of time about people like Mrs. Eddy: "Beware of the false prophets, who come to you in sheep's clothing, but inwardly are ravenous wolves. You will know them by their fruits" (Matthew 7:15, 16 NASB).

Christian Science Terms

Animal Magnetism—According to Christian Science, animal magnetism, which is wrong thinking, causes an individual to experience the illusion of evil. Malicious animal magnetism can kill those it is practiced against.

At-one-ment—In Christian Science and other gnostic cults, it is the unity between the mind of God and the mind of man as demonstrated by Christ.

Christian Science Journal—Periodical of Christian Science, used for recruitment of new members.

Christian Science Monitor—Newspaper published by Christian Science, highly regarded in the secular world, with little religious propaganda.

Christian Science Sentinel—Periodical of Christian Science, used for recruitment of new members.

Eddy, Mary Baker—Founder of Christian Science. Mrs. Eddy (her third married name) said she discovered Christian Science as a result of a miraculous healing she supposedly received after a fall. She authored the text *Science and Health with Key to the Scriptures* that Christian Scientists revere above the Bible.

Immortal Mind—God in Christian Science theology.

Mortal Mind—According to Christian Science, it is the source of the illusions of evil, sickness, sin and death.

Quimby, P. P.—Early 19th century mesmerist and psychic healer from whom Mary Baker Eddy learned the principles she later claimed were revealed from God as Christian Science.

Science and Health with Key to the Scriptures—Contains the teachings of Mary Baker Eddy, the founder of Christian Science. The book is regarded as a revelation with more authority than the Bible.

CHAPTER FIFTEEN

Unity

History

T he Unity School of Christianity was founded by Charles and Myrtle Fillmore. Charles Sherlock Fillmore was born near St. Cloud, Minnesota in 1854. He married Mary Caroline Page (or "Myrtle") in 1881.

The early years of their marriage recorded many financial ups and downs until they finally established a modest real estate office in Kansas City, Missouri. Myrtle's family had a history of tuberculosis and she herself was eventually stricken ill with the dreaded disease. She also contracted malaria and was given, by her doctor, only six months to live.

In 1886, the Fillmores went to a lecture which was to change their lives dramatically. The speaker, E. B. Weeks, said to the crowd that night, "I am a child of God and therefore I do not inherit sickness." Myrtle believed the statement and continued to recite it over and over again. Eventually she was healed.

At first, Charles refused to accept his wife's new technique but he was willing to investigate it, along with other religions. After an extensive study of the science of mind and Eastern religions, including Hinduism and Buddhism, he decided to try his wife's meditation technique. After continued meditation, his withered leg was healed, and he joined Myrtle in founding a new religious system, later called the Unity School of Christianity.

Borrowing heavily from Christian Science and New Thought, (a 19th century metaphysical healing movement developed from the system of mental healer Phineas Quimby), the Fillmores added their own interpretations, including the Eastern concept of reincarnation, and presented their teachings first to the people of Missouri and then to the world. Under pressure from Christian Science founder, Mary Baker Eddy, the Fillmores stopped using terms common to Christian Science.

They did enjoy a long relationship with the New Thought movement, but eventually chose independent status as a religious movement not affiliated with any other religion. The movement went through several names; Modern Thought (1889), Christian Science Thought (1890), and Thought (1891), and eventually took the name Unity in 1895.

Myrtle Fillmore died in 1931 whereupon Charles married Cora Dedrick, his private secretary. Charles Fillmore died in 1948. The leadership of Unity was taken over by the Fillmores' two sons, Lowell and Rickert, and subsequently experienced a rapid growth. Today, Unity has some two million adherents worldwide, with its headquarters at Unity Village, in Lee's Summit, Missouri, a suburb of Kansas City.

The Beliefs of Unity

Unity claims that beliefs and belief systems are not important. What matters is that the Unity system works, even if the practitioner doesn't believe everything Charles and Myrtle Fillmore taught. However, in actual practice Unity is a strict religious system with clear-cut beliefs to which all long-term members eventually subscribe.

It was 30 years before Charles Fillmore drew up a statement of faith which was qualified with the following: "We are hereby giving warning that we shall not be bound to this tentative statement of what Unity believes. We may change our mind tomorrow on some of the points, and if we do, we shall feel free to make a new statement" (James Dillet Freeman, *What Is Unity?*, Lee's Summit, Missouri, n.d., p. 5).

Contrary to Fillmore's statement is the Bible's continued assertion that what a person believes is important. "He who believes in the Son has eternal life; but he who does not obey the Son shall not see life; but the wrath of God abides on him" (John 3:36 NASB. See also Hebrews 11:6. [For further documentation on why right belief is vital to the Christian faith, see our work, *Answers to Tough Questions*, pp. 149-151]).

The basic world view of Unity is that of gnosticism. Gnosticism is a theological term referring to a system of belief that qualitatively separates the spirit from the material. It also believes knowledge is secret and only obtainable by a select few. Gnostics generally believe that what is spiritual is good and what is material is bad. Christian Science, another gnostic cult, goes so far as to say that the material world doesn't even exist!

According to gnosticism, God is impersonal and one's eventual goal is to reach oneness with this impersonal God. Gnostics view Jesus Christ as a human being who possessed, in some great way, the expression or presence of God. To them, Jesus refers to the man and Christ refers to the divine influence. Rather than agreeing with the Bible by declaring that Jesus is the Christ (1 John 5:1), gnostics, including Unity, separate Jesus from the Christ.

Unity is not as interested in theology as it is in prosperity and happiness. A survey of the literature of Unity will clearly show that the stress is on material and worldly happiness, not spiritual happiness.

The Bible

"We believe that the Word of God is the thought of God expressed in creative ideas and that these ideas are the primal attributes of all enduring entities in the universe, visible and invisible. The Logos of the first chapter of the Gospel of John is the God idea of Christ that produced Jesus, the perfect man. We believe the Scriptures are the testimonials of men who have in a measure apprehended the divine Logos but that their writings should not be taken as final" (Unity's *Statement of Faith*, part 27).

The Scriptures testify to the fact that it is God who is their ultimate author, "All Scripture is given by inspiration of God" (2 Timothy 3:16), ". . .When you received from us the Word of God's message, you accepted it not as the word of men, but for what it really is, the Word of God (1 Thessalonians 2:13 NASB).

God

The doctrine of God in Unity is similar to that of Christian Science and other gnostic cults. Rather than believing in the Bible's infinite and personal creator, Unity adheres to the belief that God is impersonal.

This can be readily seen by a statement from Myrtle Fillmore. "Though personal to each one of us, God is it, neither male nor female, but principle" (Myrtle Fillmore, *How to Let God Help You*, 1956, p. 25). The *Metaphysical Dictionary*, a work of Charles Fillmore states, "The Father is Principle, the Son is that Principle revealed in creative plan, the Holy Spirit is the executive power of both Father and Son carrying out the creative plan" (*Metaphysical Bible Dictionary*, p. 629). One Unity publication states, "God is all and all is God" (*Unity*, August, 1974, p. 40).

Fillmore also said, "God is not loving. . .God does not love anybody or anything. God is the love in everybody and everything. God is love. . .God exercises none of His attributes except through the inner consciousness of the universe and man" (*Jesus Christ Heals*, Unity School of Christianity, 1944, pp. 31,32).

The Fillmores and other Unity writers confuse the attributes of God with God Himself. God is more than attributes such as love. He is personal (Exodus 3:14). He is not to be equated with the impersonal "everything" for He has a separate existence apart from creation (Isaiah 44: 1-28; Romans 1:18-25). Unity would deny Him His rightful position as creator, sustainer, and Lord of the universe.

Jesus Christ

"The Bible says that God so loved the world that He gave His only begotten Son, but the Bible does not here refer to Jesus of Nazareth, the outer man; it refers to the Christ, the spiritual identity of Jesus, whom he acknowledged in all his ways, and brought forth into his outer self, until even the flesh of his body was lifted up, purified, spiritualized, and redeemed, thus he became Jesus Christ, the word made flesh.

"And we are to follow into this perfect state and become like Him, for in each of us is the Christ, the only begotten Son. We can, through Jesus Christ, our Redeemer and example, bring forth the Christ within us, the true self of all is perfect, as Jesus Christ commanded his followers to be" (*Unity*, Vol. 57, no. 5, 464, and Vol. 72, no. 2, p. 8).

The Bible states however, "Who is the liar, but the one who denies that Jesus is the Christ. . ." (1 John 2:22). Jesus was called the Christ from the time of his birth (Luke 2:11, 26). The only way one can be born of God is to believe that Jesus is the Christ (1 John 5:1).

Unity teaches that within all of us there is an "inner Christ," equated with perfection, a divine awareness (Elizabeth Sand Turner, *What Unity Teaches*, Lee's Summit, Missouri, n.d., p. 9). All of us are capable of attaining that "inner Christ," that divine awareness and perfection.

The New Testament maintains that Jesus is different from us by the fact that He is God by His very nature: "In the beginning was the Word, and the Word was with God, and the Word was God" (John 1:1). Jesus Christ is the unique Son of God (John 1:14). No one else can be the Son of God as Jesus Christ is the Son of God (John 5:18-23). He alone is the "image of the invisible God" (Colossians 1:15), the "radiance of His glory and the exact representation of His nature" (Hebrews 1:3).

Salvation

In Unity, salvation is unnecessary: "There is no sin, sickness or death" (*Unity*, Vol. 47, No. 5, p. 403). There is no need for the death of Christ on the cross to take away sin. Unity said of the atonement of Christ, "The atonement is the union of man with God the Father, in Christ. Stating it in terms of mind, we should say that the Atonement is the At-one-ment or agreement of reconciliation of man's mind with Divine Mind through the superconsciousness of Christ's mind" (*What Practical Christianity Stands For*, p. 5).

Here again we have Unity in direct contradiction to the Bible that acknowledges sin as a reality, "For *all* have sinned and come short of the glory of God" (Romans 3:23). Furthermore, "The wages of sin is death, but the gift of God is eternal life through Jesus Christ our Lord" (Romans 6:23). If a person does not come to Christ for salvation he will be lost in his sin, "For unless you believe that I am He, you shall die in your sins" (John 8:24 NASB).

Reincarnation

Unity's statement of faith shows that they believe salvation involves reincarnation. "We believe that the dissolution of spirit, soul, and body caused by death, is annulled by rebirth of the same spirit and soul in another body here on earth. We believe the repeated incarnations of man to be a merciful provision of our loving Father to the end that all may have opportunity to attain immortality through regeneration, as did Jesus. This corruptible must put on incorruption" (*Unity's Statement of Faith*, Article 22).

Reincarnation teaches that only through many lifetimes can one rid himself of the debt for all of his sins. However, the Bible teaches that through Jesus Christ we can be rid of all of our sins at one time (1 John 1:8-10). His purpose for dying on the cross was as a sacrifice for our sins (Acts 3:18, 19).

Jesus Christ is the only Savior we ever need because "He abides forever, holds His priesthood permanently. Hence, also, He is able to save forever those who draw near to God through Him, since He always lives to make intercession for them" (Hebrews 7:24, 25). We have the promise of God Himself that our salvation has been guaranteed through faith in the sacrifice of Jesus Christ on the cross (1 Peter 1:2-6).

Prosperity

Another major tenet of Unity is that no one need be poor. Charles Fillmore, in his book *Prosperity (p. 69)*, perverted the 23rd Psalm in expressing this belief.

"The Lord is my banker, my credit is good.
He maketh me to lie down in the consciousness of omnipresent abundance;
He giveth me the key to His strongbox.
He restoreth my faith in His riches;
He guideth me in the paths of prosperity for His name's sake.
Yea though I walk in the very shadow of debt,
I shall fear no evil, for Thou art with me:
Thy silver and Thy Gold, they secure me.
Thou preparest a way for me in the presence of the collector;
Thou fillest my wallet with plenty; my measure runneth over.
Surely goodness and plenty will follow me all the days of my life;
And I shall do business in the name of the Lord forever."

The message of the Bible concerns our spiritual prosperity, not our material prosperity. As Christians, our desires are to be transformed spiritually by faith in Jesus Christ and the working of the Holy Spirit in our lives. The greed and self-centeredness exhibited by Fillmore's poem is in direct contradiction to the humility and God-centeredness the Bible teaches. If one's central desire is to serve the Lord and to express His love to others, one's material needs diminish and material prosperity doesn't even matter. The Apostle Paul put it like this:

Not that I speak from want; for I have learned to be content in whatever circumstances I am. I know how to get along with humble means, and I also know how to live in prosperity; in any and every circumstance I have learned the secret of being filled and going hungry, both of having abundance and suffering need. I can do all things through Him who Strengthens me...And my God shall supply all your needs according to His riches in glory in Christ Jesus (Philippians 4:11-13,19 NAS).

Conclusion

The Unity School of Christianity has no right to use the name Christian to describe its organization, for it is decidedly not Christian. Unfortunately, many Christians read the publications of Unity without realizing it is a non-Christian cult denying the basic beliefs of Christianity.

In the first publication that proceeded from the Fillmores, the non-Christian basis was revealed when they said, "We see the good in all religions and we want everyone to feel free to find the Truth for himself wherever he may be led to find it" (*Modern Thought*, 1889, p. 42). In contrast to this, Jesus of Nazareth said, "I am the Way, and the Truth, and the Life; no one comes to the Father, but through me" (John 14:6 NASB).

It is clear that Unity and Christianity are opposed to each other on the basic issues with no possible way of reconciling Unity as being part of Christianity.

Cult Ministry Referrals

Anderson, Einar, 1124-H North Louise Street, Glendale, California 91207.
(Emphasis: Mormonism)

C.A.I., P.O. Box 3295, Chico, California 95927.
(Emphasis: Jehovah's Witnesses and Mormonism)

Ron Carlson, C.M.I., 7601 Superior Terrace, Even Prairie, Minnesota 55344.
(Emphasis: General cult and general occult)

Robert Passantino, C.A.R.I.S., P.O. Box 2067, Costa Mesa, California 92626.
(Emphasis: General cult, general occult, apologetics, and theology)

Jim Valentine, C.A.R.I.S., P.O. Box 1659, Milwaukee, Wisconsin 53201.
(Emphasis: General cult, general occult, and Eastern philosophy)

Bill Cetnar, Route 2 Wierlake, Kunkletown, Pennsylvania 18058.
(Emphasis: Jehovah's Witnesses)

Walter Martin, Christian Research Institute, P.O. Box 500, San Juan Capistrano, California 92693.
(Emphasis: General cult and general occult)

James Bjornstad, Institute for Contemporary Christianity, P.O. Box A, Oakland, New Jersey 07436.
(Emphasis: General cult, general occult, and philosophy)

Marvin Cowan, P.O. Box 21052, Salt Lake City, Utah 84121.
(Emphasis: Mormonism)

Bob Witte, Ex-Mormons for Jesus, P.O. Box 946, Safety Harbor, Florida 33572.
(Emphasis: Mormonism)

Ed Decker, Saints Alive, P.O. Box 1076, Issaquah, Washington 98027.
(Emphasis: General cult and Mormonism)

Wally Tope, Front Line, P.O. Box 1100, La Canada Flintridge, California 91011.
(Emphasis: Jehovah's Witnesses, Mormonism, and Christian Science)

Edmond Gruss, Los Angeles Baptist College, P.O. Box 878, Newhall, California 91321.
(Emphasis: General cult and general occult specializing in Jehovah's Witnesses)

Homer Duncan, Missionary Crusader, 4606 Ave. H, Lubbock, Texas 79404.
(Emphasis: Jehovah's Witnesses)

Jerald Tanner, Modern Microfilm Company, P.O. Box 1884, Salt Lake City, Utah 84110.
(Emphasis: Mormonism)

J. L. Williams, New Directions Evangelistic Association, P.O. Box 2347, Burlington, North Carolina 27215.
(Emphasis: General cult and general occult specializing in The Way International).

Kurt Van Gorden, PACE, 1944 North Tustin Ave., Suite 118, Orange, California 92665.
(Emphasis: General cult and general occult specializing in The Way International and TheUnification Church)

Personal Freedom Outreach, P.O. Box 26062, St. Louis, Missouri 63136.
(Emphasis: Jehovah's Witnesses and Mormonism)

Spiritual Counterfeits Project, P.O. Box 2418, Berkeley, California 94702.
(Emphasis: General cult, general occult, sociology, and Eastern thought)

Arthur Budvarson, Utah Christian Tract Society, P.O. Box 725, La Mesa, California 92041.
(Emphasis: Mormonism)

Duane Magnani, Witness Incorporated, P.O. Box 597, Clayton, California 94517.
(Emphasis: Jehovah's Witnesses)

Annotated
Cults Bibliography

Adair, James R. and Ted Miller, ed. *We Found Our Way Out* (Grand Rapids, Michigan: Baker Book House, 1964).

These are testimonies of people who were into cults and have come to a saving knowledge of Jesus Christ. It covers Mormonism, Jehovah's Witnesses, Christian Science, Humanism, Communism, Seventh-day Adventism, Modernism, Armstrongism, Satanism, Agnosticism, Theosophism, and Hippies.

Anderson, Einar. *The Inside Story of Mormonism* (Grand Rapids, Michigan: Kregel Publications, 1973).

This is an excellent story of a man who was a Mormon, why he got into Mormonism, what the Mormons believe, why he left it, and why he knows it is not Christian. It discusses the history of Mormonism, Mormon beginnings, Mormon Articles of Faith, and false Bible interpretations by the Mormons.

Benwar, Paul. *Ambassadors of Armstrongism* (Nutley, New Jersey: Presbyterian and Reformed Publishing Company, 1975).

A good treatment of the history and teachings of the Worldwide Church of God. Includes doctrine of Scripture, God, Holy Spirit, Christ, angels, man, sin, salvation, the church, future things, special teachings and refutes all the major doctrinal errors of the Worldwide Church of God.

Bjornstad, James. *Counterfeits at Your Door* (Ventura, California: Gospel Light Publications, 1979).

This is an excellent treatment by one of the leading authorities in cult apologetics. It discusses Jehovah's Witnesses and Mormonism. It tells basically what they believe on the major doctrines of Christianity and why they are not biblical, and how to answer them.

_____ *The Moon is Not the Son: A Close Look at the Teachings of Rev. Sun Myung Moon and the Unification Church* (Minneapolis, Minnesota: Bethany Fellowship Incorporated, 1976).

Excellent treatment of Moon's complicated theology, history and practices of the Church and good Christian responses.

Boa, Kenneth. *Cults, World Religions and You* (Wheaton, Illinois: Victor Books, a Division of Scripture Press Publications, 1977).

This book covers non-Christian religions of the east, pseudo-Christian religions of the west, the major cults—Mormonism, Jehovah's Witnesses, etc. occult religion and systems, and new religions and cults like TM, Hare Krishna, as seen from a conservative Christian point of view.

Cowan, Marvin. *Mormon Claims Answered* (Salt Lake City, Utah: Marvin Cowan Publisher, 1975).

This is a very good technical treatment of the beliefs of Mormonism. It goes into origin and history, doctrine of God, the Bible, the Book of Mormon, the church and salvation. With excellent Christian answers that show step-by-step how to witness to a Mormon who is knowledgeable.

Cowdrey, Davis, and Scales with Gretchen Passantino. *Who Really Wrote the Book of Mormon?* (Santa Ana, California: Vision House Publishers, 1977 and 1980).

This is an excellent book on the origins of the Book of Mormon. It deals briefly with Mormon history and extensively with the Book of Mormon demonstrating it is not a revelation from God. The theory also says it was not written or translated by Joseph Smith, the founder of Mormonism, but instead was plagiarized by Smith and his colleagues and stolen from a novelist named Solomon Spaulding. This is the best book on this particular theory and has great evidence to support it.

Dencher, Ted. *Why I Left Jehovah's Witnesses* (Fort Washington, Pennsylvania: Christian Literature Crusade, 1966).

Testimony of a man who was in Jehovah's Witnesses and why he left. Presents the major teachings and history of the Jehovah's Witnesses and why they are not Christian. This is an excellent book to use as a study resource for a Christian. It should not be given to a Jehovah's Witness because the author's tone of voice is sometimes sarcastic.

Edwards, Christopher. *Crazy for God: the Nightmare of Cult Life* (Inglewood, New Jersey: Prentice Hall Incorporated, 1979).

This is a story of a young man who joined the Unification Church, why he joined it, what happened to him while he was in it and how he got out of it. In the very last chapter he says he does have religious faith now, but does not go into detail.

Enroth, Ronald. *The Lure of the Cults* (Chappaqua, New York: Christian Herald Books, 1979).

Dr. Enroth is a sociologist teaching at Westmont College, department of Sociology. An excellent source for materials on the sociological aspects of the cults from the Christian perspective. This book is organized by topic, not according to cults, and he mentions many cults throughout the book. It discusses why people get involved with the cults and how one can try to teach someone who is in a cult.

————————— *Youth, Brainwashing, and the Extremist Cults* (Grand Rapids, Michigan: Zondervan Publishing House, 1977).

This book discusses case histories from Hare Krishna, Children of God,

The Alamo Foundation, The Unification Church, The Way International, and The Divine Light Mission, and then talks about the sociological factors influencing the growth and rise of the cults, again, from a conservative evangelical Christian point of view.

Fraser, Gordon. *Is Mormonism Christian?* (Chicago, Illinois: Moody Press, 1957 and 1977).
This is a good general treatment from an evangelical Christian position. It does not contain a great deal of detail on doctrinal teachings, but it contains all the essentials. It's easy to read, does not have very many footnotes, and it's not very technical.

_____ *Sects of the Church of the Latter-Day Saints* (Eugene, Oregon: Industrial Litho Incorporated, 1978).
Discusses the reorganized Church of the Latter-day Saints, and the Mormon polygamous sects. This is the best Christian treatment available on the sects of Mormonism. It is a very good book.

Gruss, Edmond. *Apostles of Denial* (Nutley, New Jersey: Presbyterian and Reformed, 1978).
This is the best single volume on Jehovah's Witnesses available today. Gruss used to be a Jehovah's Witness. He is a professor of apologetics at a Christian seminary. It is thorough and exhaustive and treats the history and all the doctrines, major and minor, in Jehovah's Witnesses from a Christian biblical perspective. It is an excellent book.

_____ *Cults and the Occults in the Age of Aquarius* (Nutley, New Jersey: Presbyterian and Reformed Publishing Company, 1974).
This is an excellent small paperback set up to be used as a study book for a Bible study. It covers Jehovah's Witnesses, Mormonism, Christian Science, the Unity Church, Herbert W. Armstrong and the Worldwide Church of God, Spiritualism, Seventh-day Adventism, Astrology, Baha'i, the occult, Scientology, and then gives a Christian response. Revised edition published in 1980.

_____ *The Jehovah's Witnesses and Prophetic Speculation* (Nutley, New Jersey: Presbyterian and Reformed Publishing Company, 1972).
This deals specifically with the Jehovah's Witnesses continual false prophecies, especially about when the end of the world is coming. It is thoroughly documented and is a good additional resource on that subject.

_____ *We Left Jehovah's Witnesses: a Non-prophet Organization* (Nutley, New Jersey: Presbyterian and Reformed Publishing Company, 1974).
This contains testimonies of several people who were Jehovah's Witnesses and became Christians. In addition to giving testimonies, the testimonies contain good information on what Jehovah's Witnesses teach and how to reach someone who is a Jehovah's Witness.

Hefley, James C. *The Youthnappers* (Wheaton, Illinois: Victor Books, A Division of Scripture Press Publications, 1977).
From an evangelical point of view it gives a brief survey of some of the

new cults: The Unification Church, Hare Krishna, Divine Light Mission, TM, Children of God, etc. This is definitely a quick overview survey. The author is a good writer and good at reviewing general movements; however, he is not an expert on the cults.

Hoekema, Anthony A. *Christian Science* (Grand Rapids, Michigan: William B. Eerdmans Publishing Company, 1963).
This is a condensation and slight revision of the section of Christian Science from his standard work, the *Four Major Cults*.

_____ *Jehovah's Witnesses* (Grand Rapids, Michigan: William B. Eerdmans Publishing Company, 1963).
This is a reprint and a slight revision of his chapter on Jehovah's Witnesses in his book the *Four Major Cults*.

_____ *Mormonism* (Grand Rapids, Michigan: William B. Eerdmans Publishing Company, 1963).
This is excerpted and revised from his classic hardcover book, the *Four Major Cults*.

_____ *The Four Major Cults* (Grand Rapids, Michigan: William B. Eerdmans Publishing Company, 1963).
This is one of the classic old-time books on the cults. It discusses Mormonism, Seventh-day Adventism, Christian Science, Jehovah's Witnesses and the distinctive traits of the cults and approaching the cultist. This is done from a conservative Christian point of view.

Hopkins, Joseph. *The Armstrong Empire: A Look at the Worldwide Church of God* (Grand Rapids, Michigan: William B. Eerdmans Publishing Company, 1974).
It has extensive history on the Worldwide Church of God and Herbert W. Armstrong. It deals extensively with British Israelism, a doctrine that says the Jews are now the Europeans. It refutes the basic Armstrong doctrines of God, Christ, the Holy Spirit, Satan, salvation and Scripture.

Hunt, Dave. *The Cult Explosion* (Eugene, Oregon: Harvest House Publishers, 1980).
This treats the spiritual aspects of the cult movements, rather than dealing systematically and theologically with specific cults. This is a good overview of the spiritual battle going on for the lives of those who are caught up in the cults. This book also has a study guide, available from the same publisher, to go with it so it can be used in classes.

Lewis, Gordon *Confronting the Cults* (Grand Rapids, Michigan: Baker Book House, 1966).
This is another classic dealing with major cults—Jehovah's Witnesses, Mormonism, Christian Science, Seventh-day Adventism, Unity and Spiritualism. It deals with the cults from an evangelical point of view and discusses the major doctrines of each of the cults and the Christian responses to them.

_____ *What Everyone Should Know About Transcendental Meditation* (Ventura, California: Gospel Light Publications, 1975).

Excellent Christian treatment of TM by an excellent Christian scholar. He is not necessarily an expert on TM but has documented facts and good documentation.

Martin, Walter. *The Kingdom of the Cults* (Grand Rapids, Michigan: Bethany Fellowship Incorporated, 1965. Revised edition 1975).

This is the classic standard text on the major non-Christian cults from an evangelical point of view. It discusses Jehovah's Witnesses, Christian Science, Mormonism, Spiritism, Father Divine, Theosophy, Buddhism, Swedenborgianism, Baha'i, Black Muslims, Unity School of Christianity, Worldwide Church of God, Seventh-day Adventism, Unitarianism, and Rosicrucians. Everybody who wants to learn about the cults should read this book.

_____ *The New Cults* (Santa Ana, California: Vision House Publishers Incorporated, 1980).

This book is probably the most comprehensive evangelical theological treatment of the new cults. It treats The Way International, Hare Krishna, TM, EST, Children of God, Silva Mind Control, Ascended Masters (I AM), Roy Masters, Church of the Living Word, Nicheren Shoshu Buddhism, Reincarnation, and the Local Church. This book documents the main beliefs of all these groups on the central doctrines of the Christian faith and the biblical responses to them.

_____ *The Rise of the Cults* (Santa Ana, California: Vision House Publishers Incorporated, 1980).

This is a condensation and revision of some of the same topics covered in the *Kingdom of the Cults*. It discusses Jehovah's Witnesses, Worldwide Church of God, Christian Science, Mormonism, Unity, Spiritism, Baha'i. This is an excellent quick reference to document what these particular cults believe on all the major doctrines of the Christian faith and why they are not Christian.

Miller, Calvin. *Transcendental Hesitation: A Biblical Appraisal of TM and Eastern Mysticism* (Grand Rapids, Michigan: Zondervan Publishing House, 1977).

This is another good treatment of TM. It includes more history and documentation.

Miller, William McElwee. *The Baha'i Faith: Its History and Teachings* (Pasadena, California: William Carey Libarary, 1974).

This is a history of the Baha'i movement, done by a conservative evangelical Christian who was a missionary for 40 years in Iran. It is the most comprehensive treatment of Baha'ism available in English.

_____ *What is the Baha'i World Faith?* (Santa Ana, California: Christian Apologetics: Research and Information Service, 1977).

This is a short booklet explaining basically what Baha'ism teaches, why it is not Christian and how to witness to someone who is a Baha'i.

Milmine, Georgine. *The Life of Mary Baker G. Eddy and the History of Christian Science* (Grand Rapids, Michigan: Baker Book House, copyright 1909 by Doubleday, reprinted 1971 by Baker Books).

This is a classic, exhaustively documented history of the founder of Christian Science. It is done by a journalist from a non-Christian point of view. It points out all the historical inaccuracies and problems in the life of Mary Baker Eddy and Christian Science. This is an excellent historical resource.

Needleman, Jacob. *The New Religions* (New York, New York: E. P. Dutton and Company Inc., 1970).

This is a non-Christian book talking about the new eastern religions and cultic movements sweeping the U.S. It's divided topically and covers the major eastern religions such as: Hinduism, Buddhism, Sufism, as well as the occult, Zen Buddhism, TM, Meher Baba, Subud, and Krishnamurti.

Passantino, Robert and Gretchen. *Answers to the Cultist at Your Door* (Eugene, Oregon: Harvest House Publishers, 1981).

This book deals with Jehovah's Witnesses, Mormons, Hare Krishna, Moonies, The Way International, and how to help your loved ones in a cult. This book is written on an easy-to-understand level. It contains testimonies of people who have left the cults. It tells specifically what the cults believe and why they are not Christian. It does not depend on the readers' knowing Greek, Hebrew, or extensive theology. It is an especially good book for a person who has not studied the cults much. It will also satisfy those with more extensive theological training.

Peterson, William J. *Those Curious New Cults* (New Canaan, Connecticut: Keats Publishers Incorporated, 1973 and 1975).

Includes why people were turned on by the new cults: Astrology, Edgar Cayce, Spiritualism, Witchcraft, Satanism, Scientology, Armstrongism, Children of God, Hare Krishna, Zen Buddhism, TM, Meher Baba, Baha'i, Gurdjieff the philosopher, The Divine Light Mission, and the Unification Church. This is a quick synopsis of some of the major features of all of these different cults. It is not in-depth. It does not deal with all of the areas of doctrinal deviation from the Bible, but it is a good Christian introduction.

Ridenour, Fritz. *So What's the Difference?* (Ventura, California: Gospel Light Publications, 1967).

This book deals with the most common cults and major religions of the world. It does treat Roman Catholicism as a cult. It is a small paperback that is easy to read.

Ropp, Harry L. *The Mormon Papers: Are the Mormon Scriptures Reliable?* (Downers Grove, Illinois: InterVarsity Press, 1977).

Another treatment of Mormon sacred writings, including the Book of Mormon, from an evangelical Christian point of view.

Rosten, Leo ed. *Religions in America* (New York, New York: Simon and Schuster, 1962-1963).

A non-Christian book. It covers 20 religious movements in the U.S., including Protestants, evangelicals, Catholics, and major cults. This is not an objective book. Each entry was submitted by a leader from that particular cult or religion.

Schnell, William. *Thirty Years a Watchtower Slave* (Grand Rapids, Michigan: Baker Book House, 1971).

This is the testimony of a man who was a Jehovah's Witness for 30 years, until he came to salvation in Jesus Christ. It tells why he was in it for so long, what held him in it, why he got out, and the freedom he then had in Jesus Christ.

Sire, James W. *Scripture Twisting: Twenty Ways the Cults Misread the Bible* (Downers Grove, Illinois: InterVarsity Press, 1980).

This is a specialized book. Written on a very simple level it discusses the way that cults try to use the Bible to support their beliefs and teachings.

Sparks, Jack. *The Mindbenders* (Nashville, Tennessee: Thomas Nelson Publishers, 1977 and 1979).

This is a standard current book on the new cults. It includes The Unification Church, The Way International, Children of God, The Local Church, TM, Divine Light Mission, Hare Krishna, People's Temple. Sparks deals with this from a sociological, psychological, and traditional church history point of view. He examines the cults' arguments theologically and gives biblical responses to them. He also points out how the Church throughout history has dealt with similar heresies.

Spittler, Russel P. *Cults and Isms: Twenty Alternatives to Evangelical Christianity* (Grand Rapids, Michigan: Baker Book House, 1962).

Discusses Mormonism, Seventh-day Adventism, Spiritualism, Christian Science, Jehovah's Witnesses, Unity, Moral Rearmament, Theosophy, Baha'i, Zen Buddhism, Anglo-Israelism, Astrology, Father Divine, Swedenborgianism, secular modernism, Humanism, Roman Catholicism, Unitarian Universalism, liberalism, and neo-orthodoxy. This book is one of the standard works. It's outdated, but does deal with cults still popular today. He examines things from a conservative Christian point of view.

Stoner, Carroll and Jo Anne Parke. *All God's Children* (Radnor, Pennsylvania: Chilton Book Company, 1977).

This book talks about the new religions, such as Unification Church and the Children of God. It discusses deprogramming, readjusting, and what to do if your child is in a cult. It discusses the upsurge in cults today. This is not a Christian book. It does contain valuable and useful information.

Tanner, Jerald and Sandra. *Mormonism—Shadow or Reality?* (Salt Lake City, Utah: Modern Microfilm Company, 1982).

This giant 600-page book contains all the documentation needed from Mormon sources on Mormon beliefs, history, and practices. It is an excellent treatise on all their historical major and minor doctrines, using primary

Mormon sources for documentation. It is written from a Christian perspective but is not a theological or doctrinal book.

_____ *The Changing World of Mormonism* (Chicago, Illinois: Moody Press, 1980).
This is a condensation for laymen of the larger book, *Mormonism — Shadow or Reality?* It is still in-depth, extensive, and technical, but more readable than *Shadow or Reality.*

Thomas, F. W. *Masters of Deception: An Exposé of the Jehovah's Witnesses* (Grand Rapids, Michigan: Baker Book House).
This is a good treatment of the major and minor doctrines of the Jehovah's Witnesses from an evangelical Christian perspective. This book is especially good for the historical treatment of the minor doctrines of Jehovah's Witnesses. Its tone, however, is often harsh.

Van Buskirk, Michael. *The Scholastic Dishonesty of the Watchtower* (Santa Ana, California: Christian Apologetics: Research and Information Service, 1976).
This is an excellent, short 44-page treatment of the Jehovah's Witnesses misuse of Greek and Hebrew scholarship. It is thorough, completely documented, and the best single source to show the Jehovah's Witnesses that the Watchtower Society has misrepresented and misused Greek and Hebrew grammar in trying to support their own position.

Williams, J. L. *Victor Paul Wierwille and The Way International* (Chicago, Illinois: Moody Press, 1979).
This is definitely the best work on the cult The Way International from a Christian perspective. An expert in the field, Williams deals with it doctrinally and historically.

Yamamoto, J. Isamu. *The Puppet Master: An Inquiry into Sun Myung Moon and the Unification Church* (Downers Grove, Illinois: InterVarsity Press, 1977).
Yamamoto is one of the leading Christian experts on the Unification Church. This book is well documented and deals extensively with Moon's doctrines and teachings.

Part II

Understanding the Occult

CHAPTER ONE

The Occult
Phenomena

I n this book we are attempting to expose the workings of Satan and the occultic realm by the standard of God's inspired Word. In doing this, it is our desire to give a balanced picture of the situation and to avoid sensationalism. Our goals include:

(1) To be a source of information as to what is and what is not an occult phenomenon by clearing up certain misconceptions;

(2) To keep those who are not now involved in the occult from becoming so;

(3) To lead those who are now dabbling in the occult out of such practices and into a personal relationship with Jesus Christ; and

(4) To inform the believer who his real enemy is and the Satanic devices used in spiritual warfare.

What is the Occult?

The word "occult" comes from the Latin word "occultus" and it carries the idea of things hidden, secret and mysterious. Hoover lists three distinct characteristics of the occult:

1. The occult deals with things secret or hidden.
2. The occult deals with operations or events which seem to depend on human powers that go beyond the five senses.
3. The occult deals with the supernatural, the presence of angelic or demonic forces.
   (David W. Hoover, *How to Respond to the Occult*, St. Louis: Concordia Publishing House, 1977, p. 8).

Under the designation occult we would class at least the following items: witchcraft, magic, palm reading, fortune telling, ouija boards, tarot cards, satanism, spiritism, demons and the use of crystal balls. To this list we could add much more.

Avoiding Extremes

C. S. Lewis once commented, "There are two equal and opposite errors into which our race can fall about the devils. One is to disbelieve in their existence. The other is to believe, and to feel an unhealthy interest in them. They themselves are equally pleased by both errors and hail a materialist or a magician with the same delight" (C. S. Lewis, *The Screwtape Letters*, New York: MacMillan Co., 1961, preface).

It is our desire to avoid such extremes that are common in dealing with the occult. We neither see the devil in everything nor completely deny his influence and workings.

Moreover, we also intend to deal with phenomena that some feel to be occultic but can be better explained either by deception, luck, or by psychological or physiological factors.

A Word of Warning

We realize that by informing people about the world of the occult, we will be exposing certain people to things and practices of which they have previously been ignorant. It is not our desire to stimulate one's curiosity in the realm of the occult to where it becomes an obsession. Seeing that mankind has a certain fascination about evil, it would be wise to take the advice of the Apostle Paul, "I want you to be wise in what is good and innocent in what is evil" (Romans 16:19, *New American Standard*).

Playing around with the world of the occult can lead to serious repercussions, both psychologically and spiritually. There is a difference between knowing intellectually that taking poison will kill you and actually taking the poison to experience what you already knew to be a fact. We need to be aware of the workings of the satanic realm but not to the point of unhealthy fascination, obsession or involvement.

The Supernatural Does Exist

We live in a day when people are looking for answers to life's basic questions, "What is the purpose of life?"; "Is there life after death?"; "Is there evidence for the existence of a supernatural God?"

In our other works we have given reasons why we believe that God exists and has revealed Himself to mankind through both the Bible and the Person of Jesus Christ.[1] This God has provided irrefutable evidence in support of the fact that He not only exists but that He is sovereign over history.

According to the Bible there is a supernatural warfare going on, "For our struggle is not against flesh and blood, but against the rulers, against the powers, against the world forces of this darkness, against the spiritual forces of wickedness in the heavenly places" (Ephesians 6:12, NASB).

This ongoing spiritual battle is between the kingdom of God and the kingdom of Satan. One purpose of Jesus Christ's coming to earth was given to us by the Apostle John, "The reason the Son of God appeared was to destroy the works of the devil" (1 John 3:8).

Although the Scriptures make it clear that the supernatural is real and that spiritual warfare is going on, there are those who would like to

[1] See *Answers to Tough Questions, Evidence That Demands a Verdict*, and *Reasons Skeptics Should Consider Christianity.*

demythologize the accounts of the devil, demons and demon possession. They contend that the supernatural references in the Scriptures are from a pre-scientific, superstitious world view. However, if one takes the supernatural out of the Scriptures, all the meaning goes out with it. John Montgomery, dean of the Simon Greenleaf School of Law and leading contemporary theologian, comments:

> Even the casual reader of the New Testament is aware of the pervasive recognition given to demonic powers. Again and again Jesus casts out demons, even engaging in dialogues with them (cf. the Gadarene demoniac incident, Luke 8); and his followers cast out demons in His name (Acts 19, etc.). Jesus' public ministry commences after He is "driven by the Spirit into the wilderness to be tempted of the devil" (Matthew 4; Mark 1; Luke 4).
>
> Central to the entire New Testament teaching concerning the end of the world is Christ's return "with all His mighty angels," God's triumph over the evil powers, and the casting of Satan into the lake of fire forever (Matthew 25; Mark 13; 2 Thessalonians 1; Revelation 19, 20).
>
> What is to be done with such material? One of my theological professors used to state flatly that the demonic in the New Testament was to be regarded as symbolic (of evil, psychosis, disease, etc.), and he became quite agitated when I asked him whether we should also regard Jesus as symbolic (of the good, of mental and physical health, etc.) since in the narrative of Jesus' temptation in the wilderness a dialogue takes place between Jesus and the devil — both evidently regarded as having comparable reality or unreality! This points up the difficulty with demythologizing of the satanic in the New Testament: They are integrally bound up with the reality of Jesus and His entire message. (John Warwick Montgomery, *Principalities and Powers*, Minneapolis: Bethany Fellowship, 1973, pp. 54, 55).

Those who would strip away the so-called myths from the Scripture are left with an empty gospel, devoid of any life-transforming power. In answer to such critics, we respond with the truth and rational claims of the whole gospel — including Satan's war against it and God's supernatural intervention and ultimate triumph. The world of the occult is real, and God's all-powerful Spirit is just as real!

Occultic Deception

Although we admit the reality of the supernatural, we must be careful not to place all unexplained phenomena into the supernatural category. There is much that goes on under the guise of the supernatural that is nothing but fakery. This pseudo-occult phenomenon has fooled many people into believing in its legitimacy.

In an excellent book entitled *The Fakers*, Danny Korem and Paul Meier expose much of this phenomenon that is taken to be supernatural. They explain the difference between what is real and what is actually deception:

> What is the difference between occult and pseudo-occult phenomena? Occult phenomena are phenomena of or relating to supernatural agencies, their effects, and knowledge of them. An example which many people consider a manifestation of occultic powers is demon possession. While the manifestation is visible, the force behind it is not. We can see the *effects* of a possession, but we cannot see the demon perpetrating the manifestation. Pseudo-occult

phenomena are events which *appear* to be caused by secretive, supernatural powers and yet are brought about by physical or psychological means.

One purpose of this book is to point out the difference between the occult and pseudo-occult. There is a great danger in treating both on equal ground. One man who had reportedly performed the act of exorcism on several demon-possessed individuals tried his hand on a young teenager. The man strapped the young lady to a chair to prevent her from harming herself and proceeded with his ritual. It turned out that the girl was not demon-possessed but was schizophrenic and needed the help of a trained psychiatrist. The girl, obviously terrified by the trauma, was left in worse shape than when she first went to see the man in question.

Misconceptions about the supernatural are legion, and it makes no difference whether one does or does not profess religious beliefs. Neither is one's level of mental competence or educational background a factor. In order for one to make qualified decisions as to whether an event is of the supernatural or not, it is helpful if one is schooled in the art of deception (Danny Korem and Paul Meier, *The Fakers*, Grand Rapids, MI: Baker Book House, 1980, pp. 15, 16).

Korem and Meier list 11 principles of deception that fakers use to imitate supernatural or occultic phenomena. These include:

1. Sleight of hand
2. Psychological principles
3. Using a stooge
4. Unseen and unknown devices
5. Mathematical principles
6. Physics
7. Physical deception
8. Mechanical deception
9. Optical illusion
10. Luck and probability
11. Combination of all the principles.
(Ibid., pp. 22-29).

Needless to say, caution must be exercised before assuming some unexplained phenomenon is demonic. While not all Christian writers would place certain phenomena under the category of deception, as Korem and Meier, the latter clearly demonstrate the need for restraint in attributing many unexplained phenomena to the occult.

What Kind of People Get Involved in the Occult?

Who gets involved in the occult and why they get involved is very important. (It is also important to remember that when we refer to the "occult," we do not mean one homogenous organization or religion. The "occult" refers to a collection of practices and beliefs generally associated with occultic phenomena. One could be in the "occult" whether he is involved in a particular occultic group or just involved with occultic practices and/or beliefs.

It is wrong to classify all occultists as either sick or on the fringe of society, for responsible professional people are practicing the occult. W. Elwyn Davies lists three characteristics which may be true of occult practitioners:

1. *Many are escapists.* It has become a cliche to say, "Satan (or the demons) made me do it." The world of the occult becomes attractive to people who find it difficult to face up to their moral responsibilities. Many dabble with "other powers," and are drawn into involvement. They often claim that they have tried "other remedies" in vain, and the alternative empowerment through the occult allures them.

2. *Many more are superstitious.* Going beyond the bounds of revelation and common sense, they profess to see demonic activity in many areas: Sickness, depression, anger, any unusual or unexplained behavior. While such may be evidence of demonic action, it should by no means be an automatic assumption. Where natural causes offer a reasonable explanation it is wise to accept them as the origin of the problem. People who jump to the conclusion that demonic influences are responsible for a wide variety of phenomena invariably become obsessed with the thought of demons-at-work, and suffer many of the disabilities commonly found in victims of demonization.

3. *All are victims.* I use the word advisedly. There is no point in being judgmental toward these people, even though as Christians we oppose and condemn all occult practices. From a biblical perspective there is no room for negotiation or compromise here. God judges and condemns all traffic with demons, and we can do no less. In the sight of God they are guilty of transgressing His law. Each one is a victim, too—the victim of powers immeasurably more powerful and knowing than he. What kind of person is he?

   (1) The curious, who experiments and plays with demonic forces, only to find eventually that they are playing with him.

   (2) The conformist, who looks around at this peer group and says, "Everyone does it," and decides to be another who "does it."

   (3) The dissatisfied, whose religious experience has left him unfulfilled and skeptical.

   (4) The sad, whose bereavement inclines him toward anything that offers knowledge of the dead.

   (5) The rebellious, who recoils from the status quo in the church and in society, and seeks a viable alternative elsewhere.

   (6) The psychically inclined, who wants to develop suspected latent powers.

   (7) The offspring of practicing occultists, who are conditioned from childhood.

   (8) The credulous, and every generation seems to produce its quota of them! (W. Elwyn Davies, in *Principalities and Powers*, edited by John Warwick Montgomery, Minneapolis, MN: Bethany Fellowship, 1976, pp. 303, 304).

CHAPTER TWO

The Occult
Explosion

W e live in a day when occult activity is rapidly increasing. The following news release reveals the widespread purchase of occultic paraphernalia, along with the modern, sophisticated methods by which it is marketed:

> . . .1980 saw another increase in occult activity in America as reflected in the marketing sophistication of occult movements.
>
> According to Craig A. Huey, president of Informat, Inc., a Rolling Hills Estates, California-based direct marketing agency, many companies prospered greatly by marketing occult books, magazines, charms, voodoo pendants and other assorted paraphernalia. The available mailing lists involved in the occult now stands at some 3,824,622 (some include the accumulation of several years). Women still constitute a majority of the buyers. The vast majority of occultists are involved in astrology. For example, one company called the American Astrological Association has some 339,660 individuals who have bought horoscopes for an average sale of between $3.50-$9.95. There are some 86,000 women mail order buyers who paid $8.40 each for a genie-in-the-bottle good luck talisman, a mystical talisman.
>
> The House of Collinwood has 92,976 buyers who purchased ankhs, pyramids, talisman amulets, zodiac medallions, occult necklaces, bracelets, rings, earrings, (mostly for women) at $12 apiece on the average.
>
> There were 208,302 buyers of the *Handbook of Supernatural Powers*, which gives directions for ancient spells and potions. Seventy percent are men, and they paid $10 each. There were 91,846 buyers of the book *Magic Power of Witchcraft* at $9.98. There are 16,842 members of the Circle of Mystic and Occult Arts Book Club of Prentice Hall Publishing.

Martin Ebon, former administrative secretary of the Parapsychology Foundation, and the author of *The Satan Trap* and *Dangers of the Occult*, gives his assessment of the upswing of interest in occult phenomena:

> Occult practices and psychic phenomena are exercising a hold on millions of Americans today. There is no single explanation for this boom, but its major causes are easy to pinpoint. To begin with, the age-old pull of the irrational remains as persistent and just about as inexplicable as, let's say, terrestrial gravity; and while traditional religious practices lose their attraction, the occult and related Eastern mysticism gain in popularity.

Two mass stimuli have contributed to this trend. One is the drug cult, which causes an interest in such matters as a "non-drug high," to be sought in meditation and similar practices, as well as in confirmation of the drug-induced feeling that mind may control matter or events. Second, a series of highly popular motion pictures created successive waves of occult or pseudo-occult involvements. With *Rosemary's Baby*, which pictured the birth of a diabolic infant, came an upswing in witchcraft practices; with *The Exorcist*, demonic possession and exorcism were dramatized to a public of millions; other films and television shows have dealt with similar themes.

These waves of interest, compounded, have indirectly drawn attention to scholarly research of parapsychology—although researchers in the field deplore the sensationalism that powers public interest. The mass-circulation tabloids, in particular the *National Enquirer*, bring a weekly potion of the magical and psychic to the check-out counters of the nation's supermarkets; stories of miraculous healings, haunted houses, visits by Unidentified Flying Objects, and exorcism abound in these periodicals. The very fact that these shrewdly edited publications find it profitable to mix the occult with jet-set gossip and anecdotes of awe and uplift illustrates public fascination with psychic subjects. Astrology, although in a category by itself, has a similar hold on a large public. ("The Occult Temptation," by Martin Ebon, *The Humanist*, January/February, 1977).

From the above it is evident that occult beliefs have now penetrated every web of our society (cf. The Gallup Poll: 1978, June 15; "Astrology and Marginality," *Journal for the Scientific Study of Religion*, 15: 157-169, by R. Wuthrow, 1976). From the media to grocery stores, one cannot turn without encountering some type of occultic literature or influence. One can find horoscopes for weight loss and horoscopes for a better sex life.

Even higher education is not exempt. The University of California at Berkeley recently awarded its first bachelor's degree in magic, and is only one of many reputable universities now offering courses in parapsychology.

Parapsychology is an attempt to give certain occultic practices scientific respectability. This often means assenting to their reality (such as mental telepathy, telekinesis) yet having no explanation for their source, or the means by which they operate.

Here is a description by someone sympathetic to the occult explosion:

The occult is no longer what it used to be. Only a few years ago, especially around the time of the Satanic film *Rosemary's Baby*, the term "occult" would have been reserved for obscure, demonic and vaguely diabolical practices alone. In San Francisco at this time Anton Szandor La Vey, who starred as the devil in the above film, was establishing his Satanic Church; Charles Manson was incarnating the Devil and Christ simultaneously; Bishop Pike was endeavouring to communicate with his suicide son through a medium; and witchcraft was thriving.

These days, we believe, the occult has a wider connotation. *The Exorcist* notwithstanding, the term "occult" today includes ESP, Kirlian photography, reincarnation, palmistry, astrology, faith healing, white magic, Tarot, and even out-of-the-body experiences. The occult, too, is no longer disreputable. Scientists at Stanford investigate psychic Uri Geller; in California, Professor Charles

Tart carries out laboratory tests on Robert Monroe, a subject who can astral-travel at will; Arthyr Koestler, previously doubtful about the powers of yogis, comes forth with a scientific rationale of the paranormal in his *Roots of Coincidence*; Colin Wilson, meanwhile coins the term "Faculty X" to describe the psychic potential of man which he believes marks the next phase of man's evolution.

In short, the occult is about man's hidden potential. Much of this, of course, relates to how he thinks and how he perceives. Many aspects of the occult dealt with in this book show how man can enlarge his consciousness (Nevill Drury and Gregory Tillett, *The Occult Sourcebook*, London: Routledge and Kegan Paul, 1978, p. ix).

Why is There Such an Interest in the Occult?

With the alarming rate at which people are becoming involved in the occult, the inevitable question of "why" comes up, Why do people who live in this enlightened age with all the marvelous scientific and technological advances become involved in occultic practices? We believe there are several factors that have contributed to the rise of occult popularity.

The Secularization of the Gospel

In recent years there has been a denial of the cardinal doctrines of the Christian faith from those occupying a position of leadership in the church. This leaves a greater spiritual vacuum in the world which invites people who have spiritual needs to go elsewhere to have them satisfied. Moreover, some of these church leaders who have forsaken the gospel have themselves become practitioners of the occult, causing a follow-the-leader mentality in many former churchgoers.

The classic example would be the Episcopal bishop, James Pike, who rejected the church's belief in the deity of Christ, His virgin birth, and other central truths. After the suicide death of his son, Pike began to consult mediums, including the famous Arthur Ford, in an attempt to contact the spirit of his dead son. Pike became a firm believer in life after death from his occultic involvement rather than from biblical doctrine and took many people with him into the dark world of the occult. When the church "waters down" the gospel of Christ, the door to occultic practice swings wide open.

Curiosity

There is a certain mystery about the occult which appeals to our curiosity. Many who get involved in occult practices do so by starting out with so-called "harmless" practices such as reading horoscopes or using a Ouija board. They afterward proceed into deeper involvement because of an increasing curiosity. Buzzard comments upon this fascination:

Our age seems to have a deep fascination with evil, the bizarre, and the inexplicable. It thrives on horror and repulsion. What makes one faint or vomit or experience nightmares has a kind of magnetic charm. Mary Knoblauch summed up this fascination in commenting on *The Exorcist:* "Perhaps the most frightening thing about *The Exorcist* is that thirst for and fascination with evil that lies buried in us all, surfacing with savage swiftness at the right incarnation." The moment of that incarnation seems to be upon us. What was buried has arisen and dances unashamedly in the streets (Lynn Buzzard, Introduction to *Demon Possession*, edited by John Warwick Montgomery, Minneapolis: Bethany Fellowship, 1976, pp. 17, 18).

Unfortunately, there is a price to pay for this curiosity about the occult. The occult is not something neutral that an individual can get in and out of without any adverse effects.

In his book *Kingdom of Darkness*, F. W. Thomas relates a story of a man-and-wife journalistic team who desired to investigate the occult in London. They joined a satanic group to obtain firsthand information, but eventually withdrew because of the frightening things which they observed. Their lives were never the same. They were troubled by many terrible experiences and incidents.

Thomas concluded, "Such was the experience of an unwise couple whose curiosity for black magic dragged them through untold anguish and despair. One cannot just pick up the dark bolts of magical fire and drop them at will without getting burned. There is always a price to pay for use of these forbidden powers, in this world as well as in the world to come" (F. W. Thomas, *Kingdom of Darkness*, cited by Clifford Wilson and John Weldon, *Occult Shock and Psychic Forces*, San Diego: Master Books, 1980, pp. 13, 14).

The Occult Offers Reality

There is a reality in the occultic experience which attracts many people to it. All of us desire some sort of ultimate answer for life's basic questions, and the world of the occult gladly supplies answers. The astrologist will chart your future. The Ouija board promises you direction, and the medium talking to the spirit of your dead relative informs you that things are fine in the next world.

Since these occultic practices do reveal some amazing things, the practitioner is lulled into thinking that he has experienced ultimate reality and no longer needs to continue his search for truth. The spiritual vacuum is filled by means of a spiritual experience, not with God, but often from the very pit of hell.

A Sign of the Times

There are many indications that we are living at the end of the age with the return of Jesus Christ on the horizon. If this is the case, then we should expect to see an increase in demonic activity as Christ's coming nears, for this is the clear teaching of Scripture: "But the Spirit explicitly says that in later times some will fall away from the faith, paying attention to deceitful spirits and doctrines of demons" (1 Timothy 4:1, NASB).

Jesus said that at the end of the age, "False Christs and false prophets will arise, and will show signs and wonders, in order, if possible, to lead the elect astray" (Mark 13:22, NASB). Thus, Scripture indicates that occultic activity would be on the rise shortly before the second coming of Jesus Christ.

The Bible and the Occult

The Bible categorically denounces any and all occultic practices:

> When you enter the land which the Lord your God gives you, you shall not learn to imitate the detestable things of those nations.
>
> There shall not be found among you anyone who makes his son or his daughter pass through the fire, one who uses divination, one who practices witchcraft, or one who interprets omens, or a sorcerer,
>
> or one who casts a spell, or a medium, or a spiritualist, or one who calls upon the dead.
>
> For whoever does these things is detestable to the Lord; and because of these detestable things the Lord your God will drive them out before you.
>
> You shall be blameless before the Lord your God.
>
> For those nations, which you shall dispossess, listen to those who practice witchcraft and to diviners, but as for you, the Lord your God has not allowed you to do so (Deuteronomy 18:9-14, NASB).

In the same manner, the New Testament condemns such workings (Galatians 5:20). In the city of Ephesus many who were practicing in the occult became believers in Jesus Christ and renounced their occultic practices. "Many also of those who practiced magic brought their books together and began burning them in the sight of all. . ." (Acts 19:19).

Another encounter with the occult can be seen in Acts 13:6-12: (NASB):

> And when they had gone through the whole island as far as Paphos, they found a certain magician, a Jewish false prophet whose name was Bar-Jesus,
>
> Who was with the proconsul, Sergius Paulus, a man of intelligence. This man summoned Barnabas and Saul and sought to hear the word of God.
>
> But Elymas the magician (for thus his name is translated) was opposing them, seeking to turn the proconsul away from the faith.
>
> But Saul, who was also known as Paul, filled with the Holy Spirit, fixed his gaze upon him.
>
> And said, "You who are full of all deceit and fraud, you son of the devil, you enemy of all righteousness, will you not cease to make crooked the straight ways of the Lord?
>
> And now, behold, the hand of the Lord is upon you, and you will be blind and not see the sun for a time. And immediately a mist and a darkness fell upon him, and he went about seeking those who would lead him by the hand.
>
> Then the proconsul believed when he saw what happened, being amazed at the teaching of the Lord.

The false prophet who called himself Bar-Jesus (Son of Jesus) was actually trying to keep the governor, Sergius Paulus, from becoming a believer, and the judgment of blindness on this man was immediate. Walter Martin makes some astute observations on the passage by listing five characteristics of those who oppose God:

1. They are in league with Satan and possess certain supernatural powers.
2. They are false prophets.
3. They seek to influence people politically and ecclesiastically, particular-

ly those in positions of power (verses 6, 7).

4. They attempt to prevent those who are seeking to hear the Word of God from learning it by opposing those who preach it (verse 8).

5. They deliberately attempt to divert prospective converts from the faith (verse 8) as their ultimate goal (Walter Martin, *The Maze of Mormonism,* Santa Ana, CA: Vision House Publishers, Inc., 1977, pp. 216, 217).

From the above, to which much could be added, we see how the Bible in the strongest terms condemns the occult and those who practice it. The road of the occult is broad and leads to destruction, while the way of Christ is narrow and leads to life eternal.

CHAPTER THREE

Astrology

T wo of the most crucial questions that haunt humanity are, "Who am I?" and "What's going to happen in the future?" Many people lose sleep at night worrying about the future, wondering what will happen tomorrow. Astrology claims to have the solution to these basic questions. They offer daily horoscopes to predict individuals' futures. "What's your sign?" crops up in many casual conversations. The ancient occultic art of astrology has become very popular in our 20th-century culture.

What Is Astrology?

Astrology is an ancient practice that assumes that the position of the stars and planets has a direct influence upon people and events. Supposedly, one's life pattern can be charted by determining the position of the stars and planets at the time of one's birth. The chart that attempts to accomplish this is known as a "horoscope." Rene Noorbergen explains how one's horoscope is charted:

> For every personal horoscope, the moment of birth is the essential starting point. This, coupled with the latitude and longitude of the individual's birthplace, provides the initial package for the usual astrological chart. While this is elementary, it is not complete; a factor known as "true local time" must also be considered. This "true" time is arrived at by adding or subtracting four minutes for each degree of longitude that your birthplace lies to the east or west of the center of your time zone of birth. Once this has been accomplished, the next step is to convert this "true" time into "sidereal" or star time. This is done with the aid of an ephemerus, a reference book showing the positions of the planets in relationship to the earth. Checking this star time in an astrological table is the last formal move, for in doing so, the theme of the individual's "ascendant"—the astrological sign that is supposed to have been rising on the eastern horizon at the moment of birth—is revealed.
>
> Once you have developed this data—these simple steps are no more difficult than solving a seventh-grade math problem—then you are ready to "chart" your horoscope. This means you align the "ascendant" with the nine-o'clock point on the inner circle of the horoscope, and from there you are prepared to "read" the various zodiacal "houses" that control your life and fortune (Rene

Noorbergen, *The Soul Hustlers*, Grand Rapids, MI: Zondervan, 1976, pp. 176, 177).

How Is It Justified?

How astrologers justify their practice is explained by Michael Van Buskirk:

> One's future can be forecast, allegedly, because astrology asserts the unity of all things. This is the belief that the Whole (or all of the universe put together) is in some way the same as the Part (or the individual component or man), or that the Part is a smaller reflection of the Whole (macrocosmic/microcosmic model). The position of the planets (the macro) influences and produces a corresponding reaction in man (the micro). This makes man a pawn in the cosmos with his life and actions pre-determined and unalterable (Michael Van Buskirk, *Astrology: Revival in the Cosmic Garden*, Costa Mesa, CA: Caris, 1976, p. 6).

Noorbergen concludes, "To believe in astrology, you must support the philosophy that you are either a 'born loser' or a 'born winner.' The stars, we are being told, do not merely forecast the course of our lives, but they also cause the events to take place. They both impel and compel. . ." (Rene Noorbergen, op. cit., pp. 178, 179).

The Problems of Astrology

The claims that astrologists have made have drawn severe criticism from the scientific community. In September, 1975, 186 prominent American scientists, along with 18 Nobel Prize winners, spoke out against "the pretentious claims of astrological charlatans," saying, among other things, that there is no scientific basis whatsoever for the assumption that the stars foretell events and influence lives. The following are some of the reasons the practice of astrology must be rejected as both unscientific and unbiblical.

The Problem of Authority

Astrologists are victims of their own system. They cannot have the objective authority necessary to explain our own world. If everything is predetermined in conjunction with the zodiac, then how can the astrologists get outside of that fatalism to accurately observe it?

What if the astrologists themselves are predetermined to explain everything by astrology? There is no way they can prove their system if they are pawns in that same system. By contrast, as Christians we can test our own world view because someone, Jesus Christ, has come from outside the "system" to tell us, objectively, what our system is like.

Conflicting Systems

The problem of authority in astrology is graphically revealed when one realizes there are many systems of astrology which are diametrically opposed to each other. Astrologers in the West would not interpret a horoscope the same way a Chinese astrologer would.

Even in the West, there is no unanimity of interpretation among astrologers, seeing that some contend for eight zodiac signs rather than

12, while others argue for 14 or even 24 signs of the zodiac.

With these different systems employed by astrologers, an individual may go to two different astrologers and receive two totally opposed courses of behavior for the same day! This is not only a possibility, it is also a reality, for a simple comparison between astrological forecasts in daily newspapers will often reveal contradictions.

Earth-Centered Viewpoint

Astrology is based upon the premise that the planets revolve around the earth, known as the "geocentric theory." This theory was shown to be in error by Copernicus, who proved that the planets revolve around the sun, not the earth. This is known as the "heliocentric theory."

Since astrology is based upon the refuted geocentric theory, its reliability is destroyed. Since the basic assumption is false, all conclusions, even if feebly reinterpreted by today's knowledge and drawn from this assumption, are likewise false.

Missing Planets

One of the major misconceptions that is the basis of astrology concerns the number of planets in our solar system. Most astrological charts are based upon the assumption that there are seven planets in our solar system (including the sun and the moon).

In ancient times, Uranus, Neptune and Pluto were unobservable with the naked eye. Consequently, astrologers based their system upon the seven planets they believed revolved around the earth. Since that time, it has been proven that the sun, not the earth, is the center of the solar system and that three other planets exist in our solar system.

According to the astrological theory, that the position of planets has a definite influence upon human behavior and events, these three previously undiscovered planets should also have an influence upon behavior and must be considered to cast an exact horoscope. Since they usually are not considered, the astrological theory breaks down, for no accurate horoscope could be charted without considering all the planets and their supposed influence.

Twins

A constant source of embarrassment for astrologers is the birth of twins. Since they are born at exactly the same time and place, they should have the same destiny. Unfortunately, this is not the case, for experience shows us that two people who are born at the same time can live totally different lives. One may turn out to be very successful, while the other ends up a failure. The fact that twins do not live out the same lives shows another flaw in the theory.

Limited Perspective

A serious problem with astrology is its limited perspective. Astrology was born in an area close to the equator and did not take into consideration those living in latitudes where the zodiac signs do not appear for the same periods of time.

As Michel Gauquelin points out, "Astrology, begun in latitudes relatively close to the equator, made no provisions for the possibility that no planet may be in sight (in the higher latitudes) for several weeks in a row" (Michel Gauquelin, *The Cosmic Clocks*, Chicago, IL: Henry Regnery Co., 1967, p. 78).

This means those living in the higher latitudes in places such as Alaska, Norway, Finland and Greenland have no planetary influence in their lives, for it is almost impossible to calculate what point of the zodiac is rising on the horizon above the Arctic circle.

Since this is the case, one of the basic pillars of astrology now crumbles, as Van Buskirk points out, "Astrology can hardly be scientifically based on its own premise that the microcosm reflects the influence of the macrocosm, when one of the microcosms (man) above the 66th latitude is left uninfluenced by the cosmos" (Michael Van Buskirk, op. cit., p. 9).

No Scientific Verification

Probably the most damaging criticism that can be leveled at astrological prediction is the fact that its scientific value is nil. Paul Couderc, astronomer at the Paris Observatory, concluded after examining the horoscopes of 2,817 musicians:

> The position of the sun has absolutely no musical significance. The musicians are born throughout the entire year on a chance basis. No sign of the zodiac or fraction of a sign favors or does not favor them.
>
> We conclude: The assets of scientific astrology are equal to zero, as is the case with commercialized astrology. This is perhaps unfortunate, but it is a fact (Paul Couderc, *L'Astrologie*, "Que Sais-je?" 508; 3rd ed.; Paris: Presses Universitaires de France, 1961, pp. 86-89, cited by John Warwick Montgomery, *Principalities and Powers*, p. 106).

The statistics to support the predictive claims of astrologers are simply not there.

Incorrect Time of Reckoning

Another major problem with astrology concerns the fact that horoscopes are cast from the time of birth, not from the time of conception. Since all the hereditary factors are determined at conception, it should logically follow that the planets could begin influencing the person's destiny immediately after conception.

The problem is, of course, trying to accurately determine when conception took place, which is nearly impossible. However, if the planets do exert an influence over a person's fate, it should start at the time of conception rather than the time of birth.

The Shifting Constellations

Astrology is unscientific because of the fact of the precession or the shifting of constellations. Boa elaborates on this problem:

> The early astronomers were not aware of precession and therefore failed to take it into account in their system. The twelve signs of the zodiac originally

correspond with the twelve constellations of the same names. But due to precession, the constellations have shifted about 30l in the last 2,000 years. This means that the constellation of Virgo is now in the sign of Libra, the constellation of Libra is now in the sign of Scorpio and so on. Thus, if a person is born on September 1, astrologers would call him a Virgo (the sign the sun is in at that date), but the sun is actually in the constellation Leo at that date. So there are two different zodiacs: one which slowly moves (the sidereal zodiac) and one which is stationary (the tropical zodiac). Which zodiac should be used? (Kenneth Boa, *Cults, World Religions, and You*, Victor Books, 1977, pp. 124, 125).

Furthermore, no constellation *ever* recurs. As Koch points out, "The most weighty factor is the astronomer's objection that no constellation in the sky ever recurs. Hence, astrological interpretations lack every basis of comparison. Hence, solstitial horoscopy rests on presuppositions which are scientifically untenable" (Kurt Koch, *Christian Counseling and Occultism*, Grand Rapids: Kregel Pub., 1973, p. 94).

The Bible and Astrology

The Bible warns people against relying on astrologers and astrology:

You are wearied with your many counsels; let now the astrologers, those who prophesy by the stars, those who predict by the new moons, stand up and save you from what will come upon you. Behold, they have become like stubble, fire burns them; they cannot deliver themselves from the power of the flame... there is none to save you (Isaiah 47: 13-15, NASB).

Other warnings can be found in such verses as Jeremiah 10:2: "Learn not the way of the heathen, and be not dismayed at the signs of Heaven; for the heathen are dismayed at them." Elsewhere, the Scripture says, "And beware, lest you lift up your eyes to heaven and see the sun and the moon and the stars, all the host of heaven, and be drawn away and worship them and serve them" (Deuteronomy 4:19, NASB).

The Book of Daniel gives us a comparison between the astologers and those dedicated to the true and living God. Chapter 1:20 reveals that Daniel and his three friends would be ten times better in matters of wisdom and understanding than the astrologers because they served the living and true God rather than the stars. When the king had a dream, the astrologers could not give an explanation for it, but rather God alone had the answer, for it is only He who can reveal the future (see Daniel 2: 27, 28).

The Scriptures make it clear that any type of astrological practice is severely condemned by God, for it attempts to understand the future through occultic means rather than through God's divinely inspired Word. The fatalistic approach of astrology, which says our lives are determined by the stars, is contradicted by Scripture, which holds us responsible for our destiny. Astrology and Christianity are simply incompatible.

Dangers of Astrology

There are some very real dangers in trying to live your life by a horoscope.

First is the attempt to try to run your life by following along in astrology. Since it is apparent a great deal of astrology has no basis in reality, you run the risk of great loss.

There can be the loss of money, both of what you may spend on astrology and what the astrologers may recommend for you to do. They may recommend you invest now, buy later, don't purchase this, etc. These recommended investments are no more certain than a fortune cookie, and you could suffer considerable financial loss.

Second, a person who continually tries to live his life by a horoscope can become very depressed as he begins to see life as fatalistic, predetermined since his birth, with no opportunity to break free. Women have even refused the medical advice of induced labor for a late pregnancy in order to have their baby born later, so as to be an Aquarius, for example.

> There is something pitiable about a lady I know who resides in a part of Europe not known for sophisticated medical practices and who refused to have the two-and-a-half-week-late birth of her child induced because she wanted him to be an Aquarius instead of whatever comes before that. I hope that the child suffers no unfortunate consequences (Samuel Hux, *The Humanist*, May/June 1978, "Parawhatsit: A Certain Incapacity to Appreciate the World," p. 32).

Numerology

Numerology is a close cousin of astrology. It too involves such aspects as a person's birth and the use of the planets. Dennis Wheatley states of numerology:

> This is closely allied to astrology and is said to have its origins in the learning of the ancient Hindus. Their priesthood was sufficiently far advanced in the science of astronomy to be aware of the precession of the equinoxes, which is completed once every 25,827 years; so one cannot lightly dismiss their belief in astrology and the potency of numbers. The belief they held was that each heavenly body is associated with a number, which partakes of its qualities.
>
> The date of a person's birth automatically associates him with one number, but that produced by substituting the above numbers for the letters of his name is considered even more important. Should the two be the same, that obviously greatly increases the influence of the planet associated with that number and adds to the potency gained when a person uses that number to further his projects (Dennis Wheatley, *The Devil and All His Works*, NY: American Heritage Press, 1971, p. 46).

Why do People Believe in Astrology?

If astrology is both unscientific and unbiblical, why do so many people believe in it?

One answer would be that it sometimes works, as one book on astrology attests: "When the late astrological genius, Grant Lewi, was asked why he believed in astrology, his blunt answer was, 'I believe in it because it works.' This is as good an answer as any. . .we say that astrology works because it is based on natural law" (Joseph Polansky, *Sun Sign Success*, New York: Warner/Destiny Books, 1977, p. 35).

There is a much better explanation for the so-called accuracy of astrological predictions. If one reads a horoscope, even in a cursory manner, he will be struck with the general and ambiguous nature of the statements, which can be pointed to as fulfilling anything and everything. *Time Magazine* observed:

> There are so many variables and options to play with that the astrologer is always right. Break a leg when your astrologer told you the signs were good, and he can congratulate you on escaping what might have happened had the signs been bad. Conversely, if you go against the signs and nothing happens, the astrologer can insist that you were subconsciously careful because you were forewarned (*Time Magazine*, March 21, 1969, p. 56).

The suggestive aspect also needs to be taken into consideration, as Koch has pointed out: "The person who seeks advice from an astrologer comes with a certain readiness to believe the horoscope. This predisposition leads to an autosuggestion to order his life according to the horoscope, and thus contribute to its fulfillment" (Kurt Koch, *Occult and Christian Counseling*, op. cit., p. 95).

Wilson and Weldon illustrate this point:

> Rachleff tells of a very interesting experiment in which an identical horoscope was mailed to over 100 persons who had given their natal information to a post office box number. The recipients had 12 different birth periods represented by their birth dates, and their varieties were as opposite as could be expected, through Leo and Cancer. Each person was told that the horoscope sent out pertained only to that one person, and basically they accepted it as such. He tells us that "many admired its pertinence and exactitude" (p. 38). The fact is, if enough information is given, we are able to find ways in which it fits our own experiences (Clifford Wilson and John Weldon, *Occult Shock and Psychic Forces*, San Diego: Master Books, 1980, p. 118).

Astrology is bankrupt both biblically and scientifically. Since it is fatalistic in its approach, it rules out the free choice of each of us, leaving man merely as a cog in the cosmic machinery. This view of reality is at odds with Scripture, which indicates all of us have both the capacity and responsibility to choose which road in life we will take.

Astrology would deny us that choice and therefore must be rejected. The Scripturee show us a better way of looking into the future, seeing that God has already told us what the future holds for each of us and for our planet.

CHAPTER FOUR

The Black Mass

T he black mass is said in honor of the devil at the witches' Sabbath. It is practiced by many satanic groups. The ritual reverses the Roman Catholic mass, desecrating the objects used in worship. Oftentimes a nude woman is stretched out upon the altar where the high priest ends the ritual by having sex with her.

Sometimes the participants drink the blood of an animal during the ceremony, along with the eating of human flesh in a mock communion ritual. Human sacrifices, though rare, are not unknown to the black mass.

The black mass contains many other repulsive practices that are unmentionable. It perverts and desecrates the true worship of God and is a blasphemous affront to all believers in Christ.

Clifford Wilson and John Weldon described a black mass as follows:

Normally, a small group of people sit in front of a table covered with a purple velvet altar cloth, lit with candles. Over the "altar" hangs a cross upside down and a picture of the devil, half-human, half-beast. A high priest stands by the table dressed in bishop's robes. On his person he wears an inverted cross. He throws a larger cross to the floor. "Shemhaforash," he shouts. This is probably the most powerful word uttered in satanic worship. According to the Talmud (a book of Jewish civil and religious laws and ethical lore) it was the secret mystic word spoken by God when He created the world. He then spits upon the cross, with an obscene gesture, and cries, "Hail Satan!" Thus begins the sickening and blasphemous ritual, as the devil worshippers repeat the Lord's prayer backwards and make mockery of the ordinances of the church. One quotation from LaVey's "The Satanic Bible" says, "Blessed are the strong, for they shall possess the earth." "If a man smite you on one cheek, smash him on the other!"

Nudity is commonly found at satanic covens. When a witch is initiated, she is symbolically "sacrificed" to the sun god, and this ceremony takes place while she is lying naked on the altar. The power of the witch is said to be heightened by the mysterious force that is within her own body, and when clothing is worn that power is supposedly obstructed. Their delusion is that they will gain pleasure and enjoyment in this world, especially of a sensual nature and that in a coming age Satan will overcome the Christians' God and return to the heaven from which he was once thrown out. Satan's earthly followers, so the delusion goes, will then share fruits of eternal power with his spirit forces (Clifford Wilson and John Weldon, *Occult Shock and Psychic Forces*, San Diego: Master Books, 1980, pp. 9, 10).

The black mass is today's perfect image of the occultism so clearly condemned by the Lord in the Old and New Testaments. It is not possible to serve Satan and Jesus Christ. Christians should have nothing to do with the black mass or any satanic or witchcraft practices. They are perversions of the true Gospel. As perversions, they bring eternal death rather than the eternal life promised by Jesus Christ.

A day will come when even Satan, his demons and those who are bound in the occult will no longer celebrate the black mass, but will be forced to bow to the Lord Jesus Christ. "At the name of Jesus every knee should bow, of those who are in heaven, and on earth, and under the earth, and that every tongue should confess that Jesus Christ is Lord, to the glory of God the Father" (Philippians 2:10, 11, NASB).

CHAPTER FIVE

Edgar Cayce and the A.R.E.

A man who has caused considerable controversy in the 20th century with his prophetic utterings was Edgar Cayce, known as the "sleeping prophet" because of the prophecies he gave while he appeared to be sleeping.

Born in Kentucky in 1877, Cayce realized at an early age that he was clairvoyant and he was determined to use his gift for the betterment of mankind. At the age of 21 Cayce was struck with paralysis of the throat, losing most of his ability to speak. After some time Cayce diagnosed his disease and prescribed a cure while in a self-induced trance. The word quickly spread of the strange ability he possessed.

Cayce began to diagnose illnesses and prescribe cures for people who were thousands of miles away. He would make remarkable diagnoses which were later verified by medical authorities. All this was accomplished in spite of the fact that Cayce had no medical training and only a grammar school education.

Sometimes during his trances he would speak about religious and philosophical issues, and occasionally he would predict the future. During his career his "readings" on medical questions totalled almost 15,000.

Cayce was active in the "Christian" church, faithfully reading his Bible from beginning to end each year for 46 years. However, at the same time, he was an occult practitioner who gained international fame for his exploits.

In 1931 Cayce formed a foundation which he named the Association of Research and Enlightenment, Inc. The purpose of the A.R.E. was the preservation and study of the readings of Edgar Cayce. Cayce's son, Hugh Lynn, assumed leadership of the organization upon his father's death in 1945. The A.R.E. did not stagnate after its founder's death, but instead used his readings and experiences as a vast resource for reaching the contemporary world.

Today's aggressively evangelistic A.R.E. claims to "offer a contemporary

and mature view of the reality of extrasensory perception, the importance of dreams, the logic of reincarnation, and a rational or loving personal concept of God, the practical use of prayer and meditation and a
deeper understanding of the Bible" (William J. Peterson, *Those Curious
New Cults*, New Canaan, CN: Keats Publishing, Inc., 1973, 1975, p. 48).
Current paid membership in the A.R.E. totals 20,000.

Cayce's Readings

The readings made by Cayce over the years reveal not only cures for
medical ailments, but also statements about God and the future. His
readings brought out the following:

- California would fall into the Pacific Ocean in the early 1970's.
- Jesus Christ was a reincarnation of Adam, Melchizedek, Joshua and other
  figures who lived before Him.
- God has in His nature a male and female principle, making Him a Father-
  Mother God.
- Mary, the mother of Jesus, was virgin-born like her Son.
- God does not know the future.
- Salvation is something man does on his own. It is not a work of God alone.
- Reincarnation occurs in many human beings.
- Jesus was tutored in prophecy on Mt. Carmel while He was a teenager. His
  teacher was a woman named Judy, a leader of the Essenes.
- Jesus grew up in Capernaum, not Nazareth.
- Luke did not write the Acts of the Apostles as traditionally believed by the
  Church. The true author was Cayce himself in a previous life as Lucius,
  Bishop of Laodicea.

Biblical Evaluation

Although the A.R.E. claims to be a study group and not a religion, the
readings made by Cayce comment on God and consequently should be
evaluated in the light of God's revealed Word, the Bible.

First and foremost, Edgar Cayce is a false prophet according to biblical
standards. He predicted many things which did not come to pass.

When a prophet speaks in the Name of the Lord, if the thing does not come
about or come true, that is the thing which the Lord has not spoken. The
prophet has spoken it presumptuously; you shall not be afraid of him
(Deuteronomy 18:22, NASB).

When Cayce said God does not know the future, he clearly contradicted
Scripture. In stark contrast to Cayce, the God of the Bible does know
the future, telling mankind of events before they come to pass.

I declared the former things long ago and they went forth from my mouth,
and I proclaimed them. Suddenly I acted, and they came to pass. . . . Therefore
I declared them to you long ago; before they took place I proclaimed them
to you, lest you should say, my idol has done them and my graven image and
my molten image have commanded them (Isaiah 48:3, 5, NASB).

The God of the Bible revealed through His prophets many things in detail before they came to pass. The predictions were specific and always accurate. Contrast that to Cayce, whose predictions were vague and often inaccurate.

There is no evidence that Jesus studied prophecy on Mt. Carmel or was a member of the Essenes. The teachings of Jesus came not from men but from God the Father: "Jesus therefore said, 'When you lift up the Son of Man, then you will know that I am He, and I do nothing on my own initiative, but I speak these things as the Father taught me' " (John 8:28, NASB).

Cayce and his followers have a low view of the Person and work of Jesus Christ. One Cayce devotee expressed it this way:

> For almost 20 centuries the moral sense of the Western World has been blunted by a theology which teaches the vicarious atonement of sin through Christ, the Son of God. . . . All men and women are sons of God. . . . Christ's giving of his life. . . is no unique event in history. . . . To build these two statements, therefore—that Christ was the Son of God and that he died for man's salvation—into a dogma, and then to make salvation depend upon believing that dogma, has been the great psychological crime because it places responsibility for redemption on something external to the self; it makes salvation dependent on belief in the divinity of another person rather than on self-transformation through belief in one's own intrinsic divinity (quoted in Phillip Swihart, *Reincarnation, Edgar Cayce and the Bible*, Downers Grove, IL: Inter-Varsity Press, 1975, pp. 27, 28).

Cayce's claim to be the reincarnated author of the book of Acts rests on his fundamental belief in reincarnation. This is one of the central doctrines and greatest attractions of the A.R.E. If one disproves reincarnation, the validity of the A.R.E. is forever destroyed. We will examine the claims of reincarnation and compare them to the truths of the Bible.

Reincarnation

One of the oldest of all religious beliefs is that of reincarnation. If one will closely study ancient religions, the teaching of reincarnation will appear frequently in a variety of different forms. The belief in reincarnation, however, is not limited to ancient religions but is widely held today by many different religions, cultic and occultic groups, including the A.R.E.

The idea behind reincarnation is that a person's soul lives a succession of lives which will eventually terminate when that person has, by his deeds, rid himself of all sin. This experience where reincarnation is no longer necessary is known as nirvana in Eastern thought, or becoming one with the divine universe. The person is born, lives and dies and comes back with a new body (hence, reincarnation). This cycle usually continues until that person reaches eternal bliss.

It needs to be mentioned that reincarnation, more a Western concept while still often held in the East, is not the same as the Eastern teaching of transmigration of the soul. The teaching of transmigration of the soul permits the person to return not only in human bodies but also in plants and animals.

While reincarnation is limited to the human body, "transmigration is still the teaching of pure Hinduism,but many offshoots of Hinduism and most Western proponents of such ideas have rejected transmigration and now embrace only reincarnation" (Walter Martin, *The New Cults*, op. cit., p. 352).

Many people turn to the Bible in an attempt to support the idea of reincarnation, but a study of the Scripture will reveal that the Bible is diametrically opposed to reincarnation. Rather than teach that we can have many deaths and rebirths, the Bible makes it clear that there is only one death per person.

But what about the various cases of alleged reincarnation which have been publicized in recent years, some sounding very convincing? One answer to this lies in the spiritual warfare spoken of in Scripture. The Bible says that "we wrestle not with flesh and blood but with principalities and powers and spiritual wickedness in high places" (Ephesians 6:12).

There is a spiritual battle going on, and if people can be convinced that there is no judgment after this life but merely a progression into the next, then they will feel no need to receive Jesus Christ as Savior. We believe it is one of the desires of Satan and his hosts to convince people they must atone for their own sins, and belief in reincarnation is one of these devices.

People experience what they believe is a regression into a past when in actuality their experience is in the realm of the occult. It is easy for demonic forces, which have been around from the beginning of the earth, to reveal to someone some past act or experience. You will always note that any so-called reincarnation experience will lead people away from the God of the Bible and the death of Christ on the cross for the forgiveness of sins.

The possibility of fraud also may be involved in so-called reincarnation experiences. The information brought out during the times of regression could be obtained by other means, such as some research about the person who supposedly is speaking. This type of fraud has been perpetrated with regard to spiritists who have "inside information" about the dead ones who allegedly speak during a scance. In reality the medium has done his homework and thus can impress the participant with little-known information about the dead. The same type of thing happens in many supposed cases of reincarnation.

Reincarnation teaches that only through many lifetimes can one rid himself of the debt for all of his sins. However, the Bible teaches that through Jesus Christ we can be rid of the penalty for all our sins at one time (1 John 1:8-10). His purpose for dying on the cross was as a sacrifice for our sins (Acts 3:18, 19).

Jesus Christ is the only Savior we ever need because "He abides forever, holds His priesthood permanently. Hence, also, He is able to save forever those who draw near to God through Him, since He always lives to make intercession for them" (Hebrews 7:24, 25, NASB). We have the promise of God Himself that our salvation has been guaranteed through faith in the sacrifice of Jesus Christ on the cross (1 Peter 1:2-6).

As Christians we look forward to resurrection, not reincarnation. Since the fall of man (Genesis 3) the entire universe has been abnormal. Man, animals, nature have all been placed under the sentence of death. God said to Adam, "By the sweat of your face you shall eat bread, till you return to the ground, because from it you were taken, for you are dust, and to dust you shall return" (Genesis 3:19, NASB).

Mankind has always looked forward to something better, namely, a resurrection into a new body on a new planet Earth that has been renovated by God. The Scriptures speak of the time when we shall all be changed:

> Behold I tell you a mystery; we shall not all sleep, but we shall all be changed, in a moment, in the twinkling of an eye, at the last trumpet; for the trumpet will sound, and the dead will be raised imperishable and we shall be changed. For this perishable must put on imperishable and this mortal must put on immortality. But when this perishable will have put on the imperishable, and this mortal will have put on immortality, then will come about the saying that is written, "Death is swallowed up in victory. O death, where is your victory? O death, where is your sting? The sting of death is sin, and the power of sin is the law; but thanks be to God, who gives us the victory through our Lord Jesus Christ" (1 Corinthians 15:51-57, NASB).

Elsewhere the Scripture says we shall be made like Him at the resurrection, "Beloved, now are we children of God, and it has not appeared as yet what we shall be. We know that, when He appears, we shall be like Him, because we shall see Him just as He is" (1 John 3:2, NASB).

Furthermore the whole creation will be made new:

> And He shall wipe away every tear from their eyes; and there shall no longer be any death; there shall no longer be any mourning, or crying, or pain; the first things have passed away. And He who sits on the Throne said, "Behold, I am making all things new" (Revelation 21:4, 5, NASB).

Thus, the Bible gives the believer the promise of a new body and a new world at the resurrection of the dead. This can be received by belief in Christ, not through a series of rebirths as taught by reincarnation.

Clifford Wilson and John Weldon show some of the differences between Christianity and reincarnation:

Christianity	Reincarnation
Believes in judgment that is eternal, following man's death.	States we have many lives, even thousands, to perfect ourselves.
God judges us.	We only judge ourselves.
Believes in the atonement of Jesus Christ for our sins.	States we need no savior, therefore denies the necessity of salvation; there is no need for it, according to the nature of "reality."
Believes in the existence of	States everyone will be "saved"

hell as a place, eternal.	(absorbed into the divine) in the end.
Believes in the deity of Christ.	Vague and contradictory views on "God." States there is no need for Jesus to be God—He was just more advanced ("He's been through more incarnations") than most.
Believes in the existence of personal devil or Satan, and fallen evil spirits—demons.	All evil is a result of man's choosing Satan is devised by human institution. Evil spirits are held to be regressed human spirits between incarnations, not demons.
Believes in the *Bible* as God's *only* Word to mankind.	Opposes biblical concepts: e.g., Hebrews 9:27. *All* religious Scriptures or writings are communications from God or the spirit world to help man.
Believes in a personal God, revealed as the Trinity of Father, Son, and Holy Spirit	Denies a personal triune God. Ultimate reality is often impersonal karmic law.
Believes in Heaven as a distinct, eternal place.	Various progressive spirit-realms.
Believes in the sinlessness of Christ.	Denies it; no one is perfect (some may say Christ has *now* reached perfection, but that He was a sinner like everyone else, beforehand).
Believes in the physical eternal resurrection of Jesus Christ.	Denies it; He will come back in another reincarnation, or He has now no need to come back at all.
Believes in personal resurrection and immortality.	The individual person is forever gone upon the next reincarnation.

(Clifford Wilson and John Weldon, *Occult Shock and Psychic Forces*, San Diego: Master Books, 1980, pp. 86, 87).

Edgar Cayce cannot be considered a prophet of God. Although he faithfully read his Bible and was active in church, his "readings" contradicted every sacred belief of Christianity. The A.R.E. which Cayce founded has continued in his anti-Christian beliefs and should also be avoided.

William Petersen gives a thought-provoking conclusion concerning Cayce's activities:

> For a good portion of his life, Cayce was a commercial photographer. He understood very well the mechanics of his trade. A blank film is developed in the dark.
>
> The nature of a photograph, whether it is a formal family picture or pornography, depends not on the film but on the photographer who uses the camera. During his trances, Cayce's mind was like a blank film that would be developed in the dark.
>
> I believe that Cayce allowed his camera to get into the wrong hands (William J. Petersen, op. cit., p. 59).

CHAPTER SIX

Demons

The Bible not only teaches the existence of the devil but also of a great company of his followers known as demons or evil spirits. These demons originally were holy but with the leader, Satan, they fell away from God. Their ultimate end will be eternal damnation when God judges Satan and his host at the Great White Throne judgment (Revelation 20:10-15).

These demons have certain characteristics revealed by the Scripture, including the following:

(1) Demons are spirits without bodies.
For our struggle is not against flesh and blood, but against the rulers, against the powers, against the world forces of this darkness, against the spiritual forces of wickedness in the heavenly places (Ephesians 6:12, NASB).

(2) Demons were originally in fellowship with God.
And angels who did not keep their own domain, but abandoned their proper abode, He has kept in eternal bonds under darkness for the judgment of the great day (Jude 6, NASB).

(3) Demons are numerous.
For He said unto him, "Come out of the man, you unclean spirit!" And He was asking him, "What is your name?" And he said to Him, "My name is Legion; for we are many" (Mark 5:8, 9, NASB).

(4) Demons are organized.
...This man casts out demons only by Beelzebub the ruler of the demons (Matthew 12:24, NASB).

(5) Demons have supernatural powers.
For they are spirits of demons, performing signs, which go out to the kings of the whole world, to gather them together for the war of the Great Day of God, the Almighty (Revelation 16:14, NASB).

(6) Demons are knowledgeable of God.
And behold, they cried out, saying, "What do we have to do with you, Son of God? Have you come here to torment us before the time?" (Matthew 8:29, NASB).

(7) Demons are allowed to roam the earth and torment unbelievers.

Now when the unclean spirit goes out of a man, it passes through waterless places, seeking rest, and does not find it. Then it says, "I will return to my house from which I came"; and when it comes, it finds it unoccupied, swept and put in order. Then it goes, and takes along with it seven other spirits more wicked than itself, and they go in and live there; and the last state of that man becomes worse than the first (Matthew 12:43-45, NASB).

(8) Demons sometimes can inflict sickness.
And as they were going out, behold a dumb man, demon possessed, was brought to Him. And after the demon was cast out, the dumb man spoke... (Matthew 9:32, 33, NASB).

(9) Demons can possess or control animals.
And He gave them permission. And coming out, the unclean spirits entered the swine; and the herd rushed down the steep bank into the sea, about two thousand of them, and they were drowned in the sea (Mark 5:13, NASB).

(10) Demons can possess or control human beings.
And also some women who had been healed of evil spirits and sicknesses; Mary who was called Magdalene, from whom seven demons had gone out (Luke 8:2, NASB).

(11) Demons sometimes can cause mental disorders.
And when He had come out of the boat, immediately a man from the tombs with an unclean spirit met Him and he had his dwelling among the tombs. And no one was able to bind him anymore, even with a chain... and constantly night and day among the tombs and in the mountains, he was crying out and gashing himself with stones (Mark 5:2, 3, 5, NASB).

(12) Demons know that Jesus Christ is God.
And just then there was in their synagogue a man with an unclean spirit; and he cried out, saying, "What do we have to do with you, Jesus of Nazareth? Have you come to destroy us? I know who you are—the Holy One of God" (Mark 1:23, 24, NASB).

(13) Demons tremble before God.
You believe that God is one. You do well; the demons also believe, and shudder (James 2:19, NASB).

(14) Demons teach false doctrine.
But the Spirit explicitly says that in later times some will fall away from the faith, paying attention to deceitful spirits and doctrines of demons (1 Timothy 4:1, NASB).

(15) Demons oppose God's people.
For our struggle is not against flesh and blood, but against the rulers, against the powers, against the world forces of this darkness, against the spiritual forces of wickedness in the heavenly places (Ephesians 6:12, NASB).

(16) Demons attempt to destroy Christ's Kingdom.
Be of sober spirit, be on the alert. Your adversary, the devil, prowls about like a roaring lion, seeking someone to devour (1 Peter 5:8, NASB).

(17) God takes advantage of the actions of demons to accomplish His divine purposes.
Then God sent an evil spirit between Abimelech and the men of

Shechem; and the men of Shechem dealt treacherously with Abimelech (Judges 9:23, NASB).

(18) God is going to judge demons at the last judgment.
For if God did not spare angels when they sinned, but cast them into hell and committed them to pits of darkness, reserved for judgment... (2 Peter 2:4, NASB).

Demon Possession

Since the release of the motion picture, "The Exorcist," there has been renewed discussion about the subject of demon possession. Can demon possession, or control of a person's will by a demon, actually occur? What are the signs of a possessed person? Is it really just superstition and ignorance to believe in demon possession? Because of the continual interest in these and other questions, we felt we should address the subject of demon possession.

The Reality of Demon Possession

The evidence from Scripture is *unmistakable* that a human being can be possessed or controlled by a demon or evil spirit (Mark 7:24-30, 9:17-29).

From the New Testament accounts of demon possession, along with other examples, we can chart some of the phenomena that can be observed during a demonic attack.

A. Change of Personality
Including intelligence, moral character, demeanor, appearance.

B. Physical Changes
1. Preternatural strength
2. Epileptic convulsions; foaming
3. Catatonic symptoms, falling
4. Clouding of consciousness, anaesthesia to pain
5. Changed voice

C. Mental Changes
1. Glossolalia; understanding unknown languages [the counterfeit gift as opposed to the biblical gift].
2. Preternatural knowledge
3. Psychic and occult powers, e.g., clairvoyance, telepathy and prediction

D. Spiritual Changes
1. Reaction to and fear of Christ; blasphemy with regret as in depression
2. Affected by prayer

E. Deliverance possible in the name of Jesus
As this is a diagnosis in retrospect it falls outside the range of pre-exorcism symptoms. (John Richards, *But Deliver Us From Evil: An Introduction to the Demonic Dimension in Pastoral Care,* London: Darton, Longman and Todd, 1974, p. 156).

Does Demon Possession Occur Today?

Granting the fact that demon possession occurred in New Testament times, the natural question arises, "Does it occur today?" After extensive study of demonology and years of observing patients, psychiatrist Paul Meier gives his professional opinion:

> I can honestly say that I have never yet seen a single case of demon posses-sion. The main thing I have learned about demon possession is how little we really know about it and how little the Bible says about it.
>
> I have had hundreds of patients who came to see me because they thought they were demon possessed. Scores of them heard "demon voices" telling them evil things to do. It was at first surprising to me that all of these had dopamine deficiencies in their brains, which were readily correctable with Thorazine or any other major tranquilizer. I discovered that all of the "demons" I was seeing were allergic to Thorazine and that, in nearly every case, a week or two on Thorazine made the "demons" go away and brought the patient closer to his real conflicts. These demons were merely auditory hallucinations. To have self-esteem, these patients were unconsciously amplifying their own un-wanted thoughts so loud they seemed like real voices. They felt less guilty when they could convince themselves that these thoughts were coming from an external source ("demons"), rather than from within themselves.
>
> Don't get me wrong, I am a strict Biblicist who believes in the inerrancy of Scripture. I believe demons really do exist because the Bible says they do. I believe that there probably are some demon possessed persons in various parts of the world (Danny Korem and Paul Meier, *The Fakers*, Grand Rapids, MI: Baker Book House, 1980, pp. 160, 161).

However, there are many others who attest to having witnessed demon possession. Kurt Koch* writes, "I was once invited by Dr. Martin Lloyd-Jones to speak before a group of psychiatrists in London. During the discussion which followed my talk, two psychiatrists stood up and stated quite dogmatically that possession as such did not exist. Immediately after this, however, two other psychiatrists present—they were both Christians—rose to their feet and said that they were not only convinc-ed that possession was a genuine phenomenon, but that they had already come across cases of it within their own practice, one of them seven cases and the other eleven" (Kurt Koch, *Demonology, Past and Present*, Grand Rapids, MI: Kregel Publications, 1973, p. 32.)

In the 19th century there were some striking cases of demon posses-sion recorded in China by missionary John L. Nevius. When Nevius first came to China, he firmly believed that demons belonged to a bygone era. When he heard firsthand accounts of demon possession, he considered it superstition. However, try as he would, he could not convince the peo-ple that what they had heard and seen was a result of their imaginations. Finally, the evidence led him to a change of mind, not only believing the demons existed but also that demon possession was in fact a present reality.

Nevius said this of his experiences:

> I brought with me to China a strong conviction that a belief in demons, and communications with spiritual beings, belongs exclusively to a barbarous and superstitious age, and at present can consist only with mental weakness and want of culture. I indulged Mr. Tu (his Chinese teacher), however, in talking on his favorite topics, because he did so with peculiar fluency and zest, and thus, elements of variety and novelty were utililzed in our severe and other-

wise monotonous studies. But Mr. Tu's marvelous stories soon lost the charm of novelty. I used my best endeavors, though with little success, to convince him that his views were not the combined result of ignorance and imagination. I could not but notice, however, the striking resemblance between some of his statements of alleged facts and the demonology of Scripture. This resemblance I account for only as apparent or accidental. . . . (John L. Nevius, *Demon Possession*, Grand Rapids, MI: Kregel Publications, 1968, pp. 9, 10).

Nevius then records his many and varied experiences with demon possessed people which eventually led to his change of mind on the matter.

Walter Martin gives a couple of examples of demon possession he has encountered:

Recently in the San Fernando Valley of California three husky clergymen tried to hold down a 120-pound girl who was possessed with multiple demons. She successfully resisted all three of them for a number of minutes, until she was finally subdued. However, she was still able to kick one man's shins until they were bloody, demonstrating tremendous supernatural power.

In Newport Beach, California, I encountered a case of demonic possession in which five persons, including myself, were involved. In this case the girl, who was about 5 feet 4 inches tall and weighed 120 pounds, attacked a 180-pound man and with one arm flipped him 5 or 6 feet away. It took four of us, including her husband, to hold her body to a bed while we prayed in the name of Jesus Christ for the exorcism of the demons within her.

During the course of the exorcism we found out that she was possessed because she had worshipped Satan, and because of that worship he had come with his forces and taken control of her. She was a perfect "tare in the wheat field," as Jesus said (Matthew 13:24-30). She had married a Christian, was a daughter of a Christian minister, had taught Sunday school in a Christian church, and had appeared on the surface to be perfectly consistent with Christian theology. But the whole time she was laughing inwardly at the church and at Christ. It was not until her exorcism that she was delivered and received Jesus Christ as her Lord and Savior. Today she and her husband are on the mission field serving the Lord Jesus Christ.

I have a psychologist friend who was present with me at an exorcism in Newport Beach, California. Before we entered the room he said, "I want you to know I do not believe in demonic possession. This girl is mentally disturbed."

I said, "That may well be. We'll find out very soon."

As we went into the room and closed the door, the girl's supernatural strength was soon revealed. Suddenly from her body a totally foreign voice said quietly, with a smirk on the face (she was unconscious—the psychologist testified to that), "We will outlast you."

The psychologist looked at me and said, "What was that?"

"That is what you don't believe in," I said.

We spent about 3½ hours exorcising what the psychologist didn't believe in!

At the end of the exorcism he was not only a devout believer in the personality of the devil, but in demonic possession and biblical exorcism as well. He now knows that there are other-dimensional beings capable of penetrating this dimension and of controlling human beings! (Walter Martin, *Exorcism: Fact or Fable*, Santa Ana, CA: Vision House Publishers, 1975, pp. 17, 18, 21).

In conclusion, although most cases of alleged demon possession turn out to be in reality something quite different, it does not negate the fact that demon possession can and does occur today. However, one should be very careful before he considers an individual demon possessed when the person's problem may be physiological or psychological.

Only a mature Christian, experienced and seasoned by the Lord in counseling and spiritual warfare, should take an active part in diagnosing or treating alleged cases of demon possession. The human body, mind and spirit is so complex and interrelated that it takes spiritual discernment coupled with a great amount of knowledge to deal responsibly with what appears to be demon possession.

If you know of someone who appears to be demon possessed and who wants help, you can and should pray for him and direct him to someone who is qualified to help. There is hope for him: God can and will set him free from whatever is binding him, be it demonic, physiological or psychological.

NOTE: The subject of the believer and demon possession will be dealt with in a later volume.

* In this volume we will refer quite often to the examples of occultic activity documented in the writings of Kurt Koch. The authors do this because Koch is the most well-known writer on the subject of the occult in the evangelical Christian world. However, citing his examples does not necessarily mean that we come to the same conclusions or agree that his examples are clear indications of occultic activity.

CHAPTER SEVEN

Jeane Dixon

I nvariably when the subject of astrology is discussed, the question of Jeane Dixon is brought up. Is Jeane Dixon a true prophetess? Do her powers come from God? What about the amazing predictions that she has made? We feel these and other questions concerning Jeane Dixon need to be addressed in light of the Bible in order to get a true picture of the situation.

Background

Jeane Dixon was born Jeane (or Lydia) Pinckert around the turn of the century in a small Wisconsin town. Her psychic abilities were either non-existent or hidden during her early years. It was not until she met a gypsy woman who gave her a crystal ball that her psychic career began.

Supposedly, this gypsy woman told her she had the makings of a psychic, destined for great things. Although she received recognition as early as the forties for her psychic powers, it was the publication of two books concerning her life, *A Gift of Prophecy* by Ruth Montgomery in 1965, and *Jeane Dixon, My Life and Prophecies* by Rene Noorbergen in 1969, that made her famous.

The Claims of Jeane Dixon

Jeane Dixon has made it clear that she believes her prophetic gift comes from God. "It is my belief God has given me a gift of prophecy for His own reasons, and I do not question them" (Jeane Dixon, *The Call to Glory*, New York: William Morrow & Company, 1972, p. 42).

Furthermore, she has stated, "The future has been shown me to 2037 A.D." (ibid, p. 175). She told her biographer, Rene Noorbergen, that, "The same spirit that worked through Isaiah and John the Baptist also works through me" (Rene Noorbergen, *The Soul Hustlers*, Zondervan, 1976, p. 114).

In the foreword of her book, *The Gift of Prophecy,* Ruth Montgomery designated Mrs. Dixon as a "modern-day psychic whose visions apparently lift the curtain of tomorrow."

Fulfilled Prophecies?

Mrs. Dixon and others have made some astounding claims as to her ability to predict the future. The introductory section of one of her books reads as follows:

> If you don't believe that anyone can predict the future with a crystal ball... then read these startling, often frightening, precognitions of events by the phenomenal Jeane Dixon.
>
> —The assassination of President Kennedy...
> —Nehru's death and his succession by Shastri
> —That China would go communistic
> —The assassination of Mahatma Ghandi
> —Russia's launching the world's first satellite
> —Eisenhower's election; his heart attack, and his recovery
> —The Kremlin shake-up ending with Krushchev's dismissal and Suslov's takeover (Ruth Montgomery, *A Gift of Prophecy*, New York: Bantam Books, 1970, Preface).

She also supposedly predicted the deaths of Carole Lombard and Marilyn Monroe and the assassinations of Robert F. Kennedy and Martin Luther King.

In the May 13, 1956 issue of *Parade Magazine*, she made this prophecy:

> As to the 1960 election, Mrs. Dixon thinks it will be dominated by labor and won by a Democrat. But he will be assassinated or die in office, though not necessarily in his first term.

With these examples of fulfilled prophecy, one might conclude that Jeane Dixon has a true prophetic gift. However, upon closer examination her "amazing" prophecies are not really that amazing. On her prophecy concerning the 1960 Presidential election, Milbourne Cristopher comments:

> As we know now, the election was not "dominated by labor." She did not name the Democrat she said would win; no date was given for the president-to-be's end; and his announced demise was qualified with Delphic ingenuity "assassinated or die in office, though not necessarily in his first term." Thus if the president served a single term, it would be within four years; if he was re-elected there was an eight-year span.
>
> Such a surmise was not illogical for anyone who has studied recent American history. William McKinley was assassinated a year after the turn of the century. Warren Gamaliel Harding and Franklin Delano Roosevelt died in office, and during Harry S. Truman's tenure an attempt was made on his life. Moreover, the normal burdens of the presidency are such that it is commonly regarded as a man-killing office. Woodrow Wilson and Dwight Eisenhower were critically ill during their terms. Unfortunately for the nation, the odds against Mrs. Dixon's prophecy's being fulfilled were not too great—7-3 based on 20th century experience (Milbourne Cristopher, *ESP, Seers and Psychics*, New York: Thomas Crowell Co., 1970, pp. 80, 81).

Moreover, before the 1960 election, Mrs. Dixon changed her mind, as Cristopher points out:

In January 1960 Mrs. Dixon changed her mind. Kennedy, then a contender for the Democrat nomination, would not be elected in November, she said in Ruth Montgomery's syndicated column. In June she stated that "the symbol of the Presidency is directly over the head of Vice-President Nixon" but "unless the Republican party really gets out and puts forth every effort it will topple." Fire enough shots, riflemen agree, and eventually you will hit the bull's-eye (ibid, p. 81).

One of the most famous of all her prophecies was received on February 5, 1962. "A child, born somewhere in the Middle East shortly after 7 a.m. (EST) on February 5, 1962 will revolutionize the world. Before the close of the century he will bring together all mankind in one all-embracing faith. This will be the foundation of a new Christianity, with every sect and creed united through this man who will walk among the people to spread the wisdom of the Almighty Power. . . He is the answer to the prayers of a troubled world."

This prophecy of a coming Messiah who would save the world received much criticism. Consequently, Mrs. Dixon revised the true identity of this child. Her biographer, Rene Noorbergen, notes:

> For several years Jeane continued to advocate that this Christ-child would guide the world in the early 1980s. The child was godly, he was divine, and he would become the salvation of the world.
> Suddenly something happened.
> While interviewing "Mrs. D" for *My Life and Prophecies*, I became aware of the inconsistencies in the revelation. Over-sensitive to criticism, Mrs. Dixon soon changed her interpretation. "There is no doubt that he will fuse multitudes into one all-embracing doctrine," she explained in her "revised version." She continued, "He will form a new 'Christianity' based on his 'almighty power,' but leading man in a direction far removed from the teachings and life of Christ, the Son." Enlarging on her new interpretation, she called the child the "Antichrist"—a far cry from her first prophetic evaluation (Rene Noorbergen, *The Soul Hustlers*, Zondervan, 1976, p. 121).

False Prophecies

Although Jeane Dixon supposedly has made some predictions that have come true, she has made many other prophecies that have failed. These include:

(1) World War III would begin in 1954;

(2) Red China would be admitted to the United Nations in 1958, yet this did not occur until 1971;

(3) The Vietnam war would end in 1966, yet it did not end until 1975;

(4) On October 19, 1968, she predicted Jacqueline Kennedy was not thinking of marriage and the next day Mrs. Kennedy married Aristotle Onassis!

(5) Union Leader, Walter Reuther, would run for President in 1964, which he did not do.

(6) In 1970, she predicted the following events which did not occur:
    (a) Castro would be overthrown from Cuba and would have to leave the island;
    (b) New facts concerning the death of President Kennedy would be

brought to light from a foreign source;
(c)   Attempts would be made on the life of President Nixon;
(7)   In 1971, she made the following predictions, neither one of which has come true:
(a)   Both Anwar Sadat of Egypt and King Hussein of Jordan would lose their thrones;
(b)   Russia would be the first nation to put men on the moon;
(8)   She has made other predictions that have not yet come true, including:
(a)   The Berlin Wall will come down;
(b)   Red China will invade Russia;
(c)   Russia will ally with the United States.

Evaluation

There are those who believe Jeane Dixon has no supernatural power whatsoever but is rather a clever fortuneteller. Danny Korem comments:

> In a given population there will be those whose "hit" ratio (a thought and an event matching up) will be higher than others simply because of the law of probability. This is true in any game of chance. When a clever fortuneteller combines good cold-reading techniques with a chance guess or two, he or she will appear to almost unerringly pick up someone's thoughts and prognosticate the future, but there will be other times when he or she will fail. My question is this: If such powers exist, why are they so fleeting, and why can't they be tested? The reason is a simple one. They don't exist. In the 12 years I have devoted to researching this subject, I have neither seen a valid case of prognostication, nor have I been confronted with hard-core documentation to substantiate a purported case (Danny Korem and Paul Meier, *The Fakers*, Grand Rapids, MI: Baker Book House, 1980, p. 115).

Whether Mrs. Dixon possesses a supernatural ability to predict the future or not, she is definitely not a prophet of God for she fails on the following counts:

(1) *The Use of Occult Artifacts.*

Jeane Dixon uses such things as a crystal ball, a deck of tarot cards and other occult artifacts to receive her prophecies. This type of practice is at odds with Scripture, for the biblical prophets received their prophecies directly from God without the use of any artifacts. The artifacts Mrs. Dixon uses are the same ones used by fortunetellers who attempt to predict the future through occultic means. A true prophet of God would never resort to using any occultic paraphernalia.

The true prophet of God spoke by the direct agency of God through the power of the Holy Spirit, not by means of any occultic devices. The words of the prophets are preserved for us in Holy Scripture (Romans 1:2) and their supreme testimony is always of Jesus Christ, the Son of God (Hebrews 1:1, 2).

(2) *Her Prophecies Do Not Exalt Jesus Christ.*

The Bible makes it clear that all true prophecy has Jesus Christ as its central theme, "...for the testimony of Jesus is the Spirit of prophecy" (Revelation 19:10, NASB).

Mrs. Dixon fails miserably in this, for there is no attempt in her prophecies to bring people to the God of the Bible and His Son, Jesus Christ. There is simply no witness to Christ in her prophecies! Moreover, many of her prophecies concern such commonplace things as what television show will be popular or the latest fashions. These are given without any spiritual meaning whatsoever and do not direct one's attention to the Gospel of Christ.

The biblical prophets always prophesied in accordance with God's will and for His glory. There is no room for frivolous and gossiping prophecy in God's Word.

Mrs. Dixon does no such thing. The biblical prophets also gave their prophecies in the Name of the Lord, something Jeane Dixon does not do. Since Jeane Dixon does not prophesy in the Name of the Lord or for the purpose of bringing individuals into a personal relationship with Christ, she cannot be considered a true prophet of God.

(3) *She Gives Prophecies That Do Not Come True.*

Mrs. Dixon also fails in the most important test of all: She utters prophecies which do not come true. The Bible makes it clear how one can know who is a true prophet of God: "And you may say in your heart, 'How shall we know the word which the Lord has not spoken?' When a prophet speaks in the Name of the Lord, if the thing does not come about or come true, that is the thing which the Lord has not spoken. The prophet has spoken it presumptuously; you shall not be afraid of him" (Deuteronomy 18:21, 22, NASB).

Mrs. Dixon, as we have already documented, has made a great many predictions that did not come to pass. To qualify for being a false prophet, a person need make only one false prophecy, for a true prophet of God will not make any mistakes in predicting the future. Jeane Dixon uses occultic artifacts in her predicting. She does not speak in the Name of the Lord, neither does she exalt Jesus Christ in her prophetic utterances. She has predicted many things that have failed to materialize. Consequently, she cannot be considered a prophet of the true and living God.

CHAPTER EIGHT

Dowsing

D owsing is the search for and location of underground springs and other objects beneath the ground by the use of a divining rod. The divining rod is a V-shaped wooden twig or piece of wire from six to eighteen inches in length which is used by the dowser, the person who possesses this ability to search for underground objects. The rod is held firmly in the hands of the dowser until the force coming from the underground object causes the rod to snap over.

Does dowsing work? Milbourne Cristopher states,

> P.A. Ongley reported in the New Zealand Journal of Science and Technology, in 1948, that fifty-eight dowsers participated in tests devised to determine their ability to make the same spots they had indicated with their eyes open when their eyes were closed, to tell if buried bottles containing water, and otherwise give evidence of their purported powers. Their scores were on pure-chance levels. Seventeen other diviners who specialize in diverse fields were observed. As in the earlier experiments in France, seven illness detectors found twenty-five diseases in a patient who doctors said was healthy, and one diviner, whose eyes were bandaged, said the leg over which he worked had varicose veins. Actually it was an artificial limb (Milbourne Cristopher, *ESP, Seers and Psychics*, New York: Thomas Y. Crowell Co., p. 140).

In his discussion of divining rods, Herbert Leventhal states:

> A second major feature of these tales is their association of dowsing with a host of other occult and supernatural phenomena. By combining the various accounts, a common pattern of American treasure-hunting magic can be discovered. The treasure is located by a divining rod, which sometimes contained mercury or was prepared at an especially propitious time; one or more protective circles, a common feature of European ceremonial magic, are drawn; magical charms, or religious verses used as charms, are recited to overcome the guardian spirits; and nails or metal rods are sometimes used to pin down the treasure because... treasure was wont to move about and attempt to escape.
>
> Some of the other stories, especially those recorded only in nineteenth-century secondary sources, may well have been influenced by the generally accepted theme for magical treasure hunting, but the existence of this theme

itself indicates a general knowledge of dowsing, and enough evidence remains to leave no doubt that dowsing for treasure, including appropriate protective measures against hostile spirits, was a not unusual occurrence in eighteenth-century America (Herbert Leventhal, *In the Shadow of the Enlightenment. Occultism and Renaissance Science in Eighteenth-Century America*, New York: New York University Press, 1976, pp. 117, 118).

Some practitioners of dowsing seem actually to have the ability to find water. How is this to be explained? Some believe that Satan empowers the dowser supernaturally to find the water or object desired. While this is possible, there seems to be a better explanation.

There are those individuals, however, who do display an uncanny ability to discover water by means of dowsing. Mr. Rawcliffe, in his book *Occult and Supernatural Phenomena* points out, after exhaustive research, that there are subtle surface clues that may allow one to discern where underground streams or pockets of water may exist. The following is only a partial list of surface clues that may subconsciously aid the dowser: (1) naturally absorbent substratum and subsoil; (2) growth of vegetation; (3) temperature of surrounding air; (4) smell of damp earth; (5) underground streams audible to the ear; and (6) ground vibrations due to underground stream. It must be noted that most clues are very subtle and, for the most part, are registered subliminally by the dowser and then translated by ideomotor action into the dipping of the rod. (Danny Korem and Paul Meier, *The Fakers*, Grand Rapids, MI: Baker Book House, 1980, p. 57).

Dowsing has never established itself as being scientifically credible because all controlled experiments do not point to any remarkable accuracy of the dowsers. Those who do seem to have an ability to find water underground are most likely responding subconsciously to the surface clues.

In addition, we should note that many people who become involved in dowsing (sometimes called water-witching) also become involved in other activities that are more directly occultic. It seems to be a step on the way to serious occultic involvement. Since it has no basis scientifically or biblically, and can be a step to occultism, Christians should definitely stay away from it.

CHAPTER NINE

Fire Walking

F ire walking is an ancient practice of someone walking barefoot across
a fiery bed of coals or stones without the slightest pain or any damage
to the person. It is still widely practiced today in Japan, India and the
Fiji Islands.

Since some magicians can duplicate fire walking by trickery, some people dismiss all fire walking as trickery. The trick is accomplished by relying upon short contact with the hot stones which prevents the walker
from being burned.

Danny Korem comments, "It has been found that one cannot take more
than four steps across a bed of coals without running the risk of being
burned. In 1937, Ahmed Hussain, another coal walker, took six steps in
2.3 seconds to cross a 20-foot pit (temperature 740 degrees Celsius) and
was severely burned. There have been other laymen, however, who have
successfully duplicated the coal-walking stunt.

"Walking on heated stones is even easier, since stone is a poor conductor of heat. You will not, however, witness a fakir walk across a heated
steel plate, as steel is an excellent conductor of heat" (Danny Korem and
Paul Meier, *The Fakers*, Grand Rapids, MI: Baker Book House, 1980, p. 89).

There are others who see fire walking not as a magician's trick but
rather as an occultic practice. This is the position of Kurt Koch, who
writes:

> In Japan a former fire walker came to me to be counseled. He confessed to
> his former activities and said that he had really deceived the audience. The
> fire had been made on a high platform down the center of which there had
> been a narrow path. Either side of this path was a fire of wood coals. The peo-
> ple around and below the platform had not been able to see the path through
> the fire. I asked this man if he thought all fire walking was faked in the same
> way. He replied, "No. Most of it is genuine. It is only faked sometimes for the
> sake of the tourists."
>
> In South Africa another fire walker confessed to his occult practice. The
> man was an Indian who worked on a sugar plantation. He told me that he
> could really walk through fire. He would prepare himself for some days through
> fasting and meditation, abstaining from alcohol and sexual intercourse, eating

only a vegetarian diet, etc. I asked him if he thought the powers he possessed over fire originated from his own subconscious mind. "That's impossible," he replied. "The devil gives this power to those who serve him." He went on to confess that when he had become a Christian he had lost his power to walk through fire.

I know that hypnosis and trance states can protect fire walkers from the pain, but they cannot protect a person from being burnt. One day in India a young mother walked through fire with her small baby. However, she was not fully prepared for the ordeal. Her baby fell from her arms into the fire and was dead within a few seconds. Before the people could reach it, its body was burnt to ashes.

Behind the phenomenon of genuine fire walking there are demonic forces at work, and newly born Christians can feel this in the atmosphere (Kurt Koch, *The Devil's Alphabet*, Grand Rapids, MI: Kregel Publications, pp. 54, 55).

Is there fire walking in the Bible? The Bible gives an account (Daniel 3:21-29) of three men of God who were supernaturally protected when they were thrown into a burning furnace. The Lord God of the Bible protected them because they were being punished for refusing to worship false gods. There are some who try to say this is an example for and justification of fire walking. By reading the account in Daniel, you can see that there is no parallel. The three men of God were preserved to bring glory and honor to the true God, not to amuse onlookers and make the performers rich. One who points to Daniel 3 as justification of fire walking makes a mockery of God's Word.

In conclusion it seems difficult to place all cases of fire walking in the category of trickery or self-hypnosis. But whatever the case may be, fire walking is an ungodly ritual attempting to get the eyes of the observers away from the true and living god. Some see this practice as Satan's imitation of God's miracle in delivering the three Jews from the fiery furnace, showing that the devil has equal power. This, as we have seen, is not the case.

Fortunetelling

F ortunetelling, the art of forecasting the future supposedly by supernatural means, is an ancient practice which is still popular today. Fortunetelling is also known as divination. The one who practices this
activity is known as a diviner. The diviner makes use of various props
to receive his supernatural knowledge, including palmistry, cartomancy,
mirror mantic and psychometry.

Kurt Koch testifies to the negative result that fortunetelling has on
peoples' lives because he sees it as being completely occultic.

> . . . People infected or burdened by fortunetelling and occult phenomena very
> frequently suffer in the following ways:
> The characters of such people reveal abnormal passions, instability, violent
> tempers, addiction to alcohol, nicotine and sexual vices, selfishness, gossip-
> ing, egotism, cursing, etc.
> Their religious lives reveal on the one hand an antagonism toward religion,
> callousness, skepticism, a vicious critical attitude and an inability to pray or
> read the Bible if they are an atheistic type of person, while on the other hand
> the pious type reveals a self-righteousness, a spiritual pride, phariseeism,
> hypocrisy and an insensitivity to the workings of the Holy Spirit.
> Medically speaking the families of those involved in fortunetelling reveal
> in a remarkable way such things as nervous disturbances, psychopathic and
> hysteric symptoms, cases of St. Vitus' dance, symptoms of paralysis, epilep-
> tics, freaks, deaf-mutes, cases of mediumistic psychoses, and a general tendency
> toward emotional and mental illnesses, etc. (Kurt Koch, *Between Christ and
> Satan*, Grand Rapids, MI: Kregel Publications, 1968, pp. 49, 50).

There are those who see fortunetelling as a con game without any
supernatural phenomena occurring. The fortuneteller, rather than making contact with the spirit world, is a con artist duping the unsuspecting
victims. Danny Korem lists certain techniques used by fortunetellers
which give realism to their readings:

(1)   Observation of sensory clues.
(2)   Prior knowledge of subject obtained secretly before reading.
(3)   Ability to think on one's feet and change direction of the reading without
      hesitation or detection.

(4) Understanding of human nature.

(5) Utilization of the cards or any other apparatus to pick up sensory clues or change the direction of the reading when off the track.

(6) An element of luck and a keen sense of playing the odds so that a well-placed guess may produce spectacular results (Danny Korem and Paul Meier, *The Fakers*, Grand Rapids, MI: Baker Book House, 1980, p. 107).

Whether all fortunetelling practice is nothing but a glorified con game remains a matter of debate. What is not debatable is the fact that any and all types of attempting to divine the future through fortunetelling is an abomination to God. God has already revealed to us in His Word the basic program for the future, and He condemns in the strongest of terms those who would try to find out what is going to occur without consulting Him.

The Bible *never* says fortunetellers can predict the future. It is their attempt to peer into the future through occultic means that is objectionable. However, whether they can do it or not really does not make that much difference, if the person having his fortune told believes that they can. The same end is accomplished. The person, instead of looking to God for direction, now consults fortunetellers to receive guidance for his life.

Satan has accomplished his purpose, which is getting people away from worshiping the true and living God. Since fortunetelling does this, it should never be practiced even for fun. It is a device of the devil which takes one further away from the Kingdom of God. 1 Chronicles 10:13, 14 (NASB) records God's punishment on Saul for going to a medium instead of God:

> So Saul died for his trespass which he committed against the Lord, because of the word of the Lord which he did not keep; and also because he asked counsel of a medium, making inquiry of it, and did not inquire of the Lord. Therefore He killed him, and turned the kingdom to David the son of Jesse.

Some would put fortunetelling in the area of the divine, insisting God had given the fortunetellers their ability. However, this could not be the case since Scripture condemns such practices.

Palmistry (Chiromancy)

Palmistry, or chiromancy, is the art of divination from the shape and markings of the hands and fingers. A proper interpretation of these signs supposedly can be used to forecast the future. It is not to be confused with chirology, which is the scientific study of the development of the shape and lines of the hand, or with graphology, which is handwriting analysis.

Kurt Koch explains chiromancy:

> Here we have fortunetelling by study of the hands. The hand is divided into areas and lines. There is a lunar mountain, the Venus belt, the Martian plain, and areas for spirit, fortune, success, fame, imagination, will and sensuousness. Further, there are four lines which dominate the surface of the palm: the head line, the heart line, the profession line and the life line. From these indica-

tions palmists claim to divine and foretell the future (Kurt Koch, *Christian Counseling and Occultism*, Grand Rapids, MI: Kregel Publications, 1972, p. 85).

Unfortunately, palmistry suffers from the same types of verification problems as does astrology. There is no testable, scientific evidence that it works. Lack of documentation and testability have led the scientific community to brand it as mere superstition. The so-called examples of palmistry being able to predict the future have never been substantiated as being right any more often than pure chance would already allow.

As far as trying to justify palmistry from the Bible is concerned, the cause is a hopeless one. The out-of-context verses used by some have nothing to do with palm reading. Moreover, the Scriptures speak loudly and clearly against trying to foretell the future using any form of divination. The following Scripture would apply to palmistry:

> There shall not be found among you anyone who makes his son or daughter pass through the fire, one who uses divination, one who practices witchcraft, or one who interprets omens, or a sorcerer, or one who casts a spell, or a medium, or a spiritist, or one who calls up the dead. For whoever does these things is detestable to the Lord; and because of these detestable things the Lord your God will drive them out before you (Deuteronomy 18:10-12, NASB).

Cartomancy (Tarot Cards)

Cartomancy forecasts the future by means of using cards. The elaborately illustrated cards used in this technique are called Tarot cards. Supposedly these cards hold the secrets to the future.

Those who use the cards extol their virtues:

> The tarot is one of the most wonderful of human inventions. Despite all the outcries of philosophers, this pack of pictures, in which destiny is reflected as a mirror with multiple facets, remains so vital and exercises so irresistible an attraction on imaginative minds that it is hardly possible that austere critics who speak in the name of an exact but uninteresting logic should ever succeed in abolishing its employment (Grillot de Givry, *Witchcraft, Magic and Alchemy*, New York: Dover Publ., 1971, p. 280).

Wheatly offers this explanation:

> Telling fortunes by cards is at the present day probably the most popuar method of predicting a person's future.
>
> There are two distinct types of pack: the Tarot, or Major Arcana, which consists of twenty-two pictorial cards, none of which has any obvious relation to the others; and the Minor Arcana, which originally had fifty-six cards (in modern times reduced to fifty-two) divided into four suits. The suits, now diamonds, hearts, spades and clubs, were originally coins, cups, swords and staffs, which represented respectively commerce, spirituality, war and agriculture. In the old packs the fourteenth card in each suit was the Knight, who has since been dropped or, if one prefers, merged with the Knave, who represents the squire of the Lord (King) and Lady (Queen).
>
> The origin of both packs is lost in mystery. Some writers have stated that the Tarot is the Book of Thoth, the God of Wisdom of the Egyptians; others connect it with the twenty-two paths of the Hebrew Cabala, and still others assert that cards were introduced into western Europe by the Bohemians (Den-

nis Wheatley, *The Devil and All His Works*, New York: American Heritage Press, 1971, p. 62).

Those who turn to Tarot readings are often insecure about the future. Not content to trust in the providence of God, they anxiously seek forbidden knowledge about the future in the hopes that such knowledge will enable them to escape some impending doom or fate.

There is nothing scientific about Tarot cards. Although fantastic claims have been made for their powers through the centuries, no one has been able to produce significant evidence that such readings are reliable. While we would agree that the majority of Tarot readings are completely fictitious, and depend more on the medium's ability to guess human nature than on spirit guides, there are some readings that appear to be genuinely supernatural.

Since these readings invariably lead a person away from the God of the Bible, and attempt to invade areas of knowledge God has determined should remain secret, we must conclude that they are demonic.

As Christians we can remain confident and peaceful, knowing that God is in full control of our unseen future. Jesus Christ is the only answer for one who is anxious about his future. He said:

> But if God so arrays the grass of the field, which is alive today and tomorrow is thrown into the furnace, will He not much more do so for you, O men of little faith? Do not be anxious then, saying, "What shall we eat?" or "What shall we drink?" or "With what shall we clothe ourselves?" For all of these things the Gentiles eagerly seek; for your heavenly Father knows that you need all these things. But seek first His kingdom and His righteousness; and all these things shall be added to you. Therefore do not be anxious for tomorrow; for tomorrow will care for itself. Each day has enough trouble of its own (Matthew 6:30-34, NASB).

Mirror Mantic

Mirror mantic uses crystal balls, mirrors, rock crystals or still water as "mirrors of the future."

> There are in existence occult text books on the subject of mirror mantic and mirror magic. The mirror magician with the help of a magic mirror may attempt to heal or to persecute through magic, to treat people at a distance or to use love and defense magic, and so on. Mirror mantic is often directed at discovering things unknown to the inquirer, in uncovering crimes or diagnosing difficult diseases, and it can embrace any physical event which happens in the world. Mirrors are not the only occult tools used in this field, but crystal balls, rock crystal and other reflecting objects all play a part. Some even use water as a reflecting surface (Kurt Koch, *Between Christ and Satan*, op. cit., p. 42).

This is an ancient method of divination. The one gazing into the crystal supposedly enters a state of clairvoyance where he can see events and things happening at the present or the future, regardless of distance from the diviner. The crystal supposedly enables the person to see a series of pictures of what is taking place or will take place, thus enabling him to peer into the unknown.

Mirror mantic has no foundation in Christianity or science. Rather than being a "window on the future," it is most often just the product of good guessing and a rich imagination on the part of the diviner. In a few cases, genuine occultic involvement appears to take place.

In either kind of instance the customer is seeking help from a medium or diviner. Throughout Scripture God condemns such practitioners and those who frequent them. They claim to speak for God but are actually frauds.

> They see falsehood and lying divination who are saying, "The Lord declares," when the Lord has not sent them; yet they hope for the fulfillment of their word. Did you not see a false vision and speak a lying divination when you said, "The Lord declares," but it is not I who have spoken? Therefore, says the Lord God, "Because you have spoken falsehood and seen a lie, therefore behold, I am against you," declares the Lord God (Ezekiel 13:6-9, NASB).

Psychometry

Psychometry can also be classed in the area of fortunetelling. The idea behind psychometry is summed up in the *Dictionary of Mysticism:*

> The psychic faculty of certain persons to divine events connected with material objects when in close contact with the latter. The material objects are considered to be acting as catalysts for the PSI faculty. Occultists call it "reading or seeing" with the inner sight (Frank Gaynor, ed., *Dictionary of Mysticism*, New York: Citadel Press, n.d., p. 148).

Psychometry consists of a person holding some material object of another in his hands and having the ability to make statements and identify characteristics of the owner of the article. He may even foretell part of the future of the owner.

Psychometry has no place in the Christian's life. We are not to depend on mediums and their paraphernalia for help in this world. Rather than depending on other men who are fallible and serving Satan rather than the Lord God, we should depend on the Holy Spirit, whose specific job is to guide us in God's will. Christians can avail themselves of the only true "medium," the Holy Spirit.

> And I will ask the Father, and He will give you another Helper, that He may be with you forever; that is the Spirit of Truth, whom the world cannot receive, because it does not behold Him or know Him... (John 14:16, 17, NASB).
>
> But the Helper, the Holy Spirit, whom the Father will send in My name, He will teach you all things, and bring to your remembrance all that I said unto you (John 14:26, NASB).
>
> And in the same way the Spirit also helps our weaknesses; for we do not know how to pray as we should, but the Spirit Himself intercedes for us with groanings too deep for words; and He who searches the hearts knows what the mind of the Spirit is, because He intercedes for the saints according to the will of God (Romans 8:26, 27, NASB).

We have no need of psychometry or any other occultic practice if we have the Holy Spirit within us.

There are other types of fortunetelling which include:

Teacup Reading—This form of divination interprets the shapes and relative positions left by tea leaves at the bottom of a cup. Fortunes are told using the same principles as are found in the oriental I CHING readings.

Geomancy—This system of divination employs a map with 12 divisions in which the symbols of geomancy are placed in conjunction with the planets.

Pyromancy—Divination by use of fire configurations.

Aeromancy—This form of divination observes atmospheric conditions or ripples on the surface of an open body of water.

Arithmancy—Divination by numbers, especially by attaching mystical significance to the numbers associated with a person, especially those numbers associated with the letters of the person's name.

Augury—"In ancient Rome, divination by the flight of birds. The word is used generally for all kinds of divination, also for any omen or sign on which divination is or can be based" (Frank Gaynor, op. cit., p. 21).

Capnomancy—This form of divination uses the smoke of an altar or sacrificial incense as a means of foretelling the future.

Rhapsodamancy—This form of divination is based upon a line in a sacred book that strikes the eye when the book is opened after the diviner prays, meditates or invokes the help of spirits.

In conclusion, there are many different names for fortunetellers or mediums. By whatever name, they are completely condemned by the Bible. God calls them detestable in Deuteronomy 18:11, 12. One who practices such things was condemned to death under the Old Testament theocracy (Leviticus 20:6, 27).

Such false prophets (Jeremiah 14:14) were sometimes called astrologers (Isaiah 47:13), mediums (Deuteronomy 18:11), diviners (Deuteronomy 18:14), magicians (Genesis 41:8), soothsayers (Isaiah 2:6), sorcerers (Acts 13: 6, 8), and spiritists (Deuteronomy 18:11).

The Lord God promises that someday he will "cut off sorceries from your hand, and you will have fortunetellers no more" (Micah 5:12).

CHAPTER ELEVEN

Ghosts

G hosts are said to be spirit apparitions through which the souls of dead persons are said to manifest themselves. All of us have heard fictionalized "ghost stories" from the time we were children. While we dismiss such stories now as figments of fertile juvenile imaginations, we cannot altogether dismiss the whole idea of genuine spirit phenomena popularly associated with ghosts, sometimes called poltergeists.

There are thousands of sophisticated, intelligent people around the world who are convinced that ghosts not only exist, but they can and do communicate with the living.

Are there actually supernatural spirit phenomena associated in a way so as to be labeled poltergeist activity? And if there are, are they adequately explained as the spirits of the deceased?

Milbourne Cristopher, known as America's foremost magician, was also a psychic researcher. Cristopher was convinced that the accounts of ghosts and haunted houses could be explained on a natural level. He offers the following account of a so-called haunted house that was found to have a natural explanation:

> There are sounds in old houses that are not made by human hands or human voices. They are heard during storms or at certain seasons of the year or in some cases on specific days and at specific times. When the sounds persist, rumors spread that houses are haunted, and they are difficult to sell or rent.
>
> An undated clipping, preserved by Houdini, reports such a story. In Union, New York, seven miles from Binghamtom, a once attractive two-story cottage was deteriorating. Paint peeled and cracked from its clapboards, grime clouded its remaining windows. Hinges, long unoiled, creaked, and the floors squeaked if a youngster, intrigued by the empty building, forced open a door and ran through the rooms. The neglected frame cottage was owned by J. W. McAdam of New York City. For two and a half years a man named Hakes had rented it. Neither he, his wife, nor his two children noticed anything peculiar during their occupancy.
>
> Edgar Williams was the next tenant. He and his wife were the first to report that something unusual was taking place. It did not happen often, Williams told the real estate agent, but whenever a high wind swept across the proper-

ty, bending the branches of trees, a wailing cry would echo through the upper floor. It was impossible to sleep then, he went on; his wife became so agitated that he thought her terror might affect her mind.

The agent went through the house, but could find nothing that might produce the weird sound. Shortly after this, the Williamses moved out. The next tenant had not been told of the strange noise. Less than a month later, he too was in to see the real estate man. He asked if anything odd had ever happened in the house. A murder, perhaps? The agent assured him that to the best of his knowledge nothing of this nature had ever taken place within the four walls. Then the tenant admitted that his wife too had heard the shrill shriek in the night; she thought it came from the garret. The agent made another trip to the house. This time he thoroughly examined the garret on the pretext that the roof might need repair. Again his search for a clue to the mystery was unsuccessful. In less than a week the house was vacant.

Three more families lived briefly in the cottage, all heard the strange, wailing cries. By now the story had spread through the area. It was impossible to rent the haunted house. Uncared for, it gradually took on an appearance that only a ghost would relish.

Early in December a man visited the real estate office and asked if the place which he had heard was haunted could be rented for a short period. The agent, delighted that interest was being expressed in a piece of property he had thought would never produce another penny, answered warily, Yes, the house was available, but as to the haunting stories, they were sheer nonsense. The stranger put him straight. He was interested in a haunted house; he was investigating spiritualism and would like a week to study the sounds the people in that part of the state attributed to a ghost. The agency gave him access to the cottage for seven days without charge. When the man returned to the real estate office again, the rental agent was expecting the same old story of cries in the night. He asked: "Have you laid the ghost?" His visitor replied: "I have, and here it is." The man reached in his pocket and took out a small metal object he had found in the garret. He displayed it on the palm of his hand. It was a toy—a child's whistle, sound, with a hole in the side.

"This had been fastened in a knothole," he said, "and was directly opposite a broken pane of glass. When the wind blew hard, it caused a draft, and the wild shrieks your tenants heard were the natural result."

Who would have guessed that one of the Hakes children, while playing in the garret, had plugged a hole with the whistle, or that a blast of wind would make it sound? Yet there are many accounts of how strange sounds in old houses have been made in the past. The whistle in Union, New York, was something new, but currents of air have accounted for other mysterious noises throughout the years (Milbourne Cristopher, *ESP, Seers And Psychics*, New York: Thomas Crowell Co., 1970, pp. 167-169).

While many such phenomena can be explained easily in natural terms, especially by means of deception, fraud and/or trickery, some poltergeist activity seems to defy natural explanation.

Allen Spraggett records the following ghost story:

Believe in ghosts? If not, how would you explain this true story?

One winter night, in northern Ontario, Canada, during the early days of World War Two, a middle-aged widow awakened from a troubled sleep to see her younger brother standing at the foot of her bed.

The eerie thing was that the woman knew her brother was in England serving with the Royal Canadian Air Force.

Yet she saw him clearly, dressed in his pilot's flying suit, his face deathly pale and solemn beyond description. The effect was horrific. The woman screamed. Abruptly the strange phantasm vanished.

When the woman's three teen-aged children rushed into the room, they found her sobbing, "He's dead, I know he's dead."

The premonition proved to be correct. Sometime later, word came that the brother's Spitfire had been shot down over the English Channel on the same day—possibly at the same hour—that the woman saw the spectral figure in her room.

This story was told to me by one of those intimately involved—the woman's son, who was a member of a church of which I was pastor (Allen Spraggett, *The Unexplained*, New York: Signet Mystic Books, 1967, p. 13).

In his excellent and extremely well-documented book, *Can We Explain the Poltergeist?* A. R. G. Owen gives some examples of genuine poltergeist (ghostly) activity. One case in particular which convinced him poltergeist activity does exist happened in Sauchie, Scotland, in 1960.

Owen goes into great detail (more than 40 pages) of the phenomena of Sauchie, which included the production of noises (tappings, knockings, sawings, bumpings) and the movement of objects. His learned conclusions were as follows:

"It is convenient to say at the outset that the evidence presented is to my mind conclusive proof of the objective reality of two types of poltergeist phenomena: production of noises... movement of objects... In my opinion the Sauchie case must be regarded as establishing beyond all reasonable doubt the objective reality of some poltergeist phenomena" (A. R. G. Owen, *Can We Explain the Poltergeist?*, New York: Garret Pubns-Helix Press, 1964, pp. 130, 169).

Examining this case of ghostly apparitions, we as Christians can use Scriptural principles to define our Christian response to such spirit phenomena.

Remember, much of what is reported as ghostly or spirit phenomena is fraudulent. It is either deliberately manufactured "evidence," or a natural explanation for the phenomena is more reasonable and probable than a supernatural explanation. We are not concerned here with such natural phenomena, but only with that which defies natural explanation.

Whatever supernatural appearance is involved in ghostly appearances, they are not the appearance of the souls or spirits of persons who are now dead. The Bible assures us that Christians who die go *immediately* to be with the Lord Jesus Christ (2 Corinthians 5:1-9; Philippians 1:21-25).

Non-Christians, on the other hand, go immediately to Hades, the spirit abode of the dead. There is active punishment for the unredeemed in Hades and no allowance is made for the dead to visit the land of the living no matter how briefly. In fact, in Luke 16:19-31, Jesus Christ presented us with the story of a non-believer who died and desired to send dead Lazarus back to the land of the living to warn his still living brothers not to reject the truth as he had done.

"But Abraham said, 'They have Moses and the prophets; let them hear them.' But he said, 'No, father Abraham, but if someone goes to them from the dead, they will repent!' But he said to him, 'If they do not listen to Moses and the prophets, neither will they be persuaded if someone rises from the dead' " (Luke 16:29-31, NASB). As a matter of fact, Jesus Christ the "firstborn from the dead" (Colossians 1:18) conquered death and was resurrected and many people still don't believe his message of good news and eternal life!

A common denominator in the most convincing ghost stories we hear is that the ghosts don't have peace. They are in some sort of torment, usually bound in some way to the place or building where they died. As we have already seen, the spirit of a Christian would go immediately to be with Jesus Christ. He would not be without peace.

In fact, the Bible promises that for the Christian, "You have not received a spirit of slavery leading to fear again, but you have received a spirit of adoption. . ." (Romans 8:15, NASB). While it is true that the non-Christian soul has no peace, his unrest is not because of what is going on in our world, but because of the torment he suffers in Hades as a direct result of his willful rejection of free salvation offered by Jesus Christ (Luke 16:23; 2 Peter 2:1).

Common ghost stories center on the departed spirit's compulsion to see his murder avenged. He cannot rest, it is said, until the crime is punished. This desire for personal vengeance, exemplified by such "hauntings," is denied to one who desires to follow the Lord. "Never take your own revenge, beloved, but leave room for the wrath of God, for it is written, 'Vengeance is mine, I will repay,' says the Lord" (Romans 12:19, NASB).

We know of no instance when a supposed ghost preached the truth of the living God. Galatians 1:8-10 warns us not to accept anyone, even an angel, who brings a gospel contrary to that revealed in God's Word. There is no need for a Christian's spirit to return to "haunt" this world. Jesus Christ conquered death and rose from the dead to prove the good news of God's love and grace extended to mankind. Surely His Word is of more value than that of a disembodied spirit!

The spirit of a non-Christian is not permitted to leave its place of torment in Hades and even if it could, it would not bring the gospel of our Lord and Master. We must reject all such messages.

We believe that the ghost experiences that defy natural explanation are demonic in origin. Hebrews 2:14 notes Satan's preoccupation with death. It would be fitting for his legions to pretend to be the spirits of the departed. The Bible even tells of a demon-possessed man who had a compulsion to roam a graveyard (Matthew 8:28; Mark 5: 2-5).

Christians have no need to fear death. Jesus Christ conquered death that He "might deliver those who through fear of death were subject to slavery all their lives" (Hebrews 2:15, NASB).

CHAPTER TWELVE

Hypnotism

D r. Nandor Fodor defines hypnotism as "a peculiar state of consciousness, artificially induced, which liberates subconscious powers in the subject, puts him in rapport with the hypnotizer, makes him accept and meticulously execute any of his suggestions, whether hypnotic or post-hypnotic, which do not conflict with deeper instincts of self-preservation and morality, and produces such strange physiological effects as anesthesia and the remarkable control over organic processes of the body. In hypnotic sleep the waking stimuli are strongly resisted, the sleeper hears and answers" (Nandor Fodor, *Encyclopedia of Psychic Science*, Secaucus, NJ: University Books, 1966, p. 77).

An objective, non-psychically oriented definition of hypnosis is "a sleeplike state that nevertheless permits a wide range of behavioral responses to stimulation. The hypnotized individual appears to heed only the communications of the hypnotist.... Even memory and awareness of self may be altered by suggestion, and the effects of the suggestions may be extended (post-hypnotically) into subsequent waking activity" (*Encyclopedia Britannica*, Chicago: Encyclopedia Britannica Publishers, 1974, Macropaedia, Vol. 9, p. 133).

Hypnotism could then be defined as a means of bringing on an artificial state of sleep or reduced consciousness.

Hypnotism is used in a variety of ways. There are those who practice self-hypnosis who attempt to rid themselves of some bad habit or to put their mind in a more restful state. Some religionists practice extreme methods of self-hypnosis in an attempt to make themselves insensitive to the pain of sticking knives through various parts of their body. Some magicians use hypnosis as a means of entertaining the public. It is not unusual for schools to allow magic shows where the magician will call up several students in order to hypnotize them.

Many physicians use hypnosis for diagnosis and therapy in treating illnesses. The idea is to alter negative aspects of a person's behavior. Another use of hypnotism, which is much too common, is the occultist who uses hypnotism, as a magic art to control the behavior of individuals.

There is a wide difference of opinion on the validity and usefulness of hypnotism. Some see hypnotism as being neutral, neither good nor bad, while others argue that hypnotism can be beneficial for diagnosis and therapy. There are yet others who see hypnotism as harmful, no matter what the case, because it is an attack on the human psyche.

Although some physicians do use hypnosis for treating certain illnesses, there is a great degree of association between hypnosis and occultism. Moreover, there are those engaged in hypnosis who have little or no training either medically or psychiatrically who use hypnosis for entertainment purposes. Both the occultic and the unprofessional use of hypnosis can have disastrous effects. Consider the following example from Kurt Koch:

> I was asked to speak at several meetings in a Baptist church in the state of Maine. The pastor of the church told me the story of his son while I was there.
>
> His son had been converted to Christ at the age of sixteen. He was baptized and became a member of his father's church. He went to college about sixty miles from his hometown.
>
> At the end of the college year, an entertainment was held for the students and teachers. The president invited a certain entertainer who performed all kinds of tricks and illusions. One thing he did was to pick out twenty-five students and bring them up to the platform to be hypnotized. One of them was given a big red potato, and it was suggested to him that it was a wonderful apple which he was now allowed to eat. The boy ate the red potato with great delight. To another boy, the entertainer suggested: "You are a baby, and here is your bottle of milk which you must drink." The boy drank the bottle of milk to the last drop. To a third, he said that it was very hot, that he was by a lake and could now bathe. The boy undressed and put on a pair of bathing trunks. All these tricks were greeted by laughter and applause from the audience. To the pastor's son he said, "You are in a horse race, and your horse has a chance of winning." The boy began to ride on a chair placed back to front as if he were sitting on a horse.
>
> When the entertainment was over, the entertainer released them from the hypnosis; all except the pastor's son, whom he could not restore to consciousness. The president became angry. But try as he might, the man was unable to bring him back from this hypnotic state. There was nothing to do but to call the hospital.
>
> An ambulance took the boy to the hospital where five specialists tried to deal with the hypnotized boy. They were unable to. The father was not informed until six days later. He drove straight to the hospital by car and took his son home. Then he remembered his local doctor who came immediately. The doctor was angry and said, "If he were my son, I would take the principal and the entertainer to court." The pastor and his wife prayed for days, but nothing happened. Suddenly, the pastor came upon the idea of commanding in the name of Jesus. He looked in spirit to the cross of Christ on Calvary and cried: "In the name of Jesus Christ, the Son of God, I command you dark powers to withdraw." At once the hypnotic spell was broken. The boy regained consciousness. At last the horse race ended (Kurt Koch, *Occult ABC*, Grand Rapids, MI: Int. Publs., n.d., pp. 97, 98).

Since there are so many examples of hypnosis which have ended in disaster, we would strongly warn people to stay away from all forms of either occultic or entertaining hypnosis. If a person allows himself to be hypnotized, it should be only under the most controlled situation by a qualified and experienced physician. The human mind is not something to play with or to let another person have control of. At best, hypnosis can have only limited use.

Even the secular *Encyclopedia Britannica* warns:

> While little skill is required to induce hypnosis, considerable training is needed to evaluate whether it is the appropriate treatment technique and, if so, how it should properly be employed. When used in the treatment context, hypnosis should never be employed by individuals who do not have the competence and skill to treat such problems without the use of hypnosis. For this reason hypnosis "schools" or "institutions" cannot provide the needed training for individuals lacking the more general scientific and technical qualifications of the healing professions. . . . Improperly used, hypnosis may add to the patient's psychiatric or medical difficulties. Thus, a sufferer of an undiscovered brain tumor may sacrifice his life in the hands of a practitioner who successfully relieves his headache by hypnotic suggestion, thereby delaying needed surgery. Broad diagnostic training and therapeutic skill are indispensable in avoiding the inappropriate and potentially dangerous use of hypnosis (*Encyclopedia Britannica*, op. cit., p. 139).

The Bible says, "All things are lawful for me, but not all things are profitable. All things are lawful for me, but I will not be mastered by anything" (1 Corinthians 6:12, NASB). We do not need to be mastered by the power of suggestion from another.

CHAPTER THIRTEEN

Magic

When we speak of magic, we are dealing with a term having a variety of meanings. People use the expression, "It's magic!" when they see something incredible. We also speak of magic being in the air when there is a particularly pleasant mood.

One of the popular uses of the word magic is in the field of show business. Magic shows entertain us when the magician saws someone in half or pulls a rabbit out of his hat. This type of magic is called sleight of hand or, as the French term it, *legerdemain*. It is the art of illusion.

Certain primitive people have a magical view of life with customs and practices based upon sheer superstition. They consider certain phenomena magic because they have not learned the natural explanation of the occurrence (for example, an eclipse of the sun).

However, the magic we are concerned with is none of the above. It is occultic in nature, an attempt to master supernormal forces in order to produce visible effects. This magic is a secretive art, and it is difficult to give a precise definition of all it includes.

Arthur S. Gregor defines magic in the following manner: "Magic is an attempt to gain control over nature by supernatural means. It consists of spells, charms, and other techniques intended to give man what he cannot achieve with his normal human powers" (Arthur S. Gregor, *Witchcraft and Magic*, New York: Charles Scribner's Sons, 1972, p. 1).

Magic, used mainly by witches, is described by Truzzi:

> For some witchcraft practitioners, especially the more orthodox or traditional ones, magic is viewed as a supernatural phenomenon. The character of magic is such that it involves special spiritual agencies (e.g., elementals, demons, etc.) which are outside the natural physical order available for study by empirical science. Thus, for some witches, magical laws are not natural laws, and they can even contradict natural laws. Supernatural agencies and mechanisms are invoked, and these are beyond scientific explanation (Marcello Truzzi, "Toward a Sociology of the Occult: Notes on Modern Witchcraft" in *Religious Movements in Contemporary America*. Irving I. Zaretsky and Mark P. Leone, eds., Princeton: Princeton University Press, 1974, p. 635).

There are different types of magic practiced today. These include:

White Magic

White magic is said to be the use of magical powers and abilities in an unselfish manner for the benefit of others. It is believed a person could be cured of bewitchment by white magic. "If a child is bewitched, we take the cradle. . . throw it three times through an enchanted hoop, ring or belt, and then a dog throws it; and then shakes the belt over the fire. . . and then throws it down on the ground till a dog or cat goes over it, so that the sickness may leave the sick person and enter the dog or cat" (R. Seth, *In the Name of the Devil*, 1969).

A witch in seventeenth-century Scotland described how white magic could be used to cure sickness:

"When we wished to heal any sore, or broken limb, we would say three times:

He put the blood to the blood, till all up stood;
The lith to the lith, till all took with;
Our Lady charmed her darling son,
With her tooth and her tongue
And her ten fingers
In the name of the Father, The Son and The Holy Ghost.

And this we say three times stroking the sore, and it becomes whole. (Roger Hart, *Witchcraft*, New York: G. P. Putnam's Sons, 1971).

Although white magic was and is used to combat evil, it still comes from an ungodly source and should in no way be practiced.

Black Magic

The opposite of white magic is the familiar black magic which can be defined as the use of magical powers to cause harm to others.

Sympathetic Magic

Sympathetic magic can be defined in the following manner:

Control of a person, animal, object, or event by either of two principles: 1) Like produces like—for example, a drawing of a deer pierced by arrows supposedly would help a tribe's real hunters repeat the scene. 2) Things that were once in contact always retain a magic connection—for example, a man supposedly could be harmed if a lost tooth fell into enemy hands (Daniel Cohen, *Superstition*, Mankato, MN: Creative Education Society, 1971, p. 115).

Sympathetic magic is based upon the principle of "like produces like"; that is, things having a resemblance to each other in shape have a magical relationship.

Liturgy of Magic

Often the rituals of magic are similar to the Christian faith. Merrill Unger compares magic liturgy and Christian worship:

A magic ceremony commonly involves the use of four elements—invocation, charm, symbolic action, and a fetish. In the case of white magic, the invocation is addressed to God the Father, God the Son, and God the Holy Spirit. If black magic is involved, the invocation is addressed to Satan and demonic powers. Such invocation is the counterpart of calling upon God through the Lord Jesus Christ. The invocation of black magic is commonly fortified by a pact with Satan in which the person signs himself over to the devil with his own blood.

The charm, which conjures the magic powers into operation, is the counterpart of the Word of God and prayer. The symbolic action, which is multifarious, mimics biblical symbolic action such as forms of prayer or imposition of hands in prayer.

Examples of charms taken from *The Sixth and Seventh Books of Moses* are (1) the transference charm of black magic. Boil the flesh of a swine in the urine of an ailing person, then feed this concoction to a dog. As the dog dies, the ailing person will recover. (2) A healing charm of white magic. Eat, unread, some walnut leaves inscribed with a Bible text. (3) A fertility charm of white magic. Place a woman's hair between two loaves of bread and feed this to cattle while saying a magic verse.

Magical symbolism and fetish. Magic symbolism is intended to give effectiveness to the magic charm and bring about occult transference. Magic symbolism, in turn, is supported by a fetish. This is a magically charmed object which is supposed to carry magical power. Any object, of the most bizarre character, can become a fetish by being magically charmed. The magical effectiveness of the fetish (amulet or talisman) is increased by inscriptions, particularly by magic charm formulas (Merrill Unger, *Demons in the World Today*, Wheaton, IL: Tyndale House Publishers, 1971, pp. 90, 91).

Lycanthropy

Lycanthropy is a form of magic which believes human beings under certain conditions can change into animals. The most well-known form of lycanthropy is: a man can change himself either permanently or temporarily into a werewolf. The following 16th century Baltic tale gives an example of this transformation:

At Christmas, a crippled boy goes around the country summoning the devil's followers, who are countless, to a general meeting. Whoever stays behind, or goes unwillingly, is beaten by another with an iron whip till the blood flows, and his traces are left in blood.

The human form vanishes, and the whole multitude become werewolves. Many thousands assemble. Foremost goes the leader armed with an iron whip, and the troop follow, firmly convinced in their imagination that they are transformed into wolves. They fall upon herds of cattle and flocks of sheep, but they have no power to slay men. When they come to a river, the leader strikes the water with his scourge, and it divides, leaving a dry path through the midst, by which the pack go. The transformation lasts twelve days. At the end of this time the wolf skin vanishes, and the human form reappears.

Although lycanthropy is considered mere legend and superstition, there have been modern reports of this phenomena occurring. The following case is cited by John Warwick Montgomery in his book, *Principalities and Powers*, wherein he is quoting from Frederick Kaigh, who alleges his statement to be based upon eyewitness testimony:

Now from the distance, out of the bush, came jackal cries, nearer and nearer. The deep growl of the male being answered by the shriller cries of the female.

Suddenly a powerful young man and a splendid young girl, completely naked, leapt over the heads of the onlookers and fell sprawling in the clearing.

They sprang up again instantly and started to dance. My God, how they danced! If the dance of the nyanga (the witch doctor) was horrible, this was revolting. They danced the dance of the rutting jackals. As the dance progressed, their imitations became more and more animal, till the horror of it brought the acid of vomit to the throat. Then, in a twinkling, with loathing unbounded, and incredulous amazement, I saw these two *turn into jackals before my eyes*. The rest of their "act" must be rather imagined than described. Suffice it to say, and I say it with all the authority of long practice of my profession (medicine), no human beings, despite any extensive and potent preparation, could have sustained the continued and repeated sexuality of that horrid mating (Frederick Kaigh, *Witchcraft and Magic of Africa*, London: Richard Lesley, 1947, p. 32).

A summary view of the two main types of magic:

This has led to a common distinction made by occultists between so-called *black* and *white* magic. In part the view on this issue depends upon the witch's relation to Christianity. For a pure Satanist, the magic he practices is black in that its power supposedly derives from the forces of evil and darkness (though he may regard Christian miracles like transubstantiation to be instances of white magic). But for the witch who has no belief in the Christian's hell or devil, magic derives from special laws in nature. Because of the common public sterotype of the witch as Satanist, however, many non-Christian witches began to speak of themselves as *white witches* and began referring to magic they did as white or beneficial. But this reference to white and black magic was meant to refer to the intentions of the magician in its invocation, not to the character of the magic itself (Truzzi, *Religious Movements*, op. cit., p. 635).

CHAPTER FOURTEEN

Ouija Boards

One of the most popular occultic devices in the world today is the Ouija board. What is the Ouija board and what does it claim to do? *The Dictionary of Mysticism* has this to say concerning the Ouija board:

> An instrument for communication with the spirits of the dead. Made in various shapes and designs, some of them used in the sixth century before Christ. The common feature of all its varieties is that an object moves under the hand of the medium, and one of its corners, or a pointer attached to it, spells out messages by successively pointing to letters of the alphabet marked on a board which is a part of the instrument (Frank Gaynor, ed., *Dictionary of Mysticism*, New York: Citadel Press, n.d., p. 132).

The Ouija board is considered by some as nothing more than a party game. Others believe that using it can reveal hidden things in the subconscious. Still others believe that, while the communications are produced supernaturally, the supernatural source is demonic rather than from "beyond the grave." One Christian authority on the occult, Kurt Koch, has strong feelings on the subject:

> . . .psychologists would have us believe that the game is harmless. They hold that it is only a matter of bringing to light things hidden in our subconscious minds. This view can swiftly be refuted. With the Ouija board, revelations from the hidden past and predictions about the future are made. These things could not possibly be stored in our subconscious minds (Kurt Koch, *Occult ABC*, Grand Rapids, MI: Int. Publs., n.d., p. 152).

Our convictions concerning the Ouija board agree exactly with those of noted cult and occult observer Edmond Gruss.

> The Ouija board should be seen as a device which sometimes actually makes contact with the supernatural for several reasons:
>
> - The content of the messages often goes beyond that which can be reasonably explained as coming from the conscious or subconscious mind of the operator. Examples of such are presented in Sir William F. Barrett's *On the Threshold of the Unseen* (pp. 176-189), and in the experiences of Mrs. John H. Curran, related in the book *Singer in the Shadows*.

- The many cases of "possession" after a period of Ouija board use also support the claim that supernatural contact is made through the board. Psychics and parapsychologists have received letters from hundreds of people who have experienced "possession" (an invasion of their personalities). Rev. Donald Page, a well-known clairvoyant and exorcist of the Christian Spiritualist Church, is reported as saying that most of his "possession" cases "are people who have used the Ouija board," and that "this is one of the easiest and quickest ways to become possessed" (*Man, Myth and Magic*, number 73, after p. 2060). While Page views these "possessions" as caused by disincarnate entities, the reality of possession is still clear. The Christian sees the invader as an evil spirit (demon).

- The board has been subjected to tests which support supernatural intervention. The testing of the board was presented in an article by Sir William Barrett, in the September 1914 *Proceedings of the American Society for Psychical Research* (pp. 381-894). The Barrett report indicated that the board worked efficiently with the operators blindfolded, the board's alphabet rearranged and its surface hidden from the sight of those working it. It worked with such speed and accuracy under these tests that Barrett concluded:

  > Reviewing the results as a whole I am convinced of their supernormal character, and that we have here an exhibition of some intelligent, disincarnate agency, mingling with the personality of one or more of the sitters and guiding their muscular movements (p. 394).

In his book, *On the Threshold of the Unseen*, Barrett referred to these same experiences and stated: "...Whatever may have been the source of the intelligence displayed, it was absolutely beyond the range of any normal human faculty" (p. 181). Similar statements could be multiplied.

The fact remains that the Ouija board works. Much phenomena is certainly through conscious and subconscious activity, but that some is of supernatural character must be accepted (Edmond Gruss, *Cults and Occult in the Age of Aquarius*, Phillipsburg, NJ: 1980, pp. 115, 116).

The magician, Danny Korem, feels there is nothing supernatural connected with the Ouija board.

I have never witnessed, read, or heard of a credible report of something of a supernatural nature taking place through the use of the Ouija board. I have seen, heard, and read, however, of many negative experiences that have entrapped people who have sought knowledge with a Ouija board. If you own a Ouija board or some similar diversion, my advice is to destroy it and never encourage others to tinker with such devices. You never know what emotional disturbances might be triggered in yourself or others through their use.

If you are still unconvinced and believe that some power might be manifested, then one should utilize the following procedure. The letters should be scattered at random, without your knowledge of their position, around the board; a bag should be placed over your head to prevent your viewing the board; and the entire letter-finding task should be viewed by a qualified magician, who would verify your lack of vision. Then and only then, if there are forces at work, will they produce something literate let alone prophetic. To save you the time and effort, let me add that this has already been tried with negative results (Danny Korem and Paul Meier, *The Fakers*, Grand Rapids, MI: Baker Book House, 1980, pp. 70, 71).

The Ouija board is not a plaything. It is another tool often used by Satan to get people to look somewhere else besides to Jesus Christ for the answers. Whether supernatural forces are at work or not, if the person using the Ouija board thinks the supernatural is at work, he will then employ it rather than looking to God for ultimate answers.

CHAPTER FIFTEEN

Parapsychology

W hile the occult generally refers to the darker side of supernatural activity, it now also involves the new discipline of parapsychology.

Parapsychology is a new branch of either the occult or psychology depending on whom you consult. It is a discipline that has aimed to put many of the supernatural phenomena associated with the occult on sound scientific footing. The attempt is to create respectability for what has been considered as foolishness.

One of the popular areas in parapsychology in recent years has been ESP (extrasensory perception). Traditional witchcraft, which assents to the supernatural, has also given way in some groups to this new scientific or paranormal explanation of occultic activity.

> Most newer witchcraft groups, however, avoid supernaturalism and prefer instead to speak of *supernormal* or *paranormal* events. Magical laws are seen as effective and within the ultimate purview of scientific understanding, but their emphasis is placed upon pragmatic knowledge of such magical laws and not on their scientific validation or understanding. In this sense, it would appear that there has been a kind of secularization of magic in adaptation to the modern scientific and naturalistic world view. Thus, what were once described in the occult literature as supernatural psychic forces are now examples of extrasensory perception of a kind basically examinable and potentially understandable in the psychologist's laboratory (Marcello Truzzi, "Toward a Sociology of the Occult: Notes on Modern Witchcraft," *Religious Movements in Contemporary America*. Irving I. Zaretsky and Mark P. Leone, eds., Princeton: Princeton University Press, 1974, pp. 635, 636).

In his book, *Parapsychology: An Insider's View of ESP,* J. Gaither Pratt, in the first chapter, "The Benign Revolution," points to a new revolution in thought, what he calls an advance in ideas, the attempt of parapsychology to gain respectability. He plots his own odyssey, how he came to embrace this revolution and the need to see parapsychology as a branch of science.

Pratt comments:

And so this book is about a revolution of human thought. Our Western culture has passed through a number of great changes in ways of thinking since the Renaissance, others are in the process of taking place, and many more will undoubtedly come in the years and centuries ahead. The advance in thinking with which this book is concerned is still in the process of taking shape. Indeed, it is even still in a very early stage of development, though not too early to be recognized and to be appreciated for what it has already accomplished as well as for its far greater potentialities yet to be appreciated.

This is the revolution of thinking embodied in the new branch of science, parapsychology. The definition of this field is quite simple: as physics is the science which deals with matter, so parapsychology is the science of mind. So simple to state, yet so far-reaching in its implications! It will be the main task of this book to present some highlights of past accomplishments in this field and the general scope and direction of present efforts — and to explore and explain the meaning of its findings (J. Gaither Pratt, *Parapsychology: An Insider's View of ESP,* New York: Doubleday & Co., 1964, pp. 2, 3).

For men such as Pratt, parapsychology demands investigation from a scientific perspective. The experiences which people have should be investigated to determine just what the possibilities are in this field of the mind.

Let us return to the main theme of the chapter: what this book is about in terms of the meaning, scope, and contents of the field itself. Earlier, I ventured to suggest that parapsychology is the science of mind. Parapsychology began when scientists frankly faced up to the questions posed by experiences from everyday life suggesting action at a distance without any sort of physical contact. These are experiences which suggest that man may be capable of gaining knowledge of distant or future events when there is no conceivable physical energy reaching any of his sense organs. If these things have any real basis in fact, then something more than the operation of the laws of physics seems to be involved (Ibid, p. 12).

In *Parapsychology and the Nature of Life,* John L. Randall comments:

As the 1960s drew to a close parapsychology won a substantial victory in its ninety-year-old battle for scientific respectability. On December 30th, 1969, Parapsychological Association was officially accepted as an affiliate member of that most distinguished body of savants, the American Association for the Advancement of Science (A.A.A.S.). The decision to grant affiliation to the parapsychologists was taken by the A.A.A.S. council, an organization composed of delegates from about 300 other affiliate scientific, medical and engineering societies; so it represented the views of a considerable cross-section of American science. For the first time in its chequered history, parapsychology had been recognized as a legitimate scientific pursuit; and from now on parapsychologists could present their papers at the bar of scientific opinion without feeling that they would be ridiculed or dismissed out of hand merely on account of their subject matter (John L. Randall, *Parapsychology and the Nature of Life,* New York: Harper and Row Publishers, p. 175).

The demand for scientific investigation is a valid quest and should and must be made. This responsibility lies with Christians too. However, in the consideration of parapsychology as science, one must be willing to embrace the most accurate explanation of the data, whether it be fraud, the occult or a valid paranormal experience.

For the most cases, one fruit in the study of parapsychology is an increasing lack of motivation to study the Scriptures. In fact, it often leads one in the direction of the paranormal or supernatural totally apart from a biblical base. In an interesting preface to his book, *Religion and the New Psychology*, Alson J. Smith writes of the story of a young woman he talked to at length doing research in parapsychology at Duke University:

> She was a quiet, intelligent girl from the middle South. She had come to Duke intending to go into some kind of religious work; she had been a "local preacher" in her home-town Methodist church and had occupied the pulpit on many occasions. At Duke, however, she had studied the various sciences and had lost most of her old, uncritical religious faith. She gave up the idea of entering religious work and lapsed into a sort of mournful agnosticism.
>
> In the course of her work in psychology, though, she had discovered parapsychology, the "venture beyond psychology," with which this book is largely concerned. It was a science in which she had learned to put her trust, and yet it spoke to her of the same spiritual world, the same spiritual forces that her old, uncritical religious faith had spoken of; in a different terminology and by a different method, it came out at the same place. The emotional void left by the loss of her religious faith was filled; her new faith (although I do not think she would call it that) satisfied her intellectually and emotionally. Her laboratory work in parapsychology became for her a sort of religious vocation (Alson J. Smith, *Religion and the New psychology*, Garden City, NY: Doubleday and Co., Inc., 1951, p.5).

Smith interestingly enough offers this explanation for the woman's change. He both attributes demise of her Christian faith and the rise of her "parapsychology faith" to the specific method:

> Her story, it seems to me, is an allegory on what is happening to millions of nominal Christians in our day. Their acceptance of the scientific method has shaken their religious faith (which, of course, has also been shaken by a great many other things), and they are not very happy about it. But they have to accept the scientific method—its accomplishments are too many and too great to be ignored.
>
> The significance of parapsychology for these millions is that it now takes the scientific method and leads men toward the spiritual world rather than away from it. Thus, a synthesis is effected between the old values and the new, authoritative method. The prestige of science is lent to religion, and the humility of true religion is lent to science as it sees that its methods can be used to underline spiritual insights that are as old as the race. Parapsychology, in a word, can make religion intellectually respectable and science emotionally satisfying. And the hope of the world in this time of crisis lies in just such a synthesis as this (Ibid, p. 6).

Not only does this new emphasis on the science of parapsychology affect the way individuals understand Christianity, it also affects the way people understand the Scriptures.

Scientists usually accept that similar phenomena occur in both the occult and parapsychology. However, many scientists disagree with the biblical explanation of such phenomena, that it is usually demonic.

Often, the new science of parapsychology will discredit any biblical interpretation of the data.

For example, in the book, *Life, Death and Psychical Research: Studies on Behalf of the Churches' Fellowship for Psychical and Spiritual Studies,* authors discredit the biblical admonition against sorcerers and mediums given in the Book of Deuteronomy. They feel this passage does not prohibit the exercise of psychical (demonic) gifts, the prohibition of which has been the historic and traditional interpretation by the church until the modern attempt to give some type, any type, of biblical credibility to the paranormal.

Consider this:

The Deuteronomic "prohibition" (Deuteronomy 18:9 to 12) has long been used by the prejudiced, the ignorant and the fearful as a reason for opposing genuine psychical research by Christian people. In the past, innocent folk have been denounced as sorcerers and witches or of being possessed by evil spirits. Others, who have exercised powers believed to come under the sacred ban, have been tortured to death.

Such attitudes still persist. Those who seek to exercise psychical gifts are often warned of the dangers of divine condemnation. Christians who encourage paranormal investigation are reminded that they are going against the teachings of the Bible and are forbidden to "dabble" in such matters (Canon J. D. Pearce, Higgens and Rev. Stanley Whitby, eds., *Life, Death and Psychical Research: Studies of the Churches' Fellowship for Psychical and Spiritual Studies,* London: Rider and Company, 1973, p. 10).

While it's true innocent people have been denounced in the past (viz., Salem witch trials), it is a logical fallacy to assume, therefore, that historical interpretation of the Scriptures by Christians on this passage has been wrong, when in fact both history and proper biblical interpretation support their position.

ESP

Extrasensory perception, or ESP as it is commonly known, has become very popular today. To know something without the help of the senses is the meaning of ESP.

Lynn Walker states of ESP:

ESP, or extrasensory perception... is the term applied to an ability to know something without the aid of the senses. It includes precognition or what is sometimes referred to as "ESP of the future"; telepathy, which is the awareness of the thoughts of a person without the use of the senses; and clairvoyance, the awareness of objects or objective events without sensory aid (Lynn Walker, *Supernatural Power and the Occult,* Austin: Firm Foundation Publishing House, n.d., p. 90).

ESP is only one major field of parapsychology. Another area of study in parapsychology is psychical research:

Systematic scientific inquiries concerning the nature, facts and causes of mediumistic phenomena (Norman Blunsdan, *A Popular Dictionary of Spiritualism,* NY: The Citadel Press, 1963, s.v. "psychical research").

However, what should be noted is that there is a difference between what is often called mental telepathy and ESP. These two often are used interchangeably, but to a parapsychologist they are different.

Mental telepathy is a branch of ESP. In fact, one of the "breakthroughs" in ESP research for parapsychologists was when they made a division between mental telepathy and clairvoyance. In mental telepathy the person is aware of mental images, say symbols on cards, and the cards are shuffled and he tries through ESP to reproduce the images seen.

Clairvoyance, on the other hand, tries to draw the symbols without any prior sense knowledge of what symbols were on the cards (Pratt, op. cit., pp. 45-54). This distinction led to a new emphasis in psychic research. The psychic researchers were able to formulate better test techniques for telepathy, and to determine precisely what was being tested, as well as what might be fraud, and from our perspective what might be strong occultic influence.

Uri Geller

One young Israeli whose name has become synonymous with the respectability of ESP is that of Uri Geller. His appearances and demonstrations around the world have made him famous and have drawn a strong spotlight to the paranormal phenomena.

Geller has supposedly demonstrated his capacity to reproduce pictorially items that he cannot see and bend things he cannot touch. Presently Geller is the center of a storm of controversy as to the validity of his claims. Although there has always been disagreement over his abilities, the catalyst for a major foray began after tests conducted at the prestigious Stanford Research Institute. Here is a brief history, beginning with positive testimony from Great Britain:

> URI SENDS BRITAIN ON A BIG BENDER, declared a *Sun* headline, while the *News of the World* ran an exclusive, front-page story entitled "Uri's Miracle Pictures," which revealed Uri's ability to take photos of himself with the lens cap still on the camera, with "no signs of trickery." And not only were the newspapers clearly persuaded about Uri's psychic powers, but a number of distintuished scientists and writers were publicly claiming that the "Geller effect" was authentic and scientifically verified.
>
> On the other hand, a number of articles appeared that expressed considerable ambivalence and even outright skepticism about Uri Geller's claims. Barbara Smoker entitled her article, published in the February 1974 issue of the *New Humanist*, "Uri Geller, the Joke's Over!" Smoker took the position that Geller was simply a clever magician.
>
> The June and July 1974 issues of *Psychology Today* contained an interesting account of Geller's abilities by Andrew Weil. Weil was initially convinced by Geller and then disillusioned when Randi (the "Amazing"), a highly talented professional stage magician and escape artist from New Jersey, duplicated all of Geller's effects and more. Andrew Weil ended his two-part article (entitled, "The Letdown") with the conclusion that questions like "Is Uri Geller a fraud?" or "Do psychic phenomena exist?" are unanswerable. "The answer is always yes and no," says Weil, "depending on who is looking and from what point of view."

This skeptical approach to Geller, however, was clearly a minority viewpoint. October 18, 1974, marked the occasion of a unique event in the history of psychic research. One of the world's most respected scientific journals, *Nature*, published an article by Russell Targ and Harold Puthoff of the Stanford Research Institute claiming verification of Geller's ESP ability (David Marks and Richard Kammann, *The Psychology of the Psychic*, Buffalo, New York: Prometheus Books, 1980, p. 74).

Targ and Puthoff had two major experiments. One had Geller draw pictures picked at random by someone else in an isolated room. The second involved Geller's pick of what face on die would be uppermost. Against the odds Geller's accuracy was incredible.

Targ and Puthoff concluded their scientific report with the conclusion that "a channel exists whereby information about a remote location can be obtained by means of an as yet unidentified perceptual modality"—in other words, that ESP is a scientifically proven reality (Ibid, p. 74).

However:

In the same week the *Nature* article appeared, another reputable British journal, *New Scientist*, published a sixteen-page report on Uri Geller by Dr. Joseph Hanlon. Hanlon's thesis was that Geller is a fraud—that he cheats, uses tricks, substitution, distraction, sleight-of-hand and all the other tools of the magician's repertoire (Ibid, p. 75).

In their book, *The Psychology of the Psychic*, the authors Marks and Kammann lay forth a study that bears close scrutiny, where they attempt to show the faulty nature of the Stanford experiments (which have come under a great deal of question by many) and a fraudulent deception on Geller's part. They also attempt to discredit the famous Kreskin, and devote a number of chapters to him as well.

Even with their study, and that of others, one cannot dismiss the work of the Stanford Research Institute lightly, nor some of the feats accomplished by Geller. In all likelihood they appear to be clever magicians' tricks. If not fraud, then possibly Geller has opened himself up to occultic powers to achieve his feats, for Geller certainly does not give credit to the God of the Bible.

University Research

The establishment of university research in the field of parapsychology and psychical study has lent much credibility for its acceptance. Universities such as Stanford and Duke have been instrumental in this regard.

In fact, Duke University has one of the most well-respected facilities for the study of parapsychology. The Duke University Parapsychology Laboratory is located in College Station, Durham, North Carolina. When Duke was founded, the Spiritualist movement was strong in the United States and their claims attracted the attention of the scientific community. Emphasis at that time was on mediumship and telepathy. Dr. J. B. Rhine brought the Laboratory to the prominence it holds today (J. B. Rhine and Associates, *Parapsychology from Duke to FRNM*, Durham, North Carolina: The Parapsychology Press, 1965, pp. 3-28).

Evaluation

How should one evaluate paranormal experiences? One must admit the possibility that such experiences may occur. Dr. J. B. Rhine of Duke University's Parapsychology Laboratory spent a lifetime in an attempt to document the reality of extrasensory perception.

It can be said that if there is some type of ESP capacity within some individuals, independent of either divine or demonic influence, its moral value would depend on its use. However, there seems to be an unlikelihood of divine use or aid.

The Scriptures have strong language about the use of such powers, where their use is referred to as not being of God. The major emphasis of such ESP experience, as has been shown, generally does not lead one toward biblical truth.

Dr. John Warwick Montgomery, in *Principalities and Powers*, takes a markedly different approach to the reality and experience of ESP than most evangelical scholars. He believes that one should not throw out all the experiences of ESP *a priori* as evil without proper investigation. After his investigation of the evidence Dr. Montgomery contends there may be a type of ESP power associated with individuals in various degrees that is not evil in origin.

Another writer, Lynn Walker, who quotes Dr. Montgomery in *Supernatural Power and the Occult*, also holds to this neutral approach, that simply to admit the existence of the power does not mean to admit evil.

In consideration of Dr. Montgomery's approach, if the power is neutral (neither divine nor demonic)—such as atomic energy is neither good nor evil, for its moral value depends on who uses it and what for (e.g., an atomic bomb dropped to murder the Nazis or a nuclear power plant built to heat a hospital)—then it would seem only limited use would be permitted by God, such as the personal experience of the individual.

For example, when a person suddenly realizes that something evil may happen to a friend or loved one, yet at the moment of realization that friend is clear around the world and he has not seen or spoken to him at all in the recent past and something does happen, then he has had a personal experience that may be best explainable at the present by ESP. But that would be the extent of the "use" by the individual.

That experience or any future experiences would not qualify him to be a prophet, for example. Yet, this limited-use idea does not seem completely consistent with the endowment of other gifts given by God, for all gifts from God (of which ESP thus would be one) are created to be used. Yet instead, here God is placing incredible restrictions on its use.

Of ESP or precognitive ability Dr. John Warwick Montgomery offers these remarks:

> Here we are evidently encountering a mental faculty (analogous to extraordinary vision) which permits some people to look through the temporal haze separating the future from the past. . . .
> Where it (precognitive ability) is used as a basis for exaggerated claims in behalf of its possessor—where, for example, the precognitive agent turns

himself into, or allows others to turn himself into, a "seer" who can pronounce on the nature of life and the meaning of the universe — precognition becomes a most dangerous quality. Moreover, used in this way, it opens the floodgates of the psyche to supernatural influences of the negative sort (John W. Montgomery, *Principalities and Powers*, Minneapolis, MN: Bethany Fellowship, 1973, pp. 125, 126).

Dr. Montgomery, in his investigation, has completed some important research that will bear close scrutiny. His work is always thorough.

Lynn Walker sums up the present situation well as he points out that today almost all forms of paranormal activity have no relation to the God of the Bible.

We must conclude that it is when man, through the influence of Satan's direct power, uses a God-given talent or ability to teach religious error (Colossians 2:8-10; 2 Corinthians 11:3, 4), to promote works of the flesh (Galatians 5:19f), to exalt self as specially endowed by God as his agent (Colossians 2:18; 2 Corinthians 10:18), to deny the God of the Bible (2 Peter 2:1), to deliberately aspire to go beyond bounds divinely set (Deuteronomy 29:29) — it is then that man has become an instrument of Satan, a tool of evil supernaturalism. Divination in its mulitplied forms and all present-day claims to revelations from God are equally Satan-inspired (Lynn Walker, *Supernatural Power*, op. cit., p. 91).

In summary, except for the unusual experiences reported above, a Christian has no reason to pursue parapsychology. This new discipline does not lead men to God and opens men up to the powers of darkness, just as participation in Maharcshi's Transcendental Meditation (TM) may harm an individual who participates in it.

Lynn Walker in *Supernatural Power and the Occult* explains the options:

If Satan did not have the power to create an ability in man, then God must have created man with all his abilities and talents; therefore, the ability to be aware of events or thoughts without the aid of the senses, ESP ability, is of God. Just as some men have, for instance, musical talent while others have none or have it in lesser degree, so do some men have ESP ability, some more, some less, some none. Almost everyone studying this lesson knows or has known someone, maybe a relative, who has at some time had a premonition or actually, with even some consistency, anticipated events or read another person's thoughts. To admit such ability does not admit an evil origin. This is not to say, however, that one's ESP ability cannot be misused (Ibid).

CHAPTER SIXTEEN

Psychic Surgery

P sychic surgery is a phenomenon which has gained quite a lot of publicity in recent years. The idea behind psychic surgery is that a psychic can perform miraculous operations on individuals by magic without traditional instruments or techniques and without leaving a scar.

The most famous instances of psychic surgery were performed in recent years by a Brazilian named Arigo, known as "the surgeon with the rusty knife." Arigo was a man with little education and absolutely no medical training. His "operations" were performed while he was in a trance.

He claimed that the actual force behind his incredible operations was a spirit that possessed him. This spirit was supposedly that of a German doctor named Adolph Fritz, who lived during the turn of the century. His methods, however, were anything but that of a qualified physician. Arigo's operations were performed with a rusty knife without using any anaesthetic or antiseptic.

His procedure included the diagnosis of the patient's disease while Arigo was in a trance. His diagnoses were usually correct. The house in which he performed many of his miracle operations had a sign which read, "Here in this house we are all Catholics." Arigo also would recite the Lord's Prayer before commencing surgery. Obviously, this is not standard operating procedure for surgeons, but the results of this illiterate miner's surgical attempts were amazing.

Kurt Koch lists some of his accomplishments:

> I have been to Brazil eight times for various tours. I have also been to Belo Horizonte. In this little town, an incredible surgical miracle was performed by Arigo. Senator Lucio Bittencourt had been holding an election meeting to which Arigo and his friends from Cogonhas had travelled. Bittencourt was suffering from lung cancer and planned to go to the U.S.A. for an operation when the election campaign was over.
>
> The Senator and Arigo were staying at the same hotel. During the night Bittencourt suddenly saw Arigo in his room, with a razor in his hand. He heard Arigo say, "You are in great danger." Then he lost consciousness. When he woke up again, he felt different in himself. He turned the light on and found that

there were clots of blood on his pajama jacket. He took the jacket off and looked at his chest in the mirror. On his chest was a fine cut. Knowing what he did of Arigo's healing skills, he hurried to Arigo's room and asked him: "Have you operated on me?"

"No, you must have drunk too much."

"I must know exactly what happened," said the Senator. "I will take the next plane and go to see my doctor in Rio."

Bittencourt told the doctor he had had his operation. The specialist took some x-ray pictures and confirmed it. "Yes. You have been operated on according to American surgical methods. We have not yet gotten so far in Brazil." Then the Senator explained what had taken place. This story caused a great sensation in the papers, and brought a flood of visitors to Arigo's clinic.

American doctors, journalists, and camera men went to Arigo's clinic. They carried out all manner of tests, but were unable to discover any deception. Arigo was willing for any test to be carried out. He even allowed his operations to be filmed. An American doctor, Dr. Puharich, even had a lipoma removed. The operation was performed with a rusty knife, without any local anaesthetic or antiseptic materials. Dr. Puharich felt no pain. This operation was also filmed (Kurt Koch, *Occult ABC*, Grand Rapids, MI: Int. Publs., n.d., p. 237).

There have been other cases recorded that have not been quite as sensational as Arigo's. Tim Timmons records the following story of a Mexican peasant woman named Carlita. Carlita always operates in a dark room with her eyes closed. Timmons states:

> Carlita's healings are strange! She does not pray over a person asking God to heal them—she actually operates on people with a dull hunting knife! Over the past fifty years, she has performed every kind of operation imaginable—on the heart, the back, the eyes, etc. A medical doctor who had observed Carlita perform many operations was present when I interviewed her. He told of one case where Carlita cut into a person's chest cavity, took the heart out for examination and handed it to him. After she closed the person up, without stitches, she suggested that he go to his hotel room and rest for three days. When the three days were up, he left Mexico City, a healthy man, with no scars from surgery. I asked the doctor what explanation he could give for such an amazing work. He replied, "There is no explanation medically. It's a miracle."

However, not everyone sees these as actual accounts of what transpired. Danny Korem says of the Timmons example,

> Carlita was very shrewd in having a physician give credence to her powers. Whether he was duped or participated in the sham is unclear. What is amusing is that she only performs her "surgery" in the dark. Of course, with few conjuring techniques at her disposal, how else could she convince her takers that she removed someone's heart with a dull hunting knife! The statement that the wound healed without scarring in three weeks is also easily explained. A slight cutting of the skin where the operation supposedly took place would heal without a scar. The cut actually gave the "surgery" some validity. The apparent healing again cannot be verified as being imaginary or psychosomatic. Is it not obvious why the psychic surgeons couldn't make the first cut for the American Medical Association? (Danny Korem and Paul Meier, *The Fakers*, Grand Rapids, MI: Baker Book House, 1980, pp. 83, 85).

Among psychic investigators there exist differing opinions about the validity of psychic surgery. Kurt Koch comments, "Let us be quite clear about this: Arigo's cures were not a trick or a swindle. They were real operations" (Kurt Koch, *Occult ABC*, op. cit., p. 238). As already stated, there are others who would vehemently disagree with this stance.

It seems difficult to put all psychic surgery in either category, as being all fake or all authentic. Whatever the case may be, it is certainly not a work of God. In the case of Arigo, he would come under the category of an angel of light. His allusions to Jesus and to the Christian religion are covering the fact that he was an instrument of Satan. The idea of being possessed by the spirit of someone else is contrary to the teaching of Scripture and if Arigo was indeed possessed, it was by a demon, not the spirit of a dead German doctor.

Psychic surgery is not the route anyone should dare take, for the spiritual and physical side effects can be fatal. It is much better to take your physical ailments to the Great Physician.

CHAPTER SEVENTEEN

Rosicrucianism

The true origin of Rosicrucianism is unknown. Today there are two groups which claim to be representative of Rosicrucianism and each claims a different origin. The Rosicrucian Fellowship is headquartered in Oceanside, California, and attempts to trace its origin back to the Chaldeans: "The founders of the Rosicrucian system were originally identical with the Chaldeans" (R. Swinburne Clymer, *The Secret Schools*, Oceanside, CA: Philos Publishing, p.16).

The rival organization, the Ancient Mystical Order Rosae Crucis (abbreviated AMORC), headquartered in San Jose, California, dubiously "traces its origin to the mystery schools or secret schools of learning established during the reign of Thutmose III, about 1500 B.C. in Egypt" (*Who and What Are The Rosicrucians?*, p. 8).

This latter group is adamant about being the faithful Rosicrucian order. One of their pamphlets states: "There is but one international Rosicrucian order operating throughout the world. . . .This organization does not sponsor a few modern publishing houses, or book propositions, operating under similar names, or selling instructions or books under the name of Rosicrucian fellowship, society, fraternity and other similar titles" (Anon., *Why Are We Here? And Why Are Our Lives Unequal?*, San Jose, California: The Rosicrucian Press, Ltd., 1952, p. 10).

The earliest authentically Rosicrucian writings come from the 17th century. These are anonymous works entitled *Fama Fraternitatis* and *The Confession of the Order*. These works set forth the travels of the alleged founder of the order, one Christian Rosenkreutz.

As the story goes, Rosenkreutz (1378-1484) learned secrets about medicine and magic while on a pilgrimage to the Near East. On his return to Europe, he attempted to share his new knowledge with the world, but his teachings were rejected by the unenlightened public. He then founded a secret fraternity whose members communicated by secret-coded writings.

Upon his death, Rosenkreutz was buried in the house in which the Order met. More than 100 years after his death his grave was opened and, along with his supposed unconsumed body, occultic writings were found. The Order was founded in 1614, based upon the supposed true wisdom and knowledge discovered by Rosenkreutz.

Most scholars agree the story is mythical, but it gives the Order the appearance of historical source. In fact, the author of the Rosenkreutz story later identified himself as Valentine Andreä and then finally admitted that the whole story was fictitious. However, this was not the end of the secret movement:

> Even this disclosure, however, did not prevent many enthusiastic persons from continuing to believe in the reality of Rosicrucian brotherhood, and professing to be acquainted with its secrets (Rev. James Gardner, *The Faiths of the World, Vol. 2*, London: A Fullarton and Co., 1874, p. 775).

What is Rosicrucianism?

The following excerpts from a Rosicrucian writing explains the Rosicrucians' purpose:

> In general terms we may announce that the primary object of Rosicrucianism is to elucidate the mysteries that encompass us in life, and reverently to raise the veil from those that await us in the dreaded dominions of death (R. Swinburne Clymer, op. cit., p. 8).

The Rosicrucian Order is syncretistic, meaning that it borrows ideas and beliefs from divergent and sometimes opposing sources, attempting to unify those ideas and beliefs into a coherent world view. Rosicrucians, for all their divergent beliefs, all unify under the central tenet that esoteric wisdom about life beyond the grave has been preserved through the ages and is revealed only to those within the secret brotherhood. Charles Braden observed:

> There are Rosicrucian societies, fraternities, orders, fellowships or lodges in most countries of the modern world. Some of them are very active; others are obscure and highly secret; some seem primarily religious in their emphasis, and some categorically deny that Rosicrucianism is a religion, holding rather that it is a philosophy, making use of the most modern scientific methods and techniques, as well as the methods of the occultist, the mystic and the seer, in the quest for truth.
>
> But, while Rosicrucianism is sectarian in character and the various branches are sometimes bitterly critical of each other, they do have common features, the central one being the purported possession of certain secret wisdom handed down from ancient times, through a secret brotherhood, an esoteric wisdom that can only be imparted to the initiated (Charles Braden, "Rosicrucianism," *Encyclopedia Britannica*, 1964 ed., XIX, p. 558).

The Teachings of Rosicrucianism

Although one of the attractions of Rosicrucianism is its claim that it is not a religion, its writings contain specific religious teaching which denies every cardinal doctrine of Christianity.

The Bible

The Rosicrucian Order does not hold the Bible in any special favor. R.

Swinburne Clymer writes, "All secret and sacred writings have truth in them, irrespective of their source, and must be judged by their inculcations rather than the source" (R. Swinburne Clymer, op. cit., p. 19).

Jesus Christ

- "Jesus was born of *Gentile* parents through whose veins flowed Aryan blood" (p. 53).
- Jesus did not die on the cross, for "an examination of the body revealed that Jesus was *not dead*. The blood *flowing from the wounds* proved that His body was not life-less . . ." (p. 265).
- The Ascension is rejected because "there is nothing in the original accounts of it to warrant the belief that Jesus arose physically or in His physical body in a cloud into the heavens" (p. 283).
- And finally, it is claimed that Rosicrucian archival records "clearly show that after Jesus retired to the monastery at Carmel He lived for many years, and carried on secret missions with His apostles. . . ." (p. 289). (H. Spencer Lewis, *The Mystical Life of Jesus*, 8th ed. 1948).

None of the above claims by the Rosicrucians concerning Jesus Christ conforms to the Bible. Matthew 1:1-18 and Luke 3:23-38 affirm the long Jewish ancestry of the human nature of Jesus Christ. Acts 2:23, 24 clearly shows that the death of Jesus Christ on the cross was according to the predetermined plan of God.

St. Paul reminds us that "if Christ has not been raised, your faith is worthless; you are still in your sins" (1 Corinthians 15:17, NASB). Finally, Acts 1:9-11 and Matthew 24:30 confirm Christ's ascension into heaven and His eventual public (not secret) return to earth. The Jesus Christ of the Rosicrucians is not the Jesus Christ of the Bible.

Salvation

Rosicrucianism does not teach that a person should trust Christ and Him *alone* for his eternal salvation. Their system is one of self-effort, their motto being, "TRY." They believe Jesus Christ never died for the sins of the world but that such teachings were added to the Bible by the Church at the Council of Nicea in 326 A.D. (see R. Swinburne Clymer, op. cit., p. 18). Clymer also states:

> Man through his own individual and consciously-made efforts must attain spiritual enlightenment and ultimate immortality (Ibid, p. 19).

The Bible doctrine of salvation states that salvation is only, and completely, by grace. In fact, Paul states, "Now to the one who works, his wage is not reckoned as a favor, but as what is due. But to the one who does not work, but believes in Him who justifies the ungodly, his faith is reckoned as righteousness, just as David also speaks of the blessing upon the man to whom God reckons righteousness apart from works" (Romans 4:4-6, NASB).

Occultic Influence

Kurt Koch cites a German Rosicrucian pamphlet, *Meisterung des Lebens* which reveals its occultic teachings.

Things are made even clearer elsewhere in the booklet. The page is entitled: "The Secret World Within Us. Abilities Which We Know of and Ought to Use." What abilities are these?

(1) "By touching letters and other objects we can become the recipients of painful messages." This is psychometry, a form of extrasensory perception.

(2) "Thoughts or sense-impressions can be transmitted at a distance." This is an occult form of mental suggestion.

(3) "Our consciousness can suddenly see far-off places and events." This is clairvoyance by means of psychic powers.

(4) "Some people reveal their true character by magnetic radiation." This is the spiritists' idea of the so-called "aura."

In this booklet *Meisterung des Lebens*, therefore, the Order of Rosicrucians encourages its members to take up psychic and occultic practices (Kurt Koch, *Occult ABC*, Grand Rapids, MI: Int. Publs., n.d., p. 193).

Rosicrucianism does not call itself a religion but rather a secret society which "expounds a system of metaphysical and physical philosophy intended to awaken the dormant, latent faculties of the individual whereby he may utilize to a better advantage his natural talents and lead a happier and more useful life" (*Who and What Are the Rosicrucians?*, op. cit., p. 3).

However, Rosicrucianism does speak about religious matters and denies every central doctrine of the Christian faith. There are strong occultic teachings in Rosicrucianism, something the Bible soundly condemns. Like Freemasonry, Rosicrucianism holds many of its practices in secret which is in contrast to Christianity, which emphasizes the open and public nature of its proclamation.

One who desires to serve Jesus Christ and His Kingdom has no business belonging to the Rosicrucian Order, working in darkness. Rather he should shout the message of Jesus Christ from the roof tops, as the Bible exhorts us:

What I tell you in the darkness, speak in the light, and what you hear whispered in your ear, proclaim upon the housetops (Matthew 10:27, NASB).

CHAPTER EIGHTEEN

Satan

K urt Koch, in his book *The Devil's Alphabet*, writes:

The devil is a many-sided and versatile demagogue. To the psychologist he says, "I will give you new knowledge and understanding." To the occultist he will say, "I will give you the keys to the last secrets of creation." To the occultist he confronts the religionist and the moralist with a mask of integrity and promises them the very help of heaven. And finally to the rationalist and the liberalist he says, "I am not there. I do not even exist."

The devil is a skillful strategist. He is the master of every tactic of the battlefield. He befogs the front. He hides behind a camouflage of empty religious talk. He operates through the use of the latest scientific method. He successfully fires and launches his arguments on the social and humane plane. And his sole aim is to deceive, to entice, and to ensnare his victims (Kurt Koch, *The Devil's Alphabet*, Grand Rapids, MI: Kregel Pub., 1971, p. 7).

Satan, or the devil, has been the subject of a multitude of books and discussions for thousands of years. Some deny his existence, saying that he is merely a mythological figure. Others seem obsessed with him, seeing him behind everything imaginable.

We will explore answers to these questions: Is there such a creature? If so, what powers does he have? Who is he? Where did he come from? Should Christians fear him?

He Does Exist

The devil is real. He is not a figment of one's imagination or a mere symbol of evil; he has personal existence! He had a beginning, he is at work now, but eventually he will be judged by God. How do we know he exists?

Since it is our firm conviction that the Bible is a supernatural revelation from the true and living God, correct in everything it affirms, we can go to the Bible and see what it says about the devil and his plans.

The evangelist Billy Sunday was once asked, "Why do you believe the devil exists?" He replied, "There are two reasons. One, because the Bible says so, two, because I've done business with him."

The Career of Satan

The career of Satan begins in the distant past. God created a multitude of angels to do His bidding. In the angelic rank there was one angel who was given the highest position, guardian to the Throne of the Most High. His name was Lucifer.

Lucifer

Information about Lucifer is revealed to us in Ezekiel 28:11-19. This passage is addressed to the prince of Tyre, a man who was vain because of the wealth he possessed and thought himself to be God. While God is rebuking the prince of Tyre for his vanity, He introduces another character called the king of Tyre, the real motivator of the prince of Tyre.

> Again the word of the Lord came to me saying, "Son of man, take up a lamentation over the king of Tyre and say to him, 'Thus says the Lord God, You had the seal of perfection, full of wisdom and perfect in beauty. You were in Eden, the garden of God; every precious stone was your covering: The ruby, the topaz, and the diamond; the beryl, the onyx, and the jasper; the lapis lazuli, the turquoise, and the emerald; and the gold, the workmanship of your settings and sockets, was in you. On the day that you were created they were prepared. You were the anointed cherub who covers; and I placed you there. You were on the holy mountain of God; you walked in the midst of the stones of fire. You were blameless in your ways from the day you were created, until unrighteousness was found in you'" (Ezekiel 28:11-15, NASB).

In his doctrinal treatise, *Satan*, Lewis Sperry Chafer comments:

> According to the Scriptures, the supreme motive of Satan is his purpose to become like the Most High and, though that purpose was formed even before the age of man, it has been his constant actuating motive from that time until now. It is also the teaching of the Scriptures that Satan is in especial authority in the present age; he being permitted the exercise of his own power in order that he, and all his followers, may make their final demonstration to the whole universe of the utter folly of their claims and of their abject helplessness when wholly independent of their Creator. This is definitely predicted in 2 Timothy 3:9 as the final outcome of the attitude of the world in its independence toward God: "They shall proceed no further: for their folly shall be manifest unto all men" (Lewis Sperry Chafer, *Satan*, Philadelphia, PA: Sunday School Times Co., 1972, p. 73).

The king of Tyre is Lucifer. He was perfect in all his ways, the highest ranking celestial being, the most beautiful and wise of all God's creation.

Lucifer, along with the other angels at this time, was in perfect harmony with God. There was no rebellion. There was not any dissent; there was only one will in the universe, the will of God. Everything was beautiful and harmonious.

The Fall of Lucifer

Everything was harmonious until one day Lucifer decided to rebel against God. The prophet Isaiah reveals the unrighteousness in Lucifer:

> How art thou fallen from heaven, O Lucifer, son of the morning! How art thou

cut down to the ground, which didst weaken the nations! For thou hast said in thine heart, "I will ascend into heaven, I will exalt my throne above the stars of God: I will sit upon the mount of the congregation, in the sides of the north: I will ascend above the heights of the clouds: I will be like the Most High" (Isaiah 14:12-14, KJV).

Donald Grey Barnhouse states concerning the fall:

The next verse in Ezekiel's account gives us the key to the origin of evil in this universe. "Thou wast perfect in thy ways from the day that thou wast created, till iniquity was found in thee" (verse 15). What this iniquity was is revealed to us in some detail in the prophecy of Isaiah, but there are already interesting indications in our passage that we may not pass by. The fact given here is that iniquity came by what we might term spontaneous generation in the heart of this being in whom such magnificence of power and beauty had been combined and to whom such authority and privilege had been given. Here is the beginning of sin. Iniquity was found in the heart of Lucifer (Donald Grey Barnhouse, *The Invisible War*, Grand Rapids, MI: Zondervan Publishing House, 1965, p. 30).

He then comments on Satan's fall in the Isaiah passage:

Comparing this passage with the one in Ezekiel, it is evident that the origin of sin in the pride of Satan was soon followed by the outward manifestation of a rebellion of his will against the will of God (Ibid., p. 41).

The Emergence of Satan

The sin of Lucifer was rebellion. Five times Lucifer said in his heart, "I will."

- I will ascend into heaven;
- I will exalt my throne above the stars of God;
- I will sit upon the mount of the congregation;
- I will ascend above the heights of the clouds;
- I will be like the Most High.

This rebellion brought the downfall of Lucifer, for when Lucifer fell he was transformed into Satan. By bringing another will into the universe, a will which was antagonistic to God, the once harmonious universe was now in disharmony. When Lucifer rebelled, many of the angels rebelled with him, attempting to overthrow the authority of God. This resulted in Lucifer and his cohorts being banished from both God's presence and His favor.

It needs to be stressed at this point that God did not create the devil. We are often asked, "Why would a good God create the devil?" The answer is, "He didn't." God created Lucifer, the highest ranking of the angels, giving him beauty and intelligence and a superior position to every other created thing. He also gave Lucifer a free will to do as he pleased.

Eventually, Lucifer decided to stage a rebellion against God, and it was at this point that he became known as the devil or the adversary. He was not created for that purpose, nor did God desire for Lucifer to act independently of His will. However, Lucifer did rebel and consequently became the enemy of God and His work.

The Creation of the Universe

After the angelic revolt God created the universe as we know it today. We are not told what things were like before God created, so all we can do is speculate. The Bible says, "In the beginning God created the heavens and the earth" (Genesis 1:1). Genesis 1 reveals God's creative efforts. The last and greatest of His creation was man.

The Creation of Man

The Bible makes it clear that man was created by God in His image: "Then God said, 'Let us make man in our image, according to our likeness; and let them rule over the fish of the sea and over the birds of the sky, and over the cattle and over all the earth, and over every creeping thing that creeps on the earth.' So God created man in His own image, in the image of God He created him: male and female He created them" (Genesis 1:26, 27, NASB).

Man was God's crown of creation. He was placed in a perfect environment with everything conceivable going for him. He was in harmony with God, nature, his fellow man and himself.

The Fall of Man

However, Satan was envious of that special relationship God had with man. In Genesis 3 there is an account of what transpired when Satan appeared to Adam and Eve in the Garden of Eden in the form of a serpent.

Now the serpent was more crafty than any beast of the field which the Lord God had made. And he said to the woman, "Indeed, has God said, 'You shall not eat from any tree of the garden'?" And the woman said to the serpent, "From the fruit of the trees of the garden we may eat; but from the fruit of the tree which is in middle of the garden, God has said, 'You shall not eat from it or touch it, lest you die.'" And the serpent said to the woman, "You surely shall not die! For God knows that in the day you eat from it your eyes will be opened, and you will be like God, knowing good and evil" (Genesis 3:1-5 NASB).

The result of the yielding to temptation was a break in that special relationship between God and man.

After the Fall

Since the Garden of Eden episode, God and Satan have been locked into one great cosmic battle with man as the prize. God is attempting to bring mankind back into a right relationship with Him, while Satan is trying to pull man away from God. Moreover, the Scripture says that unbelieving man is blinded spiritually by Satan in an effort to keep him from coming to Christ.

And even if our gospel is veiled, it is veiled to those who are perishing, in whose case the god of this world has blinded the minds of the unbelieving, that they might not see the light of the Gospel of the glory of Christ, who is the image of God (2 Corinthians 4:3, 4, NASB).

This passage is highly instructive. Satan is called the "god of this world," hiding the gospel of Christ from the minds of the unbelieving people.

He will do anything to keep people from knowing God. Besides being called "the god of this world," Satan has been given other titles in Scripture which describe his character and his methods. These include:

(1) *Devil* (John 8:44) is a Greek word meaning "the accuser and slanderer." By calling him this, one is saying that he makes a false accusation against another, one whose aim it is to harm God and man; one who will tell lies of any kind to achieve his end. The popular phrase, "The devil made me do it," (popularized by Flip Wilson) is really a cop-out. You did it because you made the choice to follow your old, sinful nature. The devil tempts!

(2) *Satan* (Matthew 12:26) is a Hebrew word meaning "the resistor or adversary." By calling him this, one is saying that he reigns oer a kingdom of darkness organized in opposition to God. In *The Bible, the Supernatural and the Jews*, McCandlish Phillips says: "Satan is a living creature. He is not corporeal. He is a spiritual being but that does not make him any less real. The fact that he is invisible and powerful greatly serves him in the pursuit of his cause. The idea that Satan is a term for a generalized influence of evil—instead of the name of a specific living personality—is a strictly anti-biblical idea...The less you know about Satan, the better he likes it. Your ignorance of his tactics confers an advantage upon him, but he prefers that you do not even cred his existence."

(3) *Tempter* (Matthew 4:3) describes the enemy's manner of acting. Not content with denouncing befor God the faults of men, he seeks to lead them into sin, because he himself is a sinner. For that reason he is called the tempter. he tempts men by promising them, as a reward for disobeying God, delights, or earthly power, or a knowledge like that of God.

(4) *Father of Lies* (John 8:44) describes one of his many tactics. To accomplish his task of tempting men by promising him things, the enemy must lie. Therefore, because he makes great use of lies, he is rightfully given this title. He is not just a liar, he is the father of lies. He hates what God loves and loves what God hates.

(5) *Lord of Death* (Hebrews 2:14). The enemy has the power of death because he can accuse sinful man. When the Son enter mankind and confronts the enemy with a human righteousness which the enemy cannot accuse, the enemy is destroyed and man is set free.

(6) *Beelzebub* (Mark 3:22, 23) ascribes to the enemy a name meaning "Lord of the dunghill" or "Lord of the flies.' The word is generally believed to be a corruption of Baalzebub, the name of a Philistine god who was considered by the Jews to be very evil (2 Kings 1:2, 3).

(7) *Belial* (2 Corinthians 6:15) is a name which originally could be applied to any wicked person. Here it is used as a synonym of the enemy. The word itself means "worthlessness," here used as the embodiment of all "worththlessness," the enemy.

(8) *Evil One* (1 John 2:13). The total effect of all the biblical references is to present the picture of the enemy as one who is the supreme evildoer. For that reason he is given this title.

(9) *Ruler of This World* (John 14:30). Since the world, according to the Bi-

ble, is mankind in opposition to God, the enemy as the inspirer and leader of that opposition is given this title, and because his power and might are operative in the present world, he is accorded this title. Similar to this, in 2 Corinthians the enemy is even called "the god of this world." The two titles should give us some idea of the tremendous scope of Satan's power and activity on the earth.

(10) *Prince of the Power of the Air* (Ephesians 2:1, 2). The enemy's power, in our age, is operative not only on the earth, but in space (David W. Hoover, *How to Respond to the Occult*, St. Louis, MO: Concordia Pub. House, 1977, pp. 13, 14).

In the *Dictionary of Satan* mention is made of various names given to Satan:

> *Malleus Maleficarum*, a fifteenth-century treatise by Heinrich Kramer and Jakob Sprenger, indicates that Satan may be invoked under several names, each with a special etymological significance:
>
> As Asmodeus, he is the Creature of Judgment. As Satan, he becomes the Adversary. As Behemoth, he is the Beast. Diabolus, the Devil, signifies two morsels: the body and the soul, both of which he kills. Demon connotes Cunning over Blood. Belial, Without a Master. Beelzebub, Lord of Flies.
>
> Here are the names by which he is generally known in various languages:

Arabic:	Sheitan
Biblical:	Asmodeus (or Belial or Apollyon)
Egyptian:	Set
Japanese	O Yama
Persian:	Dev
Russian:	Tchort
Syriac:	Beherit
Welsh:	Pwcca

(Wade Baskin, *Dictionary of Satan*, NY: Philosophical Library, 1972, p. 233).

Satan's Strategy

One of Satan's plans is to convince the world that he does not exist. Denis deRougemont makes the following insightful observation:

> Satan dissembles himself behind his own image. He chooses to don a grotesque appearance which has the sure effect of making him inoffensive in the eyes of educated people. For if the devil is simply the red demon armed with a large trident, or the faun with goatee and the long tail of popular legend, who would still go to the trouble of believing in him, or even of declaring that he does not believe in him? . . . . What appears to be incredible is not the devil, not the angels, but rather the candor and the credulity of the skeptics, and the unpardonable sophism of which they show themselves to be the victims: "The devil *is* a gent with red horns and a long tail: *therefore* I don't believe in the devil." And so the devil has them precisely where he wants them (Denis deRougemont, *The Devil's Share*, pp. 19-21, cited by D. G. Kehl in *Demon Possession*, ed., John Warwick Montgomery, Minneapolis, MN: Bethany Fellowship, 1976, p. 112).

In *The Screwtape Letters*, a fiction work by noted Christian thinker, C. S. Lewis, the demon is recorded instructing his apprentice as follows:

I wonder you should ask me whether it is essential to keep the patient in ignorance of your own existence.... Our policy, for the moment, is to conceal ourselves. Of course, this has not always been so. We are really faced with a cruel dilemma. When the humans disbelieve in our existence, we lose all the pleasing results of direct terrorism, and we make no magicians. On the other hand, when they believe in us, we cannot make them materialists and skeptics.... The fact that "devils" are predominantly *comic* figures in the modern imagination will help you. If any faint suspicion of your existence begins to arise in his mind, suggest to him a picture of something in red tights, and persuade him that since he cannot believe in that...he therefore cannot believe in you (C.S. Lewis, *The Screwtape Letters*, New York: MacMillan Publ. Co., 1961, pp.39, 40).

There are many false teachers today who encourage people to believe that they do not need to go the way of the cross. The Scriptures warn us against these individuals:

But false prophets also arose among the people, just as there will also be false teachers among you, who will secretly introduce destructive heresies, even denying the Master who bought them, bringing swift destruction upon themselves (2 Peter 2:1 NASB).

Chafer has some apt observations concerning false prophets:

False teachers usually are sincere and full of humanitarian zeal, but they are unregenerate. This judgment necessarily follows when it is understood that they deny the only ground of redemption. Being unregenerate, it is said of them: "But the natural man receiveth not the things of the Spirit of God: for they are foolishness unto him: neither can he know them, because they are spiritually discerned" (1 Corinthians 2:14). Such religious leaders may be highly educated and able to speak with authority on every aspect of human knowledge, but if they are not born again, their judgment in spiritual matters is worthless and misleading. All teachers are to be judged by their attitude toward the doctrine of the blood redemption of Christ, rather than by their winsome personalities, or by their sincerity (Chafer, *Satan*, op. cit., p. 78).

Satan will use whatever method he can to keep people from coming to Christ. If a person has done many things wrong in his life and feels guilty about them, Satan will attempt to convince that person he is not good enough for God, that God would never accept him. Many people never come to God because they do not feel God could ever forgive them.

The Bible teaches that anyone may come to Christ regardless of what he has done and receive forgiveness. The Scriptures say, "Come unto me, all who are weary and heavy-laden, and I will give you rest" (Matthew 11:28, NASB). Jesus further stated, "All that the Father gives Me shall come to Me and the one who comes to Me I will certainly not cast out" (John 6:37, NASB). The Bible teaches that forgiveness is available to all those who will come to Christ no matter what they have done.

There is another type of person who is also deceived by Satan but who has the opposite problem. That person, rather than feeling he is too bad to come to God, feels that he is too good to need God. Since he has never done anything in his life which he considers horrible, he does not feel that he needs a Savior. This person is willing to go before God based upon his own merit, on the good works he has done in his life, feeling that God will certainly accept him. However, the Scriptures say, ". . .All have sinned and fall short of the glory of God (Romans 3:23), and ". . .The wages of sin is death, but the free gift of God is eternal life in Christ Jesus our Lord (Romans 6:23, NASB).

Satan's Destiny

Satan is living on borrowed time. God has promised in His Word that Satan and his angels will receive everlasting punishment for the crimes they have committed against God and man.

> Then He will also say to those on His left, "Depart from Me, accursed ones, into the eternal fire which has been prepared for the devil and his angels" (Matthew 25:41, NASB).
> And the devil who deceived them was thrown into the lake of fire and brimstone, where the beast and false prophet are also: and they will be tormented day and night forever and ever (Revelation 20:10, NASB).

At that time Satan will be banished once and for all from God's presence without ever again being able to inflict misery on anyone. His eternal separation from God and punishment will be a just end to his inglorious career as the prince of darkness.

C. Fred Dickason in *Angels: Elect and Evil* comments on Satan's destiny.

> The Lord Jesus, the Creator and Sovereign, will judge all creatures, including evil angels (John 5:22). He defeated Satan and his demons during His career by invading Satan's territory and casting out demons from those possessed (Matthew 12:28-29). He anticipated the final defeat of Satan when His disciples returned with reports of demons being subject to them through Christ's power (Matthew 10:1, 17-20).
> Through His death and resurrection, Christ sealed the final judgment of Satan and demons. The cross reveals God's hatred and judgment of all sin. The just One had to die if the unjust ones were to be forgiven (1 Peter 3:18) (C. Fred Dickason, *Angels: Elect and Evil*, Chicago, IL: Moody Press, 1975, pp. 210, 212).

What Should Be Our Attitude Toward Satan?

The Scriptures exhort us to take the proper attitude toward Satan in order to deal effectively with his onslaughts. We urge you to observe the following biblical injunctions:

(1) *Be Aware That He Exists.* The Scriptures teach that Satan exists but that he also attempts to hide that fact from the world. "And no wonder, for even Satan disguises himself as an angel of light. Therefore, it is not surprising if his servants also disguise themselves as servants of righteousness: whose end shall be according to their deeds" (2 Corinthians 11:14, 15, NASB). We have already indicated that one of Satan's schemes is to have people believe that he is a symbolic figure of evil. He would love people to see him as an "angel of light" or even as a funny little man with a red suit and pitchfork rather than as the dangerous, evil, but ultimately doomed adversary of the Lord God and all mankind.

(2) *Be Aware of His Motives.* From the time of his rebellion until his

ultimate destruction Satan has wanted to be like the Most High. He wants adoration. He wants allegiance. He wants the service of people who rightly should be serving God. He wants people to believe that it is he who is good and it is God who is bad. However, the worship he desires is not informed worship of a god one knows and has seriously considered.

His deception has people worshipping and serving him without even being aware of what they are doing. He wants to prepare the world for his own world rule through the antichrist immediately before the Second Coming of Jesus Christ. Lewis Sperry Chafer makes the following insightful observation:

> Even fallen humanity would not at first acknowledge Satan as its object of worship and its federal head; and such a condition of society wherein Satan will be received as supreme, as he will be in the person of the first Beast of Revelation 13, must, therefore, be developed by increasing irreverence and lawlessness toward God. Thus it has been necessary for Satan to conceal his person and projects from the very people over whom he is in authority and in whom he is the energizing power. For this reason this class of humanity believes least in his reality, and ignorantly rejects its real leader as being a mythical person. When he is worshipped, it is through some idol as a medium, or through his own impersonation of Jehovah; and when he rules, it is by what seems to be the voice of a king or the voice of the people. However, the appalling irreverence of the world today is the sure preparation for the forthcoming direct manifestation of Satan, as predicted in Daniel 9; 2 Thessalonians 2; and Revelation 13 (Lewis Sperry Chafer, *Satan*, Grand Rapids, MI: Zondervan, 1919, pp. 64, 65).

(3) *Be Aware of His Methods.* The Scriptures tell us to be aware of the devices of the devil, for his desire is to destroy the believer.

> Be of sober spirit, be on the alert. Your adversary, the devil, prowls about like a roaring lion, seeking someone to devour (1 Peter 5:8, NASB).

One of his methods is deception. From the time he deceived Eve in the Garden of Eden until the present day, Satan has been a liar. The Scriptures say:

> ...The one whose coming is in accord with the activity of Satan, with all power and signs and false wonders. And with all the deceptions of wickedness for those who perish, because they did not receive the love of the truth so as to be saved (2 Thessalonians 1:9, 10, NASB).
>
> And the great dragon was thrown down, the serpent of old who is called the devil and Satan, who deceives the whole world... (Revelation 12:9, NASB).
>
> You are of your father the devil, and you want to do the desires of your father. He was a murderer from the beginning, and does not stand in the truth, because there is no truth in him. Whenever he speaks a lie, he speaks from his own nature; for he is a liar, and the father of lies (John 8:44, NASB).

His deception comes in a variety of forms. One of his favorite schemes is to try to make a person feel content without Jesus Christ. If someone does not feel a need for God, he will not turn to God. Therefore, Satan attempts to keep people satisfied just enough that they will not turn to Christ.

In many cases the alcoholic on skid row is much closer to coming to Christ than the successful businessman who thinks he has everything he wants. We often feel that the alcoholic on skid row is exactly where Satan wants him. This is not necessarily so. The alcoholic knows he has a need, knows he has a problem and may be more likely to seek help than the successful businessman who feels content. This subtle type of deception is one of the favorite ploys of the devil.

Another deception used by Satan is counterfeiting. Whatever God has done throughout history, Satan has attempted to counterfeit it. The main counterfeit is religion. Satan loves for people to be religious, to go to church, to think things stand right between themselves and God when just the opposite is true.

If a person believes in some religion without receiving Christ as his Lord and Savior, that person is lost even though he thinks things between him and God are fine. The religious man, trusting in his own works, can be an example of deception by Satan, for God has informed us that to be in a right relationship with Him we must go the way of the cross, the death of Christ for our sins.

We must also acknowledge that apart from Christ we cannot know God. Satan wants people to believe this is not so. Christians are accused of being "narrow-minded" in saying Jesus is the only way one can get to God. The Bible tells us what God thinks of those who try to play down the need for the death of Christ on the cross:

> From that time Jesus began to show His disciples that He must go to Jerusalem and suffer many things from the elders and chief priests and scribes and be killed, and be raised up on the third day. And Peter took Him aside and began to rebuke Him saying, "God forbid it, Lord! This shall never happen to you." But He turned and said to Peter, "Get behind Me Satan! You are a stumbling block to Me; for you are not setting your mind on God's interests, but man's" (Matthew 16:21-23, NASB).

The Lord was acknowledging the sharp contrast between God's ways and fallen man's ways which are actually identified with Satan's ways. Satan cannot trust in the power of God because he has rejected God. Fallen man has also rejected God (Romans 3:12) and can turn to God only through the mediating sacrifice of Jesus Christ.

Fallen man, often with the approval and help of Satan, has developed a wide variety of religious beliefs in the world as ways to achieve God's favor without submitting to God. Satan is always pleased when people trust in their religiosity rather than Jesus Christ.

(4) *Be Aware of His Limitations.* Satan, the great deceiver, sometimes tries to fool people into thinking he is greater than he actually is. One of the misconceptions that people have about Satan is that he is like God. Nothing could be further from the truth!

God is infinite while Satan is finite or limited. God can be present everywhere at once; Satan cannot. God is all-knowing, able to read our very thoughts; Satan cannot. God is all-powerful; Satan is not. God has the ability to do anything; Satan cannot. However, Satan would like people to believe he has these abilities. Unfortunately, there are too many believers who see Satan behind everything, giving him credit where no credit is due. Basil Jackson makes an appropriate comment:

> Today, I believe we are seeing a most unhealthy interest in the area of demonology so that many of our evangelical friends have, in effect, become "demonophiliacs" as a result of their fascination with the occult. They tend to see a demon under every tree and, thus, quite commonly today, we hear of demons of tobacco, alcohol, asthma, and every other condition imaginable. In this connection, it is noteworthy that, by far, the majority of cases of demon possession which are diagnosed in the deliverance ministry today are mental in phenomenology. This is in marked contrast with the only safe records we have of accurately diagnosed cases of demon possession—namely, the Gospels, in which at least half the people possessed had physical problems rather than any psychiatric difficulties (Basil Jackson in *Demon Possession*, edited by John Warwick Montgomery, Minneapolis, MN: Bethany Fellowship, 1976, p. 201).

The Scriptures tell us, "You are from God, little children, and have overcome them; because greater is He who is in you than he who is in the world" (1 John 1:4, NASB).

We need to realize that Satan is not all-powerful; he has been defeated by Christ's death on the cross. The power of sin over us is broken. Therefore, we need to respect his power but not fear it to the point of thinking he can indwell believers and make them do things they do not wish to do. The power of God is greater but the great deceiver would have you doubting that. Therefore, be aware of the limitations of Satan and the unlimited power of God.

The Bible says Christ came into the world to destroy the works of the devil (1 John 5:8). This has now been accomplished. The victory has been won. Satan has been defeated.

The Scripture exhorts us to "put on the full armor of God that you may be able to stand firm against the schemes of the devil" (Ephesians 6:11, NASB). In order to stand firm, we need to recognize that the devil exists, what his methods and motives are, and the limitations which he has. Knowing this we can intelligently combat Satan and his attacks by following the principles God has given to us:

> Put on the full armor of God, that you may be able to stand firm against the schemes of the devil. For our struggle is not against flesh and blood, but against the rulers, against the powers, against the world forces of this darkness, against the spiritual forces of wickedness in the heavenly places. Therefore, take up the full armor of God, that you may be able to resist in the evil day, and having done everything, to stand firm. Stand firm therefore, having girded your loins with truth, and having put on the breastplate of righteousness, and having shod your feet with the preparation of the gospel of peace; in addition to all, taking up the shield of faith with which you will be able to extinguish all the flaming missiles of the evil one. And take the helmet of salvation, and the sword of the Spirit, which is the Word of God (Ephesians 6:11-17, NASB).

CHAPTER NINETEEN

Satanism

The worship of Satan has deep historical roots. Known as Satanism, it is found expressed in various ways. Black magic, the Black Mass, facets of the drug culture, and blood sacrifice all have connections with Satanism.

In *Escape from Witchcraft*, Roberta Blankenship explains what two girls, both Satanists, wrote to her as part of their initiation ritual:

> They had had to go to a graveyard in the dead of night, walk across a man-sized cross, and denounce any belief in Christ. Afterwards, a ritual was performed and the girls had to drink the blood of animals that had been skinned alive (Roberta Blankenship, *Escape From Witchcraft*, Grand Rapids, MI: Zondervan Publishing House, 1972, p. 1).

Lynn Walker comments:

> In April, 1973, the battered, mutilated body of a 17-year-old boy, Ross "Mike" Cochran, was found outside of Daytona Beach, Florida. An Associated Press story said, "The verdict of police is that Cochran was the victim of devil worshippers: killed in a frenzied sacrificial ritual."
>
> Lynn McMillon, Oklahoma Christian College professor, reports, ". . .one variety of Satanism consists primarily of sex clubs that embellish their orgies with Satanist rituals. Another variety of Satanists are the drug-oriented groups" (Lynn Walker, *Supernatural Power and the Occult*, Austin, TX: Firm Foundation Publishing House, n.d., p. 1).

Traditional Satanism

Until contemporary times Satanism has had much more secretive associations than at present. In the past, the anti-religious and anti-god aspect was prevalent in all aspects of Satanism. Although this is not true of modern Satanism today, traditional Satanism still is associated with black magic and ritualism.

The worship of a personal and powerful devil is central to traditional Satanism. Those involved reject Christianity, yet choose the Lucifer of Scriptures as their god. The Occult Sourcebook comments:

> Traditionally, Satanism has been interpreted as the worship of evil, a religion

founded upon the very principles which Christianity rejects. As such, Satanism exists only where Christianity exists, and can be understood only in the context of the Christian worldview. Things are, so to speak, reversed—the Christian devil becomes the Satanist's god, Christian virtues become vices, and vices are turned into virtues. Life is interpreted as a constant battle between the powers of light and darkness, and the Satanist fights on the side of darkness, believing that ultimately this will achieve victory (Neville Drury and Gregory Tillett, *The Occult Sourcebook*, London: Routledge & Kegan Paul, Ltd., 1978, p. 149).

Satanic witchcraft is to be found under this category of Satanism, where witches are involved in the darkest side of evil.

The recent onslaught of drugs and sexual perversion associated with the devil can be found here.

Modern Satanism

Traditional Satanism is still very prevalent, and growing in society today. However, in recent times, with the growing secularization of society and decline of Judeo-Christian morality, a new humanistic Satanism has emerged and drawn a strong following. The Church of Satan is the clearest example of this new emphasis.

In modern times groups have emerged in England and Europe, and particularly in the United States, which, taking advantage of the permissiveness of modern society, have encouraged some publicity. The most famous of these has been the Church of Satan, founded in San Francisco in 1966 by Anton La Vey, which currently has a membership of many thousands, and has established itself as a church throughout the United States.

Several other groups in America have imitated it, and some groups have also been established as "black witchcraft" covens. The Manson gang, in which a bizarre mixture of Satanism and occultism was practiced, gained a great deal of unfavorable publicity for Satanism in America, but in fact this resulted in a greater public interest in the subject. With more people rejecting the traditional values of morality, the Satanist movement will inevitably have greater appeal (Drury, op. cit., p. 154).

In a chapter on Satanism today, William Petersen in *Those Curious New Cults* comments on the fact that since the mid-1960s Satanism is making a comeback. He points to the catalyst for the strong upswing as being the box office smash of "Rosemary's Baby." Of the film he states:

Anton Szandor La Vey, self-styled high priest of San Francisco's First Church of Satan and author of *The Satanic Bible*, played the role of the devil. Later, he called the film the "best paid commercial for Satanism since the Inquisition." No doubt it was (William J. Petersen, *Those Curious New Cults*, New Canaan, CT: Keats Publishing, Inc., 1973, p. 75).

Many people are becoming involved in Satanism from all walks of life. They vary in age, occupation and educational background.

Church of Satan

Although the Church of Satan sounds like a contradiction in terms, it was founded in San Francisco in 1966 by Anton Szandor La Vey. The emphasis of the Satanic church is on materialism and hedonism. Satan, to followers of this church, is more of a symbol than a reality. In this emphasis they depart from other forms of Satanism. They are interested in the carnal and worldly pleasures mankind offers.

La Vey is of Russian, Alsatian and Rumanian descent, whose past jobs have been with the circus, an organ player in nightclubs and a police photographer. All during this time La Vey was studying the occult.

Of the church La Vey declares it is:

A temple of glorious indulgence that would be fun for people. . . . But the main purpose was to gather a group of like-minded individuals together for the use of their combined energies in calling up the dark force in nature that is called Satan (Drury, *Occult Sourcebook, op. cit., p. 77).*

Of Satanism La Vey believes:

It is a blatantly selfish, brutal religion. It is based on the belief that man is inherently a selfish, violent creature, that life is a Darwinian struggle for survival of the fittest, that the earth will be ruled by those who fight to win (Ibid, p. 78).

Emphases of the Church

La Vey is currently the High Priest of the church, which espouses any type of sexual activity that satisfies your needs, be it heterosexuality, homosexuality, adultery or faithfulness in marriage. Part of La Vey's philosophy is expressed here:

I don't believe that magic is supernatural, only that it is supernormal. That is, it works for reasons science cannot yet understand. As a shaman or magician, I am concerned with obtaining *recipes.* As a scientist, you seek *formulas.* When I make a soup, I don't care about the chemical reactions between the potatoes and the carrots. I only care about how to get the flavor of soup I seek. In the same way, when I want to hex someone, I don't care about the scientific mechanisms involved whether they be psychosomatic, psychological, or what-not. My concern is with how to best hex someone. As a magician, my concern is with effectively *doing* the thing, not with the scientist's job of *explaining* it (La Vey 1968) (Marcello Truzzi, "Toward a Sociology of the Occult: Notes on Modern Witchcraft," *Religious Movements in Contemporary America,* ed. by Irving I. Zaretsky and Mark P. Leone, Princeton: Princeton University Press, 1974, p. 631).

Truzzi describes the church here:

Finally, we come to the major Satanic society operating in the United States today. This is the international Church of Satan. This group is legally recognized as a church, has a developed hierarchy and bureaucratic structure which defines it as no longer a cult, and claims over 10,000 members around the world. Most of these members are, in fact, merely mail-order and geographically isolated joiners, but there are clearly at least several hundred fully participating and disciplined members in the various Grottos (as their fellowships are called) set up around the world. Grottos are growing up rapidly around this country with about a dozen now in operation.

The church's High Priest and founder, Anton Szandor La Vey, whose headquarters are in San Francisco, has written *The Satanic Bible* (La Vey 1969) which has already reportedly sold over 250,000 copies and is now in its third paperback printing. La Vey also publishes a monthly newsletter for those members who subscribe to it, conducts a newspaper column in which he advises those who write in questions, and he has recently written a book on man-catching for the would-be Satanic witch (Ibid, p. 632).

There is a list of nine Satanic statements to which all members must agree. These are that Satan represents indulgence, vital existence, undefiled wisdom, kindness only to those who deserve it, vengeance, responsibility only to those who are responsible, the animal nature of man, all the "so-called sins," and "the best friend the church has ever had, as he has kept it in business all these years."

The Satanic Church is strongly materialistic as well as being anti-Christian. Pleasure-seeking could well describe their philosophy of life. What the world has to offer through the devil is taken full advantage of in the Church of Satan.

CHAPTER TWENTY

Spiritism (Necromancy)

S piritism (sometimes called spiritualism) is the oldest form of religious counterfeit known to man. Its roots go back to the beginning of time.

The Bible speaks of spiritistic practices going back as far as ancient Egypt. The Book of Exodus records the Egyptians' many occultic activities, including magic, sorcery and speaking to the dead (Exodus 7 and 8).

What is spiritism? A secular book, *The Dictionary of Mysticism*, defines spiritualism (spiritism) as "the science, philosophy and religion of continuous life, based upon the demonstrated fact of communication, by means of mediumship, with those who live in the spirit world. Spiritualism rejects the belief in physical reincarnation, but teaches that death is a new birth into a spiritual body, without any change in individuality and character, and without impairment of memory" (Frank Gaynor, ed., *Dictionary of Mysticism*, New York: Citadel Press, n.d., p. 174).

The main idea behind spiritism is that the spirits of the dead have the capacity to communicate with people here on earth through mediums, individuals who act as intermediaries between the material world and the spirit world. We do not use the term spiritualism because we do not believe such practices are actually "spiritual" or approved by God. We prefer the term "spiritism," since we believe authentic mediums contact evil spirits only posing as the spirits of the dead.

Mediums usually claim to have a spirit-guide who is their initial and primary contact in the spirit world. The spirit-guide supposedly puts the medium in contact with the spirits of the departed ones. The sessions conducted by the medium are known as seances.

Spiritism, also known as necromancy, is described by Dennis Wheatley:

This is foretelling the future with, supposedly, the aid of the dead.

The usual form it takes in these days is spiritualistic seances. A number of people gather in a room with a "sensitive," as a medium is called. The medium may be a man or a woman, but, as there are more women mediums than men, I will refer to the medium as "her."

The lights in the room are dimmed, the medium goes into a trance and becomes possessed. That is to say, her spirit leaves her body, which is taken over by another.

With possession the personality of the medium changes. Her voice is no longer recognizable as the one she speaks with normally. If she is a cultured woman, it may become coarse and uneducated, or vice-versa; or, quite possibly, have a foreign accent, or sound like a man's voice.

Sometimes the medium is tied to her chair, with the object of convincing the audience that she is incapable of moving. Then trumpets or tambourines are seen to float about above her head in the semi-darkness. At other times she exudes from the mouth a matter that is dough-like in appearance, and is called ectoplasm.

But the main object of the operation is for members of the audience either to ask the spirit, who is presumed to be possessing her, about the future, or to secure news, either directly or through the possessing spirit, of people dear to them who are dead (Dennis Wheatley, *The Devil and All His Works*, New York: American Heritage Press, 1971, pp. 71, 72).

In the book, *The Challenging Counterfeit*, the author, Raphael Gasson, a former medium, warns of the subtle, yet deep dangers of spiritualism. Gasson discusses the apparitions he called up which he believes were not spirits of the dead but demonic deception.

To Gasson, a spiritualist is:

(1) One who believes in life after death.
(2) One who believes in the possibility of contacting the spirits of the dead.
(3) One who considers it his duty to spread this "good news" to mankind.

While a spiritualist medium, Gasson believed the following:

As a former spiritualist minister and active medium, it is possible for me to say that at the time of my participation in the movement, I actually believed that these spirits were the spirits of the departed dead and that it was my duty to preach this to all those with whom I came into contact day by day (Raphael Gasson, *The Challenging Counterfeit*, Plainfield, NJ: Logos Books, 1970, p. 36).

On the abilities of a medium:

It is possible for the medium to give a demonstration of this gift at any seance or public meeting, in a bus, train, restaurant or park. It does not require any special lighting and can be demonstrated anywhere. No form of trance condition is necessary, only the tuning in to the spirit world by the medium, who being in a passive state of mind is open to receive messages from those who presume to be the spirits of the dead (Ibid, p. 36).

Spiritism has continued on through the ages, though sometimes waning in popularity. Over 100 years ago it experienced a rebirth which has grown and now blossomed into the modern-day spiritistic movement.

The Fox Sisters

Spiritism, in its modern form, had its beginning in the United States in 1847 through two American women, Margaret and Kate Fox. When John D. Fox and his family moved into a house in Hydeville, New York, the two youngest children, Margaret and Kate, began to hear knockings in various parts of the house.

At first it was thought this was coming from mice, but when other strange phenomena were reported, like furniture moving around by itself, natural explanations seemed inadequate. Young Kate tried to contact the "spirit" which was causing all the commotion. When she would snap her fingers, there would be a mysterious knock in response.

Kate and Margaret devised a way to communicate with the alleged spirit which would reply to their questions by coded rappings. The spirit said he was Charles Rosma, who supposedly had been murdered by a former tenant of the Fox home. When portions of a human skeleton were actually found in the cellar, worldwide attention was given to the Fox sisters.

Many groups, including scientists, who investigated the Fox sisters and the rappings went away baffled. Among those who investigated was the famous New York editor, Horace Greeley ("Go West, Young Man, Go West"). Greeley concluded that "whatever may be the origin or cause of the rappings, the ladies in whose presence they occur do not make them."

In 1886 the Fox sisters confessed that they were frauds. The raps were produced by cracking their toe joints. Margaret conducted a series of demonstrations showing how she did it. At the New York Academy of Music, Margaret Fox stood on a small pine table on the stage in her stocking feet and produced loud distinct raps that could be heard throughout the building.

Although later both Fox sisters repudiated their confessions, the natural source of the "spirit" manifestations had already been exposed. This did not stop the cause of spiritism, as Joseph Dunninger comments:

> Kate died in 1892, and Margaret in 1893, both dipsomaniacs. In spite of manifest fraud, the general contention of the spiritualists remains that they were the fountainhead of American Spiritualism, and believers have completely discounted the confessions. It is such simple-mindedness which discourages skeptics from free investigation (Harry Houdini and Joseph Dunninger, *Magic and Mystery*, New York: Weathervane Books, 1967, p. 189).

Other prominent spiritists after this period included Sir Arthur Conan Doyle (creator of Sherlock Holmes); philosopher and psychic, William James; and the "father" of British Spiritism, Sir Oliver Lodge.

Bishop Pike

Spiritism came to the forefront in the 1960s when Episcopal Bishop James Pike attempted to contact the spirit of his dead son. Pike's son had committed suicide and the Bishop consulted several mediums in an attempt to contact him.

While on television in Toronto, Canada, Pike met with famous medium, Arthur Ford, who through his spirit-guide gave the Bishop the following message from his son: "He wants you to definitely understand that neither you nor any other member of the family has any right to feel any sense of guilt or have any feelings that you failed him in any way" (James A. Pike with Diane Kennedy, *The Other Side: An Account of My Experiences With Psychic Phenomena*, New York: Doubleday, 1968, pp. 246, 247).

Pike, according to his own words, had "jettisoned the Trinity, the Virgin Birth and the Incarnation" and had become a believer in the world of departed spirits without any objective criteria by which to test the spirits. The Bishop died two years later after disappearing in the Judean Desert. The mediums in whom Pike had come to trust were giving his wife false comfort between the time he was lost and found dead, saying he was alive but sick in a cave. The Bishop's case became famous and led many into dabbling with spiritism.

The Seance

What happens at a seance? What is it that makes people believe that they are contacting the spirit world? William J. Petersen comments:

> Spiritualists say there are six types of seances: passivity, vocal reality, trumpet revelation, lights, transfiguration, and levitation. In one sitting, several of these might be witnessed. One former medium, Victor Ernest, describes it like this: "Seances are noted for quietness. As the participants enter and meditate, they block out their tensions, worries, anxieties and problems. . . . Lights are turned down at every seance. Shades are drawn in the daytime and at night."
>
> Seances always begin on time. If you come late, the spirits might be offended.
>
> After a time of meditation, an object may move. Sometimes it is a glass on the table. Sometimes it is a small board on which a message is automatically written. Then the medium may go into a trance. His body may seem to be possessed by the spirit. When he opens his mouth, the voice you hear is different from the medium's voice. In fact, the entire personality of the medium seems to have changed (William J. Petersen, *Those Curious New Cults*, New Canaan, CN: Keats Publishing Co., 1973, 1975, p. 63).

During the seance a variety of different phenomena usually occurs, including materialization, speaking through a trumpet, spirit writing, apports and the appearance of ectoplasm.

Materialization

Materialization is the term used for the appearance during the seance of the spirits of the departed in some material form. The obvious question arises, "Are these materializations real?"

The magician, Joseph Dunninger, believed all spiritistic phenomena were a result of trickery. He, like Houdini, boasted that he could explain how all so-called phenomena actually happened. One particular medium who had baffled many experts with her materializations was exposed by Dunninger. He explained it in this manner:

> There wasn't anything in the room that seemed suspicious. The furniture was ordinary, and a quick glance was sufficient to show that there were no panels in the wall, nor were there any trap doors in evidence. How was it brought about? Was this lady supernatural? Were these apparent visions of faces truly genuine? Where did the voices come from? . . . All of these things were simple to answer. Checking up the medium's history, a day or so previous, I found that she had, some twelve years back, been married to a circus ventriloquist. This gentleman was one of the supposed believers, and mingled with the rest of the guests. He not only produced the voices, but the spirits as well. These heads were painted upon the back of his vest, and in the dark, it was only necessary for him to remove his coat, and walk about the room. Although his footsteps could not be heard upon the heavy carpet, I made sure of my analysis, by placing my ear to the floor. The pitch black room made this possible. I heard footsteps clearly. As he walked

about, these spirit faces could be seen by some, but were invisible to others. They apparently vanished and reappeared, as his body assumed various positions. Upon replacing his coat, and resuming his chair, all evidence of the ghostly visions disappeared.

Madam Biederman posed as a widow. Several houses of more fashionable type, located in the more populated residential district, belonged to her. There, in all probability, she and her husband shared the harvest. It was disappointing to my newspaper friends to be enlightened, as to the *modus operandi*, which this ghost woman employed. They were quite silent after my explanation had been rendered, which was convincing, and assured me that my findings had been accepted (Houdini and Dunninger, *Magic and Mystery*, op. cit., p. 162).

Walter B. Gibson observes that materializations are infrequently used today by mediums:

The most spectacular spirit seances are those in which materializations are produced; for if it were genuine, a materialization would be the most convincing form of psychic phenomena possible. Seances of this type have a long tradition, dating back many years. But from the standpoint of the fraudulent medium, while a materialization may be desirable, it is extremely dangerous. Many mediums who have defied detection with trick methods have come to grief when they entered the field of materialization. Supposed spirits have been seized during many a seance and turned out to be living human beings. Police have raided the lairs of false mediums and brought back trick apparatus used in the seances. Most fake mediums now eliminate physical phenomena altogether, and materialization in particular (Gibson, Walter B., *Secrets of Magic*, New York: Grosset and Dunlap, 1967, p. 140).

Trumpet Speaking

A favorite device used in seances is the trumpet through which the spirit supposedly speaks. Although it sounds impressive, it is actually a clever trick. M. Lamar Keene, a former medium who exposed many of the secrets of his trade, reveals how he performed the trumpet phenomenon:

My real contribution to the science and art of mediumship was in creating an original trumpet phenomenon. The standard trumpet sitting takes place in the familiar darkness—sometimes with the red light, sometimes without—and voices heard speaking through the tin megaphone are said to be those of the spirits.

Some mediums just sit or stand in the darkness and talk through the trumpet, but these show little initiative or imagination. Our trumpets had a luminous band so that the sitters could see them whirling around the room, hovering in space, or sometimes swinging back and forth in rhythm with a hymn.

The trick was the old black art business. My partner and I, and other confederates if we needed them, wore head-to-toe black outfits which rendered us invisible in the darkness. We could handle the trumpet with impunity even in a good red light and with the luminescent bands giving off a considerable glow.

The trumpets, as I've mentioned earlier, were made in sections and were extendable to a total length of about four feet. Thus they could be swung around with considerable speed. The sitter, thinking the trumpet was only a foot long and seeing it whizzing around close to the ceiling, assumed that it had gotten up there by defying gravity.

Some skeptics, of course, suspected wires or threads, but my special trumpet effect really bamboozled them. It bamboozled everybody and may be justly described as one of the few truly original phenomena in mediumship.

The sitter's experience was of holding the trumpet in his or her hands and feeling it vibrate with voice sounds. Yet there were no wires, no cords—nothing (M. Lamar Keene, *The Psychic Mafia*, New York: St. Martin's Press, 1976, pp. 104, 105).

Spirit Writing

A popular manifestation during many seances is the appearance of writing on blank cards known as spirit writing. The writings are supposedly messages from departed spirits. Spirit writing is another trick of the mediums. M. Lamar Keene reveals:

> Among my followers a favorite phenomenon was spirit card writing. Blank cards were given to each sitter, and he or she was asked to sign his or her name. The cards were then collected and placed on a table in the center of the room, and the lights were lowered. A hymn was sung, the lights were turned on, and *voila!* the cards now bore spirit messages, signatures of dead loved ones, Bible verses, poems, personal reminiscences, and other heartwarming evidences of life after death.
>
> There were two ways of doing this. The cards signed by the sitters could be removed from the room in the dark by confederates and the messages added, then returned before the lights were turned on. The other way was to have cards prepared in advance, including look-alike forgeries of the sitters' signatures, and simply switch these for the blank cards (Ibid, p. 109, 110).

Apports

An apport is the sudden appearance of solid objects into or through other solid objects. M. Lamar Keene, explains apports:

> I was also a whiz at apports. These were gifts from the spirits: sometimes they were worthless trinkets like rings or brooches; other times, more impressively, they were (as I've already described) objects we had stolen from the sitter.
>
> The apports, as previously described, sometimes arrived in full light and other times tumbled out of the trumpet in the dark. In exotic variations I arranged for apports to turn up in a newly baked cake, in a sandwich, or inside a shoe.
>
> Once at a church function I told a woman the spirits had apported something for her into a chocolate cake, and when she cut into it and found her necklace, she screamed, "Oh my God, this was at home in my drawer when I left to come to church!"
>
> The truth was that we had pilfered it from her purse more than a month before and she evidently hadn't missed it (Ibid, p. 110).

Table Tilting

The *Dictionary of Mysticism* defines table tilting as:

> The simplest form of communicating with the spirits of the dead, using a table as the instrument of communication; the medium or all those present at the seance place their hands or fingertips on the table, which eventually begins to move on by pointing a leg at letters on a board on the floor, or by rapping according to a code, spells out the messages (Gaynor, *Dictionary,* op. cit., p. 177).

Harry Houdini, the great escape artist, who was also a psychic investigator, had this to say concerning table tilting:

The echoes by which fake mediums do their tricks would fill a volume. . . . Of course, so long as edicts insist on working in darkness or semi-obscurity, adequate investigations will be almost impossible. In the dimness, it is easy for the spirit-invoked to lift a table by means of a piece of steel projecting from his sleeve, or with a steel hook hidden in his vest (Houdini and Dunninger, *Magic and Mystery, op. cit., pp. 30, 31*).

Walter Gibson reveals other methods employed to lift or tilt tables:

There are cases where fraudulent mediums have caused a table to float all around the room while people walk with it, pressng their hands against the top of the table. Here, the medium requires a confederate at the opposite side of the table. Each has a special tube strapped to the underside of one wrist and concealed by the sleeve. A rod comes out of this tube and extends under the table while the hand is on top. When the hands are raised, up comes the table, but it must, of course, be lifted at both sides.

Another device is worn on the belt. It is a sort of hook that swings out and engages the table beneath the top. As the sitters rise from their chairs, two of them, situated at opposite sides, have attached their belt hooks. The table rises when they get up and stays there until released (Walter B. Gibson, *Secrets*, op. cit., pp. 131, 132).

There are others, such as Kurt Koch, who do not necessarily see all table lifting as trickery. "Occult literature is full of examples of table lifting. This form of spiritistic practice has found many severe critics and many convinced champions. Among the documents of critical rejection are the researches of the medical doctor, Gullat Mellenburg, who with a flash photograph has shown how the medium Kathleen Colicher lifts a little table by means of a rod held between her knees. One of the best proofs of authenticity is provided by the sessions of the physicist, Prof. Zollnek, with the American spiritist, Dr. Slade. Slade's levitations and apport phenomena aroused great amazement and could not, in spite of the most stringent checks and controls, be unmasked as a swindle or explained rationally" (Kurt Koch, *Christian Counseling and Occultism*, Grand Rapids, MI: Kregel Pub., 1972, pp. 41, 42).

Although it is not clear whether all table lifting phenomena can be explained through trickery, as Houdini believed, it is clear that the Bible has harsh words to say for anyone who would attempt to communicate with the dead:

As for the person who turns to mediums and to spiritists, to play the harlot after them, I will also set My face against that person and will cut him off from among his people (Leviticus 20:6, NASB).

Spirit Raps

It has already been mentioned that modern spiritism got its start when the Fox sisters created spirit rapping by secretly snapping their toe joints. Consequently, other mediums have felt it necessary to produce the same manifestation. There have been a variety of different methods employed to produce this desired effect, with the raps usually coming from the table where the medium is seated.

Walter B. Gibson reveals some of the way these mysterious raps are produced:

> With some tables, raps may be made by rubbing the side of a shoe against the table leg, the sound carrying up into the top of the table. There are old, creaky tables that are especially suited to imitation spirit raps because of their loose joints. The medium can produce raps in a slightly darkened room by careful pressure on the table top, causing noise like snaps to come from the table.
>
> Sound seems to magnify in the dark, especially while everyone listens intently, as at a seance. Hence a room that is dimly lighted always helps fake raps. Noticeable raps may be produced by setting the finger tips firmly against the top of a table. The left thumb presses against the table, and the right thumbnail is pushed against the left thumbnail. This produces an audible click, and there are fraudulent mediums who have caused a succession of mysterious raps in this simple manner, without detection.
>
> Mechanical table rappers make the best sounds. . . .The top of a center-legged table is hollowed out to receive an electric coil. Two wires run through the table leg and terminate in projecting points which come out of the bottom of one of the small legs. Concealed beneath the carpet, at different places in the room, are metal floor plates. Wires run from these to an adjoining room, where they are controlled by a push button. The medium takes care to place the table at one of the selected spots, and when the tiny projecting points penetrate through the carpet, a connection is formed. A confederate pushes the electric button just as he would operate a door bell, and in this manner he causes raps to come from the top of the table (Gibson, *Secrets*, op. cit., pp. 133, 134).

Spirit Photography

Most forms of psychic phenomena, although spectacular in nature, leave no lasting evidence. This is not true, however, in the case of spirit photography which supposedly offers material proof that the spirits of the dead appeared in the seance.

A spirit photograph is an ordinary photograph taken during the seance, and when developed, it reveals the faces of the dead surrounding the sitter. This photograph is offered as proof the spirits were present. However, this is another clever mediumistic trick. Walter B. Gibson reveals how this deception is accomplished:

> Back in the days of the Civil War, a photographer discovered that if an old plate was improperly cleaned, and used again, a faint trace of the original picture would remain. That was the method used in the early stages of the game, but in later years spirit photographers have allowed their subjects to bring their own plates and to watch them being developed. Still the spirit forms appear, and people pay large sums for such photographs.
>
> One neat method of producing a spirit "extra" on a visitor's own plate is by the use of a special table with a concealed electric lamp, and a developing tray with a shallow double bottom that holds a plate with small portraits already on it.
>
> The photographer takes the sitter's picture of the unprepared plate, which can be marked for later identification. He then puts the plate in the developing tray and covers it so that no light can enter. But light does get in from below, for the medium presses a hidden release and the center of the tabletop

drops in two sections like a miniature trap door. The light goes on automatically, but cannot be seen because of the covered tray.

The light causes the ghost portraits to be projected from the hidden plate in the double bottom of the tray to the sitter's original plate above. The medium presses the switch again, the light goes off, the trap closes, and the sitter's plate is removed from the tray. On the developed plate the sitter's portrait appears with faces hovering above, dim but recognizable, like spirits (Ibid, p. 146).

Ectoplasm

The *Dictionary of Mysticism* defines ectoplasm:

> *Ectoplasm:* A term coined by Professor Richet (a contraction of the Greek words *ektos*, exteriorized, and *plasma*, substance) for the mysterious protoplasmic substance which streams forth from the bodies of mediums, producing superphysical phenomena, including materializations, under manipulation by a discarnate intelligence. Ectoplasm is described as matter which is invisible and impalpable in its primary state, but assuming the state of a vapor, liquid or solid, according to its stage of condensation. It emits an ozone-like smell. The ectoplasm is considered by spiritualists to be the materialization of the astral body (Gaynor, *Dictionary*, op. cit., p. 53).

However, the production of ectoplasm can be easily manufactured by the medium. The ex-medium, M. Lamar Keene, explains how he created the ectoplasm effect:

> It's amazing what effects can be created in the dark, manipulating yards and yards of chiffon and gauze which appears to shimmer in the unearthly glow of the ruby light. What I did was what magicians call "black art." The parts of me not covered by ectoplasm were garbed totally in black and were quite invisible in the dark. (For trumpet sittings, which I'll explain next, I wore a head-to-toe black outfit, including a mask over my face which rendered me as unseen as The Shadow used to be in his famous adventures.)
>
> Standing in the seance room in my invisible outfit, I would deftly unroll a ball of chiffon out to the middle of the floor and manipulate it until eventually it enveloped me. What the sitters saw was a phenomenon: A tiny ball of ectoplasm sending out shimmering tendrils which gradually grew or developed into a fully materialized spirit. Unless you have witnessed the effect under seance conditions, you'll find it hard to grasp how eerily convincing it can be.
>
> The ectoplasmic figure could disappear the same way it appeared. I simply unwound the chiffon from my body slowly and dramatically then wadded it back into the original tiny ball. What the sitter saw was the fully formed spirit gradually disintegrate, evaporate into a puff of ectoplasm.
>
> The variations were endless... (Keene, *Psychic Mafia*, op. cit., p. 101).

In *The Dead Do Not Talk*, Julien J. Proskauer gives an historical background of the use of ectoplasm:

> Whenever gullible scientists who attend a seance witness something that they can't explain, they invent a name for it, along with a theory regarding the thing itself. In so doing, they create new targets at which mediums can aim and score a bull's-eye.
>
> For there is nothing that a smart medium likes better than a challenge, provided he is allowed full leeway. And a challenge based on a delusion is the

best of all. The medium discovers what it was that the scientist misinterpreted and cooks up an improved method of repeating the effect. The result is always more than satisfactory.

Ectoplasm was one of those scientific "finds" that really boomed the psychic business. In simple terms, ectoplasm is "ghost stuff" and it came into existence immediately after a scientific investigator reported that he saw a parcel of it emanating from a medium.

Now the curious fact is this: If spirits chose to herald themselves in ecto-plasmic style, why didn't they furnish a few samples back in the Fox cottage where the first modern manifestations began? Why didn't they float a few clouds of ectoplasm out through the windows of the cabinet in which the Davenport boys were stalling their tests because somebody had tied them with the wrong kind of knot? Why couldn't the Davenport brothers, up in the town of Chittenden, produce their Indian controls under cover of some ectoplasmic smoke, instead of waiting for evening when the scene was tempered by an abundance of standard Vermont mist?

The best answer is to consult Podmore's *Modern Spiritualism* which still rates as one of the finest samples of debunking ever written. It appeared more than fifty years after the spook business came into vogue and covers everything with a remarkable clarity and a thorough index. Yet in that index the word "ectoplasm" does not appear.

Think of it! The masters of the other plane required a half century which included such mediums as the famous Home, before they thought of releasing the great wherewithal which no Grade-A medium of today could do without (Julien J. Proskauer, *The Dead Do Not Talk*, NY: Harper & Brothers Publishers, 1946, pp. 90, 91).

Proskauer in his chapter, "Ectoplasm is Bunk," gives some excellent illustrations and examples of the fraud involved in ectoplasm (Ibid, pp. 90-98).

Automatic Writing

Automatic writing consists of producing written material by a medium who is not in control of his conscious self. The subject matter is said to be beyond any training, experience or knowledge of the medium. Mediums also claim to be able to produce automatic drawings and automatic paintings while in their trance-like state.

How can this be accomplished? Some see the answer as a matter of "disassociation," which the clever medium uses to his advantage.

According to Louis E. Bisch, the psychologist, automatic writing is largely a matter of disassociation. One need not resort to the fanciful hypothesis that a spirit is guiding the hand of the writer, says he, in discussing the writings which mediums have promulgated while apparently in a trance. Just as one can drive an automobile and think of other things, or do some familiar work and think of last night's good time, or play a familiar piece on the piano while one's mind is miles away, so is it possible to practice disassociation in writing. Of course, some can disassociate more rapidly than others — that is a matter of natural tendency.

Disassociation is common to many normals but automatic writing is liable to be displayed by people who are prone to hysteria, in which such proclivities are heightened. Give such a person a pencil, then talk to him. Such a person will answer the questions, write about something else and talk about a distinctly different matter. The curious part of it is that the subject will be afterward entirely ignorant of what he has written. With one part of his conscious mind he was talking, with the other he wrote. The medium is canny enough to take advantage of such facts of psychology and make use of them often to the detriment of the client (Houdini and Dunninger, *Magic and Mystery*, op. cit., pp. 189, 190).

Kurt Koch feels some automatic writing is a spiritist phenomenon with occultic forces at work.

In spiritist automatic writing, the medium must achieve complete inner quietness and must not concentrate on anything. Suddenly, the compulsion to write comes over the medium. One of the most versatile and powerful mediums of our day is Matthew Manning, whom we have already mentioned in another connection. A number of parapsychologists have studied Manning. Here is an example that illustrates automatic writing.

A parapsychologist visited Manning to check out some of his experiments. Manning offered to give the parapsychologist a diagnosis of his state of health. Manning took a sheet of paper and wrote the parapsychologist's date of birth at the top of the page. Then Manning waited. After a minute, his hand began to write in a quite different style of handwriting. The writing was signed at the bottom, Thomas Penn. The diagnosis that this Thomas Penn from the other side gave was also interesting. It was, "A malfunction in the epigastric region."

The parapsychologist asked Manning, "Do you know what is meant by 'the epigastric region'?" "No," said Manning, "I don't know." "It isn't altogether clear to me either," said the parapsychologist. When checked by a doctor, the diagnosis proved to be correct. This knowledge cannot therefore have come from Manning's subconscious. This is a case where extrahuman forces are at work.

Automatic drawing is on the same level. Manning takes a crayon in his hand, waits, and then suddenly starts to draw quickly. After a few minutes his style changes. He draws in the style of well-known artists. When the parapsychologist was there, Manning drew a reproduction of the rhinoceros which Albrecht Durer drew in 1515, and which is hanging in the British Museum in London. A few minutes later, Manning drew a picture of Salome with the head of John the Baptist on a table before her. The original is by Aubrey Beardsley. I have seen both drawings and know that Manning has certainly not the artistic ability to copy the drawing of Albrecht Durer or the painting of Beardsley from memory.

Manning originally believed that his subconscious mind was responsible for all these powers. He has long since given up that view. He now believes that he receives his impulses and abilities from the unseen world (Kurt Koch, *Occult ABC*, Grand Rapids, MI: Int. Publs., n.d., pp. 220, 221).

Is It All Deception?

Harry Houdini and Joseph Dunninger exposed in their day the fraudulent practices of mediums. More recently M. Lamar Keene, the famous medium, revealed how he deceived untold thousands with his gimmicks. These individuals, along with others who are well qualified in spiritistic phenomena, believe all such practice is deception.

They strongly assert that spirits of the dead do not talk to the one sitting at the seance but rather that the medium is perpetrating a con game. Although we believe the great majority of things which happen during a seance can be rationally explained as deception, we also believe that supernatural manifestation sometimes occurs.

John Warwick Montgomery makes an appropriate comment:

> Almost everyone has heard of the clever techniques of fraudulent mediums — such as inflatable rubber gloves that leave the impression of spirit hands in paraffin and then, deflated, are able to be drawn out of the hardened wax through a small hole, leaving nothing but ghostly imprints. Houdini claimed that he could duplicate by natural means any spiritistic phenomenon shown to him. And recent visitors to Disneyland have invariably been impressed by the computerized effectiveness of the "spirits" in the Haunted Mansion. Are not all occult phenomena capable of similar explanation?
>
> Doubtless the world would be a more comfortable and secure place if the answer were yes; unfortunately, however, such an answer is not possible. Innumerable instances of occult phenomena resist categorization as "humbug" or natural occurrences in disguise (John Warwick Montgomery, *Principalities and Powers*, Minneapolis, MN: Bethany Fellowship, Inc., 1973, p. 30).

Kurt Koch responds in a similar manner:

> My knowledge of spiritism is not derived from books. Counseling is the only starting point for my experience. . . . I have been dealing with these problems in counseling for forty-five years. There are fake manifestations by spiritist mediums. . . . I am not concerned with fake spiritism. I am only interested in describing genuine phenomena (Kurt Koch, *Occult ABC*, op. cit., p. 216).

Dr. Nandor Fodor, a man who spent a lifetime as a psychic investigator, attempted to present a legal case of survival after death with the following examples:

> The protagonists of survival were ready to step before the bar. Could I, as a Doctor of Laws, put forward legally acceptable evidence?
>
> I accepted the challenge without searching far and wide for the best reported case. There were many. I did not try to evaluate them comparatively. My space was restricted. So I picked the Pearl Tie-Pin case reported by Sir William S. Barrett in his book, *On the Threshold of the Unseen*, as the one. Barrett accepted it as remarkably evidential. Sir Oliver Lodge concurred with him.
>
> The message about the pearl tie-pin came through Mrs. Hester Dowden, one of the best automatic writing mediums of the time. She was the daughter of the late Professor Edward Dowden, a classical scholar of Dublin. She was a lady of culture and refinement, of a singularly critical mind. I knew her personally. Her sincerity and personal integrity have never been questioned.
>
> The message was given to Miss Geraldine Cummins, the daughter of Professor Ashley Cummins, of Cork, Ireland. Afterward, Miss Cummins herself became a remarkable automatist. This is the story as told by Sir William S. Barrett:
>
> "Miss Cummins had a cousin, an officer with our army in France, who was killed in battle a month previously to the sitting; this she knew. One day, after the name of her cousin had unexpectedly been spelt out by the Ouija board, and her name given in answer to her query, do you know who I am? the following message came:

" 'Tell mother to give my pearl tie-pin to the girl I was going to marry. I think she ought to have it.' When asked what was the name and address of the lady, both were given; the name spelt out included the full Christian and surname, the latter being a very unusual one and quite unknown to both sitters. The address given in London was either fictitious or taken down incorrectly, as a letter sent there was returned, and the whole message was thought to be fictitious.

"Six months later, however, it was discovered that the officer had been engaged, shortly before he left for the front, to the very lady whose name was given; he had, however, told no one. Neither his cousin, nor any of his own family in Ireland were aware of the fact and had never seen the lady nor heard her name until the War Office sent over the deceased officer's effects. Then they found that he had put this lady's name in his will as his next of kin, both Christian and surname being precisely the same as given through the automatist; and what is equally remarkable, a pearl tie-pin was found in his effects.

"Both the ladies have signed a document they sent me, affirming the accuracy of the above statement. The message was recorded at the time, and not written from memory after verification had been obtained."

This, indeed, is a legal case. Because of the bequest of the pearl tie-pin, it could well have been taken into court. What would have happened if the bequest had been contested? The survival of the deceased officer was as well proven as could be demanded by legal standards but to bring a verdict stating this would have been far too embarrassing to any judge, and I have no doubt that he would have used every means of persuasion at his disposal to settle the case out of court (Dr. Nandor Fodor, *The Unaccountable*, New York: Award Books, 1968, pp. 162-164).

Stan Baldwin gives the following example:

A certain medium, Mrs. Blanche Cooler, supposedly communicated with the spirit of a man killed in battle; his name was Gordon Davies. The spirit, purporting to be Davies and speaking in a voice that sounded like his, described some unusual features of a house, foretold the future, and gave accurate information that was unknown to any of the participants in the seance and therefore was not a result of thought transference from them. This time, however, events proved the communication was not from the departed Davies, because he had not departed. He turned up alive and was shown to have had nothing whatever to do with the seance! What explanation can there be for such things? The Bible teaches that there is a company of fallen spirits which, to use an especially appropriate term, bedevil men. One such spirit enabled the girl described in Acts 16 to foretell the future. Obviously, she was not a fraud, for after the spirit left her, she could no longer bring her masters gain by telling fortunes —a result that would not have come about if she were only faking from the start (Stan Baldwin, *Games Satan Plays*, Wheaton, IL: Victor Books, cited by Clifford Wilson and John Weldon, *Occult Shock and Psychic Forces*, San Diego: Master Books, 1980, p. 99).

There is also the possibility that the medium did some investigation in the life of Mr. Davies to come up with this astounding information which is, by the way, a standard practice of many fraudulent mediums. Whether the manifestation was fraudulent or was the manifestation of an evil spirit, we at least know it was not the departed spirit of Mr. Davies.

Spiritism is not confined to the spiritualistic churches, for many of the cults engage in spiritistic activities. The Mormon Church, for example, has had occultic tendencies from the beginning as the following testimony of an ex-Mormon graphically reveals:

> I began doing genealogical research even before I was baptized. From the very beginning, it was obvious that I had "help" from somewhere. Books would literally call to me from the shelves, and upon opening them I would find evidence of family lines for which Mormon Temple work needed to be done. I began teaching genealogy classes my first year as a Mormon, and was soon recognized as an expert.
>
> Once I felt the presence of a dead grandmother with me in the temple, who I had not been able to believe would accept Mormonism even in the spirit world. Yet her presence was so real that I challenged her to help me locate her mother's records, which I had been unable to find. Two hours later in the genealogical library they "turned up" miraculously.
>
> I knew others to whom dead relatives visibly appeared and spoke, telling of their conversion to Mormonism in the spirit world. One friend would see missing names written on her bedspread each night as she said her prayers. A voice once gave me a name that led me to records correcting false information I had accepted concerning an ancestor.
>
> I submitted over 200 names of ancestors and performed most of the female Temple ordinances myself. Spiritist visitations and what would otherwise have been considered occultic manifestations were accepted in the name of the Church.
>
> These supernatural experiences always came just when my testimony of the Church and Joseph Smith was wavering. For ten years I overlooked much that I knew was false and contradictory. . . convinced that if the spirits of dead ancestors were so anxious to have their genealogical work done, then the Mormon Church must be all that Joseph Smith had claimed.
>
> In appearances to many Mormons, the spirits testify that the Mormon Church is the only true church, that they have accepted the "restored" gospel of Mormonism in the spirit world, and urge the living to pursue genealogical work (Dave Hunt, *The Cult Explosion*, Irvine, CA: Harvest House Publishers, 1980, p. 147).

Can the Dead Communicate With the Living?

If there is any supernatural activity in the seance, it is most certainly *not* in the spirit of the departed one speaking through the medium. It is not possible according to the Scriptures to contact the spirits of the dead! Jesus made this very clear with the account of the rich man and Lazarus.

> Now there was a certain rich man and he habitually dressed in purple and fine linen, gaily living in splendor every day. And a certain poor man named Lazarus was laid at his gate, covered with sores, and longing to be fed with the crumbs which were falling from the rich man's table; besides, even the dogs were coming and licking his sores. Now it came about that the poor man died and he was carried away by the angels to Abraham's bosom; and the rich man also died and was buried. And in Hades he lifted up his eyes, being in torment and saw Abraham far away, and Lazarus in his bosom. And he cried out and said, "Father Abraham, have mercy on me, and send Lazarus, that he

may dip the tip of his finger in water and cool off my tongue; for I am in agony in this flame." But Abraham said, "Child, remember that during your life you received your good things, and likewise Lazarus bad things; but now he is being comforted here, and you are in agony. And besides all this, between us and you there is a great chasm fixed, in order that those who wish to come over from here to you may not be able, and that none may cross over from there to us." And he said, "Then I beg you, Father, that you send him to my father's house —for I have five brothers —that he may warn them, lest they also come to this place of torment." But Abraham said, "They have Moses and the Prophets; let them hear them." But he said to him, "No, Father Abraham, but if someone goes to them from the dead, they will repent!" But he said to him, "If they do not listen to Moses and the Prophets, neither will they be persuaded if someone rises from the dead" (Luke 16:19-31, NASB).

Two things need to be noted about this passage:

(1) There is a great gulf fixed between the abode of the righteous dead and the unrighteous dead which no one can cross. The dead, in other words, are limited in their movement.

(2) The rich man was refused permission to warn his five brothers of their impending fate if they did not repent. The passage indicates, along with the rest of Scripture, that the dead are not allowed to speak to the living on any matter. The response in this case was that the brothers needed to believe what God had said to escape their doom rather than a voice from the dead.

Jesus declared that those who harden their hearts against the very words of God through Moses and the Prophets would not listen to one returned from the dead. This is proven by those who reject the Gospel of Jesus Christ today. Jesus Christ *did* rise from the dead, any yet people still reject His Word.

Medium at Endor

A passage of Scripture often quoted in discussions of mediums is 1 Samuel 28, the story of Saul and the medium at Endor. Proponents of spiritism cite the passage to point out that the medium was able to contact Samuel's spirit.

First, it must be stated that not all Bible scholars believe it was Samuel who was called up; some believe it was a demon, and some believe that it was a trick. But the majority of evangelical scholars hold that it actually was Samuel (Joseph Bayly, *What About Horoscopes?* Elgin IL: David C. Cook Publ. Co., 1970, p. 71). This position can be substantiated and explained by studying the context.

First, the element of surprise by the medium indicates she was just as surprised as anyone at Samuel's appearance (v. 12).

Second, the Scripture clearly indicates that Samuel appeared (v. 12). There is no indication that either fraud or demonism is present, as should be the case if those were true.

Thus, the logical conclusion must be in keeping with Scripture. The Bible teaches that men have no power to call up dead spirits, yet Samuel did appear. One concludes that it was God who chose to raise up Samuel for this one occasion for His purposes, and there was no doubt who it was. Neither the powers of darkness (the medium) nor the poor representation of the Kingdom of Light (Saul) had any doubt as to the identity of who appeared.

God always does as He chooses in this area, just as He chose to bring back Moses and Elijah on the Mount of Transfiguration before Christ was resurrected. By means of analogy, it is also true that though all men are subject to death, neither Enoch nor Elijah died. Here again, the Lord made the exception.

The Beliefs of Spiritism

Some of the official writings of spiritism claim compatability with Christianity.

> How — it may be asked — should Christianity be opposed to spiritualism when the Christian religion was really born in a seance? The real beginning of Christianity, its motive power, its great impetus, came — not from the birth or death of Jesus — but from Pentecost, the greatest seance in history (R.F. Austin, *The A.B.C. of Spiritualism*, Milwaukee, WI: National Spiritualist Association of Churches, n.d., p. 23).

However, a comparison between the beliefs of spiritism and Christianity show no agreement whatsoever. The following questions and answers are taken from a booklet distributed by the National Spiritualist Association of Churches:

Is not spiritualism based upon the Bible? (Q. 11)
   No. The Bible so far as it is inspired and true is based upon mediumship and therefore, both Christianity. . . and spiritualism rest on the same basis.
   Spiritualism does not depend for its credentials and proofs upon any former revelation.

Do spiritualists believe in the divinity of Jesus? (Q. 16)
   Most assuredly. They believe in the divinity of all men. Every man is divine in that he is a child of God, and inherits a spiritual (divine) nature....

Does spiritualism recognize Jesus as one person of the Trinity, co-equal with the Father, and divine in a sense in which divinity is unattainable by other men? (Q. 17)
   No. Spiritualism accepts him as one of many Saviour Christs, who at different times have come into the world to lighten its darkness and show by precept and example the way of life to men. It recognizes him as a world Saviour but not as "the only name" given under heaven by which men can be saved.

Does not spiritualism recognize special value and efficacy in the death of Jesus in saving men? (Q. 19)
   No. Spiritualism sees in the death of Jesus an illustration of the martyr spirit, of that unselfish and heroic devotion to humanity which ever characterized the life of Jesus, but no special atoning value in his sufferings and death....

From the standpoint of spiritualism, how is the character and work of Jesus to be interpreted? (Q. 21)
   Jesus was a great Mediator, or Medium, who recognized all the fundamental principles of spiritualism and practiced them....

Does spiritualism recognize rewards and punishments in the life after death? (Q. 86)

... No man escapes punishment, no man misses due reward. The idea of an atoning sacrifice for sins which will remove their natural consequences (pardon) is simply ludicrous to the inhabitants of the spirit spheres.

Do the departed, according to spiritualism, find heaven and hell as depicted by Church teaching? (Q. 88)

Not at all.... They deny any vision of a great white throne, any manifestations of a personal God, any appearance of Jesus, or any lake of fire and torment for lost souls.... (cited by Edmond Gruss, *Cults and the Occult*, rev. ed., Grand Rapids, MI: Baker Book House, 1974, pp. 57, 58).

The Bible and Spiritism

The Scripture speaks loud and clear in its denunciation of any type of spiritistic practice.

You shall not allow a sorceress to live (Exodus 22:18, NASB).

You shall not eat anything with the blood nor practice divination or soothsaying (Leviticus 19:26), NASB).

Do not turn to mediums or spiritists; do not seek them out to be defiled by them. I am the Lord Your God (Leviticus 19:31, NASB).

As for the person who turns to mediums and to spiritists, to play the harlot after them, I will also set My face against that person and will cut him off from among his people (Leviticus 20:6, NASB).

Now a man or a woman who is a medium or a spiritist shall surely be put to death. They shall be stoned with stones, their bloodguiltiness is upon them (Leviticus 20:27, NASB).

When you enter the land which the Lord your God gives you, you shall not learn to imitate the detestable things of those nations. There shall not be found among you anyone who makes his son or his daughter pass through the fire, one who uses divination, one who practices witchcraft, or one who interprets omens, or a sorcerer, or one who casts a spell, or a medium, or a spiritist, or one who calls up the dead. For whoever does these things is detestable to the Lord; and because of these detestable things the Lord your God will drive them out before you (Deuteronomy 18:9-12, NASB).

And when they say to you, "Consult the mediums and spiritists who whisper and mutter, Should not a people consult their God? Should they consult the dead on behalf of the living?" (Isaiah 8:19, NASB).

There are many dangers involved in spiritism. The former medium, M. Lamar Keene, mentions one of them:

One of the most alarming things about the mediumistic racket is how completely some people put their lives into the hands of ill-educated, emotionally unbalanced individuals who claim a hot line to heaven. As a medium I was routinely asked about business decisions, marital problems, whether to have an abortion, how to improve sexual performance, and similar intimate and important subjects. That people who ask such questions of a medium are risking their mental, moral and monetary health is a shocking but quite accurate description of the matter (Keene, *Psychic Mafia*, op. cit., p. 22).

Attempting to contact the spirits of the dead is not only fruitless, it also leads one down the path of death. M. Lamar Keene reveals the reason he quit his profession:

... If I stayed in mediumship I saw only deepening gloom. All the mediums I've known or known about have had tragic endings.

The Fox sisters, who started it all, wound up as alcoholic derelicts. William Slade, famed for his slate-writing tricks, died insane in a Michigan sanitarium. Margery, the medium, lay on her deathbed a hopeless drunk. The celebrated Arthur Ford fought the battle of the bottle to the very end and lost. And the inimitable Mable Riffle, boss of Camp Chesterfield—well, when she died it was winter and freezing cold, and her body had to be held until a thaw for burial; the service was in the cathedral at Chesterfield. Very few attended.

Wherever I looked it was the same: mediums at the end of a tawdry life (Ibid., pp. 147, 148).

What a contrast this is to the life that is offered by Jesus Christ. Jesus promised, "... I came that they might have life, and might have it abundantly" (John 10:10, NASB). The Christian, rather than attempting the hopeless task of talking to the dead, can talk to the living God. He does not need to resort to mediums or spiritists.

Moreover, those who have died having a relationship with God are not dead but are spiritually alive in God's presence. Jesus pointed this out:

> But regarding the resurrection of the dead, have you not read that which was spoken to God saying, I am the God of Abraham, and the God of Isaac, and the God of Jacob? He is not the God of the dead but of the living (Matthew 22:31, 32, NASB).

Jesus Christ offers real hope. Spiritists offer a false hope that leads to the path of destruction. Contrast the bitter end of mediums and spiritists with that of a man of God, the Apostle Paul, who gave this dying declaration:

> I have fought the good fight, I have finished the course, I have kept the faith; in the future there is laid up for me the crown of righteousness, which the Lord the righteous Judge, will award to me on that day; and not only to me, but also to all who have loved his appearing (2 Timothy 4:7, 8, NASB).

CHAPTER TWENTY-ONE

Superstition

There are many phenomena attributed to the occult which are, in reality, nothing but superstition. Superstition is a belief or practice not based upon fact but upon fear or ignorance of the unknown. Superstition is not confined to a bygone time or to primitive people, for it is with us today. The following are some examples of superstition.

The Number 13

The number 13 is supposed to bring bad luck. This is an ancient superstition still believed by many today. Many builders skip from the 12th to the 14th floor in building construction, fearing the 13th floor will bring bad luck. Some feel it is unlucky for 13 people to dine together since supposedly one of them will die within the year. Friday the 13th allegedly brings bad luck and many people are cautious about the activities they plan. No one knows how this superstition started, as Daniel Cohen comments:

> We do not know how the number 13 got its bad reputation. "Unlucky 13" may have started with the Vikings or other Norsemen. They told the story of a great banquet for 12 guests—all of them gods. The evil god Loki, angry at not being invited, sneaked into the banquet. Now there were 13 guests. One of the gods at the banquet was killed and since that time—the story goes—the number 13 has been considered unlucky.
>
> Some think the belief started with Christianity. At the Last Supper there were 13—Jesus Christ and the 12 apostles. The Last Supper was followed by Christ's crucifixion so that again the number 13 was identified with a dreadful event. It is believed that Christ was crucified on a Friday. This explains why Friday is regarded by some superstitious people as unlucky. For example, Friday is supposed to be a bad day to start a new job, to begin a voyage, to cut one's nails, or to get married (Daniel Cohen, *A Natural History of Unnatural Things*, New York: McCall Pub. Co., 1971, pp. 5, 6).

Breaking a Mirror

Another well-known superstition involves breaking a mirror which supposedly brings the individual seven years of bad luck. This belief goes back several thousand years to when people believed the image of a person, whether a painting or a reflection, was part of that person and whatever happened to the image happened to that person.

Prayer for Sneezing

Here's a superstition we all practice without being aware of it. When a person sneezes, we say "gesundheit," which is German for "good health to you" or we might say "God bless you." Why no offer of a blessing for a cough? Why only the sneeze?

This goes back thousands of years when people believed one's spirit resided inside his head and a good sneeze might send it away! Since evil spirits were known to be lurking about trying to get into the man's head, his friends would say a prayer to keep the evil spirits away.

Daniel Cohen further illustrates the ancient idea that the spirit could get away from the body:

> When you sneeze, you are supposed to cover your nose with a handkerchief. This is just good sense because a sneeze can spread germs. But why are you supposed to cover your mouth when you yawn? Not to do so is considered very rude, yet yawning spreads few or no germs. This custom, too, started thousands of years ago. At that time, a man was afraid that his spirit might escape though his open mouth or that some evil spirit might enter. So he blocked his mouth with his hand. In modern times, this ancient belief has been changed. Some parents tell their children to cover their mouths when they yawn, or a fly might get in (Ihid, p 12).

Omens

An omen is "an event or object believed to be a sign or token portending or foretelling the evil or beneficent character of a future occurrence" (*The Dictionary of Mysticism*, op. cit., p. 130).

One medieval writer listed the following as evil omens: "If a hare cross the way at our going forth, or a mouse gnaw our clothes. If they bleed three drops at nose, the salt falls towards them, a black spot appears in their nails, etc."

Other evil omens include having a black cat cross your path and walking under a ladder.

Amulets

An amulet is an object of superstition. It can be defined as "a material object on which a charm is written or over which a charm was said, worn on the person to protect the wearer against dangers, disease, to serve as a shield against demons, ghosts, evil magic, and to bring good luck and good fortune" (Frank Gaynor, ed., *Dictionary of Mysticism*, New York: Citadel Press, n.d., p. 10).

In the ancient world, along with many present-day primitive tribes, the carrying of an amulet is a common everyday occurrence. These objects (also called fetishes, talismans, charms) supposedly ward off evil spirits or bring luck to the wearer.

CHAPTER TWENTY-TWO

Witchcraft

W itchcraft is known as the "Old Religion" and is an ancient practice
dating back to biblical times. Witchcraft can be defined as the
performance of magic forbidden by God for non-biblical ends. The
word witchcraft is related to the old English word *wiccian*, "practice of
magical arts."

It was during the Middle Ages that witchcraft experienced a great
revival. It was an age where everyone believed in the supernatural and
superstition abounded. Roger Hart expressed the climate in the following manner:

> The people of medieval Europe shared a deep belief in the supernatural. The
> kingdom of darkness, with its devils and evil spirits, was as real and personal
> as the Kingdom of Heaven: Magic could be as powerful as prayer.
> The idea of supernatural spirits was universal and ordinary folk everywhere
> believed in demons, imps, goblins, hob-goblins, poltergeists and other spirits,
> and in legendary creatures such as vampires, werewolves and unicorns (Roger
> Hart, *Witchcraft*, New York: G. P. Putnam's Sons, 1971, p. 11).

If someone wanted to become a witch, there was an initiation process.
Some of the techniques were simple and some were complicated, but
there were usually two requirements. The first requirement was that the
would-be witch must join of his or her own free will. The second requirement was that the prospective witch must be willing to worship the devil.

Witches are usually organized into covens.

> The word "coven" dates from about 1500 and is a variation of the word con-
> vent. It means simply an assembly of people, but it came to be applied especial-
> ly to the organization of the witches' society (Geoffrey Parrinder, *Witchcraft:
> European and African*, London: Faber and Faber, 1963, p. 39).

Halloween

The day witches celebrate above all others is October 31, which is All Hallows Eve or Halloween. It is believed that on this night Satan and his witches have their greatest power.

The origin of Halloween goes back 2,000 years before the days of Christianity to a practice of the ancient Druids in Britain, France, Germany and the Celtic countries. The celebration honored their god Samhain, lord of the dead. The Celtic people considered November 1st as being the day of death. This was because it was the end of autumn and the beginning of winter for them.

The time of falling leaves seemed an appropriate time to celebrate death, which is exactly what Halloween was to them: A celebration of death honoring the god of the dead. The Druids believed that on this particular evening the spirits of the dead returned to their former home to visit the living.

If the living did not provide food for these evil spirits, all types of terrible things would happen to the living. If the evil spirits did not get a treat, then they would trick the living. This ancient practice is still celebrated today where people dress up as the dead, knocking on doors and saying, "Trick or treat," not realizing the origin of that which they are practicing. Nevertheless, it is still considered by witches as the night on which they have their greatest power.

Before the introduction of Christianity to these lands, the celebration of death was not called Halloween. Halloween is a form of the designation "All Hallows Eve," a holy evening instituted by the Church to honor all the saints of Church history.

Some Church historians allow the possibility that All Saints' Eve was designated October 30 to counteract the pagan influences of the celebration of death. While All Hallows Eve began as a strictly Christian holiday, the pagan influences from earlier traditions gradually crept in while the Church's influences waned.

Today Halloween is largely a secular holiday, an excuse to get dressed up as somebody else and have a party. However, true witches and followers of witchcraft still preserve the early pagan beliefs and consider Halloween a sacred and deadly powerful time. Having turned their backs on the God of the Bible, they invoke the help of Satan, fallen from God's favor and relegated to darkness.

Witch Hunting

One of the darkest periods in European and American history was the time of the "Great Witch Hunt." Although there had been scattered instances of persecution of witches as early as the 12th century, it did not truly get started until the end of the 15th century when two significant events occurred.

The first was a papal letter (known as a Bull) issued on December 5, 1484, by Pope Innocent VIII, which instituted the beginning of official action against suspected witches. This Bull received wide circulation and in it power was granted to men who were responsible for punishing witches. These men were known as inquisitors. The Papal Bull contained the following:

> Desiring with the most profound anxiety. . . that all heretical depravity should be driven away from the territories of the faithful, we very gladly proclaim and even restate those particular means and methods whereby our Christian endeavor may be fulfilled; since. . . a zeal for and devotion to our Faith may take hold all the more strongly on the hearts of the faithful.
>
> It has recently come to our attention, not without bitter sorrow, that in some parts of northern Germany. . . many persons of the Catholic Faith, have abused themselves with devils, *incubi* and *succubi*, and by their incantations, spells, conjurations, and other accursed superstitions and horrid charms, enormities and offences, destroy the offspring of women and the young of cattle, blast and eradicate the fruits of the earth, the grapes of the vine and the fruits of trees. Nay, men and women, beasts of burden, herd beasts, as well as animals of other kinds; also vineyards, orchards, meadows, pastures, corn, wheat, and other cereals of the earth.

When a person became a witch, he or she entered into a pact with Satan to worship him. In making this covenant with the devil, the initiate promised to serve him as Christians promise to serve Christ. Moreover, Satanists had their own liturgy which was a parody of the liturgy said by Roman Catholics. The Italian scholar, Guazzo, listed some of the ancient requirements for becoming a witch:

(1) Denial of the Christian Faith: "I deny the Creator of heaven and earth. I deny my baptism, I deny the worship I formerly paid to God. I adhere to the devil and believe only in thee." Trampling the cross, which accompanied this oath, had been from very early times an important part of the ritual.

(2) Rebaptism by the devil with a new name.

(3) Symbolic removal of the baptismal chrism (the consecrated oil mingled with balm).

(4) Denial of godparents and assigning of new sponsors.

(5) Token surrender to the devil of a piece of clothing.

(6) Swearing allegiance to the devil while standing within a magic circle on the ground.

(7) Request to the devil for their name to be written in the Book of Death.

(8) Promise to sacrifice children to the devil, a step which led to the stories of witches murdering children.

(9) Promise to pay annual tribute to the assigned demon. Only black-coloured gifts were valid.

(10) Marking with the devil's mark in various parts of the body. . . so that the area marked became insensitive. The mark might vary in shape—a rabbit's foot, a toad, or a spider.

(11) Vows of service to the devil: never to adore the sacrament; to smash holy relics; never to use holy water or candles; and to keep silence on their traffic with Satan (Francesco-Maria Guazzo, *Compendium Maleficarum*, 1608, translated by Dr. R. H. Robbins).

How does one describe a witch? The popular view is that of an ugly old woman riding on a broomstick with a black cat at her side. William West, an English writer during the reign of Elizabeth I, gave the following description of a witch:

Witches: A witch or hag is she who—deluded by a pact made with the devil through his persuasion, inspiration and juggling—thinks she can bring about all manner of evil things, either by thought or imprecation, such as to shake the air with lightnings and thunder, to cause hail and tempests, to remove green corn or trees to another place, to be carried on her familiar spirit (which has taken upon him the deceitful shape of a goat, swine, or calf, etc.) into some mountain far distant, in a wonderfully short space of time, and sometimes to fly upon a staff or fork, or some other instrument, and to spend all the night after with her sweetheart, in playing, sporting, banqueting, dancing, dalliance, and divers other devilish lusts and lewd disports, and to show a thousand such monstrous mockeries (William West, *Simboleography,* 1594).

Another writer described a witch in the following manner:

Witches are those who, because of the magnitude of their crimes, are commonly called *malefici* or evil doers. These witches, by the permission of God, agitate the elements, and disturb the minds of men less trusting in God. Without administering any poison, they kill by the great potency of their charms.... For they summon devils and dare to rouse them so that everyone kills his enemies by evil stratagems. For these witches make use of the blood of victims, and often defile the corpses of the dead.... For the devils are said to love blood, and so when the witches practice the black arts, they mingle blood with water, so that by the color of blood they can more easily conjure up the devils (Gratian, *Decretum*).

Marcello Truzzi describes the traditional initiation into witchcraft:

Basically, witchcraft constitutes a set of beliefs and techniques held in secret which the novice must obtain from someone familiar with them. The normal traditional means for obtaining such information is through another witch who knows these secrets. Traditionally, this can be done through initiation into an existing witch coven or by being told the secrets of the craft by an appropriate relative who is a witch (Marcello Truzzi, "Toward a Sociology of the Occult: Notes on Modern Witchcraft," *Religious Movements in Contemporary America*, ed. by Irving I. Zaretsky and Mark P. Leone, Princeton: Princeton University Press, 1974, p. 636).

Furthermore, these wretches afflict and torment men and women, beasts of burden, herd beasts, as well as cattle of all other kinds, with pain and disease, both internal and external. They hinder men from generating and women from conceiving, whence neither husbands with their wives nor wives with their husbands can perform the sexual act.

Above and beyond this, they blasphemously renounce that Faith which they received by the Sacrament of Baptism, and at the instigation of the enemy of the human race they do not shrink from committing and perpetrating the foulest abominations and excesses to the peril of their souls, whereby they offend the Divine Majesty and are a cause of scandal and dangerous example to very many (Papal Bull, *Summis Desiderantes Affectibus 1484*, by Pope Innocent VIII).

The second event which helped cause the great witch hunt was the publication of a book called *Malleus Maleficarum* (Hammer of Witches) in 1486 by Jakob Sprenger and Prior Heinrich Kramer. This publication was a handbook for witch hunters.

The Papal Bull, along with the publication of *Malleus Maleficarum*, led to a witch panic and a 300-year nightmare. People were seeing witches everywhere. Those accused of being witches had little or no defense against their accusers. During this period more than 100,000 people in every European state were executed for supposedly being witches. The brutal methods of the inquisitors is summed up by R. H. Robbins:

(1) The accused was presumed guilty until he had proved his innocence. The inquisition adopted this pivot of Roman Imperial law; but in matters of belief, vindication was almost impossible.

(2) Suspicion, gossip, or denunciation was sufficient indication of guilt to hail a person before the Inquisition.

(3) To justify the activity of the Inquisition, the offence, whatever it might have been, was correlated with heresy. Thus, the men who killed the bigoted Inquisitor Peter Partyr in 1252 were tried not for murder but for heresy (as opponents of the Inquisition).

(4) Witnesses were not identified. Often their accusations were not made known to the defendant. In 1254 Pope Innocent IV granted accusers anonymity.

(5) Witnesses disallowed in other offences were encouraged to inform against heretics, convicted perjurers, persons without civil rights, children of tender years, and excommunicates (including condemned heretics). If a hostile witness retracted his evidence, he was prosecuted for perjury, but his testimony was allowed to stand. However, according to the Inquisitor Nicholas Eymeric (1360), if the retraction was less favourable to the accused, the judged could accept this second testimony.

(6) No witnesses were allowed to testify on behalf of the accused; nor was his previous good reputation as a citizen or Christian taken into account.

(7) The accused was permitted no counsel, since the lawyer would thereby be guilty of defending heresy. (For a short time lawyers had been allowed, especially when inquisitors were sitting on Episcopal courts, and this privilege was resumed in the 17th century.)....

(9) The judges were encouraged to trick the accused into confession. The Inquisitor Sylvestor Prierias in 1521 told how this could be done.

(10) Although technically allowed only as a last resort, the practice of torture was regularly used, and could be inflicted on any witness. Civil authorities employed torture, but the Inquisition extended and systematized its use. Torture had been sanctioned as a means to discover heresy by Pope Innocent IV in 1257, in a Bull *Ad extirpanda*, and was confirmed by later popes; it was not abolished until 1816 by Pope Pius VII....

(14) Generally no appeal was countenanced. (R. H. Robbins, *The Encyclopedia of Witchcraft and Demonology*, New York: Crown Publ., 1959, p. 180).

The Power of Witches

Witches were supposed to have a variety of different powers which kept the people in fear of them. They supposedly could cast spells which would raise storms, magically destroy crops and turn themselves into werewolves and vampires. However, the most feared power thought to be held by the witches was that of bewitchment, the ability to cause sickness and death.

Roger Hart makes an apt comment:

> It can easily be imagined how—in the days when medicine was primitive—various ailments could be mistaken for bewitchment; paralysis, lockjaw, fevers, anemia, sclerosis, epilepsy, hysteria. Such illnesses often displayed symptoms which were extremely frightening to educated and uneducated people alike (Hart, *Witchcraft*, op. cit., p. 54).

To this list we could add Huntington's Chorea and Tourette's Syndrome. Huntington's Chorea is a disease which does not show up in most of its victims until they are past 30 years of age. This disease causes the victim to behave in a peculiar manner, including involuntary body movements, fits of anger and irritability and a loss of intelligence.

The victim may make strange outbursts of laughter, cry like a baby or talk endlessly. It can easily be seen how a sufferer could be mistaken for being bewitched or being a witch. Huntington's Chorea is also an inherited disease which would convince the superstitious that the bewitchment has been passed to the children.

Tourette's Syndrome is a rare disease which usually begins in childhood. The victim experiences tics—involuntary muscle movements—throughout the body but especially in the face. The sufferer also may kick and stamp his feet. Along with making awful faces, the victim makes involuntary noises which include shouts, grunts and swearing. All of these symptoms are beyond the control of the sufferer but appear to the uneducated as a sign of being a witch, possessed by the devil.

Many today still consider victims of such diseases as demon possessed or oppressed. Research funding into such rare diseases has lagged far behind that of the major prevalent diseases of our day. Such "orphan" diseases (so named because medical and pharmaceutical interests do not want to fund research on obscure diseases whose treatment would not be profitable financially) will probably remain largely uninvestigated until comprehensive research can be funded. However, the little we do know about these diseases leads us to conclude absolutely that one should not be blamed for demonic involvement when he is in reality the victim of a truly physiological aberration.

Salem Witch Trials

America did not escape the great witch hunt. Roger Hart comments on the Salem witch trials:

> Perhaps no single witch hunt has attracted so much popular attention as that which took place at Salem in New England in the year 1692. This American witch hunt was remarkable not merely on account of the large number of people found guilty (Salem was a small community), but also because of the late

date at which it took place. No one had been executed for witchcraft in England, for example, since 1684. But above all, the Salem affair has generally been seen as a fascinating microcosm of the whole Western witchcraft delusion (Ibid, p. 109).

Although Salem was a relatively small town of about 100 households, the percentage of those tried for being witches was enormous. As historian R. H. Robbins reports:

All in all, the toll of Salem, a township of a hundred-odd households, was enormous. During the hysteria, almost 150 people were arrested. A search of all the court records would no doubt add to this number. Because of the time taken to convict each prisoner, only thirty-one were tried in 1692, not including Sarah Churchill and Mary Warren, two accusers who briefly recanted. The court of Oyer and Terminer (hear and determine) sentenced to death all thirty-one, of whom six were men. Nineteen were hanged. Of the remaining twelve, two (Sarah Osborne and Anne Foster) died in jail; one (Giles Cory) was pressed to death; one (Tituba) was held indefinitely in jail without trial. Two (Abigail Faulkner and Elizabeth Proctor) postponed execution by pleading pregnancy and lived long enough to be reprieved. One (Mary Bradbury) escaped from jail after sentencing; and five made confessions which secured reprieves for them (Robbins, op. cit., p. 185).

Fourteen years later one of the accusers, Anne Putnam, retracted her charges, stating she and others carried the guilt of innocent blood.

Comment on Witch Hunting

The great witch hunt of the Middle Ages is remarkable for a number of reasons. First, it is remarkable because it lasted some 300 years and took hundreds of thousands of lives. It is also remarkable because it took place during a time of renewed interest in learning.

The people who participated in this craze were not all irrational individuals but were rather some of the most brilliantly educated people of that day. Scientists, philosophers and lawyers were among those who participated in the great witch hunt, showing that superstition knows no educational bounds.

It is also unfortunate that much of the persecution came from professing Christians doing it in the Name of God. The passages which were used to justify the witch hunt were misread and taken totally out of context. The legal penalties of such Old Testament crimes were part of the then-operating theocracy in Israel.

The Lord God was the King in Israel; He had the right to determine the crimes and punishments against His holy and sovereign state. One who participated in witchcraft was aligning himself with Satan, the foe of God. Such an alignment was treason against the government of Israel, a government directed personally by the Lord God.

Even today treason is often punished by death. However, since no nation today is a theocracy, a nation governed directly by God, the penalties instituted then are not applicable. Witchcraft is still evil and is still rebellion against God. It is not treason. Jesus Christ warned that physical death was not the ultimate punishment anyway.

Those who practice witchcraft, displaying their rejection of Jesus Christ, should heed His warning: "And do not fear those who kill the body, but are unable to kill the soul; but rather fear Him who is able to destroy soul and body in hell" (Matthew 10:28, NASB).

Witchcraft Today

Although witch hunting and witch trials no longer occur, the practice of witchcraft continues. The modern witch does not fit the stereotype of the old hag, for many people who are practicing this art are in the mainstream of society. The question is why? Why a renewed interest in this ancient art among both the educated and the ignorant? Daniel Cohen lists a couple of possible reasons:

> First, there is the eternal appeal of magic, the promise, however muted, that there are secrets available that will give a person power, money, love, and all those things he or she desires but cannot seem to obtain. Second, witchcraft is a put-down and a revolt against some of the establishment beliefs in organized religion, science, and rational thinking. The historic connection between witchcraft and drugs and sex also has undoubted appeal. Here is a set of beliefs that claim to be part of an extremely ancient religion. Yet this is a religion in which drugs and free sexuality are not condemned, but might be encouraged.
>
> Despite all the publicity and all the witch covens that have been organized, witchcraft still is not taken seriously (Daniel Cohen, *A Natural History of Unnatural Things*, New York: McCall Pub. Co., 1971, pp. 31, 32).

Modern witchcraft bears little resemblance to the witchcraft of the Middle Ages or to witchcraft in still primitive, preliterate societies. Modern witchcraft is a relatively recent development (the last 200 years), embraces hundreds of beliefs and practices and has hundreds of thousands of adherents. The one common theme running through modern witchcraft is the practice of and belief in things forbidden by God in the Bible as occultic.

> Up until a couple of decades ago, and for previous centuries, there were no admitted witches anywhere. Most people have thought of witchcraft as something that only the superstitious gave any credence to. Witch hunts and broomsticks were filed away together in a little-used corner of the mind.
>
> Today, in a massive spin-off from the culture-wide interest in the occult, this has all changed. Tens of thousands across America—some of them with university degrees—are dabbling in witchcraft, Satanism, voodoo, and other forms of black and white magic. Witches appear openly on television. Every high school is said to have its own witch. In Cleveland you can rent a witch to liven up a party. There are some 80,000 persons practicing white magic in the United States, with 6,000 in Chicago alone.
>
> Some of this is a fad. But unfortunately, much of it isn't. Murder after murder has been linked to the craze, with the murderers openly admitting to police or to reporters that they worshipped Satan. Police, more and more frequently are finding grim evidence of both animal and human sacrifice (George Vandeman, *Psychic Roulette*, Nashville, TN: Thomas Nelson, Inc., 1973, pp. 99, 100).

Witchcraft is not dead today as can be observed by an article appearing in the *Los Angeles Times* concerning the goddess movement:

> ...Eerie monotones... reverberated on the UC Santa Cruz campus. Cheers and whoops went up for the goddesses of yore—Isis, Astara, Demeter, Artemis, etc.
>
> ...The event was indicative of a burgeoning spiritual dimension to the women's liberation movement in America....
>
> Christine Downing, head of San Diego State University's religious studies department, estimates that many—if not most—spiritually sensitive women in the women's movement are willing to replace the biblical God with a frankly pagan and polytheistic approach.
>
> Witchcraft is aiding the women in their search for roots and rituals—without the connotations of evil usually associated with witchcraft.
>
> A Santa Cruz woman... said, "Some of the women think of themselves as witches, but not all."
>
> A brief, unscheduled appearance—met with enthusiastic applause—was made by Z Budapest. A self-described witch... the goddess movement knows her more as a leader of the Susan B. Anthony Coven No. 1 in Los Angeles and a charismatic spokeswoman for a feminist brand of Wicca, an ancient women's religion (witchcraft).
>
> The goddess movement, also called the women-spirit movement, apparently considers its first major gathering to have been a conference attended by about 1,200 women at the University of Massachusetts in late 1975....
>
> The ancient Mediterranean world, pagan Europe, Native America and Hindu tradition are all sources for goddess imagery...
>
> A religious phenomenon virtually unknown outside feminist circles, "goddess consciousness" will be widely known in three to five years (*Los Angeles Times*, April 10, 1978).

The Bible and Witchcraft

Both the Old and New Testaments make repeated references to the practice of witchcraft and sorcery, and whenever these practices are referred to they are always condemned by God. The Bible condemns all forms of witchcraft, including sorcery, astrology and reading human and animal entrails. The following passages describe the various forms of witchcraft which are condemned by God.

> You shall not allow a sorceress to live (Exodus 22:18, NASB).
>
> You shall not eat anything with the blood, nor practice divination or soothsaying (Leviticus 19:26, NASB).
>
> Do not turn to mediums or spiritists; do not seek them out to be defiled by them. I am the Lord your God (Leviticus 19:31, NASB).
>
> Now a man or a woman who is a medium or a spiritist shall surely be put to death. They shall be stoned with stones, their bloodguiltiness is upon them (Leviticus 20:27, NASB).
>
> You shall not behave thus toward the Lord your God, for every abominable act which the Lord hates they have done for their gods; for they even burn their sons and daughters in the fire to their gods (Deuteronomy 12:31, NASB).
>
> There shall not be found among you anyone who makes his son or his daughter pass through the fire, one who uses divination, one who practices witchcraft, or one who interprets omens, or a sorcerer, or one who casts a spell, or a medium, or a spiritist, or one who calls up the dead.... For those na-

tions, which you shall dispossess, listen to those who practice witchcraft and to diviners, but as for you, the Lord your God has not allowed you to do so (Deuteronomy 18:10, 11, 14, NASB).

For rebellion is as the sin of divination, and insubordination is as iniquity and idolatry. Because you have rejected the word of the Lord, He has also rejected you from being king (1 Samuel 15:23, NASB).

Then they made their sons and their daughters pass through the fire, and practiced divination and enchantments, and sold themselves to do evil in the sight of the Lord, provoking Him (2 Kings 17:17, NASB).

And he made his son pass through the fire, practiced witchcraft and used divination, and dealt with mediums and spiritists. He did much evil in the sight of the Lord provoking Him to anger (2 Kings 21:6, NASB).

Moreover, Josiah removed the mediums, and the spiritists and teraphim and the idols and all the abominations that were seen in the land of Judah and in Jerusalem, that he might confirm the words of the law which were written in the book that Hilkiah the priest found in the house of the Lord (2 Kings 23:24, NASB).

So Saul died for his trespass which he committed against the Lord, because of the word of the Lord which he did not keep; and also because he asked counsel of a medium, making inquiry of it, and did not inquire of the Lord. Therefore He killed him, and turned the kingdom to David the son of Jesse (1 Chronicles 10:13, NASB).

And when they say to you, "Consult the mediums and the spiritists who whisper and mutter," should not a people consult their God? Should they consult the dead on behalf of the living? (Isaiah 8:19, NASB).

Then the spirit of the Egyptians will be demoralized within them; and I will confound their strategy, so that they will resort to idols and ghosts of the dead, and to mediums and spiritists (Isaiah 19:3, NASB).

Stand fast now in your spells and in your many sorceries with which you have labored from your youth; perhaps you will be able to profit, perhaps you may cause trembling. You are wearied with your many counsels; let now the astrologers, those who prophesy by the stars, those who predict by the new moons, stand up and save you from what will come upon you (Isaiah 47:12, 13, NASB).

But as for you, do not listen to your prophets, your diviners, your dreamers, your soothsayers, or your sorcerers, who speak to you, saying, "You shall not serve the king of Babylon." For they prophesy a lie to you, in order to remove you far from your land; and I will drive you out, and you will perish (Jeremiah 27:9, 10, NASB).

"Then I will draw near to you for judgment; and I will be a swift witness against the sorcerers and against the adulterers and against those who swear falsely, and against those who oppress the wage earner in his wages, the widow and the orphan, and those who turn aside the alien, and do not fear Me," says the Lord of Hosts (Malachi 3:5, NASB).

And when they had gone through the whole island as far as Paphos, they found a certain magician, a Jewish false prophet whose name was Bar-Jesus, who was with the proconsul, Sergius Paulus, a man of intelligence. This man summoned Barnabas and Saul and sought to hear the word of God. But Elymas the magician (for thus his name is translated) was opposing them, seeking to turn the proconsul away from the faith. But Saul, who was also known as Paul, filled with the Holy Spirit, fixed his gaze upon him, and said, "You who are full of all deceit and fraud, you son of the devil, you enemy of all righteousness, will you not cease to make crooked the straight ways of the Lord?" (Acts 13:6-10, NASB).

Now the deeds of the flesh are evident, which are: immorality, impurity, sensuality, idolatry, sorcery, enmities, strife, jealousy, outbursts of anger, disputes, dissensions, factions, envying, drunkenness, carousing, and things like these, of which I forewarn you just as I have forewarned you that those who practice such things shall not inherit the kingdom of God (Galatians 5:19-21, NASB).

But for the cowardly and unbelieving and abominable and murderers and immoral persons and sorcerers and idolaters and all liars, their part will be in the lake that burns with fire and brimstone, which is the second death (Revelation 21:8, NASB).

CHAPTER TWENTY-THREE

Conclusion

T he existence of an evil, supernatural realm, led by Satan and supported by his legions of demons, is a reality. Satan's devices are many, and his methods are as varied as his devices. We as believers never are called to investigate all of these occult phenomena. Preoccupation with Satan's methods is not the best means of approaching our foe, our enemy, the accuser of the brethren. However, this does not mean we are to do nothing.

Rather, as believers, we are exhorted in three major areas. First, we are called to *understand*—understand that Satan has already been defeated. Christ's death and resurrection sealed Satan's fate and destruction. That fact became reality for us when we trusted Christ.

Second, we are called to *know*—know Satan's strategy. Not to know all his methods, but rather his means of operation. This includes his being disguised as an angel of light. Satan's *modus operandi*, aside from a direct assault of lies, also includes the more subtle and often used art of deception. He seeks to lure through the things of the world and the temptations of the flesh. Satan's desire is to replace God's plan with his counterfeit, just as he attempted to do in the Garden of Eden.

Third, besides having a good defense of knowing our position in Christ and recognizing Satan's strategy, we must *be on the offensive* in what we do. This means knowing God and making Him known. When we get closer to our Lord and share the gospel with others, it pierces Satan as with a knife—the Lord uses us to advance His Kingdom and bring Satan's domain to ruin. For our mastery over Satan is not in our power, but in God's power and through His plan—sharing the gospel. This is why Jesus said in Luke that we should not rejoice because we have power over demons but because our names are in the book of life (Luke 10:17-20).

Paul clearly states, "For I am not ashamed of the gospel, for it is the power of God for salvation to everyone who believes" (Romans 1:16 NASB). Communicating the gospel *is* our goal, even amid all the conflicts that Satan and the world attempt to throw at us. The command to believers is to grow in the gospel and to share it with others.

This is graphically and clearly illustrated in chapter six of Paul's epistle to the Ephesians. The whole point of this chapter is often overlooked, as the emphasis is usually placed on the "armor of God." That is not Paul's point. The whole reason for Paul's emphasis on the armor to stand against the powers of darkness is the need to get the gospel out (Ephesians 6:18-20 NASB).

In this section, Ephesians 6:10-20, Paul points out that the true battle stems from the evil forces in the heavenlies, and that his purpose for life is to spread the gospel. His very prayer at the end of the book, which comes in the context of this section on the armor of God, is for him to be able to *make known the gospel.* He places that prayer there by design and not by accident. As Paul saw fit to end his discussion of the forces of darkness in that way, so do we:

> Finally, be strong in the Lord, and in the strength of His might. Put on the full armor of God, that you may be able to stand firm against the schemes of the devil. For our struggle is not against flesh and blood, but against the rulers, against the powers, against the world forces of this darkness, against the spiritual forces of wickedness in the heavenly places. Therefore take up the full armor of God, that you may be able to resist in the evil day, and having done everything to stand firm. Stand firm therefore, having girded your loins with truth, and having put on the breastplate of righteousness, and having shod your feet with the preparation of the gospel of peace; in addition to all, taking up the shield of faith with which you will be able to extinguish all the flaming missiles of the evil one. And take the helmet of salvation, and the sword of the Spirit, which is the word of God. With all prayer and petition pray at all times in the Spirit, and with this in view, be on the alert with all perseverance and petition for all the saints, and pray on my behalf, that utterance may be given to me in the opennng of my mouth, to make known with boldness the mystery of the gospel, for which I am an ambassador in chains; that in proclaiming it I may speak boldly, as I ought to speak (Ephesians 6:10-20 NASB).

Magic and the Occult in Literature

M any Christians have legitimate questions about the use of fairies, witches, goblins, etc., in literature, and what should be our Christian response. Should we enjoy and condone writings which elevate supernatural powers only related to the God of the Bible? What of Gandalf in Tolkien's *Lord of the Rings?* Or of Galadriel and the palantir? What of C. S. Lewis, G. K. Chesterton or even Superman?

Another question arises. Should Christians celebrate Halloween? This type of question is so commonly asked by Christians, and deals with the ramifications of the occult on such a practical level, we thought it should be addressed.

Literature

Some believe that literature which elevates beings of supernatural powers should not be accepted and read by Christians. The literature is often accused of condoning such occultic practices as white magic— magic used for good purposes.

However, this is not the case. First, although white magic is sometimes used for the good, its foundation is usually the world of nature without God. The true God through Christ is never their basis for supernatural power. Behind the world of fairies in Lewis, Tolkien and others is a Supreme Being of good, and often some type of lesser but superpowerful being of evil, who is manifested in various ways, but usually defeated by the Good.

The second issue is that of motive. The literature often seeks to honor and promote values associated with the attributes of the God found in Scripture, such as love, justice, truth, and faith in a trustworthy object. White magic does not have this objective. There is a vast difference between the supernatural in literature and white magic both in purpose and in practice.

Dr. John Warwick Montgomery, one of the few Christian authors to address this important topic, and one who is well-qualified because of his interest and expertise in this area, offers this excellent analysis:

> Like Tarot symbolism, the imagery of Faerie strikes to the archetypal level, thus driving us closer to Christ or leaving us in hatred or despair. Samuel Roberts, a noted Welsh scholar, said that he "believed such things (fairies) existed and that God allowed them to appear in times of great ignorance to convince people of the existence of an invisible world." It is in this spirit that C. S. Lewis, by way of his seven Narnian Chronicles, and J. R. R. Tolkien, in *The Hobbit, The Lord of the Rings,* and his short stories ("Leap by Niggle," "Farmer Giles of Ham," etc.), have employed the motifs of Faerie to bring sensitive readers to face spiritual reality—archetypally in their own souls and factually in terms of the "existence of an invisible world" (John W. Montgomery, *Principalities and Powers,* Minneapolis, MN: Bethany Fellowship, 1973, p. 136).

Participation in Halloween

The history of Halloween has already been discussed, but the celebration of it has not. What should a Christian's attitude be toward this occasion? This is an often-asked, practical question involving one aspect of the occult.

Halloween has held an association with the occult throughout its history, and to a degree that stigma still exists today. While we don't feel that any hard and fast rules should be made about participation in Halloween festivities, we do feel that people, especially parents, should use discretion in regulating their degree of involvement. Rather than totally ignoring this occasion we would encourage Christians to develop creative alternatives to the traditional Halloween celebration.

The guiding principle from Scripture concerning areas that are not directly addressed is found in Paul's statement, "Let every man be fully persuaded in his own mind" (Romans 14:5 NASB). In other words, whatever you do, do not violate your conscience. If you are not sure you— or your children—should participate in an activity such as Halloween, then you should not enter into it. Your judgment in these areas must be guided by the Holy Spirit.

The Authority
of the Believer

A t the center of the occult, either openly or disguised as an "angel of
light," is Satan. Peter exhorts believers concerning our chief foe when
he writes, "Be of sober spirit, be on the alert. Your adversary, the devil,
prowls about like a roaring lion, seeking someone to devour" (1 Peter 5:8,
NASB).

Christians often have the tendency to "blame it all on the devil," when
in fact it was their own carelessness or fleshly nature which led to the
sin or error. It can also be said, however, that even when it is our fleshly
nature or the world which draws us from the Lord—and not the devil
directly—it is nevertheless true that Satan and his army of demons desire
that we be drawn to the world's standards.

Satan is the one who ultimately desires that we pursue the lusts of
the flesh, and it is he who sits as the "god of this world" (Ephesians 2:1-10).
Though not always directly involved, Satan's prime objective is the defeat
of God, and for us that means our defeat.

The authority of the believer spells out the authority a believer has
over Satan and his efforts to thwart God's desire for our lives and his attempt to defeat us.

For the rest of your life, one of the most important Scriptural messages
you'll ever consider is found here.

As you study the Old Testament, you see that men and women were
in a constant struggle with Satan, fighting many spiritual battles. As you
study the life of Christ, and Paul, and the other Apostles, you see a constant spiritual struggle. Christians today face many spiritual battles.

I'm so glad I learned the authority of the believer before I went to South
America. The authority of the believer is a possession that belongs to
every true child of God. And it gives so much authority over the enemy
that Satan has tried to blind most believers to the authority they have.

During Easter week at Balboa, I first learned of the authority of the believer. About 50,000 high school and college students came down for Easter. With André Kole, the illusionist, we packed out a big ballroom several nights in a row—for two or three meetings a night. So many people were coming to our meetings, in fact, that many of the bars were empty. It really irritated some of the people. The second night, one of the men from a night club came over to break up our meeting. They figured if they broke up one of them, that would finish it for us.

As André was performing, this guy pulled up with his Dodge Dart all souped up. With a deafening sound, he popped the clutch and went roaring down the street. Everyone inside, of course, turned around and looked out to see the commotion. Finally, André got them settled down.

Then the guy went around the block again. As he stopped out front, he revved it up again and roared down the street. By this time everyone was whispering and wondering what was going on. Some stood up, trying to look out the window.

When the guy went back around the block again, I knew that if he repeated his performance one more time, it would break up the meeting. Turning to Gene Huntsman, one of our staff members, I said, "I think Satan is trying to break up this meeting. Let's step out in the doorway and exercise the authority of the believer." So we stepped out and prayed a very simple prayer.

When the guy came back, he started to rev it up again, and as he popped the clutch—pow! The rear end of his car blew all over the street. By that time, we just thanked the Lord and went over and pushed him off the street. As I shared the *Four Spiritual Laws* with him, it reminded me that Jesus said all authority is given to the believer in heaven and in earth.

Now, to point out what the authority is, let's look at Luke 10:19: "Behold, I give unto you power to tread on serpents and scorpions, and over all the power of the enemy: and nothing shall by any means hurt you" (KJV).

Two separate Greek words are used for *power* here, but one English translation. The first one should be translated *authority*, not *power*. The Lord is saying, "Behold, I give you authority over the power of the enemy." The Christian does not have *power* over Satan; he has *authority* over Satan. Let me give you an illustration.

I used to live in Argentina. Buenos Aires, the second largest city in the western hemisphere, has six subway lines, one of the longest streets in the world—almost 60 miles long, and one of the widest streets in the world—25 lanes, almost three blocks wide. One street is called Corrente, which means *current*. It is a solid current of traffic—sometimes considered one of the longest parking lots in the world.

One intersection is so busy, about the only way you can make it across is to confess any unknown sin, make sure you are filled with the Spirit, commit your life to the Lord and dash madly! But one day we approached, and an amazing thing took place.

Out in the center of the intersection was a platform, on which stood a uniformed policeman. About 20 of us waited at the corner to cross. All of a sudden, he blew his whistle and put up his hand. As he lifted his hand, all those cars came to a screeching halt. With all of his personal power he couldn't have stopped one of those cars, but he had something far better; he was invested with the authority of the police department. And the moving cars and the pedestrians recognized that authority. So, first, we see that authority is delegated power.

Second, let's examine the source of this authority. Paul writes, "And what is the surpassing greatness of His Power toward us who believe. These are in accordance with the working of the strength of His might which He brought about in Christ, when He raised Him from the dead, and seated Him at His right hand in the heavenly places, far above all rule and authority and power and dominion, and every name that is named, not only in this age, but also in the one to come. And He put all things in subjection under His feet, and gave Him as head over all things to the Church, which is His Body, the fullness of Him who fills all in all" (Ephesians 1:19-23, NASB).

When Jesus Christ was raised from the dead, we see the act of the resurrection and the surrounding events as one of the greatest workings of God manifested in the Scriptures. So powerful was the omnipotency of God that the Holy Spirit, through the Apostle Paul, used four different words for power.

First, the greatness of his power—in the Greek—is *dunamis*, from which comes the English word *dynamite*. Then comes the word *working—energios*, where *energy* comes from—a working manifestation or activity. The third word is *strength—kratous*—meaning to *exercise strength*. Then comes *might*, or *esquai*—a great summation of power.

These four words signify that behind the events described in Ephesians 1:19-23 are the greatest workings of God manifested in the Scriptures—even greater than creation. This great unleashing of God's might involved the resurrection, the ascension and the seating of Jesus Christ. "When He had disarmed the rulers and authorities, He made a public display of them, having triumphed over them through Him" (Colossians 2:15, NASB). Satan was defeated and disarmed. All of this unleashing of God's might in the resurrection, the ascension and the seating of Jesus Christ was for you and me—that we might gain victory right now over Satan. The source of our authority over Satan is rooted in God and His power.

Third, what are the qualifications you must have to be able to be consistent in exercising the authority of the believer?

First, there must be knowledge, a knowledge of our position in Christ and of Satan's defeat. At the moment of salvation we are elevated to a heavenly placement. We don't have to climb some ladder of faith to get there. We are immediately identified in the eyes of God—and of Satan—with Christ's crucifixion and burial, and we are co-resurrected, co-ascended and co-seated with Jesus Christ at the right hand of the Father, far above all rule and power, authority and dominion and above every name that is named.

The problem is that, though both God and Satan are aware of this, most believers are not. And if you don't understand who you are, you will never exercise that authority which is the birthright of every true believer in Jesus. So the first step is knowledge.

The second qualification is belief. A lot of people really don't comprehend one of the primary aspects of belief, which is "to live in accordance with." This is not merely mental assent, but it leads to action. You could say it like this: That which the mind accepts, the will obeys. Otherwise you are not really a true believer. Do we actually believe that we've been co-resurrected, co-ascended, co-seated with Jesus Christ? If we do, our actions will be fervent.

We should wake up each morning and say, "Lord, I accept my position. I acknowledge it to be at the right hand of the Father, and today, through the Holy Spirit, cause it to be a reality to me, that I might experience victory." You talk about space walking! A Christian who is filled with the Holy Spirit and who knows his position with Christ is walking in the heavenlies. I put it this way: Before you can be any earthly good, you have to be heavenly minded. Your mind should be set at the right hand of the Father, knowing who you are.

Often, when I wake up in the morning, while my eyes are still closed, I go over my position in Christ, thanking the Holy Spirit for indwelling me, etc. But every morning, I acknowledge my position in Christ. I don't have to drum it up—I ask the Holy Spirit to make my position real in my experience.

The third qualification is humility. While belief introduces us to our place of throne power at the right hand of the Father, only humility will ensure that we can exercise that power continuously. Let me tell you, ever since Mr. and Mrs. Adam occupied the garden of Eden, man has needed to be reminded of his limitations. Even regenerated man thinks he can live without seriously considering his total dependence upon God.

Yet, humility to me is not going around saying, "I'm nothing, I'm nothing, I'm nothing. I'm just the dirt under the toenail. When I get to heaven all I want is that little old dinky cabin, that's enough for me." That's an insult to Christ. It's not humility—it's pride. Humility is knowing who you are and knowing who made you who you are and giving Him the glory for it. Sometimes, when I hear a person claim he's nothing, I say, "Look sir, I don't know about you, but I'm someone." I *am* someone. On December 19, 1959, at 8:30 at night, Jesus Christ made me a child of God, and I'm sure not going to say I'm nothing. Maybe I'm not all I should be, but I am more than I used to be, and God's not finished with me yet. I know He has made me, and I won't insult what God has made.

The next qualification, the fourth one, is boldness. Humility allows the greatest boldness. True boldness is faith in full manifestation. When God has spoken and you hold back, that is not faith, it is sin. We need men and women who have set their minds at the right hand of the Father and who fear no one but God. True boldness comes from realizing your position in Jesus Christ and being filled with the Holy Spirit.

The fifth and final qualification is awareness, a realization that being at the right hand of the Father also puts you in the place of the most intense spiritual conflict. The moment your eyes are open to the fact that you are in that place, that you have been co-resurrected, co-ascended and co-seated with Christ, Satan will do everything he possibly can to wipe you out, to discourage you. You become a marked individual. The last thing Satan wants is a Spirit-filled believer who knows his throne rights. Satan will start working in your life to cause you not to study or appropriate the following principles which show you how to defeat him.

Going through all of the above was necessary to lay a foundation on which you can exercise the authority of the believer. Here is how I do it. Remember, authority is delegated power. Usually I speak right out loud and address Satan directly, "Satan, in the name of the Lord Jesus Christ. . ." I always use this point first because those three names—Lord, Jesus and Christ—describe His crucifixion, burial, resurrection and seating, and His victory over Satan. "Satan, in the name of the Lord Jesus Christ and His shed blood on the cross, I command you to stop your activities in this area." Or, "Satan, in the name of the Lord Jesus Christ and His shed blood on the cross, I acknowledge that the victory is Jesus' and all honor and glory in this situation go to Him." I speak to Satan in various ways, but I always use those beginning phrases because they remind him that he is already defeated.

Next, I realize there is nothing I can do. I have no power over Satan, I only have authority. And the more I learn of the power behind me, the force behind me, the greater boldness I have in exercising the authority of the believer.

Once the authority of the believer is exercised, though, we must be patient. Never have I exercised that authority that I did not see Satan defeated, but I have had to learn to wait.

Some time ago, for example, I was to speak in a university in South America. Because of the university's Marxist leanings, I was the first American to speak there in four years, and it was a tense situation. Big photographs of me had been posted all over campus and the Communist students, trying to influence the other students to stay away from the meeting, had painted "CIA Agent" in red letters across the posters. I thought CIA meant "Christ in Action." Anyway, it backfired. Most of the students had never seen a CIA agent, so they came to the meeting to see what one looked like, and the room was packed. However, as is often the case when someone speaks in that part of the world, professional Marxist agitators had also come, and their intent was to disrupt the meeting.

When I go to another country I like to speak as well as possible in the language of that country. So I pointed out to the audience that I was learning their language and that night I would be lecturing in it. Well, I started, and, oh, it was horrible! My back was against the wall—the chairs were about five inches from me. And one after another, these agitators would jump up and throw accusations at me, call me "a filthy pig," etc., and hurl words at me that I didn't even know. Right in front of the audience they twisted me around their little fingers. I couldn't answer them; I didn't even know what they were saying. I felt so sorry for the Christians who were there because they had looked forward so eagerly to my coming to the campus and to seeing people come to Christ.

After 45 minutes of this heckling, I just felt like crying. I literally wanted to crawl under the carpet. My wife asked me one time, "Honey, what's the darkest situation you've ever been in?" And I said, "It was that one."

By this time I was ready to give up. Every time I even mentioned the name of Jesus they laughed. I had exercised the authority of the believer, and now I thought, "God, why aren't you doing something? Why? Isn't Satan defeated?" Well, I wasn't walking by faith. You see, God works when it brings the greatest honor and glory to His name, not to ours.

Finally, God started to work. The secretary of the Revolutionary Student Movement stood up, and everyone else became silent. I figured she must be someone important.

She was quite an outspoken woman, and I didn't know what to expect. But this is what she said. "Mr. McDowell, if I become a Christian tonight, will God give me the love for people that you have shown for us?"

Well, I don't have to tell you what happened. It broke just about everyone's heart who was there, and we had 58 decisions for Christ.

I've learned to exercise the authority of the believer and then to walk by faith and to wait. Sometimes I have had to wait six months or a year, but in the long run, when I look back on a situation and see how God has been glorified, it is beautiful.

And I never repeat the exercise of the authority of the believer in a given situation. Satan only needs one warning. God will take care of it from there. Jesus said, "All authority has been given to me in heaven and earth. Go therefore, and make disciples of all nations."

Part III

Understanding Non·Christian Religions

CHAPTER ONE

Hinduism

H induism is not only one of the oldest of all religious systems, it is also one of the most complex. During its history Hinduism has spawned a variety of sects holding diverse beliefs; therefore, it is difficult to get an accurate picture of Hinduism without considering a vast array of history and commentary. John B. Noss states:

> It is not one religion, but rather a family of religions... Hinduism is fluid and changing....Hinduism is the whole complex of beliefs and institutions that have appeared from the time when their ancient (and most sacred) scriptures, the vedas, were composed until now....Hindus have an extraordinarily wide selection of beliefs and practices to choose from: they can (to use Western terms) be pantheists, polytheists, monotheists, agnostics, or even atheists (John B. Noss, *Man's Religions*, New York: MacMillan Company, 1969, p. 88).

Joseph Gaer lists some of the complexities of Hinduism:

> Just as the attributes of the Hindu Triad multiplied until there were millions of them, and the castes divided and subdivided from the original four to a very large number, so also has this extremely old religion given rise to many sects.
> There are sects who worship Vishnu as the god of space and time.
> There are sects who worship Shiva (or Lord Siva) as a god of song and healing.
> There are sects who worship Durga, the Divine Mother (goddess of motherhood).
> And there are many others. But all the various sects believe in:
> *Brahman*, the eternal Trimutri, or Three-in-One God: *Brahma*, the Creator; *Vishnu*, the Preserver; and *Shiva*, the Destroyer;
> *Submission to Fate*, since man is not outside, but part of Brahman;
> The *Caste System*, determined by the Laws of Manu;
> The *Law of Karma*, that from good must come good, and from evil must come evil;
> *Reincarnation*, as a chain of rebirths in which each soul, through virtuous living, can rise to a higher state;
> *Nirvana*, the final stage reached upon the emancipation of the soul from the chain of rebirths;
> *Yogas*, the disciplines which enable the individual to control the body and the emotions; and

Dharma, the Law of Moral Order, which each individual must find and follow to reach nirvana (Joseph Gaer, *What the Great Religions Believe*, New York: Dodd, Mead, and Company, 1963, p. 35).

Because of its many complexities, Hinduism seemingly is impossible to summarize, as John Bowker observes:

> To summarize the thought of any religion is difficult, but in the case of Hinduism it is impossible. It is the essence of Hinduism that there are many different ways of looking at a single object, none of which will give the whole view, but each of which is entirely valid in its own right. A statue may be viewed from many angles. Each aspect helps to convey what the statue is like, but no single aspect is able to comprehend the statue as a whole, still less does the act of viewing it from one particular angle or another constitute "the statue itself" (John Bowker, *Problems of Suffering in Religions of the World*, London: Cambridge University Press, 1970, p. 193).

Hinduism as a Universal Religion

Hinduism is tolerant of other religions because Hindus see a sameness in all of them:

> The truth, which is the kernel of every religion, is one and the same; doctrines, however, differ considerably since they are the applications of the truth to the human situation. . . Rites, ceremonies, systems and dogmas lead beyond themselves to a region of utter clarity and so have only relative truth. . . Every work, every concept is a pointer which points beyond itself. The sign should not be mistaken for the thing signified. The sign-post is not the destination (S. Radhakrishnan, *East and West, The End of Their Separation*, New York: Alen & Uniwin, Humanities Press, 1954, p. 164).

> Different religious leaders have belonged to different schools, and most Hindus are rather proud of the fact that there have not been any violent conflicts or persecution, thanks to mutual tolerance. This is a field where no one theory can claim to explain all the mysteries, and tolerance may well be the path to wisdom rather than that to confusion (K. M. Sen, *Hinduism*, London: Gannon Publ., 1963, pp. 84 ff).

Hindu Scriptures

The Hindu scriptures, written over a period of 2,000 years (1400 B.C.-500 A.D.) are voluminous. They reflect the practices and beliefs which arose during the different long periods of Hindu history. Bruce Nichols explains:

> The Hindu scriptures are divided into two classes—*sruti* and *smriti*. Sruti, or "what is heard," refers to the eternal truths of religion which the *rishis* or seers saw or heard. They are independent of any god or man to whom they are communicated. They are the primary and final authority of religious truth. Using the analogy of the reflection of an image in a mirror or on the surface of a lake, the intellect of the ancient *rishis* was so pure and calm that it perfectly reflected the entirety of eternal truth. Their disciples recorded this truth and the record of it is known as the *vedas*. *Smriti*, or "what is remembered," possess a secondary authority, deriving their authority from the *sruti* whose principles they seek to expand. As recollections they contain all the sacred texts other than the *vedas*. These are generally understood to include the law books, the two great epics, the *Ramayana* and the *Mahabharata*, and the *Puranas*, which are largely collections of myths, stories, legends and chronicles of great events.

Also included are the *aqamas*, which are theological treatises and manuals of worship, and the *sultras*, or aphorisms, of the six systems of philosophy. There is also a vast treasury of vernacular literature largely of a *bhakti* or devotional type, which continues to inspire the masses of religious Hindus and which different sects accept as *smriti* (Bruce Nichols in *The World's Religions*, Sir Norman Anderson, ed., Grand Rapids: Wm. B. Eerdmans Publishing Company, 1976, pp. 137, 138).

The Vedas

The word *veda* literally means wisdom or knowledge. It is the term applied to the oldest of the Hindu scriptures, originally transmitted orally and then subsequently preserved in written form. The vedas contain hymns, prayers and ritual texts composed over a period of one thousand years, beginning about 1400 B.C.

The term vedas (plural) refers to the entire collection of these wisdom books, also known as the *samhitas*, which include the *rig-veda*, the *sama-veda*, the *yajur-veda* and the *athara-veda*. Each of these texts consists of three parts: (1) the *mantras*, hymns of praise to the gods; (2) the *brahmanas*, a guide for practicing ritual rights, and (3) the *upanishads*, the most important part of which deals with teachings on religious truth or doctrine.

The *samhitas* are the basis of vedic Hinduism, the most significant of the group being the *rig-veda*. This collection of hymns, originally composed in Sanskrit, praises the various Hindu deities, including Indra, Soma, Varuna and Mitra.

The *yajur-veda* consists of a collection of mantras borrowed from the rig-veda and applied to specific ritual situations carried out by the executive priest and his assistants.

The *sama-veda* in the same manner borrows mantras from the rig-veda. These hymns are chanted.

The *athara-veda* consists of magical spells and incantations carried out by the priests.

The Upanishads

The *upanishads* are a collection of speculative treatises. They were composed during the period 800 to 600 B.C., and 108 of them are still in existence. The word *upanishad* conveys the idea of secret teaching. Its treatises mark a definite change in emphasis from the sacrificial hymns and magic formulas in the vedas to the mystical ideas about man and the universe, specifically the eternal Brahman, which is the basis of all reality, and the *atman*, which is the self or the soul. The upanishads reportedly had an influence upon Gautama Buddha, the founder of Buddhism, as can be observed in some basic similarities between the upanishads and the teachings of Mahayana Buddhism.

Ramayana

The *Ramayana* is one of the two major epic tales of India, the other being the *Mahabharata*. Authorship is ascribed to the sage-poet Valmiki. The work consists of 24,000 couplets based upon the life of Rama, a righteous king who was supposedly an incarnation of the god Vishnu.

Although the story has some basis in fact, much of it is layered folklore added throughout the centuries. Besides Valmiki, other poets and writers have contributed to the complexities of the story. Edward Rice gives a brief synopsis of the account:

> Rama, a warrior and wanderer in the great tradition (one might equate him to Gilgamesh and Odysseus), is faced with a series of challenges and tests, some of which involve battles with other kings, or with demons; his wife Sita is kidnaped by a demon king and carried off in an air chariot to Ceylon; his chastity and faithfulness are tested; great battles ensue; the ending is a happy one, with Rama restored to the throne of Ayodha, and eventually he and Sita, after more trials, are united, not on earth but in the celestial abodes.
>
> By the time the innovators have finished the story, Rama and Sita are not only avatars of Vishnu but also exemplars of all the mundane and spiritual qualities with which the cosmos is endowed. The work has special interest to historians and ethnologists, for many elements depict the social conditions of the peninsula during that period. It is involved in the conflict of the Aryans with the aborigines and the Aryanization of the latter; the monkeys and bears who were allies of Rama were actually aborigines who bore animal names as totems, as they still do today (Edward Rice, *Eastern Definitions*, Garden City, NJ: Doubleday, 1980, p. 296).

The Mahabharata

The *Mahabharata* is the second epic, an immense story of the deeds of Aryan clans. It consists of some 100,000 verses and was composed over an 800-year period beginning about 400 years B.C. Contained within this work is a great classic, the *Bhagavad Gita*, or the "Song of the Blessed Lord."

Bhagavad Gita

This work is not only the most sacred book of the Hindus, it is also the best known and most read of all Indian works in the entire world, despite the fact it was added late to the Mahabharata, sometime in the first century A.D. The story, in short, consists of a dialogue between Krishna, the eighth Avatar of Vishnu, and the warrior Arjuna, who is about to fight his cousins. The question Arjuna asks Krishna is. How can he kill his blood relatives?

> Krishna! as I behold, come here to shed
> Their common blood, yon concourse of our kin,
> My members fail, my tongue dries in my mouth,
> A shudder thrills my body, and my hair
> Bristles with horror; hardly may I stand.
>   ...What rich spoils
> Could profit; what rule recompense; what span
> Of life seem sweet, bought with such blood?
> Seeing that these stand here, ready to die,
> For whose sake life was fair, and pleasure pleased,
> And power grew precious: — grandsires, sires, and sons,
> Brothers, and fathers-in-law, and sons-in-law,

Elders and friends!
So speaking, in the face of those two hosts,
Arjuna sank upon his chariot-seat,
And let fall bow and arrows, sick at heart (*The Bhagavad Gita*, 1:28-47).

The story revolves around man's duty, which if carried out will bring nothing but sorrow. The significance this story has on Hindu belief is its endorsement of bhakti, or devotion to a particular god, as a means of salvation, since Arjuna decides to put his devotion to Vishnu above his own personal desires. The Gita ends with Arjuna devoted to Vishnu and ready to kill his relatives in battle.

This poem has inspired millions of Hindus who have identified Arjuna's dilemma with their own situation. The poem offers hope, through the way of devotion, to all people no matter what their caste or sex. The poor and downtrodden, who could not achieve salvation through the way of works or the way of knowledge, can now achieve it through the way of devotion.

These two epic stories, the Ramayana and the Mahabharata, depict characters who have become ideals for the people of India in terms of moral and social behavior.

The Puranas

The Puranas are a very important source for the understanding of Hinduism. They include legends of gods, goddesses, demons and ancestors. They describe pilgrimages and rituals to demonstrate the importance of bhakti, caste and dharma. This collection of myths and legends, in which the heroes display all the desirable virtues, has made a significant contribution to the formation of Hindu moral codes.

Hindu Teachings (Doctrine)

To achieve a proper understanding of the world view held by the Hindus, it is necessary to present some of the basic concepts they hold to be true.

Brahman

Brahman, the ultimate reality for the Hindu, is a term difficult if not impossible to define completely, for its meaning has changed over a period of time. Edward Rice explains it in the following manner:

The Supreme Reality conceived of as one and undifferentiated, static and dynamic, yet above all definitions; the ultimate principle underlying the world, ultimate reality: "Without cause and without effect, without anything inside or outside," according to the sage Yajñavalkya. "Brahman is he whom speech cannot express, and from whom the mind, unable to reach him, comes away baffled," states the *Taittiriya Upanishad*. Brahman is now of interest more as a philosophic concept of past ages than as an active principle—to be meditated upon, but not adored or worshiped (*Ibid*, p. 71).

The enigmatic concept of Brahman is illustrated in this famous passage from the Bhagavad-Gita:

"Place this salt in water and come to me tomorrow morning."
Svetaketu did as he was commanded, and in the morning his father said to
him: "Bring me the salt you put into the water last night."
Svetaketu looked into the water, but could not find it, for it had dissolved.
His father then said: "Taste the water from this side. How is it?"
"It is salt."
"Taste it from the middle. How is it?"
"It is salt."
"Taste it from that side. How is it?"
"It is salt."
"Look for the salt again, and come again to me."
The son did so, saying: "I cannot see the salt. I only see water."
His father then said: "In the same way, O my son, you cannot see the spirit.
But in truth he is there. An invisible and subtle essence is the Spirit of the
whole universe. That is Reality. That is Truth. THOU ARE THAT!"

Moksha

Moksha, also known as *mukti*, is the Hindu term used for the liberation of the soul from the wheel of karma. For the Hindu, the chief aim
of his existence is to be freed from *samsara* (the binding life cycle) and
the wheel of karma with its endless cycle of births, deaths and rebirths.
When one achieves this liberation, he enters into a state of fullness or
completion. This state can be attained through death or preferably while
one is still living.

Moksha can be achieved through three paths: (1) knowledge, or *jnana*;
(2) devotion, or *bhakti*, or (3) ritual works, or *karma*. One who achieves
moksha before death is known as jivanmukta.

Atman

Atman is another Hindu term which is difficult to define. It refers to
the soul or true self, the part of each living thing that is eternal. The
Taittiriya Upanishad says atman is "that from which speech, along with
the mind, turns away—not able to comprehend." Oftentimes, it is used
synonymously with Brahman, the universal soul, seeking mystical union
together, or moksha.

Maya

A central concept in Hindu thought is that of *maya*. Huston Smith
expands upon the meaning of this key concept as follows:

This word is often translated "illusion," but this is misleading. For one thing
it suggests that the world need not be taken seriously. This the Hindu would
deny, pointing out that as long as it appears real and demanding to us we must
accept it as such. Moreover, it does have a kind of qualified reality; reality
on a provisional level.

Were we to be asked if dreams are real, our answer would have to be qualified.
They are real in the sense that we have them, but they are not real in the sense
that the things they depict necessarily exist in their own right. Strictly speaking,
a dream is a psychological construct, something created by the mind out of
its particular state. When the Hindus say the world is maya, this too, is what
they mean. Given the human mind in its normal condition, the world ap-

pears as we see it. But we have no right to infer from this that reality is in itself the way it so appears.

A child seeing a motion picture for the first time will assume that the objects he sees—lions, kings, canyons—are objectively before him; he does not suspect that they are being projected from a booth in the rear of the theater. It is the same with us; we assume the world we see to be in itself as we see it whereas in actuality it is a correlate of the particular psycho-physical condition our minds are currently in. (Huston Smith, *The Religions of Man*, New York: Harper and Row, 1958, pp. 82, 83.)

Karma

The word *karma* literally means *action* and has reference to a person's actions and the consequences thereof. In Hinduism, one's present state of existence is determined by his performance in previous lifetimes. The law of karma is the law of moral consequence, or the effect of any action upon the performer in a past, a present or even a future existence. As one performs righteous acts, he moves towards liberation from the cycle of successive births and deaths.

Contrariwise, if one's deeds are evil, he will move further from liberation. The determining factor is one's karma. The cycle of births, deaths and rebirths could be endless. The goal of the Hindu is to achieve enough good karma to remove himself from the cycle of rebirths and achieve eternal bliss.

Samsara

Samsara refers to transmigration or rebirth. It is the passing through a succession of lives based upon the direct reward or penalty of one's karma. This continuous chain consists of suffering from the results of acts of ignorance or sin in past lives. During each successive rebirth, the soul, which the Hindus consider to be eternal, moves from one body to another and carries with it the karma from its previous existence.

The rebirth may be to a higher form; i.e., a member of a higher caste or god, or down the social ladder to a lower caste or as an animal, since the wheel of karma applies to both man and animals. Accordingly, all creatures, both man and beast, are in their current situations because of the actions (karma) of previous lives.

The Caste System

The caste system is a unique feature of the Hindu religion. The account of its origin is an interesting story. Brahma created Manu, the first man. From Manu came the four different types of people, as the creator Brahma determined. From Manu's head came the Brahmins, the best and most holy people. Out of Manu's hands came the Kshatriyas, the rulers and warriors. The craftsmen came from his thighs and are called Vaisyas. The remainder of the people came from Manu's feet and are known as Sudras. Therefore, the structure of the caste system is divinely inspired.

The Brahmins are honored by all the people, including the royal family. Their jobs as priests and philosophers are subsidized by the state and involve the study of their sacred books.

The Kshatriyas are the upper middle class involved in the government and professional life, but they are lower in status than the Brahmins.

The Vaisyas are the merchants and farmers below the Brahmins and Kshatriyas but above the rest of the population in their status and religious privileges.

The Sudras are the lowest caste whose duty is to serve the upper castes as laborers and servants. They are excluded from many of the religious rituals and are not allowed to study the vedas.

The caste system became more complicated as time went on, with literally thousands of subcastes coming into existence. Today the caste system is still an integral part of the social order of India, even though it has been outlawed by the Indian government.

Swami Vivekananda gives the rationale for the caste system:

> Caste is a natural order. I can perform one duty in social life, and you another; you can govern a country, and I can mend a pair of old shoes, but there is no reason why you are greater than I, for can you mend my shoes? Can I govern the country? I am clever in mending shoes, you are clever in reading, vedas, but there is no reason why you should trample on my head...Caste is good. That is the only natural way of solving life. Men must form themselves into groups, and you cannot get rid of that. Wherever you go there will be caste. But that does not mean that there should be these privileges. They should be knocked on the head. If you teach vedanta to the fisherman, he will say, I am as good a man as you, I am a fisherman, you are a philosopher, but I have the same God in me as you have in you. And that is what we want, no privileges for any one, equal chances for all; let every one be taught that the Divine is within, and every one will work out his own salvation... (*The Complete Works of Swami Vivekananda Almora*, Hollywood, CA: Vedanta Press, 1924-32, III: 245 f., 460).

Salvation

Salvation, for the Hindu, can be achieved in one of three ways: the way of works, the way of knowledge, or the way of devotion.

1. *The Way of Works.* The way of works, *karma marga*, is the path to salvation through religious duty. It consists of carrying out the prescribed ceremonies, duties and religious rites. The Hindu believes that by doing these things he can add favorable karma to his merit. Moreover, if he does them religiously, he believes it is possible to be reborn as a Brahmin on his way toward liberation from the wheel of karma.

   The performance of these practices is something non-intellectual and emotionally detached, since it is the mechanical carrying out of prescribed laws and rituals. A basic concept in Hinduism is that one's actions, done in sincerity, must not be done for gain but must be done unselfishly.

2. *The Way of Knowledge.* Another way of achieving salvation—in the Hindu sense—is *jnana marga*, the way of knowledge. The basic premise behind the way of knowledge is the cause of human suffering based upon ignorance. This mental error concerning our own nature is at the root of mankind's problems. The error in man's thinking is this: man sees himself as a separate and real entity. The truth of the matter, Hindus say, is this: the only reality is Brahman, there is no other. Therefore, man, rather than

being a separate entity, is part of the whole, Brahman.

Selfhood is an illusion. As long as man continues seeing himself as a separate reality he will be chained to the wheel of birth, death and rebirth. He must be saved from this wrong belief by the proper understanding that he has no independent self. This knowledge is not merely intellectual but experiential, for the individual reaches a state of consciousness where the law of karma is of no effect. This experience comes after much self-discipline and meditation. The way of knowledge does not appeal to the masses but rather to an intellectual few who are willing to go through the prescribed steps.

3. *The Way of Devotion.* The way of devotion, *bhakti marga,* is chronologically the last of the three ways of salvation. It is that devotion to a deity which may be reflected in acts of worship, both public and private. This devotion, based upon love for the deity, will also be carried out in human relationships; i.e., love of family, love of master, etc. This devotion can lead one to ultimate salvation. The *Bhagavad Gita* is the work which has devoted special attention to this way of salvation. This path to salvation is characterized by commitment and action.*

The Sacred Cow

From early times the Hindus revered the cow and considered it a possessor of great power. The following verses from the *atharva veda* praise the cow, identifying it with the entire visible universe:

> Worship to thee, springing to life, and worship to thee when born!
> Worship, O Cow, to thy tail-hair, and to thy hooves, and to thy form!
> Hitherward we invite with prayer the Cow who pours a thousand streams,
> By whom the heaven, by whom the earth, by whom these waters are preserved....
> Forth from thy mouth the songs came, from thy neck's nape sprang strength, O Cow.
> Sacrifice from thy flanks was born, and rays of sunlight from thy teats.
> From thy fore-quarters and thy thighs motion was generated, Cow!
> Food from thine entrails was produced, and from thy belly came the plants....
> They call the Cow immortal life, pay homage to the Cow as Death.
> She hath become this universe, Fathers, and Rishis, hath become the Gods, and men, and Spirits.
> The man who hath this knowledge may receive the Cow with welcoming.
> So for the giver willingly doth perfect sacrifice pour milk....
> The Cow is Heaven, the Cow is Earth, the Cow is Vishnu, Lord of Life.
> The heavenly beings have drunk the out-pourings of the Cow,
> When these heavenly beings have drunk the out-pourings of the Cow,
> They in the Bright One's dwelling-place pay adoration to her milk.
> For Soma some have milked her; some worship the fatness she hath poured.

---

*We have combined *bhakti yoga* (devotion) and *raja yoga* (meditation). Some treat the two aspects as separate ways of salvation.

They who have given a Cow to him who hath this knowledge have gone up to the third region of the sky.
He who hath given a Cow unto the Brahmans winneth all the worlds.
For Right is firmly set in her, devotion, and religious zeal.
Both Gods and mortal men depend for life and being on the Cow.
She hath become this universe: all that the Sun surveys is she (*Atharva Veda* X:10).

Hinduism and Christianity

A comparison between Hinduism and Christianity shows the wide divergence of belief between the two faiths.

On the subject of God, Hinduism's supreme being is the undefinable, impersonal Brahman, a philosophical absolute. Christianity, on the other hand, teaches that there is a Supreme Being Who is the infinite-personal Creator. The God of Christianity, moreover, is loving and keenly interested in the affairs of mankind, quite in contrast to the aloof deity of Hinduism.

The Bible makes it clear that God cares about what happens to each one of us. "And call upon Me in the day of trouble; I shall rescue you, and you will honor Me" (Psalm 50:15 NASB). "Come to Me, all who are weary and heavy laden, and I will give you rest" (Matthew 11:28 NASB).

The Hindu views man as a manifestation of the impersonal Brahman, without individual self or self-worth. Christianity teaches that man was made in the image of God with a personality and the ability to receive and give love. Although the image of God in man has been tarnished by the fall, man is still of infinite value to God. This was demonstrated by the fact that God sent His only-begotten Son, Jesus Christ, to die to redeem sinful man, even while man was still in rebellion against God.

The Bible says, "For while we were still helpless, at the right time Christ died for the ungodly. For one will hardly die for a righteous man; though perhaps for the good man someone would dare even to die. But God demonstrates His own love toward us, in that while we were yet sinners, Christ died for us" (Romans 5:6-8 NASB). "Namely, that God was in Christ reconciling the world to Himself, not counting their trespasses against them, and He has committed to us the word of reconciliation. Therefore, we are ambassadors for Christ, as though God were entreating through us; we beg you on behalf of Christ, be reconciled to God. He made Him who knew no sin to be sin on our behalf, that we might become the righteousness of God in Him" (2 Corinthians 5:19-21 NASB).

In Hinduism there is no sin against a Holy God. Acts of wrongdoing are not done against any God but are mainly a result of ignorance. These evils can be overcome by following the guidelines of one's caste and way of salvation. To the contrary, Christianity sees sin as a real act of rebellion against a perfect and Holy God.

All acts of transgression are ultimately acts of rebellion against the laws of God.

The Scripture states, "Against Thee, Thee only, I have sinned, and done what is evil in Thy sight, so that Thou art justified when Thou dost speak, and blameless when Thou dost judge" (Psalm 51:4 NASB). "For all have sinned and fall short of the glory of God" (Romans 3:23 NASB).

Salvation in Hinduism can be attained in one of three general ways: the way of knowledge, knowing one is actually a part of the ultimate Brahman and not a separate entity; the way of devotion, which is love and obedience to a particular deity; or the way of works, or following ceremonial ritual. This salvation is from the seemingly endless cycle of birth, death, and rebirth. By contrast, in Christianity salvation is from a potentially eternal separation from God and cannot be obtained by any number of good deeds, but rather is given freely by God to all who will receive it.

The Bible says, "For by grace you have been saved through faith; and that not of yourselves, it is the gift of God; not as a result of works, that no one should boast" (Ephesians 2:8,9 NASB). "He saved us, not on the basis of deeds which we have done in righteousness, but according to His mercy, by the washing of regeneration and renewing by the Holy Spirit" (Titus 3:5 NASB). "He who believes in the Son has eternal life; but he who does not obey the Son shall not see life, but the wrath of God abides on him" (John 3:36 NASB).

Hinduism views the material world as transitory and of secondary importance to the realization of Brahman, while Christianity sees the world as having objective reality and its source in the creative will of God. Hindus see the world as an extension of Brahman, part of the absolute, while Christianity views the world as an entity eternally different in nature from God: not part of some universal or monistic One.

The Bible says that in the beginning God created the heavens and the earth (Genesis 1:1). Since the earth, therefore, was created by God, it is not to be identified with Him or His eternal nature.

These contradictions represent major diversities between the two religions. Many other differences remain which we cannot discuss in this small space. However, even with this limited spectrum of differences, one readily can see that the two faiths of Hinduism and Christianity never can be reconciled. The basic foundations on which both are built are mutually exclusive.

Hindu Terms

Agni—The Vedic god of the altar fire who mediates between the gods and men. Mentioned in the Rig Veda.

Atman—The real self, the eternal and sometimes universal life principle.

Bhagavad-Gita—The "Song of the Lord," the most well-known of all Hindu scriptures. Contains a philosophical dialogue between the warrior Arjuna and the Lord God Krishna.

Brahma—The creator god, the first member of the Hindu triad, consisting of Brahma, Shiva, and Vishna.

Brahman—Ultimate Reality, the supreme essence of the universe, the all-prevading deity.

Brahmin—(or Brahman) A member of the priestly caste, the highest and most noble class.

Darhma—The teachings of virtue and principle. A term by which Hindus refer to their own religion.

Ganesa—The god of prudence and wisdom represented as being a short red or yellow man with an elephant's head.

Hanuman—The monkey god, lord of the winds. He helped Rama in battle.

Indra—The Vedic god of rain and thunder, originally the god of light and once considered (during the Vaidic period) as a member of the Hindu triad. Not as important today as in the past.

Karma—The culminating value of all of one's life actions, good and bad, which together determine one's next rebirth after death.

Krishna—The eighth or ninth incarnation of Vishnu, one of the most widely worshipped deities. Krishnaites believe Krishna is the supreme deity, incarnating as Vishnu.

Lakshma—Goddess of beauty and wealth, concubine of Krishna (and/or Vishnu). (Also *Laksmi*.)

Mahabharata—One of the national epics of India. Contained in the Mahabharata is the famous Bhagavad Gita.

Maya—The power that produces the transient phenomena of physical existence.

Moksha—The term for liberation from the bondage of finite existence.

Parvati—The goddess who is believed to be the daughter of the Himalayas. A consort of Shiva.

Puranas—Part of the Hindu scriptures consisting of myths and legends mixed with historical events.

Ramayana—One of the national epics of India based upon the story of the good king Rama, who was purported to be an incarnation of the god Vishnu.

Rishi—First, an inspired poet or holy sage; later, any wise man.

Samsara—The cyclical transmigration or rebirth of souls passing on from one existence to another until release can be achieved.

Sarasvati—The goddess of learning, music and speech; the consort of Brahma.

Soma—The soma plant is a leafless vine from Western India that yields an intoxicating juice. The personification of soma was once worshipped as a god.

Upanishads—Part of the Hindu sacred scriptures containing speculative treatises on the nature of ultimate reality and the way to achieve union with the absolute.

Varuna—Hindu god, considered as ruler and guardian of the cosmic order.

Veda—The oldest of the Hindu scriptures, consisting of four collections of sacred writings.

Vishnu—The preserver, second god of the Hindu triad.

Yoga—The Hindu path of union with the divine. Any sort of exercise (physical, mental, or spiritual) which promotes one's journey to union with Brahma.

Yogi—A devotee of yoga.

Hinduism Bibliography

Almore, Swami Vivekananda, *The Complete Works of Swami Vivekananda Almore*, Hollywood, CA: Vedanta Press, 1924, 1932, III.

Bowker, John, *Problems of Suffering in Religions of the World*, London: Cambridge University Press, 1970.

Gaer, Joseph, *What the Great Religions Believe*, New York: Dodd, Mead, and Company, 1963.

Nichols, Bruce in *The World's Religions*, Sir Norman Anderson, ed., Grand Rapids, MI: William B. Eerdmans Publishing Company, 1976.

Noss, John B., *Man's Religions*, New York: MacMillan Company, 1969.

Radhakrishnan, S., *East and West, the End of Their Separation*, New York: Allen & Unwin, Humanities Press, 1954.

Rice, Edward, *Eastern Definitions*, Garden City, NJ: Doubleday, 1980.

Sen, K. M., *Hinduism*, London: Gannon Publ., 1963.

Smith, Huston, *The Religions of Man*, New York: Harper and Row, 1958.

CHAPTER TWO

Jainism

H induism gave birth to three religious factions: Jainism, Buddhism and Sikhism. Jainism was its first offspring and though, like any child, it appears in a certain light to be somewhat like its mother, it eventually established itself as a new religion. Within the Hindu religion, Jainism started as a reformation movement but soon found itself as an independent religion based upon the teachings of its founder, Mahavira. Although relatively small in its number of adherents (3 million Indian followers) compared to other religions, Jainism has had an influence disproportionate to its size.

Founder Mahavira

Jainism, in contrast to Hinduism, is based upon a founder and leader known as Mahavira. This name actually is an honorific title signifying "great man." Tradition places the birth of Mahavira at 599 B.C. in northeastern India, which would make him a contemporary of Buddha. Tradition also relates that Mahavira was the second son of a rajah living in luxurious surroundings. He married and had one daughter.

When his parents died, Mahavira decided at the age of 30 to live a life of self-denial, pledging to deny himself the care of his body and not to speak for 12 years. After a short time, Mahavira put off the robe he wore and wandered naked through India receiving injuries from both man and beast. He wandered for 12 years until he reached enlightenment at the age of 42.

The *Sacred Books of the East* record, "During the thirteenth year, in a squatting position...exposing himself to the heat of the sun...with knees high and the head low, in deep meditation, in the midst of abstract meditation he reached nirvana, the complete and full, the unobstructed, infinite absolute" (F. M. Mueller, ed., *Sacred Books of the East*, Vol. 22, Oxford: Krishna Press, 1879-1910, p. 201).

After reaching enlightenment, Mahavira stopped living by himself and took on disciples, preaching his new-found belief. So he continued to live until the end of his life, at which time he was said to have over 14,000 monks in his brotherhood (Maurice Rawlings, *Life-Wish: Reincarnation: Reality or Hoax*, Nashville: Thomas Nelson Inc., 1981, p. 63).

Jainism's Debt to Hinduism

It must be stressed that Jainism did not appear in a religious vacuum. Jainism began as an heretical movement within Hinduism, but now can only be viewed as a distinct religion with reference to Hinduism. Mahavira held firmly to such Hindu beliefs as the law of moral retribution or karma and the transmigration of souls after death. There were, however, many points of disagreement between the two religions at the inception of Jainism. Herbert Stroup lists some of the differences between Hinduism and Jainism:

1. The doctrine of karma, the law of causation as applied to the moral sphere, seemed to him too rigid and restrictive, for within Hinduism its rule is absolute. He sought to lessen this rigidity and to find a practical measure of release from it.

2. The Hindu conception of rebirth came to mean, especially in the Upanishadic period, that individual souls do not possess real individuality. According to Hindu doctrine souls do not remain individualized in eternity, but become absorbed in Brahma. Mahavira strongly asserted the independence or autonomy of the individual soul.

3. Hinduism taught caste. In Mahavira's time these lines of social organization were still in the making, and he benefited to a considerable extent personally from the system. But he was strongly democratic, believing in the worth of all individuals. He taught the importance of a casteless society.

4. The priestly caste, as a result of the solidifying caste system, was clearly becoming the most influential group in Indian life. Mahavira was a member of the second or warrior caste. This had much to lose as the priesthood became dominant in the society, and a good deal of the impact of early Jainism was in opposition to the prominence of the priestly caste.

5. Particularly in the Vedic and Brahmanic periods, Hinduism was polytheistic. One hymn in the Vedic literature suggests that the gods may number as many as 3,333. Mahavira, in the simplicity of his character, was repelled by the extremes of Vedic polytheism. In fact, he did not teach the existence of a god at all.

6. Hinduism in the Vedic and Brahmanic period also taught the importance of animal sacrifices. These ceremonial occasions became complex affairs with large numbers of animals slaughtered. Mahavira may well have developed his emphasis upon harmlessness (*ahimsa*) to all living things in response to the excesses of animal sacrifice in his time (Herbert Stroup, *Four Religions of Asia*, New York: Harper and Row, 1968, p. 99).

Jainism and Belief in God

Mahavira was vehemently opposed to the idea of acknowledging or worshipping a supreme being. He once said:

A monk or a nun should not say, "The god of the sky!" "The god of the thunderstorm!" "The god who begins to rain!" "May rain fall!" "May the crops grow!" "May the king conquer!" They should not use such speech. But, knowing the nature of things, he should say, "The air." "A cloud is gathered, or come down." "The cloud has rained." This is the whole duty (F. M. Mueller, ed., *op. cit.*, vol. 22, p. 152).

Later Jainism, however, did acknowledge and worship a deity: Mahavira himself became their object of worship.

Deification of Mahavira

Although Mahavira denied that any God or gods existed to be worshipped, he, like other religious leaders, was deified by his later followers. He was given the designation as the 24th Tirthankara, the last and greatest of the savior beings. Mahavira was regarded as having descended from heaven without sin and with all knowledge.

He descended from heaven...The venerable ascetic Mahavira descended from the Great Vimana (palace of the gods) (*Ibid.*, pp. 189, 190).

Having wisdom, Mahavira committed no sin himself...He meditated, free from sin and desire (*Ibid.*, p. 86, 87).

He possessed supreme, unlimited, unimpeded knowledge and intuition (*Ibid.*, p. 257).

Self-Denial

Jainism is a religion of asceticism involving rigid self-denial. Salvation or liberation could be achieved only by ascetic practices. These practices for the monks are listed in the "Five Great Vows" and include the renunciation of: (1) killing living things, (2) lying, (3) greed, (4) sexual pleasure, and (5) worldly attachments.

The monks, according to Mahavira, were to avoid women entirely because he believed they were the cause of all types of evil:

Women are the greatest temptation in the world. This has been declared by the sage. He should not speak of women, nor look at them, nor converse with them, nor claim them as his own, nor do their work (*Ibid.*, p. 48).

These five great vows could be fulfilled completely only by those Jains who were living the monastic life. Consequently, the laymen who practiced Jainism were given a more modified code to follow.

Non-violence

Central to Jainism is the practice of non-violence or *ahimsa*. The dedicated Jain is constrained to reverence life and is forbidden to take life even at the lowest level. The obvious consequence of this belief is strict vegetarianism. Farming is frowned upon since the process would inevitably involve killing of lower forms of life. Ahimsa has been summed up in the following statement:

This is the quintessence of wisdom: not to kill anything (*Ibid.*, Vol. 45, p. 247).

The Principles of Jainism

Among the sacred books of Jainism, the 12 *angas* hold the foremost position. In the second anga, called *sutra-keit-anga*, the following sayings are contained which give insight into the nature of Jainism:

> Know what causes the bondage of the soul; and knowing, try to remove it.
> All things are eternal by their very nature.
> As imprisoned birds do not get out of their cage, so those ignorant of right or wrong do not get out of their misery.
> There are three ways of committing sins: by our actions; by authorizing others, and by approval.
> A sage leads a life as far removed from love as from hate.
> All living beings hate pain: therefore do not injure them or kill them. This is the essence of wisdom: not to kill anything.
> Leave off pride, anger, deceit and greed.
> Men suffer individually for the deeds they themselves have done.
> The wise man should consider that not he alone suffers; all creatures in the world suffer.
> Conceit is a very thin thorn; it is difficult to pull out.
> No man should seek fame and respect by his austerities.
> A man should treat all creatures in the world as he himself would like to be treated.
> He who is purified by meditation is like a ship in the water that avoids all dangers until it reaches the shore.
> Do not maintain that there is no such thing as good or evil, but that there is good and evil.

The reason most Jains are wealthy is that their devotion to ahimsa precludes their assuming most manual jobs. They were left to run such non-life-threatening occupations as finance, commerce, and banking.

Jainism and Christianity

Jainism is a religion of legalism, for one attains his own salvation only through the path of rigid self-denial. There is no freedom in this religion, only rules. In contrast to this system which teaches salvation in the Hindu sense of the word (through self-effort), the biblical salvation sets one free through Jesus Christ, who said:

> If therefore the Son shall make you free, you shall be free indeed (John 8:36, NASB).
> Come to Me, all who are weary and heavy-laden, and I will give you rest. Take My yoke upon you, and learn from Me, for I am gentle and humble in heart; and you shall find rest for your souls. For My yoke is easy, and My load is light (Matthew 11:28-30, NASB).

The faith Jesus taught alleviates the burdens of people, while Jainism only adds to them.

Any concept of God in a personal sense is missing from Jainism. Mahavira and early Jainism rejected the idea of the existence of a supreme being. Although prayer and worship were not advocated by Mahavira himself, after his decease Jainism took to worshipping Mahavira and the Hindu deities.

The Bible condemns the worship of any other god apart from Yahweh.

"I am the Lord your God, who brought you out of the land of Egypt, out of the house of slavery. You shall have no other gods before Me" (Exodus 20:2,3, NASB).

The doctrine of ahimsa, which is central to the Jain belief, is impossible to practice fully since there is no way to avoid killing millions of micro-organisms every time even a glass of water is drunk. This in turn should produce bad karma and thereby make any salvation virtually impossible.

Furthermore, there is no established source of authority for Jain beliefs in light of existing disputes over which of the various books are to be considered authoritative. These books did not even take any permanent form until 1,000 years after the death of Mahavira.

Contrast that with the evidence for the authority of the biblical documents, especially the New Testament. Sir Frederic Kenyon, former director and principal librarian of the British Museum, wrote this about the New Testament:

> "The interval between the dates of original composition (of the New Testament) and the earliest extant evidence becomes so small as to be in fact negligible, and the last foundation for any doubt that the Scriptures have come down to us substantially as they were written has now been removed. Both the authenticity and the general integrity of the books of the New Testament may be regarded as finally established" (Sir Frederic Kenyon, *The Bible and Archaeology*, New York: Harper and Row, 1940, pp. 288, 289).

The failure of Jainism to advance much beyond certain areas of India speaks to the fact that it does not meet universal human need. This can be contrasted to Jesus Christ, whose impact is universal.

> Turn to Me, and be saved, all the ends of the earth; For I am God and there is no other (Isaiah 45:22, NASB).

Jesus sent his disciples out with these words:

> Go into all the world and preach the gospel to all creation (Mark 16:15, NASB).

> ...you shall be my witnesses both in Jerusalem, and in all Judea and Samaria, and even to the remotest part of the earth (Acts 1:8, NASB).

Griffith Thomas sums up the universal appeal of Christianity: "Other religions have had their ethical ideal of duty, opportunity, and even of love, but nowhere have they approached those of Christ, either in reality or in attractiveness or in power. Christ's message is remarkable for its *universal adaptation.* Its appeal is universal; it is adapted to all men from the adult down to the child; it makes its appeal to all times and not merely to the age in which it was first given. And the reason is that it emphasizes a threefold ethical attitude toward God and man which makes a universal appeal as nothing else does or perhaps can do. Christ calls for repentance, trust and love" (Griffith Thomas, *Christianity Is Christ*, Chicago: Moody Press, 1965, p. 35).

Comparison of Hinduism, Buddhism and Jainism

Hinduism, the mother religion, and its offshoots, Buddhism and

Jainism, have much in common. However, on certain issues they sharply disagree. Robert E. Hume lists both the areas of agreement and disagreement between the faiths:

Points of Agreement between All Three Religions

General pessimism concerning the worth of human life in the midst of the material and social world.

The specific worthlessness of the human body.

The specific worthlessness of human activity.

The specific worthlessness of the individual as such.

A common tendency to ascetic monastic orders.

A common tendency to sectarian subdivisions.

No program of organized social amelioration.

A common ideal of the greatest good as consisting in subservience, quiescence or passivity, certainly not universally beneficial.

A common ideal of salvation to be obtained by methods largely negative or repressive, certainly not self-expressive.

A common appreciation of a certain religious value in sufferings borne, even voluntarily self-imposed, for self-benefit.

A common belief in many prophets in the same religion, teaching the same eternal doctrines of that particular system.

A common belief in karma and transmigration.

Points of Disagreement among the Three Religions

	NATURE OF EVIL	METHOD OF OVERCOMING EVIL	RESULTING SALVATION
Philosophic Hinduism:	Intellectual—ignorance of Brahma	By knowledge of pantheism	Mystical reabsorption into the Infinite
Jainism:	Physical—encumbrance of body	By asceticism of body	Freedom of soul from worldly attachments
Fundamental Buddhism:	Emotional—unsatisfied desires	By suppression of desires	Passionless peace, nirvana

	MATERIAL WORLD	INDIVIDUAL SOUL	SUPREME SOUL
Philosophic Hinduism:	Unreal, an illusion	Unreal, a temporary emanation	The only Real, the All
Jainism:	Real	Real	Unreal
Fundamental Buddhism:	Unreal	Unreal	Unreal

	VALUE OF ASCETICISM	VALUE OF MORALITY
Philosophic Hinduism:	Optional, though theoretically unnecessary	Unimportant; ultimately illusory
Jainism:	Obligatory; the chief means of salvation	Relatively unimportant; list of prohibitions
Fundamental Buddhism:	Of desires, rather than of only the body	Quite important; yet distinctly subordinate

[Robert E. Hume, *The World's Living Religions*, New York: Charles Scribner's Sons, rev. ed., 1959, pp. 82-84].

Jainistic Terms

Ahimsa—The practice of non-violence and reverence for life. Ahimsa forbids the taking of animal life at any level.

Digambaras—The sect of Jainism that insists on going naked, as did the Mahavira, when duty called for it.

Five Great Vows—The principle of self-denial, central to Jain belief, which includes the renunciation of (1) killing living things, (2) lying, (3) greed, (4) sexual pleasure, (5) worldly attachments.

Jains—The designation for the disciples of Mahavira the Jina (the Conqueror).

Jina—Literally, "the conqueror." The designation given to Mahavira for his achievement of victory over his bodily desires. His disciples were thus named Jains.

Mahavira—An honorific title meaning "great man," given to the founder of Jainism.

Nirgrantha—Literally, "naked one." A person who practices asceticism in accordance with Jain principles.

Sallakhana—The rite of voluntary self-starvation which, according to tradition, took the life of Mahavira's parents.

Shvetambaras—"The white clad," one of the two main sects of Jainism. The Shvetambaras are the liberal wing who believe in wearing at least one garment in contrast to the Digambaras, who insist on wearing nothing when duty demands.

Sthanakvasis—A Jain sect that worships everywhere, not allowing for idols or temples.

Tirthankara—A savior being. According to Jain belief, Mahavira is the 24th Tirthankara, the last and greatest of the savior beings.

Twelve Angas—The part of the sacred scriptures of Jainism which holds the foremost position.

Venerable One—One of the titles given to the Mahavira by his later disciples.

Jainism Bibliography

Hume, Robert E., *The World's Living Religions*, New York: Charles Scribner's Sons, rev. ed., 1959.

Mueller, F. M., ed., *Sacred Books of the East*, vol. 22, Oxford: Krishna Press, 1879-1910.

Rawlings, Maurice, *Life-Wish: Reincarnation: Reality or Hoax*, Nashville: Thomas Nelson Inc., 1981.

Stroup, Herbert, *Four Religions of Asia*, New York: Harper and Row, 1968.

CHAPTER THREE

Buddhism

B uddhism began in India about 500 years before the birth of Christ. The people living at that time had become disillusioned with certain beliefs of Hinduism including the caste system, which had grown extremely complex. The number of outcasts (those who did not belong to any particular caste) was continuing to grow.

Moreover, the Hindu belief of an endless cycle of births, deaths and rebirths was viewed with dread. Consequently, the people turned to a variety of beliefs, including the worship of animals, to satisfy this spiritual vacuum. Many different sects of Hinduism arose, the most successful being that of Buddhism, which denies the authority of the vedas.

The Buddha

Buddhism, unlike Hinduism, can point to a specific founder. However, in Buddhism, like so many other religions, fanciful stories arose concerning events in the life of the founder, Siddhartha Gautama (fifth century B.C.):

> Works devoted to the exposition of philosophical doctrines or religions usually begin with the biography of the founder. Most of these biographies are, however, largely if not wholly mythical. The piety of the average disciples has never failed to make the sages whom they celebrate perform such impossible deeds as are calculated to increase their renown in the eyes of the people, so that often enough within a few years of their death many of these masters are already seen to be transformed into mythological figures.
>
> The Buddha was no exception. Archaeological discoveries have proved, beyond a doubt, his historical character, but apart from the legends we know very little about the circumstances of his life (Alexandra David-Neel, *Buddhism: Its Doctrines and Its Methods*, New York: St. Martin's Press, 1977, p. 15).

Though Buddha, as well as other religious leaders, was deified by later disciples, this was not the case with Jesus of Nazareth. The accounts of His miracles and His claims as to being God in human flesh were recorded from eyewitness testimony rather than having been developed over a long period of time. (See 1 John 1:1-3 and 2 Peter 1:16.)

Early Biography

The Buddha, or "enlightened one," was born about 560 B.C. in north-eastern India. His family name was Gautama, his given name Siddhartha. Siddhartha was the son of a rajah, or ruler. His mother died when he was just a week old and Siddhartha was cared for by his mother's sister, who was also the rajah's second wife. There was supposedly a prophecy given at the time of his birth by a sage at his father's court.

The prophecy said that the child would be a great king if he stayed at home, but if he decided to leave home, he would become a savior for mankind. This bothered his father, for he wanted his son to succeed him as king. Therefore, to keep him at home, his father surrounded him with wealth and pleasures and kept all painful and ugly things out of his sight.

Siddhartha eventually married and had a son but was still confined to the palace and its pleasures. One day he informed his father that he wished to see the world. This excursion would forever change his life, for it was during this journey that he saw "the four passing sights."

Although his father ordered the streets to be cleansed and decorated and all elderly or infirmed people to stay inside, there were those who did not get the message. The first troubling sight Siddhartha saw was that of a decrepit old man. When Siddhartha asked what happened to this man, he was told that the man was old, as everyone someday would become.

Later, he met a sick man and was told that all people were liable to be sick and suffer pain like that individual.

He then saw a funeral procession with a corpse on its way to cremation, the followers weeping bitterly. When asked what that meant, the prince was informed that it was the way of life, for sooner or later both prince and pauper would have to die.

The last sight was that of a monk begging for his food. The tranquil look on the beggar's face convinced Siddhartha that this type of life was for him. Immediately he left the palace and his family in search of enlightenment. The night that he left his home to seek enlightenment became known as the Great Renunciation.

The former prince, now a beggar, spent his time wandering from place to place seeking wisdom. Unsatisfied by the truths taught in the Hindu scriptures, he became discouraged but continued on his quest. He tried asceticism but this gave him no peace. The fateful day in his life came while he was meditating beneath a fig tree.

Buddha's Enlightenment

Deep in meditation, he reached the highest degree of God-consciousness, known as nirvana. He supposedly stayed under the fig tree for seven days, after that, the fig tree was called the bodhi, or the bo tree, the tree of wisdom. The truths he learned he would now impart to the world, no longer as Siddhartha Gautama, but as the Buddha, the enlightened one.

When the Buddha emerged from his experience under the bo tree, he met with five monks who had been his companions. It was to these monks that the Buddha began his teaching ministry with the sermon at Benares. The sermon contained the following:

> These two extremes, monks, are not to be practiced by one who has gone forth from the world. What are the two? That conjoined with the passions and luxury, which is low, vulgar, common, ignoble, and useless; and that conjoined with self-torture, which is painful, ignoble, and useless. Avoiding these two extremes the Blessed One has gained the enlightenment of the Middle Path, which produces insight and knowledge, and leads to calm, to higher knowledge, enlightenment, nirvana.
>
> And what, monks, is the Middle Path...? It is the noble Eightfold Path: namely, right view, right intention, right speech, right action, right livelihood, right effort, right mindfulness, right concentration...
>
> Now this, monks, is the noble truth of pain (dukkha): birth is painful, old age is painful, sickness is painful, death is painful, sorrow, lamentation, dejection, and despair are painful. Contact with unpleasant things is painful, not getting what one wishes is painful. In short the five components of existence are painful.
>
> Now this, monks, is the noble truth of the cause of pain: the craving, which tends to rebirth, combined with pleasure and lust, finding pleasure here and there; namely, the craving for passion, the craving for existence, the craving for non-existence.
>
> Now this, monks, is the noble truth of the cessation of pain, the cessation without a remainder of craving, the abandonment, forsaking, release, nonattachment.
>
> Now this, monks, is the noble truth of the path that leads to the cessation of pain: this is the noble Eightfold Path (E. A. Burtt, ed., *The Teachings of the Compassionate Buddha*, New York: New American Library, 1955, pp. 29, 30).

After the sermon at Benares, the Buddha started to spread his teachings to the people of India. The Indian people, disillusioned with Hinduism, listened intently to this new doctrine. By the time of Buddha's death, at age 80, his teachings had become a strong force in India.

The Death of Buddha

The following discourse is from the Tripitaka. The dying Buddha is instructing a young monk against craving, one of the major doctrines of Theravada Buddhism:

> I am old now, Ananda, and full of years: my journey nears its end, and I have reached my sum of days, for I am nearly eighty years old. Just as a worn out cart can only be kept going if it is tied up with thongs, so the body of the Tathagata can only be kept going by bandaging it.
>
> Only when the Tathagata no longer attends to any outward object, when all separate sensations stops and he is deep in inner concentration, is his body at ease.
>
> So, Ananda, you must be your own lamps, be your own refuges. Take refuge in nothing outside yourselves. Hold firm to the truth as a lamp and a refuge, and do not look for refuge to anything besides yourselves. A monk becomes his own lamp and refuge by continually looking on his body, feelings, perceptions, moods, and ideas in such a manner that he conquers the cravings and

depressions of ordinary men and is always strenuous, self-possessed, and collected in mind. Whoever among my monks does this, either now or when I am dead, if he is anxious to learn, will reach the summit.

The Four Noble Truths and the Eightfold Path

The First Noble Truth is the existence of suffering. Birth is painful, and death is painful; disease and old age are painful. Not having what we desire is painful, and having what we do not desire is also painful.

The Second Noble Truth is the cause of suffering. It is the craving desire for the pleasures of the senses, which seeks satisfaction now here, now there; the craving for happiness and prosperity in this life and in future lives.

The Third Noble Truth is the ending of suffering. To be free of suffering one must give up, get rid of, extinguish this very craving, so that no passion and no desire remain.

The Fourth Noble Truth leads to the ending of all pain by way of the Eightfold Path.

The first step on that path is *Right Views:* You must accept the Four Noble Truths and the Eightfold Path.

The second step is *Right Resolve:* You must renounce the pleasures of the senses; you must harbor no ill will toward anyone and harm no living creature.

The third step is *Right Speech:* Do not lie; do not slander or abuse anyone. Do not indulge in idle talk.

The fourth is *Right Behavior:* Do not destroy any living creature; take only what is given to you; do not commit any unlawful sexual act.

The fifth is *Right Occupation:* You must earn your livelihood in a way that will harm no one.

The sixth is *Right Effort:* You must resolve and strive heroically to prevent any evil qualities from arising in you and to abandon any evil qualities that you may possess. Strive to acquire good qualities and encourage those you do possess to grow, increase and be perfected.

The seventh is *Right Contemplation:* Be observant, strenuous, alert, contemplative, free of desire and of sorrow.

The eighth is *Right Meditation:* When you have abandoned all sensuous pleasures, all evil qualities, both joy and sorrow, you must then enter the four degrees of meditation, which are produced by concentration.

The Veneration of The Buddha

Some time after his death, the Buddha was deified by some of his followers. The following description of him is typical of the adulation he was given:

1. The countenance of the Buddha is like the clear full moon,
   Or again, like a thousand suns releasing their splendour.
   His eyes are pure, as large and as broad as a blue lotus.
   His teeth are white, even and close, as snowy as white jade.

2. The Buddha's virtues resemble the boundless great ocean.
   Infinite wonderful jewels are amassed within it.
   The calm, virtuous water of wisdom always fills it.
   Hundreds and thousands of supreme concentrations throng it.

3. The marks of the wheel beneath his feet are all elegant—
   The hub, the rim, and the thousand spokes which are all even.
   The webs on his hands and his feet are splendid in all parts—
   He is fully endowed with markings like the king of geese.

4. The Buddha-body's radiance is like a golden mountain's;
   It is clear, pure, peculiar, without equal or likeness,
   And it too has the virtues of beauty and loftiness.
   Therefore I bow my head to the Buddha, king of mountains.

5. His marks and signs are as unfathomable as the sky.
   And they surpass a thousand suns releasing their splendour.
   All like a flame or a phantom are inconceivable.
   Thus I bow my head to him whose mind has no attachments
   (Richard Robinson, trans., *Chinese Buddhist Verse*, London: Greenwood
   Publ., 1954, p. 48).

Such veneration of the Buddha is against the basic teachings of Buddha
himself.

Theravada and Mahayana Buddhism

Early Buddhism was confined largely to India and is usually referred
to as Theravada Buddhism. Later Buddhism, which became very popular
outside of India (notably in China and Japan), became known as
Mahayana Buddhism:

> By the time of King Asoka (c. 236-232 B.C.), Indian Buddhism had split into
> a number of groups generally referred to as Theravada schools. Again, around
> the beginning of the Christian era, Mahayana Buddhism arose, being distin-
> guished from Theravada Buddhism primarily by its enlargement of the bod-
> hisattva ideal, according to which certain compassionate beings or bodhi-
> sattvas defer their own emancipation in order to save others, and by its conse-
> quent enlargement of the offer of salvation, making it available not only to
> those who enter monastic orders but to all who trust in a bodhisattva.
>
> For several centuries Buddhism continued to evolve in India, developing in
> interaction with the various Indian religions and philosophies, but due to the
> Islamic invasion of the thirteenth century, it ceased to exist in the land of
> its birth (Agency for Cultural Affairs, *Japanese Religion: A Survey*, Tokyo, New
> York and San Francisco: Kodansha International Ltd., 1972, 1981, p. 48).

As we can see from the comparative chart below, Mahayana Buddhism
had many qualities which differed from Theravada Buddhism but which
were very attractive to new converts:

Theravada	*Mahayana*
Man as an individual	Man as involved with others
Man on his own in the universe (emancipation by self-effort)	Man not alone (salvation by grace)
Key virtue: wisdom	Key virtue: *karuna,*

	compassion
Religion: a full-time job	Religion: relevant to life
(primarily for monks)	in the world (for laymen as well)
Ideal: the Arhat	Ideal: the Bodhisattva
Buddha: a saint	Buddha: a savior
Eschews metaphysics	Elaborates metaphysics
Eschews ritual	Includes ritual
Confines prayer to	Includes petitionary
meditation	prayer
Conservative	Liberal

(Huston Smith, *The Religions of Man*, New York: Harper and Row, 1958, p. 138).

Nirvana

A key concept in Buddhism is nirvana, the final goal for the Buddhists. Donald K. Swearer gives insight to this important concept.

Nirvana has been a troublesome idea for students of Buddhism. Just what is it? The term itself does not offer much help. Like not-self (*an-atta*), nirvana is a negative term. Literally, it means the "blowing out" of the flame of desire, the negation of suffering (*dukkha*). This implies that nirvana is not to be thought of as a place but as a total reorientation or state of being realized as a consequence of the extinction of blinding and binding attachment. Thus, at least, nirvana implies that the kind of existence one has achieved is inconceivable in the ordinary terms of the world (Donald K. Swearer, *Buddhism*, Niles, IL: Argus Communications, 1977, p. 44).

The following texts mention nirvana:

Dispassion is called the Way. It is said: "Through dispassion is one freed." Yet, in meaning, all these (words: stopping, renunciation, surrender, release, lack of clinging) are synonyms for nirvana. For, according to its ultimate meaning, nirvana is the Aryan Truth of the stopping of suffering (Edward Conze, et. al, *Buddhist Texts Through the Ages*, New York: Philosophical Library, 1954, "Path of Purity 507," p. 100).

"Venerable Nagasena, things produced of karma are seen in the world, things produced of cause are seen, things produced of nature are seen. Tell me, what in the world is born not of karma, not of cause, not of nature" (*Ibid.*, "The Questions of King Milinda," p. 97).

There is, monks, that plane where there is neither extension nor. . . motion nor the plane of infinite space. . . nor that of neither-perception-nor-non-perception, neither this world nor another, neither the moon nor the sun. Here, monks, I say that there is no coming or going or remaining or deceasing or uprising, for this is itself without any support. . .

There is, monks, an unborn, not become, not made, uncompounded, and. . . because there is,. . . an escape can be shown for what is born, has become, is made, is compounded (*Ibid.*, "Udana 81," pp. 94, 95).

Swearer comments on these passages:

These three passages point to different aspects of the concept of nirvana. The first passage illustrates our initial claim about nirvana, namely, that it is the negation of attachment and suffering (dukkha). The second, a question from King Milinda, is answered, as you probably guessed, by nirvana. Nirvana, then, is the one thing that is not caused by anything else. The third quotation pushes this idea even further. Nirvana as the Absolute Truth cannot be adequately expressed in words. Nonetheless, the term implies that there is a goal to be reached and that this goal surpasses anything experienced in this world of conventional understanding (Swearer, *op. cit.*, p. 45).

Sacred Scriptures

In Theravada Buddhism there are three groups of writings considered to be holy scripture, known as "The Three Baskets" (Tripitaka). The Vinaya Pitaka (discipline basket) contains rules for the higher class of Buddhists; the Sutta Pitaka (teaching basket) contains the discourses of the Buddha; and the Abidhamma Pitaka (metaphysical basket) contains Buddhist theology. The total volume of these three groups of writings is about 11 times larger than the Bible.

In Mahayana Buddhism the scriptures are much more voluminous, as Clark B. Offner reveals:

"A Mahayanist is one who reads Mahayana scriptures" is the definition given by one ancient Buddhist scholar. In contrast to the comparatively limited scope of the Pali canon used by Theravada Buddhists, Mahayana scriptures have multiplied to the point where standard editions of the Chinese canon encompass over 5,000 volumes. While the oldest scriptures are based on Sanskrit and contain much that is parallel to the Pali canon, other scriptures which have no Sanskrit prototypes have been written in Nepalese, Tibetan and Chinese.

Since there are no clear limits to the Mahayana "canon," comparatively recent works by later innovators are often given *de facto* canonical status in the sects which adhere to their teachings. As there are such a number and such a variety of scriptures, most Mahayana sects have chosen certain favourite ones to which they refer exclusively. The fact is that some such selection is necessary, for this extreme bulk and breadth of the scriptures make it impossible for believers to be acquainted with, let alone understand and practise, the often contradictory teachings found in them (Clark B. Offner, in *The World's Religions*, Sir Norman Anderson, ed., Grand Rapids: William B. Eerdmans Publishing Company, 1976, p. 181).

The Laity

Conze explains how the laity can gain religious merit:

The layman's one and only religious task at present can be to increase his store of merit. The Buddhist religion offers him four avenues for doing so:

1. He must observe the five precepts, or at least some of them. On feast days, every fortnight, he may add to them another three, i.e., he fasts, avoids worldly amusements, and uses neither unguents nor ornaments. A few observed still two more precepts, i.e., they did not sleep on a high, big bed and they accepted no gold or silver.

2. He must have devotion for the Three Treasures and faith is the virtue apposite to a householder's state of life. But this faith is not an exclusive one and does not entail a rejection of his ancestral beliefs and of the Brahmanic religious usages of his social environment. The Triple Jewel is not a jealous God and is not displeased by the worship of the deities of a man's country or caste.

3. He must be generous, especially to the monks, and give as much as possible to them, not only for their upkeep, but also for religious buildings inhabited by no one. To some extent the merit produced by gifts depends on the spiritual endowments of the recipient, and therefore the sons of Sakya muni, and in particular the Arhats, are the best possible "field for planting merit."

4. He may worship the relics of the Buddha. The actual attitude of the Buddhists to these teeth and bones is difficult to describe in terms readily understood in the West. It is obviously impossible for them to "pray" to the Buddha, for the reason that He is no longer there, being in nirvana, i.e., extinct as far as this world is concerned (Edward Conze, *A Short History of Buddhism*, London: George Allen and Unwin Ltd., 1980, p. 39).

Buddhist Precepts

There are five precepts taught by Buddhism that all Buddhists should follow:

1. Kill no living thing (including insects).
2. Do not steal.
3. Do not commit adultery.
4. Tell no lies.
5. Do not drink intoxicants or take drugs.

There are other precepts that apply only to monks and nuns. These include:

6. Eat moderately and only at the appointed time.
7. Avoid that which excites the senses.
8. Do not wear adornments (including perfume).
9. Do not sleep in luxurious beds.
10. Accept no silver or gold.

A Buddhist Creed

In 1981, Colonel H. S. Olcott, one of the founding presidents of the Theosophical Society, proposed a common platform for all Buddhist schools of thought. Various representatives of different Buddhist persuasions reviewed his work and found it to be satisfactory. It was published as an appendix to his *Buddhist Catechism*. The fundamental Buddhistic beliefs are:

1. Buddhists are taught to show the same tolerance, forbearance, and brotherly love to all men, without distinction; and an unswerving kindness towards the members of the animal kingdom.

2. The Universe was evolved, not created; and it functions according to law, not according to the caprice of any God.

3. The truths upon which Buddhism is founded are natural. They have, we believe, been taught in successive kalpas, or world periods, by certain illuminated beings called Buddhas, the name Buddha meaning "enlightened."

4. The fourth teacher in the present kalpa was Sakya Muni, or Gautama Buddha, who was born in a royal family in India about 2,500 years ago. He is an historical personage and his name was Siddhartha Gautama.

5. Sakya Muni taught that ignorance produces desire, unsatisfied desire is the cause of rebirth, and rebirth the cause of sorrow. To get rid of sorrow, therefore, it is necessary to escape rebirth; to escape rebirth, it is necessary to extinguish desire; and to extinguish desire, it is necessary to destroy ignorance.

6. Ignorance fosters the belief that rebirth is a necessary thing. When ignorance is destroyed the worthlessness of every such rebirth, considered as an end in itself, is perceived, as well as the paramount need of adopting a course of life by which the necessity for such repeated births can be abolished. Ignorance also begets the illusive and illogical idea that there is only one existence for man, and the other illusion that this one life is followed by states of unchangeable pleasure or torment.

7. The dispersion of all this ignorance can be attained by the persevering practice of an all-embracing altruism in conduct, development of intelligence, wisdom in thought, and destruction of desire for the lower personal pleasures.

8. The desire to live being the cause of rebirth, when that is extinguished rebirths cease and the perfected individual attains by meditation that highest state of peace called nirvana.

9. Sakya Muni taught that ignorance can be dispelled and sorrow removed by the knowledge of the four Nobel Truths, viz:

   1. The miseries of existence;
   2. The cause productive of misery, which is the desire ever renewed of satisfying oneself without being able ever to secure that end;
   3. The destruction of that desire, or the estranging of oneself from it;
   4. The means of obtaining this destruction of desire. The means which he pointed out is called the Noble Eightfold Path, viz: Right Belief; Right Thought; Right Speech; Right Action; Right Means of Livelihood; Right Exertion; Right Remembrance; Right Meditation.

10. Right Meditation leads to spiritual enlightenment, or the development of that Buddha-like faculty which is latent in every man.

11. The essence of Buddhism as summed up by the Tathagata (Buddha) himself is:
    > To cease from all sin,
    > To get virtue,
    > To purify the heart

12. The universe is subject to a natural causation known as "karma." The merits and demerits of a being in past existences determine his condition in the present one. Each man, therefore, has prepared the causes of the effects which he now experiences.

13. The obstacles to the attainment of good karma may be removed by the observance of the following precepts, which are embraced in the moral code of Buddhism, viz: (1) Kill not; (2) Steal not; (3) Indulge in no forbidden sexual pleasure; (4) Lie not; (5) Take no intoxicating or stupefying drug or liquor. Five other precepts, which need not here be enumerated, should be observed by those who would attain more quickly than the average layman the release from misery and rebirth.

14. Buddhism discourages superstitious credulity. Gautama Buddha taught it to be the duty of a parent to have his child educated in science and literature. He also taught that no one should believe what is spoken by any sage, written in any book, or affirmed by a tradition, unless it accord with reason.

Drafted as a common platform upon which all Buddhists can agree (Cited by Christmas Humphreys, *Buddhism*, London: Penguin Books, 1951, pp. 71-73).

Sayings of the Buddha

The following extracts are from the Dhammadada, which contains a collection of sayings attributed to the Buddha:

VIGILANCE is the way of immortality (the Deathless). Heedlessness is the way of death. Those that are vigilant do not die. Those that are heedless are already as though dead.

Those who know these things, those who know how to meditate, they take this delight in meditation, and in the knowledge of the noble.

By meditation and perseverance, by tireless energy, the wise attain to nirvana, the supreme beatitude.

He who meditates earnestly, he who is pure in conduct and mindful of every action, he who is self-restrained and righteous in his life, the fame of such a one shall increase.

By diligent attention, by reflection, by temperance, by self-mastery, the man of understanding makes for himself an island that no flood can overwhelm.

Do not give yourselves over to heedlessness. Have naught to do with the lusts of the flesh. The vigilant man, who is given to meditation, he will attain to abundant happiness.

When the wise man in his vigilance puts away heedlessness and ascends the tower of wisdom, he looks down, being free from sorrow, upon the sorrow-laden race of mankind. As from a mountain-top, the wise man looks down upon the foolish men in the valley.

Vigilant among the heedless, waking among those who slumber, as a fleet courser outstrips a sorry nag, so the wise go their way.

By yourselves must the effort be made: the Tathàgatas do but make known the way.

Conquer wrath with benevolence, overcome evil with good. Confound the niggardly with liberality, and with truth the speaker of falsehoods.

Even as a solid rock is unshaken by the wind, so are the wise unmoved by praise or by blame.

Whoso seeks his own welfare by devising injury to another, he is entangled in hatred, and does not attain to freedom.

Let your words be truth, and give not way to anger; give of your little to him that asks of you; by these three things men go to the realm of the gods.

He who refrains from action when it is the time to act, he who in his youth and strength, gives himself over to idleness, he whose will and whose spirit are feeble, this slothful man shall never find the way that leads to Wisdom.

Stem the torrent with all thy might, O Brahmana. Having understood how the formations (*samskaras*) are dissolved, thou wilt understand that which is not formed (which is not a group of impermanent elements).

It is not plaited hair, nor birth, nor wealth that makes the Brahmana. He in whom truth and justice reside, he is happy, he is a Brahmana.

Of what avail thy plaited hair, O witless one? Of what avail thy goatskin garment? Within there is disorder: thou carest only for the outer man.

I do not call him "a Brahmana" who is born of such a family or such a mother. He may be arrogant, he may be rich. He who is poor and detached from all things—him I call a Brahmana.

He who has shattered all bonds, he who is inaccessible to fear, he who is free from all servitude and cannot be shaken—him I call a Brahmana.

He who has broken the thong, the cord, and the girth, he who has destroyed all obstacles, he who is the Awakened—him I call a Brahmana.

He from whom the delights of the senses fall away as water from the petal of the lotus or a mustard seed from the point of a needle—him do I call Brahmana.

He who in this world has been able to set a term to his suffering, he who has set down his burden, he whom nothing can trouble, him do I call a Brahmana.

He whose knowledge is profound, he who possesses wisdom, who discerns the right path from the wrong, who has attained the highest aim, him do I call a Brahmana.

He who holds himself apart, both from laymen and from monks, who contents himself with little and does not beat upon other men's doors—him do I call a Brahmana.

He who uses no violence, whether to the weak or the strong, who neither slays nor causes to be slain—him do I call a Brahmana.

He who is tolerant with the intolerant, gentle with the violent, without greed among the grasping—him do I call a Brahmana.

He from whom envy, hatred, pride and hypocrisy have fallen away like a mustard-seed placed on the point of a needle—him do I call a Brahmana.

He whose speech is instructive and truthful and without harshness, offending none—him do I call a Brahmana.

He who no longer covets aught, whether in this world or another, he who is unattached and inaccessible to trouble—him do I call a Brahmana.

He who is free from all ties, whom knowledge preserves from questioning, who has attained to the depths where death is not—him do I call a Brahmana.

He who in this world has shaken off the two chains; the chain of Good and the chain of Evil; who is pure and exempt from suffering and passion—him do I call a Brahmana.

He who in his serenity, his purity, his changeless peace is radiant as the flawless moon, who has dried up within him the source of all joy—him do I call a Brahmana.

He who has traversed the miry path, the inextricable world, so difficult to traverse, and all its vanities, he also, having achieved the passage, and has reached the further shore, who is meditative, unshaken, exempt from doubts, unattached and satisfied—him do I call a Brahmana.

He who, putting off all human ties, has risen above all divine ties, who has liberated himself from every tie—him do I call a Brahmana.

He who has rejected that which causes pleasure and that which causes suffering, he who is impassive, liberated from all germs, the hero who has raised himself above all the worlds—him do I call a Brahmana.

Nichiren Shoshu Buddhism

One form of Buddhism that has seen a revival of sorts in the past 50 years is a Japanese mystical sect known as Nichiren Shoshu. Its recent growth has been astounding, as chronicled by Walter Martin:

> Nichiren Shoshu continued as a small sect of Buddhism until the founding in Japan of the Soka Gakkai (Value Creation Society), by Makiguchi Tsunesaburo in 1930. Known first as Soka Kyoiku Gakkai and founded by Makiguchi Tsunesaburo and Josei Toda, Soka Gakkai is the Japanese lay organization of Nichiren Shoshu and has become the evangelistic arm of the religion.
>
> When the Japanese government attempted to unify all of Japan under Shinto Buddhism in 1940, only Nichiren Shoshu refused to obey. (NSB claims to be the only orthodox sect among the many sects claiming Nichiren Daishonin as their founders.) In 1940 there were only 21 members, all of whom were arrested. Nineteen of those members converted to Shintoism and were released. Leader Makiguchi died in prison, and the only remaining member, Josei Toda, was released from prison in 1945, shortly before the end of World War Two.
>
> Under Toda's leadership, the movement began growing and elected Toda the second president of Soka Gakkai. In 1960 Daisaku Ikeda was inaugurated president over 1.3 million members. Ikeda expanded NSB's evangelism in foreign countries, opening a branch in the United States in 1960. The quickly growing branch of the sect held its first convention in 1963 in Chicago, with representatives from ten chapters. By 1973, membership was more than 250,000. From 1960 to 1973, NSB in the United States increased three-hundredfold! Japanese growth was even faster. The number of practicing Japanese families grew from three thousand in 1951 to more than seven million in 1971 (Walter Martin, ed., *The New Cults*, Santa Ana, CA: Vision House Publishers Inc., 1980, p. 323).

The origins of Nichiren Shoshu go back to a Japanese reformer named Nichiren Daishonon, who lived in the 13th century A.D.

Nichiren

Nichiren was born the son of a fisherman in Japan in A.D. 1222 (and died in A.D. 1282) during a time of turmoil in Japan. Christmas Humphreys sets the historical background of the time of Nichiren's birth:

> In the last half of the twelfth century, the Kyoto Government had so degenerated that civil war broke out. After fifty or more bloody years of strife, in which Buddhist monasteries were more than once engaged, a few of the stronger feudal lords gained power, and after fighting each other to a standstill left the Minamoto family, with the great Yorimoto at its head, in control at the new capital of Kamakura. Thereafter, until 1868, the Emperor was more or less a puppet, and Japan was ruled by hereditary Shoguns.
>
> The civil wars had developed and perfected the cult of Bushido, the eastern equivalent of the western cult of knighthood, and the cult was ripe for spiritual guidance. The existing Buddhist sects, discredited to some extent by participation in the political wars of Kyoto, were not suited to the needs of the new capital, and the people as a whole, as well as their feudal overlords, needed

new forms of Buddhism. The need produced the supply, and within a century three new schools arose, the *Jodo* of China, elaborated in Japan into *Jodo-Shin* or *Shin*, the Chinese *Ch'an*, now to be known as *Zen*, and the School of the firebrand Nichiren (1222-1282) (Christmas Humphreys, *op. cit.*, pp. 174, 175)

Nichiren studied the various schools of Buddhism until deciding upon which of the teachings were true. He was convinced that the true faith was taught by Dengyo Daishi (named Saicho before his death) who had introduced Tendai Buddhism to Japan in the eighth century. Dengyo Daishi taught that only one scripture was of supreme authority, the Lotus Sutra. Nichiren believed if he could get his people back to the Lotus Sutra, which he believed was the true interpretation of the words of Buddha, the country could be saved.

Nichiren went about preaching his newly discovered truth, condemning all others as false religions. This did not go over well with the authorities, making Nichiren the object of persecution. Nichiren was both arrested and exiled for his preaching, many times narrowly escaping with his life. At the time of his death in 1282 he had attracted many followers to his rediscovered truth.

The Lotus Sutra

Nichiren believed that the Lotus Sutra contained the true teaching of the Buddha, but the facts contradict his belief. The Lotus Sutra was composed somewhere between the second century B.C. and the second century A.D. The work differs in several aspects from traditional Buddhist beliefs. Edward Rice elaborates:

> The work stresses the eternal Buddha-principle, represented in innumerable forms to work out the salvation of all suffering humanity. In the Lotus Sutra, Buddha is the eternal, omniscient, omnipotent, omnipresent; creator-destroyer, re-creator of all worlds—concepts borrowed from Hinduism and carried over into Mahayana Buddhism...*Its central thesis is that of universal salvation: Everyone and everything have within the potentiality of Buddhahood (Edward Rice, *Eastern Definitions*, New York: Doubleday, 1980, p. 238).

The following is an extract from the Lotus Sutra:

> Those among the living beings,
> Who have come into contact with former Buddhas,
> And have learned the Law and practiced charity,
> Or have held on to discipline and endured forbearance and humiliation,
> Or have made serious efforts at concentration and understanding,
> Or have cultivated various kinds of blessing and wisdom—
> All such beings as these
> Have already achieved Buddhahood...
> Men who possess a tender heart....
> Those who have offered relics,
> Or have built hundreds of millions of pagodas.....
> Those who have had pictures of the Buddha embroidered,

---

*See our earlier section on the two main branches of Buddhism.

Expressing the great splendor
Which he achieved from a hundred merits and blessings,
Whether embroidered by himself or by others,
Have all achieved Buddhahood.
Even boys at play
Who have painted Buddha figures
With straws, wooden sticks, brushes, or finger nails—
All people such as these,
By gradual accumulation of merits
And with an adequate sense of compassion,
Have already achieved Buddhahood.

Worship

Central to Nichiren Shoshu belief is the "gohonzon." The gohonzon is a black wooden box containing the names of important people in the Lotus Sutra and is used as a private altar. The gohonzon supposedly contains universal forces that control the devotee's life. There is, they believe, a direct connection between events in a person's life and the treatment of the gohonzon.

The worship ritual practiced by Nichiren Shoshu members is called "gongyo." The practice consists of kneeling before the gohonzon, the recitation of passages from the Lotus Sutra, then the rubbing of rosary-type beads while chanting the daimoku—"nam-myoho-renge-kyo."

The chief object of worship in Nichiren Shoshu Buddhism is a shrine known as the Dai-gohonzon located at the base of Mount Fuji in Japan. The individual gohonzons are mystical representations of the Dai-gohonzon.

Missionary Emphasis

Nichiren Shoshu's recent accelerated growth (1970 figures by the Japanese Office of Cultural Affairs put membership at over 16 million*) can be attributed directly to its missionary emphasis. Their members practice a proselytizing method called "Shakubuku," their goal being to convert the world to the one true faith:

> Soka Gakkai regards itself as not only the one true Buddhist religion, but the one true religion on earth. Its principal aims are the propagation of its gospel throughout the world, by forced conversion if necessary, and the denunciation and destruction of all other faiths as "false" religions. . . Soka Gakkai is unmistakably a church militant in Japan geared for a determined march abroad. Its significance to America and all nations cannot be ignored. Its target is world domination (Richard Okamoto, "Japan," *Look*, September 10, 1963, p. 16).

Zen Buddhism

Zen is a branch of Mahayana Buddhism that has become widely known in the West.

---

*Agency for Cultural Affairs, *op. cit.*, p. 208.

The Chinese added to the many schools of Buddhism a new school, whose name reveals its history. Dhyana is the Indian word for meditation; it was changed in China to Chan and in Japan to Zen, which is now the best-known title of this sect (Elizabeth Seeger, *Eastern Religions*, New York: Crowell, 1973, p. 145).

The exact origin of Zen is unknown. Legend has it that Zen's teaching was derived from Bodhidharma, a wandering Buddhist master living in India 600 years before Christ. Bodhidharma supposedly told a Chinese emperor that the basic tenets of Buddhism are not dependent upon the scriptures; its teachings were directly transmitted from mind to mind and do not need to be explained in words. This sums up Zen's unorthodox approach to its teaching, for they have no sacred literature which they use for their instruction but employ any writings, Buddhistic or not, they deem necessary to further their religion. Bodhidharma summed up the Zen viewpoint with this famous saying:

A special tradition outside the scriptures,
No dependence on words,
A direct pointing at man,
Seeing into one's own nature and the attainment of wisdom

Development

Zen actually developed about one thousand years after the death of the Buddha. However, it contains Buddha's emphasis on meditation which led to his enlightenment. One statement attributed to the Buddha has become a frequent reference by Zen teachers: "Look within, you are the Buddha."

This goes along with Buddha's deathbed statement that his disciples must find their own ways through self-effort. This self-effort is the foundation of Zen practice, for only through disciplined individual work can one attain enlightenment, known in Zen as "Kensho" or "Satori."

Zen has found great popularity in the West, with a large selection of literature available on the subject, including such titles as *Zen and the Art of Motorcycle Maintenance, The Zen of Seeing*, and *Zen and Creative Management*. The list of titles is long and varied.

One famous story tells about a man who desired to be a Zen master. He asked to be taught Zen. The Zen master did not speak but began to pour a cup of tea for his visitor, using a cup that was already filled. The extra tea overflowed and ran across the table to drip to the rice-mat-covered floor. Still the Zen master kept pouring until the pot was empty. He finally spoke: "You are like this cup," he said. "You are full. How can I pour Zen into you? Empty yourself and come back."

Zazen

Central to Zen practice is *zazen*. Zazen is the method of sitting in Zen meditation, which is done daily at specific times with occasional periods of intense meditation lasting one week. The goal is final enlightenment. The practice of zazen is done under the guiding hand of a master (roshi). Nancy Wilson-Ross elucidates:

The very heart of Zen practice lies in zazen, or sitting meditation done at specific times daily, with longer and more intensive periods on occasions of sesshin, in which concentrated "sitting" may endure for as long as a week. Zazen is a formalized procedure which consists of active meditation interspersed with the chanting of sutras. In this daily Zen chanting the sutra known as the *Prajna Paramita* is always included. The actual sitting itself is preceded by prescribed use of bells, wooden clappers and the exchange of formal bows. Practitioners sit facing a wall or the center of the zendo, depending on the tradition of the specific sect to which the group belongs or the preference of the presiding Zen roshi.

The usual zazen posture is the full lotus or half-lotus cross-legged sitting position on a specific type of round cushion. The position of the hands is strictly specified: they are held in front of the abdomen, the back of the left in the palm of the right, the thumbs lightly touching. The eyes are not closed, although the gaze is directed downward and is fixed a little in advance of the sitter. Zazen is terminated by the sound of wooden clappers, the ringing of a bell three times and the chanting of the Four Great Vows. Periods of formal sitting may be interspersed by walking meditation, known as *kinhin*. This is essentially a method for giving the body relief from the prolonged sitting posture, but it serves also as a way of practicing concentration, whether during a slow circling of the zendo or in a brisk walk outside (Nancy Wilson-Ross, *Buddhism: A Way of Thought*, New York, Alfred A. Knopf, Inc., 1980, p. 143).

The Koan

The master, in attempting to aid his pupil toward enlightenment, gives him a verbal puzzle known as a *koan*. Solving the koan supposedly leads the pupil into greater self-awareness. Commonly used koans by Zen masters number about 1,700, each of which may have hundreds of "answers" depending upon the exact circumstances of the students' training, Knowing the answer is not nearly as important as experiencing or realizing the answer. The following are some examples of koans:

A master, Wu Tsu, says, "Let me take an illustration from a fable. A cow passes by a window. Its head, horns, and the four legs all pass by. Why did not the tail pass by?"

What was the appearance of your face before your ancestors were born?

We are all familiar with the sound of two hands clapping. What is the sound of one hand? (If you protest that one hand can't clap, you go back to the foot of the class. Such a remark simply shows you haven't even begun to get the point.)

Li-ku, a high government officer of the T'ang dynasty, asked a famous Ch'an master: "A long time ago a man kept a goose in a bottle. It grew larger and larger until it could not get out of the bottle anymore. He did not want to break the bottle, nor did he wish to hurt the goose; how would you get it out?"
The master called out, "O Officer!"
"Yes," was the response.
"There, it's out!"

A monk asked Chao-chou, "What is the meaning of Bodhidharma's visit to China?" "The cypress tree in the courtyard," replied Bodhidharma.

A monk asked Thich Cam Thanh, "What is Buddha?" "Everything." The monk then asked, "What is the mind of Buddha?" "Nothing has been hidden." The monk said again, "I don't understand." Cam Thanh replied, "You missed!"

Satori

In Zen the sudden illumination or enlightenment is known as *satori*. Satori is an experience beyond analyzation and communication, bringing the practitioner into a state of maturity. The experience of satori comes abruptly and momentarily, but it can be repeated. It cannot be willed into existence.

Evaluation

Huston Smith gives an insightful evaluation of Zen belief:

> Entering the Zen outlook is like stepping through Alice's looking glass. One finds oneself in a topsy-turvy wonderland in which everything seems quite mad — charmingly mad for the most part but mad all the same. It is a world of bewildering dialogues, obscure conundrums, stunning paradoxes, flagrant contradictions, and abrupt non sequiturs, all carried off in the most urbane, cheerful and innocent style (Huston Smith, *op. cit.*, p. 140).

Part of Zen's attraction is that one is not required to be responsible in evaluating anything in the world or even in his own thoughts. One loses his capacity to think logically and critically. While the Bible commands Christians to test *all* things (1 Thessalonians 5:21, 22), Zen mocks critical analysis.

Buddhism and Christianity

There are radical differences between Buddhism and Christianity that make any attempt of reconciliation between the two faiths impossible. The Buddhistic world view is basically monistic. That is, the existence of a personal creator and Lord is denied. The world operates by natural power and law, not divine command.

Buddhism denies the existence of a personal God.

> Any concept of God was beyond man's grasp and since Buddhism was a practical approach to life, why not deal with practical things? India, where Buddhism was born, had so many Hindu gods that no one could number them. They were often made in the image of men, but Buddhism was made in the image of concepts, great concepts about life and how life should be lived. If the truth were known, you often tell yourself, Buddhism has no God in the Hindu or Christian sense, nor does it have a saviour or a messiah. It has the Buddha. And he was the Enlightened One, the Shower-of-the Way (Marcus Bach, *Had You Been Born in Another Faith*, Englewood Cliffs, NJ: Prentice-Hall, 1961, p. 47).

There are those who deify the Buddha but along with him they worship other gods. The Scriptures make it clear that not only does a personal God exist, but He is to be the only object of worship. "'You are My witnesses,' declares the Lord, 'And My servant whom I have chosen, in order that you may know and believe Me, and understand that I am

He. Before Me there was no God formed, and there will be none after Me'" (Isaiah 43:10 NASB). "Thus says the Lord, the King of Israel and His Redeemer, the Lord of hosts: 'I am the first and I am the last, and there is no God besides Me'" (Isaiah 44:6 NASB). "'I am the Lord your God, who brought you out of the land of Egypt, out of the house of slavery. You shall have no other gods before Me'" (Exodus 20:2, 3 NASB). "Then Jesus said to him, 'Begone, Satan! For it is written, "You shall worship the Lord your God, and serve Him only""'" (Matthew 4:10 NASB). "Jesus therefore said to them again, 'Truly, truly, I say to you, I am the door of the sheep. All who came before Me are thieves and robbers; but the sheep did not hear them. I am the door; if anyone enters through Me, he shall be saved and shall go in and out, and find pasture'" (John 10:7-9 NASB).

There is no such thing in Buddhism as sin against a supreme being. In Christianity sin is ultimately against God although sinful actions also affect man and his world. The Bible makes it clear, "against thee, thee only, I have sinned, and done what is evil in thy sight" (Psalm 51:4, NASB). Accordingly man needs a savior to deliver him from his sins.

The Bible teaches that Jesus Christ is that Savior and He offers the gift of salvation to all those who will believe, "The next day he saw Jesus coming to him, and said, 'Behold, the Lamb of God who takes away the sin of the world!'" (John 1:29 NASB). "And she will bear a Son; and you shall call His name Jesus, for it is he who will save His people from their sins" (Matthew 1:21 NASB). "For the wages of sin is death, but the free gift of God is eternal life in Christ Jesus our Lord" (Romans 6:23 NASB).

According to Buddhist belief, man is worthless, having only temporary existence. In Christianity man is of infinite worth, made in the image of God, and will exist eternally. Man's body is a hindrance to the Buddhist while to the Christian it is an instrument to glorify God.

The Scriptures reveal, "Then God said, 'Let us make man in our image, according to our likeness; and let them rule over the fish of the sea and over the birds of the sky and over the cattle and over all the earth, and over every creeping thing that creeps on the earth'" (Genesis 1:26 NASB). "Or do you not know that your body is a temple of the Holy Spirit who is in you, whom you have from God, and that you are not your own?" (1 Corinthians 6:19 NASB).

Another problem with Buddhism is the many forms it takes. Consequently, there is a wide variety of belief in the different sects with much that is contradictory. John B. Noss makes an appropriate comment:

"The rather odd fact is that there ultimately developed within Buddhism so many forms of religious organization, cultus and belief, such great changes even in the fundamentals of the faith, that one must say Buddhism as a whole is really, like Hinduism, a family of religions rather than a single religion" (John B. Noss, *Man's Religions*, New York: Macmillan Company, 1969, p. 146).

With these and other differences, it can be seen readily that any harmonization of the two religions simply is not possible.

Buddhistic Terms

An-Atta—Literally, "not self." A concept in Theravada Buddhism denying the permanent existence of self as contained by physical and mental attributes.

Bhikkhu—A Buddhist monk who wanders about depending upon others for his basic necessities.

Bodhi—A Buddhist term for the wisdom by which one attains enlightenment.

Bodhisattva—In Mahayana Buddhism, one who postpones attaining nirvana in order to help others achieve this goal. In Theravada Buddhism, it is one who is on the way to becoming a Buddha. Gautama was called a Bodhisattva before he attained enlightenment.

Buddha—"The enlightened one." This title was given to Siddhartha Gautama, the founder of Buddhism, upon his enlightenment. Likewise, a person can attain this position through following the fourfold path to enlightenment.

Buddhism—The religion based upon the teachings of the Buddha (Siddhartha Gautama). The Buddha's main teaching revolved around the causes for human suffering and the way to salvation from this suffering could be achieved. The two main branches of Buddhism are called Mahayana and Theravada or Hinayana.

Dalai Lama—The title of the head of the hierarchal system of Tibetan Buddhism. Worshipped as the reincarnation of Bodhisattva Chenresi.

Dhamma—The teachings of the Buddha. Related to the Sanskrit *Dharma*, or virtuous principles.

Dukkha—Suffering, which is rooted in desire and attachment.

Gohonzon—A small black wooden box used as an object of religious devotion, an altar, in Nichiren Shoshu Buddhism.

Heart Sutra—One of the most important scriptures to Zen Buddhists.

Koan—A verbal puzzle in Zen Buddhism which aids the pupil in loosing himself from this world and moving toward enlightenment.

Mahayana—The form of Buddhism prevalent in China, Japan, Korea and Vietnam. Literally translated, means "the great vehicle."

Maya—In Buddhism, the mother of Siddhartha Gautama (the Buddha). (See under *Hindu Terms* for additional meanings.)

Nirvana—A difficult, if not impossible, word to define. In Buddhism, it is basically a blissful spiritual condition where the heart extinguishes passion, hatred and delusion. It is the highest spiritual plane one person can attain.

Pitaka—Literally, "basket." Refers to the "three baskets" (Tripitaka) of sacred Buddhist writings.

Pure Land—Refers to a teaching in the Lotus Sutra which emphasizes faith in the Buddha of immeasurable light (Buddha Amitabha) and the goal of rebirth in his heaven of the pure land. Emphasizes easy attainment of nirvana. There are also Chinese and Japanese Pure Land sects.

Pure Land Buddhism—A sect that bases its faith in the Amida Buddha (the Buddha of the infinite light) as its saviour who will lead his followers into a celestial paradise. Salvation is achieved by repeating Amida's name (the Nembutsu).

Samsara —The cycle of birth, suffering, death and rebirth.

Sangha —The Buddhist monastic order literally translated as "group" or "community." May be the oldest order in Buddhism.

Satori —The term for enlightenment in Zen Buddhism.

Soka Gakkai —The Creative-Value Study Society. The modern revival of a thirteenth century Buddhist sect, Nichiren Shoshu.

Stupas —Originally, burial mounds, now used as relic chambers or memorials, especially of the Buddha.

Theravada —Literally the "teachings of the elders." The form of Buddhism that arose early among Buddha's disciples. Also called Hinayana Buddhism. Prevails in Southeast Asia.

Tibetan Buddhism (Lamaism) —A sect of Buddhism that began in Tibet in the seventh century A.D. It combined Buddhist principles with the occult religion of Tibet, producing Lamaism. The priests are all called Lamas and at the head is the Dalai Lama, a man who is worshipped as the reincarnated Bodhisattva Chenresi (Avalokita).

Tripitaka —See Pitaka.

True Sect of the Pure Land —A sect emphasizing the teachings of Pure Land (see above entry), founded in the thirteenth century by Shinran. Today it is the largest of any Buddhist sect in Japan.

Vinaya —The first of the three parts of the Pitaka, or scriptures of Buddhism, containing the rules of discipline of the Buddhist monastic order.

Zazen —Zen meditation, concentrating on a problem or koan (see below).

Buddhism Bibliography

Agency for Cultural Affairs, *Japanese Religion: A Survey*, Tokyo, New York, and San Francisco: Kodansha International Ltd., 1972, 1981.

Bach, Marcus, *Had You Been Born in Another Faith*, Englewood Cliffs, NJ: Prentice-Hall, 1961.

Burtt, E. A., ed., *The Teachings of the Compassionate Buddha*, New York: New American Library, 1955.

Conze, Edward, *A Short History of Buddhism*, London: George Allen and Unwin Ltd., 1980.

Conze, Edward, et. al, *Buddhist Texts Through the Ages*, New York: Philosophical Library, 1954.

David-Neel, Alexandra, *Buddhism: Its Doctrines and Its Methods*, New York: St. Martin's Press, 1977.

Humphreys, Christmas, *Buddhism*, London: Penguin Books, 1951.

Martin, Walter, ed., *The New Cults*, Santa Ana, CA: Vision House Publishers Inc., 1980.

Noss, John B., *Man's Religions*, New York: MacMillan Company, 1969.

Offner, Clark B. in *The World's Religions*, Sir Norman Anderson, ed., Grand Rapids, MI: William B. Eerdmans Publishing Company, 1976.

Rice, Edward, *Eastern Definitions*, New York: Doubleday, 1980.

Robinson, Richard, trans., *Chinese Buddhist Verse*, London: Greenwood Publ., 1954.

Ross, Nancy Wilson, *Buddhism: A Way of Thought*, New York, Alfred A. Knopf, Inc., 1980.

Seeger, Elizabeth, *Eastern Religions*, New York: Crowell, 1973.

Smith, Huston, *The Religions of Man*, New York: Harper and Row, 1958.

Swearer, Donald K., *Buddhism*, Niles, IL: Argus Communications, 1977.

CHAPTER FOUR

Confucianism

C onfucianism, a religion of optimistic humanism, has had a monumental impact upon the life, social structure and political philosophy
of China. The founding of the religion goes back to one man, known
as Confucius, born a half-millenium before Christ.

History

The Life of Confucius

Although Confucius occupies a hallowed place in Chinese tradition,
little is verifiable about his life. The best source available is *The Analects*,
the collection of his sayings made by his followers. Long after his death
much biographical detail on his life surfaced, but most of this material
is of questionable historical value. However, there are some basic facts
that can be accepted reasonably to give an outline of his life.

Confucius was born Chiu King, the youngest of 11 children, about 550
B.C., in the principality of Lu, which is located in present-day Shantung.
He was a contemporary of the Buddha (although they probably never met)
and lived immediately before Socrates and Plato. Nothing is known for
certain concerning his ancestors except the fact that his surroundings
were humble.

As he himself revealed: "When I was young I was without rank and
in humble circumstances." His father died soon after his birth, leaving
his upbringing to his mother. During his youth Confucius participated
in a variety of activities, including hunting and fishing; but, "On reaching
the age of 15, I bent my mind to learning."

He held a minor government post as a collector of taxes before he
reached the age of 20. It was at this time that Confucius married.
However, his marriage was short-lived, ending in divorce; but he did produce a son and a daughter from his unsuccessful marriage. He became
a teacher in his early twenties, and that proved to be his calling in life.

His ability as a teacher became apparent and his fame spread rapidly,
attracting a strong core of disciples. Many were attracted by his wisdom.
He believed that society would not be changed unless he occupied a public

office where he could put his theories into practice.

Confucius held minor posts until age 50, when he became a high official in Lu. His moral reforms achieved an immediate success, but he soon had a falling out with his superiors and subsequently resigned his post. Confucius spent the next 13 years wandering from state to state, attempting to implement his political and social reforms. He devoted the last five years of his life to writing and editing what have become Confucian classics.

He died in Chüfou, Shantung, in 479 B.C., having established himself as the most important teacher in Chinese culture. His disciples referred to him as King Fu-tzu or Kung the Master, which has been latinized into Confucius.

China Before Confucius

It is important to understand life in China at the time of Confucius in order to develop a better appreciation of the reforms he was attempting to institute. The age in which Confucius lived was characterized by social anarchy. Huston Smith gives insight into the condition of China during this difficult period:

> By Confucius' day, however, the interminable warfare had degenerated a long way from this code of chivalrous honor toward the undiluted horror of the Period of the Warring States. The horror reached its height in the century following Confucius' death. The chariot, arm of the tournament, gave way to the cavalry with its surprise attacks and sudden raids. Instead of nobly holding their prisoners for ransom, conquerors put them to death in mass executions. Soldiers were paid upon presenting the severed heads of their enemies. Whole populations unlucky enough to be captured were beheaded, including women, children, and the aged. We read of mass slaughters of 60,000, 80,000, 82,000, and even 400,000. There are accounts of the conquered being thrown into boiling caldrons and their relatives forced to drink the human soup (Huston Smith, *The Religions of Man*, New York: Harper and Row, 1965, p. 166).

It is easy to see how the need arose for someone like Confucius to provide answers for how the people could live together harmoniously. Although the conduct of Chinese officials was exceedingly corrupt, Confucius believed the situation was not hopeless, for the general population had not reached the point of total corruption.

Confucius believed China could be saved if the people would seek for the good of others, a practice of their ancestors. The role Confucius would play was not as a savior or messiah but as one who would put the people back in touch with the ancients: "I transmit but do not create. I believe in and love the ancients. I venture to compare myself to our old P'eng (an ancient official who liked to tell stories)."

The Veneration of Confucius

Like many great religious leaders, Confucius was eventually deified by his followers. The following chart traces the progress which led to his ultimate deification:

B.C.

195   The Emperor of China offered animal sacrifice at the tomb of Confucius.

A.D.

1   He was given the imperial title "Duke Ni, All-complete and Illustrious."

57   Regular sacrifice to Confucius was ordered at the imperial and provincial colleges.

89   He was raised to the higher imperial rank of "Earl."

267   More elaborate animal sacrifices to Confucius were decreed four times yearly.

492   He was canonized as "The Venerable, the Accomplished Sage."

555   Separate temples for the worship of Confucius were ordered at the capital of every prefecture in China.

740   The statue of Confucius was moved from the side to the center of the Imperial College, to stand with the historic kings of China.

1068-1086   Confucius was raised to the full rank of Emperor.

1906   December 31. An Imperial Rescript raised him to the rank of Co-assessor with the deities Heaven and Earth.

1914   The worship of Confucius was continued by the first President of the Republic of China, Yuan Shi Kai (Robert E. Hume, *The World's Living Religions*, New York: Charles Scribner's Sons, rev. ed., 1959, pp. 117, 118).

The Life of Mencius

One of the central figures in Confucianism is Meng-tzu (Latinized into Mencius) who became second only to Confucius in the history of Confucian thought. Mencius, born in the state of Ch'i in 371 B.C., studied with a disciple of Confucius' grandson, Tzu-Ssu.

Like his master, Mencius spent most of his life traveling from state to state, seeking those in leadership who would adopt the teachings of Confucius. The feudal order in China had become worse than in the days of Confucius, and the attempts of Mencius to reverse this trend were of no avail.

Mencius, rejected by the politicians of his day, turned to teaching and developing Confucian thought. Among his accomplishments was the clarification of a question that Confucius left ambiguous: the basic nature of man. Mencius taught that man is basically good. This is still a basic presupposition of Confucian thought.

In his classic example, Mencius compared the potentiality of the goodness of man to the natural flow of water. Though water naturally flows downward, it can be made to flow uphill or splashed above one's head, but only as a result of external force. Likewise man's nature is basically good but can be forced into bad ways through external pressure.

This teaching, which is diametrically opposed to the biblical doctrine of original and universal sin, has made the proclamation of the Gospel that much more difficult among the people in China who accept the ideas of Mencius concerning the nature of man.

Confucius and Lao-tzu

There are reports, perhaps untrue, that Confucius met with Lao-tzu (var. sp.: Lao-tze), the founder of Taoism. Confucius had heard about the old archivist with strange philosophical beliefs and decided to investigate. The meeting was anything but amiable, however. Confucius, still a young man, had become famous because of his teachings and wisdom, and Lao-tzu was annoyed with him.

Joseph Gaer records what is believed to have taken place:

Confucius had prepared a number of questions he wished to ask of Lao-tze concerning his doctrines. But before he could even begin on the topic, Lao-tze questioned Confucius about his interests.

Confucius replied that he was interested in the history of the Ancients, especially as recorded in *The Book of Annals (Shu K'ing)*.

"The men of whom you speak are long since dead and their bones are turned to ashes in their graves." Lao-tze interrupted.

Their talk continued, with Lao-tze asking the questions and Confucius answering them deferentially and politely. It was his belief, Confucius explained, that man is by nature good, and that knowledge can keep him good.

"But why study the Ancients?" Lao-tze asked impatiently.

Confucius tried to explain his belief that new knowledge must be based upon old knowledge.

Lao-tze interrupted him, saying: "Put away your polite airs and your vain display of fine robes. The wise man does not display his treasure to those he does not know. And he cannot learn justice from the Ancients."

"Why not?" asked Confucius.

"It is not bathing that makes the pigeon white," was Lao-tze's reply. And he abruptly ended the interview (Joseph Gaer, *What the Great Religions Believe*, New York: Dodd, Mead, and Company, 1963, p. 76).

Whether or not this meeting occured, the account amply illustrates the difference between the two men and the religions which proceeded from them.

The Sources of Confucianism

During his teaching career Confucius collected ancient manuscripts which he edited and on which he wrote commentaries. He arranged these manuscripts into four books to which he also added a fifth book of his own. These works are known as the *Five Classics*.

The Five Classics

The Five Classics as we have them today have gone through much editing and alteration by Confucius' disciples, yet there is much in them that can be considered the work of Confucius. *The Five Classics* are:

1. *The Book of Changes (I Ching)* The I Ching is a collection of eight triagrams and 64 hexagrams which consist solely of broken and unbroken

lines. These lines were supposed to have great meaning if the key were discovered.

2. *The Book of Annals (Shu K'ing)* This is a work of the history of the five preceding dynasties. The example of the ancients was crucial to Confucius' understanding of how the superior man should behave.

3. *The Book of Poetry (Shih Ching)* The book of ancient poetry was assembled by Confucius because he believed the reading of poetry would aid in making a man virtuous.

4. *The Book of Ceremonies (Li Chi)* This work taught the superior man to act in the right or traditional way. Again Confucius stressed doing things in the same way as the ancients.

5. *The Annals of Spring and Autumn (Ch'un Ch'iu)* This book, supposedly written by Confucius, gave a commentary on the events of the state of Lu at Confucius' time.

The Teachings of Confucius

None of these works contain the unique teaching of Confucius but are rather an anthology of works he collected and from which he taught. Confucius' own teachings have come down to us from four books written by his disciples. They include:

1. *The Analects.* This is the most important source we have on Confucius. *The Analects* are sayings of both Confucius and his disciples.

2. *The Great Learning.* This work which deals with the education and training of a gentleman comes not from the hand of Confucius but rather from a later period (about 250 B.C.).

3. *The Doctrine of the Mean.* This work deals with the relationship of human nature to the order of the universe. Authorship is uncertain (part of it may be attributed to Confucius' grandson Tzu-Ssu), but it does not come from Confucius.

4. *The Book of Mencius.* Mencius wrote the first exposition of Confucian thought about 300 B.C. by collecting earlier teachings and attempting to put them down systematically. This work, which has had great influence and gives an idealistic view of life, stresses the goodness of human nature.

The Doctrines of Confucianism

Ancestor Worship

A common feature of Chinese religion prevalent at Confucius' time was the veneration of ancestors. Ancestor worship is the veneration of the spirits of the dead by their living relatives. Supposedly the continued existence of the ancestors in spirit is dependent upon the attention given them by their living relatives. It is also believed that the ancestors can control the fortunes of their families.

If the family provides for the ancestors' needs, then the ancestors will in turn cause good things to happen to their relatives. However, if the ancestors are neglected, it is believed that all sorts of evil can fall upon the living. Consequently, the living sometimes live in fear of the dead.

Richard C. Bush expands upon this thought:

> The veneration of ancestors by royal families and common people alike reveals several reasons for ancestor worship. People wanted their ancestors to be able to live beyond the grave in a manner similar to their life-style on earth; hence the living attempted to provide whatever would be necessary. A secondary motive lurks in the background: if not provided with the food and weapons and utensils needed to survive in the life beyond, those ancestors might return as ghosts and cause trouble for the living. To this day people celebrate a Festival of the Hungry Ghosts, placing food and wine in front of their homes to satisfy those ancestral spirits or ghosts whose descendants have not cared for them and who therefore may wander back to old haunts. A third motive is to inform the ancestors of what is going on at the present time, hopefully in such a way that the ancestral spirits may be assured that all is well and therefore may rest in peace. Finally, ancestor worship expresses the hope that ancestors will bless the living with children, prosperity, and harmony, and all that is most worthwhile (Richard C. Bush, *The Story of Religion in China*, Niles, IL: Argus Communications, 1977, p. 2).

Filial Piety

A concept that was entrenched in China long before the time of Confucius is that of filial piety (*Hsaio*) which can be described as devotion and obedience by the younger members of the family to the elders. This was particularly the case of son to father. This loyalty and devotion to the family was the top priority in Chinese life. Such duty to the family, particularly devotion to the elders, was continued throughout one's life.

This was expressed in *The Classic of Filial Piety*: "The services of love and reverence to parents when alive, and those of grief and sorrow to them when dead—these completely discharge the fundamental duty of living men" (Max Mueller, ed., *Sacred Books of the East*, Krishna Press, 1879-1910, Vol. III, p. 448).

Confucius stressed this concept in his teachings, and it was well received by the Chinese people, both then and now. In *The Analects*, Confucius said:

> The master said, "A young man should be a good son at home and an obedient young man abroad, sparing of speech but trustworthy in what he says, and should love the multitude at large but cultivate the friendship of his fellow men" (I:6).
>
> Meng Wu Po asked about being filial. The master said, "Give your father and mother no other cause for anxiety than illness" (II:6).
>
> Tzu-yu asked about being filial. The master said, "Nowadays for a man to be filial means no more than that he is able to provide his parents with food. Even hounds and horses are in some way provided with food. If a man shows no reverence, where is the difference?" (II:2).

Doctrinal Principles

Confucianism's doctrines can be summarized by six key terms or ways. *Jen* is the golden rule; *Chun-tzu* the gentleman; *Cheng-ming* is the role-player; *Te* is virtuous power; *Li* is the standard of conduct; and *Wen* encompasses the arts of peace. A brief discussion of the six principles reveals the basic doctrinal structure of Confucianism.

1. *Jen*. *Jen* has the idea of humaneness, goodness, benevolence or man-to-manness. *Jen* is the golden rule, the rule of reciprocity; that is to say, do not do anything to others that you would not have them do to you.

   "Tzu-Kung asked, 'Is there a single word which can be a guide to conduct throughout one's life?' The master said, 'It is perhaps the word "Shu." Do not impose on others what you yourself do not desire'" (Confucius, *The Analects*, XV:24).

   This is the highest virtue according to the Confucian way of life; if this principle could be put into practice, then mankind would achieve peace and harmony.

2. *Chun-tzu*. *Chun-tzu* can be translated variously as the gentleman, true manhood, the superior man, and man-at-his-best. The teachings of Confucius were aimed toward the gentleman, the man of virtue.

   Huston Smith observes, "If *Jen* is the ideal relationship between human beings, *Chun-tzu* refers to the ideal term of such relations" (Smith, *op. cit.*, p. 180). Confucius had this to say about the gentleman:
   > (Confucius:) He who in this world can practice five things may indeed be considered man-at-his-best.
   > What are they?
   > Humility, magnanimity, sincerity, diligence, and graciousness. If you are humble, you will not be laughed at. If you are magnanimous, you will attract many to your side. If you are sincere, people will trust you. If you are gracious, you will get along well with your subordinates (James R. Ware, trans., *The Sayings of Confucius*, New York: New American Library, 1955, p. 110).

   It is this type of man who can transform society into the peaceful state it was meant to be.

3. *Cheng-ming*. Another important concept according to Confucius was *Cheng-ming*, or the rectification of names. For a society to be properly ordered, Confucius believed everyone must act his proper part. Consequently, a king should act like a king, a gentleman like a gentleman, etc.

   Confucius said, "Duke Ching of Ch'i asked Confucius about government. Confucius answered, 'Let the ruler be a ruler, the subject a subject, the father a father, the son a son. . . .'" (*The Analects*, XII:11).

   He said elsewhere, "Tzu-lu said, 'If the Lord of Wei left the administration (*cheng*) of his state to you, what would you put first?' The master said, 'If something has to be put first, it is perhaps the rectification of names'" (*The Analects*, XIII:3).

4. *Te*. The word *te* literally means "power," but the concept has a far wider meaning. The power needed to rule, according to Confucius, consists of more than mere physical might. It is necessary that the leaders be men of virtue who can inspire their subjects to obedience through example. This concept had been lost during Confucius' time with the prevailing attitude being that physical might was the only proper way to order a society.

   Confucius looked back at history to the sages of the past, Yao and Shun, along with the founders of the Chou dynasty, as examples of such virtuous rule. If the rulers would follow the example of the past, then the people would rally around the virtuous example.

5. *Li*. One of the key words used by Confucius is *li*. The term has a variety of meanings, depending upon the context. It can mean propriety,

reverence, courtesy, ritual or the ideal standard of conduct. In the Book of Ceremonies (*The Li Chi*), the concept of *li* is discussed:

> Duke Ai asked Confucius, "What is this great *li*? Why is it that you talk about *li* as though it were such an important thing?"
>
> Confucius replied, "Your humble servant is really not worthy to understand *li*."
>
> "But you constantly speak about it," said Duke Ai.
>
> Confucius: "What I have learned is this, that of all the things that people live by, *li* is the greatest. Without *li*, we do not know how to conduct a proper worship of the spirits of the universe; or how to establish the proper status of the king and the ministers, the ruler and the ruled, and the elders and the juniors; or how to establish the moral relationships between the sexes; between parents and children, and between brothers; or how to distinguish the different degrees of relationships in the family. That is why a gentleman holds *li* in such high regard" (Lin Yutang, *The Wisdom of Confucius*, New York: Random House, 1938, *Li Chi* XXVII, p. 216).

6. *Wen*. The concept of *Wen* refers to the arts of peace, which Confucius held in high esteem. These include music, poetry and art. Confucius felt that these arts of peace, which came from the earlier Chou period, were symbols of virtue that should be manifest throughout society.

Confucius condemned the culture of his day because he believed it lacked any inherent virtue. He had this to say:

> The master said, "Surely when one says, 'The rites, the rites,' it is not enough merely to mean presents of jade and silk. Surely when one says 'music, music,' it is not enough merely to mean bells and drums. . . ." The master said, "What can a man do with the rites who is not benevolent? What can a man do with music who is not benevolent?" (*The Analects*, XVII:11, III:3).

Therefore, he who rejected the arts of peace was rejecting the virtuous ways of man and heaven.

Ethical Doctrines

The *Book of Analects* (*Lun Yu*) contains the sayings of Confucius which present his ethical principles. The following excerpts are from *The Analects* and give an example of the teachings of Confucius:

Men of superior minds busy themselves first getting at the root of things; when they succeed, the right course is open to them.

One excellent way to practice the rules of propriety is to be natural.

When truth and right go hand in hand, a statement will bear repetition.

Sorrow not because men do not know you; but sorrow that you do not know men.

To govern simply by statute and to maintain order by means of penalties is to render the people evasive and devoid of a sense of shame.

If you observe what people take into their hands, observe the motives, note what gives them satisfaction; then will they be able to conceal from you what they are?

When you know a thing, maintain you know it; when you do not, acknowledge it. This is the characteristic of knowledge.

Let the leader of men promote those who have ability, and instruct those who have it not, and they will be willing to be led.

To see what is right and not to do it, that is cowardice.

The superior man is not contentious. He contends only as in competitions of archery; and when he wins he will present his cup to his competitor.

A man without charity in his heart, what has he to do with ceremonies? A man without charity in his heart, what has he to do with music?

He who has sinned against Heaven has none other to whom his prayer may be addressed.

Tell me, is there anyone who is able for one whole day to apply the energy of his mind to virtue? It may be that there are such, but I have never met with one.

If we may learn what is right in the morning, we should be content to die in the evening.

The scholar who is intent upon learning the truth, yet is ashamed of his poor clothes and food, is not worthy to be discoursed with.

The superior man thinks of his character; the inferior man thinks of his position; the former thinks of the penalties for error, and the latter, of favors.

One should not be greatly concerned at not being in office, but rather about the requirements in one's self for that office. Nor should one be greatly concerned at being unknown, but rather with being worthy to be known.

The superior man seeks what is right, the inferior one what is profitable.

The superior man is slow to promise, prompt to fulfill.

Virtue dwells not in solitude; she must have neighbors.

In my first dealings with a man, I listen to his avowals and trust his conduct; after that I listen to his avowals and watch his conduct.

These are the four essential qualities of the superior man: he is humble, he is deferential to superiors, he is generously kind, and he is always just.

Those who are willing to forget old grievances will gradually do away with resentment.

I have not yet seen the man who can see his errors so as in a day to accuse himself.

Where plain naturalness is more in evidence than fine manners, we have the country man; where fine manners are more in evidence than plain naturalness, we have the townsman; where the two are equally blended we have the ideal man.

Better than the one who knows what is right is he who loves what is right.

To prize the effort above the prize, that is virtue.

What you find in me is a quiet brooder and memorizer, a student never satiated with learning, an unwearied monitor to others.

These things weigh heavily upon my mind: failure to improve in the virtues, failure in discussion of what is learned, inability to walk always according to the knowledge of what is right and just, inability to reform what has been amiss.

Fix your mind on truth; hold firm to virtue; rely upon loving-kindness; and find your recreation in the arts.

With coarse food to eat, water to drink, and a bent arm for a pillow, happiness may still be found.

Let there be three men walking together, and in them I will be sure to find my instructors. For what is good in them I will follow; and what is not good I will try to modify.

Sift out the good from the many things you hear, and follow them; sift out the good from the many things you see and remember them.

Without a sense of proportion, courtesy becomes oppressive; calmness becomes bashfulness; valor becomes disorderliness; and candor becomes rudeness.

Even if a person were adorned with the gift of the Duke of Chau, if he is proud and avaricious, all his other qualities are not really worth looking at.

Learn as if you could never overtake your subject, yet as if apprehensive of losing it.

When you have erred, be not afraid to correct yourself.

It is easier to carry off the chief commander of an army than to rob one poor fellow of his will.

We know so little about life, how can we then know about death?

If a man can subdue his selfishness for one full day, everyone will call him good.

When you leave your house, go out as if to meet an important guest.

Do not set before others what you yourself do not like.

The essentials of good government are: a sufficiency of food, a sufficiency of arms, and the confidence of the people. If forced to give up one of these, give up arms; and if forced to give up two, give up food. Death has been the portion of all men from of old; but without the people's trust, nothing can endure.

A tiger's or a leopard's skin might be a dog's or a sheep's when stripped of its hair.

Hold fast to what is good and the people will be good. The virtue of the good man is as the wind; and that of the bad man, as the grass. When the wind blows, the grass must bend.

Knowledge of man, that is wisdom.

The superior man feels reserved in matters which he does not understand.

Let the leader show rectitude in his personal character, and things will go well even without directions from him.

Do not wish for speedy results nor trivial advantages; speedy results will not be far-reaching; trivial advantages will matter only in trivial affairs.

The superior man will be agreeable even when he disagrees; the inferior man will be disagreeable even when he agrees.

Confucius was asked, "Is a good man one who is liked by everybody?" He answered, "No." "Is it one who is disliked by everybody?" He answered, "No. He is liked by all the good people and disliked by the bad."

In a country of good government, the people speak out boldly and act boldly.

Good men speak good words, but not all who speak good words are good. Good men are courageous, but not all courageous men are good.

The Supernatural

Confucianism is not a religion in the sense of man relating to the Almighty but is rather an ethical system teaching man how to get along with his fellow man. However, Confucius did make some comments on the supernatural which give insight into how he viewed life, death, heaven, etc. He once said, "Absorption in the study of the supernatural is most harmful" (Lionel Giles, *Sayings of Confucius, Wisdom of the East Series,* London: John Murray Publ., 1917, II:16, 94). When asked about the subject of death, he had this to say, "Chi-lu asked how the spirits of the dead and the gods should be served. The master said, 'You are not able to serve man. How can you serve the spirits?' 'May I ask about death?' 'You do not understand even life. How can you understand death?'" (Confucius, *The Analects,* D. C. Lau, trans., London: Penguin Books, 1979, Book XI, 12).

John B. Noss comments, "His position in matters of faith was this: whatever seemed contrary to common sense in popular tradition, and whatever did not serve any discoverable social purpose, he regarded coldly" (John B. Noss, *Man's Religions,* New York: MacMillan Company, 1969, p. 291).

Confucius did, however, feel that heaven was on his side in the ethical teachings that he espoused, as can be observed by the following comment:

"The master said, 'At fifteen I set my heart on learning; at thirty I took my stand; at forty I came to be free from doubts; at fifty I understood the decree of heaven; at sixty my ear was attuned; at seventy I followed my heart's desire without overstepping the line'" (*The Analects,* II:5).

Is Confucianism a Religion?

Since Confucianism deals primarily with moral conduct and the ordering of society, it is often categorized as an ethical system rather than a religion. Although Confucianism deals solely with life here on earth rather than the afterlife, it does take into consideration mankind's ultimate concerns.

One must remember the outlook of the people during the time of Confucius. Deceased ancestors were thought to exercise power over the living, sacrifice to heaven was a common occurrence, and the practice of augury, or observing the signs from heaven (thunder, lightning, the flight of birds, etc.), all were prevalent. Huston Smith makes an appropriate comment:

> In each of these three great features of early Chinese religion—its sense of continuity with the ancestors, its sacrifice, and its augury—there was a common emphasis. The emphasis was on Heaven instead of Earth. To understand the total dimensions of Confucianism as a religion, it is important to see Confucius (a) shifting the emphasis from Heaven to Earth (b) without dropping Heaven out of the picture entirely (Huston Smith, *op. cit.,* p. 189).

The emphasis in Confucianism was on the earthly, not the heavenly; but heaven and its doings were assumed to be real rather than imaginary. Since Confucianism gradually assumed control over all of one's life, and it was the presupposition from which all action was decided, it necessarily permeated Chinese religious thought, belief and practice as well.

The Impact of Confucianism

The impact Confucianism has had on China can hardly be overestimated. Huston Smith observes:

> History to date affords no clearer support for this thesis than the work of Confucius. For over two thousand years his teachings have profoundly affected a quarter of the population of this globe. Their advance reads like a success story of the spirit. During the Han Dynasty (206 B.C.-A.D. 20), Confucianism became, in effect, China's state religion. In 130 B.C. it was made the basic discipline for the training of government officials, a pattern which continued in the main until the establishment of the Republic in 1912. In 59 A.D. sacrifices were ordered for Confucius in all urban schools, and in the seventh and eighth centuries temples were erected in every prefecture of the empire as shrines to him and his principal disciples. To the second half of the twelfth century his *The Analects* remained one of the classics. But in the Sung Dynasty it became not merely a school book but *the* school book, the basis of all education. In 1934 his birthday was proclaimed a national holiday (*Ibid.*, p. 192).

Marcus Bach in a similar way relates:

> One thing that the Communist regime will never be able to do is to get Confucius out of China. Some say it has not been tried. Others contend there is no use trying. China's. . .people know Confucius as well as America's millions know the Christ. We do not have a state religion, but we are predominantly Christian. China does not have a state religion, but it is predominantly Confucian (Marcus Bach, *Major Religons of the World*, Nashville: Abingdon, 1970, p. 81).

Confucianism and Christianity

The ethical system taught by Confucius has much to commend it, for virtue is something to desire highly. However, the ethical philosophy Confucius espoused was one of self-effort, leaving no room or need for God.

Confucius taught that man can do it all by himself if he only follows the way of the ancients, while Christianity teaches that man does not have the capacity to save himself but is in desperate need of a savior. Confucius also hinted that human nature was basically good. This thought was developed by later Confucian teachers and became a cardinal belief of Confucianism.

The Bible, on the other hand, teaches that man is basically sinful and left to himself is completely incapable of performing ultimate good. Contrast what the Bible says about human nature and the need of a savior against Confucianism.

> "The heart is more deceitful than all else and is desperately sick; Who can understand it?" (Jeremiah 17:9, NASB). "For all have sinned and fall short of the glory of God" (Romans 3:23, NASB). "For by grace you have been saved through faith; and that not of yourselves, it is the gift of God: not as a result of works, that no one should boast" (Ephesians 2:8, 9, NASB). "He saved us, not on the basis of deeds which we have done in righteousness, but according

to His mercy, by the washing of regeneration and renewing by the Holy Spirit" (Titus 3:5, NASB).

Since Confucianism lacks any emphasis upon the supernatural, this religious system must be rejected. It must be remembered that Confucius taught an ethical philosophy that later germinated into a popular religion, though Confucius had no idea that his teachings would become the state religion in China. Nevertheless, Confucianism as a religious system is opposed to the teachings of Christianity and must be rejected summarily by Christians.

Confucianistic Terms

Analects, The—One of the *Four Books* containing the sayings of Confucius. *The Analects* are considered the best source of determining the sayings and wisdom of Confucius.

Ancestor Worship—the Chinese practice of worshipping the spirits of their dead relatives in order to appease them from causing trouble with the living.

Cheng Ming—The concept of rectification of names, meaning that one should act in accordance with his position in life (king as a king, father as a father, etc.).

Chun-tzu—"Man-at-his best," the superior man. The type of man, according to Confucius, who could transform society into a peaceful state.

Confucius—"Kung the Master," the title for Chiu King, the founder of Confucianism.

Feng Shui—The Chinese name for geomancy, a branch of divination to determine appropriate sights for houses or graves.

Filial Piety—The Chinese practice of loyalty and devotion by the younger members of the family to their elders.

Five Classics—Along with the *Four Books*, the Five Classics are the authoritative writings of Confucianism. The Five Classics were collected and edited by Confucius. They include: *The Book of Changes, The Book of Annals, The Book of Poetry, The Book of Ceremonies*, and *The Annals of Spring and Autumn.*

Four Books—The Four Books are a collection of the teachings and sayings of Confucius. They include: *The Analects, The Great Learning, The Doctrine of the Mean, The Book of Mencius.*

Jen—The golden rule in Confucianism, "Do not do to others what you would not have them do to you."

Li—The concept denoting the ideal standard of conduct.

Mandate of Heaven—The authorization of power to Chinese emperors and kings believed traditionally to issue from heaven.

Mencius—A later disciple of Confucius who is credited with developing and systematizing Confucian thought.

Te—The virtuous power needed to properly rule the people.

Wen—The arts of peace, which include poetry, music, and art.

Confucianism Bibliography

Bach, Marcus, *Major Religions of the World*, Nashville: Abingdon, 1979.

Bush, Richard C., *The Story of Religion in China*, Niles, IL: Argus Communications, 1977.

Confucius, *The Analects*, D. C. Lau, trans., London: Penguin Books, 1979.

Gaer, Joseph, *What the Great Religions Believe*, New York: Dodd, Mead, and Company, 1963.

Giles, Lionel, *Sayings of Confucius, Wisdom of the East Series*, London: John Murray Publ., 1917.

Hume, Robert E., *The World's Living Religions*, New York: Charles Scribner's Sons, rev. ed., 1959.

Mueller, Max, ed., *Sacred Books of the East, Fifty Volumes*, London: Krishna Press, 1879-1910.

Noss, John B., *Man's Religions*, New York: MacMillan Company, 1969.

Smith, Huston, *The Religions of Man*, New York: Harper and Row, 1965.

Ware, James R., trans., *The Sayings of Confucius*, New York: New American Library, 1955.

Yutang, Lin, *The Wisdom of Confucius*, New York: Random House, 1938.

CHAPTER FIVE

Taoism

A t the same time Confucius' teachings were spreading through China, another religion was also having its beginning. In contrast to the humanistic, ethical teachings of Confucius, the mystical, enigmatic beliefs of Taoism (pronounced "Dowism") appeared. Behind this enigmatic religion is itself an enigmatic figure named Lao-tzu.

History

Lao-tzu, the Founder

Taoism has its roots in a shadowy figure named Lao-tzu, of whom little or nothing is verifiable. Many scholars feel that Lao-tzu never existed at all. His date of birth is uncertain, being put variously between 604 and 570 B.C. One legend said that he was never young but rather was born old with white hair, a long white beard and wrinkled skin.

Another story has him named Plum-Tree-Ears by his mother because he was born under the shadow of a plum tree and his ears were unusually long. However, he was known to the people as Lao-tzu, meaning "the old philosopher." He supposedly held an important post as curator of the imperial archives at Loyang, the capital city in the state of Ch'u.

His government position became tiresome, for Lao-tzu disapproved of the tyranny of the rulers and the idea of government itself. Lao-tzu came to believe that men were meant to live simply without honors and without a fruitless search for knowledge. Consequently, he resigned his post and returned home.

Since his opinions had gathered unwanted students and disciples, Lao-tzu left his house to seek privacy from curiosity seekers. He bought a cart and a black ox and set out toward the border of the province, leaving corrupt society behind. However, at the crossing of the border the guard, his friend Yin-hsi, recognized him and would not allow him to pass.

Yin-hsi exhorted Lao-tzu, "You have always kept to yourself like a hermit and have never written down your teachings. Yet many know them. Now you wish to leave and retire beyond our borders. I will not let you cross until you have written down the essentials of your teachings."

Lao-tzu returned after three days with a small treatise entitled *The Tao Te King*, or *The Way and Its Power* (sometimes translated as *The Way and Moral Principle*). Then he mounted a water buffalo and rode off into the sunset, never to be heard of again. Another version of the story has the gatekeeper Yin-hsi begging Lao-tzu to take him with him after he read *The Tao Te King*. Whatever the case may be, the little book was left behind and became the basis for a new religion.

Lao-tzu, the Book

The Tao Te King, also known as the *Lao-tzu*, is a small book of approximately 5,500 words instructing rulers in the art of government. It teaches that the less government, the better, and that a ruler should lead by non-action.

Needless to say, no ruler in the history of China has taken the political section seriously. However, there is a philosophical side to *The Tao Te King* that has had enormous impact. The work teaches individuals how to endure life against the terrible calamities that were common in China. It advocates a low-key approach of non-ambition and staying in the background which will help one's odds of survival.

There is an ongoing debate as to when *The Tao Te King* was composed. The traditionalist point of view has the work composed by Lao-tzu, a contemporary of Confucius, in the sixth century B.C. The basis for holding this traditional date is the biography of Lao-tzu in the *Shih-chi (Records of the Historian)* about 100 B.C.

The modernists view the work as having been formally compiled about 300 B.C. because of the similarity of style to works composed in that period. The historical setting, they argue, fits more with this turbulent era than with the earlier one claimed by the traditionalists, although the modernists do believe many of the sayings actually come from a much earlier time.

Chuang-tzu

Apart from Lao-tzu, the most important figure in Taoism is Chuang-tzu, a disciple of the famous Lao-tzu. Chuang-tzu was a prolific author living during the fourth century B.C. who wrote some 33 books. Chuang-tzu was a clever writer, popularizing the teachings of Lao-tzu as Mencius did with his master, Confucius.

The following excerpts from the writings of Chuang-tzu give insight into the philosophical side of Taoism which he helped popularize:

> Once I, Chuang Chou, dreamed that I was a butterfly and was happy as a butterfly. . . . Suddenly I awoke, and there I was, visibly Chou. I do not know whether it was Chou dreaming that he was a butterfly or the butterfly dreaming it was Chou. Between Chou and the butterfly there must be some distinction. This is called the transformation of things (Wing-Tsit Chan, ed., *A Sourcebook in Chinese Philosophy*, Princeton, NJ: Princeton University Press, 1963, p. 190).

Upon hearing the news of the death of his wife, Chuang-tzu responded:

When she died, how could I help being affected? But as I think the matter over, I realize that originally she had no life; and not only no life, she had no form; not only no form, she had no material force. In the limbo of existence and non-existence, there was transformation and the material force was evolved. The material force was transformed to become form, form was transformed to become life, and now birth has transformed to become death. This is like the rotation of the four seasons, spring, summer, fall, and winter. Now she lies asleep in the great house (the universe). For me to go about weeping and wailing would be to show my ignorance of destiny. Therefore I desist (*Ibid.*, p. 209).

Taoist History Review

Robert E. Hume charts some of the highlights in the history of Taoism:

B.C.

212 Emperor Shi Huang Ti burned Confucian books, and established Taoism; sent naval expeditions to Fairy Islands to discover the herb of immortality.

A.D.

1 The leading Taoist in China endeavored to compound a pill of immortality.

156 **Emperor Hwan of China first sacrificed to Lao-tzu.**

574-581 Emperor Wu arranged order of precedence, viz., Confucianism, first; Taoism, second; and Buddhism, third; but soon became disgusted with Taoism and Buddhism and ordered their abolition. The next emperor, Tsing, re-established both non-Confucian religions.

650-684 Lao-tzu canonized as an emperor; his writings included among subjects for government examinations.

713-742 Emperor Kai Yuen distributed copies of the *Tao-Te-King* throughout the empire; took a dose of Taoist "gold-stone" medicine; magicry increased.

825-827 Emperor Pao-li banished all Taoist doctors on account of their intrigues and pretensions away to the two southernmost provinces of China.

841-847 Emperor Wu Tsung ordered all Taoist and Buddhist monasteries and nunneries closed. Later he restored Taoism to imperial favor, and stigmatized Buddhism as "a foreign religion." Took Taoist medicine to etherealize his bones, so as to fly through the air like the fairies.

1661-1721 Emperor Kang Hsi ordered punishment not only of the Taoist quacks, but also of the patients; forbade Taoist assemblies and processions; endeavored to suppress the various Taoist sects.

1900 The Boxer Uprising originated in a sect of specially ardent Taoists who believed their bodies would be immune against foreigners' bullets, trusting the exact words of the founder: "When coming among solders, he need not fear arms and weapons..." (Robert E. Hume, *The World's Living Religions*, New York: Charles Scribner's Sons, rev. ed., 1959, pp. 147, 148).

The Teachings of Taoism

The Tao

In *The Tao Te King*, the central concept is that of the Tao. Finding the proper definition of the term is no easy task, for while the word "Tao" literally means "way" or "path," the concept goes far beyond that. The opening words of *The Tao Te King* express the thought that the Tao that can be understood is not the real Tao. The name that can be named is not the real name.

A famous Taoist saying is, "Those who know don't say and those who say don't know." It is a mysterious term beyond all our understanding, imagination and senses. Yet it is the way of ultimate reality, the ground of all existence. It is the way of the universe, the way by which one should order his life.

> The cosmic Tao is invisible, inaudible, unnamable, undiscussable, inexpressible (Max Mueller, ed., *Sacred Books of the East*, London: Krishna Press, 1879-1910, 40:68, 69).
>
> The perfect man is peaceful like the Tao (*Ibid.*, 39: 1992-193).
>
> The ideal condition is a by-gone utopian simplicity in a state of nature (*Ibid.*, 39:278).
>
> Vacancy, stillness, placidity, tastelessness, quietude, silence, non-action— this is the level of Heaven and Earth, and the perfection of the Tao (*Ibid.*, 39:331).

The question arises, how does one get his life in harmony with the Tao? If mankind's chief aim is to conform his existence to the way of the Tao, what must he do to accomplish this? *The Tao Te King* teaches this can be done by practicing the basic attitude of *Wu Wei*, which literally means inaction.

This principle calls for the avoidance of all aggressiveness by doing that which is natural and spontaneous. Mankind should live passively, avoiding all forms of stress and violence to properly commune with nature. In doing this, his life will flow with the Tao.

Yin and Yang

A concept that has been accepted in Confucianism, as well as philosophical and religious Taoism, is that of the *yin* and *yang*. Although all things emanate from the Tao, there are those elements that are contrary to each other, such as good and evil and life and death. The positive side is known as the "yang" and the negative side the "yin." These opposites can be expressed in the following manner:

Yang	Yin
Male	Female
Positive	Negative
Good	Evil
Light	Darkness
Life	Death

Summer	Winter
Active	Passive

These concepts are interdependent and find themselves as expressions of the Tao. The concept of yin and yang is used to explain the ebb and flow in both man and nature. According to Taoism, "to blend with the cycle (of the universe) without effort is to become one with the Tao and so find fulfillment" (Maurice Rawlings, *Life-Wish: Reincarnation: Reality or Hoax*, Nashville, TN: Thomas Nelson Inc., 1981).

A broader Chinese concept regarding yin and yang is that the harmonious life can be achieved with the proper interaction of these forces. Richard C. Bush expands this idea:

> An understanding of the world had emerged: there were powers from above associated with Heaven such as rain and sun, and powers of the earth below such as the fertility of the soil. It follows naturally that the forces of heaven and earth should be in a state of interaction and that all of life flows from this interaction. All people have observed this process in nature, have planted and harvested their crops accordingly, and therefore developed a rhythm of life. The ancient Chinese sensed beneath this rhythm the movement of two basic forces called yang and yin. Yang is above, male, light, warm and aggressive; yin is below, female, dark, cold, and passive. Harmonious life is a complementary interaction of male and female, darkness and light. Rain and sun (yang) fall on the earth (yin) and crops grow. The passive yields to the aggressive but, by yielding, absorbs and overcomes. The result is a philosophy of continual change which is believed to explain the rise and fall of dynasties as well as the change from day to night and back to day again. The goal of this process is a harmony between ruler and subject, among the members of the family, and in society as a whole becomes the goal of life, both in ancient China and among many Chinese today (Richard C. Bush, *The Story of Religion in China*, Niles, IL: Argus Communications, 1977, pp. 6, 7).

Excerpts from the Tao Te King: Principles of Taoism

The following excerpts from The *Tao Te King* demonstrate the basic thought of Taoism (translation by James Legge):

Chapter I: The Tao That Can Be Trodden

The Tao that can be trodden is not the enduring and unchanging Tao. The name that can be named is not the enduring and unchanging name.

Conceived of as having no name, it is the Originator of heaven and earth; conceived of as having a name, it is the Mother of all things.

Always without desire we must be found,
If its deep mystery we would sound;
But if desire always within us be,
Its outer fringe is all that we shall see.

Under these two aspects, it is really the same; but as development takes place, it receives the different names. Together we call them the Mystery. Where the Mystery is the deepest is the gate of all that is subtle and wonderful.

Chapter LVI: He Who Knows the Tao

He who knows the Tao does not care to speak about it; he who is ever ready to speak about it does not know it.

He who knows it will keep his mouth shut and close the portals of his nostrils. He will blunt his sharp points and unravel the complications of things; he will temper his brightness, and bring himself into agreement with the obscurity of others. This is called "the Mysterious Agreement."

Such a one cannot be treated familiarly or distantly; he is beyond all consideration of profit or injury; of nobility or meanness—he is the noblest man under heaven.

Chapter LXIII: It Is the Way

It is the way of the Tao to act without thinking of acting;
To conduct affairs without feeling the trouble of them;
To taste without discerning any flavor;
To consider what is small as great, and a few as many; and
To recompense injury with kindness.

The master of it anticipates things that are difficult while they are easy, and does things that would become great while they are small.

All difficult things in the world are sure to arise from a previous state in which they were easy, and all great things from one in which they were small. Therefore the sage, while he never does what is great, is able on that account to accomplish the greatest things.

He who lightly promises is sure to keep but little faith; he who is continually thinking things easy is sure to find them difficult. Therefore the sage sees difficulty even in what seems easy, and so never has any difficulties.

Chapter XXV: There Was Something

There was something undefined and complete, coming into existence before Heaven and Earth. How still it was and formless, standing alone, and undergoing no change, reaching everywhere and in no danger of being exhausted! It may be regarded as the Mother of all things.

I do not know its name, and I give it the designation of the Tao (the Way or Course). Making an effort further to give it a name I call it The Great.

Great, it passes on in constant flow. Passing on, it becomes remote. Having become remote, it returns. Therefore the Tao is great; Heaven is great; Earth is great; and the sage king is also great. In the universe there are four that are great, and the sage king is one of them.

Man takes his law from the Earth; the Earth takes its law from Heaven; Heaven takes its law from the Tao. The law of the Tao is its being what it is.

So, in their beautiful array,
Things form and never know decay.

How know I that it is so with all the beauties of existing things? By this nature of the Tao.

Chapter LI: All Things

All things are produced by the Tao, and nourished by its outflowing operation.

They receive their forms according to the nature of each, and are completed according to the circumstances of their condition.

Therefore all things without exception honor the Tao, and exalt its outflowing operation.

This honoring of the Tao and exalting of its operation are not the result of any ordination, but always a spontaneous tribute.

Thus it is that the Tao produces all things, nourishes them, brings them to their full growth, nurses them, completes them, matures them, maintains them, and overspreads them.

It produces them and makes no claim to the possession of them;

It carries them through their processes and does not vaunt its ability in doing so;

It brings them to maturity and exercises no control over them;

This is called its mysterious operation.

The Way is like an empty vessel which is the ancestry from which come all things in the world.

The value of an act is judged by its timing.

Thirty spokes unite in the hub, but the worth of the wheel will depend on the void where the axle turns.

What gives a clay cup value is the empty space its walls create.

Usefulness is to be found in non-existence.

If you know righteousness, though you die, you shall not perish.

If you trust people not enough, they may trust you not at all.

Get rid of your preachers and discard your teachers, and the people will benefit a hundredfold. Root out your schemers and renounce your profiteers, and thieving will disappear.

Between "yes" and "no" how small the difference; between "good" and "evil" how great the difference.

He who is not a competitor, no one in the whole world can compete with him.

If you work by the Way, you will be of the Way.

Little faith is put in those who have little faith.

There is something that existed before the earth and the sky began and its name is the Way.

Man conforms to the earth; the earth conforms to the sky; the sky conforms to the Way; the Way conforms to its own nature.

As for those who would take the whole world to tinker with as they see fit, observe that they never succeed.

The wise reject all extremes.

Those who are on the Way might be compared to rivulets flowing into the sea.

He who understands others is wise; he who understands himself is enlightened.

He who conquers others is strong; he who conquers his own will is mighty.

If you would take, you must first give, this is the beginning of intelligence.

Absence of desires brings tranquility.

A cart is more than the sum of its parts.

The Way is nameless and hidden, yet all things gain their fulfillment in it.

To the good I would be good, and to the bad I would be good; in that way all might become good.

Wars are best waged by stratagem; but people are best governed by forthrightness.

The more prohibitions, the more poverty; the more laws, the more crimes; the more skills, the more luxuries; the more weapons, the more chaos.

In serving Heaven and in ruling men use moderation.

Everything difficult must be dealt with while it is still easy.

A thousand-mile journey can be made one step at a time.

Three things prize above all: gentleness, frugality and humility. For the gentle can be bold, the frugal can be liberal and the humble can become leaders of men.

If you cannot advance an inch, retreat a foot.

Philosophical and Religious Taoism

Philosophical

Taoism has historically taken two different roads. Taoism as a philosophy, or philosophical Taoism, began around 300 B.C. Emphasizing the Tao as the source of ultimate reality, philosophical Taoism attempted to put man in touch with the harmony of nature by allowing him to exercise freely his instincts and imaginations.

Religious Taoism began forming around the second century A.D. when the emperor Huan ordered a temple built in honor of Lao-tzu, with offerings also being made to him. However, as a formal religion Taoism did not actually make an appearance until the seventh century. John B. Noss explains why this occurred:

> By this time Buddhism had made its appearance as a great and significant factor in Chinese religious life. Neither Confucianism, the rather stiff and formal mode of thought and behavior known chiefly to the literati and officials, nor Taoism, still the preoccupation either of intellectuals on the one hand or of students of the esoteric and the occult on the other, was wholly satisfactory to the unlearned and lowly masses. Hinayana Buddhism was no better in the eyes of these unlettered but spiritually hungry souls, but the Mahayana was another matter. The beneficent Bodhisattvas who gave aid in daily life and the Dhyani Buddhas who admitted one to paradise, were soon being plied with gifts and prayers by millions.
>
> As Buddhism swept across China and into Korea, the Taoists, struck with amazement and yet sure that China had her own resources, so to speak, in the way of gods and spirits, began to look into their own heritage, and finding much to value, they began to ape the powerful faith brought in from India (John B. Noss, *Man's Religions*, New York: MacMillan Company, 1969, p. 272).

Religious

Religious Taoism had sacred scripture, a priesthood, temples and disciples. There was also an eschatological belief that a new age would come about, overthrowing the old established order. As time went on, gods were brought into the religious system along with belief in heaven and hell and eventually the deification of Lao-tzu.

Noss reports on the present state of Taoism:

> Taoism has for many years been in decline. According to the latest reports, as a religion it is now dead. The government frowns upon it and is determined to suppress it. But many still cling to it as magic, no matter how secret they must be about it nor how carefully they must try to elude the vigilant eye of the Communist district leaders (*Ibid.*, p. 274).

Taoism and Christianity

In his book *The World's Living Religions*, Robert E. Hume lists the following weaknesses in Taoism:

> Its not sufficiently personal and responsible Supreme Being.
> Its founder's positively ignoble example of withdrawing from difficulty; not organizing for reform.
> Its inadequate recognition of the evils in the world.

Its inadequate appreciation of physical facts and resources, discouraging to scientific inquiry.

Its over-emphasis on inactivity *(Wu-Wei)*, belittling to human effort.

Its lack of a commanding enthusiastic principle for living; mostly negative advice.

Its ethical ideal of indifference and irresponsibility.

Its inadequate conception of immortal life; merely a protracted existence.

Its lack of a program for the uplift of society; only a return to an uncivilized simplicity.

Its relapse into polytheism, demonolatry, and practice of magic (Hume, *op. cit.*, p. 151).

Although Taoism may have run its course in China, it is a very real threat in the West. With the hippie generation the United States saw the advent of the "tune out, drop out" mentality, a mentality completely suited to Taoist philosophy.

We can rest assured, however, that even though the Tao may have a temporary appeal, it ultimately cannot fulfill its disciples. The impersonal Tao is in stark contrast to the personal loving God of Christianity, who is both willing and able to meet the deepest needs we all have.

The Bible says, "Come to Me, all who are weary and heavy laden, and I will give you rest. Take My yoke upon you, and learn from Me, for I am gentle and humble in heart; and you shall find rest for your souls. For My yoke is easy, and My load is light" (Matthew 11:28-30 NASB).

Taoism has no real answer to the problem of evil, for the Taoist "solution" of ignoring or withdrawing from the ills of society does nothing to cure those very real ills.

Jesus, on the other hand, taught His disciples to get involved with the problems of the world. "Go therefore and make disciples of all the nations, baptizing them in the name of the Father and the Son and the Holy Spirit" (Matthew 28:19 NASB). "But you shall receive power when the Holy Spirit has come upon you; and you shall be My witnesses both in Jerusalem, and in all Judea and Sumaria, and even to the remotest part of the earth" (Acts 1:8 NASB).

God, through Jesus Christ, got involved with the problems we all face and provided a once-and-for-all solution by His death on the cross. The near extinction of the religious side of Taoism is a testimony to the fact that it doesn't meet our deepest needs. God in Jesus Christ made the ultimate identification with our suffering and by it, secured our salvation from it.

"Since then the children share in flesh and blood, He Himself likewise also partook of the same, that through death He might render powerless him who had the power of death, that is, the devil; and might deliver those who through fear of death were subject to slavery all their lives. . . Therefore, He had to be made like His brethren in all things, that He might become a merciful and faithful high priest in things pertaining to God, to make propitiation for the sins of the people. For since He Himself was tempted in that which He has suffered, He is able to come to the aid of those who are tempted" (Hebrews 2:14, 15, 17, 18 NASB).

Taoistic Terms

Chuang tzu—A later disciple of Lao-tzu who wrote some 33 books which helped popularize Taoism.

Lao-tzu—Chinese sage and philosopher who founded Taoism.

Tao Te King—Literally translated, "The Way and Its Power." This small book, supposedly written by Lao-tzu, is the sacred scripture of Taoism. The work advocates enduring the hardships of the world through non-involvement, thereby giving the individual a better chance for survival. Sometimes called *Lao-tzu*, after its supposed author.

The Tao—Literally, the "Way" or "Path." The Tao is the inexpressible way of ultimate reality by which one should order his life.

Wu Wei—The concept of inaction, taught in the *Tao Te King*. By practicing *Wu Wei*, one can get his life in harmony with the Tao and live as he is meant to live.

Yin-Yang—The Yin and Yang represent elements in the universe that are contrary to each other, such as life and death, light and darkness, good and evil. The Yang represents positive elements, the Yin the negative elements.

Taoism Bibliography

Bush, Richard C., *The Story of Religion in China*, Niles, IL: Argus Communications, 1977.

Chan, Wing-Tsit, ed., *A Sourcebook in Chinese Philosophy*, Princeton, NJ: Princeton University Press, 1963.

Hume, Robert E., *The World's Living Religions*, New York: Charles Scribner's Sons, rev. ed., 1959.

Mueller, Max, ed., *Sacred Books of the East*, London: Krishna Press, 1879-1910.

Noss, John B., *Man's Religions*, New York: MacMillan Company, 1969.

Rawlings, Maurice, *Life-Wish: Reincarnation: Reality or Hoax*, Nashville: Thomas Nelson Inc., 1981.

CHAPTER SIX

Shintoism

S hinto, the national religion of Japan, is one of the oldest of all the world's religions. It is unlike other religions inasmuch as it is basically not a system of beliefs. It has been variously defined. John B. Noss' definition states:

> It is basically a reverent loyalty to familiar ways of life and familiar places. . . it is true to say that for the masses in Japan love of country, as in other lands, is a matter of the heart first, and of doctrinal substance second (John B. Noss, *Man's Religions*, New York: MacMillan Company, 1969, p. 316).

Clark B. Offner defines Shinto in the following manner:

> Shinto denotes "the traditional religious practices which originated in Japan and developed mainly among the Japanese people along with the underlying life attitudes and ideology which support such practices." Various implications can immediately be derived from this statement of a modern Shinto scholar. First, Shinto does not refer to an organized, clearly-defined body of doctrine nor to a unified, systematized code of behaviour. The origins of Shinto are lost in the hazy mists enshrouding the ancient period of Japanese history, but from the time the Japanese people became conscious of their own cultural character and traditions, the practices, attitudes and ideology that eventually developed into the Shinto of today were already included within them (Clark B. Offner, in *The World's Religions*, Sir Norman Anderson, ed., Grand Rapids: William B. Eerdmans Publishing Company, 1976, p. 190).

Shinto History

Shinto is purely a Japanese religion, the origins of which are buried in antiquity. The Japanese are a people who love their land and believe the islands of Japan were the first divine creation. This idea of the divine origin of their land is very old and goes hand-in-hand with the beliefs of Shinto. This national idealism, the love of their country, is basically why Shinto has been limited to Japan. John B. Noss comments:

> The Japanese came early to the belief that their land was divine, but late to the nationalistic dogma that no other land is divine, that the divinity of Japan is so special and unique, so absent elsewhere, as to make Japan "center of this phenomenal world" (John B. Noss, *op. cit.*, p. 316).

The Japanese name for their country is *Nippon,* which means "sun origin." Until the end of World War II, Japanese children were taught at school that the emperors were descendants of the sun-goddess, *Amaterasu. Amaterasu* had allegedly given the imperial house the divine right to rule. In 1946, in a radio broadcast to the Japanese people, Emperor Hirohito repudiated his divine right to rule.

Early Development

Shinto's history can be divided into a number of stages. The first period was from prehistoric times to 552 A.D. when Shinto reigned supreme among the people of Japan without any serious competition.

In 552 A.D. Buddhism started gaining in popularity among the Japanese people. In the year 645 A.D., the Emperor Kotoku embraced Buddhism and rejected Shinto.

From A.D. 800 to 1700, Shinto became combined with other religions, mixing with both Buddhism and Confucianism and forming what is called *Ryobu Shinto,* or dual-aspect Shinto. Shinto, by itself, experienced a considerable decline during this period.

Revival

Around 1700 Shinto experienced a revival when the study of archaic Japanese texts was reinstituted. One of the most learned Shinto scholars of the period was Hirata, who wrote:

> The two fundamental doctrines are: that Japan is the country of the Gods, and her inhabitants are the descendants of the Gods. Between the Japanese people and the Chinese, Hindus, Russians, Dutch, Siamese, Cambodians and other nations of the world there is a difference of kind, rather than of degree.
>
> The Mikado is the true Son of Heaven, who is entitled to reign over the four seas and the ten-thousand countries.
>
> From the fact of the divine descent of the Japanese people proceeds their immeasurable superiority to the natives of other countries in courage and intelligence. They "are honest and upright of heart, and are not given to useless theorizing and falsehoods like other nations" (Cited by Robert E. Hume, *The World's Living Religions,* New York: Charles Scribner's Sons, rev. ed., 1959, p. 172).

These ideas revitalized Shinto among the Japanese people since it reestablished the divine origin of the land and the people of Japan.

State Religion

Japanese Emperor Meiji established Shinto as the official religion of Japan in place of Buddhism. However, since the people continued to embrace both religions, in 1877 Buddhism was allowed to be practiced by the people, with total religious liberty granted two years afterward.

State Shinto, which is to be regarded as a patriotic ritual by the citizens irrespective of their religion, paid homage to the Emperor, and was established in 1882. This soon became, for all intents and purposes, the state religion. After the military victories of Japan in World War I, the idea of the divinity of the Emperor became solidly entrenched again in the people. It was not until the defeat of World War II that state Shinto was abolished as the religion of the Japanese people. With the fall of state Shinto, the shrines no longer came under government control and are now supported by private means.

Meaning of Shinto

The word Shinto comes from the Chinese word *Shen-tao,* which means "the way of the gods." This term was not applied to the religion until the sixth century A.D., in order to distinguish it from Buddhism. A major feature of Shinto is the notion of *kami. Kami* is a difficult term to define precisely but it refers basically to the concept of sacred power in both animate and inanimate objects. Ninian Smart elaborates upon the idea of *kami* in the following manner:

> Shintoism displayed, and still displays, a powerful sense of the presence of gods and spirits in nature. These spirits are called *kami,* literally "superior beings," and it is appropriate to venerate them. The kami are too numerous to lend themselves to a systematic ordering or stable hierarchy, but among the many the sun goddess Amaterasu has long held a central place in Shinto belief. According to the myth found at the beginning of the *Kojiki,* the earliest of the celestial gods who came into being instructed Izanagi and Izanami, male and female deities of the second generation of gods, to create the world, and in particular the islands of Japan (the two were in effect identified).
>
> Through the process of sexual generation they produced the land, and the kami of the mountains, trees, and streams, the god of the wind and the god of fire, and so on. Eventually. . . the goddess Amaterasu, the great kami of the Sun, came into being. Possibly, prior to the mythological account of her origin she was the mother goddess of the Yamato clans; the mythology may reflect the way in which the other deities were successively replaced in the earliest period, and then were put under the dominance of the chief kami of the Yamato. But the line between kami and human is not a sharp one, however exalted some of the deities may be.
>
> The Japanese people themselves, according to the traditional myths, are descended from the kami; while the line of emperors traces its descent back to Amaterasu. Amaterasu sent her son Ni-ni-gi down to rule Japan for her, and thence the imperial line took its origin (this tradition in recent times was given exaggerated emphasis in order to make Shinto into an ideology justifying a nationalistic expansionist policy). The line, too, between the personal and impersonal in the kami is fluid. Some of the spirits associated with particular places or things are not strongly personalized, though the mythology concerned with the great gods and goddesses is fully anthropomorphic (Ninian Smart, *The Religious Experience of Mankind,* New York: Charles Scribner's Sons, 1969, pp. 192, 193).

Sacred Books

Although Shinto does not consider any one volume as the wholly inspired revelation on which its religion is based, two books are considered sacred and have done much to influence the beliefs of the Japanese people. These works are *Ko-ji-ki,* the "records of ancient matters," and *Nihongi,* the "chronicles of Japan." They were both composed around 720 A.D. and in that they report events occurring some 1300 years earlier in the history of Japan, they are to be considered late works.

The *Ko-ji-ki* is the oldest existing written record in Japanese. The work contains myth, legend and historical narrative in relating the story of Japan, the imperial ancestors and the imperial court. The work was compiled around 712 A.D.

The *Nihon-gi*, compiled around 720 A.D., chronicles the origin of Japan up until 700 A.D.

Types of Shinto

Since Shinto has neither a founder, sacred writings, nor any authoritative set of beliefs, there are great diversities in the two types of Shinto practiced and the beliefs held. Some Shinto groups do claim a founder, authoritative scriptures, and specific doctrine. These groups are designated sects of Shinto. However, the majority of practitioners have no such set beliefs but worship freely at various shrines located throughout Japan. This practice of *Shrine Shinto* is usually identified with the term *Shinto*.

Worship

The basic place for worship in Shinto is at one of the numerous shrines covering the country of Japan. Although many Shintoists have built altars in their homes, the center of worship is the local shrine. Since Shinto has a large number of deities, a systematic worship of all such deities is impossible. The Shinto religious books acknowledge that only a few deities are consistently worshipped, the chief being the sun-goddess, *Amaterasu.*

There is a grand imperial shrine dedicated to the worship of *Amaterasu* at Ise, some 200 miles southwest of Tokyo. This centralized place of worship is the most sacred spot in all of Japan. The practice of worshipping at this particular spot has its roots before the time of Christ. It is here that the Shintoists make a pilgrimage to worship at the outer court, while the inner court is reserved for the priests and government officials.

Amaterasu is the chief deity of Shinto and is feminine rather than masculine. That the highest object of worship from whom the divine ancestors arose is a female rather than a male deity is unique among the larger world religions.

A Shinto Prayer

The following Shinto prayer, found in the *Yengishiki*, shows the Shintoists' intermingling of their spiritual feeling with nature:

> I declare in the great presence of the From-Heaven-shining-great-deity who sits in Ise.
> Because the Sovereign great goddess bestows on him the countries of the four quarters over which her glance extends,
> As far as the limit where Heaven stands up like a wall,
> As far as the bounds where the country stands up distant,
> As far as the limit where the blue clouds spread flat,
> As far as the bounds where the white clouds lie away fallen—

The blue sea plain as far as the limit whither come the prows of the ships without drying poles or paddles,
The ships which continuously crowd on the great sea plain,
And the roads which men travel by land, as far as the limit whither come the horses' hoofs, with the baggage-cords tied tightly, treading the uneven rocks and tree-roots and standing up continuously in a long path without a break—
Making the narrow countries wide and the hilly countries plain,
And as it were drawing together the distant countries by throwing many tens of ropes over them—
He will pile up the first-fruits like a range of hills in the great presence of the Sovereign great goddess, and will peacefully enjoy the remainder.

Shinto and Christianity

The religion of Shinto is in opposition to Christianity. The fact that Shinto in its purest form teaches the superiority of the Japanese people and their land above all others on earth is diametrically opposed to the teaching of the Bible. According to the Bible, the Jews are God's chosen people through whom He entrusted His words.

"Then what advantage has the Jew? or what is the benefit of circumcision? Great in every respect. First of all, that they were entrusted with the oracles of God" (Romans 3:1, 2, NASB). However, though the Jews are God's chosen people, they have never been designated better than any other people (Galatians 3:27) and they have never been taught that they were direct descendants of the gods, as Shinto teaches.

Shintoism fosters a pride and a feeling of superiority in the Japanese people. This type of pride is condemned by God, who says, "There is none righteous, not even one" (Romans 3:10, NASB). The same lesson was learned by the Apostle Peter who concluded: "I most certainly understand now that God is not one to show partiality, but in every nation the man who fears Him and does what is right, is welcome to Him" (Acts 10:34, NASB).

Since Shinto teaches the basic goodness and divine origin of its people, there is no need for a Savior. This is the natural consequence of assuming one's race is of celestial origin.

Christianity teaches that all of us need a savior because our sins need to be punished. God, through Jesus Christ, took that punishment on Himself so that all mankind could be brought back into a proper relationship with Him. "Namely, that God was in Christ reconciling the world to Himself, not counting their trespasses against them, and He has committed to us the word of reconciliation. Therefore, we are ambassadors for Christ, as though God were entreating through us; we beg you on behalf of Christ, be reconciled to God. He made Him who knew no sin to be sin on our behalf, that we might become the righteousness of God in Him" (2 Corinthians 5:19-21, NASB).

Furthermore, the *Ko-ji-ki* and *Nihon-gi*, as the basis of the Shinto myth, are found to be hopelessly unhistorical and totally unverifiable. The stories and legends contained in these works are a far cry from the historically verifiable documents of both the Old and New Testaments.

The concept of *kami* is both polytheistic and crude, surrounded by much superstition. This is in contrast to the God of the Bible whose ways are righteous and beyond reproach. Immorality abounds in the stories of Shinto while the Bible is quick to condemn acts of immorality.

> The Bible deals very frankly with the sins of its characters. Read the biographies today, and see how they try to cover up, overlook or ignore the shady side of people. Take the great literary geniuses; most are painted as saints. The Bible does not do it that way. It simply tells it like it is:
>
> The sins of the people denounced—Deuteronomy 9:24
>
> Sins of the patriarchs—Genesis 12:11-13; 49:5-7
>
> Evangelists paint their own faults and the faults of the apostles—Matthew 8:10-26; 26:31-56; Mark 6:52; 8:18; Luke 8:24, 25; 9:40-45; John 10:6; 16:32
>
> Disorder of the churches—1 Corinthians 1:11; 15:12; 2 Corinthians 2:4, etc.
>
> (Josh McDowell, *Evidence That Demands a Verdict*, San Bernardino, CA: Campus Crusade for Christ International, 1972, p. 23).

Shinto finds little acceptance apart from Japan since everything of Japanese origin is exalted and that which is non-Japanese is abased. Shinto is a textbook example of a religion invented by man to explain his ancestry and environment while taking no consideration of anyone but himself.

Shintoistic Terms

Amaterasu—The sun-goddess, the chief deity worshipped in Shintoism.

Bushido Code—Literally, "the warrior-knight-way." The code practiced by the military class of the feudal period (Samurai) which has held a fascination with the Japanese people throughout its history. The code is an unwritten system of behavior stressing loyalty to emperor and country.

Emperor Meiji—The Japanese emperor who established Shinto as the state religion of Japan.

Harakiri—The ceremonial suicide committed by the Bushido warrior performed as an atonement for failure or bad judgment. The warrior believed death was to be preferred to disgrace.

Hondon—The inner sanctuary of a Shinto shrine in which is housed the Shintai, or "god body."

Izanagi—The "female-who-invites." The female deity who, according to the Shinto myth, gave birth to the eight islands of Japan.

Izanami—The "male-who-invites." The male deity who, along with the female deity Izanagi, helped produce the Japanese islands and the Japanese people.

*Jigai*The method of suicide consisting of cutting the jugular vein. It is committed by females as an atonement for their sins.

Kami—The sacred power found in both animate and inanimate objects. This power is deified in Shintoism.

Kami Dama—"The god shelf" which is found in most private homes on which are placed memorial tablets with the names of an ancestor or deity ty inscribed on it.

Ko-Ji-Ki—The "records of ancient matters" composed in 712 A.D., charting the imperial ancestors and the imperial court.

Mikado—A term used by foreigners to designate the emperor of Japan.

Nihon-Gi—The "chronicles of Japan" composed around 720 A.D. This work is a history of Japan from its origin until 700 A.D.

O-Harai—"The Great Purification." The greatest of all Shinto ceremonies by which the people go through a national purging of their sins.

Ryobu Shinto—Also known as, "dual aspect Shinto." The term refers to the mixing of Shintoism with Buddhism and Confucianism.

Shintai—An object of worship housed in the inner sanctuary of a Shinto shrine. The Shintai is usually an object of little value, such as a sword or mirror, but it supposedly contains magical powers and consequently is viewed as a good-luck charm.

Shinto—The term *Shinto* is derived from the Chinese term, *Shen-tao*, meaning the "way of the higher spirits." *Shinto* is the designation for the religion that has long characterized Japan and its people.

Shinto Myth—The belief that the islands of Japan and the Japanese people are of divine origin.

State Shinto—The patriotic ritual, established in 1882, which worshipped the emperor as the direct descendant of the gods. State Shinto was abolished at the end of World War II.

Shintoism Bibliography

Hume, Robert E., *The World's Living Religions*, New York: Charles Scribner's Sons, rev. ed., 1959.

Noss, John B., *Man's Religions*, New York: MacMillan Company, 1974.

Offner, Clark B. in *The World's Religions*, Sir Norman Anderson, ed., Grand Rapids, MI: William B. Eerdmans Publishing Company, 1976.

Smart, Ninian, *The Religious Experience of Mankind*, New York: Charles Scribner's Sons, 1969.

CHAPTER SEVEN

Zoroastrianism

Z oroastrianism, a unique religion which stresses the eternal battle of good versus evil, has had a larger impact than its small number of followers (100,000) would suggest. It is the religion of one man who lived some 600 years before the birth of Christ. His name was Zoroaster. The religiously fertile area of Babylonia (modern Iraq and Iran) was his home.

History

Zoroaster

The founder of Zoroastrianism was the man Zoroaster (a Greek corruption of the old Iranian word *Zarathushtra*). His time and place of birth are unknown, but it is generally believed that he was born around 650 B.C. in Persia (present-day Iran). However, as Richard Cavendish observed, there is much doubt as to when and where Zoroaster was born:

> The early history of Zoroastrianism is much in dispute. The religion was founded by Zoroaster (the Greek form of his name, which is Zarathushtra in Persian), but it is not certain when he lived, where he lived or how much of later Zoroastrianism came from him. Tradition puts him in western Iran in the sixth century B.C., a little earlier than the Buddha in India, but it is now thought that he lived in northeastern Iran, in the area on the borders of modern Afghanistan and Turkmenistan. An alternative theory dates him much earlier, somewhere in the period from 1700 to 1500 B.C., and places him in the plains of Central Asia, perhaps before the first groups of Aryans moved south from the plains into Iran and India (Richard Cavendish, *The Great Religions*, New York: Arco Publishing Company, 1980, p. 125).

Tradition says that Zoroaster was the son of a camel merchant and grew up at a time when his fellow Persians worshipped many gods. While growing up he had a keen interest in religion, pondering the mysteries of life. At an early age he became known for his compassionate nature, especially toward the elderly.

Zoroaster had an excellent education, studying with some of the best teachers in Persia. Yet he became restless, and at age 20 he left his father and mother in a search for answers to life's deepest questions. He would seek, from all those whom he met, answers to his religious questions.

During this time of Zoroaster's religious quest, it is said he used his medical ability to help heal those ravaged by the ongoing wars. It was at age 30 that Zoroaster received enlightenment. As the account goes, Zoroaster received a vision on the banks of the Daitya River when a large figure appeared to him. This personage identified himself as *Vohu Manah*, or "good thought." This figure took Zoroaster into the presence of the wise lord *Ahura-Mazda*, who instructed Zoroaster in the true religion.

Zoroaster spent the next ten years proclaiming his newly discovered truth but had little success. The movement began to grow after Zoroaster converted a prince named Vishtaspa, who helped propagate his new-found faith. During the ensuing years the faith spread rapidly. Zoroastrian tradition records two holy wars which were fought over the faith, the second of which took the life of Zoroaster at age 77. However, though the prophet died, the faith remained alive. Zoroastrianism quickly destroyed the magic and idol worship prevalent then and established its own belief in one god, a heaven, and a hell (see Maurice Rawlings, *Life-Wish: Reincarnation: Reality or Hoax*, Nashville: Thomas Nelson Inc., 1981, p. 63).

The Deification of Zoroaster

As is true with many religious leaders, the later disciples of Zoroaster, far removed in time from their master, made him an object of veneration. Thus, Zoroaster became an object of worship along with the deity *Ahura-Mazda*. He is lauded in the following terms:

Head of the two-footed race; the wisest of all beings in the perfection of his holiness; the only one who can daunt evil (Max Mueller, ed., *Secret Books of the East*, Oxford: Krishna Press, 1897-1910, 23:190, 229, 275).

The chieftainship of all things was from Zoroaster; the completely good, the righteous Zoroaster (*Ibid.*, 5:88; 18:90).

Incomparable among mankind through his desire for righteousness, and his understanding the means of defeating the destroyer, and teaching creatures (*Ibid.*, 37:241).

A heavenly radiance "came down from the endless light" to the grandmother of Zoroaster for his birth from a radiantly wonderful virgin mother (*Ibid.*, 47:18-20, 138-139).

He was pre-existent, 3,000 years before his physical birth, and during the interval he remained with the archangels equal to the archangels (*Ibid.*, 47:21, 22, 122).

Present-day Status

Richard Cavendish sums up the present-day status of Zoroastrianism:

The principal religions of the world count their adherents in the millions, and on this scale it almost needs a microscope to see Zoroastrianism at all. There are about 100,000 Zoroastrians in India and Pakistan, where they are called Parsis. They do not accept converts and their numbers are steadily diminishing. There are also a few thousand Zoroastrians in Iran, and smaller communities in North America, Britain, East Africa and Hong Kong. Despite its comparative poverty in numbers, however, Zoroastrianism is enormously rich in ideas, which have had an influence far beyond its own ranks (Richard Cavendish, *op. cit.*, p. 125).

Because of the influence it exerts, Zoroastrianism is still a religion to be reckoned with.

The Avesta

The sacred scripture of the Zoroastrians is known as the *Avesta*, originally written in an old Iranian language called *Avestan*. Of the original work only a small fraction has survived, with the total size about one-tenth that of the Bible. The *Avesta* contains hymns, prayers and ritual instruction. It is divided into three major sections, the oldest of which is called *Yasna*.

Within the *Yasna* there is a group of five hymns known as the *Gathas*, which are composed in a more archaic dialect than the remainder of the *Avesta*. These hymns are generally assumed to be the closest account we have of the very words of Zoroaster.

The *Gathas* stress the lordship of *Ahura-Mazda* as the only supreme God, along with an exhortation to righteous living. The *Gathas* also reveal that the righteous will receive a reward at the end of this present age.

The second major section is called the *Yashts* and contains hymns to various deities. The third section is known as the *Videvdāt* (or *Vendīdād*) and is a section written much later, containing the law against the demons along with other codes and regulations.

The priests of Zoroastrianism are called *magi* and use magic in their communion with God. This is the source for our English word "magic."

Ahura-Mazda

According to Zoroaster, there is one true deity to be worshipped. His name is *Ahura-Mazda* (wise lord). The opening lines of the *Avesta* exalt this deity:

> Ahura-Mazda, the creator, radiant, glorious, greatest and best, most beautiful, most firm, wisest, most perfect, the most bounteous spirit! (Max Mueller, ed., *op. cit.*, 31:195-196).

The *Gathas* attribute the following characteristics to *Ahura-Mazda*:

Creator: (*Yasna*, 31:7, 11; 44:7; 50:11; 51:7.)
All-seeing: (*Yasna*, 31:13; 44:2.)
All-knowing: (*Yasna*, 31:13; 45:3; 48:2-3.)
Most mighty, greatest:(*Yasna*, 28:5; 33:11; 45:6.)
Friendly: (*Yasna*, 31:21; 44:2; 4:2.)
Father of Justice or Right, *Asha*: (*Yasna*, 44:3; 47:2.)
Father of Good Mind, *Vohu Manah*: (*Yasna*, 31:8; 45:4.)
Beneficent, *hudae*: (*Yasna*, 45:6; 48:3.)
Bountiful, *spenta*: (*Yasna*, 43:4, 5, 7, 9, 11, 13, 15; 44:2; 45:5; 46:9; 48:3; 51:10.)
Most bountiful spirit, *spenishta mainyu*: (*Yasna*, 30:5.)

Angra Mainyu

Although *Ahura-Mazda* is the supreme deity, he is opposed by another powerful force known as *Angra Mainyu*, or *Ahriman*, "the bad spirit." From the beginning of existence these two antagonistic spirits have been at odds with each other:

> Now the two primal Spirits, who revealed themselves in vision as Twins, are the Better and the Bad in thought and word and action. And between these two the wise once chose aright, the foolish not so. And when these twain Spirits came together in the beginning, they established Life and Not-Life, and that at the last the Worst Existence (Hell) shall be to the followers of the Lie, but the Best Thought (Paradise) to him that follows Right. Of these twain Spirits he that followed the Lie *chose* doing the worst things; the holiest Spirit *chose* Right (James Hope Moulton, *Early Zoroastrianism*, London: Constable and Company, 1913, *Yasna* 30:3-5, p. 349).

These two powers have been co-equal from the beginning of time and will continue to battle each other until the end of the world. As Zoroastrian doctrine developed, both *Ahura-Mazda* and *Angra Mainyu* were given seven attributes (known as the *Amesha-stentas*) which were corresponding opposites:

Ahura-Mazda	*Angra Mainyu*
Ahura-Mazda (God of light, wisdom)	*Angra Mainyu* (Prince of darkness)
Asha (right, justice)	*Druj* (falsehood)
Vohu monah (good mind)	*Akem* (evil mind)
Kshathra (power)	*Dush-kshathra* (cowardice)
Armaiti (love)	*Taromaiti* (false pretense)
Haurvatat (health)	*Avetat* (misery)
Ameretat (immortality)	*Merethyn* (annihilation)

Future Judgment

Zoroastrianism was one of the earliest religions to teach an ultimate triumph of good over evil. There would be punishment in the end for the wicked and reward for the righteous. The following portions of the *Gathas* present this doctrine:

> *Yasna* 30:2, 4, 9-11; 31:8, 19; 32:6, 15; 33:3, 5; 43:12; 45:7; 46:12; 48:4; 51:6; 53:7-9

Influence Upon Other Religions

One of the claims made by some religious scholars is that Zoroastrianism has had a profound effect in shaping the doctrines of three major religions: Judaism, Islam and Christianity. Consider the following assertions:

> The importance of Zoroastrianism has always been qualitative rather than quantitative. Its highest significance lies in the influence it has exercised on the development of at least three other great religions. First, it made contributions to Judaism, for between 538 B.C. (when the Persians under Cyrus captured Babylonia and set free the Jews exiled in that land) and 330 B.C. (when

the Persian Empire was destroyed by Alexander) the Jews were directly under the suzerainty of the Zoroastrians. And it was from the suzerains that the Jews first learnt to believe in an Ahriman, a personal devil, whom they called in Hebrew, Satan. Possibly from them, too, the Jews first learnt to believe in a heaven and hell, and in a Judgment Day for each individual (Lewis Browne, *This Believing World*, New York: MacMillan Company, 1926, pp. 216, 217).

Influence on the Bible

Of all the other nine extra-Biblical living religions, Zoroastrianism is the only one from which a definite religious belief has been borrowed and included in the Bible. Consistently throughout the Old Testament down to and including the Isaiah of the Exile, the ultimate source of everything, including evil, is represented as the God Jehovah. But a distinct change took place after the Exile. A comparison of two parallel accounts of a certain experience of King David will show that a post-exilic document (1 Chronicles 21:1) substitutes "Satan" for "Jehovah" in the pre-exilic account (2 Samuel 24:1). Thus Satan is not an original feature of the Bible, but was introduced from Zoroastrianism.

Perhaps certain other innovations besides the idea of a Satan were adopted from Zoroastrianism by the Hebrews after they had come into direct contact with that religion in the Babylonian Exile: for example, the ideas of an elaborate angelology and demonology, of a great Saviour or Deliverer to come, of a final resurrection and divine Judgment, and a definitely picturable future life. Certainly Jesus' word "Paradise" (Greek, *paradeisos*, Luke 23:43) was, at least etymologically, derived form Persian origin (Avestan, *pairidaeza*)(Robert E. Hume, *The World's Living Religions*, New York: Charles Scribner's Sons, rev. ed., 1959, p. 200).

Although many teach that Zoroastrianism has had a profound influence upon the teachings of the Bible, we believe this is not the case at all.

In other works *(Answers, Reasons)* we have demonstrated that Christianity is not a man-made religion, as many assume, but it is rather the one true faith supernaturally revealed by the true and living God. The Bible claims to be God's unique revelation of Himself, and we have shown the evidence that leads one in that direction. If this be true, then the practices of other religions, including Zoroastrianism, could not have affected Biblical doctrine as is claimed.

Those who claim Zoroastrianism has had an effect on the Bible begin with the inherent assumption that the Old Testament was written later than the traditional evidence shows. Many books, such as the Pentateuch (Genesis-Deuteronomy), Job and Isaiah chapters 40-66, are wrongly dated during or after the exile (ca 536 B.C.) instead of as early as 1300 B.C. Consequently, when these concepts appear in certain biblical books, they are given a late date because they are already assumed to have been influenced by other religions.

In *More Evidence That Demands a Verdict* (written by Josh McDowell), we see that these assumptions of the late dating of the Old Testament are anything but assured. If one accepts the traditional dating of the Old Testament, then the proverbial shoe is on the other foot. It is not Zoroastrianism that influenced biblical doctrine when the Jews were in exile under Persian rule; it is the Bible that influenced Zoroastrianism!

Moreover, the ideas that are suposed to have influenced New Testament doctrine (resurrection, final judgment, a messiah) were either taught in the Old Testament before the rise of Zoroastrianism or come from later Zoroastrian teachings which first appeared *after* the birth of Christ. Therefore, we stongly believe if there was any influencing on one by the other, it is Zoroastrianism that has been influenced by the Bible, not the opposite.

Zoroastrianism and Christianity

Although Zoroastrianism has been thought to have exerted an influence over some of the beliefs of Christianity, there is much in Zoroastrianism that is incompatible with Christianity.

The God of Zoroastrianism is similar to the God revealed in the Bible; however, there are some major differences. *Ahura-Mazda* is not an all-powerful God but is only equal in strength to *Angra Mainyu*. They are co-equal and co-eternal.

According to the Bible, God is the only all-powerful Being, with His archenemy, Satan, a created being.

> "'You are My witnesses,' declares the Lord, 'And My servant whom I have chosen, in order that you may know and believe Me, and understand that I am He'" (Isaiah 43:10, NASB). Speaking of Satan, the Scripture says, "You were blameless in your ways from the day you were created, until unrighteousness was found in you" (Ezekiel 28:15, NASB).

Satan is not the opposite of God, for he is neither all-powerful nor eternal. (See our previous volume in this series, *Understanding the Occult,* on the character and abilities of Satan).

Zoroastrianism believes that a person earns favor with God by his good works. There is no answer to the sin problem of mankind, for the difference between a good man and a bad man is considered to be only relative. According to the Bible, there is no one who is good enough on his own to make it to heaven. This is why Jesus Christ had to die on the cross, to solve the problem of sin. The Bible makes this very clear:

> As it is written, There is none righteous, not even one (Romans 3:10, NASB).
>
> For all have sinned and fall short of the glory of God (Romans 3:23, NASB).
>
> For the wages of sin is death, but the free gift of God is eternal life in Christ Jesus our Lord (Romans 6:23, NASB).
>
> For by grace you have been saved through faith, and that not of yourselves, it is the gift of God; not as a result of works, that no one should boast (Ephesians 2:8, 9, NASB).
>
> He saved us, not on the basis of deeds which we have done in righteousness, but according to His mercy, by the washing of regeneration, and renewing by the Holy Spirit (Titus 3:5, NASB).

The practice of Zoroastrianism involves much that is occultic and superstitious, something resoundingly condemned in the Scripture. The practice of drinking *haoma* (*soma* in India), a hallucinogenic, has become a central rite in Zoroastrian worship.

Any type of involvement in occultic practices is strongly forbidden by the Bible. "There shall not be found among you anyone who makes his son or his daughter pass through the fire, one who interprets omens, or a sorcerer, or one who casts out a spell, or a medium, or a spiritist, or one who calls up the dead. For whoever does these things is detestable to the Lord; and because of these detestable things the Lord your God will drive them out before you" (Deuteronomy 18:10-12, NASB).

Worship in Zoroastrianism is legalistic and impersonal, reflecting the view of its impersonal god, *Ahura-Mazda.* In Christianity, God is to be worshipped personally with all one's heart, since His nature is personal.

Psalm 100 reflects the proper attitude with which to approach the God of the Bible. "Shout joyfully to the Lord, all the earth. Serve the Lord with gladness; come before Him with joyful singing. Know that the Lord Himself is God; it is He who has made us, and not we ourselves; we are His people and the sheep of His pasture. Enter His gates with thanksgiving, and His courts with praise. Give thanks to Him; bless His name. For the Lord is good; His loving-kindness is everlasting, and His faithfulness to all generations" (Psalm 100, NASB).

Zoroastrianism may resemble something of Christianity on the surface, but a close comparison of the two will reveal the contradictory differences between them.

Zoroastrianism Terms

Ahura-Mazda—The supreme deity, creator of the world, the principle of good.

Amesha-Spenta—One of the seven archangels.

Angra Mainyu—The evil creator, archenemy of *Ahura-Mazda.*

Avesta—The sacred scriptures of Zoroastrianism.

Dakhmas—The towers of silence where the Zoroastrians dispose of their dead by leaving the bodies partially uncovered to be eaten by vultures. This practice keeps the soil and water from being contaminated with dead flesh.

Fire Temple—The place where fire worship is carried on. An important practice in present-day Zoroastrianism.

Gabras—The name given Zoroastrians by Muslims. The term denotes an infidel.

Vivedat (Venidad)—A portion of the *Avesta* containing magic spells and prescriptions for purification.

Vohu Manah—the archangel also known as *good thought.*

Yasna—The most important portion of the *Avesta,* Zoroastrianism's sacred scripture.

Zend-Avesta—A third century A.D. commentary on the Zoroastrian scriptures *(Avesta)* is known as the *Zend.* The combining of the two is called the *Zend-Avesta.*

Zoroastrianism Bibliography

Browne, Lewis, *This Believing World*, New York: MacMillan Company, 1926.

Cavendish, Richard, *The Great Religions*, New York: Arco Publishing Company, 1980.

Hume, Robert E., *The World's Living Religions*, New York: Charles Scribner's Sons, rev. ed., 1959.

Moulton, James Hope, *Early Zoroastrianism*, London: Constable and Company, 1913.

Mueller, Max, ed., *Sacred Books of the East*, Oxford: Krishna Press, 1879-1910.

Rawlings, Maurice, *Life-Wish: Reincarnation: Reality or Hoax*, Nashville: Thomas Nelson Inc., 1981.

CHAPTER EIGHT

Judaism

T o Christians, Judaism is unique among world religions. It is to historic Judaism, the Judaism of the Old Testament, that Christianity traces its roots. Christianity does not supplant Old Testament Judaism; it is the fruition of Old Testament Judaism.

One cannot hold to the Bible, Old and New Testaments, as God's one divine revelation without also recognizing and honoring the place God has given historic Judaism. As the apostle Paul recited, these are some of the blessings God has given to the Jewish people:

> ...to whom belongs the adoption as sons and the glory and the covenants and the giving of the Law and the temple service and the promises, whose are the fathers, and from whom is the Christ according to the flesh, who is over all, God blessed forever. Amen (Romans 9:4, 5, NASB).

Judaism has undergone many changes throughout its long history. At times it has been very close to the true God, serving Him in spirit and in deed. At other times it has ranged far from the will of God, forsaking its promises to Him, while He has remained faithful to Israel.

The true God, the Yahweh of the Old Testament, the God of Christianity, is the God of historic Judaism, the same Master, the people of Israel have long occupied a special place in God's divine plan, and Christians should not overlook this rich spiritual heritage.

Although Judaism as a whole has rejected God's greatest revelation and gift in the Person of Jesus Christ our Lord, Christians cannot deny Judaism's vital contributions to our faith. We should earnestly pray that the physical descendants of Abraham will recognize that their spiritual heritage is also in Abraham and will return to it (see Romans 11:17-24).

History of Judaism

Judaism had its origin when a man named Abram received a divine call from the one true God to leave his idolatrous people in "Ur of the Chaldees" and go to the land of Canaan. This call is recorded in Genesis 12:1-3 (NASB).

Now the Lord said to Abram,
Go forth from your country,
And from your relatives
And from your father's house,
To the land which I will show you;
And I will make you a great nation,
And I will bless you,
And make your name great;
And so you shall be a blessing;
And I will bless those who bless you,
And the one who curses you I will curse.
And in you all the families of the earth shall be blessed.

The promise made to Abram, whose name was later changed to Abraham, included the fact that his descendants would inherit a land which would belong forever to them. This covenant was repeated to Abraham's son Isaac and likewise to Isaac's son Jacob. The family of Jacob, whose name was changed to Israel, migrated to Egypt to escape a severe famine. They were soon enslaved and forced to build mighty cities for the pharaoh. During the years of bondage they continually cried out for a deliverer.

Moses

God eventually raised up a man from among His people to deliver them out of the bondage of Egypt; his name was Moses. Moses led the children of Israel in the exodus from Egypt through the miraculous power of God, which included parting the Red Sea to allow them to escape from the Egyptians. Because of unbelief the people did not immediately enter into the land but wandered in the desert for 40 years. It was during this time of wandering that God gave the Law, including the Ten Commandments, to Moses.*

The Promised Land

Under the leadership of Moses' successor, Joshua, the Jews entered into the promised land but had to conquer the inhabitants before settling down. After Joshua, the nation of Israel was governed by judges for 350 years. During this time they were engaged in numerous battles with the neighboring nations, falling in and out of subjugation to those nations.

After the time of the judges, the Israelites pleaded with God (through the prophet Samuel) for a king to rule them. Although it was not God's desire, He gave them their first king, Saul. Saul did not follow the Lord but almost ruined the nation of Israel. When he died, he had been abandoned by the people and by God.

David, called a man after God's own heart, and divinely appointed to lead the nation, was the second king. He conquered Jerusalem and established it as Israel's capital. David's son Solomon, upon becoming

---

* See Josh McDowell's previous works, *Evidence that Demands a Verdict* and *More Evidence that Demands a Verdict*, for information on the validity of the Old Testament record and for an affirmation of the validity of miracles.

king, built a magnificent temple to the Lord.

During the reign of Solomon, Israel prospered greatly, becoming a leader of nations. Upon the death of Solomon, the nation was divided into two kingdoms, the southern, known as Judea with Jerusalem as its capital, and the northern kingdom of Israel, of which Samaria became the capital.

The Captivity

Both the northern and southern kingdoms were constantly threatened by other nations and each eventually was overcome. The Assyrians conquered the northern kingdom in 721 B.C. and the Babylonians defeated the southern kingdom in 606 B.C. When the southern kingdom was captured, Solomon's temple was destroyed.

During the years the southern kingdom was in exile (606 B.C. to 536 B.C.), changes took place with regard to Jewish worship. Since the temple could not be used as a central place of worship, houses of prayer, called synagogues, were established. The teacher of the synagogue, known as the rabbi, grew in importance to the Jewish people and simultaneously the priests lost importance. By the time the Jews returned to their land, the synagogue had become firmly established as the place of worship (but not sacrifice).

The Restoration

During the period of the restoration, the Jews became exposed to Greek culture (Hellenism) when Alexander the Great conquered the world (336-323 B.C.). Upon Alexander's death, the land fell under the rule of the Ptolemies of Egypt. The Hellenic influence was so strong during this time that many Jews no longer understood biblical Hebrew. Aramaic and Greek became the dominant languages in Palestine. During this period the Old Testament was translated into Greek (this text is commonly called the Septuagint, abbreviated as LXX), for the benefit of those Jews who did not read Hebrew.

The Revolt

The people soon became part of the Syrian Kingdom, and when one of the kings, Antiochus IV Epiphanes, tried to suppress the Jewish religion, the people revolted. In 167 B.C. a rebellion led by Judas Maccabaeus resulted in the independence of the Jewish nation, celebrated to this day by the festival of Hanukkah.

The Roman Rule

The independence was short-lived because the Roman general Pompey made Israel a vassal state of Rome in 63 B.C., placing puppet leaders over the people. Rome dominated the people and the land, causing unrest and rebellion among the people. The Roman general Titus destroyed the city of Jerusalem in 70 A.D., scattering the inhabitants. Several rebellions arose after that in an effort to reconquer the land, the last being the Bar Kokhba Rebellion (A.D. 132-135).

Later History

When Christianity became the state religion of the Roman Empire (325 A.D.), the Jews were seen as an accursed race and the center of Jewish life soon moved to Babylonia, a non-Christian country. The Jews did not regain an independent homeland in Israel until 1948 after a long history of persecution which reached its height in the Holocaust of World War II.

The Land

The land of Israel has a very special place in the history of the Jewish people. Leo Trepp comments:

> From the very beginning of history, Jewish destiny has remained inextricably linked to that of the land of Israel. To the Jew, his history starts as Abraham is bidden to migrate to the promised land, for only there can he fulfill himself as the servant and herald of God. The land of Israel always remained the promised land. Only there could Torah be translated freely into the life of an independent nation (Leo Trepp, *Judaism: Development and Life*, Belmont, CA: Dickenson Publishing Company, 1966, pp. 4, 5).

Statement of Faith

One of the great figures in Jewish history was Moses Maimonides, a Spanish Jew who lived in the 12th century A.D. Maimonides, a systematic thinker, tried to condense basic Jewish beliefs into the form of a creed. Although criticized afterward by some, his creed is still followed by the traditional forms of Judaism. The creed is expressed in these 13 basic beliefs:

1. I believe with perfect faith that the Creator, blessed be His Name, is the Creator and Guide of everything that has been created; and He alone has made, does make, and will make all things.
2. I believe with perfect faith that the Creator, blessed be His Name, is One, and that there is no unity in any manner like unto His, and that He alone is our God, who was, and is, and will be.
3. I believe with perfect faith that the Creator, blessed be His Name, is not a body, and that He is free from all the properties of matter, and that He has not any form whatever.
4. I believe with perfect faith that the Creator, blessed be His Name, is the first and the last.
5. I believe with perfect faith that to the Creator, blessed be His Name, and to Him alone, it is right to pray, and that it is not right to pray to any being besides Him.
6. I believe with perfect faith that all the words of the prophets are true.
7. I believe with perfect faith that the prophecy of Moses, our teacher, peace be unto him, was true, and that he was the chief of the prophets, both of those who preceded and of those who followed him.
8. I believe with perfect faith that the whole *Torah*, now in our possession, is the same that was given to Moses, our teacher, peace be unto him.
9. I believe with perfect faith that this Torah will not be changed, and that there will never be any other Law from the Creator, blessed be His Name.
10. I believe with perfect faith that the Creator, blessed be His Name, knows every deed of the children of men, and all their thoughts, as it is said.

It is He that fashioned the hearts of them all, that gives heed to all their works.

11. I believe with perfect faith that the Creator, blessed be His Name, rewards those that keep His commandments and punishes those that transgress them.

12. I believe with perfect faith in the coming of the Messiah; and, though he tarry, I will wait daily for his coming.

13. I believe with perfect faith that there will be a revival of the dead at the time when it shall please the Creator, blessed be His Name, and exalted be His Fame for ever and ever.

For Thy salvation I hope, O Lord.

Jewish Holy Days

The cycle of Jewish holy days is called the sacred round. Based on the ancient Jewish calendar, these holy days serve to remind Jews regularly of significant historical events in which God displayed his covenant with them and to give them regular opportunity to display their commitment to God.

The Sabbath

This is a holy day of rest, in commemoration of God's completed work of creation and in His later liberation of the Israelites from the bondage in Egypt. It is a day of joy and thanksgiving to God for His many blessings.

Passover

Passover (*Pessah*), the festival of spring, is celebrated one month after Purim. It constitutes the beginning of the time of harvest; therefore, it is a time of celebration. However, there is a deeper reason for the people to observe this holiday, as the Scriptures plainly reveal. This feast celebrates the deliverance of the children of Israel from the bondage of Egypt.

The story of the Passover is given in Exodus 12: God sent the final plague on the Egyptians; the death of the firstborn. However, those who put blood on their doorposts were passed over by the angel of death. This plague was instrumental in convincing the pharaoh to allow the children of Israel to leave. Consequently, it is to be celebrated as a permanent memorial by the Jewish people. Deuteronomy 16:1-4 (NASB) tells how it is to be observed:

Observe the month of Abib and celebrate the Passover to the Lord your God, for in the month of Abib the Lord your God brought you out of Egypt by night.

And you shall sacrifice the Passover to the Lord your God from the flock and the herd, in the place where the Lord chooses to establish His name.

You shall not eat leavened bread with it; seven days you shall eat with it unleavened bread, the bread of affliction (for you came out of the land of Egypt in haste), in order that you may remember all the days of your life the day when you came out of the land of Egypt.

For seven days no leaven shall be seen with you in all your territory, and none of the flesh which you sacrifice on the evening of the first day shall remain overnight until morning.

Shabuot

Shabuot, the feast of weeks, comes seven weeks after the Passover. Shabuot commemorates the giving of the Ten Commandments. During ancient times the farmer would bring his firstfruits to the temple on Shabuot and offer them to God. The day is also celebrated by the reading of the Ten Commandments and the recitation of the book of Ruth.

Rosh Hashanah

Rosh Hashanah literally means "head of the year." It is the Jewish New Year, celebrated on the first two days of the month of Tishai (September-October). It is a solemn day of reflection on both the deeds of the past year and the hopes of the upcoming one.

The ram's horn (*shofar*) is sounded in daily worship for an entire month before Rosh Hashanah, calling the people to repentance. Moses Maimonides, the great Jewish theologian and philosopher, explained the message of the day:

> Wake up, ye sleepers, from your sleep; and ye that are in a daze, arouse yourselves from your stupor. Reflect on your actions and return in repentance. Remember your Creator. Be not as those who forget truth in their chase after shadows, wasting their year wholly in vanities which neither help nor bring deliverance. Look into your soul, and mend your ways and deeds. Let everyone forsake his evil ways and worthless thoughts (*Teshubah* 3, 4).

Yom Kippur

Yom Kippur is the holiest day of the year, the day of atonement. It is celebrated ten days after Rosh Hashanah and is devoted to confession of sins and reconciliation with God. Problems with enemies must be reconciled before one can be right with God, and forgiving and forgetting is the order of the day. The day is spent without touching food or drink, the mind being devoted to God on this holiest of days. During this day of confession of sin and fasting, the following passage from Isaiah is read:

> Is it a fast like this which I choose, a day for a man to humble himself? Is it for bowing one's head like a reed, and for spreading out sackcloth and ashes as a bed? Will you call this a fast, even an acceptable day to the Lord? Is this not the fast which I chose, to loosen the bonds of wickedness, to undo the bands of the yoke, and to let the oppressed go free, and break every yoke? Is it not to divide your bread with the hungry, and bring the homeless poor into the house, when you see the naked, to cover him; and not to hide yourself from your own flesh? (Isaiah 58:5-7, NASB)

Yom Kippur has a long Jewish and biblical tradition and is the most important Jewish holy day. Usually even liberal or non-practicing Jews consider the day holy and devote themselves to contrite contemplation and prayer on this day.

Milton Steinberg effectively summarizes the Jewish concept of Yom Kippur:

> . . .Yom Kippur, the day of Atonement, a solemn white fast, during which from dusk to dusk the faithful partake of neither food nor drink in token of penitence,

but through prayer and confession scrutinize their lives, abjure their evil-doing, and seek regeneration, a returning to God and goodness (Milton Steinberg, *Basic Judaism*, New York: Harcourt Brace Jovanovich, 1947, 1975, pp. 130, 131).

Sukkoth

Sukkoth is the feast of tabernacles, or booths. This festival, which commemorates the ingathering of the harvest, is one of the three pilgrim feasts in ancient times where yearly trips were made to the Temple of Jerusalem. It is known as the feast of booths because the people lived in tabernacles, or temporary shelters, during its duration (Exodus 34:18-26). In modern times the people, for the most part, only take their meals in these tabernacles rather than living in them for the duration of the feast.

Hanukkah

Hanukkah, observed for eight days in midwinter, is the only major feast that does not have its source in the Bible. The feast is based upon the story of the Maccabees, recorded in the Apocrypha. When Antiochus IV Epiphanes in 167 B.C. introduced the worship of the Greek gods as the state religion, a small group of Jews led by Judas Maccabee staged a revolt.

Antiochus, who, among other things desecrated the temple by slaughtering a pig in the Holy of Holies, was finally overthrown and freedom of religion returned to the land. Hanukkah is celebrated in observance of the heroic acts of the Maccabees.

The eight-branched candlestick, the Menorah, is integral to Hanukkah worship and commemorates a miracle that took place when the temple was cleansed from the idolatrous acts of Antiochus IV Epiphanes. The tradition states that only enough holy oil was found in the temple to light the lamp for one night. However, because of the providence of God and as a sign that He blessed the Jewish cleansing and rededication of the temple, God miraculously kept the lamp burning for eight days and nights.

Since Hanukkah is celebrated near the Christian Christmas holiday, it has borrowed some ideas from Christmas, including the giving of gifts (traditionally one to each child each of the eight nights), and family gatherings. Especially among non-practicing and reform (liberal) Jews, Hanukkah is a very important holiday.

The Three Branches of Judaism

Very simply stated, modern-day Judaism can be divided into three groups: Orthodox, Conservative and Reform.

Orthodox

Orthodox Judaism designates the traditionalists who are united in their upholding of the Law. The *Encyclopedia of Jewish Religion* says:

> Though Orthodoxy is widely diversified among its many religious groupings and nuances of belief and practice, all Orthodox Jews are united in their belief in the historical event of revelation at Sinai, as described in the Torah; in their acceptance of the Divine Law, in its Written and Oral forms, as immutable

and binding for all times; in their acknowledgment of the authority of duly qualified rabbis—who themselves recognize the validity of the Talmud and all other traditional sources of the Halakhah—to interpret and administer Jewish Law (*Encyclopedia of Jewish Religion*, New York: Holt, Rhinehart and Winston, 1966, p. 293).

Orthodox Judaism observes most of the traditional dietary and ceremonial laws of Judaism. It adheres to the inspiration of the Old Testament [although greater authority is given the Torah (Law), the first five books, than to the rest].

Conservative

Conservative Judaism is sort of a happy medium between Orthodox and Reform Judaism. Founded in the 19th century, the Conservative movement quickly gained strength in both Germany and the United States.

In 1918, six months after the Balfour Declaration, the Conservative movement announced:

We hold that Jewish people are and of right ought to be at home in all lands. Israel, like every other religious communion, has the right to live and assert its message in any part of the world. We are opposed to the idea that Palestine should be considered *the home-land* of the Jews. Jews in America are part of the American nation.

The ideal of the Jew is not the establishment of a Jewish state—not the reassertion of Jewish nationality which has long been outgrown. We believe that our survival as a people is dependent upon the assertion and the maintenance of our historic religious role and not upon the acceptance of Palestine as a home-land of the Jewish people. The mission of the Jew is to witness to God all over the world.

Reform

Reform Judaism is the liberal wing of Judaism. Leo Trepp traces its development:

Abraham Geiger (1810-1874) stands out as the towering genius of Reform Judaism, and is essentially its founder. To him the scientific man cannot accept revelation, for science offers no proof of any revelation. Mendelssohn had seen Judaism as *revealed* law; Geiger rejected this idea, as he equally rejected any revealed doctrines. He refuted the hope for a return to the Land, for the land of citizenship is the land of the Jew. This was an attack on the validity of Torah, of Mitzvot, and of the Land. What remained, then, was the deep-seated sense of kinship with the Jewish *people* (a feeling of which Geiger himself may have been unaware, but which kept him from suggesting the dissolution of Judaism in favor of a general religion of ethical conduct).

Thus, Torah to him becomes a source of ethics, performance of Mitzvot becomes a matter of individual decision, but not binding, the *Talmud* and *Shulhan Arukh* have no power of commitment, and the messianic hope has been fulfilled in Jewish Emancipation. However, the genius of the Jewish people as teachers of ethics was strongly emphasized. The Hebrew language of prayer was to be retained in part, at least, for its emotional appeal. Education, sermon, and worship now were to form Torah in this new interpretation, and Mitzvot were to be understood as the missionary ideal of spreading ethics throughout the world. For these the Jew must live. The effect of Geiger's Reform

Judaism was to be strongly felt, especially in America (Leo Trepp, *op. cit.*, pp. 50, 51).

Reform Judaism is so culture- and race-oriented that it easily can neglect the spiritual and religious side of Jewish life. Rather than assuming that the religious life produces and molds the culture, Reform Judaism assumes that the cultural and racial heritage of the Jews produced and molded the religious life. While belief and doctrine may be changeable or even dispensable, the cultural history of the race is vital to any continuation of Jewishness. There is little concensus on doctrinal or religious belief in Reform Judaism.

Doctrine

Judaism and the Messiah

While Christianity recognizes that the promise of a personal, spiritual savior is the core of biblical revelation, Judaism has long vacillated in its concept of messiahship. That Jesus Christ, the true Messiah predicted in God's Word, would be rejected by the Jews of the first century shows that even at that time there was divergence of opinion on the meaning and authority of messianic passages in Scripture.*

In the course of Jewish history the meaning of the Messiah had undergone changes. Originally it was believed that God would send His special messenger, delivering Israel from her oppressors and instituting peace and freedom. However, today, any idea of a personal messiah has been all but abandoned by the majority of Jews. It has been substituted with the hope of a messianic age characterized by truth and justice.

Within the history of Judaism, from the time of Jesus of Nazareth until Moses Hayyim Luzatto (died A.D. 1747), there have been at least 34 different prominent Jews who have claimed to be the Messiah (James Hastings, *Encyclopedia of Religion and Ethics*, Vol. 8, New York and London: Scribner's and T. & T. Clark, 1919, pp. 581-588).

Carrying on one Jewish tradition, most of these self-proclaimed messiahs promised salvation from political, economic and cultural oppression, rather than spiritual salvation. Only Jesus of Nazareth perfectly fulfilled the Old Testament passages concerning the Messiah and only He validated His claims by His victory over death, displayed in His glorious resurrection from the dead (Acts 2:22-36).

God

The orthodox Jewish concept of God is based upon the Old Testament. The Hebrew scholar Samuel Sandmel summarizes the biblical teaching:

> The heritage from the Bible included a number of significant components about the Deity. God was not a physical being: He was intangible and invisible. He was the Creator and Ruler, indeed, the Judge of the World. He and He alone was truly God; the deities worshipped by peoples other than Israel were not God. Idols were powerless and futile; they were unworthy of worship; and in-

---

* For a discussion of Old Testament prophecies concerning the messiahship of Jesus, see Josh McDowell's *Evidence that Demands a Verdict*, pp. 144 ff.

deed, to worship what was not God was a gross and sinful disrespect of Him.

Scripture contains an abundance of divine terms: Elohim, El, El Elyon, Shaddai. Insofar as God might be thought of as having a name, that name was Yahve. But so holy and awesome was He that His name Yahve itself had force and power, and it was unbecoming or even sinful for men to pronounce it, as was expressed in the words "You shall not take the name of Yahve your God in vain" (Exod. 20:7, Deut. 5:11). Only the High Priest might pronounce it, and only on one day in the year, that on the Day of Atonement.

God was, as it were, above and over the world. His dwelling was in heaven. At high moments, such as at Sinai, He had descended to reveal Himself. Accordingly, He was both in the world and also over and above it. He had very early revealed Himself to the patriarchs; He had later revealed Himself to the prophets. To some of these prophets, such as Zechariah, He had disclosed His divine will and intention by sending an angel to bring His desires from the distance to earth. Apart from sending an angel, He could, and did, pour His "holy" spirit onto selected men. In heaven there were a host of beings, subordinate to Him, who constituted His heavenly council. Among these was Satan who could with divine consent test a man such as Job; a lying spirit who could on occasion delude a presumptuous king or prophet (Samuel Sandmel, *Judaism and Christian Beginnings*, London: Oxford University Press, 1978, pp. 168, 169).

The sacred scriptures of Judaism consist of documents arranged in three groups known as the Law, the Prophets, and the Writings. These books were originally written in Hebrew, except for parts of Daniel and Ezra and a verse in Jeremiah which were composed in Aramaic. These books are synonymous with the 39 books of Christianity's Old Testament. Their composition was over a period of some one thousand years, from 1400-400 B.C.

The Jews do not hold each part of their writings in equal importance. *The Law*, the Torah, is the most authoritative, followed by *the Prophets*, which have lesser authority, and lastly *the Writings*.

Salvation in Judaism

Judaism, while admitting the existence of sin, its abhorrence by God, and the necessity for atonement, has not developed a system of salvation teaching as found in Christianity. Atonement is accomplished by sacrifices, penitence, good deeds and a little of God's grace. No concept of substitutionary atonement (as in Christianity in the Person of Jesus Christ) exists.

Scholar Michael Wyschogrod explains the difference:

A Jew who believes that man is justified by works of the law would hold the belief that man can demand only strict justice from God, nothing more. Such a man would say to God: "Give me what I deserve, neither more nor less; I do not need your mercy, only your strict justice."

If there are Jews who approach God in this spirit, I have never met nor heard of them. In the morning liturgy that Jews recite daily, we find the following: "Master of all worlds: It is not on account of our own righteousness that we offer our supplications before thee, but on account of thy great compassion. What are we? What is our life? What is our goodness? What is our virtue? What is our help? What our strength? What our might?"

The believing Jew is fully aware that if he were to be judged strictly according to his deeds by the standards of justice and without mercy, he would be doomed. He realizes that without the mercy of God there is no hope for him and that he is therefore justified—if by "justified" we mean that he avoids the direst of divine punishments—not by the merit of his works as commanded in the Torah, but by the gratuitous mercy of God who saves man in spite of the fact that man does not deserve it (Tanenbaum, Wilson, and Rudin, eds., *Evangelicals and Jews in Conversation on Scripture, Theology, and History*, Grand Rapids, MI: Baker Book House, 1978, pp. 47, 48).

So then, Jews do believe in the mercy of God but they do not believe in any substitutionary atonement that once and for all time cleanses them from all sin. Contrast this with the great passage of assurance in Hebrews 7:22-28 (NASB):

So much the more also Jesus has become the guarantee of a better covenant. And the former priests, on the one hand, existed in greater numbers, because they were prevented by death from continuing, but He, on the other hand, because He abides forever, holds His priesthood permanently. Hence, also, He is able to save forever those who draw near to God through Him, since He always lives to make intercession for them. For it was fitting that we should have such a high priest, holy, innocent, undefiled, separated from sinners and exalted above the heavens; who does not need daily, like those high priests, to offer up sacrifices, first for His own sins, and then for the sins of the people, because this He did once for all when He offered up Himself. For the Law appoints men as high priests who are weak, but the work of the oath, which came after the Law, appoints a Son, made perfect forever.

Original Sin

Judaism holds no concept of original sin. According to Christian belief, all human beings are born into the world with a sinful nature because of the transgression of Adam (Romans 5:12-21). Judaism's emphasis is not on original sin but original virtue and righteousness. Although Judaism acknowledges that man does commit acts of sin, there is not a sense of man being totally depraved or unworthy as is found in Christian theology.

Atonement for sin is achieved by works of righteousness, which include repentance, prayer and the performing of good deeds. There is no need for a savior, as is emphasized in Christianity.

J.H. Hertz writes:

Note that the initiative in atonement is with the sinner (Ezekiel 18:31). He cleanses himself on the Day of Atonement by fearless self-examination, open confession, and the resolve not to repeat the transgressions of the past year. When our Heavenly Father sees the abasement of the penitent sinner, He sprinkles, as it were, the clean waters of pardon and forgiveness upon him. And again: On the Day of Atonement the Israelites resemble the angels, without human wants, without sins, linked together in love and peace. It is the only day of the year on which the accuser Satan is silenced before the throne of Glory, and even becomes the defender of Israel. . . . The closing prayer (on the Day of Atonement) begins: "Thou givest a hand to transgressors, and Thy right hand is stretched out to receive the penitent. Thou hast taught us to make confession unto Thee of all our sins, in order that we may cease from the violence of our hands and may return unto Thee who delightest in the repentance of the wicked." These words contain what has been called "the Jewish doctrine of salvation" (J. H. Hertz, *The Pentateuch and the Haftorahs*, London: Socino Press, 1938, p. 523 f).

A Common Heritage

Although there are marked differences in many areas of belief and practice between Judaism and Christianity, there is a common heritage that both religions share. The Jewish writer, Pinchas Lapide, comments:

We Jews and Christians are joined in brotherhood at the deepest level, so deep in fact that we have overlooked it and missed the forest of brotherhood for the trees of theology. We have an intellectual and spiritual kinship which goes deeper than dogmatics, hermeneutics, and exegesis. We are brothers in a manifold "elective affinity"

—in the belief in one God our Father,
—in the hope of His salvation,
—in ignorance of His ways,
—in humility before His omnipotence,
—in the knowledge that we belong to Him, not He to us,
—in love and reverence for God,
—in doubt about our wavering fidelity,
—in the paradox that we are dust and yet the image of God,
—in the consciousness that God wants us as partners in the sanctification of the world,
—in the condemnation of arrogant religous chauvinism,
—in the conviction that love of God is crippled without love of neighbor,
—in the knowledge that all speech about God must remain in a stammering on our way to Him (Pinchas Lapide *Israelis, Jews and Jesus*, Garden City, NJ: Doubleday and Company, 1979, p. 2).

The book of Galatians gives us God's view of Jews and Gentiles today. Chapter 3 shows forcefully that God's blessings on the Jews were a means of showing His grace, which was fully expressed in the sacrifice of His son, Jesus Christ, on the cross for the sins of all, Jewish or Gentile. The gospel was preached beforehand to Abraham, the Father of the Jews (5:8) and was given to the Gentiles in Jesus Christ (5:14).

The heritage of the Old Testament, preserved for all mankind by the Jews, points all of us, Jewish or Gentile, to Jesus Christ (5:22-24). Each man, whether of Jewish or Gentile heritage, must come to God through Jesus Christ. There is no other way to true peace with God. As Galatians 3: 26-29 concludes, "For you are all sons of God through faith in Christ Jesus. For all of you who were baptized into Christ have clothed yourselves with Christ. There is neither Jew nor Greek, there is neither slave nor free man, there is neither male nor female; for you are all one in Christ Jesus. And if you belong to Christ, then you are Abraham's offspring, heirs according to promise."

Judaistic Terms

Diaspora—The dispersion of the Jews after the Babylonian Captivity.

Gemarah—The commentary based upon the Mishnah.

Hannukah—The feast of dedication celebrating the Maccabean victory in 167 B.C.

Midrash—A commentary of the Hebrew scriptures, especially the Torah.

Mishnah—Oral law in general to be distinguished from scripture.

Passover—An annual feast commemorating the deliverance of the firstborn in Egypt when the angel of death took all those who did not have blood on the doorpost.

Pentateuch—The first five books of the Old Testament.

Pentecost—The feast of weeks observed fifty days after the Passover. Also called Shabuoth.

Purim—The feast commemorating Esther's intervention on behalf of the Jews when they were in Persia.

Rosh Hashanah—The Jewish New Year.

Seder—The festival held in Jewish homes on the first night of the Passover commemorating the Exodus from Egypt.

Sukkoth—The feast of tabernacles celebrating the harvest.

Torah—Refers to the first five books of the Old Testament (The Law). It also can refer to the entire corpus of the Jewish law.

Shofar—The ram's horn that is blown during services on Rosh Hashanah.

Talmud—The Jewish library of oral law and tradition consisting of Mishnah and Gemara.

Judaism Bibliography

Encyclopedia of Jewish Religion, New York: Holt, Rhinehart and Winston, 1966.

Hastings, James, *Encyclopedia of Religion and Ethics, Vol. 8*, New York and London: Scribner's and T. & T. Clark, 1919.

Hertz, J. H., *The Pentateuch and the Haftorahs*, London: Socino Press, 1938.

Lapide, Pinchas, *Israelis, Jews and Jesus*, Garden City, NJ: Doubleday and Company, 1979.

Sandmel, Samuel, *Judaism and Christian Beginnings*, London: Oxford University Press, 1978.

Steinberg, Milton, *Basic Judaism*, New York: Harcourt Brace Jovanovich, 1947, 1975.

Tanenbaum, Marc, and Wilson, and Rudin, eds., *Evangelicals and Jews in Conversation on Scripture, Theology, and History*, Grand Rapids, MI: Baker Book House, 1978.

Trepp, Leo, *Development and Life*, Belmont, CA: Dickenson Publishing Company, 1966.

CHAPTER NINE

Islam

I n recent years, Islam has been in the spotlight because of the heightened tension in the Middle East. This has served to put its culture under the microscope of world attention. Islam is indeed a major part of Middle Eastern culture, but it is much more.

The Muslim (var. sp.: Moslem) faith is a major driving force in the lives of many of the nations in the Middle East, West Asia and North Africa. The impact of this faith on the world has been increasing steadily. Today, Islam is the fastest-growing religion in the world. In large part, the Arab-Israel tension can be traced back to the Islam-Judaism conflict.

Not only does Islam collectively wield a strong sword in world conflict as Muslims threaten war with Israel, but Islamic sects also threaten even greater unrest in the fragile Middle East and could be catalysts for greater conflict. Right-wing Islamic fundamentalists were responsible for both the takeover of Iran and the assassination of Egyptian President Anwar el-Sadat.

The vast majority of Muslims, however, are not of this militant variety. The contrast between the moderate and progressive Islam of Egypt and the fundamentalistic and reactionary Islam of Iran is marked. Islam has had a great deal of positive impact on many countries where it is a strong force. But positive influence is no reason to follow any religion with one's life-commitment. One must examine the teachings of Islam along with one's faith and ascertain what is true and why.

The very impact of Islam in history also makes it worthy of study. Sir Norman Anderson capsulizes it this way:

> The religion of Islam is one of the outstanding phenomena of history. Within a century of the death of its founder, the Muslim Empire stretched from Southern France through Spain, North Africa, the Levant and Central Asia to the confines of China; and, although Islam has since been virtually expelled from Western Europe and has lost much of its political power elsewhere, it has from time to time made notable advances in Eastern Europe, in Africa, in India, and in Southeast Asia. Today it extends from the Atlantic to the Philippines and numbers some three hundred million adherents drawn from races

as different as the European from the Bantu, and the Aryan Indian from the primitive Philippine tribesmen; yet it is still possible to speak of the "World of Islam" (Sir Norman Anderson, ed., *The World's Religions*, Grand Rapids, MI: William B. Eerdmans Publishing Company, 1976, p. 52).

Today, there are an estimated 450 million members of Islam which dominate more than three dozen countries on three continents. The word *Islam* is a noun which is formed from the Arabic verb meaning "to submit, surrender or commit oneself." *Islam* means submission or surrender, and with the translation comes the idea of action, not simple stagnation. The very act of submissive commitment is at the heart of Islam, not simply a passive acceptance and surrender to doctrine. *Muslim*, another noun form of the same verb, means "the one who submits."

History of Islam

The early history of Islam revolves around one central figure, Muhammad (var. sp.: Muhammed, Mohammed). Although the teaching of Islam is an interesting mixture of different religions, the origin of the faith is found historically in the one person of Muhammad.

Muhammad

Born around 570 A.D. in the city of Mecca in Arabia, Muhammad's father died before his birth. His mother died when he was six. He was raised first by his grandfather and later by his uncle. Muhammad's early background is not well known. Some scholars believe he came from a well-respected family, but this is not certain. What is clear is that he was of the Hashimite clan of the *Al Qu'raysh* tribe. At the age of 25, he married a wealthy 40-year-old widow named Khadijah. Of his life Anderson relates:

> There is evidence in a tradition which can scarcely have been fabricated that Muhammad suffered in early life from fits. Be that as it may, the adult Muhammad soon showed signs of a markedly religious disposition. He would retire to caves for seclusion and meditation; he frequently practiced fasting; and he was prone to dreams. Profoundly dissatisfied with the polytheism and crude superstitions of his native Mecca, he appears to have become passionately convinced of the existence and transcendence of one true God. How much of this conviction he owed to Christianity or Judaism it seems impossible to determine. Monophysite Christianity was at that time widely spread in the Arab Kingdom of Ghassan; the Byzantine Church was represented by hermits dotted about the Hijaz with whom he may well have come into contact; the Nestorians were established at al Hira and in Persia; and the Jews were strongly represented in al Madina, the Yemen and elsewhere. There can be no manner of doubt, moreover, that at some period of his life he absorbed much teaching from Talmudic sources and had contact with some form of Christianity; and it seems overwhelmingly probable that his early adoption of monotheism can be traced to one or both of these influences (*Ibid.*, p. 54).

The character of Muhammad was quite a mosaic, as Anderson summarizes:

> For the rest, his character seems, like that of many another, to have been a strange mixture. He was a poet rather than a theologian: a master improvisor

rather than a systematic thinker. That he was in the main simple in his tastes and kindly in his disposition there can be no doubt; he was generous, resolute, genial and astute: a shrewd judge and a born leader of men. He could, however, be cruel and vindictive to his enemies; he could stoop to assassination; and he was undeniably sensual (*Ibid.*, p. 60).

Robert Payne also brings this out in his book, *The Holy Sword:*

It is worthwhile to pause for a moment before the quite astonishing polarity of Muhammad's mind. Violence and gentleness were at war within him. Sometimes he gives the appearance of living simultaneously in two worlds, at one and the same moment seeing the world about to be destroyed by the flames of God and in a state of divine peace; and he seems to hold these opposing visions only at the cost of an overwhelming sense of strain. Sometimes the spring snaps, and we see him gazing with a look of bafflement at the world around him, which is neither the world in flames nor the world in a state of blessedness, but the ordinary day-to-day world in which he was rarely at home (Robert Payne, *The Holy Sword*, New York: Collier Books, 1962, p. 84).

The Call

As Muhammad grew, his views changed. He came to believe in only one God, Allah, a monotheistic faith. He rejected the idolatrous polytheism of those around him. By the age of 40, the now religious Muhammad had his first vision. These revelations are what are recorded in the *Qur'an (Koran)*.

Muhammad was at first unsure of the source of these visions, whether divine or demonic. His wife, Khadijah, encouraged him to believe they had come from God. Later she became his first convert. However, his most important early convert was a wealthy merchant named Abu Bakr, who eventually became one of his successors.

The Cambridge History of Islam comments on Muhammad's revelations:

Either in the course of the visions or shortly afterwards, Muhammad began to receive "messages" or "revelations" from God. Sometimes he may have heard the words being spoken to him, but for the most part he seems simply to have "found them in his heart." Whatever the precise "manner of revelation"—and several different "manners" were listed by Muslim scholars—the important point is that the message was not the product of Muhammad's conscious mind. He believed that he could easily distinguish between his own thinking and these revelations.

The messages which thus came to Muhammad from beyond his conscious mind were at first fairly short, and consisted of short verses ending in a common rhyme or assonance. They were committed to memory by Muhammad and his followers, and recited as part of their common worship. Muhammad continued to receive the messages at intervals until his death. In his closing years the revelations tended to be longer, to have much longer verses and to deal with the affairs of the community of Muslims at Medina. All, or at least many, of the revelations were probably written down during Muhammad's lifetime by his secretaries (P.M. Holt, ed., *The Cambridge History of Islam*, Vol. II, London: Cambridge University Press, 1970, pp. 31, 32).

Alfred Guillaume states:

Now if we look at the accounts of his call, as recorded by the early biographers, some very interesting parallels with Hebrew prophets come to light. They say that it was his habit to leave the haunts of men and retire to the mountains to give himself up to prayer and meditation. One night as he was asleep the angel Gabriel came to him with a piece of silk brocade whereon words were written, and said "Recite!" He answered "What shall I recite?" The order was repeated three times, while he felt continually increasing physical pressure, until the angel said:

> Recite in the name of thy Lord who created
> Man from blood coagulated.
> Recite! Thy Lord is wondrous kind
> Who by the pen has taught mankind
> Things they knew not (being blind).

When he woke these words seemed to be written on his heart (or, as we should say, impressed indelibly on his mind). Then the thought came to him that he must be a *sha'ir* or possessed, he who had so hated such people that he could not bear the sight of them; and he could not tolerate the thought that his tribesmen would regard him as one of them—as in fact they afterwards did. Thereupon he left the place with the intention of throwing himself over a precipice. But while on his way he heard a voice from heaven hailing him as the Apostle of God, and lifting up his eyes he saw a figure astride the horizon which turned him from his purpose and kept him rooted to the spot. And there he remained long after his anxious wife's messengers had returned to report that they could not find him (Alfred Guillaume, *Islam*, London: Penguin Books, 1954, pp. 28, 29).

Sir Norman Anderson discusses how Muhammad at first thought he was possessed by the demons, or Jinn, as they were called, but later dismissed the idea:

> It seems, however, that Muhammed himself was at first doubtful of the source of these revelations, fearing that he was possessed by one of the Jinn, or sprites, as was commonly believed to be the case with Arab poets and soothsayers. But Khadijah and others reassured him, and he soon began to propound divine revelations with increasing frequency (Anderson, *op. cit.*, p. 55).

These visions mark the start of Muhammed's prophetic call by Allah. Muhammed received these visions during the following 22 years, until his death in 632 A.D.

The Hijira

The new faith encountered opposition in Muhammed's home town of Mecca. Because of his rejection in Mecca and the ostracism of his views, Muhammed and followers withdrew to the city now known as *Medina*, which means in full, "City of the Prophet," renamed from its original *Yathrib*.

The Hijira, which means "flight," marks the turning point in Islam. All Islamic calendars mark this date, July 16, 622, as their beginning. Thus, 630 A.D. would be 8 A.H. (in the year of the Hijira).

In his early years in Medina, Muhammed was sympathetic to both the Jews and Christians as well. But they rejected him and his teaching. Upon that rejection, Muhammed turned from Jerusalem as the center of worship of Islam, to Mecca, where the famous black stone Ka'aba was enshrined. Muhammed denounced all the idols which surrounded the Ka'aba and declared it was a shrine for the one true God, Allah.

With this new emphasis on Mecca, Muhammed realized he must soon return to his home. The rejected prophet did return in triumph, conquering the city.

John B. Noss details some of Muhammed's actions upon his return to Mecca:

> One of his first acts was to go reverently to the Ka'aba; yet he showed no signs of yielding to the ancient Meccan polytheism. After honoring the Black Stone and riding seven times around the shrine, he ordered the destruction of the idols within it and the scraping of the paintings of Abraham and the angels from the walls. He sanctioned the use of the well Zamzam and restored the boundary pillars defining the sacred territory around Mecca. Thenceforth no Muslim would have cause to hesitate about going on a pilgrimage to the ancient holy city.
>
> Muhammed now made sure of his political and prophetic ascendency in Arabia. Active opponents near at hand were conquered by the sword, and tribes far away were invited sternly to send delegations offering their allegience. Before his sudden death in 632 he knew he was well on the way to unifying the Arab tribes under a theocracy governed by the will of God (John B. Noss, *Man's Religions*, New York: MacMillan Publishing Company Inc., 1974, p. 517).

Between the return to Mecca and Muhammad's death, the prophet zealously and militantly propagated Islam, and the new faith quickly spread throughout the area.

After Muhammad's Death

When Muhammad died he had not written a will instructing the leadership in Islam about determining his successor. Sir Norman Anderson comments:

> Muhammad died, according to the best-supported view, without having designated any successor (Khalifa or Caliph). As the last and greatest of the Prophets he could not, of course, be replaced. But the community he had founded was a theocracy with no distinction between Church and State, and someone must clearly succeed, not to give but to enforce the law, to lead in war and to guide in peace. It was common ground, therefore, that a Caliph must be appointed: and in the event 'Umar ibn al Khattab (himself the second Caliph) succeeded in rushing the election of the aged Abu Bakr, one of the very first believers. But the question of the Caliphate was to cause more divisions and bloodshed than any other issue in Islam, and almost from the first three rival parties, in embryo at least, can be discerned. There were the Companions of the Prophet, who believed in the eligibility of any suitable "Early Believer" of the tribe of Quraysh; there was the aristocracy of Mecca, who wished to capture the Caliphate for the family of Umayya; and there were the "legitimists," who believed that no election was needed, but that 'Ali, the cousin and son-in-law of the Prophet, had been divinely designated as his successor (Anderson, *op cit.*, p. 64).

Abu Bakr died less than two years after his designation as Caliph. Upon his death, 'Umar became successor, and under him the borders of the Islamic empire were considerably expanded.

Eventually a power struggle developed as different factions believed their own methods of establishing a successor were better than their rivals. The major eruption came between those who believed the Caliph should be elected by the Islamic leadership and those who believed the successor should be hereditary, through 'Ali, Muhammad's son-in-law, married to his only daughter, *Fatima*. This struggle, along with others, produced the main body of Islam known as the Sunnis (followers of the prophet's way) as well as numerous sects.

The Sunnis

Along with the Caliphate controversy, conflict raged on another front, that of law and theology. Through this conflict eventually four recognized, orthodox schools of Islamic thought emerged. All four schools accepted the *Qur'an* (Koran), the *Sunna*, or the practice of the Prophet as expressed in the *Hadith* (traditions) and the four bases of Islamic Law *(Shari'a):* the *Qur'an*, the *Hadith*, the *Ij'ma'* (consensus of the Muslim community) and the *Q'yas* (use of analogical reason). These four groups came to be called the Sunnis.

Noss explains:

> The rapid expansion of Islam confronted Muslims with other crucial, and even more complex, decisions concerning Muslim behavior. Situations early appeared in areas outside of Arabia where the injunctions of the Qur'an proved either insufficient or inapplicable. The natural first step in these cases was to appeal to the *sunna* (the behavior or practice) of Muhammad in Medina or to the Hadith that reported his spoken decisions or judgments. In the event that this proved inconclusive, the next step was to ask what the sunna and/or consensus of opinion *(Ijmā)* of the Medina community was, in or shortly after the time of Muhammad. If no light was yet obtainable, the only recourse was either to draw an analogy *(Qiyās)* from the principles embodied in the Qur'an or in Medinan precedents and then apply it, or to follow the consensus of opinion of the local Muslim community as crystallized and expressed by its Qur'anic authorities.
>
> The Muslims who took this way of solving their behavioral problems were, and are to this day, called Sunnites (Noss, *op. cit.*, p. 530).

The Majority of Islam today is Sunni.

The Shi'a

The fourth Caliph to follow Muhammed was an early convert and also his son-in-law, *'Alī*. He was eventually murdered by *Mu'awiya*, who claimed the Caliphate for himself.

> The tragedy that befell the House of 'Alī, beginning with the murder of 'Alī himself and including the deaths of his two sons, grandsons of Muhammad, has haunted the lives of "the party *(Shi'a)* of 'Ali." They have brooded upon these dark happenings down the years as Christians do upon the death of Jesus. A major heretical group, they have drawn the censure and yet also have had the sympathy of the Sunnis and Sufis. They were among the sects whose radical

elements al-Ghazāli attacked as guilty of resting their claims on false grounds and sinfully dividing Islam. And yet, although agreeing with this indictment, the Muslim world at large has suppressed its annoyance at them, because their movement goes back to the very beginnings of Islam and has a kind of perverse justification, even in orthodox eyes. Their critics agree that there is little sense in it, yet it has an appeal of its own.

The partisans of 'Ali only gradually worked out the final claims made by the various Shi'ite sects. In the beginning there was simply the assertion—which as events unfolded became more and more heated—that only Muhammad's direct descendants, no others, could be legitimate caliphs; only they should have been given first place in the leadership of Islam. This "legitimism" could be called their political and dynastic claim, and at first this seems to have been all that they were interested in claiming. But this was not enough for adherents of their cause in Iraq, who over the years developed the religious theory, perhaps as an effect of Christian theories about God being in Christ, that every legitimate leader of the 'Alids, beginning with 'Ali, was an *imām mahdi*, a divinely appointed and supernaturally guided spiritual leader, endowed by Allah with special knowledge and insight—an assertion that the main body of Muslims, significantly enough called *ghuluw*, "exaggeration," rather than heresy (Noss, *op. cit.*, p. 540).

Today, the Shi'ites completely dominate Iran; their most prominent present leader is the Ayatollah Khoumeni.

The Sufis

In any strong, legalistic, religious system, worship can become mechanical and be exercised by rote, and God can become transcendent. Such an impersonal religion often motivates people to react. Such is the case with Islam, as the Sufis, the most well-known Islamic mystics, have arisen in response to orthodox Islam and to the often loose and secularist view of Islamic leadership during some of its early days under the *Ummayad* and *Abbasid* dynasties.

Despite the claims of the Law, another aspect of Islam has been almost equally important for the rank and file of the faithful—this is Sūfism: mysticism, as it is usually translated.

The Sūfis are those Muslims who have most sought for direct personal experience of the Divine. While some of them have been legalists of the most fundamentalist stamp, their emphasis on direct religious experience has more often led the Sūfis into tension with the legalists, and their attitude toward the Law has ranged from patronizing irony to outright hostility (John Alden Williams, *Islam*, New York: George Braziller, 1962, p. 136).

Describing the emergence of the Sufis, Noss states:

Millions of Muslims had within themselves the natural human need to feel their religion as a personal and emotional experience. Islam had no priests, then or now, ordained and set apart for a life dedicated to the worship of God and the pursuit of holiness, and yet everyone knew that Muhammad had been a true man of God, wholly dedicated to his mission, who in the period before the revelations came had retired at times from the world to meditate in a cave. It was thus that he had become an instrument of God's truth.

It was the popular yearning for the presence among them of unworldly men dedicated to God, asceticism, and holiness that encouraged the eventual emergence of Islamic mysticism (Noss, *op. cit.*, p. 535).

The Sūfis exist today and probably are best known through their Dervish Orders (e.g., "the whirling Dervish").

There are many other sects and divergent groups among Islam, too numerous to detail here. One might mention that the Baha'i Faith, although significantly different from Islam today, had its roots in Islam.

Contemporary Islam

The rise of Israel as a prominent power has brought renewal to a once-anemic Islamic faith. Nationalism, coupled with the Islamic faith, has served as a raison d'etat for many in the Arab world as they stand against Israel, their enemy. At various times in the recent past, Arab alliances have been conceived, discussed and then have died. There was the United Arab Republic and later an alliance discussed between Egypt, Libya and Syria.

Grunebaum comments:

> The spectacular success of the Arab Muslims in establishing an empire by means of a small number of campaigns against the great powers of the day has never ceased to stimulate the wonderment and the admiration of the Muslim world and Western scholarship (G.E. von Grunebaum, *Modern Islam*, Berkeley: University of California Press, 1962, p. 1).

Neill amplifies:

> It is not surprising that the Islamic world has caught the fever of nationalism that is raging everywhere among the peoples of Asia and Africa. The special intensity and vigour of Islamic, and especially Arab, nationalism springs from a complex of causes—memories of past splendour, resentment over Muslim weakness and Christian strength, above all that obscure sense of malaise, the feeling that in some way history has gone awry, that somehow the purposes of God are not being fulfilled as the Muslim has a right to expect.
>
> The achievments of the post-war period have been considerable. Egyptian self-assertion has made the Middle East one of the chief problem areas in the world. Libya became independent after the war. Morocco and Tunis have since won their independence. In Algeria the story of detachment from France was long and painful. But here too, in 1962, the goal of total independence was attained. And so the story goes on (Stephen Neill, *Christian Faith and Other Faiths*, London: Oxford University Press, 1970, pp. 43, 44.

However, much of this discussion has been quelled with the Camp David accords which saw peace rise out of the Middle East between Israel and Egypt. Yet on another front, committed Islamic fundamentalists have drawn world attention to Iran, and also in Egypt where they allegedly assassinated President Anwar Sadat. Nationalism is a strong sweeping movement in nations with majority Muslim populations.

In addition, secularism has increased as the practices of the West infiltrate nations. Some of these Western transfusions have been sudden—many Arab countries are accumulating new and previously unknown wealth in the form of petro-dollars. However, the secularism has also had a backlash effect as many of the Muslim countries, in an attempt to preserve their identity, are holding the line on imported Western customs.

Since Islam embraces not only religion but also culture, the future of the faith will be very much dependent on the state of the nations it thrives in today. With Arab nations prospering, this could turn out to be both a curse and a blessing to the Islamic faith. It may be good for its culture, but its faith could be seriously compromised.

> Islam is a rapidly spreading religion for several reasons. It is the state religion of Moslem countries and this gives it a strong cultural and political base. It has the appeal of a universal message because of its simple creed and tenets. Anyone can enter the *Ummah*, the community of faithful Muslims. There are no racial barriers and thus it spreads quickly among the black communities of Africa, and more recently, of America. Its five doctrines and five pillars can be easily communicated. In the West it is making appeals to the universal brotherhood of man, world peace, temperance, and the uplifting of women (Kenneth Boa, *Cults, World Religions, and You*, Wheaton, IL: Victor Books, 1977, p. 56).

The supremacy of Islam in the political and social (as well as religious) arenas is exemplified by the following quote from the Koran:

> Believers, have fear of Allah and stand with those who uphold the cause of truth. No cause have the people of Medina and the desert Arabs who dwell around them to forsake Allah's apostle or to jeopardize his life so as to safeguard their own; for they do not expose themselves to thirst or hunger or to any ordeal on account of the cause of Allah, nor do they stir a step which may provoke the unbelievers. Each loss they suffer at the enemy's hands shall be counted as a good deed in the sight of Allah: He will not deny the righteous of their recompense. Each sum they give, be it small or large, and each journey they undertake, shall be noted down, so that Allah may requite them for their noblest deeds.
>
> It is not right that all the faithful should go to war at once. A band from each community should stay behind to instruct themselves in religion and admonish their men when they return, so that they may take heed.
>
> Believers, make war on the infidels who dwell around you. Deal courteously with them. Know that Allah is with the righteous (N.J. Dawood, trans., *The Koran*, London: Penguin Books, 1956, p. 333).

The Teachings of Islam

Faith and Duty

The teachings of Islam are comprised both of faith *(imam)* and practice or duty *(din)*. Sir Norman Anderson explains:

> The faith and practice of Islam are governed by the two great branches of Muslim learning, theology and jurisprudence, to both of which some reference has already been made. Muslim theology (usually called "Tawhid" from its central doctrine of the Unity of the Godhead) defines all that a man should believe, while the law (Shari'a) prescribes everything that he should do. There is no priesthood and no sacraments. Except among the Sufis, Islam knows only exhortation and instruction from those who consider themselves, or are considered by others, adequately learned in theology or law.
>
> Unlike any other system in the world today the Shari'a embraces every detail of human life, from the prohibition of crime to the use of the toothpick, and

from the organization of the State to the most sacred intimacies — or unsavoury aberrations — of family life. It is "the science of all things, human and divine," and divides all actions into what is obligatory or enjoined, what is praiseworthy or recommended, what is permitted or legally indifferent, what is disliked or deprecated, and what is forbidden (Anderson, op. cit., p. 78).

These practices are mainly true of Sunni Islam, not of the divergent sects.

The Law: Shari'a

Islamic law (Shari'a) plays a central role in all Islamic culture. The structure of the law is that civil law rather than common law is generally practiced in England and the United States.

It must be emphasized that the Shari'a has been central to Islamic doctrine:

> The most important and fundamental religious concept of Islam is that of the shari'a which literally means a "path to the watering place" but in its religious application means the total way of life as explicitly or implicitly commanded by God. The word has been used in the Koran, which sometimes suggests that different religions have different shari'as but at other times that all religions have fundamentally one shari'a.
>
> The concept as formulated by Muslim religious teachers, includes both the doctrine or belief, and practice or the law. But historically the formulation and systemization of the law took place earlier than the crystallization of the formal theology. This, as shown below, had far-reaching consequences for the future development of Islam (Encyclopedia Britannica, s.v. "Islam," Chicago: William Benton Publishing Company, 1967, p. 664).

The controversy surrounding the law and theology and the fourfold division of the Shari'a led to the formulation and distinction of the Sunni and Shi'ite sects in Islam. Guillaume explains:

> In Chapter 5 a sketch of the sources of Muslim law and of the formation of the four main schools has been given. In certain countries certain matters have been taken out of the purview of the shari'a and now come within the scope of secular courts; but, broadly speaking, no change comparable with that which has taken and is taking place in Islamic countries today has been seen within Islam for a thousand years or more. Turkey, as everyone knows, has abolished the shari'a altogether. Officially it is a secular State, though actually the influence of Islam on the population, especially in Asia, is very considerable, and shows signs of becoming stronger under the new democratic government.
>
> In a series of articles in The Moslem World and elsewhere my colleague, Mr. J.N.D. Anderson, has shown how in the Arab countries, too, the shari'a is undergoing revision. Egypt, the Sudan, Syria, Lebanon, Jordan, and Iraq are all on the move. The changes which are being made illustrate how a definite attempt to relate the shari'a to the conditions of modern life and to a more liberal view of human relations is being realized in positive legislation (Guillaume, op. cit., pp. 166, 167).

He then comments on one of the differences of the Shi'ites and the Sunnis:

> In theory, the Shi'ite conception of the supreme authority in law is utterly different from that of the Sunnis, though in practice the difference does not

amount to very much. They reject the four schools and the doctrine of *ijma* because their Hidden Imam has the sole right of determining what the believer shall do and believe. Therefore their duly accredited doctors can still exercise the power of *ijtihad* or personal opinion. This power the Sunnis lost a thousand years ago or more (Guillaume, *op. cit.*, p. 103).

Qur'an

The basis for Islamic doctrine is found in the Qur'an (Koran). Boa describes the central place of the Qur'an in the Islamic faith as well as the supplementary works:

> The Koran is the authoritative scripture of Islam. About four-fifths the length of the New Testament, it is divided into 114 surahs (chapters). Parts were written by Mohammed, and the rest, based on his oral teaching, was written from memory by his disciples after Mohammed's death.
>
> Over the years a number of additional sayings of Mohammed and his early disciples were compiled. These comprise the *Hadith* ("tradition"), the sayings of which are called *sunna* ("custom"). The Hadith supplements the Koran much as the Talmud supplements the Law in Judaism (Kenneth Boa, *op. cit.*, p. 52).

The Qur'an is the Word of God in Islam, the holy scriptures. As the authoritative scripture, it is the main guide for all matters of faith and practice. The Qur'an was revealed to Muhammad as the Word of God for mankind.

Other revelations include the *Torat* (of Moses), the *Suhuf* (books of the prophets), *Zabur* (psalms of David), *Injil* (gospel of Jesus). The Qur'an supercedes all other revelations and is the only one of which we still have the original text. All of the others have been corrupted, almost beyond recognition.

Islam, for example, would not consider our New Testament to be the Injil (gospel of Jesus). It is not the words of Jesus, it is others' words *about* Jesus. His original words have been corrupted and many have been lost. Only the Qur'an is infallible. Muhammad and the Qur'an are that which Islam is to follow.

Neill comments:

> It is well known that at many points the Qur'an does not agree with the Jewish and Christian Scriptures. Therefore, from the Muslim point of view, it follows of necessity that these Scriptures must have been corrupted. Historical evidence makes no impression on the crushing force of the syllogism. So it is, and it can be no other way. The Muslim controversialist feels no need to study evidence in detail. The only valid picture of Jesus Christ is that which is to be found in the pages of the Qur'an (Stephen Neill, *op. cit.*, p. 64).

The Qur'an is comprised of 114 *surahs*, or chapters, all attributed to Muhammad. The surahs are arranged in the Qur'an by length—the longer in front, the shorter in back.

> For the Muslims, the Koran *(q.v.)* is the Word of God, confirming and consummating earlier revealed books and thereby replacing them; its instrument or agent of revelation is the Prophet Mohammed, the last and most perfect of a series of messengers of God to mankind—from Adam through Abraham to Moses and Jesus, the Christian claims for whose divinity are strongly rejected.

Indeed there is no people to whom a prophet has not come. Although Mohammed is only a human creature of God, he has nevertheless an unequaled importance in the Koran itself which sets him only next to God as deserving of moral and legal obedience. Hence, his sayings and deeds (Sunna) served as a second basis, besides the Koran, of the belief and practice of Islam.

The Koran (which, for the Muslim, is the miracle par excellence of Mohammed, unsurpassable in form as well as in content) is a forceful document basically expressing an *élan* of religious and social justice. The early chapters (surahs) of the Koran, reflecting Mohammed's grim struggle against the Meccans, are characterized by grave warnings of the imminent judgment, while the later surahs, of the Medina period, are chiefly directed to regulating the internal and external affairs of the young Muslim community-state, besides narrating the stories of the earlier prophets.

The koranic theology is rigorously monotheistic: God is absolutely unique— "there is nothing like him"— omnipotent, omniscient, merciful. Men are exhorted to obey his will (*i.e.*, to be Muslim) as is necessarily done by all inorganic objects. Special responsibility is laid on man who willingly, although with his characteristically foolish pride, accepted "the trust," refused by all creation. Besides human beings and angels, the Koran speaks of the jinn, both good and evil, to whom sometimes the devil is represented as belonging (*Encyclopedia Britannica*, op. cit., p. 663).

In modern times, the Qur'an has faced many of the same dilemmas as the Bible. A major issue is the inspiration of the Qur'an. Islamic scholars do not agree as a whole on how the Qur'an came to be true or how much is true, although conservative Islamic scholars accept it *all* as literally true. John Alden Williams comments:

> The Qur'an, then, is the Word of God, for Muslims. While controversies have raged among them as to the sense in which this is true—whether it is the created or uncreated Word, whether it is true of every Arabic letter or only of the message as a whole, that it *is true* has never been questioned by them (John Alden Williams, *op. cit.*, p. 15).

The Qur'an was revealed and written in the Arabic language. Because of this, and the fact it was revealed by God, Muslims deplore translations of the Qur'an into other languages. There is, then, no *authoritative* translation for the Qur'an. Anyone familiar with the reading of translations of any work would be sympathetic to this demand. However, as rich as Arabic is, the translations still provide a close original which can and must be evaluated for its validity, not simply its reliability.

The Qur'an came into written form shortly after Muhammad's death.

> All the sûrahs of the Koran had been recorded in writing before the Prophet's death, and many Muslims had committed the whole Koran to memory. But the written sûrahs were dispersed among the people; and when, in a battle which took place during the Caliphate of Abû Bakr—that is to say, within two years of the Prophet's death—a large number of those who knew the whole Koran by heart were killed, a collection of the whole Koran was made and put in writing. In the Caliphate of Othmân, all existing copies of sûrahs were called in, and an authoritative version, based on Abû Bakr's collection and the testimony of those who had the whole Koran by heart, was compiled exactly in the present form and order, which is regarded as traditional and as the ar-

rangement of the Prophet himself, the Caliph Othmân and his helpers being Comrades of the Prophet and the most devout students of the Revelation. The Koran has thus been very carefully preserved (Mohammed Marmaduke Pickthall, trans., *The Meaning of the Glorious Koran*, New York: Mentor Books, n.d., p. xxviii).

On the origin of the Qur'an, Guillaume comments:

From the books of tradition we learn that the prophet was subject to ecstatic seizures. He is reported to have said that when inspiration came to him he felt as it were the painful sounding of a bell. Even in cold weather his forehead was bathed in sweat. On one occasion he called to his wife to wrap him in a veil. At other times visions came to him in sleep. Religious ecstasy is a world-wide phenomenon in one stage of human society, and in its early stages Muhammad's verses were couched in the Semitic form of mantic oracular ut-terance. The veiling of the head and the use of rhymed prose were marks of the Arabian soothsayer, while the feeling of physical violence and compul-sion, and the outward appearance of "possession" which seemed to the onlookers to indicates madness or demonic possession were sometimes record-ed by, or observed in, the Hebrew prophets.

The Qur'an as we have it now is a record of what Muhammad said while in the state or states just mentioned. It is beyond doubt that his hearers recognized the symptoms of revelation, otherwise his *obiter dicta* which the literature of tradition purports to record would be included in the Qur'an (Guillaume, *op. cit.*, p. 56).

Five Articles of Faith

The five articles of faith are the main doctrines of Islam. All Muslims are expected to believe these tenets.

1. *God.* There is only one true God and his name is Allah. Allah is all-knowing, all-powerful and the sovereign judge. Yet Allah is not a personal God, for he is so far above man in every way that he is not personally knowable. Noss states:

In the famous Muslim creedal formula the first part reads: *lā ilāha illa Allāh*, "(There is) no god but God." This is the most important article in Muslim theology. No statement about God seemed to Muhammad more fundamental than the declaration that God is one, and no sin seemed to him so unpardonable as associating another being with God on terms of equality. God stands alone and supreme. He existed before any other being or thing, is self-subsistent, omniscient, omnipotent ("all-seeing, all-hearing, all-willing"). He is the creator, and in the awful day of judgment he is the sole arbiter who shall save the believer out of the dissolution of the world and place him in paradise (Noss, *op. cit.*, p. 517).

This doctrine, which makes God different from His creatures, is strong in Islam. Allah is so different that it makes it (1) difficult to really know very much about him, and (2) unlikely that he is affected by his creatures' attitudes or actions. Although Allah is said to be loving, this aspect of his nature is almost ignored, and his supreme attribute of justice is thought to overrule love (Anderson, *op. cit.*, p. 79).

The emphasis of the God of Islam is on judgment, not grace; on power, not mercy. He is the source of both good and evil and his will is supreme.

2. *Angels.* The existence of angels is fundamental to Islamic teaching. Gabriel, the leading angel, appeared to Muhammad and was instrumental in delivering the revelations in the Qur'an to Muhammad. Al Shaytan is the devil and most likely a fallen angel or jinn. Jinn are those creatures between angels and men which can be either good or evil.

Angels do not perform any bodily functions (sexual, eating, etc.) as they are created of light. All angels have different purposes, such as Gabriel, or Jibril, who is the messenger of inspiration. Each man or woman also has two recording angels—one who records his good deeds, the other, his bad deeds.

3. *Scripture.* There are four inspired books in the Islamic faith. They are the *Torah* of Moses, the Psalms *(Zabin)* of David, the Gospel of Jesus Christ *(Injil)* and the *Qur'an.* Muslims believe the former three books have been corrupted by Jews and Christians. Also, since the Qur'an is god's most recent and final word to man, it supercedes all the other works.

4. *Prophets.* In Islam God has spoken through numerous prophets down through the centuries. The six greatest are: Adam, Noah, Abraham, Moses, Jesus and Muhammad. Muhammad is the last and greatest of all Allah's messengers.

5. *Last Days.* The last day will be a time of resurrection and judgment. Those who follow and obey Allah and Muhammad will go to Islamic heaven, called Paradise, a place of pleasure. Those who oppose them will be tormented in hell.

> The last day (the resurrection and the judgment) figures prominently in Muslim thought. The day and hour is a secret to all, but there are to be twenty-five signs of its approach. All men will then be raised; the books kept by the recording angels will be opened; and God as judge will weigh each man's deeds in the balances. Some will be admitted to Paradise, where they will recline on soft couches quaffing cups of wine handed them by the Huris, or maidens of Paradise, of whom each man may marry as many as he pleases; others will be consigned to the torments of Hell. Almost all, it would seem, will have to enter the fire temporarily, but no true Muslim will remain there forever (Anderson, *op. cit.*, p. 81).

Finally there is a sixth article of faith which is considered by many to belong to the five doctrines. Whether this is one of the articles or not, it is a central teaching of Islam—the belief in God's decrees or Kismet, the doctrine of fate. This is a very rigid view of predestination that states all good or evil proceeds from divine will.

This strong fatalism has played a central role in Muslim culture. "To this the lethargy and lack of progress which, until recently at least, has for centuries characterized Muslim countries, can be partially attributed" (Anderson, *op. cit.*, p. 82). From this concept comes the most common Islamic phrase, roughly translated, "It is Allah's will."

Five Pillars of Faith

Besides the five major beliefs or doctrines in Islam, there are also "five pillars of faith." These are observances in Islam which are foundational practices or duties every Muslim must observe. The five are: The Creed, Prayers, Almsgiving, Fasting and the Pilgrimage to Mecca.

1. *The Creed. (Kalima).* "There is no God but Allah, and Muhammad is the Prophet of Allah," is the bedrock of Muslim belief. One must state this aloud publicly in order to become a Muslim. It is repeated constantly by the faithful.

2. *Prayer (Salat).* Prayer as ritual is central to a devout Muslim. Boa comments:

> The practice of prayer *(salat)* five times a day (upon rising, at noon, in midafternoon, after sunset, and before retiring). The worshipper must recite the prescribed prayers (the first surah and other selections from the Koran) in Arabic while facing the Ka'aba in Mecca. The Hadith (book of tradition) has turned these prayers into a mechanical procedure of standing, kneeling, hands and face on the ground, and so forth. The call to prayer is sounded by the *muezzin* (a Muslim crier) from a tower called a *minaret* which is part of the *mosque* (the place of public worship) (Boa, *op. cit.*, p. 53).

3. *Almsgiving (Zakat).* Muhammad, himself an orphan, had a strong desire to help the needy. The alms originally were voluntary, but all Muslims are legally required to give one-fortieth of their income for the destitute. There are other rules and regulations for produce, cattle, etc. Freewill offerings also can be exercised.

Since those to whom alms are given are helping the giver to salvation, they feel no sense of debt to the giver. On the contrary, it is the giver's responsibility and duty to give and he should consider himself lucky he has someone to give to.

4. *Fasting (Ramadan).* Faithful Muslims fast from sunup to sundown each day during this holy month. The fast develops self-control, devotion to God and identity with the destitute. No food or drink may be consumed during the daylight hours; no smoking or sexual pleasures may be enjoyed, either. Many Muslims eat two meals a day during Ramadan, one before sunrise and one shortly after sunset.

5. *The Pilgrimage (Hajj).* The pilgrimage is expected of all Muslims at least once in their lifetimes. It can be extremely arduous on the old or infirm, so in their cases they may send someone in their places. The trip is an essential part in Muslims' gaining salvation. It involves a set of ceremonies and rituals, many of which center around the Ka'aba shrine, to which the pilgrimage is directed. Of the Ka'aba, Muhammad M. Pickthall comments in *The Meaning of the Glorious Koran:*

> The Meccans claimed descent from Abraham through Ishmael, and tradition stated that their temple, the Ka'aba, had been built by Abraham for the worship of the One God. It was still called the House of Allah, but the chief objects of worship there were a number of idols which were called daughters of Allah and intercessors (Pickthall, *op. cit.*, p. ix).

The idols were destroyed by Muhammad on his return to Mecca in power following the *Hijira* (exile).

When the pilgrim is about six miles from the holy city, he enters upon the state of *ihram:* he casts off, after prayers, his ordinary clothes and puts on two seamless garments; he walks almost barefooted and neither shaves, cuts his hair nor cuts his nails. The principle activity consists of a visit to the Sacred mosque *(al-Masjid al-Haram);* the kissing of the Black Stone *(al-Hajar al-Aswad);* seven circumambulations of the Ka'aba three times running and four times slowly; the visit to the sacred stone called Maqam Ibrahim; the ascent of and running between Mt. Safa and Mt. Marwa seven times; the visit to Mt. Arafat; the hearing of a sermon there and spending the night at Muzdalifa; the throwing of stones at the three pillars at Mina and offering sacrifice on the last day of Ihram, which is the *'id* of sacrifice *('Id al-Adha) (Encyclopedia Britannica, op. cit.,* p. 664).

This Muslim pilgrimage serves to heighten and solidify Islamic faith.

There is a sixth religious duty associated with the five pillars. This is *Jihad,* the Holy War. This duty requires that when the situation warrants, men are required to go to war to spread Islam or defend it against infidels. One who dies in a *Jihad* is guaranteed eternal life in Paradise (heaven).

Cultural Expression

Islam, like Judaism, is both a religion and a cultural identity which cannot be separated from the people. In many countries the Islamic faith, though not strictly practiced, is woven into the web of society at every facet.

The Cambridge History of Islam comments on this phenomenon:

Islam is a religion. It is also, inseparably from this, a community, a civilization and a culture. It is true that many of the countries through which the Qur'anic faith spread already possessed ancient and important cultures. Islam absorbed these cultures, and assimilated itself to them in various ways, to a far greater extent than it attempted to supplant them. But in doing this, it provided them with attributes in common, with a common attitude toward God, to men and to the world, and thus ensured, through the diversities of language, of history and of race, the complex unity of the *dār al-Islām,* the "house" or "world" of Islam.

The history of the Muslim peoples and countries is thus a unique example of a culture with a religious foundation, uniting the spiritual and the temporal, sometimes existing side by side with "secular" cultures, but most often absorbing them by becoming very closely interlinked with them (P. M. Holt, *op. cit.,* Vol. I, p. 569).

Language and the Arts

To doctrine which serves as both a religious and social foundation, the Arabic language can be added as another unifying factor which helps weld Islamic peoples together.

There is an abundance of Arabic poetry and prose in which the Islamic faith is placed in high regard. Muslim art and architecture also have a highly developed style. Many of the mosques and minarets are tremendous works of art decorated with intricate arabesque ornamentation.

The Family

The family is very important in the social economy of Islam. Marriage is required for every Muslim, even the ascetics. Muhammed commanded men to marry and propagate the race. Men may not have more than four wives, yet many cohabit with as many concubines as they choose.

Although the act of marriage is important, the sanctity of the union is not as highly regarded. A Muslim may divorce his wife at any time and for any reason. On the whole, women in Islamic culture do not enjoy the status or the privileges of the men and are very dependent on their husbands. While this sounds cruel and sexist to Westerners, it was a humane innovation in Muhammad's time. Islamic law requires what was then unheard of: each wife must be treated equally.

Other practices include the veiling of women, circumcision, abstention from alcohol, gambling and certain foods. Many of the above, such as alcohol and gambling, are seen as vices of the West.

Islam and Christianity

Many of the Muslim beliefs come from the Bible. The historical foundation for the Qur'an comes from the Old Testament. Yet even though there has been influence and there are similarities, the differences in the beliefs of the two faiths are striking.

God

Islam teaches the unity of God's essence and personality, explicitly excluding the Trinity as taught in the Bible.

This emphasis on the unity of God comes across in other ways. Islam has God divorced from His creation, so unified to Himself that He cannot be associated with creation. His transcendence is so great that He acts impersonally.

Because of their doctrine of predestination and the fact that both evil and good came from Allah, it makes their God very capricious. Whatever Allah chooses becomes right; this makes any true standard of righteousness or ethics hard to discern if not impossible to establish.

This is unlike the God of the Bible who is righteous. The very word righteous means, "a standard."

The Muslim finds it difficult to divorce the concept of father from the physical realm. To them it is blasphemous to call Allah or God your father. To do so is the same as saying that your mother and Allah had sexual intercourse to produce you!

In addition, while calling God "Father" is to evoke thoughts of love, compassion, tenderness and protectiveness to Christians, it is not so to the Muslim mind. To him, a father is strict, shows no emotion, never expresses love, and is bound to his family by duty and for what his family can provide for him, not by devotion.

Allah is also very deficient in such attributes as love, holiness and grace. Grace, of course, is rooted in the character of God (Ephesians 2).

The Bible

As mentioned before, the Muslim holy books include the sayings of Moses, the prophets, David, Jesus and Muhammad. However, all of the previous sayings have been lost or corrupted. Only the Qur'an, the words of Muhammad, have been preserved free of error. They also supercede the previous revelations. Remember, the holy books mentioned in Islam are *not* exactly like our biblical Scriptures.

One would presuppose that since the teachings of Christianity and Islam are clearly different, it would follow that the practical and social consequences of the doctrine would also be vastly different. This is precisely the case. As Guillaume mentions, this is nowhere better illustrated than in the status of women:

> The Qur'an has more to say on the position of women than on any other social question. The guiding note is sounded in the words, "Women are your tillage," and the word for marriage is that used for the sexual act. The primary object of marriage is the propagation of children, and partly for this a man is allowed four wives at a time and an unlimited number of concubines. However, it is laid down that wives are to be treated with kindness and strict impartiality; if a man cannot treat all alike he should keep to one.
>
> The husband pays the woman a dowry at the time of marriage, and the money or property so alloted remains her own. The husband may divorce his wife at any time, but he cannot take her back until she has remarried and been divorced by a second husband. A woman cannot sue for divorce on any grounds, and her husband may beat her. In this matter of the status of women lies the greatest difference between the Muslim and the Christian world.
>
> Since Muslim propagandists in this country persistently deny that women are inferior to men in Islam it is worthwhile to set out the facts. Surah 4:31 says: "Men have authority over women because God has made the one superior to the other and because they spend their wealth [to maintain them]. So good women are obedient, guarding the unseen [parts] because God has guarded [them]. As for those from whom you fear disobedience admonish them and banish them to beds apart and beat them; then if they obey you seek not occasion against them (Guillaume, *op. cit.*, pp. 71, 72).

Christ

In Islam the person and work of Jesus Christ are not seen in the same way as in Christianity. For the Christian the resurrection of Jesus Christ as the incarnate Son of God is the vital cornerstone of faith, yet the Muslim does not hold to either of these truths—that Christ is the Son of God or that he rose from dead. In fact, Muslims do not even believe Jesus was crucified; rather, many believe Judas was crucified in His place. Some, however, believe it was Christ on the cross but that He did not die.

Islam does believe Jesus was a sinless prophet although not as great as Muhammad. While Surah 3:45-47 in the Qur'an speaks of the virgin birth of Christ, it is not the same biblical virgin birth. Jesus is certainly *not* the only begotten Son of God, and an angel—rather than the Holy Spirit—was the agency of God's power in the conception. However, the idea that Allah had a son is repugnant to them. Surah 4:171 states, "Jesus... was only a messenger of Allah... Far is it removed from His transcendent majesty that He should have a son."

John states concerning Christ, "And the Word became flesh, and dwelt among us, and we beheld His glory, glory as of the only begotten from the Father, full of grace and truth . . . And I have seen, and have borne witness that this is the Son of God" (John 1:14, 34).

Christ's claim for His own deity and Sonship are unequivocal. In John 10:30 He claims equality with the Father when He states, "I and the Father are one." For not only is the Sonship of Christ important per se, but the deity of Christ is also an important point of difference between Christianity and Islam since Islam denies the doctrine of the Trinity.

Of the crucifixion, the Qur'an states in Surah 4:157, "They slew him not nor crucified, but it appeared so unto them . . ." Most Muslims believe Judas was put in the place of Christ, and Christ went to heaven. The Bible teaches that Christ went to the cross to pay the penalty for man's sins, died, and was raised from the dead, appeared to the disciples and *then* ascended to heaven.

Paul recounts the events this way: "For I delivered to you as of first importance what I also received, that Christ died for our sins according to the Scriptures, and that He was buried, and that He was raised on the third day according to the Scriptures, and that He appeared to Cephas and then to the twelve. After that He appeared to more than five hundred" (2 Corinthians 15:3-6, NASB).

Of the importance of the resurrection, Paul states, "And if Christ has not been raised, your faith is worthless; you are still in your sins" (2 Corinthians 15:17, NASB).

Max Kershaw, in *"How to Share the Good News with Your Muslim Friend,"* states:

> In this regard, the Muslim view of Jesus is significant. The Qur'an presents Jesus as one of the great prophets. He is called the Messiah. He is declared to have been born of the virgin Mary. He lived a sinless life (Surah 19:19). He accomplished many wonderful miracles, such as the giving of sight to the blind, healing of lepers and the raising of the dead (3:49). He is going to return to the earth again to establish Islam throughout the earth. He is called "the Word of God" (3:45) and "the Spirit from God" (4:171). Thus, Muslims have a high view of Jesus.
>
> But they are adamant in declaring that Jesus is not the **Son of God** and **Savior.** In fact, they believe that equating anyone with God is blasphemy, the unforgiveable sin. More than this, they do not believe that he was crucified. Instead, God took him to heaven without dying, and someone else died in his place. One particular passage in the Qur'an (4:156-158) seems to say this, but it is not clear. In fact, other Qur'anic passages speak of the death of Jesus (19:33) (Max R. Kershaw, *How to Share the Good News with Your Muslim Friend,* Colorado Springs: International Students, Inc., 1978).

Boa comments:

> Unlike the God of the Bible, Allah has done nothing for man that cost him anything. Islam makes no real provision for sin. One's salvation is never certain since it is based on a works system and on complete surrender ("Islam") to the will of Allah. This religion rejects the biblical teaching of the crucifix-

ion and resurrection of Jesus, though it concedes that He was a sinless prophet. Mohammed did not rise from the dead, and there is no basis for a resurrection in Islam (Boa, *op. cit.*, p. 55).

Neill states with respect to Islam and the person of Christ:

It is perfectly true that the central concern of Jesus was with the kingdom of God. But everything depends on the meaning that is put into the word "God." Here is perhaps the very heart of our differences. Islam conceives the possible relationship of man to God in one way, and the Gospel in another.

While God was the exclusive source of the revelation to Muhammad, God himself is not the content of the revelation. Revelation in Islamic theology does not mean God disclosing himself. It is revelation *from* God, not revelation *of* God. God is remote. He is inscrutable and utterly inaccessible to human knowledge. . . . Even though we are his creatures whose every breath is dependent upon him, it is not in inter-personal relationship with him that we receive guidance from him.

At this central point the teaching of Jesus diverges from what the Muslim believes to be the essential prophetic witness. His God is a God who cares for his creatures, who is prepared to enter into fellowship with them, and is concerned that they should love him in response to his love. Under the law man was in the position of a slave; now under the Gospel he is called to freedom, to the freedom of grown-up sons in their Father's house. The Qur'an never uses the word "Father" of God. Jesus taught his disciples to address him as "Our Father." The whole of the Gospel is summed up in these two words.

If the possibility is admitted that God might be such as Jesus declared him to be, the incarnation presents itself no longer as a blasphemous and irrational impossibility, but as something that appears even appropriate, in the light of this new perception of what the fatherhood of God might be.

The death of Christ at the hands of the Jews is rejected by Muslims on *a priori* grounds, which are absolutely convincing if the major premise is admitted. It is impossible that God should so desert a prophet in the fulfillment of his mission. It would be contrary to His justice to permit the suffering of an innocent on behalf of others. It would be contrary to His omnipotence not to be able to rescue a prophet in danger. Therefore Jesus cannot have been left helpless in the hands of his enemies (Neill, *op. cit.*, pp. 66, 67).

Sin and Salvation

The previous differences between Islam and Christianity find fruit in the teachings of salvation. Neill comments:

At the heart of the Muslim-Christian disagreement, we shall find a deep difference in the understanding of the nature of sin. It is not true to say that the Muslim has no sense of sin or of the need for forgiveness. He has both. But sin reveals its deadly nature only when it is seen in its effects on personal relationships; and such an understanding of it is almost necessarily excluded, as we have seen, by the Muslim's concept of the possible relationship between the believer and his God. The believer may sin against the law and the majesty of God, and if he does so he deserves to be punished. The idea that man by his sin might break the heart of God is not yet within the spectrum of the Muslim understanding of reality (Neill, *op. cit.*, pp. 68, 69).

The Muslim operates under a legalistic system and must earn his salvation. He holds to the *Articles of Faith* and follows the *Pillars of Faith*.

For the Muslim, sin is lack of obedience to Allah. Thus, man is sinful by act only, not by nature.

The Bible teaches that man is sinful by nature. Paul writes to the Romans, "For all have sinned and fall short of the glory of God" (Romans 3:23, NASB).

These are historical roots which tie Islam to Christianity, yet this is where the similarity ends. Islam rejects the key doctrines of the Christian faith—the Trinity, the deity of Christ, Christ's crucifixion and resurrection, and the sin of man and his salvation by grace alone through faith in Christ.

They also reject the Bible as the only authoritative book on which to base all matters of doctrine, faith and practice. When Islam rejects the truth of the written Word of God, they are left not only different from Christianity, but opposite from Christianity on all counts. Islam was founded by a dead prophet; Christianity was founded by the risen Savior.

Conclusion

Islam is one of the driving forces among world religions today, its growth closely tied to nationalism. But growth does not mean truth.

The God of Islam is a very capricious one, too far removed from people to be personally involved or concerned. Not only is he impersonal, but he also emphasized judgment to the exclusion of love, and he motivates people by fear rather than by grace.

Muhammad, the founder, has based his teaching on inaccurate and untrue interpretations of the Bible. There is no historical evidence to support Muhammad's contentions that either the Jewish or Christian scriptures have been corrupted. In addition, his teaching in the Qur'an is based on revelations which he initially believed were demonic in origin.

Islam is an aggressive and impressive world religion. It appeals to those who welcome a religious world view which permeates every facet of life. However, it is ultimately unfulfilling. The Islamic God of strict judgment, Allah, cannot offer the mercy, love, and ultimate sacrifice on mankind's behalf that the Christian God, incarnate in Jesus Christ, offers to each man even today.

Islamic Terms

Abu Bakr—(Reign: 632-634 A.D.) The first Moslem caliph, according to Sunni Muslims. The Shi'ite Muslims reject this and instead consider the fourth caliph, 'Ali, as the first true successor to Mohammad.

Allah—The Supreme Being. The name of God, derived from the Arabic *Al-Ilah*.

Caliph—The title given to office of the spiritual and political leadership which took over after Mohammad's death.

Fatima—The daughter of Mohammad and his first wife; and the wife of 'Ali, the fourth Caliph.

Hadith—The sacred sayings of Mohammad, handed down by oral tradition, for generations after Mohammad's death until finally transcribed.

Hajj—A pilgrimage to Mecca. One of the five pillars of the Islamic faith.

Hegira—Mohammad's flight from Mecca to present day Medina in 622 A.D.

Imam—A Moslem who is considered by Sunnis to be an authority in Islamic law and theology or the man who leads the prayers. Also refers to each of the founders of the four principal sects of Islam. The Shi'ites accept 12 great Imams.

Islam—Literally, "submission to the will of Allah."

Ka'Aba—A small stone building located in the court of the great mosque at Mecca containing the black stone (a meteorite) supposedly given to Abraham by Gabriel.

Koran (Qur'an)—Said to be the final and complete inspired word of God transmitted to the prophet Mohammad by the angel Gabriel.

Mahdi—"The guided one." A leader who will cause righteousness to fill the earth. The Sunnites are still awaiting his initial appearance while the Shi'ites hold that the last Imam, who disappeared in 874 A.D. will someday reappear as the Mahdi.

Mecca—The birthplace of Mohammad. This city, located in Saudi Arabia, is considered the most holy city by the Moslems.

Medina—A holy city of Islam named for Mohammad. It was previously named Yathrib. It is the city to which Mohammad fled in 622 A.D.

Mohammad—The prophet and founder of Islam. Born around 570 A.D., died 632 A.D.

Moslem (Muslim)—A follower of Mohammad. Literally, "one who submits."

Mosque—An Islamic place of worship.

Muezzlin—A Moslem crier who announces the hour of prayer.

Mulla—A teacher of Islamic laws and doctrines.

Omar—According to the Sunnites, the second Moslem caliph and principal advisor to the first caliph, Abu Bakr.

Purday—A veil or covering used by Moslem women to ensure them privacy against public observation, and to indicate their submission.

Ramadan—The ninth month of the Moslem year, when Mohammad received the Qur'an from heaven, and now devoted to fasting.

Salat—The Moslem daily prayer ritual. One of the five pillars of Islamic faith.

Shi'ites—A Moslem sect which rejects the first three caliphs, insisting that Mohammad's son-in-law 'Ali was Mohammad's rightful initial successor.

Sufis—Iranian (Persian) philosophical mystics who have largely adapted and reinterpreted Islam for themselves.

Sunnites—The largest Moslem sect which acknowledges the first four caliphs as Mohammad's rightful successors.

Surahs—What the chapters of the Qur'an are called.

Islam Bibliography

Anderson, Sir Norman, *The World's Religions*, Grand Rapids, MI: William B. Eerdmans Publishing Company, 1976.

Boa, Kenneth, *Cults, World Religions, and You*, Wheaton, IL: Victor Books, 1977.

Davood, N. J., trans., *The Koran*, London: Penguin Books, 1956.

Holt, P. M., and Lambton, and Lewis, eds., *The Cambridge History of Islam*, London: Cambridge University Press, 1970.

Encyclopedia Britannica, s.v. "Islam," Chicago: William Benton Publisher, 1967.

Grunebaum, G. E. von, *Modern Islam*, Berkeley: University of California Press, 1962.

Guillaume, Alfred, *Islam*, London: Penguin Books, 1954.

Kershaw, Max R., *How to Share the Good News with Your Muslim Friend*, Colorado Springs: International Students Inc., 1978.

Neill, Stephen, *Christian Faith and Other Faiths*, London: Oxford University Press, 1970.

Noss, John B., *Man's Religions*, New York: MacMillan Publishing Company Inc., 1974.

Payne, Robert, *The Holy Sword*, New York: Collier Books, 1962.

Pickthall, Muhammed Marmaduke, trans., *The Meaning of the Glorious Koran*, New York: Mentor Books, n.d.

Williams, John Alden, *Islam*, New York: George Braziller, 1962.

CHAPTER TEN

Sikhism

S ikhism is a religion all but unknown to western civilization. Its
adherents are to be found for the most part in the Punjab province of
India. A fairly recent religion, Sikhism is an attempt to harmonize
two of the world's greater religions, Hinduism and Islam. Sikhism is the
third major branch of Hinduism and was founded by a man named Nanak.
It also owes much to Islam.

History of Sikhism

Nanak: the Founder

Nanak was born in the Indian village of Talwandi, some 30 miles
southwest of Lahore, capital of Punjab. The date of his birth is given as
1469 A.D. His parents were common people who embraced the Hindu
religion. There are folk stories of Nanak's youth which depict him charg-
ing a Hindu teacher to know the true name of God.

At an early age, Nanak supposedly gave religious instruction to certain Brahman priests concerning the material sacrament. Whether these
stories are true or not, his life was devoted more to meditation and religion
than to work. The occupations chosen for him by his parents were not
satisfying and caused him to be somewhat of a black sheep within his
family. He eventually took a government position which was offered him
by his brother-in-law in another town. However, Nanak remained unhappy
and continued his constant search for religious truth.

At the age of 33 he was said to have received his divine call.

One day after bathing, Nanak disappeared into the forest and was taken in
a vision to God's presence. He was offered a cup of nectar, which he gratefully
accepted. God said to him: "I am with thee. I have made thee happy, and also
those who shall take thy name. Go, and repeat Mine, and cause others to do
likewise. Abide uncontaminated by the world. Practice the repetition of my
Name, charity, ablutions, worship, and meditation... My Name is God, the
primal Brahma. And thou are the divine Guru" (M. A. McAuliffe, *Sikh Religion:
Its Gurus, Sacred Writings, and Authors*, London: Oxford University Press,
1909, pp. 33-35).

Three days later Nanak returned from the forest and after remaining silent for one day, he pronounced, "There is no Hindu and no Musalman" (*Ibid.*, p. 37). In India, Muslims are known as "Musalmans."

Nanak, along with his minstrel friend Mardana, proceeded to proclaim his new-found message with relatively little success until they returned to Punjab. Disciples were now gathered around him and the newly found faith continued to grow throughout his life. Around age 70 Nanak died, but not without first appointing a successor to continue his mission. The choice was his trusted disciple Angad. According to tradition, even in death, Nanak appeased both Hindu and Muslim.

> The Musalmans, who had received God's name from the Guru, said they would bury him after his death. His Hindu followers, on the contrary, said they would cremate him. When the Guru was invited to decide the discussion, he said: "Let the Hindus place flowers on my right, and the Musalmans on my left. They whose flowers are found fresh in the morning, may have the disposal of my body." Guru Nanak then ordered the crowd to sing: "O my friends, pray for me that I may meet my Lord." The Guru drew a sheet over him, made obeisance to God, and blended his light with Guru Angad's [his successor]. . . . When the sheet was removed the next morning, there was nothing found beneath it. The flowers on both sides were in bloom. All the Sikhs reverently saluted the spot on which the Guru had lain. . . at Kartepur in the Punjab. The Sikhs erected a shrine, and the Muhammadans a tomb in his honour on the margin of the Ravi. Both have since been washed away by the river (*Ibid.*, pp. 190, 191).

Development of Sikhism

Prior to his death, Nanak appointed a ropemaker named Lahina as his successor. It was Lahina who thereafter changed his name to Angad (bodyguard), and who introduced the doctrine of Nanak's equality with God. A series of different gurus followed Angad, one of whom was Guru Arjan, who compiled the *Granth Sahib* during his leadership.

After the tenth guru in the line of succession died in 1708, the loyalty of the Sikhs was transferred from the personal authority of the guru to the sacred book, the *Granth Sahib*, and so it remains today.

The Teachings of Sikhism

The teachings of Sikhism are a syncretism of the doctrines of Islam and Hinduism. Rather than borrowing from the Hindu and Islamic scriptures, the Sikhs wrote their own scripture based upon their interpretation of certain ideas taught in Hinduism and Islam. Sikhism actually rejects some of the teachings of Hinduism and Islam. The result is an interesting combination of both Hindu and Moslem theology.

Scripture

The sacred scriptures of Sikhism are known as the *Granth Sahib* or "Lord's Book." This work was composed by several dozen authors, some living prior to Nanak and having only a distant relationship to Sikhism. It contains a collection of poems of various lengths and totals some 29,480 rhymed verses. The contents center on extolling the name of God and exhortations on daily living.

A unique feature of this work is the number of languages utilized in its composition. The *Granth Sahib* is written in six different languages and several dialects. It is therefore nearly impossible for even the learned Sikh to study these scriptures in their entirety, much less so for the unlearned.

Undoubtedly, there are only a handful of people in the entire world capable of reading the volume in its totality. There has never been any extensive system of scriptural study made by the Sikhs. The average Sikh devotee knows very little about the *Granth Sahib*, and it is for this reason non-essential to Sikh religious training. Although most Sikhs do not know the contents of their sacred book, they do treat it with reverence, almost to the point of idolatry.

God

According to Sikh belief there is one God who is absolute and sovereign over all things. Nanak's first statement after receiving his call became the opening sentences of the *Granth Sahib:*

> There is but one God, whose name is true, creator, devoid of fear and enmity, immortal, unborn, self-existent, great and bountiful. The True One was in the beginning (*Ibid.*, p. 35).

The usual name given to the Sikh deity is *"sat nam"* which means "true name," although god may be called many different names since He takes on various manifestations. The *Granth Sahib* records:

> Thou, O Lord, art One. But many are thy manifestations (*Ibid.*, p. 310).

Although God is basically a unity, according to Sikh doctrine, He is not considered personal but rather is equated with truth and reality. K. Singh observes:

> In equating God with the abstract principle of truth or reality, Nanak avoided the difficulty encountered by religious teachers who describe God only as the Creator of the Father... but Nanak's system has its own problems. If God is truth, what is truth? Nanak's answer was that in situations when you cannot decide for yourself, let the guru be your guide (K. Singh in *Abingdon Dictionary of Living Religions*, Keith Grim, general editor, Nashville: Abingdon Press, 1981, p. 691).

Salvation

Robert E. Hume comments upon the Sikh idea of salvation:

> The Sikh religion teaches that salvation consists in knowing God, or in obtaining God, or being absorbed into God. The general method of salvation is fairly consistent with the supremacy of an inscrutable God, and with the accompanying doctrines of the worthlessness of the world and the helplessness of man... This method of obtaining salvation by a pantheistic merging of the individual self with the mystical world soul is identical with the method of salvation which had been taught in the Hindu Upanishads" (Robert E. Hume, *The World's Living Religions*, New York: Charles Scribner's Sons, rev. ed., 1959, pp. 102, 103).

Hume lists the points of agreement and disagreement between Sikhism and the Hinduism and Islamic doctrines:

A COMPARISON OF SIKHISM WITH HINDUISM

(1) *Points of Agreement*

Theoretically, belief in a mystical Supreme Unity.

Practically, great variety of designations for deity.

A certain theistic application of pantheism, even as in some of the Hindu *Upanishads* and the *Bhagavad Gita*.

Salvation by faith in the grace of God.

The doctrine of Karma.

Transmigration of souls.

(2) *Points of Disagreement*

Hindu polytheism repudiated, in favor of a monistic pantheism.

Hindu pilgrimages, ritualism, and hermit asceticism repudiated, in favor of pure worship of the Pure One.

Hindu scriptures repudiated, in favor of the Sikh scriptures.

Hindu degradation of women repudiated, in favor of a higher regard for women.

Hindu infanticide repudiated, in favor of a more vigorous populating.

Hindu vegetarianism repudiated, in favor of a more vigorous meat-eating.

COMPARISON OF SIKHISM WITH ISLAM

(1) *Points of Agreement*

Unity of the Supreme Personal Being.

Sovereignty of the Supreme Absolute Ruler.

A certain mercifulness attributed to the inscrutable deity, along with an uncomplainable arbitrariness.

Salvation through submission to God.

Worship through repetition of the name of the deity.

Great importance in repeating prescribed prayers.

Devotion to the founder as God's prophet.

Extreme reverence for sacred scripture.

The first section in the sacred scripture, a kind of Lord's Prayer, composed by the founder at a crisis in his early life when seeking for God, and subsequently prescribed for daily repetition by all his followers.

A series of subsequent leaders after the original founder.

A long, powerful, militaristic church state.

Unity among believers, despite subsequent sects.

A very important central shrine—Mecca and Amritsar.

Vehement denunciation of idolatry.

(2) *Points of Disagreement*

Sikhism's founder not so ruthless or violent as Islam's.

Sikhism's deity not so ruthless or violent as Islam's.

Sikhism's sacred scriptures ascribed to many teachers, at least thirty-seven; not to one, as in Islam.

No fasting prescribed to Sikhs, as to Muslims in month of Ramadan.
No decisive judgment-day in Sikhism, as in Islam. (*Ibid.*, pp. 108-110).

Sikhism and Christianity

The basic premise of Sikhism, uniting different religions, is foreign to the teachings of the Bible. Sikhism attempts to unify the contradictory faiths of Islam and Hinduism. Christianity teaches that it is the only true religion and demonstrates that its world view is consistent with reality.

Jesus Christ pointed out that those who do not believe in Him as their Savior will not receive everlasting life. "I said therefore to you, that you shall die in your sins; for unless you believe that I am He, you shall die in your sins" (John 8:24 NASB). "Jesus said to him, 'I am the way, and the truth, and the life; no one comes to the Father, but through Me'" (John 14:6 NASB).

The concept of God which Nanak obtained by uniting certain features from both Hinduism and Islam is abstract and impersonal, in contradistinction to the biblical concept of a personal, caring God.

The God who is revealed in the Bible is intimately involved with the actions of mankind. "O Lord, Thou hast searched me and known me. Thou dost know when I sit down and when I rise up. Thou dost understand my thought from afar. Thou dost scrutinize my path and my lying down, and art intimately acquainted with all my ways. Even before there is a word on my tongue, behold, O Lord, thou dost know it all" (Psalm 139:1-4 NASB).

The Bible makes it clear that Jehovah God cannot be reconciled with any other so-called god of another religion:

> "You are My witnesses," declares the Lord, "and My servant whom I have chosen, in order that you may know and believe Me, and understand that I am He. Before Me there was no God formed, and there will be none after Me" (Isaiah 43:10 NASB).

Sikhistic Terms

Angad—A disciple of Nanak who became the first in a line of ten successors as the leader of Sikhism. Angad introduced the teaching that Nanak was equal to God.

Granth Sahib—The "Lord's Book." The sacred scripture of Sikhism.

Guru Arjan—The compiler of the *Granth Sahib*, the sacred scripture of Sikhism.

Mardana—The minstrel friend of Nanak who was his sole companion in the early years of the spreading of Sikhism.

Nanak—The 15th century A.D. religious leader who founded Sikhism.

Sat Nam—The "true name." This is the usual designation for God in Sikhism.

Sikh—Literally, "disciple." The designation for followers of Sikhism.

Sikhism Bibliography

Hume, Robert E., *The World's Living Religions*, New York: Charles Scribner's Sons, rev. ed., 1959.

McAuliffe, M. A., *Sikh Religion: Its Gurus, Sacred Writings, and Authors*, London: Oxford University Press, 1909.

Singh, K. in the *Abingdon Dictionary of Living Religions*, Keith Grim, general editor, Nashville: Abingdon Press, 1981.

Annotated
Cults Bibliography

Agency for Cultural Affairs. *Japanese Religions: A Survey by the Agency for Cultural Affairs.* Tokyo, Japan: Kodansha International, Ltd., 1972 and 1981.
   A non-Christian book concentrating on Buddhism but covering all the religions in Japan.

Anderson, Sir Norman, ed. *The World's Religions.* Grand Rapids, MI: William B. Eerdmans Publishing Co., 1975.
   A Christian book discussing religions of Pre-literary societies; Judaism; Buddhism; Islam; Hinduism; Shintoism; Confucianism; and concluding with a Christian approach to comparative religions.

Azzam, Abd-Al-Rahman. *The Eternal Message of Muhammad.* New York: The New American Library, 1964.
   A non-Christian book tracing some of the history of Islam.

Boa, Kenneth. *Cults, World Religions, and You.* Wheaton, IL: Victor Books, 1977.
   A Christian book covering major non-Christian religions of the East, major pseudo-Christian religions of the West, occult religions and systems, new religions and cults. Contains a good bibliography.

Burks, Thompson. *Religions of the World.* Cincinnati, OH: Standard Publishing Co., 1972.
   A Christian book designed for use as an adult education course in Sunday school. Covers Judaism, Islam, Hinduism, and Christianity.

Chang, Lit-Sen. *Zen-Existentialism: The Spiritual Decline of the West.* Nutley, NJ: Presbyterian and Reformed Publishing Co., 1969.
   Christian, probably the most in-depth view on Zen-Buddhism, especially as to how it affects American thought today.

Drummond, Richard. *Gautama the Buddha, An Essay in Religious Understanding.* Grand Rapids, MI: William B. Eerdmans Publishing Co., 1974.

Discusses the life of Buddha and his teachings. Includes theological interpretations and a Christian criticism.

Eastman, Roger, ed. *The Ways of Religion.* San Francisco, CA: Harper & Row Publishers, Inc., 1975.

An anthology in comparative religions combining pertinent and interesting primary sources and expository materials. College textbook, non-Christian.

Hesselgrave, David, J., ed. *Dynamic Religious Movements.* Grand Rapids, MI: Baker Book House, 1978.

Covers world religions in Africa, Europe, the Far East, the Middle East, North America, South America and Southeast Asia. A Christian book.

Heydt, Henry J. *A Comparison of World Religions.* Fort Washington, PA: Christian Literature Crusade, 1967.

Designed for use in a Sunday school or Bible class. A Christian book with good Christian perspectives. Historical survey of Judaism, Christianity, Hinduism, Zoroastrianism, Shintoism, Taoism, Jainism, Buddhism, Confucianism, Islam, and Sikhism, with a discussion of the sacred literature of each. Includes a topical comparison of the religions plus the distinctives of Christianity.

Marsh, C. R. *Share Your Faith with a Muslim.* Chicago, IL: Moody Press, 1975.

Contains the history of Islam, the five pillars of Islamic faith, Islamic teachings on essential Christian doctrines, and Christian answers to them.

Martin, Walter, ed. *The New Cults.* Santa Ana, CA: Vision House Publishers, Inc., 1980.

Although this deals mostly with new cults such as the Unification Church and Transcendental Meditation, it also contains information on Hinduism and Nichiren Shoshu Buddhism. A Christian book.

Miller, William McElwee. *The Baha'i Faith: Its History and Teachings.* Pasadena, CA: William Carey Library, 1974.

The most comprehensive, thorough and excellent treatment of Baha'ism available anywhere, written by a man who was a Christian missionary in Iran for over 40 years.

_____. *A Christian Response to Islam.* Nutley, NJ: Presbyterian and Reformed Publishing Co., 1976.

This is the best single small book on a Christian approach to Islam. Contains the history of Islam, beliefs and practices of Muslims, and differences between Islam and Christianity. Gives testimonies of people converted from Islam, tips for presenting the Gospel to Muslims, and an excellent bibliography.

_____. *Ten Muslims Meet Christ.* Grand Rapids, MI: William B. Eerdmans Publishing Co., 1969.

Testimonies of Muslims who came to Christ and who are from Islamic countries.

Needleman, Jacob. *The New Religions.* New York: E. P. Dutton, 1970.
A non-Christian book. Discusses some of the traditional world religions, as well as some new religions including the new American forms of Zen-Buddhism, Meher Baba, Subud, Transcendental Meditation, Krishna Murdi, Tibetan ideas in America, etc.

Neil, William, ed. *Concise Dictionary of Religious Quotations.* Grand Rapids, MI: William B. Eerdmans Publishing Co., 1974.
List of quotations by subject. Has a source index and subject index.

Palmer, Bernard. *Understanding the Islamic Explosion.* Beaver Lodge, Alberta, Canada: Horizon House Publishers, 1980.
Discusses contemporary Islam; the positions of women in Islamic tradition; the Koran versus the Bible; the prophet Mohammed; and the roots of Islam. Includes tips for sharing Christ with a Muslim.

Parrinder, Geoffrey. *A Dictionary of Non-Christian Religions.* Philadelphia, PA: The Westminster Press, 1971.
A comprehensive dictionary of the major terms of all the major religions. Good detail in a short space. Written from a Christian perspective but does not include Christianity as a world religion.

Pickthall, Mohammed Marmaduke, trans. *The Meaning of the Glorious Koran.* New York: New American Library, 1959.
Not a Christian book but an expository translation of the Koran. Since Islam teaches that the Koran is perfect and holy in Arabic, there is no authorized translation, but this is a good popular work.

Richardson, Don. *Eternity in Their Hearts.* Ventura, CA: Gospel Light Publications, 1981.
Written from a Christian perspective on the development of primitive religions. Though not very well documented, it does contain some good ideas.

Ridenour, Fritz. *So What's the Difference?* Ventura, CA: Gospel Light Publications, 1967 and 1979.
Deals with world religions and written from a Christian perspective. Includes Roman Catholicism; the major religions of the world: Judaism, Islam, Hinduism, Buddhism; and major cults: Unitarianism, Jehovah's Witnesses, Christian Science, and Mormonism. A pocket book, a little outdated, but contains good information.

Ringgren, Helmer. *Religions of the Ancient Near East.* Philadelphia, PA: The Westminster Press, 1973.
Covers Samarian religions, Babylonian and Assyrian religions, and West Semitic Religions. Deals with the major beliefs of those systems.

Jackson, Samuel Macauley, editor-in-chief. *The New Schaff-Herzog En-*

cyclopedia of Religious Knowledge, 15 volumes. Grand Rapids, MI: Baker Book House, updated in 1955.

Written from a Christian standpoint, though not always conservative. Covers all major issues in religious knowledge and world religions. A standard reference work, essential for serious study of religion. See also new revised edition (1980).

Sharpe, Eric J. *50 Key Words in Comparative Religions*. London: Lutterworth Press, 1971.

Alphabetical listing of subjects such as: ancestor worship, animism, astrology, mystery, mysticism, myth, phenomenology of religion, shaman, sin, soul, spirit, syncretism, witchcraft and worship.

Smith, Huston. *The Religions of Man*. New York: Harper and Row Publishers, 1958.

A widely quoted classic. Not necessarily the most reliable or the most up-to-date, but one of the first thorough treatments of Hinduism, Buddhism, Confucianism, Taoism, Islam, Judaism and Christianity.

Steinberg, Milton. *Basic Judaism*. New York: Harcourt Brace Jovanovich, Inc., 1975.

Excellent overview of general Judaism. Written from a Jewish perspective, covers the Torah, God, the good life, Israel and the nations, practices, law, institutions, and the world to come. Does not necessarily distinguish between the three major branches of Judaism.

Sumrall, Lester. *Where Was God When Pagan Religions Began?* Nashville, TN: Thomas Nelson Publishers, 1980.

Covers the cause and effect of pagan religions, animism, the religions of fear, Egyptian religion, a pattern for America, Babylonian religion, the roots of astrology, Hinduism, Buddhism, Shintoism, Confucianism, Taoism, Islam and end-time paganism. Written from a Christian perspective.

Tanenbaum, Marc H., Marvin Wilson and A. James Rudin, eds. *Evangelicals and Jews in Conversation*. Grand Rapids, MI: Baker Book House, 1978.

Divided into seven parts in which evangelical Christians and Jews share perspectives on the Messiah, Israel, interpretation of Scripture, response to moral crises and social problems, religious pluralism and the future. An excellent source book on the differences between Judaism and Christianity and how Jews interact with Christians.

Vos, Johannes G. *A Christian Introduction to Religions of the World*. Grand Rapids, MI: Baker Book House, 1965.

A fairly old book and somewhat out of date, but a good, brief, and simple introduction to the major world religions, written from a Christian perspective.

Part IV

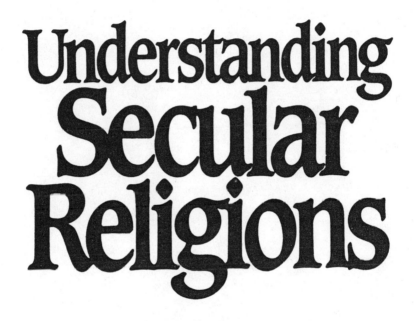

Understanding
Secular
Religions

CHAPTER ONE

Atheism, Agnosticism, and Skepticism

W hile it might seem odd at first to include atheism, agnosticism, and skepticism in a series on religion, these three systems of thought should be addressed here. Religion is sometimes defined as whatever about which a man is deeply concerned,[1] and it is to such concerns that we now turn. Everyone, even the nontheist attempts to make sense of and explain the reality around him. While those who believe in some form of God attribute this world's existence in some way to that God (or gods); the atheist, agnostic, and skeptic form an alternative naturalistic explanation for this world.

Since our space is limited, we usually will refer to the three views as one, recognizing the great overlap among them. Where their distinctions are important we will point them out. After defining the three terms we will review briefly the history of the nontheist (apart from God) movement. Then we will discuss five kinds of objections which represent most of the arguments brought by nonbelievers against a belief in God. These five objections include problems in the areas of language, knowledge, moral concepts, scientific method, and logic. Since this is to be a survey of nontheistic religions, and not a presentation of Christianity, we will not present systematic proofs for the existence of God, but we will present short theistic resolutions to the five problems mentioned. We have included the names of the major philosophers whose writings would be helpful in understanding these areas of belief.

Definitions

Atheism

The word *atheism comes from the Greek prefix a-* (no or non-) and the noun *theos* (god or God). An *atheist* is one who believes that there

---

[1]Richard Purtill, *Reason to Believe*, Grand Rapids, MI: William B. Eerdmans Publishing Company, 1974, p. 10.

exists positive evidence that there is no God. To the atheist, all of existence can be explained naturally rather than supernaturally. An atheist is convinced that all religious belief, evidence, and faith are false.

Popular authors and philosophy professors William and Mabel Sahakian explain it as follows:

> Unlike Agnostics, the Atheist takes a definite stand, arguing that proof regarding God's existence or nonexistence is available, but that the evidence favors the assumption of nonexistence (William and Mabel Sahakian, *Ideas of the Great Philosophers*, New York: Harper and Row, Publishers, 1966, p. 100).

Bishop Charles Gore summarizes atheistic belief as presupposing

> that we see in the world of which we form a part no signs of anything corresponding to the mind or spirit or purposes which indisputably exist in man—no signs of a universal spirit or reason with which we can hold communion, nothing but blind and unconscious force (Charles Gore, *The Reconstruction of Belief*, London: John Murray, 1926, pp. 45,46).

Historically, *atheism* sometimes refers to a rejection of only particular gods or a particular God. Hans Schwarz informs us that

> When the Greek philosopher Anaxagoras, for instance, declared that the sun was an incandescent stone somewhat larger than the Peloponesus, he was accused of impiety or atheism and forced to leave his hometown Athens (Hans Schwarz, *The Search for God*, Minneapolis, MN: Augsburg Publishing House, 1975, p. 16).

Plato in his *Laws X* (c. 352-350 B.C.) defined two basic kinds of atheists: those who are sincerely convinced God (or gods) does not exist; and those who assert that there is no place for God (or gods) in this world. The first kind of atheist is considered moral and upright while the second kind is seen as an anarchistic (without law) threat to society.[2] Socrates may have been put to death for being this second kind of atheist. Again, Schwarz notes,

> . . .when Socrates was indicted for "impiety" in 399 B.C. on grounds that he had corrupted the young and neglected the gods during worship ceremonies ordered by the city and had introduced religious novelties, he was sentenced to death and was condemned to drink the hemlock within twenty-four hours. But Socrates' position and that of other atheists was far from being atheistic in the modern sense (ibid., p. 17).

Agnosticism

Agnosticism comes from the Greek prefix *a-* (no or non-) and the noun *gnosis* (knowledge, usually by experience). An agnostic is one who believes there is insufficient evidence to prove or disprove the existence or nonexistence of God or gods. Agnostics criticize the theist and the atheist for their dogmatism and their presumption of such knowledge.

William and Mabel Sahakian say that agnosticism "refers to a neutralist view on the question of the existence of God; it is the view of the person who elects to remain in a state of suspended judgment" (Sahakian and Sahakian, *Ideas*, p. 100).

---

[2] Edith Hamilton and Huntington Cairns, eds., *Plato: The Collected Dialogues*, Princeton, NJ: Princeton University Press, 1961, pp. 1463-1465.

The Runes *Dictionary of Philosophy* defines agnosticism as:

1. (epist.) that theory of knowledge which asserts that it is impossible for man to attain knowledge of a certain subject-matter. 2. (theol.) that theory of religious knowledge which asserts that it is impossible for man to attain knowledge of God (Dagobert D. Runes, ed., *Dictionary of Philosophy*, Totowa, NJ: Littlefield, Adams & Company, 1960, 1962, p. 7).

This is complemented by Peter Angeles' *Dictionary of Philosophy*, which defines agnosticism as:

1. The belief (a) that we cannot have knowledge of God and (b) that it is impossible to prove that God exists or does not exist. 2. Sometimes used to refer to the suspension of judgment... about some types of knowledge such as about the soul, immortality, spirits, heaven, hell, extraterrestrial life (Peter Angeles, *Dictionary of Philosophy*, New York: Harper Row, Publishers, 1981, p. 20).

There are two types of agnostics. One type says there is insufficient evidence but leaves open the possiblility of sometime obtaining enough evidence to know with certainty. The second type is convinced that it is objectively impossible for anyone to ever know with certainty the existence or non-existence of God or gods.

William and Mabel Sahakian add this distinction to their definition of agnosticism (see above):

One group of Agnostics assumes that it merely lacks the facts necessary to form a judgment and defers any conclusion pending the acquisition of such facts; another group assumes a more dogmatic position, contending that facts are not available because it is impossible now (and will continue to be impossible) to obtain these facts—a view exemplified in Immanuel Kant's attacks upon the traditional arguments for the existence of God (Sahakian and Sahakian, *Ideas*, p. 100).

Christian authors Norman Geisler and Paul Feinberg also point out the distinction between the two kinds of agnostics:

One form of agnosticism claims that we *do not* know if God exists; the other insists that we *cannot* know. The first we'll call "soft" and the second "hard" agnosticism. We are not here concerned about "soft" agnosticism, since it does not eliminate in principle the possibility of knowing whether God exists. It says in effect, "I do not know whether God exists but it is not impossible to know. I simply do not have enough evidence to make a rational decision on the question." We turn, then, to the "hard" form which claims that it is impossible to know whether God exists (Norman Geisler and Paul Feinberg, *Introduction to Philosophy: A Christian Perspective*, Grand Rapids, MI: Baker Book House, 1980, p. 296).

Skepticism

Skepticism is derived from the Latin *scepticus* (inquiring, reflective, doubting). The Latin in turn comes from the Greek *scepsis* (inquiry, hesitation, doubt). The Greeks used the word to refer to a certain school of philosophical thought, the Skeptics[3] (see *History* below), who taught that because real knowledge is unattainable, one should suspend judg-

---

[3]Skepticism is capitalized when used as the title of a school of philosophy; and is in lower case when used to describe a general concept.

ment on matters of truth. This meaning is carried in Runes' *Dictionary of Philosophy*:

> A proposition about a method of obtaining knowledge: that every hypothesis should be subjected to continual testing; that the only or the best or a reliable method of obtaining the knowledge of one or more of the above kinds is to doubt until something indubitable or as nearly indubitable as possible is found; that wherever evidence is indecisive, judgment should be suspended; that knowledge of all or certain kinds at some point rests on unproved postulates or assumptions (Runes, *Philosophy*, p. 278).

This is confirmed by B. A. G. Fuller's *A History of Philosophy*, where he reminds us that the "role of skepticism is to remind men that knowing with absolute certainty is impossible" (B. A. G. Fuller, *A History of Philosophy*, New York: Holt, Rinehart and Winston, 1955, vol. II, p. 581).

Peter Angeles shows in his definition of *skepticsm* that there is a range of belief within the system. He writes,

> 1. A state of doubting. 2. A state of suspension of judgment. 3. A state of unbelief or nonbelief. Skepticism ranges from complete, total disbelief in everything, to a tentative doubt in a process of reaching certainty (Angeles, *Philosophy*, p. 258).

While skepticism is sometimes synonymous with certain definitions of agnosticism, other writers distinguish between skepticism and agnosticism as does Warren Young, who writes:

> Skepticism carries the negative attitude a step farther than agnosticism, denying the possibility of human knowledge. Truth in an objective sense is unattainable by any means within man's reach (Warren Young, *A Christian Approach to Philosophy*, Grand Rapids, MI: Baker Book House, 1954, p. 61).

Keeping in mind Geisler and Feinberg's two kinds of agnosticism (see above under the definition of agnosticism), their comments on the differences between agnosticism and skepticism are important. They write,

> The skeptic neither affirms nor denies God's existence. And in contrast to the (hard) agnostic, the skeptic does not say it is impossible to know. For (hard) agnosticism too is a form of dogmatism—negative dogmatism. The skeptic claims to take a much more tentative attitude toward knowledge. He is not sure whether a man can or cannot know God. In fact, the complete skeptic is not sure of anything (Geisler and Feinberg, *Philosophy*, p. 299).

Because of the overlap of definitions for atheism, agnosticism, and skepticism, it is at times difficult and even unnecessary to distinguish one's usage of the terms. What is most important to remember is that most non-religious people, while they may label themselves with one of the three terms, usually have no clear understanding of how their own views fit one category but not the others. A person may be regarded as an atheist but, in actual practice, fall under the common definition of an agnostic. Another person may be regarded as a skeptic but admit to the possibility of change to accept some universal truths. If someone questions everything, the title "skeptic" can be applied. But since certainty might be found someday it would be appropriate to be seen as an agnostic. However, if at this time that person does not believe in God, is "atheist" the proper term? While the three terms are useful to us (as in reading other philosophy works), the terms are relatively unimportant in most personal encounters. If we can establish what someone believes about knowledge, about obtaining knowledge, and about the ultimate meaning of existence, then we can deal with that person on the level at which he is comfortable. In such a situation, the label of atheist, agnostic, or skeptic is unimportant.

History

As we look at brief histories of atheism, agnosticism, and skepticism, we will reverse our order of discussion to reflect the chronological development of these three areas of philosophical thought. There have been skeptics, atheists, and agnostics throughout the history of mankind, and we will treat skepticism first, then atheism, and finally agnosticism.

Skepticism

The Greek schools of Skepticism began around 365 B.C. The first skeptic philosopher of note was Pyrrho of Elis (365-275 B.C.). The Pyrrhonic School held that skepticism was so pervasive that even their theory of skepticism was not certain. Skepticism was adopted as a way to avoid mental and emotional distress caused by conflictng data.

> ...the central idea of the early Skeptics was to avoid mental insecurity or doubt by abstaining from judgment on issues; suspension of judgment (*epoche*) became the fundamental theory of Skepticism. The policy of withholding judgment applied not only to metaphysical and logical questions, but also to value judgments pertaining to right conduct, the good, and the desirable. . . .
>
> The Skeptics, who were called the doubters, suspenders of judgment, and inquirers, based their philosophy on the premise that since we can know nothing of ultimate reality, then such basic things are matters of indifference to us, and they must be treated as inconsequential (William Sahakian, *History of Philosophy*, New York: Harper & Row, Publishers, 1968, pp. 48,49).

A second school of Skepticism is called Academic Skepticism, or the Middle Academy. Its leaders were Arcesilaus of Pitane in Aeolia (315-241 B.C.), Carneades of Cyrene (214-129 B.C.), and Clitomachus (187-109 B.C.). The basic premise of Academic Skepticism is summarized well by Sahakian:

> The Academic Skeptics set forth the fundamental premise that they could know only one thing, namely, that nothing is knowable (ibid., pp. 49,50).

The Academics spent most of their efforts attacking the teachings of the Stoics,[4] and their presentation of Skepticism was often done in

---

[4]*Stoics*—an Athenian school of philosophy founded around 305 B.C. by Zeno of Citium in Cyprus. *Stoicism*—"For Stoicism virtue alone is the only good and the virtuous man is the one who has attained happiness through knowledge, as Socrates had taught. The virtuous man thus finds happiness in himself and is independent of the external world which he has succeeded in overcoming by mastering himself, his passions and emotions. As for the Stoic conception of the universe as a whole, their doctrine is pantheistic. All things and all natural laws follow by a conscious determination from the basic World-Reason, and it is this rational order by which, according to Stoicism, the wise man seeks to regulate his life as his highest duty" (Runes, *Philosophy*, p. 301).

direct contrast to Stoicism. Arcesilaus stated that, while one could not know, even about ethics, one could judge probability and that, in fact, one should order his life by probability. He was followed by Carneades, who postulated three degrees of probability.

> 1. In the first place, we have mere probability, where we act with little or no observation of simlar situations to help us, and where the chances therefore are about fifty-fifty, but seem worth taking in view of what we shall gain if we win.
> 2. Secondly, we have undisputed probability, where empirical observation shows us that other people have repeatedly taken the same chances successfully and to their advantage, and have never lost. Here the face-value of the probable truth and reliability of an impression is backed up by all the other impressions and notions related to it.
> 3. Finally, we may be able to act upon chances that not only look worth taking on a fifty-fifty basis and are uncontradicted and backed up by the experiences of other people, but have been thoroughly investigated and found to have solid reasons for taking them. In other words, we may be able to discover a "system" for life's gamble that mathematically, so to speak, ought to work. Then, says Carneades, we have a basis for action that is probable, undisputed, and tested (Fuller, *Philosophy*, pp. 277,278).

Clitomachus (sometimes spelled Cleitomachus) was the third leader. He attacked the three degrees of probability, opting for a more uniform system of Skepticism.

Sensationalistic Skepticism was the last of the classical schools of Skepticism. Its two most prominent leaders were Aenesidemus of Gnossus (first century B.C.) and Sextus Empiricus (200 A.D.). Aenesidemus exposed what he felt were fallacious tests for truth: sensation and confirmed opinion. He felt that these were subjective tests and could not be trusted. However, he had no objective tests for truth and instead was a confirmed skeptic, viewing life and existence as uncertain but livable on the basis of custom and probability. Sextus Empiricus was a doctor, from the empiricist school of doctors, and he put forth the maxim that life should be ordered by observation, or empiricism. Loyal to skepticism, Sextus promoted the study of Socrates' remark, "All that I know is that I know nothing." Sextus set forth his skepticism as follows:

> The *archē*, or motive, for skepticism was the hope of reaching *ataraxia*, the state of "unperturbedness." ... Sextus Empiricus' skepticism had three stages: antithesis, *epochē* (suspension of judgment), and *ataraxia*. The first stage involved a presentation of contradictory claims about the same subject. These claims were so constructed that they were in opposition to one another, and appeared equally probable or improbable.... The second state is *epochē*, or the suspension of judgment. Instead of either asserting or denying any one claim about the subject at hand, one must embrace all mutually inconsistent claims and withhold judgment on each of them. The final stage is *ataraxia*, a state of unperturbedness, happiness, and peace of mind. When that occurs one is freed from dogmatism. He can live peacefully and undogmatically in the world, following his natural inclinations and the laws or customs of society (Geisler and Feinberg, *Philosophy*, pp. 85,86).

Skepticism died out for the most part during the ascendency of Christianity. It did not become a noticeable philosophical movement again until the post-Reformation period of western European thought with Bishop John Wilkins (1614-1672) and Joseph Glanvill (1636-1680). They are sometimes called "mitigated skeptics." While clinging tenaciously to one area of skepticism, they compromised by not embracing skepticism as the answer to all knowledge problems in all fields. They distinguished between two types of knowledge. The first type, which they agreed was unreliable, was called "infallibly certain knowledge." Nothing, in other words, could be known infallibly and certainly. However, the second type of knowledge, by which one could order life, was called "indubitably certain knowledge." This was knowledge that one had no reason, experience, evidence, or report by which to doubt its veracity. Using this knowledge, Wilkins and Glanvill developed their own system of determining truth within the limits of "reasonable doubt."

Rene Descartes (1596-1650) wrote at the same time as Wilkins and Glanvill, although he is not considered to be a "mitigated skeptic." As a Christian theist, he used skepticism as a tool to prove the existence of God. Rather than seeing skepticism as an end in itself, he saw it as the way to begin to show the undeniability of the existence of God.

> For Descartes, skepticism was not the conclusion of some argument, but the method whereby all doubt could be overcome. Descartes claimed that it is possible to arrive at indubitable knowledge through the rigorous and systematic application of doubt to one's beliefs (ibid., p. 91).

From the time of Descartes, the majority of such thinkers have been atheists or agnostics. We will treat some of these skeptical thinkers more thoroughly in the historical sections on atheism and agnosticism. However, we will mention them briefly here.

David Hume (1711-1776) is known as a metaphysical[5] skeptic. He believed that it was impossible to have any accurate knowledge about anything metaphysical. He pointed out that standards of probability for beliefs go beyond our immediate experience and must be accepted with some measure of faith.

Nicholas Horvath in his book, *Philosophy,* explains that:

> Hume claimed that only sense-knowledge based on experience is possible. Ideas are mere copies of sense impressions. Impressions and ideas constitute the human intellect. Ideas are not entirely unconnected; there is a bond of union between them and one calls up another. This phenomenon is called association of ideas.
>
> Neither material nor spiritual substances exist in reality; their ideas are purely imaginative concepts, being nothing other than a constant association of impressions. Likewise there is nothing in man's experience that justifies a notion of necessary connection or causation; cause and effect designate merely a regular succession of ideas. Since the principle of causality is mere expectation due to custom, no facts outside consciousness are known to man.
>
> Granted the negation of substance, the existence of God and the immor-

---

[5]In this context, "metaphysical" means that which is unable to be tested by the senses.

tality of the human soul are only hypothetical. Freedom of will is an illusion; virtue is that which pleases, and vice is that which displeases (Nicholas A. Horvath, *Philosophy*, Woodbury, NY: Barron's Educational Series, Inc., 1974, pp. 88,89).

More recently, A. J. Ayer (1910-1970), a limited skeptic, taught that any talk about metaphysics is meaningless. In addition, Albert Camus (1913-1960), one of the most important of the so-called "irrational" skeptics asserted that there is no meaning, no knowledge that is objectively true, and no objective value. The entire history of skepticsm has the same basic theme. Is suspends judgment about truth. At various times skeptics have said that even their statement of skepticism is doubtful. At other times they have said that the one non-skeptical statement is the same statement, that skepticism is doubtful.

Atheism

Although the term *atheism* as a reference to the belief that God (or gods) does (do) not exist dates from the late sixteenth century, Niccolo Machiavelli (d. 1527) had already promoted a social ethic which did not depend on belief in, or the existence of, a supreme God. In his satirical essay, *The Prince*, he taught that the ruler ought to rule wisely and justly in order *to secure his position and to satisfy his ego*, rather than to satisfy some divine mandate. Machiavelli was one of the first to champion the then novel idea that "the end justifies the means." He argued that a ruler should not burden his subjects too much, not because it would be morally wrong to do so, but because it would not be expedient, for his oppressed subjects would then be more likely to revolt, depose him, and perhaps even kill him for his cruelty. Although Machiavelli cannot be termed an actual atheist, his system for successful governorship does not depend on, or presuppose, any divine order to this world.

Ideas from many philosophers, not all of whom were actually atheists, helped shape the atheistic philosophy of today.

During the enlightenment of the eighteenth century, the Baron P. H. T. d'Holbach referred to an atheist as

> a man who destroys the dreams and chimerical beings that are dangerous to the human race so that men can be brought back to nature, to experience, and to reason (*Enclyclopaedia Britannica*, Chicago, et. al.: Encyclopaedia Britannica, Inc., 1978, *Macropaedia*, II, p. 259).

As a brief and circumscribed overview of the history of atheism, we will review some of the contributions to modern atheism made by Hegel, Feuerbach, Marx, Comte, Nietzsche, Jaspers, and Sartre. Ideas from philosophers such as Bayle, Spinoza, Fichte, and Hume, although not mentioned here, also contributed to the development of modern atheistic thought.

Georg W. F. Hegel (1770-1831) was the man whose writings became an inspiration for the modern atheistic movement. He was one of the first prominent philosophers to advance the idea that God[6] was dependent upon the world at least as much as the world was dependent upon God. He said that without the world God is not God. In some way, God needed his creation. This was the first step in saying that, since God was not sufficient in Himself, he was then unnecessary and ultimately imaginary.

Ludwig Feuerbach (1804-1872) was an early prominent atheistic philosopher. He denied all supernaturalism and attributed all talk about God to talk about nature. Man, he said, is dependent not on God, but on nature. Feuerbach promoted what is sometimes referred to as the wish-fulfillment idea of God. He postulated that the idea of God arose as a result of men desiring to have some sort of supernatural Being as an explanation for their own existence and the events they observed around them. This wish, or desire, is the seed from which the God-myth grew. Feuerbach thought this hypothesis proved that God actually did not exist.

Hegel and Feuerbach strongly influenced Karl Marx (1818-1883) and his English collaborator, Frederich Engels (1820-1895). Marx, an avowed atheist, preached that religion is the opiate of the people and the enemy of all progress. Part of the task of the great proletariat revolution is the destruction of all religion.

Auguste Comte (1798-1857) was an early contemporary of Marx and Engels. He believed that God was an irrelevant superstition. As a result, Comte divided human development into three main stages:

"The Theological, or fictitious," "the Metaphysical, or abstract" and "the Scientific, or positive." In the first the human mind looks for first causes and "supposes all phenomena to be produced by the immediate action of supernatural beings." The second is a transitional stage where the mind searches for "abstract forces" behind phenomena. But in the third and ultimate stage man's mind applies itself to the scientific study of the laws according to which things work. God and the supernatural are left behind as irrelevant superstition (Colin Brown, *Philosophy and the Christian Faith*, Downers Grove, IL: InterVarsity Press, 1968, pp. 241, 142).

Friedrich Nietzsche (1844-1900) is often called the Father of the Death of God School. He laid the cornerstone for later nihilists by teaching that since God does not exist, man must devise his own way of life.

Karl Jaspers (1883-1969) and Martin Heidegger (1889-1971) were two

---

[6]Hegel thought of God as Spirit. His concept of God is described by Vincent Miceli: "But Hegel questioned whether the philosophers or the theologians had succeeded in attaining the real God. He protested that the God of Christian experience was an inadequate, a premature, not-yet-developed God. Hegel set himself the task of completing the good news of the Gospels; he would go beyond Christianity by demonstrating that the only valid God was dialectically evolving Thought or Spirit Which gradually, inevitably attains and reveals Itself in conceptual clarity and complete self-consciousness through the entire scope of cosmic and human history. Hegel set himself the mission of rescuing the God of Christianity from the vagueness of imagery, the symbolism of myths, the simplistic charm of parables" (Vincent P. Miceli, *The Gods of Atheism*, New Rochelle, NY: Arlington House, 1971, pp. 21, 22).

prominent existentialist thinkers who discussed the ambiguous (and therefore meaningless) nature of religious transcendence. In addition, Heidegger stressed that one's salvation lay in his own independence as an individual separated from every other individual, including, of course, any sort of God.

Jean-Paul Sartre (1905-1981) was the most popular proponent of existentialism. He argued that man not only creates his own destiny, each man has only himself as the sole justification for his existence. There is no ultimate, objective, eternal meaning to life. An individual simply exists without reference to others.

A good example of atheistic perspective is contained in the *Humanist Manifesto* (1933). It was composed and signed by leading secular humanists who declared, in part, that "Humanism is faith in the supreme value and self-perfectability of human personality." Although there have been many other important thinkers in the history of atheism, these are representative of the most influential contributors shaping modern atheistic thought. Other modern atheistic thinkers are discussed in some of the references mentioned in the bibliography.

Agnosticism

Although agnosticism is a very broad field, we have chosen to limit our historical discussion of it to three of the most influential philosophers in its recent expressions. As we stated before, there is some overlap among atheism, agnosticism and skepticism, and many of the philosophers important in the development of one are also important to the others.

David Hume (1711-1776), known for promoting metaphysical skepticism, showed the close marriage between skepticism and agnosticism. As a British Empiricist, he declared that the probabalistic standards for beliefs go beyond our immediate experience. We act on faith, then, not on knowledge. We do not know for sure: we are agnostic. However, we still act, having chosen to trust faith while at the same time being prepared for faith to let us down. Belief is not to be confused with ultimate truth, which is unknowable.

Immanuel Kant (1724-1804), although a theist, developed Hume's skepticism into metaphysical agnosticism. He believed it was impossible to know reality and consequently impossible to know metaphysical reality.

Colin Brown credits T. H. Huxley (1825-1895) with the term *agnostic*.

> The word agnosticism is of much more recent coinage. It is generally ascribed to T. H. Huxley, the Victorian scientist and friend of Charles Darwin, who devised it to describe his own state of mind. He used it, not to deny God altogether, but to express doubt as to whether knowledge could be attained, and to protest ignorance on 'a great many things that the -ists and the -ites about me professed to be familiar with' (ibid., p. 132).

Hume, Kant and Huxley represent a short history of contemporary agnosticism, which is distinguished by its assertion that one cannot know. Other prominent agnostics include Charles Darwin and Bertrand Russell.

Arguments Against the Existence of God

We will now summarize five types of arguments most nontheists use against the existence of God, and then give a Christian response to each. Space limitations preclude direct quotes, but some of the most important thinkers on these arguments include Immanuel Kant and Georg Hegel in addition to those we refer to.

It is not important here to distinguish atheism, agnosticism, and skepticsm from each other since nonbelievers of all three persuasions can use each of the arguments in various forms. But an understanding of these five arguments will give the reader useful principles for responding to many of the arguments against God's existence.

These areas of our divisions (languages, knowledge, moral concepts, scientific method, and logic) are not strictly demarcated nor are they generally accepted philosophical categorizations, but they are simply made as a convenience to the reader. They will help you find that area of argument in which you are most particularly interested.

Language

EXAMPLE: *Talking about God is meaningless.*

"There are only two kinds of meaningful statements. A statement can be purely definitional (all triangles have three sides) without telling us about the real world (whether triangles actually exist). Or, a statement can be about reality by containing empirically verifiable (testable by the senses) information (this is a triangle). To talk about God in purely definitional statements does not tell us if He actually exists. However, because He is not empirically verifiable, we cannot make empirically verifiable statements about Him. Since purely definitional and empirically verifiable statements are the only kinds of meaningful statements there are, to talk of God's existence is meaningless or [as it is often put] nonsense."

This argument does not actually deny that God exists, but declares all talk about Him futile. Leading thinkers on this subject include A. J. Ayer, Paul van Buren, and Ludwig Wittgenstein.

Knowledge

EXAMPLE: *We can't know the real.*

"We can know about things in the real world through the use of our senses and our mind. However, since our senses are imperfect and selective, and our mind is affected by all it has experienced previously, our perception of a thing is thereby affected. Therefore, we can know a thing as it is to us,* but not as it is in itself."**

This does not argue specifically against God's existence, but can be used to deny that one can know objectively about God. Immanuel Kant and David Hume were instrumental in developing this theory of knowledge.

---

*Kant termed this the "phenomenal world."

** Kant termed this the "noumenal world."

Moral Concepts

EXAMPLE: *The Christian God could not allow evil.*

"If there were an all-powerful God, then He could destroy all evil. If He were all-good, then He would want to destoy all evil. If your all-powerful, all-good God existed, then He would have had to destroy all evil. Evil exists. Therefore, your all-powerful, all-good God must not exist. Or, if He exists, He is not able to do away with evil."

This idea does not argue against the existence of all gods, but only against this "all-powerful, all-good God." From this basis the other problems of evil emerge. Among those issues are the suffering of innocents, natural calamities, etc. One of the earliest proponents of this idea was Epicurus. More modern thinkers were David Hume and J. L. Mackie.

Scientific Methods

EXAMPLE 1: *God is man's wish.*

"Man feels inadequate in himself. He wishes for Someone who is big enough to rescue him from life's tragedies. He desires God to exist. God arises from man's mind. Therefore, God has no objective reality. He does not exist."

Leading supporters of this idea included Ludwig Feuerbach, Friedrich Nietzsche, and Sigmund Freud.

EXAMPLE 2: *God is a result of superstitious belief (sociology).*

"Primitive man could not explain the world around him in natural terms. He invented God to explain the unknown. Today science has shown us the natural laws governing our world. Natural laws explain everything. We no longer need belief in God to explain things. Therefore, God does not exist."

Some of those instrumental in developing this argument included David Hume, Sir James George Frazer, Sir Edward Burnett Tylor, and Bertrand Russell.

Logic

EXAMPLE 1: *God's all-powerfulness is contradictory.*

"There cannot be an omnipotent (all-powerful) God. Such a God would be stuck with the following contradictory questions (antimonies):

1. Can God create a rock too heavy for Him to lift?
2. Can God make $2 + 2 = 6$?
3. Can God make Himself go out of existence and then pop back into existence?
4. Can God make a square circle?

If God is all-powerful, He should be able to do these things. But, in doing them, He is thwarting His own omnipotence. He must not exist."

EXAMPLE 2: *God's attributes contradict each other.*

"How can one being possess both love and wrath? How can God be all-loving (giving man free will) but be all-knowing (predestining man's actions by His foreknowledge)? How can God be absolutely good and yet absolutely free (able to choose evil)? Because God's attributes contradict each other logically, He must not exist."

Christian Responses

Encountering a variety of arguments against the existence of God at one time can be overwhelming. Many Christian students who are unfamiliar with secular philosophy sometimes are at a loss to answer those arguments when they are first confronted with them. We have presented a few of the most common arguments which are representative of the skeptical/agnostic/atheistic attitude prevalent in many secular circles today. (For further discussion of such arguments, see the books referred to in the Bibliography.) We have found that most arguments against the existence of God can be answered by the simple principles we will present below. Due to space limitations the arguments and our responses have been simplified. However, we are confident that the reader can establish a reasonable defense against such arguments with the following principles and personal study.

Refutation of Skepticism

Skepticism is a powerful tool in the hands of an agnostic or atheist. As we saw in our definition and history sections, skepticism is utilized in many areas of nontheistic thought. It often is presupposed or asserted openly as part of an argument against the existence of God. For this reason, we shall deal with the claims of skepticism before we deal with the specific arguments raised above.

Skepticism is ultimately meaningless. It refutes itself. If one declares, "You can never be sure about anything," he is catching himself in his own trap. If we can be sure of nothing, then we cannot be sure of the statement, "nothing is certain." But, if that statement is objectively true, then we can be sure about one thing, the statement. But, if we can be sure about the statement, then the statement must be false. If the statement is false, then we cannot be sure. The inexorable fate of the skeptic is to be condemned by his own sentence.

The Sahakians comment:

> Nihilism and Skepticism are both self-contradictory and self-defeating philosophies. If truth does not exist (Nihilism), then the posited truth of Nihilism could not exist. If knowledge is impossible (Skepticism), how could we ever come to know that? Apparently some things can be known.
>
> Even the less extreme view of Protagoras is self-defeating, as demonstrated by Plato's charming argument in the following paragraphs. . . .
> PROTAGORAS: Truth is relative, it is only a matter of opinion.
> SOCRATES: You mean that truth is mere subjective opinion?
> PROTAGORAS: Exactly. What is true for you is true for you, and what is true for me, is true for me. Truth is subjective.
> SOCRATES: Do you really mean that? That my opinion is true by virtue of its being my opinion?
> PROTAGORAS: Indeed I do.
> SOCRATES: My opinion is: Truth is absolute, not opinion, and that you, Mr. Protagoras, are absolutely in error. Since this is my opinion, then you must grant that it is true according to your philosophy.
> PROTAGORAS: You are quite correct, Socrates. (Sahakian and Sahakian, p. 28.)

Geisler and Feinberrg continue in the same vein:

> ... The skeptic's assertion that we cannot know anything is itself a claim about knowledge. If the skeptic's claim is false, then we need not worry about the skeptic's charge. On the other hand, if it is true, then his position is self-contradictory, because we know at least one thing—that we cannot know anything.
>
> ...But suppose that the skeptic responds by saying that we have misunderstood his claim. He is not claiming that the sentence, "You cannot know anything" is either true or false. . .The skeptic's position is shown to be necessarily false, for his is still a claim about knowledge: "For all sentences, we know that we cannot know whether they are true or false." Therefore, total or complete skepticism is rationally inconsistent (Geisler and Feinberg, *Philosophy*, p. 94).

Christians who often encounter non-believers (agnostics or atheists) find that many arguments against the existence of God or the claims of Christianity are basically claims that one cannot know. They are essentially skeptical arguments and are self-refuting. This one principle is sufficient for answering several anti-theistic arguments.

Refutation of Language Argument

The language argument is self-refuting, just as skepticism is self-refuting. To say that one cannot talk meaningfully about God is to talk meaningfully about God. Either one's statement ("One cannot talk meaningfully about God") is meaningful, in which case it gives us meaningful information about God, or it is, itself, meaningless, in which case we need not heed it. As Geisler puts it,

> ...the principles of empirical verifiability as set forth by Ayer is self-defeating. For it is neither purely definitional nor strictly factual. Hence, on its own grounds it would fall into the third category of non-sense statements. . . . the attempt to limit meaning to the definitional or to the verifiable is to make a truth claim that must itself be subject to some test. If it cannot be tested, then it becomes an unfalsifiable view (Norman Geisler, *Christian Apologetics*, Grand Rapids, MI: Baker Book House, 1976, p. 23).

Refutation of Knowledge Argument

One who adheres completely to the idea that we cannot know the real is another example of one who refutes himself. Reasonably we could say that we do not know *everything* about the real, but it is self-defeating to say one knows *nothing* about the real. If one really knows nothing about the real, then his statement ("I know nothing about the real") is false: he really knows the truth of his statement. His statement cannot be true unless, contradictorily, it is also false. The Christian philosopher Warren Young put it this way:

> The basis of the possibility of knowing rests on a belief in the rationality of the human mind. Apart from belief in rationality, knowledge is impossible. Unless the organizing ability of the mind be granted, it is impossible to know. The data organized by reason are the data of human experience. In spite of the skeptic's rejection of the reliability of experience, his answer is not final. Man is not only deceived by his senses, but in almost all cases he *knows* that

he is being deceived. His reason leads him to compensate for possible deception, to interpret sense data properly, and so he is able to know (Young, *Philosophy*, p. 62).

Geisler also discusses this dilemma with his analysis of complete agnosticism. He writes,

Complete agnosticism is self-defeating; it reduces to the self-destructing assertion that "one knows enough about reality in order to affirm that nothing can be known about reality." This statement provides within itself all that is necessary to falsify itself. For if one knows *something* about reality, then he surely cannot affirm in the same breath that *all* of reality is unknowable. And of course if one knows nothing whatsoever about reality, then he has no basis whatsoever for making a statement about reality. It will not suffice to say that his knowledge about reality is purely and completely negative, that is, a knowledge of what one cannot meaningfully affirm that something is *not*— that it follows that total agnosticism is self-defeating because it assumes some knowledge about reality in order to deny any knowledge of reality (Geisler, *Apologetics*, p. 20).

Refutation of Moral Concepts Argument

The argument of the problem of evil and its various forms and development is probably the most frequently used argument against the existence of God. Whole books are devoted to a Christian reconciliation of the problem. Whole books are devoted to exploring the ideas of non-Christian proponents of the concept. Many sub-arguments against God's existence come from this basic argument. Why does God allow babies to suffer and die? Why are there murder victims? Why does God allow natural calamities?, etc. By understanding the basic problems with the view, one can learn the principles for answering the different forms the view takes.

A good way to find answers to such arguments is to look at each step of the argument and see whether or not it tells the truth. If even one step of the argument is invalid or untrue, then the weight of the entire argument crashes down. When we examine this argument, we find little disagreement with its first step (premise): "If there were an all-powerful God, He could destroy all evil." We begin to have problems with the second premise: "If He were all-good, He would want to destroy all evil." There are two problems here. First, an all-good God may have beneficent uses for evil. Second, the arguer has not taken into consideration the element of time. What if God were to use evil for a time and *then*, ultimately, destroy it? That would allow for a good God and yet also allow evil at this present time.

Richard Purtill sums it up this way:

Now on this view there can be a problem of evil, since some things that happen in the world seem to be contrary to what a loving God would permit. But the problem must somehow be soluble, since the events we condemn and the moral law by which we condemn them are both traceable to the same Source. If God is what Christianity says he is, he is the God of Love and Justice, and also the God who permits apparently useless suffering. It must be, then, that there is a reconciliation. (Perhaps the suffering is *not* useless, for example.)

Thus evil is a problem for Christianity, but not an objection to it. The view that admits a problem holds out the hope of a solution (Purtill, *Reason*, p. 52).

Geisler and Feinberg point out some of the problems:

The theist responds by first pointing out that (the) premise... places an unjustified time limit on God. It says, in effect, that since God has not yet done anything to defeat evil we are absolutely sure He never will. But this cannot be known for certain by any finite mind. It is possible that God will yet defeat evil in the future. This is indeed what Christians believe, for it is predicted in the Bible (Revelation 20-22) (Geisler and Feinberg, pp. 274,275).

Refutation of Scientific Methods Arguments

To say that man's wish for God to exist proves that God does *not* exist is completely illogical. Because I wish for my children to grow up as strong Christians is no proof that they will grow up as atheists. My wishing does not make things exist, nor does it preclude things from existing. The arguments for the existence of God must be taken on their own merits, regardless of whether men have wished for God to exist. Does the fact that atheists wish for God *not* to exist prove that He *does* exist? Of course not. One must look at the evidence.

In the same manner, the idea that man (or at least some men) derived their belief in God from superstition says nothing about whether or not that God actually exists. In *Ideas of the Great Philosophers*, this is identified as the genetic fallacy in logic:

... According to this argument, religion was spawned in fear, superstition, and ignorance; and fear of the unknown, at a time of ignorance concerning scientific causes, drove man to superstition.

Logicians criticize the preceding argument as an example of a *genetic fallacy*, the error of assuming that a point has been proved merely because it has been traced to its source. It may be of interest, and definitely is of interest to at least the psychologist and the historian, to ascertain how our religious beliefs emerged and what gave them their initial impetus, but so far as proof of Atheism is concerned, such factors are irrelevant. Thus, evidence that a particular science grew out of magic or alchemy does not imply that science today is invalid (Sahakian and Sahakian, *Ideas*, p. 102).

Richard Purtill quickly took apart the argument when he wrote:

Let us begin with the accusation that Christianity represents a pre-scientific, "magical" view of the world. Of course Christianity is pre-scientific in the sense that it began before modern science began. So, for that matter, did mathematics, logic, history, and a great many other things. But that Christianity is *opposed* to a genuinely scientific view of the universe we will deny. As for the accusation that Christianity represents a "magical" view of the universe, "magical" here either just means un- or antiscientific, or else it has some connection with historical beliefs in magic. This is a confusion. Magic, as believed in for many centuries, was an attempt to exert power over nature by means of words, ceremonies, mixtures of materials, etc. It was essentially an attempt of a sort of technology, an attempt to master forces that would give men power, wealth, and secret knowledge. Insofar as it was an attempt to satisfy curiosity and give power over nature, it was the ancestor of science rather than of religion.

Christianity, on the other hand, believes that certain wonderful events have occurred, sometimes as an answer to prayer. But these events are the result of the will of the Person who created nature and its laws, and could not be predicted, demanded, or forced. The effects of these events may sometimes be beneficial to men but their purpose is to reveal something about God or to authenticate such a revelation. The whole attitude and atmosphere of magic and Christianity are opposed. On the one hand you have the magician, with his secret knowledge, forcing certain things to occur by his spells or potions. On the other hand you have the Christian saint with his message for all men, praying that God's will be done, and sometimes finding a marvelous response to his prayer. The two things are poles apart (Purtill, *Reason*, pp. 38,39).

Refutation of Logic Arguments

Arguments which attempt to make the Christian God self-contradictory are many. However, almost all of them concern God's attributes. The most popular target is God's omnipotence or all-powerfulness. We listed just a few of the arguments that supposedly argue against the omnipotence of God. What does it mean when we can say that God is all-powerful? Do we mean that he can do anything we can imagine?

No. When we say that God is all-powerful, we mean that anything which is capable of being done, God can do. He cannot do the logically or intrinsically impossible. The Christian theologian James Oliver Buswell, Jr. writes,

> . . .omnipotence does not mean that God can do anything, but it does mean that He can do with power anything that power can do. He has all the power that is or could be.
>
> Can God make two plus two equal six? This is a question which is frequently asked by skeptics and by children. We reply by asking how much power it would take to bring about this result. The absurdity of the question is not too difficult to see. Would the power of a ton of dynamite make two plus two equal six? or the power of an atom bomb? or of a hydrogen bomb? When these questions are asked it is readily seen that the truth of the multiplication tables is not in the realm of power. Power has nothing to do with it. When we assert that God is omnipotent, we are talking about power (James Oliver Buswell, Jr., *A Systematic Theology of the Christian Religion*, Grand Rapids, MI: Zondervan Publishing House, 1962, pp. 63,64).

Sahakian and Sahakian point out that this sort of logical argument is logically inconsistent. It is known as the fallacy of contradictory premises.

> . . .When contradictory premises are present in an argument, one premise cancels out the other. It is impossible for one or the other of the two premises to be true, but not for both to be simultaneously true. Note the contradictory premises in the following questions: "If God is all-powerful, can he put himself out of existence, then come to life with twice the power he had originally?" "Can God make a stone so heavy that he cannot lift it?" "Can God make a round square?" "What would happen if an irrestible force met an immovable object?" (One student's answer: "An inconceivable smash!") (Sahakian and Sahakian, *Ideas*, p. 23).

The principle is spelled out clearly in Thomas Warren's words:

Rather than saying that God *cannot* do the things just referred to, it would be more in harmony with the truth to say simply that such things *cannot be done at all!* God is infinite in power, but power meaningfully relates only to that which *can* be done, to what is *possible* of accomplishment—*not* to what is *impossible!* It is absurd to speak of any power (even infinite power) being able (having the power) to do what simply *cannot* be done. God *can* do whatever is *possible* to be done, but he *will* do only what is in harmony with *his* nature. Rather than saying that God *cannot* make a four-sided triangle, one would more accurately (or, perhaps, more meaningfully) say (in the light of the fact that the word "triangle" means a *three*-sided figure and cannot refer to any *four*-sided figure) that the making of four-sided triangles simply cannot be done (Thomas B. Warren, *Have Atheists Proved There is No God?*, Nashville, TN: Gospel Advocate Company, 1972, pp. 27,28).

With the preceding thorough refutation of the problems with God's omnipotence, it seems hardly worthwhile to examine the other claims to God's self-contradictions. However, a quick look will show that such purported contradictions are not contradictions at all. The Christian God has a unified nature of complementary attributes. None cancel out any others.

If we simply examine the presuppositions of the arguments, we can see their problems. For example, the skeptic is presupposing that God's love and his wrath (the pouring-out of his justice) are mutually exclusive. We would answer by bringing it to a human level. No one would argue that a father's discipline of his child or a judge's punishment of a criminal proves that the father or judge have no love. On the contrary, their justice should work with their love.

While we would agree that it is loving for God to give man free will, we would not agree that foreknowledge causes predestination. Merely knowing the future does not predetermine it. Finally, freedom for the infinitely good and eternal (never changing) God does not have to include the ability to choose evil to be genuine freedom. Freedom does not mean freedom to contradict one's nature. God's nature is immutably good, holy, and perfect. (By perfect we mean complete). His will is the self-expression of His nature and as such His will is necessarily good, holy, and perfect.

Geisler sums up the unity of God's attributes in the following way:

Perfections such as love and justice are not incompatible in God. They are different, but not everything different is incompatible. What is different, and sometimes at least seemingly incompatible in this world, is not necessarily incompatible in God. For example, there can be such a thing as just-love or loving-justice. Likewise, God can be all-knowing and all-loving, for his infinite knowledge may be exercised in allowing men the freedom to do evil without coercing them (in accordance with his love) against their will so that through it all he may achieve (by infinite power) the greatest good for all (in accordance with his justice) (Geisler, *Apologetics*, p. 229).

Conclusion

While we have just touched the surface of the broad fields of atheism, agnosticism, and skepticism, we have given viable Christian responses to some of the most signficant arguments against the existence of God. We urge the reader to check the bibliography for more intensive study of the subject.

As Christians in a non-Christian world we alternately defend the gospel (1 Peter 3:15) and aggressively proclaim the truth (Acts 2:14-39). God is no stranger to logic and philosophy. His Word will endure long after the thoughts of men have turned to ashes (1 Peter 1:25).

The apostle Paul was not afraid to preach Jesus Christ among the non-believing philosophers of his day. He proclaimed to them:

> For while I was passing through and examining the objects of your worship, I also found an altar with this inscription, "TO AN UNKNOWN GOD." What therefore you worship in ignorance, this I proclaim to you.
>
> The God who made the world and all things in it since He is Lord of heaven and earth, does not dwell in temples made with hands; neither is He served by human hands, as though He needed anything, since He Himself gives to all life and breath and all things... that they should seek God, if perhaps they might grope for Him, though He is not far from each one of us (Acts 17:23-25,27 NASB).

Atheism Extended Bibliography

Note: The Bibliography is divided into three parts. The first part lists general references. The second part lists books and authors from a generally nontheistic position. The third part lists books and authors which can be used to support a general theistic position. Not all of the authors listed in this third section are evangelical Christians.

General Reference

Angeles, Peter, *Dictionary of Philosophy.* NY: Harper and Row, Publishers, 1981.

Avey, Albert E., *Handbook in the History of Philosophy.* NY: Harper and Row, Publishers, 1954.

Frost, S. E., Jr., *Basic Teachings of the Great Philosophers.* Garden City, NY: Doubleday and Company, Inc., 1942, 1962.

Fuller, B. A. G., *A History of Philosophy.* NY: Holt, Rinehart and Winston, 1955.

Hook, Sidney, ed., *Philosophy and History: A Symosium.* NY: New York University Press, 1963.

Horvath, Nicholas A. *Philosophy.* Woodbury, NY: Barron's Educational Series, Inc., 1974.

Joad, C. E. M., *Guide to Philosophy.* London: Victor Gollancz, Ltd., 1955.

Runes, Dagobert D., ed., *Dictionary of Philosophy.* Totowa, NJ: Littlefield, Adams and Company, 1960, 1962.

Sahakian, William, *History of Philosophy.* NY: Harper and Row, Publishers, 1968.

Sahakian, William and Mabel, *Ideas of the Great Philosopher's.* NY: Harper and Row, Publishers, 1966.

Nontheistic

Ayer, A. J., *Language, Truth, and Logic*. NY: Dover Publications, 1946.

Dewey, John, *A Common Faith*. New Haven, CT: Yale University Press, 1934.

Feuerbach, Ludwig, *The Essence of Christianity*. NY: Harper and Row, Publishers, 1957.

Flew, Antony, *God and Philosophy*. NY: Dell Books, 1966.

Freud, Sigmund, *The Future of an Illusion*. NY: Doubleday and Company, 1927.

Kaufmann, Walter, *Critique of Religion and Philosophy*. NY: Harper and Row, Publishers, 1958.

_____, ed., *The Portable Nietzsche*. NY: The Viking Press, 1954.

Madden, Edward H., and Peter H. Hare, *Evil and the Concept of God*. Springfield, IL: Charles C. Thomas, Publishers, 1968.

Marx, Karl, and Friedrich Engels, *On Religion*. NY: Schocken Books, 1964.

Matson, Wallace I., *The Existence of God*. Ithaca, NY: Cornell University Press, 1965.

Nielson, Kai, *Contemporary Critiques of Religion*. NY: Seabury Press, 1972.

_____, *Ethics without God*. Buffalo, NY: Prometheus Books, 1973.

_____, *Skepticism*. NY: St. Martin's Press, 1973.

Russell, Bertrand, *Religion and Science*. NY: Oxford University Press, 1935.

_____, *Why I Am Not a Christian*. NY: Simon and Schuster, 1957.

Sartre, Jean-Paul, *Existentialism and Human Emotions*. NY: Philosophical Library, 1957.

Theistic

Adler, Mortimer J., *How to Think about God: A Guide for the 20th-Century Pagan*. NY: Macmillan Publishing Company, Inc., 1980.

Baillie, John, *Our Knowledge of God*. NY: Charles Scribner's Sons, 1959.

Benignus, Brother, *Nature, Knowledge and God: An Introduction to Thomistic Philosophy*. Milwaukee, WI: The Bruce Publishing Company, 1947.

Bowne, Borden P., *Theism*. NY: American Book Company, 1887, 1902.

Brown, Colin, *Philosophy and the Christian Faith*. Downers Grove, IL: InterVarsity Press, 1968.

Buswell, James Oliver, Jr., *A Systematic Theology of the Christian Religion*. Grand Rapids, MI: Zondervan Publishing House, 1962.

Carnell, Edward J., *A Philosophy of the Christian Religion*. Grand Rapids, MI: William B. Eerdmans Publishing Company, 1952.

Custance, Arthur C., *Evolution or Creation?* Grand Rapids, MI: Zondervan Publishing House, 1976.

Fairbairn, A. M., *The Philosophy of the Christian Religion.* NY: Macmillan Publishing Company, Inc., 1903.

Fitch, William, *God and Evil: Studies in the Mystery of Suffering and Pain.* Grand Rapids, MI: William B. Eerdmans Publishing Company, 1967.

Flint, Robert, *Agnosticism.* NY: Charles Scribner's Sons, 1903.

_____, *Anti-Theistic Theories.* London: William Blackwood and Sons, 1899.

Geisler, Norman, *Christian Apologetics.* Grand Rapids, MI: Baker Book House, 1976.

_____, *Philosophy of Religion.* Grand Rapids, MI: Zondervan Publishing House, 1974.

_____, and Paul Feinberg, *Introduction to Philosophy: A Christian Perspective.* Grand Rapids, MI: Baker Book House, 1980.

Gerstner, John, *Reasons for Faith.* NY: Harper and Row, Publishers, 1960.

Gore, Charles, *The Reconstruction of Belief.* London: John Murray, 1926.

Hackett, Stuart, *The Resurrection of Theism.* Chicago, IL: Moody Press, 1957.

Hick, John, *Arguments for the Existence of God.* NY: Herder and Herder, 1971.

Jay, Eric G., *The Existence of God.* London: Society for Promoting Christian Knowledge, 1946.

Lewis, C. S., *Mere Christianity.* NY: Macmillan Publishing Company, Inc., 1952.

_____, *Miracles.* NY: Macmillan Publishing Company, Inc., 1947, 1960.

_____, *The Problem of Pain.* NY: Macmillan Publishing Company, Inc., 1943.

Mascall, E. L., *Existence and Analogy.* London: Longmans, Green and Company, Ltd., 1949.

_____, *The Openness of Being: Natural Theology Today.* Philadelphia, PA: The Westminster Press, 1971.

_____, *Words and Images.* NY: The Ronald Press Company, 1957.

Mavrodes, George I., *Belief in God: A Study in the Epistemology of Religion.* NY: Random House, 1970.

Miceli, Vincent P., *The Gods of Atheism.* New Rochelle, NY: Arlington House, 1971.

Plantinga, Alvin, *God, Freedom, and Evil.* NY: Harper and Row, Publishers, 1974.

Purtill, Richard, *Reason to Believe.* Grand Rapids, MI: William B. Eerd mans Publishing Company, 1974.

Ross, James F., *Philosophical Theology.* NY: Bobbs-Merrill, 1969.

—————————, *Introduction to the Philosophy of Religion.* NY: Macmillan Publishing Company, Inc., 1972.

Schwarz, Hans, *The Search for God.* Minneapolis, MN: Augsburg Publishing House, 1975.

Sillen, Edward, *Ways of Thinking About God.* NY: Sheed and Ward, 1961.

Taylor, Richard, *Metaphysics.* Englewood Cliffs, NJ: Prentice Hall, 1974.

Warren, Thomas B., *Have Atheists Proved There is No God?* Nashville, TN: Gospel Advocate Company, 1972.

Young, Warren, *A Christian Approach to Philosophy.* Grand Rapids, MI: Baker Book House, 1954.

CHAPTER TWO

Marxism

M arxism, and its descendant, modern communism, presents a strong
challenge to Christianity. Marxism in its various expressions rules
a greater number of people in today's world than any other single
system. What Vincent P. Miceli observed in 1971 about Marxism is still
true today, and now many more are victims of Marxist rule:

> Indeed, today more than one billion persons are ruled by governments that
> openly profess and practice the doctrine of Marx. And millions of other per-
> sons are ruled by governments that fearfully sway to the winds of communist
> policies. In an age of unprecedented and proliferating crises, there is scarcely
> a turmoil anywhere in the world in which the catalyzing power of communism
> may not be discovered. Atheistic communism is a sword of division; it cuts
> asunder families, communities, nations, empires. It has, indeed, succeeded,
> directly or indirectly, by action or example, in keeping the world in a state
> of military conflict since its seizure of power in 1917 (Vincent P. Miceli, *The
> Gods of Atheism*, New Rochele, NY: Arlington House, 1971, pp. 92, 93).

Marxism is not just politics and economics. Marxism is also a world
view, a way of looking at and *explaining* the world. As such, it encompasses philosophy and religion, while paradoxically and vigorously asserting its atheism and contempt for philosophy. The *Encyclopaedia Britannica* points out this quasi-religious nature of Marxism:

> Marxism, which provides remarkable evidence of the power of dominant key
> ideas to inspire and direct man, is undoubtedly one of the greatest challenges
> to traditional religious belief. . . the thinking of Marx had religious overtones,
> whether from his own Jewish background or from a Christian atmosphere,
> not least in Britain where he lived from 1849 to 1883. Second, Marxism can
> be called a quasi-religion insofar as it calls from its followers a devotion and
> a commitment that in their empirical character greatly resemble commitment
> and devotion that characterize religious people. Marxism has undoubtedly fired
> the spirit of man and given to revolutions, whether in Russia or China, a power-
> ful direction that has maintained stability and avoided anarchy. Furthermore,
> like a religion, it has provided themes of fulfillment and hope—a revolution
> interpreted as the initiation of a Communist world society that would be a
> final consummation. There are many logical similarities between the doctrine

of the Marxist millenium and the Christian doctrine of Christ's Second Coming (*Encyclopaedia Britannica III, Macropaedia*, "Philosophy of Religion," Chicago, IL: William Benton, Publisher, 1978, vol. 15, p. 598).

It is the job of philosophy and religion to answer the "why" questions about existence, to give explanations rather than only observing phenomena. While Marx often strongly stressed that his system was *scientific*, and not *philosophical*, he could not excape the realm of philosophy. Because the world view of Marxism attacks the world view of Christianity, we are here addressing that challenge.

In this chapter we will review Karl Marx, the man and his life; briefly discuss thinkers before him who had the most profound effect upon him; and examine those parts of his system which are at root philosophical and atheistic. We will face the atheistic challenge of Marxism in its major manifestations today. Also we will review briefly Marxism's political and economic impact and will see the cohesive Christian world view as presented in the Bible. We will not attempt to present a systematic discussion of Marx's entire system: it has taken others whole volumes to attempt such a task. We shall focus on the core of the system which categorically denies the Christian world view.

Christians cannot remain silent about or, worse, embrace Marxism:

> Marxism and its offspring, Russian Communism, have always maintained world domination as one of their goals. Believing as they do in the inevitability of world revolution and believing that this revolution must be aided and abetted by violence, it is against the very nature of the system for Communists to "live and let live." It is this aspect of domination which poses a grave threat to the world, especially that part of the world that treasures its traditions and inheritance of democratic, constitutional government. The very existence of the church is sharply challenged. . . .
>
> For Christianity, the conflict becomes most basically a spiritual conflict. In Christianity, Christ becomes the motivating force of all action and is the center of the culture of believers. Marxism and its proponents—though usually referred to as atheistic—have set up their own guiding force which is history itself. This becomes their god, and the motivation for all activity around this is materialistic. Thus they deny God and Christ and spiritual power in history and culture (Thomas O. Kay, *The Christian Answer to Communism*, Grand Rapids, MI: Zondervan Publishing House, 1961, pp. 11, 12).

Karl Marx

The name of Karl Marx is probably the best known name of any founder of a political or economic system. While he made little difference in the societies in which he lived, his system of thought has, in the last hundred years, exerted tremendous influence on the governments and economies of hundreds of countries. The two largest nations in the world, Russia and China, claim him as their ideological father. His ideas have flourished for years, showing a greater strength and stability than the man himself, who spent most of his life in poor health, precarious psychological balance and financial insecurity.

Karl Marx was born in Trier, an ancient German city in the Rhineland (sometimes claimed by France, and known as Treveri). His ancestors, Jewish on both his mother's and father's sides, were rabbis. His father, Heinrich, had converted to Protestantism in 1816 or 1817 in order to continue practicing law after the Prussian edict denying Jews to the bar. Karl was born in 1818 and baptized in 1824, but his mother, Henriette, did not convert until 1825, when Karl was 7. While the family did not appear religious at all—it was said that not a single volume on religion or theology was in Heinrich's modest library—Karl was raised in an atmosphere of religious toleration. There was some discrimination against Jews in the area, but general religious tolerance was the standard. Karl was sent to religious school primarily for academic rather than religious training. On the whole, the family was not committed to either evangelical Protestantism or evangelical Judaism. Vincent Miceli notes:

> The family lived as very liberal Protestants, that is, without any profound religious beliefs. Thus, Karl grew up without an inhibiting consciousness of himself as being Jewish. In changing his credal *allegience*, or course, the father, newly baptized Heinrich, experienced the alienation of turning his back on his religious family and traditions. Thus, though politically emancipated and socially liberated from the ghetto, the experience of being uprooted and not completely at home in the Germany of the nineteenth century did affect the Marx family (Miceli, *Atheism*, pp. 94, 95).

Marx attended the gymnasium (high school) from 1830-1835 and then attended Bonn University (1835-1836). He worked on his doctorate at Berlin University (1836-1841). During this time he met and associated with the Young Hegelians (see below our discussion of Hegel's contributions to Marx's thinking) and suffered a nervous breakdown (1837). His doctoral dissertation was in philosophy and was titled *The Difference between Democritean and Epicurean Philosophy of Nature*. It was accepted by Jena University. His father died in 1838.

Marx's professed atheism and his radical views may have made it difficult for him to be hired as a professor at Prussian-dominated schools and his attention turned to political involvement. His life pattern of revolutionary involvement and intense political activism began to emerge. In 1842 he became the editor of the *Reinische Zeitung*, which was said to be a business periodical. However, this publication had strong radical political views. Marx's philosophy of dialectical materialism and class struggle was already being developed, and often appeared in the pages of the *Reinische Zeitung*.

The year 1843 was an important one for young Marx (25 years old). He met for the first time with Frederich Engels, who was to become his closest friend, benefactor, collaborator, and philosophical and political "soul-mate." He also married Jenny von Westphalen, a baroness to whom he was devoted (in spirit if not always in deed) for the rest of his life. During that same year he wrote two of his early works and they typify his thinking at the time: the "Critique of Hegel's Philosophy of Law," and "On the Jewish Question."

(It is debated whether Marx was specifically anti-semitic or only anti-semitic in the sense that his economic theories had no room for Jewish free enterprise and his presupposed atheism had no room for Jewish religion. Space precludes our discussion of the different sides of this matter. Further discussion can be found in the books listed in the bibliography. Our showing his basic atheistic presuppositions later in this chapter indicate that he at least did reject Judaism.)

That same year also saw the demise of the *Reinische Zeitung*—it became a victim of Prussian censorship—and the expulsion of Marx and his bride from Germany. They moved to Paris in October of 1843.

Carrying his political zeal with him, Marx published the *Deutsche Französische Jahrbücher* in Paris in 1844. This fiery publication earned him expulsion from France, and he moved to Brussels in January-February of 1845.

Marx jumped enthusiastically into the communist activity of Brussels. In 1847 he wrote for the *Deutsche-Brüssler-Zeitung* and organized the *German Communist League* and *German Worker's Association*. At the request of the Brussels communists, Marx and Engels wrote their famous *Communist Manifesto* in 1848. It has become the creed and catechism of Marxist Communism.

Early in 1848 Marx and Jenny were expelled from Brussels, spent a short time in Paris, and returned to Germany as revolutionaries in April. Throwing his entire energies into the workers' fight against the repressive Prussian government, Marx began to publish the *Neue Reinische Zeitung* in June. Less than a year later he was again expelled from Prussia, spent a month in Paris, was expelled from there and moved himself and his family to London (August 24, 1849). For nearly 30 years Marx called London his home. It was there, where he had much more literary freedom than in any country before, that he wrote his monumental work *Das Kapital* which criticized, among other things, British capitalism.

Most of the time they were in London, his family was wretchedly poor. Three of his children died, their illnesses complicated by inadequate shelter, food, and medicine. Although he loved his wife and children devotedly, it was unequal to the passion he felt for his political writing and involvement. Stumpf records:

> While his poverty was deeply humiliating, he was driven with such single-mindedness to produce his massive books that he could not deviate from this objective to provide his family with more adequate facilities. In addition to his poverty, he was afflicted with a liver ailment and, as Job, was plagued with boils. In this environment his six-year-old son died and his beautiful wife's health failed (Samuel Enoch Stumpf, *Socrates to Sartre: A History of Philosophy*, New York: McGraw-Hill Book Company, 1966, p. 425).

Marx and his wife made many trips to friends and relatives to beg and borrow enough money to pay their debts, feed their children, and finance Marx's political activities. He recognized the sad position in which he put his family, but seemed unable to turn from his profitless writing and organizing to work at any physical labor or occupation that could have provided better for his family. In later years he looked back with regret on the hardships he had made his family endure, commenting:

> You know that I have sacrificed my whole fortune to the revolutionary struggle. I do not regret it. Quite the contrary. If I had to start my life over again, I would do the same. But I would not marry (Saul K. Padover, *Karl Marx: An Intimate Biography* (abridged edition), New York: New American Library, 1978, 1980, p. 280).

In 1851 his illegitimate son, Frederick Demuth, was born to his wife's maid. His wife and children were not told that Frederick was Karl's son. Instead, benefactor, confidant and collaborator Engels was appointed the boy's "father." Not until after her parents' death did Karl's daughter, Eleanor ("Tussy"), learn the truth from Engels.

The years 1849-1853 were times of desperate financial straits for the family but a time when Marx rose to the top of the exiled German communist movement. A personal description of him by a Prussian spy recorded in 1853 reveals the two tensions, poverty and politics, in the Marx household.

> In private life he is a highly disorderly, cynical person, a poor host; he leads a gypsy existence. Washing, grooming, and changing underwear are rarities with him; he gets drunk readily. Often he loafs all day long, but if he has work to do, he works day and night tirelessly. He does not have a fixed time for sleeping and staying up; very often he stays up all night, and at noon he lies down on the sofa fully dressed and sleeps until evening, unconcerned about the comings and goings around him...
>
> Marx lives in one of the worst, and thus cheapest, quarters in London. He lives in two rooms, the one with a view on the street is the living room, the one in the back is the bedroom. In the whole lodging not a single piece of good furniture is to be found; everything is broken, ragged and tattered; everything is covered with fingerthick dust; everywhere the greatest disorder. In the middle of the living room there is a big old table covered with oilcloth. On it lie manuscripts, books, newspapers, the childrens' toys, the scraps of his wife's sewing, tea cups with broken rims, dirty spoons, knives, forks, candlesticks, inkwell, drinking glasses, Dutch clay pipes, tobacco ashes—in a word, everything piled up helter-skelter on the same table...(ibid, pp. 155-157).

As destitute as the family was, Karl and Jenny did not neglect the education of their daughters (no legitimate son lived to adulthood), paying for their education in the classics, language, music, art, business, and social graces. While they lived like Marx's beloved proletariat, their daughters were groomed to join the hated bourgeois.

While exiled from Germany, Marx resumed publication of the *Neue Reinische Zeitung*. He wrote it in London and it was printed and distributed in Germany.

From 1852 to 1862 Marx was also a foreign correspondent for the New York *Daily Tribune*. He wrote his "Critique of Political Economy" in 1859. This work served as the prologue to his later *Das Kapital*. In 1860 he studied the writings of Charles Darwin and wrote of *Natural Selection*, "it is the book that contains the natural-history basis of our philosophy" (ibid., p. 366). He sent a copy of the first volume of *Das Kapital* to Darwin and later requested Darwin's permission to dedicate volume two to him. (Darwin turned him down.)

Work on *Das Kapital* began in earnest in 1861. In 1864, in very poor health, Marx temporarily suspended work on it and devoted his failing energy to the founding of the communist *International Working Men's Association*. The first draft of *Das Kapital* was finished in 1865 and the book was finally published in Germany on September 14, 1867. His finances became somewhat stabilized and he began to join the ranks of the very class his new book condemned. During his stay in Germany for the release of *Das Kapital*, his hostess remarked to him, "I cannot think of you in a leveling society, as you have altogether aristocratic tastes and habits." Marx replied, "I cannot either. That time will come, but we will be gone by then" (ibid., pp. 201, 202).

On December 2, 1881, his beloved wife Jenny died, probably from stomach cancer, and the already-ill Marx never fully recovered from losing her. In declining health, he received the news of the death of his daughter, also named Jenny, in 1883. He went into a deep depression; his health finally failed him, and he died of an abscessed lung on March 14, 1883.

Karl Marx's personal life was an intricate pattern of conflicts, interweaving his passion for his political system with his love for his family and his middle-class upbringing. It makes a fascinating backdrop against which to picture his philosophy, his world view and his system of thought. His personal life shows that he was not a monster incarnate as some detractors would make him. Nor was he the perfect Christ-figure as others see him. He was a complicated and often contradictory man whose all-consuming interest was the philosophical system we will now consider in brief.

Philosophy

Marx never claimed to possess a "philosophy." It is true that he never developed a complete system of philosophical thought covering all of the main brances of philosophy. However, as a thinking man vitally concerned with explaining man's existence and with finding the causes for events in history, Marx was a philosopher. His disdain for traditional philosophy was related to his zeal for political and social revolution. To Marx, a person doesn't have time to be an armchair philosopher: he should be out in the streets, living his philosophy.

> Philosophy, he said, was a symptom of social malaise and would disappear when revolution put society on a healthier foundation. The young Marx thought that this would happen because revolution would "realize" philosophy, would give solid reality to the ideal phantoms of reason, justice, and liberty that philosophers in sick societies consoled themselves with. The older Marx thought that revolution would destroy philosophy, would simply make it unnecessary, by bringing men back to the study of "the real world." Study of that world is to philosophy "what sexual love is to onanism." In either case Marx never varied in the opinion that the reign of philosophy over men's minds was drawing to a close. Thus, he naturally would not have contributed to its sur-

vival by writing a "Marxist philosophy" (Paul Edwards, ed., *The Encyclopedia of Philosophy*, New York: Macmillan Publishing Company, Inc., 1967, vol. 5&6, p. 173).

Regardless of Marx's dislike of traditional philosophy, he philosophized and he received great inspiration from two prominent philosophers who began writing before him.

Georg Wilhelm Hegel

Hegel (d. 1831) developed a system to explain change which is called *dialectics*. Change and progression are accomplished through a process of thesis, antithesis, and synthesis.

Hegel himself rarely used the terms *thesis, antithesis,* and *synthesis* (see Frederick Copleston, *A History of Philosophy*, Garden City, NY: Doubleday and Company, Inc., 1963, vol. 7, Part 1, p. 215). However, traditional interpretations of Hegel recognize this preoccupation with triads in Hegel's philosophy and note his debt to his predecessor, Fichte, with whom the three terms were commonplace.

There are those who protest such a generalization of Hegel's dialectic, seeing the interpretations of Marx and others as misinterpretations of Hegel (see Gustav E. Mueller, "The Hegel Legend of 'Thesis-Antithesis-Synthesis,'" in the *Journal of the History of Ideas*, vol. XIX, no. 3, June 1958, pp. 411-441; and Winfried Corduan, "Transcendentalism: Hegel," in *Biblical Errancy*, Norman Geisler, ed., Grand Rapids, MI: Zondervan Publishing Company, 1981, pp. 81-104). However, most general authorities recognize the traditional designation of Hegel's dialectic. H. B. Acton, in the *Enclyclopedia of Philosophy*, (Paul Edwards, ed., New York: Macmillan Publishing Company, Inc. 1967, vol. 3, p. 436) remarks, "It should first be noted that Hegel set out his systematic writings in dialectical triads comprising a thesis, antithesis, and synthesis." Colin Brown notes that the traditional interpretation of Hegel's dialectic must be dealt with:

> It is customary to describe Hegel's view of the outworking of Spirit as a Dialectic (which is simply another word for process or dynamic pattern) of Thesis, Antithesis and Synthesis. But it has been pointed out that although Hegel makes occasional use of these latter terms, they are in fact more characteristic of Fichte. However, the basic idea is there, and the notion of Dialectic is paramount. Hegel saw the Dialectic of the Spirit in everything (Colin Brown, *Philosophy and the Christian Faith*, Downers Grove, IL: InterVarsity Press, 1968, p. 121).

It is to this traditional interpretation of Hegel's dialectic, the same understanding modified by Marx, that we will address ourselves. Regardless of the "true" interpretation of Hegel's dialectic, a Christian who would critique Marx must understand Marx's interpretation of Hegel, which is compatible with the traditional interpretation.

The three dialectical principles of thesis, antithesis, and synthesis mark all of existence, all of life, all of thinking. It is not only the process through which we go to gain knowledge, it is the process through which all of existence passes. It is illustrated by Hegel's "basic triad" of *Being, Not-Being,* and *Becoming*.

The most all-embracing concept of our minds would seem to be that of *being*. It is the least common denominator to which all things may be reduced. But pure unspecified *being* without a particular content of some sort is equivalent to nothing at all. It is indistinguishable from *not-being*. To assert, then, as a *thesis* that the Absolute is unqualified *being* is also to assert the *antithesis* of our statement, and to say that the Absolute is non-existent.

Can we then find some further concept that will overcome this contradiction and prove to be a *synthesis* of the ideas of *being* and *not-being*? Hegel finds such a concept in that of *becoming*. When a thing *changes*, it *is* what is it *was not* a moment before, and it *will be* in another instant what it *is not* now. But, if it is to remain the *same* object throughout its changes, what it *is* must be somehow *identical* with what it *was not*, and with what it *will be*. In a *process* then, the seemingly mutual exclusion of *being* and *non-being* by each other is overcome in a higher synthesis (B. A. G. Fuller, *A History of Philosophy*, New York: Holt, Rinehart and Winston, 1955, vol. 2, p. 313).

Marx accepted Hegel's process of dialectics, seeing Reality as a process that can be understood by the mind and that proceeds by the dialectic of thesis, antithesis, and synthesis.

. . . the general view, which Marx took over from Hegel, that all development, whether of thought or things, is brought about through a conflict of opposing elements or tendencies. This doctrine, as we have already seen, is two-sided. It is a description of the way in which things come into being, develop and behave, and it is a description of the way in which we come to learn the truth about them. For Hegel the two processes, the development of things and the discovery of truth, were aspects of the same reality; but whereas he gave logical priority to the second, Marx, holding, as we shall see, that thought is in some sense a reflection of things, emphasised the priority of the first (C. E. M. Joad, *Guide to Philosophy*, London: Victor Gollancz Ltd., 1955, p. 466).

To his triad of thesis, antithesis, and synthesis Hegel added the goal of absolute Spirit. Every process was leading to the ultimate existence, fully self-conscious Thought. The material was secondary to the spiritual.

In Hegel the driving force of the dialectical process was engendered by the developing ideas themselves (ibid., p. 467).

However, Marx flatly rejected Hegel's Spirit-goal, adopting instead a thorough-going materialism.

Hegel believed that by this process one eventually reached the highest synthesis possible, Absolute Spirit, which includes all possible experience. His system might be called idealistic or spiritualistic pantheism. However, Karl Marx, using the same method, concluded that the ultimate synthesis was *matter*, not Spirit, so that his system is called *dialectical materialism* (Warren Young, *A Christian Approach to Philosophy*, Grand Rapids, MI: Baker Book House, 1954, p. 33).

Karl Marx received the keys to his communist kingdom from his German masters Hegel and Feuerbach. Hegel gave him the keys of the unhappy conscience and the dialectical method of analyzing history. History, according to Hegel, is the contradictory unfolding of Reason itself from less to more rational forms, to the utmost rational form of existence—fully self-conscious Thought—God Himself. . . . But Marx, his most famous follower, interpreted this action to be revolutionary action, the sole way of development for matter and man. Thus the Hegelian philosophical impulse to give a scientific analysis of history became the Marxian revolutionary action to create history (Miceli, *Atheism*, p. 96).

Marx, then was an absolute materialist (seeing ultimate reality only in matter) and believed that all process occurred through a dialectical system.

> He rejected flatly the latter's view that these characteristics of the world-process indicated that it was the teleological unfolding of a design or Idea in the experience of an Absolute Mind or Spirit. The behavior of the world-process, he maintained, did not suggest guidance by a moral plan or purpose. Above all, its material and physical aspects could not be reduced to conscious content and regarded as mental in their essential character. On the contrary, they could only be explained on the supposition that matter in motion, extended in space and time, and existing in and by itself, independent of any mental awareness of or reflection upon it, underlay the phenomenal world (Fuller, *Philosophy*, p. 371).

This concept is very important to remember because it forms the basis for his view of history and the future. Because only the material is fundamental, and everything (even mind) proceeds from the material, and progress can only occur through dialectic change, Marx easily concludes that class reform (dealing with the material) is man's basic priority and that such reform can occur only through revolution (dialectics). How sharply this differs from Christian teaching, where the intangible is most important, where God can and does intervene for our good, and where social reform is accomplished through the transformation of individual souls from darkness into light!

Ludwig Feuerbach

Feuerbach (d. 1872) was one of the shapers of Marx's ideas about religion. His *Essence of Christianity* (1841) reduced Christianity to man's fulfillment of his desires. There is no objective religion, no objective God, no objective Jesus Christ. All religious belief is subjective, projected from man's inner needs and desires. It is because of man's miserable existence that he feels the need to invent God.

> In other words, predicate and object of theology is man's imagination, and the religious objects, such as eternal life, God's goodness, and the like are projections of his own desires. If man had no desires, despite his fantasy, he would have no religion and no gods....Religion, in short, is the true characteristic of man. It shows the feeling of man's imperfections and the desire to overcome them. But religion does not indicate that man would have cognitions of anything or anyone beyond himself (Hans Schwarz, *The Search for God*, Minneapolis, MN: Augsburg Publishing House, 1975, pp. 24, 25).

> Ludwig Feuerbach, with the publication of his *The Essence of Christianity*, supplied Marx with the key of a humanist, materialistic humanism. By revealing God to be the "fictitious" creation of man's sick conscience, Feuerbach denied the reality of God, of any transcendent, of spirit. He argued that God did not create man but that man created God out of his warped imagination. Hence only matter, nature and man exist. And man is to regain his own

glory by knowing and controlling matter, of which he himself is the highest product (Miceli, *Atheism*, pp. 96, 97).

Marx went further than Feuerbach. In his typical demarcation between "philosophers" who merely observed and "revolutionaries" who acted, Marx called for revolution to bring man to the place where he no longer needed religion. He was not content to wait for man to grow out of a need for God. He was ready to join the fight himself. Marx, then, was not passive when it came to religion. The active destruction of religion and promotion of atheism was part of his plan to fulfill man through his dialectical materialism (matter is the ultimate reality and change occurs through a dialectic process).

Marx faulted him (Feuerbach) for overlooking the fact:

> that the chief thing still remained to be done. The religious projection and contradiction of the actual human situation demands a removal of the factors that make this projection necessary. According to Marx, Feuerbach was still too "pious." He had not recognized that the "religious sentiment" is not a truly anthropological phenomenon which makes man truly human. It is a *social product* and belongs to a particular form of society.
>
> . . .Thus the abolition of religion as the illusory happiness is required in order to gain real happiness. The demand to give up the illusion is the demand to give up a condition which needs illusions. "The criticism of religion is therefore in embryo the criticism of the vale of woe, the halo of which is religion." Religion is the opiate of the people and is a tool of the capitalists to comfort the suppressed working class with the prospect of a better beyond. Yet Marx demands that the working class should establish its happiness here on earth instead of projecting it into an imaginary beyond. . . .Marx is not satisfied with philosophers like Feuerbach, who have only interpreted the world in various ways. The task is to change the world (Schwarz, *Search*, pp. 25, 26).

Marx modified Feuerbach's idea as he modified Hegel's idea. He fit both into his basic materialistic world view. With the establishment of his dialectical materialism (with its roots, as we see, in Hegel and Feuerbach) he was ready to propose radical and revolutionary change into the society around him. To the downtrodden, the workers, his "proletariat," he offered dialectical materialism as a beacon of hope. To the oppresive ruling classes, the "bourgeois," dialectical materialism was to be the means of their execution.

Against Religion

Since dialectical materialism is the basis for the whole Marxist system, it is no wonder, and in fact, follows necessarily, that Marxism is thoroughly atheistic. There is no room for God in Marx's system.

Marx eagerly anticipated the day when men everywhere would recognize the face in their mirror of religion as their own.

> That is, if a man is a reality seeker and should he discover that religion is but a projection of his own imagination, he will turn to the human reality instead of worshiping the mirror that reflects it (Norman Geisler, *Philosophy of Religion*, Grand Rapids, MI: Zondervan Publishing House, 1974, p. 70).

William S. Sahakian has accurately summarized Marx's attitude toward religion:

> Marxists reject religious doctrines about spiritual values, the soul, immortality, and God, asserting that religion is an illusion, and that the illusory happiness based on it must be condemned. "Religion is the sign of the oppressed creature, the heart of the heartless world, just as it is the spirit of a spiritless situation. It is the opium of the people." God does not create man; rather, man creates invalid religion with its mythical God. Religion functions as a police force, as a bourgeois technique to dissuade the masses from revolting by promising them a better, happier existence after death than their exploiters allow them to enjoy during their lifetime on earth (William S. Sahakian, *History of Philosophy*, New York: Harper and Row, Publishers, 1968, p. 251).

Marx saw two compelling reasons to abolish religion and promote atheism: first, his materialism denied the existence of the supernatural; and second, the very structure of organized religion had, through the ages, condoned and supported the bourgeois suppression of the proletariat.

> As he saw it, Christianity had to be extirpated root and branch, not only because dialectical materialism denied the existence of anything but matter in motion and its products, and was therefore opposed to all supernaturalistic systems, religious and philosophical, but also because Christianity, and for that matter all religions, had not only tolerated but sanctioned the existing social and economic organization of society, which was about to be overthrown (Fuller, *Philosophy*, p. 377).

We must make this clear: abolishment of religion is an integral part of Marx's dialectical materialism.

There are some who try to synthesize Marxism and Christianity. "Liberation Theology" proponents in various areas of South America are examples. Usually such quasi-Marxists are motivated by strong social concerns. They see inequity and suffering in the world and they want to do something about it. Too often, the Marxists are the only ones who appear to be working to relieve such suffering.

Former British communist Douglas Hyde was studying to become a missionary when he was drawn to communism in just such a way after World War I in England. He joined his first Communist sponsored Party after reading a book by a Quaker who embraced communism and extolled its virtues in *The Challenge of Bolshevism*. Young Hyde recounted his reaction to the book:

> It did for my generation of communists what the Dean of Canterbury by his books and lectures does today. It lulled my doubts about the Marxists' militant atheism. It provided a bridge by means of which the man with some religious belief could cross with a clear conscience into the camp of unbelief.
>
> The author's case was that the communists had found the Christian answer to an utterly un-Christian, bourgeois system of society. "Let the atheists of Russia speak the *language* of blasphemy: is it more than the echo of the blasphemy which has so long been embodied in the social order we uphold?"
>
> In communism this sincere Quaker found honesty of purpose, intellectual integrity, a higher morality and a system which would prepare the way for

a Christianity purified and reborn. And, of course, the communists used the book for all they were worth.

It was exactly what I needed at the time. It resolved a crisis for me, clarified my position and accelerated my progress towards communism. It was the link between my Christian past and my atheist future. I was able now to read with an "open mind" Engels' *Anti-Duhring*, the *A. B. C. of Communism*, the works of Lenin and others which formerly I would have rejected because of their atheism (Douglas Hyde, *I Believed*, London: William Heinemann Ltd., 1951, pp. 22, 23).

However, as Hyde discovered, one *cannot* remain true to othodox Marxism and orthodox Christianity at the same time. Hyde quickly abandoned all faith in God and was as militantly atheistic as any other communist for more than two decades, until his disillusionment with communism drove him to Christ. Again, one cannot be an orthodox Marxist and an an orthodox Christian. Even the liberal theologian Hans Küng recognizes this when he says:

But at this point we can hear the dogmatic response: Marxism is *necessarily atheistic*. Is this true?
It is true of *orthodox Marxism*. For Marx and the classical Marxist authors, Engels, Lenin and Stalin—in their personal life, in their culture, in their system and in their practice—atheism was and remained of central importance and essentially connected with their theory of society and history. In their view, religion and science are two mutually exclusive methods of grasping reality (Hans Küng, *Does God Exist?* NY: Random House, 1978, 1980, p. 257).

For orthodox Marxism to embrace orthodox Christianity is to emasculate Marxism of its foundation: dialectical materialism. For orthodox Marxism to embrace orthodox Christianity is to emasculate Christianity of its ultimate source and sustenance in the deity, person, and work of Jesus Christ. Marx saw it this way:

To achieve the real happiness of the people, it is necessary to abolish the illusory religious one. This involves the elimination of conditions that require such illusions. *The first step in this direction must be an attack on religion*. "*Criticism of religion is the prelude of all criticism*" (Padover, *Karl Marx*, p. 80).

The Soviet Communist leader Nikolai Lenin showed that he had learned well from his teacher, Marx, when his contempt for religion and religious people prompted unmentionable atrocities against thousands of innocent people, who were guilty only of believing in God. Lenin wrote:

Every religious idea, every idea of god, every flirtation with the idea of god is unutterable vileness. . . Any person who engages in building a god, or who even tolerates the idea of god-building, disparages himself in the worst possible fashion (Nikolai Lenin, *Selected Works*, London: Lawrence and Wishart, Ltd., 1939, vol. XL, pp. 675, 676).

Some have taken various elements from Marxism and formed what they term Christian Marxism, Christian socialism, or Christian communism.

A revised Marxism could be nonatheistic if it distinguished between dispensable and indispensable elements. The critique of religion is then no longer the precondition of all criticism. It would then no longer be—as with the classical atheistic writers—a central element in Marxism but marginal and open to modification. Such an understanding of Marxism—denounced in Moscow as "revisionist"—is found in fact today even among individual Communist parties, among individual less-orthodox party theorists, and not least in Europe and South America among those forces that are aiming at a practical alliance between Christians and Marxists. The Communist Party of Italy, like other Eurocommunist parties, rejects not only the idea of a Catholic state but also Soviet state atheism—at least for the sake of winning votes...(Küng, *Does God Exist?* p. 257).

Remember, though, that this is not orthodox Marxism. The Christian "socialist" *must* reject those elements of Marxism that oppose the Christian world view.

> ...whatever his attitude to these questions, a person will in any case be taken seriously as a Christian only if Christ and not Marx is for him the ultimate, decisive authority in such questions as class struggle, use of force, terror, peace, justice, love (ibid, p. 259).

So that there can be no confusion on this point, we reiterate that atheism is an integral part of orthodox Marxism.

> It becomes evident, then, that precisely because and, in as much as it is a humanism, communism is necessarily an atheism. Atheism is not an accidental accretion to communist humanism. It is intrinsic and essential to both its creed and conduct. Atheism is as inseparable from a vital communism as the soul is inseparable from a living man. Atheism is the reverse side of communist humanism (Miceli, *Atheism*, p. 102).

In fact, Douglas Hyde expressed in his biography his belief that communist organizations that appear to be compatible with Christianity are not honest. He states that in the British Party, open atheism and hatred for the clergy was practiced before 1931, but that then there was a shift in *public* policy. He stated:

> It was all very thorough but very phoney, for we went back on none of the fundamentals; we simply put some into cold storage and found new methods of dishing up the rest.
>
> That is still the tactic today, and in the intervening years the technique has been developed to a point where the communists' public propaganda never at any time bears any relation whatsoever to their real aims as expounded in their text-books and as taught in the privacy of their members' study classes.
>
> Communism has, in fact, become a gigantic hoax, a deliberate and total deception of the public (Hyde, *I Believed*, p. 57).

Whether or not the British Communist Party is as portrayed by Hyde, the fact remains that he perceived it that way. For almost 15 years he was a leading British communist and news editor for the communist *Daily Worker*.

Hyde did not finish his life as a communist. On the contrary, his dynamic conversion from communism to Christianity is related in his moving *I Believed*. He tells of his growing disillusionment with communism and the reawakening of his conscience, which took place over a period of years. One of the turning points came when he realized:

It was not sufficient now to tell myself that the end justified the means. Once a Marxist begins to differentiate between right and wrong, just and unjust, good and bad, to think in terms of spiritual values, the worst has happened so far as his Marxism is concerned (ibid., p. 243).

He chronicles how he and his wife searched and how they accepted Christianity intellectually before they were reborn spiritually.

We had come to accept the intellectual case for God, to see that without it not only Catholicism but the universe itself made nonsense. We had discovered with some surprise that the great thinkers and philosophers of the Church had made out a better case for God's existence than Marx and Engels had done for His non-existence.

Yet we realised that that was not enough. Belief meant being able to *feel* the existence of the spiritual, to *know* God and not just to know *about* Him. Christians even said they loved Him, they talked to Him and listened to Him. That was still outside our experience and, in moments of depression, we feared that it would remain so (ibid., p. 248).

Hyde and his wife made personal commitments to Jesus Christ and found the faith they had yearned for. His story ends:

I lost my communism because I had been shown something better. I did not find it easy to get to know my new God. And the love of God did not even then come automatically. Just as one has first to get to know a man or woman, and love comes later on the basis of common interest shared and intimacies exchanged, so, slowly, I came to know that love. But one thing is certain: my God has not failed (ibid., p. 303).

We are not trying to say that all communists are dishonest, immoral, and bereft of any positive characteristics or attributes. Most people are drawn to communism first because they see it as a way to help the suffering in the world, or, if they are suffering, to help themselves. Hyde, with inside knowledge, summed up the typical convert to communism:

Most, beyond doubt, had come to communism because of the good that was in them. They had come with idealism, with anger at bad social conditions; fundamentally they had, in most cases, come because no one had ever shown them anything better. What had happened to them afterwards, as they were turned into the new Marxist men, the steel-hardened cadres which the Party makes and moulds, was another matter. I wished I could stay and make them see what I now saw, could share with them the truths which I had found. . . .

Life is so much more complex, and so are men's motives, I would say that the majority who come to communism do so because, in the first instance, they are looking for a cause which will fill the void left by unbelief, or, as in my own case, an insecurely held belief which is failing to satisfy them intellectually and spiritually (ibid., pp. 274, 290).

The Loss of the Individual

A complete acceptance of Marx's dialectical materialism and theories of class struggle leads one inexorably to the denial of individual human worth. History and its march toward perfection is the Marxist god. In the struggle for the classless society, those who stand in the way must be eliminated. Absolute materialism leads to a form of practical totalitarianism. As Thomas O. Kay points out:

> If there is no God or other absolute beyond the existence of matter, then there is no source of eternal, abiding, absolute truth upon which an objective system of law and order can be based. All becomes relative to time and place. The expedient becomes the good and true. Matter itself is not able to provide this absolute because of its ever-changing character.
>
> Since there is no soul and since all goodness and truth are relative to time and place, it follows that there can be no abiding value attributed to man as an individual. He has no worth within himself. This makes man a tool of his environment. Furthermore it brings him under the subjection of the group. At a given moment the good of the group becomes all-embracing. The individual thus may be sacrificed for the good of the group.
>
> It is at this point that one readily observes the relationship between materialism and totalitarianism. Totalitarianism is based upon the assumption that the individual is of little or no importance and his will can be made subservient to that of another individual, a group, or the state (Kay, *Christian Answer*, p.92).

Such a totalitarianism denies the worth and freedom of the individual and cuts at the heart of the gospel message. The individual is so important to God that He sent his only begotten Son to die for our sins, that we may be reconciled to fellowship with God, on an individual basis. Marx sought to elevate man. His system only served to degrade the individual. Marx saw evil someplace out in the material world, someplace other than in the heart of free-will, moral, and personal agents. By attacking the evil he saw in society with class struggle, he hoped to eradicate evil from mankind. He and his philosophical descendents did not succeed. Sin is not man divorced from his social potential; it is man in willful alienation from himself and God.

> Sin is his self-alienation, not the projection from himself of an illusory God, as Feuerbach taught Marx. The attempt to become God in himself, by himself, is the self-alienation, a personal, subjective, self-inflicted alienation....Sin corrupts, disrupts man who then corrupts and disrupts human conditions and relationships....
>
> Marx makes the fundamental mistake of equating the alienation of private property, his source for all alienations, with original sin; sin is an economic evil for him; it calls for an economic saviour. The Catholic Church teaches that sin is a spiritual evil, an insult by man against God; it calls for a divine saviour, since a limited creature cannot atone for an infinite offense against an infinite Being. Yet it also calls for a human saviour, if humanity is to atone for its own offense against both God and man. Communist humanism holds that the redemption of man is achieved by the sufferings of the sacrificial lamb and economic saviour, the proletariat, whose crucifixion and resurrection in rebellion emancipates all men into the socialist heaven....The truth of the matter is, as the Church teaches, that man is reconciled to God, his fellow man and himself by One who is at once fully Man and fully God....The sufferings of proletarians are the sufferings of mere creatures; the sufferings of Christ "knock down the wall of separation" that sin erected (Miceli, *Atheism*, pp. 125, 126).

As the reader can see, there is a sharp distinction between the goal and plan of Marxism and the goal and plan of Christianity. Christianity also works toward a transformed society. This working is in two major areas. Christianity recognizes that sin, within man, is action perpetrated by personal agents. It is not some nasty by-product of social birth-pangs. Christianity seeks to change those personal agents through the life-transforming power of the Lord Jesus Christ. Then, once that personal and individual transformation has taken place, that redeemed individual shows his faith through his actions by working toward social, economic, political, and religious parity among his fellow men.

> The sharp contrast between the Communist approach and the Christian approach to the problems of society is found in comparing the life of Karl Marx with that of Lord Shaftesbury, British statesman of the nineteenth century. While Marx criticized society and fomented revolutions, Shaftesbury—an evangelical Christian—worked for the bettermen of conditions often at great personal sacrifice (Kay, *Christian Answer*, p. 19).

True freedom for mankind is possible only when the individual is considered valuable and when the root causes of injustice are removed. Such change is not brought about by violent revolution at the expense of others nor is it based on a philosophy which sees man valuable only as a member of a classless society.

> Communist humanism does not liberate man; it delivers man into his own hands to do with himself what he will; this is slavery. For, once man rejects God, he has no place to go but back into himself and there lies the agony of isolation. Thus, the revolt against God is the prelude to all serfdom. For the essence of man's freedom is that he be able to transcend himself, the material things of earth and choose to live in companionship with God. Indeed, it was in order that man might enjoy freedom that God, Absolute Liberty Himself, made man in His own image and likeness. He made him a little less than the angels. But communist humanism, in delivering man into his own hands, really renders man captive to the material world below man. Communist humanism, by ripping man down from God, the source of all freedom, makes man less than man (Miceli, *Atheism*, p. 139).

"It was for freedom that Christ set us free; therefore keep standing firm and do not be subject again to a yoke of slavery" (Galatians 5:1 NASB).

Appendix

Marxist Economics and Politics

Our aim in this chapter was to treat the religious and anti-religious aspects of Marxism. It was not our aim to deal extensively with Marx's complicated philosophical and political system as a whole. Below we have produced a short summary of the major principles of Marxism with a short critique.

Our brief description of Marxist theory will present six economic/political themes that are integral to the Marxist system and which together represent its basic thrust. These six themes include 1) dialectical materialism; 2) the four epochs of human history; 3) economic "determinism;" 4) the class struggle; 5) revolution (with a subsequent temporary proletariat dictatorship); and 6) the final "Utopia," the classless society.

1. Dialectical Materialsim

We previously discussed dialectical materialism, citing it as the foundation of Marxist thought. Dialectical materialism is, in fact, the basis of all Marxist philosophy. To Marx, dialectical materialism was the ultimate Reality. As we discussed before, Marx developed his dialectical materialism from Hegel (dialectics) and Feuerbach (materialism).

Dialectical materialism says that reality is grounded in materialism and that all progress in reality (history) occurs through a process of opposing matters clashing together and then forming a new synthesis which is progressively better than either of its forebears.

When we say that Marx was a materialist, we are not saying that he denies the relative existence of anything metaphysical, such as the mind. However, he believed that anything metaphysical, like the mind, arose *from* the material world and depended *on* the material world for its existence. He would say that matter produced mind, rather than saying that mind produced matter (or, as Christians would say, the Ultimate God, being Spirit, produced matter, the creation, from nothing).

> . . . *dialectical materialism*, that is, matter arguing with itself causes historical progress. These two polysyllables are a formidable verbal whip in the hands of the Marxist, but they are simply a shorthand for one explanation of history among many (Lester DeKoster, *Communism and Christian Faith*, Grand Rapids, MI: William B. Eerdmans Publishing Company, 1956, p. 29).

2. The Four Epochs of Human History

Marx simplistically divided all of human history into four epochs: the primitive, the ancient, the feudal, and the bourgeois (middle-class) or modern.* He felt that all previous cultures and societies could be categorized into one of the four epochs. Capitalism, the economic "god" of Marx's London residence, was the motivating force in the bourgeois epoch. Below we will mention the fifth epoch, the "classless society" which in Marx's day was a future dream.

3. Economic "Determinism"

Marxism taught that, generally speaking, economic forces controlled all of human social life. This is popularly called Marx's theory of "economic determinism." However, this term is sometimes misleading because it tends to give the impression that man has no free will and that no change can possibly come from any but an economic source. Kay summarizes:

> Marx concludes then that these economic forces determine by virtue of the dialectic the course of all human history (Kay, *Christianity*, p. 16).

However, such a statement can be misleading. Marx's economic determinism was not a rigid predestination or fate. It was precisely because he believed economics could be influenced by forceful human interven-

*See Kay, *Christian Answer* p. 17.

tion that he advocated revolution to achieve quick change.

> Dialectical materialists criticise doctrines often designated as economic determinism on the ground that they are too narrow and assert only a one-way causal influence (from economic base to other institutions), whereas causal influence, they hold, proceeds both ways. They (often) refer to their own theory as historical materialism or the materialist conception of history (Dagobert D. Runes, ed., *Dictionary of Philosophy*, Totowa, NJ: Littlefield, Adams and Company, 1977, p. 87).

In fact, his economic "determinism" was practiced during each of the four epochs of history mentioned above, with the economics of the age directing all other social functions. It was the deliberate intervention of men through revolution that brought about the end of one epoch and the beginning of the next. Marx believed that the flow of history along his fivefold pattern was inexorable. Society was bound through its economics to pass through the four epochs and eventually arrive at the fifth, the classless society and eventual freedom. The revolutionaries of each epoch were to hurry the process along. Marx saw it as the job of the communist proletariat to instigate the revolution which would terminate the epoch of the bourgeois and usher in the ultimate classless society.

Economic determinism involves Marx's whole detailed analysis of economics. Under this heading we find him discussing "the labor theory of value," i.e., a product's value is determined only by the amount of labor required to produce it.

> ...only *labor*—manual and mental—creates value; and, what is more specifically Marx's contribution to the theory, only *socially necessary* labor creates *real value*. The fact that under capitalism the employment of labor is spent upon luxuries long before all necessities have been met, means for Marx that capitalism is not the best form for the selective use of a nation's labor force (DeKoster, *Communism*, p. 16).

The Marxist "demon" of "surplus value" also comes under this heading. "Surplus value" represents the insurmountable obstacle separating the employer and employee from peace.

> Profit, which is the motive force of capitalism, arises only out of *surplus value*, that is out of paying the workman for *less* value than his labor creates (ibid., p. 20).

When Marx talks of economic determinism, he lays out his whole view of human history. He discusses "modes of production," "property relations," "fair wages," etc. (For more than this quick overview of economic determinism, please see the books in the bibliography, especially August Thalheimer's *Introduction to Dialectical Materialism: The Marxist World-View*, NY: Covici, Friede, Publishers, 1936).

4. Class Struggle

Accepting Marx's dialectical materialism leads one to accept his view of history, which reveals his economic determinism. The acceptance of the presupposition of economic determinism draws one to the conclusion that the only way to achieve change in one's society is through class struggle. History, to Marx, is a record of continual struggle (dialectics) between different classes. He sets this forth in the *Communist Manifesto*. After its preamble, the *Communist Manifesto* opens with the words, "The history of all hitherto existing society is the history of class struggles" (Harold J. Laski, ed., *The Communist Manifesto* by Karl Marx and Friedrich Engels, NY: New American Library, 1967, p. 129).

To Marx, this class struggle has always been in existence and is present at all times in every society. However, it will not be present in the classless society Marx advocates. When dialectical conditions are just right, and the downtrodden class can take no more, the struggle will explode into revolution, paving the way for the next epoch. The final class struggle will be between the proletariat (working class) and the bourgeois (commercial class).

> ...the current class struggle in capitalist society would be the last and was by far the greatest of all. The proletariat (working class) was the antithesis of the bourgeois (commercial or middle-class) capitalist and would eventually bring about the downfall of capitalist society and the establishment of a new society on the basis of the new modes of production (Kay, *Christian Answer*, p. 17).

5. Revolution

As mentioned earlier, Marx saw the bridge between two epochs of history as revolution, triggered by class struggle. Such revolution is necessary and vital to the evolution of society toward the eventual, economically determined, communist state of the classless society.

> Although Marx held that the inevitable outcome of history was the emergence of the communist society, he felt that because of the great problems in this last stage there was a role which man could play in aiding the course of history (ibid., p. 17).

The *Communist Manifesto* was Marx's blueprint for the leadership of the coming revolution. In it he and Engels laid down their plans for overthrowing capitalism and ushering in history's final epoch, the classless society. As with the other themes of Marxism, note that the concept of revolution is a *necessary* consequence of Marx's dialectical materialism. Revolution *must* occur.

Marx recognized that after this final revolution not everyone (namely, the bourgeois) would welcome the classless society. In addition, the entire capitalistic system, with its modes of production, would have to be dismantled and retooled to fit the classless society. During this "short" interim, it would be necessary to have a proletariat dictatorship. This was seen as a temporary and necessary hardship that all proletariats would welcome because of the vital work the dictatorship would do to develop the final classless society.

6. The Classless Society

The final and fifth epoch of human social history would be the classless society, the Marxist "Utopia," its "heaven." In this ideal, no-class society, hard-won by thousands of years of class struggle, revolution, and temporary dictatorship, there would be no class struggles. With no class struggles, there would be no end to the paradise.

The communist society would be the classless society. (Remember that what we call "communist countries" today have not yet reached this classless state. They are still in the "temporary" proletariat dictatorship.) The communist society would have abolished private ownership, the "stifling" family unit, the delusion of religion, and all other "capitalistic" institutions. There will be no need for government or law. The natural law of dialectical materialism will have reached its goal in producing the perfect society.

> What would become of history itself, which was propelled by the energies released by class struggle? Strictly speaking, it would cease. Time would pass, of course, but the only economic changes to be reflected in society would be those leading to ever greater production, ever more leisure for all, and so history in the present tense would, with the dialectic, be transformed into universal tranquility and peace. The economic law would be, in the words of Marx: "From each according to his ability, and to each according to his need." The millennium would be ushered in, on earth and in time. Evil, which is the fruit of class struggle, would be done away. The development of science would bring man ever closer to the control of natural catastrophe. Art and culture could flourish. A temporal heaven would have been brought to earth (DeKoster, *Communism*, p. 34).

This is the final of the six major themes of Marxism.

General Critique

Rather than picking Marxism's themes apart piece by piece, we will offer here a general critique of the system. We urge the reader to obtain a comprehensive critique of Marxism by referring to the books in the bibliography, especially to William O. Kay's *The Christian Answer to Communism* and Lester DeKoster's *Communism and Christian Faith*.

From a Christian perspective, the most ominous flaw in Marxism is its broad anti-supernaturalistic foundation. One cannot accept thoroughgoing and classical dialectical materialism and orthodox Christianity at the same time.

Marx's economic theory is simplistic and thus inadequate, unable to correctly diagnose contemporary economic ills or correctly prognosticate concerning the future of economics. He overemphasizes the role of economic factors in the course of history.

His description of history and how it advances is also inadequate. The historical divisions are artificial and no longer supportable in any real sense when one views contemporary understandings of history.

Orthodox Marxism ignores the fact that some change does take place without struggle, and that often, when change takes place as a result of struggle, it does not result in an entire economy being completely gutted and replaced.

Orthodox Marxism has no guideline for limiting the duration of the "temporary" proletariat dictatorship after the final revolution. Are there perhaps Russians who feel that a "temporary" dictatorship which spans their whole lifetimes is no better than a "permanent" dictatorship?

Orthodox Marxism also presupposes that man is basically good. Marxism sees evil as a product of a sick society. Cure the society (or shoot it and replace it with a new one) and evil disappears. Human history and God's Word, the Bible, say differently.

Finally, Marxism ignores the greatest human freedom there is: personal freedom. Economic freedom is not the most important freedom of all. God has given mankind personal freedom, the freedom to choose his own destiny. This personal freedom has been recognized and enhanced in those societies that are politically and religiously democratic.

> (Marx) also held that it was society that determined the consciousness of man rather than man of society. But what is society without the individual? Marx has given us a rationale that is non-existent in actuality (Kay, *Christian Answer*, p. 19).

We shall conclude this brief look at Marxist theory with two quotes which appear as fitting criticisms of a powerful system that is, nevertheless, inadequate to meet men's needs. The first quote is from a modern communist who classifies himself as an "unorthodox" Marxist. Here is his analysis of classical Marxism:

> The orthodox theory does little to explain the complex dynamics of human behavior and personality. Historical materialism, the orthodox theory of history and social change, focuses our attention on too few needs, makes a fetish of production, and overlooks too many aspects of capitalist everyday life. It seeks fundamental contradictions where none are to be found. It misses the complex dynamics of how societies maintain their stability, and of how revolution occurs as well.
>
> The orthodox Marxism which is still quite prevalent and at the root of almost all socialist organizational activity, insufficiently recognizes the multiplicity of groups and issues central to social change. Economic aspects continually exclude concerns of a more social and cultural nature; ownership relations exclude more complex sex, race, and authority relations. In short, orthodox Marxism is vulgar. It clings to so-called fundamentals and in doing so misses the broader picture. The modern orthodox Marxist sees reality through a set of insufficient concepts. Reality's fullness is obscured. Facts are made to conform with the theory rather than the reverse. The person as subject/object of history is lost to view (Michael Albert and Robin Hahnel, *UnOrthodox Marxism*, Boston, MA: South End Press, 1978, p. 6).

Our final quote is from the astute ex-communist leader and editor, Douglas Hyde:

> It has been taken for granted by those attracted to communism that the man who can see and denounce the evils of a social system is thereby qualified also to lay down the lines of a better one and, in due course, to administer it. Experience shows that there is little to warrant this assumption. For one evil thing to attack another is normal enough. It does not make either the attacker or that which is attacked less evil because one is attacked by the other.
>
> The communist may be able to put his finger on what is bad in our society but only the Christian is fitted to expound the good (Hyde, *I Believed*, p. 300).

Marxism Extended Bibliography

Albert, Michael and Robin Hahnel, *UnOrthodox Marxism*. Boston: South End Press, 1978.

Andrews, William G., ed., *European Political Institutions*. Princeton, NJ: D. Van Nostrand Company, Inc., 1962, 1966.

Avey, Albert E., *Handbook in the History of Philosophy*. NY: Harper and Row, Publishers, 1954, 1961.

Angeles, Peter A., *Dictionary of Philosophy*. NY: Harper and Row, Publishers, 1981.

Bottomore, T. B., trans., *Karl Marx: Selected Writings in Sociology and Social Philosophy*. NY: McGraw-Hill Book Company, 1956.

_____, trans., *Karl Marx: Early Writings*. NY: McGraw-Hill Book Company, 1963.

Brown, Colin, *Philosophy and the Christian Faith*. Downers Grove, IL: InterVarsity Press, 1968.

Carlebach, Julius, *Karl Marx and the Radical Critique of Judaism*. London: Routledge and Kegan Paul, 1978.

Corduan, Winfried, "Transcendentalism: Hegel," in *Biblical Errancy*, Norman Geisler, ed., Grand Rapids, MI: Zondervan Publishing Company, 1981, pp. 81-104.

Dean, Thomas, *Post-Theistic Thinking*. Philadelphia: Temple University Press, 1975.

DeKoster, Lester, *Communism and Christian Faith*. Grand Rapids, MI: William B. Eerdmans Publishing Company, 1956.

Dupre, Louis, *The Philosophical Foundations of Marxism*. NY: Harcourt, Brace and World, Inc., 1966.

Edwards, Paul, ed., *The Encyclopedia of Philosophy, 8 Vols*. NY: Macmillan Publishing Company, Inc., 1967.

Encyclopaedia Britannica III, Macropaedia, "Philosophy of Religion." Chicago, IL: William Benton, Publisher, 1978, vol. 15.

Flew, Antony, *A Dictionary of Philosophy*. NY: St. Martin's Press, 1982.

Fuller, B. A. G., *A History of Philosophy*. NY: Holt, Rinehart and Winston, 1955.

Geisler, Norman, *Philosophy of Religion*. Grand Rapids, MI: Zondervan Publishing House, 1974.

Hyde, Douglas, *I Believed*. London: William Heinemann, Ltd., 1951.

Joad, C. E. M., *Guide to Philosophy*. London: Victor Gollancz, Ltd., 1955.

Kamenka, Eugene, *The Ethical Foundations of Marxism*. London: Routledge and Kegan Paul, 1962, 1972.

Kay, Thomas O., *The Christian Answer to Communism*. Grand Rapids, MI: Zondervan Publishing House, 1961.

Koren, Henry J., *Marx and the Authentic Man*. Pittsburgh, PA: Duquesne University Press, 1967.

Küng, Hans, *Does God Exist?* NY: Random House, 1980.

Laski, Harold J., *The Communist Manifesto by Karl Marx and Friedrich Engels*. NY: New American Library, 1967.

Lee, Francis Nigel, *Communist Eschatology*. Nutley, NJ: The Craig Press, 1974.

Lenin, Nikolai, *Selected Works*. London: Lawrence and Wisehart Ltd., 1939, Vol. XL.

McFadden, Charles J., *The Philosophy of Communism*. New York: Benziger Bros., 1963.

McLellan, David, *Marxism after Marx*. Boston: Houghton Mifflin Company, 1979.

Marsden, George and Frank Roberts, *A Christian View of History?* Grand Rapids, MI: William B. Eerdmans Publishing Company, 1975.

Miceli, Vincent P., *The Gods of Atheism*. New Rochelle, NY: Arlington House, 1971.

Montgomery, John Warwick, *The Shape of the Past*. Minneapolis: Bethany Fellowship, Inc., 1975.

_____, *Where is History Going?* Minneapolis: Bethany Fellowship, Inc., 1969.

Mueller, Gustav E., "The Hegel Legend of 'Thesis-Antithesis-Synthesis'," in the *Journal of the History of Ideas*, June 1958, pp. 411-441.

Niebuhr, Reinhold, *Marx and Engels on Religion*. NY: Schocken Books, 1964.

North, Gary, *Marx's Religion of Revolution*. Nutley, NJ: The Craig Press, 1968.

Padover, Saul K., *Karl Marx: An Intimate Biography*. NY: New American Library, 1978, 1980 (abridged ed.).

Parsons, Howard L., *Humanism and Marx's Thought*. Springfield, IL: Charles C. Thomas Publisher, 1971.

Payne, Robert, *The Unknown Karl Marx*. NY: New York University Press, 1971.

Runes, Dagobert D., *Dictionary of Philosophy*. Totowa, NJ: Littlefield, Adams and Company, 1977.

_____, *Philosophy for Everyman*. Totowa, NJ: Littlefield, Adams and Company, 1974.

Sahakian, William S., *History of Philosophy*. NY: Harper and Row, Publishers, 1968.

————————, and Mabel Lewis Sahakian, *Ideas of the Great Philosophers*. NY: Harper and Row, Publishers, 1966.

Schwarz, Hans, *The Search for God*. Minneapolis: Augsburg Publishing House, 1975.

Stumpf, Samuel Enoch, *Socrates to Sartre: A History of Philosophy*. NY: McGraw-Hill Book Company, 1966.

————————, *Philosophy: History and Problems*, 2nd edition (new title). NY: McGraw-Hill Book Company, 1966.

Taylor, A. J. P., *Karl Marx/Friedrich Engels: The Communist Manifesto*. NY: Penguin Books, 1967.

Thalheimer, August, *Introduction to Dialectical Materialism: The Marxist World-View*. NY: Covici, Friede, Publishers, 1936.

Titus, Harold H., *Living Issues in Philosophy*. NY: American Book Company, 1964.

Trueblood, D. Elton, *Philosophy of Religion*. Grand Rapids, MI: Baker Book House, 1957.

Tucker, Robert C., *Philosophy and Myth in Karl Marx*. Cambridge: University Press, 1972.

Young, Warren C., *A Christian Approach to Philosophy*. Grand Rapids, MI: Baker Book House, 1954.

CHAPTER THREE

Secular Humanism

O ne of the most organized, most challenging and most clearly non-
Christian philosophies of today is *secular humanism*. It is ably
represented and defended by a core of prominent scientists and
philosophers at the forefront of new scientific and philosophical thought.
Secular humanism has its own meetings, its own "clergy" of spokesmen,
its own "creed" called *The Humanist Manifesto*, and its own goals toward
which it desires all of humanity to work. Because of its cohesive world
view and strong threat to biblical Christianity, it needs to be examined
and answered in this book.

First, let's examine some popular ideas of what humanism can represent. The term *humanism* by itself is not automatically anti-God or pro-
God, as many have tried so often to maintain. Historically, during
Renaissance times, the word emphasized the importance of man, not to
the exclusion of God, but simply with little emphasis on God.

Sometimes humanism is defined as the study of the worth and dignity of man as such worth is given him by God. As Christians, we must
be careful not to build a false case about all use of the word humanism
and then attempt to refute that false case. In fact, this is what some
secular humanist writers do when they unfairly paint a caricature of
Christianity and then attempt to tear that down.

We will make a working definition of secular humanism, adapting it
from the ancient Greek philosopher Protagoras, who said, "Man is the
measure of all things." Today this view holds that man is the ultimate
standard by which all life is measured and judged. Thus values, law,
justice, good, beauty, and right and wrong all are to be judged by man-
made rules with no credence to either God or the Bible. We identify this
as secular (non-theistic) humanism (in distinction to the ambiguous and
broad term humanism).

Secular humanism is a collection of ideas which bind together into
a coherent system. Because of this, some humanistic ideas can affect and
be adapted to many different disciplines such as existentialism and communism. Thus, while we can define humanism generally, we will be

careful to recognize that there is some measure of latitude in the system and our definition can be modified as necessary. Peter Angeles, in his *Dictionary of Philosophy*, defines philosophical humanism as follows:

> A philosophy that (a) regards the rational individual as the highest value; (b) considers the individual to be the ultimate source of value; and (c) is dedicated to fostering the individual's creative and moral development in a meaningful and rational way without reference to concepts of the supernatural (Peter Angeles, *Dictionary of Philosophy*, NY: Harper & Row, Publishers, 1981, p. 116).

As rational theists and evangelical Christians, our argument with secular humanism centers on its denial of the supernatural, especially as that precludes any idea of God. In this chapter we will examine, from secular humanistic literature itself, the main tenets of secular humanism and give brief Christian responses to its sweeping claims. By defining secular humanism, we as Christians see the need for evaluating it. Rejection of God, the Bible and the gospel of Jesus Christ compels us to defend the gospel through open discussion, evaluation, and refutation of these tenets of secular humanism. Support of this creed denies the heart of Christianity. (We refer the reader to the chapter on atheism for a closer look at arguments against the existence of God).

Historical Perspective

One can trace the roots of modern secular humanism back to the renewed emphasis on man during the Renaissance. This revival of classical learning and emphasis on man did not exclude God as man's Maker, but it focused attention away from Him, as man made great strides on his own.

Later God was de-emphasized to the point where He was no longer seen as an intimate worker in creation and Father to mankind, and before long, deism became a prominent view. Deism affirmed belief in God, but a God who was not involved in the affairs of men. Deism soon gave way to naturalism, a world view which dismissed God completely from the scene.

One can trace secular humanism from the Renaissance to the present. Humanism entered the nineteenth century through the French philosopher, Comte, who was committed to the secularization of science, and through British utilitarianism via English deism. These serve as a backdrop for twentieth century naturalism and pragmatism. Through such men as Schiller and especially Dewey, the modern tenets of secular humanism began to take their expressed form.

Today this self-centered system of ideas exerts influence in all of our lives. Its assumptions and dogmas continue to be adopted by more and more people, and as a result, many secular humanist organizations are in existence both in Europe and in America, some of which have been around for a long time. Two prominent organizations, *The American Humanist Association* and *The British Humanist Association*, are both front-runners in the secular humanist cause. Another secular humanist-oriented organization is *The Aspen Institute for Humanistic Studies* (see

The Aspen Idea by Sidney Hyman, Norman, OK: University of Oklahoma Press, 1975). *The Aspen Institute* is a motivator for thought and action on cultural issues affecting man and society. Committed to and rooted in a secular humanistic approach, it seeks solutions to local, national, and international problems. Another organization is *The Sex Information and Education Council* (see *The Siecus Circle: A Humanist Revolution*, Claire Chambers, Belmont, MA: Western Islands Publishing Company, 1977). *The Sex Information and Education Council* is humanistic in its outlook and policy. The periodical *The Humanist*, a bimonthly publication, is a leading outlet in America for secular humanist doctrine.

The Humanist Manifesto I

Unlike some of the quasi-religious secular movements we discuss in this book, secular humanism is a well-organized movement with unified beliefs, goals, and presuppositions. More than most modern movements, it represents an organized corporate unity.

In 1933 secular humanists, drawn together by like beliefs, ideas, and dreams, drafted a manifesto which became the creed of secular humanism. Drafter and philosopher Paul Kurtz explains the background of the *Humanist Manifesto I*:

> In the twentieth century, humanist awareness has developed at a rapid pace; yet it has to overcome powerful anti-humanist forces that seek to destroy it.
>
> In 1933 a group of thirty-four liberal humanists in the United States defined and enunciated the philosophical and religious principles that seemed to them fundamental. They drafted *Humanist Manifesto I*, which for its time was a radical document. It was concerned with expressing a general religious and philosophical outlook that rejected orthodox and dogmatic positions and provided meaning and direction, unity and purpose to human life. It was committed to reason, science, and democracy (Paul Kurtz, ed., *Humanist Manifesto I and II*, Buffalo, NY: Prometheus Books, 1973, p. 3).

The *Humanist Manifesto I* reflected the general optimism of the time immediately after World War I. Mankind was convinced that it had ably weathered, in the war, the greatest evil imaginable, and that the future perfecting of humanity was now possible. Mankind had proved that it could triumph over evil.

In summary, the *Humanist Manifesto I* dealt with 15 major themes, or convictions, of secular humanism. It asserted that the universe was self-existing and not created; that man is a result of a continuous natural process; that mind is a projection of body and nothing more; that man is molded mostly by his culture; that there is no supernatural; that man has outgrown religion and any idea of God; that man's goal is the development of his own personality, which ceases to exist at death; that man will continue to develop to the point where he will look within himself and to the natural world for the solution to all of his problems; that all institutions and/or religions that in some way impede this "human development" must be changed; that socialism is the ideal form of economics; and that all of mankind deserves to share in the fruits from following the above tenets.

The conclusion to the *Humanist Manifesto I* clearly reflects the anti-supernatural and optimistic, self-centered aims of its signers:

> Though we consider the religious forms and ideas of our fathers no longer adequate, the quest for the good life is still the central task for mankind. Man is at last becoming aware that he alone is responsible for the realization of the world of his dreams, that he has within himself the power for its achievement. He must set intelligence and will to the task (Kurtz, *Manifesto*, p. 10).

The Humanist Manifesto II

World War II and Adolph Hitler rudely contradicted the unmitigated optimism of the secular humanists who signed the 1933 *Manifesto*. Not only had World War I failed to rout evil, but evil had reared its ugly head much more powerfully through the Nazi atrocities of World War II. Having rejected the supernatural and a higher Judge in favor of the basic goodness and perfectibility of man, the secular humanists turned toward modifying their previous statements. Drafters Paul Kurtz and Edwin H. Wilson explained the need for a new *Manifesto*:

> It is forty years since *Humanist Manifesto I* (1933) appeared. Events since then make that earlier statement seem far too optimistic. Nazism has shown the depths of brutality of which humanity is capable. Other totalitarian regimes have suppressed human rights without ending poverty. Science has sometimes brought evil as well as good. Recent decades have shown that inhuman wars can be made in the name of peace. The beginnings of police states, even in democratic societies, widespread government espionage, and other abuses of power by military, political, and industrial elites, and the continuance of unyielding racism, all present a different and difficult social outlook. In various societies, the demands of women and minority groups for equal rights effectively challenge our generation.
>
> As we approach the twenty-first century, however, an affirmative and hopeful vision is needed. Faith, commensurate with advancing knowledge, is also necessary. In the choice between despair and hope, humanists respond in this *Humanist Manifesto II* with a positive declaration for times of uncertainty.
>
> As in 1933, humanists still believe that traditional theism, especially faith in the prayer-hearing God, assumed to love and care for persons, to hear and understand their prayers, and to be able to do something about them, is an unproved and outmoded faith. Salvationism, based on mere affirmation, still appears as harmful, diverting people with false hopes of heaven hereafter. Reasonable minds look to other means for survival.
>
> Those who sign *Humanist Manifesto II* disclaim that they are setting forth a binding credo; their individual views would be stated in widely varying ways. The statement is, however, reaching for vision in a time that needs direction. It is social analysis in an effort at consensus. New statements should be developed to supersede this, but for today it is our conviction that humanism offers an alternative that can serve present day needs and guide humankind toward the future (ibid., p. 13).

The thrust of the new *Manifesto*, published in 1973, is much more aggressive than that of the first. No longer content to let basically good mankind evolve naturally toward his zenith, the secular humanists now have a consuming drive to help accomplish that transformation as quickly as possible, thwarting the evil of the few evil men. The introduction to the resolutions in the second creed declares:

> Humanity, to survive, requires bold and daring measures. We need to extend the uses of scientific method, not renounce them, to fuse reason with compassion in order to build constructive social and moral values. Confronted by many possible futures, we must decide which to pursue. The ultimate goal should be the fulfillment of the potential for growth in each human personality—not for the favored few, but for all of humankind. Only a shared world and global measures will suffice.
>
> A humanist outlook will tap the creativity of each human being and provide the vision and courage for us to work together. This outlook emphasizes the role human beings can play in their own spheres of action. The decades ahead call for dedicated, clear-minded men and women able to marshal the will, intelligence, and cooperative skills for shaping a desirable future. Humanism can provide the purpose and inspiration that so many seek; it can give personal meaning and significance to human life (ibid., pp. 14, 15).

Humanism is the new religion, the new God who gives meaning to life as the old one never could. This is the interloper into divinity which the Christian must challenge and answer.

The Secular Humanist Creed

The belief system of secular humanists is clearly spelled out in the *Humanist Manifesto II*. It is very easy to see just what the humanists have committed themselves to and just what they desire for us as Christians to embrace instead of our Lord and Savior, Jesus Christ. In order to understand and deal with the claims of humanism in such a small space, we have elected to reproduce each resolution of *Manifesto II* and below it our comments from an evangelical perspective. These resolutions may be found on pages 13-24 of the previously mentioned *Humanist Manifesto I and II*, edited by Paul Kurtz. This is not meant to be an exhaustive examination and refutation of secular humanism, but it will serve to acquaint the reader with humanist thought and will give the reader a Christian background to the subject. Since much of *Manifesto II* deals with a denial of the existence of God and the supernatural, the reader is referred to the chapter on atheism and its bibliography of Christian books for further information. The subject will not be dealt with extensively here.

A study of *Manifesto II* reveals that its 17 propositions can be categorized into six groups and we will present them within those groupings of Religion, Philosophy, Mankind, Society, One-World Government, and Science.

Religion

Religion is the topic of the first two resolutions. We quote a portion of the first resolution and the entire (shorter) second resolution:

> First:...We believe, however, that traditional dogmatic or authoritarian religions that place revelation, God, ritual, or creed above human needs and experience do a disservice to the human species. Any account of nature should

pass the tests of scientific evidence; in our judgment, the dogmas and myths of traditional religions do not do so. Even at this late date in human history, certain elementary facts based upon the critical use of scientific reason have to be restated. We find insufficient evidence for belief in the existence of a supernatural; it is either meaningless or irrelevant to the question of the survival and fulfillment of the human race. As non-theists, we begin with humans not God, nature not deity. Nature may indeed be broader and deeper than we now know; any new discoveries, however, will but enlarge our knowledge of the natural. . . .

But we can discover no divine purpose or providence for the human species. While there is much that we do not know, humans are responsible for what we are or will become. No deity will save us; we must save ourselves.

Second: Promises of immortal salvation or fear of eternal damnation are both illusory and harmful. They distract humans from present concerns, from self-actualization, and from rectifying social injustices. Modern science discredits such historic concepts as the "ghost in the machine" and the "separable soul." Rather, science affirms that the human species is an emergence from natural evolutionary forces. As far as we know, the total personality is a function of the biological organism transacting in a social and cultural context. There is no credible evidence that life survives the death of the body. We continue to exist in our progeny and in the way that our lives have influenced others in our culture.

Traditional religions are surely not the only obstacles to human progress. Other ideologies also impede human advance. Some forms of political doctrine, for instance, function religiously, reflecting the worst features of orthodoxy and authoritarianism, especially when they sacrifice individuals on the altar of Utopian promises. Purely economic and political viewpoints, whether capitalist or communist, often function as religious and ideological dogma. Although humans undoubtedly need economic and political goals, they also need creative values by which to live.

The world view of humanism, as expressed by these first two tenets, is diametrically opposed to Christianity. While the humanists start and end with man, the Bible starts and ends with God. It was God who was in the beginning (Genesis 1:1, John 1:1-3), not impersonal, self-creating nature, from which man gradually evolved. The Bible consistently teaches that it is upon the infinite God that this finite world depends for its existence. For primordial, nonintelligent mass to produce human intelligence assumes, contrary to reason, that an effect is greater than its cause. To account for that human intelligence by a higher intelligence in whose image the human was made, and who sustains the very life of the human and his world, is reasonable, and biblical. When the apostle Paul argued with the Greek philosophers of his day he testified about this sustaining God:

The God who made the world and all things in it, since He is both Lord of heaven and earth, does not dwell in temples made with hands; neither is He served by human hands, as though He needed anything, since He Himself gives to all life and breath and all things; . . . for in Him we live and move and exist, as even some of your own poets have said, 'For we also are His offspring' (Acts 17: 24-28, NASB).

For the humanists to blithely dismiss all religious philosophy and all evidence in support of the existence of God in two simple propositions does not settle the matter of God's existence. As evangelical Christians we believe that our reasoning ability was given to us by God, in whose image we were created, and that responsible use of our reasoning ability to understand the world around us can lead us to sound evidence for the existence of God. Christian philosopher Richard Purtill expressed it this way:

> . . . if we begin to ask fundamental questions about the universe, and follow the argument where it leads us, then it will lead us to belief in God; that if we examine tne evidence of history and of human experience, we will be compelled to acknowledge that the only satisfactory explanation of the evidence leads us to Christianity. Such Christians acknowledge that there is still a gap between intellectual assent and commitment to a Christian way of life, but they believe that reason is neither opposed to such a commitment nor irrelevant to it—rather, it is the best possible ground for it (Richard Purtill, *C. S. Lewis's Case for the Christian Faith*, San Francisco: Harper and Row, Publishers, 1981, pp. 12, 13).

Our chapter on atheism deals with this subject more in depth, and we also refer the reader to our other works, *Evidence That Demands a Verdict*, *The Resurrection Factor*, and *More Than a Carpenter* by Josh McDowell, and *Answers* and *Reasons* by Josh McDowell and Don Stewart. We believe that God has given sufficient evidence as to His existence and His purpose in this world for man.

The French philosopher Pascal stated the matter plainly:

> The evidence of God's existence and his gift is more than compelling, but those who insist that they have no need of Him or it will always find ways to discount the offer (Blaise Pascal, *Pense's No. 430*, translated by H. F. Stewart, NY: Random House, n.d., n.p.).

When *Manifesto II* says that it can find no design or purpose or providence for the human species, it devaluates man to a level below that on which God places Him as His highest creation. The humanists pretend to esteem the human being above all else. In reality, as *Manifesto II* shows, the humanist takes away all worth from mankind. Unless our worth is rooted and grounded in something objective and outside ourselves, we are of value only to ourselves, and can never rise above the impermanence of our own short lives. The God of Christianity is outside our finite and transitory universe and His love for us gives us a value which transcends not only ourselves but our finite universe as well.

Humanist Manifesto II states that we must save ourselves. While we believe this statement was made somewhat tongue-in-cheek, since humanists do not believe man needs saving from anything, we do still need to comment on the statement. We believe it is not possible for an individual to save himself in all circumstances. In fact, given the biblical definition of salvation, it is an operation undertaken because the individual *cannot* help himself. While we would grant that a man could "save himself" from falling after a slip by grabbing a railing, for example, it is not always possible. Picture a man in the middle of a large lake. He has fallen from his boat, which is now hopelessly out of reach. He has been in the frigid water for two hours. He can no longer keep himself afloat. His body temperature is falling rapidly. He is becoming delirious. Would he find solace and genuine help in a bystander's admonition to "save himself"? Of course not. Without *outside* intervention, he will die. The spiritual (moral) condition of man is such that he is past the point of "saving himself." He needs *outside* intervention. Christians believe that intervention is from God. He alone is able to save man.

If there really is a God, and if man really is in the state of decay in which he finds himself because of his deliberate sin (offense) against God, then he must turn to God for his salvation. To use another human illustration, if one man hits another, he cannot rectify the situation by saying, "So-and-So isn't angry with me anymore for my hitting him, because I forgave myself." No, So-and-So is the one offended, and he is the only one who can extend forgiveness to his attacker. That is the biblical picture of sin and salvation. Ephesians 2:8-10 reminds us:

> For by grace you have been saved through faith; and that not of yourselves, it is the gift of God; not as a result of works, that no one should boast. For we are His workmanship, created in Christ Jesus for good works, which God prepared beforehand, that we should walk in them (NASB).

Contrary to humanist declarations, Christianity gives true worth and dignity to man and secular humanism makes all human dignity subjective and self-centered. Francis Schaeffer comments:

> I am convinced that one of the great weaknesses in evangelical preaching in the last few years is that we have lost sight of the biblical fact that man is wonderful. We have seen the unbiblical humanism which surrounds us, and, to resist this in our emphasis on man's lostness, we have tended to reduce man to a zero. Man is indeed lost, but that does not mean he is nothing. We *must* resist humanism, but to make man a zero is neither the right way nor the best way to resist it. . . .
>
> In short, therefore, man is not a cog in a machine; he is not a piece of theater; he really can influence history. From the biblical viewpoint, *man is lost, but great* (Francis Schaeffer, *Death in the City*, Downers Grove, IL: InterVarsity Press, 1969, pp. 80, 81).

Secular humanism rejects the idea of life after death, dogmatically asserting that it is impossible to prove. On the contrary, the resurrection of Jesus Christ from the dead is a fact of history, verifiable by standard historical tests. His resurrection becomes the seal and the hope of every Christian. In addition to the works previously cited in what we have written before on this subject, we here quote Michael Green:

> The evidence points unmistakably to the fact that on the third day Jesus rose. This was the conclusion to which a former Chief Justice of England, Lord Darling, came. At a private dinner party the talk turned to the truth of Christianity, and particularly to a certain book dealing with the resurrection. Placing his fingertips together, assuming a judicial attitude, and speaking with a quiet emphasis that was extraordinarily impressive, he said, 'We, as Christians, are

asked to take a very great deal on trust; the teachings, for example, and the miracles of Jesus. If we had to take all on trust, I, for one, should be skeptical. The crux of the problem of whether Jesus was, or was not, what He proclaimed Himself to be, must surely depend upon the truth or otherwise of the resurrection. On that greatest point we are not merely asked to have faith. In its favour as living truth there exists such an overwhelming evidence, positive and negative, factual and circumstantial, that no intelligent jury in the world could fail to bring in a verdict that the resurrection story is true' (Michael Green, *Man Alive*, Downers Grove, IL: InterVarsity Press, 1968, pp. 53, 54).

Philosophy

The second major division in *Manifesto II* covers propositions three and four and relates mostly to philosophy.

Third: We affirm that moral values derive their source from human experience. Ethics is *autonomous and situational*, needing no theological or ideological sanction. Ethics stems from human need and interest. To deny this distorts the whole basis of life. Human life has meaning because we create and develop our futures. Happiness and the creative realization of human needs and desires, individually and in shared enjoyment, are continuous themes of humanism. We strive for the good life, here and now. The goal is to pursue life's enrichment despite debasing forces of vulgarization, commercialization, bureaucratization, and dehumanization.

Fourth: Reason and intelligence are the most effective instruments that humankind possesses. There is no substitute: neither faith nor passion suffices in itself. The controlled use of scientific methods, which have transformed the natural and social sciences since the Renaissance, must be extended further in the solution of human problems. But reason must be tempered by humility, since no group has a monopoly of wisdom or virtue. Nor is there any guarantee that all problems can be answered. Yet critical intelligence, infused by a sense of human caring, is the best method that humanity has for resolving problems. Reason should be balanced with compassion and empathy and the whole person fulfilled. Thus, we are not advocating the use of scientific intelligence independent of or in opposition to emotion, for we believe in the cultivation of feeling and love. As science pushes back the boundary of the known, one's sense of wonder is continually renewed, and art, poetry, and music find their places, along with religion and ethics.

These two tenets of secular humanism are concerned with philosophy, or the way the world is viewed. They are specifically concerned with ethics first and then with reason. Again, developing from the secular humanistic presupposition of the autonomy and self-sufficiency of man, these two humanistic concerns are wholly exhausted within the framework of man.

The humanists are right to point out that their ethics (morals) are situational. Since they are based in and come forth from the individual, they are necessarily self-centered and subjective. They have no objective basis or root. On the surface, this appears to promote one's idea of the importance and power of man.

However, upon closer examination, we find flaws with this view. If moral values are determined from human experience, there is no objective basis for calling anything right or wrong. There is no such thing as intrinsic good or intrinsic evil. Whether something is good or not depends on the context of the individual or the group of like-minded individuals — the society. On this basis, could we condemn the society of Nazi Germany for judging the moral value of Jewish life as worthless? Would we have the right to call it bad? What if happiness in one society is eating one's enemy instead of convincing him to surrender?

Because humanism does not offer any absolute value system, mankind has no absolute system of right and wrong. In such an instance, why should I believe and accept the value system of the group (society) of men who drafted and signed *Manifesto II*? What compelling reason can they give me for accepting their dogmatic ethical assertion that "vulgarization, commercialization, bureaucratization, and dehumanization" are "debasing?" What if I happen to believe that it is *good* to promote vulgarization, commercialization, bureaucratization, and dehumanization?

Christianity asserts that there is absolute good and absolute evil. Our moral values are patterned after the nature and attributes of our creator, God. He is the absolute standard by which everything else is judged. Hitler's Germany was wrong because our God has declared that all human life is sacred and of equal value, whether it is the human life of a Jew, a German, and unborn child, or a senile old man, crippled and bedridden.

The fourth article of *Manifesto II* concerns the role of reason in determining man's future. We believe that the main fault with this view of reason, that it can direct all human development, is that the humanist has no valid reason for accepting his own reason.

If mankind is actually a product of long evolutionary development from simpler life forms, having its ultimate origin in impersonal matter, how can a man know today that he is reasonable? Is impersonal matter a sufficient cause for personal mind (reason)? And even if this mindless Nature did produce a self-cognizant (personal) being, how could that self-cognizant being know that his thinking process is rational, i.e., reasonable?

The Christian does not see reason rising from within man, the biological machine. The Christian believes that man's reason was created by God and patterned after (in the image of) God. Man's reason can make sense of the world in which he lives because someone who is outside this world has equipped him with the critical apparatus necessary.

Although science and technology, manipulated by man's reason, have made amazing strides in solving problems, they have not answered the ultimate questions of life. They may be able, some day, to answer the "how" of life. They can never answer the "why" of life. Os Guiness comments:

> If "evolution is good," then evolution must be allowed to proceed and the very process of change becomes absolutized. Such a view can be seen in Julian Huxley's *Evolutionary Ethics* or in the writings of Teilhard de Chardin. But in ever more areas, science is reaching the point of "destructive returns"; and the attempt to use evolution as a basis for morals and ethics is a failure. If evolutionary progress is taken as an axiom, then the trend toward convergence (social and evolutionary "unanimization") becomes a value, as suggested by Teilhard

de Chardin. But this militates against the value of individuality and can be used to support totalitarianism. Bertrand Russell was typical of a growing majority who admit that science can be no more than neutral and does not speak directly into the area of moral choice (Os Guiness, *The Dust of Death*, Downers Grove, IL: InterVarsity Press, 1973, pp. 15, 16).

Mankind

Assumptions five and six of *Manifesto II* concern the nature of man, mankind. This is one of the most popular features of secular humanism, which is itself a form of the word human and so stresses continually the place of mankind in its philosophy.

Fifth: The preciousness and dignity of the individual person is a central humanist value. Individuals should be encouraged to realize their own creative talents and desires. We reject all religious, ideological, or moral codes that denigrate the individual, suppress freedom, dull intellect, dehumanize personality. We believe in maximum individual autonomy consonant with social responsibility. Although science can account for the causes of behavior, the possibilities of individual *freedom of choice* exist in human life and should be increased.

Sixth: In the area of sexuality, we believe that intolerant attitudes, often cultivated by orthodox religions and puritanical cultures, unduly repress sexual conduct. The right to birth control, abortion, and divorce should be recognized. While we do not approve of exploitive, denigrating forms of sexual expression, neither do we wish to prohibit, by law or social sanction, sexual behavior between consenting adults. The many varieties of sexual exploration should not in themselves be considered "evil." Without countenancing mindless permissiveness or unbridled promiscuity, a civilized society should be a *tolerant* one. Short of harming others or compelling them to do likewise, individuals should be permitted to express the sexual proclivities and pursue their life-styles as they desire. We wish to cultivate the development of a responsible attitude toward sexuality, in which humans are not exploited as sexual objects, and in which intimacy, sensitivity, respect, and honesty in interpersonal relations are encouraged. Moral education for children and adults is an important way of developing awareness and sexual maturity.

The secular humanist position on relative moral values is almost the watershed for critiquing humanistic tenets. With no absolute ethic, why should we accept the humanists' moral value that the individual person is precious and deserves dignity in his own right? The Marxist, for example, argues that the individual only has worth as a member of society. It is permissible, indeed necessary, to expend the individual for the society. Why isn't the Marxist right? How can the humanist infringe on the Marxist's individual preciousness and dignity by telling him his view of mankind is wrong?

The term "social responsibility" is an empty one since each society differs in what it considers responsible behavior. The rule of the society can change at any moment.

Furthermore, is there objective evidence for this unmitigated optimism concerning man's ability to direct his own development and fulfillment? Os Guiness points out that many don't think so:

A persistent erosion of man's view of himself is occurring. The fact that man has made so many significant scientific discoveries points strongly to the significance of man, yet the content of these same scientific discoveries underscores his insignificance. Man finds himself dwarfed bodily by the vast stretches of space and belittled temporally by the long reaches of time. Humanists are caught in a strange dilemma. If they affirm the greatness of man, it is only at the expense of ignoring his aberrations. If they regard human aberrations seriously, they have to escape the dilemma raised, either by blaming the situation on God (and how often those most strongly affirming the non-existence of God have a perverse propensity to question his goodness!) or by reducing man to the point of insignificance where his aberrations are no longer a problem. During World War II, Einstein, plagued by the mounting monstrosity of man against man, was heard to mutter to himself, "After all, this is a small star." He escaped the dilemmas of man's crime and evil but only at a price of undermining man's significance. A supreme characteristic of men today is the high degree of dissatisfaction with their own views of themselves. The opposition to determinism is growing not because determinism explains nothing but because it explains too much. It is a clutching constriction on that which man feels himself to be. Arthur Koestler attacks it as "ratomorphic," Vicktor Frankl as "modern nihilism" and Norman Chomsky as "the flat earth view of man."

Mortimer Adler's *The Difference of Man and the Difference It Makes* is one book which probes deeply in this area and is scrupulously objective in its extensive analysis. He warns that if man continues to recognize no fundamental difference in kind between himself and the world of animals and machines, then his view of himself in terms of his moral dilemma or his metaphysical being must alter irretrievably. Anything left of contemporary concepts of morality and identity will be reduced to the level of the illusory, and the implications for individuals and for civilization are far-reaching (ibid., pp. 16, 17).

Humanist Manifesto II has a contradictory statement about human sexuality. While championing the autonomy of individual sexual rights, the statement also contradictorily makes bold universal moral assertions about some kinds of sex. What right do the humanist signers of this *Manifesto* have to say they do not approve of "exploitive, denigrating forms of sexual expression" or "mindless permissiveness or unbridled promiscuity"? What if an individual *likes* such sexual activity? If the humanists were to reply that such activity denies the rights of other parties, we must ask, what right have the humanists to say that those others' rights should come before the particular individual's rights?

In short, without an absolute standard of ethics by which one's sexual attitudes are determined, one cannot successfully argue for the universal adoption of his own subjective ethics. The secular humanists may have decided among themselves that certain forms of sexual behavior are "wrong," but they have no right to enforce their ideas on anyone who disagrees.

As Christians we believe that God is the source of our ethical system. Because He commands us to have respect and love for others, it is therefore wrong to engage in exploitive and denigrating forms of sexual expression. A Christian's sexual ethics should follow from God's character, expressed to man.

The Bible also strongly disagrees with any taking of human life, even if such murder is disguised with the empty word "abortion." Doesn't abortion exploit and denigrate the unborn child who is its victim?

Society

Articles seven through eleven of *Humanist Manifesto II* deal with the secular humanist view of and hope for society. These articles touch on politics, sociology, and economics.

Seventh: To enhance freedom and dignity the individual must experience a full range of civil liberties in all societies. This includes freedom of speech and the press, political democracy, the legal right of opposition to governmental policies, fair judicial process, religious liberty, freedom of association, and artistic, scientific, and cultural freedom. It also includes a recognition of an individual's right to die with dignity, euthanasia, and the right to suicide. We oppose the increasing invasion of privacy, by whatever means, in both totalitarian and democratic societies. We would safeguard, extend, and implement the principles of human freedom evolved from the Magna Charta to the Bill of Rights, the Rights of Man, and the Universal Declaration of Human Rights.

Eighth: We are committed to an open and democratic society. We must extend participatory democracy in its true sense to the economy, the school, the family, the workplace, and voluntary associations. Decision-making must be decentralized to include widespread involvement of people at all levels — social, political, and economic. All persons should have a voice in developing the values and goals that determine their lives. Institutions should be responsive to expressed desires and needs. The conditions of work, education, devotion, and play should be humanized. Alienating forces should be modified or eradicated and bureaucratic structures should be held to a minimum. People are more important than decalogues, rules, proscriptions, or regulations.

Ninth: The separation of church and state and the separation of ideology and state are imperatives. The state should encourage maximum freedom for different moral, political, religious, and social values in society. It should not favor any particular religious bodies through the use of public monies, nor espouse a single ideology and function thereby as an instrument of propaganda or oppression, particularly against dissenters.

Tenth: Human societies should evaluate economic systems not by rhetoric or ideology, but by whether or not they increase economic well-being for all individuals and groups, minimize poverty and hardship, increase the sum of human satisfaction, and enhance the quality of life. Hence the door is open to alternative economic systems. We need to democratize the economy and judge it by its responsiveness to human needs, testing results in terms of the common good.

Eleventh: The principle of moral equality must be furthered through elimination of all discrimination based upon race, religion, sex, age, or national origin. This means equality of opportunity and recognition of talent and merit. Individuals should be encouraged to contribute to their own betterment. If unable, then society should provide means to satisfy their basic economic, health, and cultural needs, including, wherever resources make possible, a minimum guaranteed annual income. We are concerned for the welfare of the aged, the infirm, the disadvantaged, and also for the outcasts — the mentally retarded, abandoned or abused children, the handicapped, prisoners, and addicts — for all who are neglected or ignored by society. Practicing humanists should make it their vocation to humanize personal relations. . . .

We deplore racial, religious, ethnic, or class antagonisms. Although we believe in cultural diversity and encourage racial and ethnic pride, we reject separations which promote alienation and set people and groups against each other; we envision an integrated community where people have a maximum opportunity for free and voluntary association.

We are critical of sexism or sexual chauvinism — male or female. We believe in equal rights for both women and men to fulfill their unique careers and potentialities as they see fit, free of invidious discrimination.

Rather than picking these articles apart piece by piece, we will offer some general observations in criticism. Our two major criticisms go back to two of the most basic presuppositions of secular humanism: relative morals and the basic goodness of mankind.

Because the secular humanists state that all ethics/morals/values are subjective and situational, they cannot support their system consistently and yet retain absolute values. However, many statements in these five articles do assume absolute values. We are told (article seven) that the individual "must experience a full range of civil liberties" to "enhance freedom and dignity." What's so great about freedom and dignity? Why should we accept the humanists' dogmatic assertion that human freedom and dignity are values all men should strive for? We are told that the individual has the "right to die with dignity, euthanasia, and the right to suicide." How can relativistic secular humanists make such a value judgment? Why have the secular humanists decided that it is universally wrong to kill someone else (murder), but it is morally right to choose to kill yourself (suicide)?

As Christians we are not asked, nor do we ask others, to support an arbitrary, finite system of absolute values just on the basis of our having proposed it. We believe that there are absolute values and morals because God, the framer and sustainer of this world, has designed the world to work in accordance with His intrinsic attributes of goodness, love, etc., and to malfunction (as in the fall) when its members do not harmonize with God's will.

As Christians we are dedicated to the freedom of man as an individual because God demonstrated the importance of that freedom in the freedom he gave man, a freedom that includes rejecting man's very Maker and his provision of peace and eternal joy. As Christians we believe that life is sacred because it is a gift from God, its origin and sustainer. It is not for man to decide the time of death, for another person or for himself. Christianity has an absolute standard of values based on the Creator of all things.

Secular humanism and Christianity are diametrically opposed on the moral bent of mankind. Secular humanism assumes that everyone is basically good (with a few exceptions) and that evil comes from outside people and societies, rather than from within. This is somewhat like the naive view of Marxism, which taught that if the evils of society were only eradicated, evil men would cease to exist.

While Christians should applaud secular humanism's commitment to racial, social, and sexual integration, we should not lose sight of the fact that removing the trappings of bigotry does not remove the evil seeds of that bigotry from within the individual. Society will never be transformed by tampering with the mechanics of social intercourse. Neither will it be reshaped into Utopia by temporarily forcing evil men to act like good men. The only way to change society is to transform the individuals within that society.

Christianity teaches that all of mankind made its choice for evil in the person of Adam at the fall. The Bible says that man is not basically good, but basically bad (see Romans 3:10, 23, 30; 6:23). Only through the freewill appropriation of the atoning work of Jesus Christ on the cross can a man be turned from evil to good. The Christian works to transform the individuals who compose society. This alone will bring about true change in the society.

One-World Government

Many people in Western society are turning toward the idea of a one-world government as the solution to the problems of mankind. This idea does not belong to the secular humanists alone. A great number of those who are oriented toward Eastern philosophy and religion believe that world unity will be accomplished only in this way. In fact, the Bible itself teaches that God eventually will establish a one-world government. However, under discussion here is the secular humanist view of a one-world system, as described in *Manifesto II*, articles twelve, thirteen, fourteen and fifteen.

> Twelfth: We deplore the division of humankind on nationalistic grounds. We have reached a turning point in human history where the best option is to transcend the limits of national sovereignty and to move toward the building of a world community in which all sectors of the human family can participate.Thus we look to the development of a system of world law and a world order based upon transnational federal government. This would appreciate cultural pluralism and diversity. It would not exclude pride in national origins and accomplishments nor the handling of regional problems on a regional basis. Human progress, however, can no longer be achieved by focusing on one section of the world, Western or Eastern, developed or underdeveloped. For the first time in human history, no part of humankind can be isolated from any other. Each person's future is in some way linked to all. We thus reaffirm a commitment to the building of world community, at the same time recognizing that this commits us to some hard choices.
>
> Thirteenth: This world community must renounce the resort to violence and force as a method of solving international disputes. We believe in the peaceful adjudication of differences by international courts and by the development of the arts of negotiation and compromise. War is obsolete. So is the use of nuclear, biological, and chemical weapons. It is a planetary imperative to reduce the level of military expenditures and turn these savings to peaceful and people-oriented uses.
>
> Fourteenth: The world community must engage in cooperative planning concerning the use of rapidly depleting resources. The planet earth must be con-

sidered a single ecosystem. Ecological damage, resource depletion, and excessive population growth must be checked by international concord. The cultivation and conservation of nature is a moral value, we should perceive ourselves as integral to the sources of our being in nature. We must free our world from needless pollution and waste, responsibly guarding and creating wealth, both natural and human. Exploitation of natural resources, uncurbed by social conscience, must end.

Fifteenth: The problems of economic growth and development can no longer be resolved by one nation alone; they are worldwide in scope. It is the moral obligation of the developed nations to provide—through an international authority that safeguards human rights—massive technical, agricultural, medical, and economic assistance, including birth control techniques, to the developing portions of the globe. World poverty must cease. Hence extreme disproportions in wealth, income, and economic growth should be reduced on a worldwide basis.

We believe that men live by absolute ethics even if they claim to believe only in relative ethics. One may say that all ethics and moral values are relative to one's society or to the individual conviction, but one rarely lives by such a maxim. This we find with the secular humanists who drafted *Humanist Manifesto II.*

The beginning of *Manifesto II* declares that morals and values are relative and largely governed by society. Yet in these four articles we find such absolute moral values as "the best option is to transcend the limits of national sovereignty," belief in "peaceful adjudication of differences by international courts and by the development of the arts of negotiation and compromise," "the cultivation and conservation of nature is a moral value," and "it is the moral obligation of the developed nations to provide...massive...assistance,...to the developing portions of the globe."

Christians would not necessarily disagree with the above moral values. But Christians have an absolute ground for their ethics. Christian morality does not depend on the shifting subjective standards of any particular society or vocal group of people. Biblical Christianity depends on the Sovereign of the universe for its moral values.

In the twelfth article the humanists say that adopting a one-world government would commit us to "some hard choices." Unfortunately for the layman, those choices are not identified. We would worry that, in their zeal to establish Utopia, secular humanists might consider it a hard but necessary choice to sacrifice certain dissident individuals for the better choice of promoting the one-world Utopian government. Isn't this just the sort of "choice" we Westerners decry as human rights violations in many Marxist countries today? (See the chapter on Marxism for a discussion of the role—or lack of role— of the individual in the struggle for the classless society.) The Christian cannot endorse article twelve without knowing just what "hard choices" face the one-world government advocate.

According to God's Word, just before the second coming of Jesus Christ to establish His kingdom, the forces of Satan will attempt to set up a one-world system, implementing worship and submission to Satan's representative, the Anti-Christ. (See Matthew 24, 1 and 2 Thessalonians and the book of Revelation.) The secular humanists, at least in that day, will get their wish of a one-world government. But it will not usher in Utopia, rather it will bring on Armageddon.

As we discussed previously, the secular humanists diverge sharply from the Christian perspective by assuming that mankind is basically good. Many of the goals of a one-world government are lofty and not in opposition to Christianity. However, the feasibility of implementing such changes is almost non-existent given the biblical presupposition that man is basically bad instead of good.

It sounds good to say that the "world community must renounce the resort to violence and force" and that "war is obsolete." However, a proclamation by itself never altered reality. Just how do the secular humanists propose to guarantee that everyone in a position of power will give up the use of force? And if even one person with power chooses to use it to force his own views, what will the humanist recourse be? Will he sweet-talk the offender? Or use force to teach him not to use force?

Christianity does not advocate the use of force to spread one's values and beliefs. However, Christianity recognizes that self-centered men will use force. Christianity sees the ultimate "weapon" against force as being an individual whose life has been transformed by the power of the Holy Spirit and whose will has been surrendered to the Lord Jesus Christ. Only when men are changed will violence cease. The Bible tells us the time will come when there will be no more violence. Such a world will not come about by proclamation of secular humanism, but by the divine command, judgment and forgiveness of the Lord (Revelation 20, 21).

In the meantime, the Bible specifically places responsibility for self-defense on the individual. We have a God-given obligation to protect those who depend on us. We must ensure the safety of our families. Christians may disagree about what sort of resistance is meant in the Bible. Whether or not a Christian allows for the use of force to safeguard those for whom he is responsible, he understands the serious charge God has given him and recognizes through it the measure of the value God places on each human life.

The use of abortion appears to be allowed by both articles fourteen and fifteen of *Manifesto II*. Article fourteen states that "excessive population growth must be checked" and article fifteen calls birth control techniques a "human right." Taken with the previous *Manifesto II* statement in article six regarding abortion as a human right, we can see that it is very likely that the secular humanists, if given the chance, would solve population booms with, among other things, abortions. We repeat what we said earlier: does it contribute to the dignity and value of the individual human life to murder it if it is inconvenient, if it doesn't fit into the world plan for conservation of resources and if it just happens not to have been born yet? Christians cannot agree to taking innocent human life in the name of any world plan.

Article fifteen presents a socialistic world economy as the only society of value. How is this new society to be obtained? It is easy to say "disproportions in wealth, income, and economic growth should be reduced on a worldwide basis." But how is this to be accomplished? Do the secular humanists actually think it likely that the wealthy of this world will, en masse and without exception, give up their wealth and distribute it to the poor? If so, why hasn't it already happened? If mankind is basically good, society should need no impetus such as a *Humanist Manifesto II* for the wealthy to share with the poor.

Perhaps the secular humanists are not so naive as that. What then, is their solution? Should they use force to relieve the rich of their "economic burdens" and then bless the poor with the wealth taken from the rich? It seems the humanists will break either article thirteen banning violence or article fifteen banning private wealth. Marxism and socialism have similar economic goals. A look at the "freedom" of contemporary Marxist and Socialist societies show us that these goals are not realistic.

Science

The last two propositions by the secular humanists offer the tools for implementing the grand scheme: science and its workhorse, technology. Somewhere in science, they say, lies the solution to the problems of mankind.

> Sixteenth: Technology is a vital key to human progress and development. We deplore any neo-romantic efforts to condemn indiscriminately all technology and science or to counsel retreat from its further extension and use for the good of humankind. We would resist any moves to censor basic scientific research on moral, political, or social grounds. Technology must, however, be carefully judged by the consequences of its use; harmful and destructive changes should be avoided. We are particularly disturbed when technology and bureaucracy control, manipulate, or modify human beings without their consent. Technological feasibility does not imply social or cultural desirability.

> Seventeenth: We must expand communication and transportation across frontiers. Travel restrictions must cease. The world must be open to diverse political, ideological, and moral viewpoints and evolve a worldwide system of television and radio for information and education. We thus call for full international cooperation in culture, science, the arts and technology, across ideological borders. We must learn to live openly together or we shall perish together.

When all else is said, it appears that the humanists rely on science and its evolution to provide the magic formulas needed to materialize the new world order envisioned by the humanists. Christianity is not intrinsically antagonistic to science. In fact, it is the Christian God who created the world around us and who determined its laws and functions, which have been categorized by what we call science. Colossians 1:16-17 reminds us that it is to the Lord Jesus Christ that we owe our existence:

> For in Him all things were created, both in the heavens and on earth, visible and invisible, whether thrones or dominions or rulers or authorities—all things have been created through Him and for Him. And He is before all things, and

in Him all things hold together (NASB).

Science does not create laws of nature, it discovers them. When science does discover one of those laws,it is no surprise to God. However, science is no substitute for God. All science can do is discover and describe, it cannot create reality *ex nihilo* (out of nothing).

While we would not dismiss out of hand any particular advance of science, we would question the humanists' assertion that all science will be used "for the good of humankind" and that "carefully judged by the consequences of its use; harmful and destructive changes should be avoided." We return to the same but still valid critique: who is to determine what the "good of humankind" is, and who is to enforce the judgments of whomever has been chosen to determine that good? The spectre of George Orwell's *1984* looms threateningly as we think of the abuses, intentional or not, to which such judgment and enforcement could be put.

Finally, we agree with the last sentence of proposition seventeen: "We must learn to live openly together or we shall perish together." This is exactly what the Bible has to say. However, the Bible states that because man is basically self-centered and sinful, he will forever be unable to live peaceably with his fellow man on his own initiative. It takes the supernatural intervention of God to transform individuals into selfless, caring, loving people who really will sacrifice their own desires for the sake of their fellow men. Universal peace will come only with the intervention of Almighty God. We see expressed in 2 Peter 3:3-14 the biblical vision of the future, a future cleansed of evil by judgment and restored in love by the Lord Jesus Christ:

> Know this first of all, that in the last days mockers will come with their mocking, following after their own lusts, and saying, 'Where is the promise of His coming? For ever since the fathers fell asleep, all continues just as it was from the beginning of creation.' For when they maintain this, it escapes their notice that by the word of God the heavens existed long ago and the earth was formed out of water and by water, through which the world at that time was destroyed, being flooded with water. But the present heavens and earth by His word are being reserved for fire, kept for the day of judgment and destruction of ungodly men. But do not let this one fact escape your notice, beloved, that with the Lord one day is as a thousand years, and a thousand years as one day. The Lord is not slow about His promise, as some count slowness, but is patient toward you, not wishing for any to perish but for all to come to repentance. But the day of the Lord will come like a thief, in which the heavens will pass away with a roar and the elements will be destroyed with intense heat, and the earth and its works will be burned up. Since all these things are to be destroyed in this way, what sort of people ought you to be in holy conduct and godliness, looking for and hastening the coming of the day of God, on account of which the heavens will be destroyed by burning, and the elements will melt with intense heat! But according to His promise we are looking for new heavens and a new earth, in which righteousness dwells. Therefore, beloved, since you look for these things, be diligent to be found by Him in peace, spotless and blameless (NASB).

Humanism Bibliography

Angeles, Peter A., *Dictionary of Philosophy*. NY: Harper and Row, Publishers, 1981.

Edwards, Rem. B., *Reason and Religion*. NY: Harcourt Brace Jovanovich, Inc., 1972.

Flew, Antony, *A Dictionary of Philosophy*. NY: St. Martin's Press, 1982.

Geisler, Norman, *Is Man the Measure: An Evaluation of Contemporary Humanism*. Grand Rapids, MI: Baker Book House, 1982.

Green, Michael, *Man Alive*. Downers Grove, IL: InterVarsity Press, 1968.

Guiness, Os, *The Dust of Death*. Downers Grove, IL: InterVarsity Press, 1973.

Horvath, Nicholas A., *Philosophy*. Woodbury, NY: Barron's Educational Series, 1974.

Kurtz, Paul W., *The Humanist Alternative*. London: Pemberton Press, 1973.

_____ ed., *Humanist Manifesto I and II*. Buffalo, NY: Prometheus Books, 1973.

Lamont, Corliss, *Freedom of Choice Affirmed*. NY: New Horizon Publishers, 1967.

_____, *The Independent Mind*. NY: New Horizon Publishers, 1951.

Maritain, Jacques, *True Humanism*. Westport, CT: Greenwood Press, 1970.

Pascal, Blaise, *Pense's No. 430*. Trans. H. F. Stewart, NY: Random House, n.d.

Purtill, Richard, *C. S. Lewis's Case for the Christian Faith*. San Francisco: Harper and Row, Publishers, 1981.

Runes, Dagobert D., ed., *Dictionary of Philosophy*. Totowa, NJ: Littlefield, Adams and Company, 1977.

Sahakian, William S., *History of Philosophy*. NY: Harper and Row, Publishers, 1968.

_____, and Mabel L. Sahakian, *Ideas of the Great Philosophers*. NY: Harper and Row, Publishers, 1966.

Schaeffer, Francis, *Death in the City*. Downers Grove, IL: InterVarsity Press, 1969.

Sire, James, *The Universe Next Door*. Downers Grove, IL: InterVarsity Press, 1976.

Stumpf, Samuel Enoch, *Socrates to Sartre: A History of Philosophy*. NY: McGraw-Hill Book Company, 1966.

Young, Warren C., *A Christian Approach to Philosophy*. Grand Rapids, MI: Baker Book House, 1954.

CHAPTER FOUR

Existentialism

E xistentialism, a difficult system to define, has been developing over the last fifty years. As it evolved it attracted followers from many different backgrounds. Today its influence has subtly affected much popular thought and expression. As F. H. Heinemann observes

> Among contemporary philosophies none has made a greater impact on religion and theology than existentialism (F. H. Heinemann, *Existentialism and the Modern Predicament*, NY: Harper and Row, Publishers, 1953, p. 219)

Because of its pervasive influence and incompatibility with orthodox Christianity, existentialism should be answered in a Christian response to secular religion.

The Difficulty of Definition

One of existentialism's problems is that it is difficult to define or categorize concisely. Philosopher Walter Kaufmann comments:

> Existentialism is not a philosophy but a label for several widely different revolts against traditional philosophy. Most of the living "existentialists" have repudiated this label, and a bewildered outsider might well conclude that the only thing they have in common is a marked aversion for each other. To add to the confusion, many writers of the past have frequently been hailed as members of this movement, and it is extremely doubtful whether they would have appreciated the company to which they are consigned. In view of this, it might be argued that the label "existentialism" ought to be abandoned altogether.
>
> Certainly, existentialism is not a school of thought nor reducible to any set of tenets. The three writers who appear invariably on every list of "existentialists"—Jaspers, Heidegger, and Sartre—are not in agreement on essentials. Such alleged precursors as Pascal and Kierkegaard differed from all three men by being dedicated Christians; and Pascal was a Catholic of sorts while Kierkegaard was a Protestant's Protestant. If, as is often done, Nietzsche and Dostoevsky are included in the fold, we must make room for an impassioned anti-Christian and an even more fanatical Greek-Orthodox Russian imperialist. By the time we consider adding Rilke, Kafka, and Camus, it becomes plain that one essential feature shared by all these men is their perfervid individualism.

The refusal to belong to any school of thought, the repudiation of the adequacy of any body of beliefs whatever, and especially of systems, and a marked dissatisfaction with traditional philosophy as superficial, academic, and remote from life — that is the heart of existentialism (Walter Kaufmann, *Existentialism from Dostoevsky to Sartre*, NY: The World Publishing Company, 1956, pp. 11, 12).

Others echo Kaufmann's sentiment:

Every existentialist develops his own terminology because he finds everyday language inadequate, in the same way he rebels against a day-to-day view of the world. . . . if one reads the existentialists without exasperation, one is almost certainly misreading them (I. M. Bochenski, *Contemporary European Philosophy*, Berkeley and Los Angeles: University of California Press, 1956, p. 154, note 5).

Bochenski goes on to say:

. . .existentialism must not be identified with any one body of existentialist doctrine, for example, that of Sartre, for as we shall see there are profound differences between individual points of view (ibid., p. 156).

Existentialism Defined

Existentialism may be explained according to the themes and concerns of its proponents. Existentialists are concerned with existence, change, freedom and self-cognizance, among other things. William and Mabel Sahakian describe existentialism in the following manner:

Existentialists accept the conclusion that "existence precedes essence," and some go even further and affirm that essence does not exist, that only existence has reality. All Existentialists emphasize the person as subject. The subject exists, and for some, he alone exists; that is to say, if any essence whatever exists, it is the individual's subjective state of existence (William S. Sahakian and Mabel L. Sahakian, *Ideas of the Great Philosophers*, NY: Barnes and Noble, Inc., 1966, p. 167).

Philosopher B. A. G. Fuller recognizes the problems in defining existentialism, but also recognizes certain existential theses:

There is no single existentialist position. The philosophy varies with its proponents, some of whom insist that they are not existentialists at all. But there is a common fund of doctrine that identifies them, nevertheless, and indicates quite clearly their relation to the classical philosophic tradition. Their major and differentiating thesis is the metaphysical pronouncement that "existence is prior to essence," while in the established tradition "essence is prior to existence." What this means for the existentialist is that human nature is determined by the course of life rather than life by human nature (B. A. G. Fuller, *A History of Philosophy*, NY: Holt, Rinehart and Winston, 1955, p. 603).

I. M. Bochenski, in his book *European Philosophy* relates six of the common existential themes:

1) The commonest characteristic among the various existentialist philosophies of the present is the fact that they all arise from a so-called existential *experience* which assumes a different form in each one of them. It is found by Jaspers, for instance, in awareness of the brittleness of being,

by Heidegger through experiencing "propulsion toward death," and by Sartre in a general "nausea." The existentialists do not conceal the fact that their philosophies originate in such experiences. That is why existentialist philosophy always bears the stamp of personal experience, even in Heidegger.

2) The existentialists take so-called existence as the supreme object of inquiry, but the meaning which they attach to the word is extremely difficult to determine. However, in each case it signifies a peculiarly human mode of being. Man—a term which is rarely used and is generally replaced by "thereness" (Dasein), "existence," "ego," "being for oneself"—is unique in possessing existence; more precisely, man does not *possess*, but he *is* his existence. If man has an essence, either this essence is his existence or it is the consequence of it.

3) Existence is conceived as absolutely *actualistic*; it never *is* but freely *creates* itself, it becomes; it is a pro-jection; with each instant it is more (and less) than it is. The existentialists often support this thesis by the statement that existence is the same as temporality.

4) The difference between this actualism and that of life-philosophy is accounted for by the existentialists' regarding man as pure *subjectivity* and not as the manifestation of a broader (cosmic) life process in the way that Bergson does, for example. Furthermore, subjectivity is understood in a *creative* sense; man creates himself freely, and *is* his freedom.

5) Yet it would be thoroughly misguided to conclude from this that the existentialists regard man as shut up within himself. On the contrary, man is an incomplete and open reality; thus his nature pins him tightly and necessarily to the world, and to other men in particular. This double dependence is assumed by all representatives of existentialism, and in such a way that human existence seems to be inserted into the world, so that man at all times not only faces a determinate situation but *is* his situation. On the other hand they assume that there is a special connection between men which, like the situation, gives existence its peculiar quality. That is the meaning of Heidegger's "togetherness," Jasper's "communication," and Marcel's "thou."

6) All existentialists repudiate the distinction between subject and object, thereby discounting the value of *intellectual knowledge* for philosophical purposes. According to them true knowledge is not achieved by the understanding but through experiencing reality; this experience is primarily caused by the dread with which man becomes aware of his finitude and the frailty in that position of being thrust into the world and condemned to death [Heidegger] (Bochenski, *European Philosophy*, pp. 159, 160).

To summarize Bochenski, he identifies six major themes of existentialism: 1) experience as the ground of discovery; 2) existence as the supreme object of inquiry; 3) existence preceding essence; 4) man as pure subjectivity and not part of a cosmic life process; 5) the interdependence of man and his world; and 6) a devaluation of intellectual knowledge.

Finally, we will turn to philosopher Samuel Stumpf for his recognition of the fact that existentialists reject traditional philosophy:

Whether they were theists or atheists, the existentialists all agreed that traditional philosophy was too academic and remote from life to have any adequate meaning for them. They rejected systematic and schematic thought in favor of a more spontaneous mode of expression in order to capture the authentic concerns of concrete existing individuals. Although there is no "system" of existentialist philosophy, its basic themes can, nevertheless, be discovered in some representative existentialist thinkers (Samuel Enoch Stumpf, *Socrates to Sartre*, NY: McGraw-Hill, 1966, p. 455).

The Scope of Our Study

Our aim is to simplify an admittedly complex subject. Because of the intricate and sometimes contradictory assertions made among existentialists, we have decided to examine the themes of their reasoning as described by six leading philosophers often cited as shapers of existentialist thought. This method of treating the subject will avoid the sweeping and often erroneous generalizations made about this school of thought, but may result in some oversimplification.

Existentialism is more far-reaching than these six representative writers indicate. Moreover, some of these individuals would repudiate the label existentialist, finding it stultifying, although they deal with the same general themes from some of the same perspectives. We conclude with a Christian perspective on the thematic presuppositions of existentialism.

Religious Existentialists

Many Christians have never studied philosophy formally and are unfamiliar with the mainstream of existentialist thought. However, they have heard of a stream of existential thought that appears to be paradoxical. It is known as religious or Christian existentialism. Many Christians have at least a vague familiarity with some of the ideas of Karl Barth, Paul Tillich, and Rudolph Bultmann. We will not argue whether or not one can be religious and an existentialist at the same time. There are competent observers on both sides of the question. Almost every knowledgable observer, from either side, will agree that religious existentialism is not the same as orthodox existentialism. Even the term "orthodox existentialism" is a problem since the field is so diverse and the prominent existential thinkers don't agree about what existentialism is. Nevertheless, religious existentialists are concerned with some of the same themes as are non-religious existentialists. They just address them from different (religious) perspectives.

The Sahakians separate these two types of existentialists in much the same way as we will. They write:

> Two main schools of Existentialist philosophy may be distinguished; the first is religious as delineated by the father of Existentialism, Soren Aabye Kierkegaard (1813-1855); the second is atheistic, as expounded by its most articulate contemporary spokesman, Jean-Paul Sartre. A number of outstanding Existentialists in each of these schools disclaim the Existentialist label; some adherents of the religious view prefer to be known as Neo-Orthodox philosophers (Sahakian and Sahakian, *Ideas*, p. 167).

Fuller confirms this view, expanding on the perspectives of the religious existentialists:

> In its theistic form, existentialism has been an important factor in the neo-orthodox awakening that has marked theology since the first war. Its emphasis on the negative qualities of man, on human estrangement and the tragedy of

human existence, have supported the resurgence of the dogma of original sin and the entire structure of eschatological theology (Fuller, *Philosophy*, pp. 603, 604).

Christian philosopher Milton Hunnex reveals how existentialism has penetrated modern theological circles:

> Unable to assimilate either the naturalism of Aristotle or that of the scientific revolution, Protestant theology eventually turned to idealism as the modern philosophy best adapted to Christian belief. Modern liberalism made its home among the idealists during the nineteenth century. After World War I it became apparent that idealism was ill suited to the twentieth century, and theologians as well as philosophers abandoned it. They turned instead to existentialism as the kind of philosophy that did appear to fit the mood and needs of the twentieth century. Existentialism seemed to be the best philosophy for getting at the problems of men caught up in swift-moving change (Milton D. Hunnex, *Existentialism and Christian Belief*, Chicago: Moody Press, 1969, pp. 13, 14).

Although we have chosen to examine this religious existentialist view of the controversy, we recognize that there are those who see no compromise between existentialism and religious belief. While we believe that they make some valid points, we feel the claims of the so-called religious existentialists still need to be dealt with, even if they do arise from a misunderstanding of existentialism and religion. Hazel Barnes recognizes the two sides of the controversy:

> I confess that I sympathize with the fundamentalist ministers who argue that whatever else it may be, this new religion is not Christianity and should be given some other name. (Hazel Barnes, *An Existentialist Ethics*, Chicago, IL: University of Chicago Press, 1978, p. 383).

We agree that historic Christianity cannot embrace the presuppositions and core of existentialist concern. However, there is much that claims the name "Christian" today that is not truly Christian in the biblical sense, but that must be dealt with by the biblically-centered Christian. We agree with Hazel Barnes that Sartrean existentialism (atheistic) cannot ever be reconciled with any form of theistic belief. She comments:

> I do not believe that religious existentialism is compatible with a position based on Sartrean premises. I do not find in Tillich's Being-itself a concept which is logically tenable or a reality existentially meaningful. I cannot see that Heidegger's Being is a valid or more valuable alternative to Sartre's Being-in-itself (ibid., p. 382).

As a final qualification, we recognize the distinction between theologians or religious thinkers who have existential orientations (existential theologians) and a true *existential theology*, which, almost by definition, cannot exist. We conclude, with Heinemann, who draws the general conclusion, that:

> *Existentialist Theology does not exist.* But the question remains to be answered: Can it exist? I am afraid the answer must be: No. The principle of existence is a call, an appeal (Jaspers), or in Kantian terminology, a regulative principle. It appeals to people to care for their inner life, for their freedom,

their true self, their authentic existence, for their neighbours and their predicament. It admonishes us never to forget in thought and action the primacy of human persons as ends in themselves. It is not a constitutive principle, it defends the person against the menace of any kind of system and cannot therefore itself be the basis of a system. Existential Theology does not and cannot exist, but *existential theologians* should exist, that is theologians whose chief interest does not lie in dogmatics and in the external observance of rituals, but in the souls of men, in their predicament and in the willingness to help them. *Existential theologians have always existed* (Heinemann, *Existialism*, p. 225).

With the above factors in mind, we will look at three "religious existentialists," Soren Kierkegaard, Paul Tillich, and Gabriel Marcel.

Soren Kierkegaard (1813-1855)

Soren Aabye Kierkegaard was born in Copenhagen, Denmark, and was raised in an unusual religious family. His father had a morose obsession that God had cursed and doomed him and his family. The young Soren spent his youth convinced that continual, almost debilitating, depression was his fate. Of his youth he wrote:

> From a child I was under the sway of a prodigious melancholy, the depth of which finds its only adequate measure in the equally prodigious dexterity I possessed of hiding it under an apparent gaiety and *joie de vivre*. So far back as I can barely remember, my one joy was that nobody could discover how unhappy I felt (Soren Kierkegaard, *The Point of View for My Work as An Author: A Report to History*, NY: Harper and Row, Publishers, 1962, p. 76).

When Kierkegarrd entered the University of Copenhagen in 1830, he bowed to the wishes of his father and studied theology. However, his first love was philosophy, in which he excelled. He began to believe that he was predestined or chosen to change people for the better through philosophy. Late in life he reflected on his life, which he saw as developing dialectically,* and traced the path made "by the hand of God":

> About my *vita ante acta* (i.e. from childhood until I became an author) I cannot expatiate here at any length, however remarkable, as it seems to me, was the way I was predisposed from my earliest childhood, and step by step through the whole development, to become exactly the sort of author I became....
>
> An observer will perceive how everything was set in motion and how dialectically: I had a thorn in the flesh, intellectual gifts (especially imagination and dialectic) and culture in superabundance, an enormous development as an observer, a Christian upbringing that was certainly very unusual, a dialectical relationship to Christianity which was peculiarly my own, and in addition to this I had from childhood a training in obedience, obedience absolute, and I was armed with an almost foolhardy faith that I was able to do anything....Finally, in my own eyes I was a penitent. The impression this now makes upon me is as if there were a Power which from the first instant had been observant of this and said, as a fisherman says of a fish, Let it run awhile, it is not yet the moment to pull it in. And strangely enough there is something that reaches far back in my recollection, impossible as it is for me

---

*See chapter on Marxism for a discussion of dialectics.

to say when I began this practice or why such a thing ever occurred to me: I prayed to God regularly, i.e. every day, that He would give me zeal and patience to perform the work He would assign me.

Thus I became an author (ibid., pp. 76, 82, 83).

Even in his most despondent moments, Kierkegaard said, he still had faith in God. But although he believed God existed and controlled the universe, he also believed he was doomed to depression. Speaking of his early beliefs, cultivated by his despondent father, he wrote:

What wonder then that there were times when Christianity appeared to me the most inhuman cruelty—although never, even when I was farthest from it, did I cease to revere it, with a firm determination that (especially if I did not myself make the choice of becoming a Christian) I would never initiate anyone into the difficulties which I knew and which, so far as I have read and heard, no one else has alluded to. But I have never definitely broken with Christianity nor renounced it. To attack it has never been my thought. No, from the time when there could be any question of the employment of my powers, I was firmly determined to employ them all to defend Christianity, or in any case to present it in its true form (ibid., pp. 76,77).

In 1836, on the brink of suicide, he experienced the first of several religious encounters. The power of this experience led him to develop a system of morals (ethics) by which he determined to live his life.

In 1838 he had another religious experience that turned him toward a greater Christian commitment. He was also engaged to be married, but broke it off, feeling that marriage would interfere with his "mission" in life.

In later life, Kierkegaard viewed his writings as representing the three phases of human commitment: the aesthetic, the ethical, and the religious. His works, he believed, were in one way autobiographical, showing his own dialectical growth through the three stages. In another way, his writings were prototypical of the life experience that should be sought by each human being. And in still a third way, portions of his writings were not meant to represent his viewpoints at all, but were meant to encourage the reader to expand his own thinking patterns, entertain new belief systems, and thus dialectically grow toward the ultimate religious commitment, where he would find true peace. Most of Kierkegaard's writings were published under pseudonyms as part of his technique to encourage new thought. In 1843 he published *Either/Or* which, as he described it, expressed "the fact that I had become thoroughly aware how impossible it would be for me to be religious only up to a certain point. Here is the place of *Either/Or*. It was a poetical catharsis, which does not, however, go farther than the "ethical" (ibid., p. 18). In 1844 he published *The Concept of Dread and Philosophical Fragments*; in 1845 *Stages of Life's Way*; in 1846 *Concluding Unscientific Postscript*; in 1848 *Anti-Climacus* and *Christian Discourses*; and *The Point of View* was published after his death. These are the major writings of Kierkegaard.

Kierkegaard's writings had only limited influence during his lifetime. However, they were translated into other languages, mostly after his death, and his influence became tremendous. Because of this great later influence and his concerns with the existential themes of existence and the "authenticated" man, he became known as "the Father of Existentialism." Remember though, that he consistently referred to himself as a religious and even Christian thinker and would definitely not have aligned himself with the atheistic existentialists such as Sartre had he been alive in the twentieth century. His faith did not conform to historical and biblical Christianity, but it was religious faith nonetheless.

Kierkegaard's Philosophy

William S. Sahakian has concisely summarized Kierkegaard's main tenets:

> The essence of Kierkegaard's philosophy can be seen in his doctrine that there are three stages of life experience: (1) aesthetic, (2) ethical, and (3) religious. These represent three attitudes toward life, three philosophies of life. Some of us progress from one stage to the next, while others never go beyond the first stage. Kierkegaard sometimes fused the second and third stages, referring to them as the religio-ethical. The third stage is superior to the other two stages. All of them reflect man's attempt to win salvation, to gain satisfaction for life's greatest good, while it is still within reach. Kierkegaard discussed the three stages in a number of his writings, but he devoted a most famous work, *Either/Or*, to a detailed analysis of the first two stages (William S. Sahakian, *History of Philosophy*, NY: Barnes and Noble Company, Inc., 1968, p. 343).

I. The Aesthetic

The man in the first stage, the aesthetic, is looking for fulfillment from his outside activities and from within himself. He may seek romance, pleasure, or intellectual pursuits as means to satisfy himself. However, these activities are not enough. They are not ultimately satisfying. The man becomes bored with himself and his activities. This boredom turns to despair. If not checked, the despair ends in suicide.

II. The Ethical

What is the remedy for this aesthetic despair? Kierkegaard replied that commitment gives meaning to life. Commitment to some arbitrary absolute, and the ordering of one's life around that commitment, brings one out of the aesthetic stage and into the second or ethical stage. The person achieves selfhood through commitment. The individual becomes aware. His choices are made with passion and emotional commitment. The person now chooses and acts, thereby establishing his selfhood and integrity. He is a man of duty. This is the type of person described by psychotherapist Viktor Frankl, who revolutionized European psychoanalytic theory after World War II. He calls the ethical urge the "will to meaning" and says:

> Man's search for meaning is a primary force in his life and not a "secondary rationalization" of instinctual drives. This meaning is unique and specific in that it must and can be fulfilled by him alone; only then does it achieve a

significance that will satisfy his own will to meaning. There are some authors who contend that meanings and values are "nothing but defense mechanisms, reaction formations and sublimation." But as for myself, I would not be willing to live merely for the sake of my "defense mechanisms," nor would I be ready to die merely for the sake of my "reaction formations." Man, however, is able to live and even to die for the sake of his ideals and values! (Viktor E. Frankl, *Man's Search for Meaning: an Introduction to Logotherapy,* NY: Simon and Schuster, Inc., 1963, pp. 154, 155).

III. *The Religious*

The third and greatest stage, the stage where man finally finds contentment, is the religious stage. The person commits himself, as in the second stage, and is looking for fulfillment, as in the first stage, but in this religious stage his commitment is to One who is able to satisfy completely: God. In this stage man is finally content because of his commitment to God. Selfhood cannot be achieved ultimately and completely within the self. The self must be committed to the One beyond, to God.

Kierkegaard and Hegel

Kierkegaard's philosophy was in opposition to that of the German philosopher Hegel, although they both used a system of dialectics. Samuel Stumpf points out:

> At the University of Copenhagen Kierkegaard was trained in Hegel's philosophy and was not favorably impressed by it. When he heard Schellings's lectures at Berlin, which were critical of Hegel, Kierkegaard agreed with this attack upon Germany's greatest speculative thinker. "If Hegel had written the whole of his Logic and then said...that it was merely an experiment in thought," wrote Kierkegaard, "then he could certainly have been the greatest thinker who ever lived. As it is, he is merely comic." What made Hegel comic for Kierkegaard was that this great philosopher had tried to capture all of reality in his system of thought, yet in the process lost the most important element, namely, *existence.* For Kierkegaard, the term *existence* was reserved for the individual human being. To exist, he said, implies being a certain kind of individual, an individual who strives, who considers alternatives, who chooses, who decides, and who, above all, commits himself. Virtually none of these acts were implied in Hegel's philosophy (Stumpf, *Socrates,* p. 455).

William Sahakian made some good contrasts between the concerns of Hegel and the concerns of Kierkegaard:

> Kierkegaardian philosophy is fundamentally in direct antithesis to Hegelianism. Whereas Hegel placed the emphasis on speculative thought, Kierkegaard placed it on existence. Hegel discerned truth in the rational system, Kierkegaard in paradox. The former sought the universe, the latter the individual or particular. The former saw in logic a mediation of anitheses or formulated an unbroken logic (Hegelian dialectic); the latter replaced it with the leap or logical gap (qualitative dialectic). *Either/Or* was the Kierkegaardian answer to the Hegelian synthesis or mediation. Hegel found truth in the Absolute and objectivity, while Kierkegaard found it in the relative and subjective. Hegel emphasized necessity, Kierkegaard freedom. Other Kierkegaardian concepts, which replaced Hegelian ones were: repetition for recollection,

concealment for openness, possibility for actuality, indirect communication (Socratic maimetic) for direct communication, transcendence of God for the immanence of God, and mediacy (or reflection) or immediacy (Sahakian *Philosophy*, p. 347).

Kierkegaard and Truth

Kierkegaard defined truth as "subjectivity." For him it was paradoxically the only thing one could be sure about and yet the one thing one was anxious about. Sahakian explains:

> Truth is subjectivity; the highest expression of subjectivity is passion. To think Existentially is to think with inward passion. Objectivity accents *what* is said, but subjectivity accents *how* it is said. The inward *how* is passion; decision is found only in subjectivity. Subjectivity is the truth; truth is defined as "an objective uncertainty held fast in an appropriation-process of the most passionate inwardness." Uncertainty creates anxiety which is quieted by an exercise of faith. The preceding definition of truth also serves as a definition of faith. There is no faith without risk, choice, passion, and inwardness; nor is there truth without them. Uncertainty always accompanies subjectivity, calling for the leap of faith (ibid., p. 348).

The Christian philosophers Norman Geisler and Paul Feinberg point out a very important feature of Kierkegaardian "truth." They note that Kierkegaard never denies such a thing as *objective* truth: he merely denies its importance over what he calls *"subjective"* truth.

> While not denying that there is such a thing as *objective* scientific truth, the existentialist does not consider that kind of truth important, at least not nearly as important as *subjective* truth. Indeed, Kierkegaard declared "truth is subjectivity." By that he did not mean that any subjective belief is true, but that unless one believes something subjectively and passionately he does not possess the truth. Truth is always personal and not merely propositional. One never gains truth by mere observation, but by obedience: never by being a spectator, but only by being a participator in life. Truth is found in the concrete, not in the abstract: in the existential, not in the rational. In fact, one places himself in the truth only by an act of his will, by a "leap of faith." It is not deliberation of the mind but a decision of the will by which one comes to know truth (Norman L. Geisler and Paul D. Feinberg, *Introduction to Philosophy*, Grand Rapids, MI: Baker Book House, 1980, p. 46).

In summary, Kierkegaardian philosophy is much more complicated than at first meets the eye. One especially must be aware that common and philosophical vocabularies take on new definitions for Kierkegaard. The evangelical Christian who declares that Jesus Christ is the truth means something quite different from what Kierkegaard means. Kerkegaard's three-fold path to personal fulfillment sounds good until it is examined from within the context of the claims of the Bible or until attempts are made to authenticate it by history and objective reason.

Paul Tillich (1886-1965)

One of the most influential liberal theologians of the twentieth century was Paul Tillich. Because of his orientation in both existentialist themes and Christian tradition, he rightly can be called an existential theologian. F. H. Heinemann notes:

> The title 'existentialist theologian' would fit. . . Paul Tillich. His unique case is that of a philosopher-theologian who started as a religious socialist and ends up as an existential theologian. Being a philosopher as well as a theologian, he tries to correlate philsophy and religion, embraces existentialism as the true philosophy whose task it is to penetrate the structure of human existence (Heinemann, *Existentialism*, p. 219).

Alston and Nakhnikian give some of Tillich's Lutheran, liberal theology, and philosophical background:

> Paul Tillich is one of the most influential Christian thinkers of our time — perhaps the most influential in English-speaking countries. Born in a small village in eastern Germany in 1886, the son of a Lutheran pastor, he received a theological and philosophical education, and was ordained in the Evangelical Lutheran Church in 1912. After serving as an army chaplain during World War I, Tillich taught theology and philosophy at several German universities — Berlin, Marburg, Dresden, and Frankfurt. He incurred the wrath of the Nazis, and when Hitler came to power in 1933 he emigrated to the United States. On his arrival in America he became a Professor of theology at Union Theological Seminary. From this post Tillich has exercised an enormous influence on religious thought in this country. (William P. Alston and George Nakhnikian, *Readings in Twentieth Century Philosophy*, NY: The Free Press, 1963, p. 723).

Anxiety

Anxiety is one of the very important themes in existentialism. Although different existentialists handle the theme in different ways, Tillich's discussion of anxiety in his *Systematic Theology* gives a very thorough discussion of the subject from an existential point of view. Philosopher B. A. G. Fuller summarizes Tillich's discussion:

> *Anxiety.* Accepting the familiar description of the post-war era, both for Europe and America, as an "age of anxiety," Tillich describes anxiety as fundamentally the "existential awareness of nonbeing," the "awareness that nonbeing is a part of one's own being." The awareness of one's own transitoriness and of one's own having to die produces a natural anxiety, an anxiety of ultimate nonbeing. Naked anxiety, which belongs to the nature of being as such and is an experience of unimaginable horror, strives vainly to convert itself into fear, because fear has an object and can therefore be met and overcome by courage. But anxiety itself has no object.
>
> *The Anxiety of Fate and Death.* Anxiety appears in three forms, dependent upon the direction in which "nonbeing threatens being." The *anxiety of fate and death* proceeds from the threat of nonbeing against man's "ontic" affirmation. It is basic, universal, and entirely inescapable. The contingency of man, that the causes which determine him are without any rationality or ultimate necessity, yields the relative anxiety of fate. The fact of death, present with man during every moment of life as well as at the moment of dying, produces an absolute anxiety of nonbeing. The basic question of courage is whether there is a *courage to be* in the face of this absolute threat against being.

The Anxiety of Emptiness and Meaninglessness.   The second type of anxiety is in its relative form the *anxiety of emptiness* and in its absolute form the *anxiety of meaninglessness.* Emptiness is the product of a threat to participation in creativity. Meaninglessness, which lies always in the background of emptiness as death lies always behind fate, is the loss of a spiritual center for life, the loss of an ultimate concern, of the meaning fundamental to all meanings. This anxiety is the threat of nonbeing to the spiritual life, a threat that follows from man's finitude and estrangement and leads to despair. To escape it, one attempts an escape from his own freedom and thereby sacrifices his genuine existence.

The Anxiety of Guilt and Condemnation.   The third type of anxiety issues from the threat of nonbeing against man's self-affirmation, in its relative form, the *anxiety of guilt;* in its absolute form, the *anxiety of condemnation.* Man as finite freedom is free to determine himself in the fulfillment of his destiny. The anxiety of guilt and condemnation is produced by the failure to realize one's potentiality. It is a self-rejection, a despair in the loss of proper identity. Despair is the product of the three anxieties, interrelated to foster and support one another. Despair is the complete absence of hope. By suicide one might escape the anxiety of death, but he would be caught in the anxiety of guilt and condemnation.

Anxiety and Cultural History.   Life, Tillich holds, is largely an attempt to avoid despair. From it there is no escape, yet most people experience it in its intensity only infrequently if at all. In the history of western culture the three types of anxiety have always been present, but each has dominated one of the three major eras. The classical era, the era of absolutism and tyranny, was characterized by the anxiety of fate and death, and ended with the attempt to achieve the Stoic courage. The Middle Ages, under the influence of the Judeo-Christian (Moral) religion, was brought to a close under the domination of the anxiety of guilt and condemnation, induced by the breakdown of the unity of religion. Today it is the anxiety of emptiness and meaninglessness that casts its shadow over a world that has lost its spiritual content. (B. A. G. Fuller, *Philosophy*, pp. 609-610).

God

Tillich's definition of God was much more broad than that of evangelical Christianity or the Bible. In fact, Tillich's concept of God was not even first and foremost personal. God for Tillich was "the ground of all being," "the source of your being," "your ultimate concern." As such, Tillich saw no room for atheists or agnostics, for he believed that it was impossible for one to have no ultimate concerns. In his *The Shaking of the Foundations* he stated:

The name of this infinite and inexhaustible depth and ground of all being is *God.* That depth is what the word *God* means. And if that word has not much meaning for you, translate it, and speak of the depths of your life, of the source of your being, of your ultimate concern, of what you take seriously without any reservation....If you know that God means depth, you know much about Him. You cannot then call yourself an atheist or unbeliever. For you cannot think or say: Life has no depth! Life itself is shallow. Being itself is surface only. ...The name of this infinite and inexhaustible ground of history is *God.* That is what the word means, and it is that to which the words *Kingdom of God* and *Divine Providence* point. And if these words do not have much meaning for you, translate them and speak of the depth of history, of the ground and aim of our social life, and of what you take seriously without reservation in your moral and political activities. Perhaps you should call this depth *hope*, simply hope (Paul Tillich, *The Shaking of the Foundations*, NY: Charles Scribner's Sons, 1953, pp. 57, 59).

As is true with most themes in existentialism, Tillich's idea of God is deeply colored by the existential theme of subjectivity. Subjectivity is so important in existentialism that it almost becomes the most important theme, affecting all other existential thought.

Grace

Tillich not only redefined the traditional view of God, but he also put an existential interpretation to the concept of grace. His grace is universal, subjective, and flows from and to each individual. When he talks of the "acceptance" of grace, he is not talking about the forgiveness of God made possible by the sacrifice of Jesus Christ upon the cross. He is talking about the subjective experience of acceptance that one feels during a crisis.

Grace strikes us when we are in great pain and restlessness...It strikes us when we feel that our separation is deeper than usual, because we have violated another life, a life which we loved, or from which we were estranged. It strikes us when our disgust for our own being, our indifference, our weakness, our hostility, and our lack of direction and composure have become intolerable to us....Sometimes at that moment a wave of light breaks into our darkness, and it is as though a voice were saying: "You are accepted. *You are accepted,* accepted by that which is greater than you, and the name of which you do not know. Do not ask for the name now; perhaps you will find it later.... *Simply accept the fact that you are accepted!*" In the light of this grace we perceive the power of grace in our relation to others and to ourselves....We experience the grace of being able to accept the life of another, even if it be hostile and harmful to us, for, through grace, we know that it belongs to the same Ground to which we belong, and by which we have been accepted (ibid., pp. 161, 162).

In summary, we can see that Tillich's concerns (just a few of which have been highlighted here) are common to existential themes and that his applications of those themes to religion change the very essence or fundamentals of Christian belief. It cannot be denied that he was a religious existentialist. But it is also true that he was not an evangelical Christian, committed to the biblical fundamentals of our faith.

Gabriel Marcel (1889-1973)

Another religious philosopher who had strong influence in the growth of French existentialism was Gabriel Marcel (1889-1973). Marcel, a French Catholic existentialist, criticized many of his fellow existentialists. His primary philosophical loyalty to existentialism seemed to be the stress he placed on the value of the individual. Philosopher Anthony Flew comments:

...Marcel considered existentialism to be compatible with Christian doctrines. The aim of life is "communication" between men as well as between man and God, but relationships must be based on and retain the freedom and uniqueness of individuals, not be dependent on the joint acceptance of rules and goals (Anthony Flew, ed., *A Dictionary of Philosophy*, NY: St. Martin's Press, 1982, p. 204).

Jean T. Wilde and William Kimmel make the following additional appraisal of Marcel:

> Gabriel Marcel, a Christian existentialist, shares with the atheist existentialist Sartre the responsibility for the further development in France of that trend in philosophy represented by this anthology. A convert to Roman Catholicism, Marcel has nevertheless maintained a philosophical independence from the official philosophy of the church and has developed original avenues of thought that bear the unmistakable stamp of their author's temperament and spirit. He is not only a philosopher but also a successful dramatist and a fine musician (Jean T. Wilde and William Kimmel, eds., trans., *The Search for Being*, NY: The Noonday Press, 1962, p. 417).

It is important to remember that while Wilde and Kimmel, as well as Flew, note Marcel's alignment with Christianity, they also note that this alignment was not with historic Christianity. Marcel actually denied those doctrines evangelicals consider vital.

Marcel's philosophy was much less systematic than other existentialists such as Tillich, so we will just touch on some of his concerns. Marcel was more of an observer than a shaper of philosophy or theology. His greatest concerns were those which were involved in existentialism and which earned him a place among existentialist thinkers.

> Rather than systematic discourses, Marcel's works are collections of observations and notes. Avoiding the traditional metaphysical categories and principles, his thought revolves around a number of root ideas which are not so much ideas as modes of concrete experience: estrangement, nostalgia, and homecoming; presence and absence; appeal and response; fidelity and betrayal; availability and unavailability; despair, recollection, courage, and hope. It is within the framework of these modes of experience that human life unfolds and it is here, rather than in the abstract manipulations of technical reason, that Being as personality and community can reveal itself. In reflection upon these dimensions of experience, Marcel evokes a sense of the mystery that envelops and unfolds within experience, that informs, illumines and fulfills experience, the mystery that is not alien to existence because it is itself that from which existence has its being. By recovering this inner bond between existence and mystery, one uncovers the source of his own meaning and creative power (ibid., p. 419).

I. M. Bochenski gives an excellent discussion of the basic ideas of Marcel. He has done such a good job of summarizing Marcel that we will quote from him extensively:

> Marcel holds that being-an-object and existence are two entirely different dimensions of being. This is seen most clearly in the fundamental problem of embodiment (*incarnation*). The relation between my body and myself cannot be described as either being or having. I *am* my body, yet I cannot identify

myself with it. The question about embodiment has led Marcel to a rigorous distinction between the *problem* and the *mystery.* A problem concerns what lies wholly before me, something which I scan objectively as an observer. A mystery, on the other hand, is "something in which I am involved *(engagé).*" Only mysteries are of any philosophic relevance and thus philosophy must be transobjective, personal, dramatic, indeed tragic. "I am not witnessing a spectacle": we should remind ourselves of this every day, says Marcel. The possibility of suicide is the point of departure of every genuine metaphysics. Such a metaphysics must be neither rational or intuitive. It is the result of a kind of second reflection *(réflexion seconde).*

Marcel has not worked out this metaphysics, but he has adumbrated its methodology. It is to give an answer to the basic ontological demand, namely, that there must be being, there must be something which cannot be explained away in some easy way as, for example, psychoanalysis explains away psychic phenomena. We are certain that there is being through the mysterious reality of the "I am"—not through *cogito ergo sum.* In this way the opposition of subject and object, of idealism, is overcome. Human reality reveals itself as the reality of a *homo viator,* of being which is always in process of becoming. Every philosophy which misinterprets this truth, which tries to explain man by means of a system, is incapable of understanding man.

We are led to the understanding of human being above all through the study of human relationships which are signified by judgments in the second person, in the *thou.* These unobjective thou-relationships are creative, for through them I create myself and also help another to create his own freedom. Here Marcel is close to the Jewish philosopher Martin Buber (b. 1878) who had enunciated similar theses even before Marcel. The center of the thou-relationship is faithfulness *(fidélité).* It appears as the embodiment of a higher free actuality, since the faithful one creates himself in freedom. Hope is even more basic than faithfulness, for the latter is built upon hope. Marcel holds that hope has ontological significance. It shows that the victory of death in the world is merely apparent and not final. Marcel regards his doctrine of hope as the most important result of his work. Here he departs radically from Sartre and Heidegger and apparently even from Jaspers.

The human thou can also be objectivized and become an it. But for this there is a definite limit, behind which stands the absolute thou which can no longer be taken as an object, namely God. We cannot through reason prove the existence of God. One encounters God on the same plane as the other, the plane of the thou, in loving and in honoring through participation in true being which may already take its rise in the questioning attitude of the philosopher (Bochenski, *Eurpoean Philosophy,* p. 183, 184).

The Secular Existentialists

By far the largest group of thinkers categorized as extentialists are those with no religious orientation at all, the secular existentialists. Some of them ignore religion completely, others are forcefully atheistic. The secular existentialists are concerned with the same themes as the religious existentialists, but their presuppostions and belief systems preclude any supernatural or any idea of God.

In our overview, we will examine three secular existentialists: Martin Heidegger, Karl Jaspers and Jean-Paul Sartre.

Martin Heidegger (1889-1976)

Martin Heidegger was one of the most influential promoters of contemporary existentialism. He wrote in German but his works have been translated into English. His most famous, *Being and Time*, has become one of the most popular expressions of English/American existentialism in the philosophical world. Alston and Nakhnikian note the scope of Heidegger's spreading influence:

> In Latin America and Europe, excluding, of course, the Soviet Union and her European satellites, one of the dominant contemporary philosophers is Heidegger. Heidegger's influence ranges widely over philosophers, theologians (including Paul Tillich), and certain psychotherapists. In the English-speaking world, too, there are philosophers who regard Heidegger with as much respect as do his Continental and Latin-American admirers (Alston and Nakhnikian, *Readings*, p. 679).

Heidegger's writings had a great effect on both the religious existentialist Rudolph Bultmann, who attempted to build a theology from Heideggerian existentialism, and Jean-Paul Sartre, the French secular existentialist and novelist.

Heidegger studied under the philosopher Edmund Husserl before he became rector of Freiburg University in 1933. His main treatise, *Sein und Zeit(Being and Time)*, was published in 1927. Although *Being and Time* reflected the influence Husserl and Kierkegaard made on Heidegger, it also showed he differed from those men in some important ways.

Heidegger's existentialism is unique and complex. It is difficult for even professional philosophers to understand:

> Heidegger is an extremely original thinker. The problem of his historical affiliations is not of primary concern here and we need only mention that he borrows his method from Husserl, that he is in many ways influenced by Dilckey, and that his general thesis is largely inspired by Kierkegaard. Heidegger is equipped with an unusual knowledge of the great philosophers of the past, among whom he frequently quotes Aristotle, although he interprets him in very arbitrary fashion. A stir was caused by the volume which he devoted to Kant, *Kant und das Problem der Metaphysik* (1929).
>
> Few philosophers are so hard to understand as Heidegger (Bochenski, *European Philosophy*, p. 161).

Because Heidegger's philosophy is so difficult to understand, interpretations of his thought vary and even contradict one another. Philosopher/historian A. Robert Caponigri remarks:

> Heidegger's thought has given rise to extensive interpretations, varying much among themselves and frequently at variance with the line of exegesis which Heidegger himself has suggested. From the point of view of doctrine and interests, his thought falls into two phases. The line of demarcation is drawn (but not too sharply),...by the Holderlin lecture in 1936. The first phase centers about the great work of 1927: *Sein und Zeit*. This work is still considered as presenting the essential Heidegger. It most clearly exhibits his originality as a thinker in his "existential analysis" of human behavior with respect to the "unveiling of truth" and his "ontological" mode of treating

phenomenology. It is the basis for the wide influence he has enjoyed. The second phase possesses no strict unity but shows Heidegger's concern with a number of themes, both historical and analytical, stemming from his main concern: being and truth (A. Robert Caponigri, *A History of Western Philosophy: Philosophy from the Age of Positivism to the Age of Analysis,* Notre Dame, in: University of Notre Dame Press, 1971, p. 264).

Along with the difficulty in understanding Heidegger, and the added difficulty of interpretation, we find that Heidegger did not view himself as an existentialist!

Heidegger believes that the term "existentialist" does not apply to his philosophy. . .Heidegger grants that "existentialism" is an apt label for what Sartre represents, but not for his own position. Heidegger is interested in Being. He approaches the problem of Being through the study of *Dasein*, Heidegger's word for human existence, "the being of what we ourselves are" (Alston and Nakhnikian, *Readings*, p. 680).

Because of these problems, we will not deal extensively with Heidegger although he bears mentioning because of his influence on other existentialists. Recognizing our limits of space and purpose, we will confine our discussion to three concerns of Heidegger: *Dasein, angst,* and *death.* The reader is referred to the bibliography for books that deal more extensively with Heidegger.

Dasein

The most important concept unique to Hcidegger's system is *Dasein* (a word Heidegger used to refer to the human being, or the existing-ness of the human, which causes or becomes his essence). William Sahakian describes *Dasein*:

Dasein. The idea of Being is an old one to a philosopher grounded in Scholasticism, as Heidegger was. But Heidegger was interested in the meaning of Being, its sense, or its purpose—i.e., what renders it intelligible. Furthermore, he was interested primarily in the *human* Being, for the nature of the human Being leads to other levels of Being or reality. Only *Dasein* (his term for the human Being) can be said to have or not to have meaning; hence *Being* is meaningful solely in terms of human existence.

Dasein (being-there), that is, the human Being or the human existent, Heidegger identified as: (1) concern (*Sorge*), (2) being-toward-death (*Sein zum Tode*), (3) existence (*Existenz*), and (4) moods (*Stimmungen*). The human Being's essence is in his existence, for numerous possibilities are open to him whereby he may choose differnent kinds of Being for himself. The possibilities of what he may become are the pivotal points by which the human Being is oriented. Heidegger was greatly interested in interpreting time in terms of temporality; consequently, in addition to the problem of Being (*Dasein*), time is of utmost importance. Accordingly, his interest was in the Being and temporality of *Dasein* (human existence) (Sahakian, *Philosophy*, p. 349).

Angst

Angst is another term with heavy existential meaning for Heidegger. The German word refers to anxiety, dread and hopeless fear of the future. This concept is important to Heidegger because it forms the impetus for much of human metaphysical development. It is the goad toward human existential encounter.

> In existentialist philosophy, (angst is) the dread occasioned by man's realization that his existence is open towards an undetermined future, the emptiness of which must be filled by his freely chosen actions. Anxiety characterizes the human state, which entails constant confrontation with possibility and the need for decision, with the concomitant burden of responsibility (Flew, *Philsophy*, p. 13).

Death

As it is with most existential thought, death is important in Heidegger's system. His secular (non-supernatural) presuppositions, and his commitment to existence preceding essence give Heidegger no view of reality for an individual before birth or after death. According to his scheme, the man who recognizes this fact, freely accepts its inevitability, and seeks nothing beyond, is then free to choose his own existence. He is no longer bound by fear of death or imaginary retributive punishment after death. He is able to choose his actions, thereby choosing his existence and ultimately his essence. This is man with dignity.

> For Heidegger, man is the being that knows he is going to die. He dies not only at the end of life, but every day of it. Death is certain, yet indefinite. Because it is inevitable it marks the contingency of life. Life is cast up between nothing and nothing. Death is its boundary and is its supreme possibility. To freely accept death, to live in its presence, and to acknowledge that for it there is no substitute and into it one must go alone, is to escape from all illusions and to achieve genuine dignity and authentic existence (Fuller, *Philosophy*, p. 608).

Jean-Paul Sartre (1905-1980)

The man who most popularized an atheistic brand of existentialism was the French philosopher, Jean-Paul Sartre. Sartre's major work, *Being and Nothingness*, was written in 1943 while he was a prisoner of the Germans during World War II. Some of his other writings, including *Existentialism is Humanism* and the novel, *No Exit*, reflect an indebtedness to both Kierkegaard and Heidegger. Sartre's great ability enabled him to have a clear understanding of the history of philosophy. Marjorie Greene reports:

> [Sartre] does indeed use the thinkers of the past (and present) for his own ends, but at the same time he sees them with extraordinary clarity. In his references, say, to Kant or Spinoza, he not only uses their thought as a springboard for his own, but also exhibits a solid and scholarly penetration into their principles and views. His relation to Marx is less straightforward, as we shall see, but in general one finds in his philosophical works an interweaving of themes in which the original strands stand out for themselves with unusual distinctness, while at the same time they are being worked into a characteristically Sartrean pattern (Marjorie Green, *Sartre*, NY: Franklin Watts, Inc., 1973, p. 33).

Absurdity

One major tenet of Sartre's existentialism is that life is absurd. In his novel, *Nausea*, Sartre brings out the absurdity of life through his main character, Roquentin. Robert Davidson writes,

The story of Roquentin, the hero of *Nausea*, is not told as an end in itself. Actually it expresses Sartre's own view concerning human existence. This story provides a descriptive or phenomenological account of a man's growing realization of the absurdity of human life in itself, and of his awakening to the fact that if a man's life is to have any meaning or purpose, the individual himself must confer that meaning upon it. A sense of the absurd, the absurdity of life and of man himself, permeates Sartre's early existentialism. In *Nausea* he portrays this as an immediate insight in one's own experience. As he sat in a public park one day, staring at the long black roots of an old chestnut tree, Roquentin became acutely aware of the absurdity of his own existence:

"Absurdity was not an idea in my head nor the sound of a voice. It was this long, lean, wooden snake curled up at my feet—snake or claw or talon or root, it was all the same. Without formulating anything I knew that I had found the clue to my existence, to my nausea to my life. And indeed everything I have ever grasped since that moment comes back to this fundamental absurdity" (Robert F. Davidson, *Philosophies Men Live By*, NY: Holt, Rinehart and Winston, Inc., 1974, p. 362).

Man is Autonomous

The absurdity of the universe leads Sartre to another major tenet of existentialism; namely, that man is autonomous. Sartre wrote:

The existentialist, on the contrary, thinks it very distressing that God does not exist, because all possibility of finding values in a heaven of ideas disappears along with Him; there can no longer be an *a priori* Good, since there is no infinite and perfect consciousness to think it. Nowhere is it written that the Good exists, that we must be honest, that we must not lie: because the fact is we are on a plane where there are only men. Dostoevsky said, 'If God didn't exist, everything would be possible.' That is the very starting point of existentialism. Indeed, everything is permissible if God does not exist, and as a result man is forlorn, because neither within him nor without does he find anything to cling to. He can't start making excuses for himself. In other words, there is no determinism, man is free, man is freedom. On the other hand, if God does not exist, we find no values or commands to turn to which legitimize our conduct. So, in the bright realm of values, we have no excuse behind us, nor justification before us. We are alone, with no excuses (Jean-Paul Sartre, *Existentialism and Human Emotions*, NY: The Citadel Press, n.d., pp. 22, 23).

Freedom

Man comes into the scene and defines himself. He lives in absolute freedom. Sartre states:

That is the idea I shall try to convey when I say that man is condemned to be free. Condemned, because he did not create himself, yet, in other respects is free; because, once thrown into the world, he is responsible for everything he does. The existentialist does not believe in the power of passion. He will never agree that a sweeping passion is a ravaging torrent which fatally leads a man to certain acts and is therefore an excuse. He thinks that man is responsible for his passion (ibid., p. 23).

Existence Before Essence

Another major tenet of Sartre's existentialism is that existence precedes essence. This means that man, by his own choices, defines his character, his essence and the person he is becoming. His choices determine his make-up. Sartre argues:

Atheistic existentialism, which I represent, is more coherent. It states that if God does not exist, there is at least one being in whom existence precedes essence, a being who exists before he can be defined by any concept, and that this being is man, or as Heidegger says, human reality. What is meant here by saying that existence precedes essence? It means that, first of all, man exists, turns up, appears on the scene, and, only afterwards, defines himself. If man, as the existentialist conceives him, in indefinable, it is because at first he is nothing. Only afterward will he be something, and he himself will have made what he will be. Thus, there is no human nature, since there is no God to conceive it. Not only is man what he conceives himself to be, but he is also only what he wills himself to be after this thrust toward existence (ibid., pp. 15-16).

In *Being and Nothingness*, Sartre states

Human freedom precedes essence in man and makes it possible. The essence of the human being is suspended in freedom (Jean-Paul Sartre, *Being and Nothingness*, NY: Philosophical Library, Inc., 1956, p. 25).

He continues with the remifications of this assertion:

[It is that] choice that is called "will." But if existence really does precede essence, man is responsible for what he is. Thus, existentialism's first move is to make every man aware of what he is and to make the full responsibility of his existence rest on him. And when we say that a man is responsible for himself, we do not only mean that he is responsible for his own individuality, but that he is responsible for all men (ibid., p. 16).

Fulfillment

Sartre believed that man could receive his own self-fulfillment, as Sahakian reports:

Notwithstanding the pessimistic views in most of Sartre's writings his existentialism ends on a note of optimism, for his *Existentialism is Humanism* concludes with the declaration that existentialism does not plunge man into despair but is an optimistic doctrine of action, that man is his own lawmaker, a creator of values, living in a human universe of human subjectivity, and capable of self-fulfillment (Sahakian, *Philosophy*, p. 357).

Thus, man makes his own fulfillment. Those who try to accomplish this through religion are guilty of bad faith, as Flew defines:

Bad faith. In the existentialism of Sartre, a form of deception of self and others; the attempt to rationalize human existence through religion, science, or any belief in operative forces that impose meaning and coherence. Man shapes his own destiny through a succession of free choices for which he is totally responsible. In 'bad faith' he denies the necessity of relying on his own moral insight and fallible will, trying to escape the burden of responsibility by regarding himself as the passive subject of outside influences, and his actions as being predetermined by these rather than freely chosen by himself (Flew, *Philosophy*, p. 35).

Forlornness

One of the major themes Sartre dealt with is also (not surprisingly) one for which he is perhaps best known, the theme of forlornness. It arises out of existential individuality and subjectivity. In some ways, it resembles Kierkegaard's second and unsatisfying stage, where man realizes he is alone, determines an ethic, but has nothing on which to depend. Sartre himself presented a moving description of this forlornness in the previously cited *Existentialism and Human Emotion*:

> To give you an example which will enable you to understand forlornness better, I shall cite the case of one of my students who came to see me under the following circumstances: his father was on bad terms with his mother, and moreover, was inclined to be a collaborationist; his older brother had been killed in the German offensive of 1940, and the young man, with somewhat immature but generous feelings, wanted to avenge him. His mother lived alone with him, very much upset by the half-treason of her husband and the death of her older son; the boy was her only consolation.
>
> The boy was faced with the choice of leaving for England and joining the Free French Forces—that is, leaving his mother behind—or remaining with his mother and helping her to carry on. He was fully aware that the woman lived only for him and that his going-off—and perhaps his death—would plunge her into despair. He was also aware that every act that he did for his mother's sake was a sure thing, in the sense that it was helping her to carry on, whereas every effort he made toward going off and fighting was an uncertain move which might run aground and prove completely useless; for example, on his way to England he might, while passing through Spain, be detained indefinitely in a Spanish camp; he might reach England or Algiers and be stuck in an office at a desk job. As a result, he was faced with two very different kinds of action: one, concrete, immediate, but concerning only one individual; the other concerned an incomparably vaster group, a national collectivity, but for that very reason was dubious, and might be interrupted en route. And, at the same time, he was wavering between two kinds of ethics. On the one hand, an ethics of sympathy, of personal devotion; on the other, a broader ethics, but one whose efficacy was more dubious. He had to choose between the two.
>
> Who could help him choose? Christian doctrine? No. Christian doctrine says, "Be charitable, love your neighbor, take the more rugged path, etc., etc." But which is the more rugged path? Whom should he love as a brother? The fighting man or his mother? Which does the greater good, the vague act of fighting in a group, or the concrete one of helping a particular human being to go on living? Who can decide *a priori*? Nobody. No book of ethics can tell him. The Kantian ethics says, "Never treat any person as a means, but as an end." Very well, if I stay with my mother, I'll treat her as an end and not as a means; but by virtue of this very fact, I'm running the risk of treating the people around me who are fighting, as means; and, conversely, if I go to join those who are fighting, I'll be treating them as an end, and, by doing that, I run the risk of treating my mother as a means.
>
> If values are vague, and if they are always too broad for the concrete and specific case that we are considering, the only thing left for us is to trust our instincts. That's what this young man tried to do; and when I saw him, he

said, "In the end, feeling is what counts. I ought to choose whichever pushes me in one direction. If I feel that I love my mother enough to sacrifice everything else for her—my desire for vengeance, for action, for adventure—then I'll stay with her. If, on the contrary, I feel that my love for my mother isn't enough, I'll leave.

But how is the value of a feeling determined? What gives his feeling for his mother value? Precisely the fact that he remained with her. I may say that I like so-and-so well enough to sacrifice a certain amount of money for him, but I may say so only if I've done it. I may say "I love my mother well enough to remain with her" if I have remained with her. The only way to determine the value of this affection is, precisely, to perform an act which confirms and defines it. But, since I require this affection to justify my act, I find myself caught in a vicious circle. (Sartre, *Existentialism*, pp. 24-27).

From this we can see the futility inherent in Sartre's existential thought. Since "existence precedes essence," and the individual is enveloped within "subjectivity" and must find his essence of "authenticity," he is truly alone. Many people have embraced existentialism for a time, sincerely thinking that its view of life is accurate. However, many leave existentialism because it offers a solution, meaning, and commitment which is not truly satisfying. Even Sartre, toward the end of his life, swung very close to theistic commitment. The magazine *National Review* reported it this way:

Throughout his mature career, the philosopher Jean-Paul Sartre was a militant atheist. Politically, although he quarreled with Marxist materialism, his rhetoric was often indistinguishable from the most heavy-handed Stalinist boiler-plate.

However, during the philosopher's last months there were some surprising developments. In 1980, nearing his death, by then blind, decrepit, but still in full possession of his faculties, Sartre came very close to belief in God, perhaps even more than very close.

The story can be told briefly, and perhaps reverently. An ex-Maoist, Pierre Victor, shared much of Sartre's time toward the end. In the early spring of 1980 the two had a dialogue in the pages of the *ultra-gauchiste Nouvel Observateur*. It is sufficient to quote a single sentence from what Sartre said then to measure the degree of his acceptance of the grace of God and the creatureliness of man: "I do not feel that I am the product of chance, a speck of dust in the universe, but someone who was expected, prepared, prefigured. In short, a being whom only a Creator could put here: and this idea of a creating hand refers to God."

Students of existentialism, the atheistic branch, will note that in this one sentence Sartre disavowed his entire system, his *engagements*, his whole life. Voltaire converted on his deathbed; one never knows, the brilliant old rascal is supposed to have said. Sartre did not convert, at least outwardly, but came to understand. Everything ought to be forgiven him.

The epilogue is much less edifying. His mistress, Simone de Beauvoir, behaved like a bereaved widow during the funeral. Then she published *La cérémonie des adieux* in which she turned vicious, attacking Sartre. He resisted Victor's seduction, she recounts, then he yielded. "How should one explain this senile act of a turncoat?" she asks stupidly. And she adds: "All my friends, all the Sartrians, and the editorial team of *Les Temps Modernes* supported me in my consternation."

Mme. de Beauvoir's consternation v. Sartre's conversion. The balance is infinitely heavier on the side of the blind, yet seeing, old man. (*National Review*, June 11, 1982, p. 677).

Karl Jaspers (1883-1969)

Karl Jaspers began his academic career by studying law at Heidelberg and Munich. He later studied medicine at several German universities and soon made important contributions to pathological and psychiatric research. He was professor of philosophy at Heidelberg from 1921 until the Nazis came into power. After World War II he returned to Heidelberg and in 1948 he moved to Basel. He was one of the foremost representatives of existentialism.

B. A. G. Fuller comments upon those who influenced Jaspers' thought:

His philosophical activity was influenced from the beginning by careful studies of Kant and Hegel, but Kierkegaard and Nietzsche have dominated his thought by directing it constantly upon the problem of the human condition. His philosophy has been more than anything else an attempt to answer their question of the nature of human existence. His answers reflect his Kantianism. (Fuller, *Philosophy*, p. 604).

One aspect of Jaspers' philosophy is that it is more balanced than that of some of his existentialist comrades. I. M. Bochenski reports

The thought of Karl Jaspers is on the whole much more balanced than that of the majority of his fellow existentialists, for example, he critically analyzes their view of science, to which he accords a far more important place than they do. His books contain a wealth of remarkable analyses and are written in comparatively simple language free from the characteristic neologisms which make the other authors so difficult to read. An obvious concern for metaphysics and a sort of natural theology also serve to distinguish him from the others who share the same label. Even so, he exhibits the fundamental attitudes and convictions common to all existentialists (Bochenski, *European Philosophy*, p. 185).

His Method

In 1932 Jaspers completed a major philosophical work entitled, *Philosophie*. In it he examined in depth the common philosophical method, relating it to his own brand of existentialism. Robert A. Caponigri comments:

Jaspers' philosophical thought proper begins to emerge with the work *Philosophie* and is developed in the subsequent works. These works do not, however, constitute a progressive movement toward a systematic position. Jaspers' thought is thematic, not systematic. The basic themes of his thought are three: 1) science and its relation to man's understanding of himself, 2) existence, and 3) transcendence. The most fruitful approach to Jaspers' thought lies in the exploration of his meditative enrichment of these themes. (Caponigri, *Philosophy*, p. 257).

His Philosophy

Jean T. Wilde and William Kimmel sum up the philosophy of Karl Jaspers:

For Jaspers philosophy is not the attempt to give definitive form to a body of knowledge about man in his universe. Philosophy is rather a way, an activity of the human mind moving toward the ultimate truth which can never become an object of knowledge, but which can be encountered in that process of thought which he calls "transcending thinking." Truth is always on the way, always in movement and never becomes final, not even in its most wonderful crystallizations. Thought is never at rest in its own content.

God, Man, and the World, while they may become objects of our attention can never become objects of knowledge. Their authentic being, their fundamental reality, always recedes beyond the limits of objectification, defying confinement and circumscription. They are, therefore, objects of encounter during the process of reflective thinking but encountered at the limits or boundaries of knowledge. The objects of knowledge or reflection, whether the products of scientific, aesthetic, mythical, philosophical, psychological, or merely common-sense experience are not ends and results but limiting forms whose reality lies not in their positive form or content but in their power to point beyond themselves toward Transcendence—the goal of philosophical thought.

But just as God—Transcendence, the all encompassing One in which and from which all things have their being and meaning—transcends objectification, so also the Self in its authenticity, its *Existenz*, can never become an object for itself. One encounters the Self at the "boundary situations" of existence, at the limits of knowledge and action, at those points where all knowledge and action fails, or founders—in the presence of absolute chance, conflict, suffering, guilt, death. At these boundary situations of finite existence one is driven either to despair or to a discovery of authentic Selfhood in freedom. In other words, in the concrete situation, where the forms of knowledge fail, the formulas do not apply, the path is no longer predetermined, one is forced to decide, and in this free decision out of the Self one discovers the true Self, the Being which one is.

Between the Being that I am (*Existenz*) and the Being that is the all (*Transcendence*) lies the World embodied in the constructed and interpreted forms of knowledge. This World, however, is also evanescent and, in a sense, unstable, but its forms serve as a mediation between the Self that I am and the Transcendence toward which my thought moves. As *forms* of mediation the forms of knowledge of the World are indispensable; but as forms of *mediation* none is final or absolute or binding. Their status is that of "cyphers," symbols that are open to Transcendence and through which reflection can encounter Transcendence. Only when they are "interpreted" as a cypher-script of Being rather than accepted as self-sufficient objects of knowledge is their status and that of the World they embody understood. But the interpretation itself is never final or accomplished. Nor can there be an interpretation for man-in-general. Each individual in his encounter with the World must interpret them anew, for only in the act of interpretation does the Transcendence which hovers around the forms reveal itself through them. There is necessary, then, both the expectant receptivity of the Self to the cypher and the recognition of the forms of knowledge as being cyphers of Being.

True philosophy, then, for Jaspers, is a hovering (*Schweben*) of the mind around the given forms of knowledge and the forming forms of one's own thought, a gliding of thought in expectant search for that truth about the Self, the World and God which reveals itself as the Being that is for the Being that I am (Wilde and Kimmel, *Search*, p. 451-3).

Jaspers and Sartre

F. H. Heinemann has compared the existential philosophies of Jaspers and Sartre, and he shows some interesting differences between them:

Jaspers	Sartre
Keep space open for the Comprehensive.!	There is no Comprehensive.
Do not identify yourself with an object of your knowledge!	Commit yourself!
Do not reject any form of the Comprehensive!	Reject all those forms which restrict your liberty!
Do not accept any defamation of existence!	Describe reality in its ugliness, absurdity and obscenity!
Do not allow yourself to be cut off from the Transcendent!	You are cut off from the Transcendent, for it is non-existent.

(Heinemann, *Existentialism*, p. 129).

Despite the differences between Jaspers and Sartre (and, in fact, among many existentialists), there are common themes that run throughout their philosophies.

Christian Response

The themes of existentialism are themes that the God of the Bible addresses in His Word. God is concerned about individuals. God is concerned about an individual's happiness, contentment and inner peace. God is concerned about an individual's fulfillment. However, existentialism is not biblical Christianity. Though not a Christian, philosopher Hazel Barnes notes that distinction:

> My first objection to the theological claims of Tillich, Robinson, Bonhoeffer, and Bultmann—to use them as examples and speaking of what they share in common without implying that they are in full agreement—is that they claim to be Christian while denying what has been essential in Christianity whereas they subtly retain Christian assumptions when they profess to establish philosophical truths independent of sectarian commitments.
>
> In their plea for a revolution in Christian thought, these theologians seem at times to argue for a position scarcely discernible from naturalism. The idea of a God "out there" somewhere in or beyond space, or the concept of any Being which is separate from us and the world is as offensive to Bishop Robinson as the medieval God who dwelt "up there" in Dante's three-level universe. Tillich argues against all use of "supernatural" concepts of God. Bultmann urges that we must "demythologize." Bonhoeffer suggests that Christianity should advance to the point where it no longer needs the "religious premise," that the Christian must "plunge himself into the life of a godless world, without attempting to gloss over its ungodliness with a veneer of religion or trying to transfigure it" (Barnes, *Ethics*, pp. 382, 383).

Bochenski gives another slant to a critical look at existentialism. He talks about some of the philosophical problems posed but not answered by the usual existential concepts:

> As often happens, existentialism has gone too far in the rejection, inherently

justified, of the past. For many existentialist philosophers there seems to be nothing in principle worth considering except those...questions of fate we have already alluded to. Their whole philosophy seems to center on death, suffering, failure. Thereby they neglect another essential factor in European culture, namely that sense of the objective and scientific which the Greeks had in such eminent degree. Often existentialism goes so far...that it seems to be more an Indian than a European philosophy, that is, a kind of thought which seems to be exclusively, even in its logic, a kind of therapeutic device. It is for such reasons that existentialism encounters justified reproach among many, perhaps most, serious European philosophers.

Another unique trait of existentialist philosophy...is its definite technical philosophical character. Here many valuable insights and results are discernible. Unquestionably philosophy has been enriched by numerous superior analyses in psychology and phenomenology, and some fields have in fact been subjected to study for the first time through these efforts, for example, pure personal relationships between human beings —"being-with-another," "being-for-another," "thou," "communication." A study of problems has thus arisen which constitutes a definite advancement in philosophy. Equally fundamental are the critical attacks on positivism and on idealism by the existentialists. Against the first they have successfully defended the irreducibility of human existence to matter, and respecting the second they have asserted with great power and conviction the priority of existence to thought. They have occupied themselves with ontology in various ways and some have not only worked it out in detail but have capped their efforts with a metaphysics (Bochenski, *European Philosophy*, p. 199).

Christianity is based on a completely different set of presuppositions from those of existentialism. While existentialism stresses subjective inner experience, Christianity links subjective inner experience with objective and testable supernatural events in history (such as the resurrection of Jesus Christ) and with God-given and God-developed reason. Biblical Christians have faith. Existentialists also have faith. But faith, however sincere, is not enough. Faith must have an object and that object must be worthy of faith. Jesus Christ alone, the creator and sustainer of the universe and every individual in it, is worthy of ultimate faith.

We have dealt with the historicity of the Christian faith and its reasonableness in previous works (see, for example, Josh's *Evidence, More than a Carpenter,* and *The Resurrection Factor;* and Josh and Don's *Reasons* and *Answers*). Christianity presents a cohesive world view which fits the reality around us. Existentialism does not. We are convinced that Christianity alone makes the greatest sense out of the world we live in and out of our own inner thoughts and feelings. Christian philosopher Richard Purtill has capably summarized our perspective:

...reason is on the side of Christianity....If we begin to ask fundamental questions about the universe, and follow the argument where it leads us, then it will lead us to belief in God; that if we examine the evidence of history and of human experience, we will be compelled to acknowledge that the only satisfactory explanation of the evidence leads us to Christianity. Such Christians admit that there is still a gap between intellectual assent and commitment to a Christian way of life, but they believe that reason is neither opposed to such a commitment or irrelevant to it—rather, it is the best possible ground for it (Richard Purtill, *C. S. Lewis's Case for the Christian Faith*, San Francisco: Harper and Row, Publishers, 1981, pp. 12, 13).

Existentialism Bibliography

Alston, William P. and George Nakhnikian, *Readings in Twentieth Century Philosophy.* NY: The Free Press, 1963.

Angeles, Peter A., *Dictionary of Philosophy.* NY: Harper and Row, Publishers, 1981.

Avey, Albert E., *Handbook in the History of Philosophy.* NY: Barnes and Noble, Inc., 1961.

Barnes, Hazel E., *An Existentialist Ethics.* Chicago: University of Chicago Press, 1978.

Bochenski, I. M., *Contemporary European Philosophy.* Berkeley and Los Angeles: University of California Press, 1954.

Brown, James, *Kierkegaard, Heidegger, Buber and Barth.* NY: Collier Books, 1955.

Caponigri, A. Robert, *A History of Western Philosophy: Philosophy from the Age of Positivism to the Age of Analysis.* Notre Dame, IN: University of Notre Dame Press, 1971.

Collins, James, *The Existentialist.* Chicago: Henry Regnery Co., 1952.

Davidson, Robert F., *Philosophies Men Live By.* NY: Holt, Rinehart and Winston, Inc., 1974.

Edwards, Rem B., *Reason and Religion.* NY: Harcourt Brace Jovanovich, Inc., 1972.

Flew, Antony, *A Dictionary of Philosophy.* NY: St. Martin's Press, 1982.

Frankl, Viktor E., *Man's Search for Meaning.* NY: Pocket Books, 1963.

Frost, S. E., Jr., *Basic Teachings of the Great Philosophers.* Garden City, NY: Doubleday and Company, Inc., 1962.

Fuller, B. A. G., *A History of Philosophy.* NY: Holt, Rinehart and Winston, 1955.

Geisler, Norman L. and Paul D. Feinberg, *Introduction to Philosophy.* Grand Rapids, MI: Baker Book House, 1980.

Greene, Marjorie, *Sartre.* NY: Franklin Watts, Inc., 1973.

Heidegger, Martin, *On Time and Being.* NY: Harper and Row, Publishers, 1972.

Heinemann, F. H., *Existentialism and the Modern Predicament.* NY: Harper and Row, Publishers, 1953.

Herberg, Will, *Four Existentialist Theologians*. Garden City, NY: Doubleday and Company, Inc., 1958.

Horvath, Nicholas A., *Philosophy*. Woodbury, NY: Barron's Educational Series, 1974.

Hunnex, Milton D., *Existentialism and Christian Belief*. Chicago, IL: Moody Press, 1969.

James, William, *The Varieties of Religious Experience*. NY: The New American Library, Inc., 1958.

Kaufmann, Walter, *Existentialism from Dostoevsky to Sartre*. NY: The World Publishing Co., 1956.

_____, *Existentialism, Religion and Death*. NY: The New American Library, Inc., 1976.

Kierkegaard, Soren, *Attack upon Christendom*. Princeton, NJ: Princeton University Press, 1944, 1968.

_____, *The Point of View for My Work as An Author*. NY: Harper and Row, Publisher, 1962.

Marias, Julian, *History of Philosophy*. NY: Dover Publications, Inc., 1967.

Purtill, Richard L., *C. S. Lewis's Case for the Christian Faith*. San Francisco: Harper and Row, Publishers, 1981.

_____, *Thinking About Ethics*. Englewood Cliffs, NJ: Prentice-Hall, Inc., 1976.

Runes, Dagobert D., ed., *Dictionary of Philosophy*. Totowa, NJ: Littlefield, Adams and Company, 1977.

Sahakian, William S., *Ethics: An Introduction to Theories and Problems*. NY: Harper and Row, Publishers, 1974.

_____, *History of Philosophy*. NY: Harper and Row, Publishers, 1968.

_____, and Mabel L. Sahakian, *Ideas of the Great Philosophers*. NY: Harper and Row, Publishers, 1966.

Sartre, Jean-Paul, *Existentialism and Human Emotions*. NY: The Citadel Press, n.d.

Stumpf, Samuel Enoch, *Socrates to Sartre: A History of Philosophy*. NY: McGraw-Hill Book Company, 1966.

Thomas, Henry, *Understanding the Great Philosophers*. Garden City, NY: Doubleday and Companny, Inc., 1962.

Tillich, Paul, *The Shaking of the Foundations*. NY: Charles Scribner's Sons, 1953.

Wild, John, *Existence and the World of Freedom*. Englewood Cliffs, NJ: Prentice-Hall, Inc., 1963.

Wilde, Jean T., and William Kimmel, eds. and trans., *The Search for Being.* NY: The Noonday Press, 1962.

Young, Warren C., *A Christian Approach to Philosophy.* Grand Rapids, MI: Baker Book House, 1954.

Part V

A Christian Approach

to

Comparative Religions

A Christian Approach
to Comparative Religions

Norman Anderson*

The study of comparative religion, fascinating though it is, leaves many with a sense of bewilderment. Such diverse beliefs are held by multitudes whose sincerity cannot be questioned that the student may easily fall into the logical absurdity of wondering whether any ultimate truth exists in matters of religion, or into the resigned pessimism of doubting whether any firmly founded conviction in such matters can be attained by man. Should not all religions be regarded, then as vain attempts to solve the insoluble or alternatively, as different roads, however devious, to one grand but distant goal? Admittedly, most of the world's faiths seem to the unprejudiced enquirer to be a patchwork of good and bad, or at least of the desirable and the less desirable; but cannot the mind which eschews fanaticism accept the postulate which seems in some sense common to all, that there is a Principle or a Person beyond and behind the material universe, which to recognize, or whom to worship, meets some craving of the human heart? As for the rest—the details of dogma and worship—may not each individual work out for himself an eclectic faith chosen from what seems best in all the great religions?

There are however, decisive reasons which preclude the Christian from adopting such an attitude. He will be vitally concerned, of course, with what millions of his fellow creatures believe, and their convictions will command not only his interest, but also his study and respect. More, he will find much in those who follow other religions which will rebuke, instruct and inspire him—as, for instance, the Muslim's fidelity in prayer and fast, the Buddhist's dignified self-discipline, and the Sadhu's detachment from the things of time and sense. But these things concern matters of observance rather than teaching, of practice rather than dogma, noble—and, in its context, valid—though much non-Christian dogma undoubtedly is. With the basic content of his faith, however, the Christian will neither want, nor dare, to meddle—although he will retain an insatiable longing to enter into a much deeper understanding of the revelation on which it rests and an ever richer experience of the God who thus reveals himself.

* From Sir Norman Anderson, ed., *The World's Religions*, Grand Rapids, MI: William B. Eerdmans Publishing Company, 1976. Used with permission from the publisher.

But how can the Christian be so confident that his faith does in fact rest on a uniquely authoritative self-revelation of God? The history of the Christian church is so darkened by the sin, intolerance, frailty and divisions of generations of its adherents that it is easy to understand the cynicism with which it is often regarded. Even the Christian religion, as it has been elaborated, expounded and embodied down the centuries, has been so fraught with human error that this, too, stands under the judgment of God. What is it, then, which gives the Christian his confident conviction in the essential truth and unique authority of the divine revelation which it is his duty and privilege to proclaim?

It is to Jesus himself that the Christian will continually return. Behind him, of course, stands the long history of Israel, and God's progressive revelation of himself through Abraham, Moses and a succession of prophets. But the Old Testament is always looking forward—whether through promise, prediction or prefiguration—to One who was to come. Then at last, as the apostle Paul puts it: 'When the time had fully come, God sent forth his Son, born of woman, born under the law, to redeem those who were under the law, so that we might receive adoption as sons' (Galatians 4:4, 5). And the whole New Testament bears witness to that unique event and its essential implications.

About the historicity of Jesus, about his basic teaching and the impact he made on his contemporaries, and about his death on a Roman gibbet, there can surely be no serious question. Nor is there any room for doubt that, after his death, something happened which transformed his little band of dejected and dispirited followers into a company of witnesses whom no persecution could silence, and who 'turned the world upside down.' One and all, moreover, they testified that what had happened was that the crucified Jesus had been raised from the dead and had appeared to them and many other witnesses. As Paul wrote to the Corinthians in a letter which is unquestionably authentic: 'I delivered to you first of all (or as a matter of first importance) what I also received, that Christ died for our sins in accordance with the scriptures, that he was buried, that he was raised on the third day in accordance with the scriptures, and that he appeared to Cephas, then to the twelve. Then he appeared to more than five hundred brethren at one time. . .' (1 Corinthians 15:3-5). Now Paul must himself have received this tradition, at least in outline, immediately after his own conversion, within between two and (at most) five years of the crucifixion; and he must certainly have received it in its fullness, with the appended list of the principal witnesses, on his first visit to Jerusalem (which he describes in the first chapter of his letter to the Galatians) just three years later. In all probability, then, he received it within five years of the alleged event. He tells us, moveover, that this was the common message of all the apostles (cf. 1 Corinthians 15:11). And he goes out of his way to assert that the majority of those five hundred witnesses to having seen the risen Christ were still alive when he wrote to the Corinthians some twenty years later. As C. H. Dodd put it: 'No statement could be more emphatic or unambiguous. In making it Paul is exposing himself to the criticism of resolute opponents who would have been ready to point to any flaw in his credentials or in his presentation of the common tradition.[1] So the addition of this comment can only have meant: 'If you don't believe me, there are a very large number of witnesses still alive to whom you can turn for confirmation of what I say.'

It is perfectly true—as critics have not been slow to emphasize—that there is no explicit reference to the empty tomb in this earliest piece of historical evidence. But what oriental Jew of the first century could possibly have written that Christ died (physically, of course), that he was buried (physically, of course), and that he was later 'raised again on the third day' unless he had believed that *something* had happened to the body which had been laid in the sepulchre? When, from the very first, the early Christians—as C. H. Dodd again insists—said that 'He rose again from the dead,' they 'took it for granted that his body was no longer in the tomb. If the tomb had been visited it would have been found empty. The gospels supplemented this by saying, it *was* visited, it *was* found empty.'[2] And that this was an authentic part of the original apostolic tradition seems to me beyond any reasonable doubt.

But while it was the joyful certainty that Jesus was risen and still alive which was, unquestionably, the dominant note in the earliest apostolic proclamation, they soon began to put an equal emphasis on his atoning death. It was in the same letter to the Corinthians that Paul insisted that the gospel must be so preached that the cross of Christ should not 'be emptied of its power. For the word of the cross is folly to those who are perishing, but to us who are being saved it is the power of God' (1 Corinthians 1:17, 18). And in his second letter to the same church he explained this by saying, 'What I mean is, that God was in Christ reconciling the world to himself, no longer holding men's misdeeds against them, and that he has entrusted us with the message of reconciliation' (2 Corinthians 5:19, NEB). And the basis of this reconciliation was that, at the cross, God 'for our sake. . . made him to be sin who knew no sin, so that in him we might become the righteousness of God' (verse 21). This indeed, was the united testimony of the apostolic church, which they saw as the fulfilment of the fifty-third chapter of Isaiah and other Old Testament prophecies.[3]

It is for this reason that the Christian can allow no compromise, syncretism or theological relativism to obscure the inevitable intolerance—not in its spirit, but in its essential nature—of the gospel to which he is committed. It is not that he denies that there is any revelation of God's 'eternal power and Godhead' in the wonders of nature (cf. Romans 1—20) or in those glimpses of the truth which God has vouchsafed to many seeking souls. But if God could have *adequately* revealed himself in any other

---

[1]C. H. Dodd, "The Appearances of the Risen Christ," in *Studies in the Gospels*, D. E. Nineham, ed., Naperville, IL: Allenson, 1955, p. 28.

[2]C. H. Dodd, *The Founder of Christianity*, New York: MacMillan Company, 1970, p. 166.

[3]*Cf.* Mark 10:45; Luke 22:37; 1 Peter 2:24; *etc.*

way, is it reasonable to suppose that he would have taken the almost incredible road to the incarnation and the passion? And if it had been possible to deal with the problem of man's sin and its consequences in any other way whatever, is it conceivable that God would not have 'spared his own Son' the physical, mental and spiritual agony of Calvary—an agony in which he himself was so intimately involved? Surely that would not make sense.

If, then, the basic Christian message is true—and for this the evidence seems wholly convincing—it must follow that, as Stephen Neill puts it:

> 'Simply as history the event of Jesus Christ is unique. Christian faith goes a great deal further in its interpretation of that event. It maintains that in Jesus the one thing that needed to happen has happened in such a way that it need never happen again... Making such claims, Christians are bound to affirm that all men need the Gospel. For the human sickness there is one specific remedy, and this is it. There is no other. Therefore the Gospel must be proclaimed to the ends of the earth and to the end of time. The Church cannot compromise on its missionary task without ceasing to be the Church. If it fails to see and to accept this responsilibily, it is changing the Gospel into something other than itself... Naturally, to the non-Christian hearer this must sound like crazy megalomania, and religious imperialism of the very worst kind. We must recognize the dangers; Christians have on many occasions fallen into both of them. But we are driven back ultimately on the question of truth.'[4]

If many different groups of pathologists, let us suppose, were all seeking earnestly to discover the cause and cure of cancer, and one group—through no brilliance of their own—were to light upon the secret, would it constitute 'crazy megalomania' for them to share what they had found with their fellows? Would it not, rather, be criminal folly for them to keep the secret to themselves?

To what conclusion, then, does this lead us in regard to the attitude of the Christian to other religions as systems and to the eternal destiny of those who follow them? In regard to both these questions Christian opinion has been—and still is—widely divided. There have been many, all down the centuries, who have regarded most, if not all, of the non-Christian religions as a sort of *praeparatio evangelica*—as, indeed, all Christians would say of Old Testament Judaism. Some of those who take this view find the secret of the elements of truth in other religions in terms of an original divine revelation, the traces and influence of which have never been wholly lost or forgotten—or even in some cross-fertilization of ideas from one religion to another. Others, again, discern in them the influence of the 'cosmic Christ' who, as the eternal Logos or revealer of the Godhead, is the 'light that enlightens every man.' This view was taken by Justin Martyr and the Christian philosophers of Alexandria in the early centuries of the Christian era, and was summed up by William Temple when he wrote: 'By the word of God—that is to say by Jesus Christ—Isaiah and Plato, Zoroaster, Buddha, and Confucius ut-

---

[4]Stephen C. Neill, *Christian Faith and Other Faiths*, London: Oxford University Press, 1970, pp. 17f.

tered and wrote such truths as they declared. There is only one Divine Light, and every man in his own measure is enlightened by it.'[5]

Other Christians have adopted, at times, a diametrically opposite attitude. Instead of giving prominence to the elements of truth to be found in other religions they have emphasized the darker side of their ethical teaching and the less persuasive of their theological tenets, and have concluded that they emanate from the devil, rather than from God. In particular, those who take this view insist that these other religions clearly deny, whether by explicit statement or implicit teaching, the unique claims of the 'Word made flesh' and the fundamental need for the atonement that he alone could—and did—effect. Those elements of truth which can unquestionably be found in these other religions should therefore be explained, they feel, in terms of the fact that even Satan himself not infrequently appears as an angel of light—as, indeed, he might be expected to do in any religion designed to capture, and hold, men's allegiance and to constitute a substitute for, or an alternative to, the Christian gospel.

Yet a third view regards these other religions as not emanating primarily from either God or the devil, but as representing a variety of human attempts to explain the phenomena of life, to reach out after ultimate reality and to construct some system of thought, behaviour and religious observance which will satisfy man's needs. Those who founded and developed these religions were, like the rest of us, a compound of good and evil, of sincere aspiration after truth and of self-seeking; and they were also exposed to supernatural influences—both from God and Satan. It is scarcely to be wondered at, then that the non-Christian religions commonly represent such a diverse amalgam of truth and falsehood. All that is true must surely come from God, whether directly or indirectly; and all that is false must, presumably, owe its ultimate origin to the 'father of lies,' although its immediate source can usually be found in the sincere, but mistaken, conclusions of some human teacher.

The Christian preacher, then, will not feel that he can commend the non-Christian religions (other than Old Testament Judaism) as divinely inspired preparations for the gospel—although he will frequently, like the apostle Paul, use some element in their teaching or practice as a bridge by means of which he can reach the minds and hearts of their followers and bring to them the message he longs to communicate in an intelligible way. Nor will he—normally, at least—feel at liberty to speak against (or, still less, to ridicule) what other men sincerely, if mistakenly, believe, although he may at times be forced to speak out plainly about some particular point. His characteristic stance, however, will be positive rather than negative; and his habitual message will be to plead with all men to consider—or, in some cases, to reconsider—Jesus Christ. But far from any personal sense of superiority he will freely and frankly acknowledge that he is himself no better than anyone else; and he will do his best to present the essential Good News in a way which is stripped bare of

---

[5]W. Temple, *Readings in St. John's Gospel*, New York: St. Martin's Press, 1945, I, p.10.

accretions derived from the thought and culture of his own race or background. The truth as it is revealed in Jesus will be his one criterion, and the need of all men, without exception, for the forgiveness, reconciliation and new life which Jesus died to bestow will be the message he lives to proclaim.

But this means that he must listen quite as much as he speaks, for he needs to learn how someone from another religion and culture sees things. It is only then that the Christian 'may be given access to the dark places of that stranger's world—the things that really make him ashamed or anxious or despairing.' And then, at last, he will see the Saviour and Lord of that other world, his own Lord Jesus, yet not as he has known him hitherto. Instead he will 'understand how perfectly he matches all the needs and all the aspirations and all the insights of that other world— He who is the unique Lord and Saviour of all possible worlds.'[6] For every man, whatever his religion, race or moral virtue, is a sinner; and sin always and necessarily, alienates men from a holy God. So all of us alike need forgiveness, and all of us stand in need of a Saviour—since a sinful man can never save either himself or anyone else. It is precisely at this point, moreover, that the New Testament is at its most unequivocal, for Jesus himself is reported as saying, 'I am the way, and the truth, and the life; no one comes to the Father, but by me' (John 14:6)—or, in the Synoptic tradition, 'no one knows the Father except the Son and any one to whom the Son chooses to reveal him' (Matthew 11:27; cf. Luke 10:22). And the apostles in their turn reiterated this truth when they asserted that 'there is salvation in no one else, for there is no other name under heaven given among men by which we must be saved' (Acts 4:12).

Inevitably, however, this raises in an acute form the question of the eternal destiny of those who, for example, have never so much as heard the truth as it is in Jesus. This is usually through no fault of their own, but rather through the failure of Christians to take sufficiently seriously the commission to preach the gospel to every creature. But if all men are sinners, and alike stand in need of forgiveness; if sinful men can never save either themselves or one another; and if there is only one Saviour— then what hope can any man have? Does this mean that they are inevitably lost? That would, indeed, be an agonizing conclusion to those whose basic belief is that 'God is love'; but is there really any alternative?

It is at this point, as I see it, that the Old Testament throws a ray of light on our darkness, for who can doubt that Abraham, Moses, David and a host of others enjoyed both forgiveness and fellowship with God? Yet they did not know Jesus and the salvation he was to effect—except as a vague hope of the future which they proclaimed but only dimly understood. And what of that multitude of more ordinary Jews who, convicted of sin by God's Spirit, turned to him in repentance and faith, brought the prescribed sacrifices, and threw themselves on his mercy? Were they not, too, forgiven and accepted—not because they had merited salvation, for no man can do this; nor on the basis of their animal

---

[6]J.V. Taylor, *The Go-between God*, Philadelphia: Fortress Press, 1973, p. 189.

sacrifices, which could never atone for human sin; but, rather, on the basis of what the God of love was going to do in the unique 'Lamb of God' who was still to come, and of that atoning death to which all the Old Testament sacrifices were designed to point. For this supreme event, although it certainly—and necessarily—happened at one particular time and place in human history, is timeless in its divine efficacy. And that this alone was the ultimate ground on which the transgressions and sins of Old Testament believers were forgiven seems to be clearly taught by New Testament verses such as Romans 3:25 and Hebrews 9:15.[7]

May this not provide us with a guideline to the solution of the burning problem of those in other religions who have never heard—or never heard with understanding—of the Saviour? It is not, of course, that they can earn salvation through their religious devotion or moral achievements, great though these sometimes are—for the New Testament is emphatic that no man can ever earn salvation. But what if the Spirit of God convicts them, as he alone can, of something of their sin and need; and what if he enables them, in the darkness or twilight, somehow to cast themselves on the mercy of God and cry out, as it were, for his forgiveness and salvation? Will they not then be accepted and forgiven in the one and only Saviour? And if it be asked how this can be when they have never so much as heard of him, then the answer must be that they will be accepted on the basis of what the God of all grace himself did in Christ at the cross; for it is on that basis, alone, that a God who is light as well as love, just as well as merciful, can welcome and forgive repentant sinners.

It cannot be claimed that this is the clear and unequivocal teaching of the New Testament, where the primary emphasis is on the Christian's duty to share the Good News of God's love with the whole world. But how else can we understand Peter's words in the house of Cornelius: 'I now see how true it is that God has no favourites, but that in every nation the man who is godfearing and does what is right is acceptable to him' (Acts 10:34, 35, NEB)? This cannot mean that the man who does his best to be religious and moral will earn salvation, for the whole of the New Testament, as we have seen denies this possibility. But may it not mean that the man who realizes something of his need, and who casts himself on the mercy of God with a sincerity that shows itself in his life, will find that mercy where it is always available—at the cross where Jesus died?

If such a person should subsequently hear and understand the gospel, he would presumably be among the company of those (whom the Christian does meet, sometimes, in non-Christian lands) who accept it at once, and even say: 'Why didn't you come and tell me this before? It is what I have been waiting for all my life.' And if he never hears it in this life, then I believe he will wake up, as it were, on the other side of the grave to worship the One in whom, without understanding it, he had found

---

[7]There are also, of course, many verses which refer to the preincarnate Christ, through whom all things were created and in whom they are held together, whose atoning death was an essential part of the eternal counsel of God.

the mercy of God.

This, it should be understood, is totally different from what has been termed the doctrine of the 'second chance'. In the latter it is the opportunity to choose, and the subsequent decision of faith, which are deferred to the after-life, while what I suggest happens to such a man beyond the grave is that he will come into the light of a joyful understanding of the salvation to which the Spirit of God has brought him through the repentance and faith which he inspired—faltering, it may be, and unenlightened, certainly—during the days of his earthly pilgrimage.

But if this is true—as I myself believe—then it certainly does not lessen the Christian's missionary responsibility. To begin with, his Master's last commission and command was that he should go and tell the Good News, and that should be quite enough. If, moreover, he reflects how he himself was brought to the point of no longer trying to earn salvation, but accepting it as a gift, he will almost certainly conclude that this was through hearing the gospel story and its implications; so how can he deny this privilege to others? Any who are enabled by the Holy Spirit to turn to God, in the twilight, in repentance and faith, would still, moreover, lack what assurance, conscious companionship and confident message which come only from a knowledge that Christ died to justify his people, rose again to manifest himself to them in the 'power of an endless life' and has commissioned them as his ambassadors to appeal to others to be reconciled to God. So it is our manifest duty to share this knowledge, and these privileges, with all mankind.

The question remains, however, whether the non-Christian religions may be said in any way to represent a 'saving structure which serves to point men to the cosmic Christ.' This is certainly the contention of Raymond Panikkar, who believes that the 'good and *bona fide* Hindu is saved by Christ and not by Hinduism, but it is through the sacraments of Hinduism, through the message of morality and the good life, through the mysterion that comes down to him through Hinduism, that Christ saves the Hindu normally.'[8] Somewhat similarly, W. Cantwell Smith, writing of more than one non-Christian religion in the light of fellowship with their adherents, insists that we must recognize these religions as 'channels through which God Himself comes into touch with these His children.'[9] But it seems to me that both Panikkar and Cantwell Smith here go much too far. It is not through other religions as 'saving structures', as I see it, but rather through the basic fact of God's general revelation, vouchsafed in nature and in all that is true (including, of course, the truth there is in other religions), and the equally fundamental fact of our common humanity, that the Spirit of God, or the 'cosmic Christ', brings home to men and women something of their need. It is this, I think, which helps to explain what Lesslie Newbigin terms an 'element

---

[8]R. Panikkar, *The Unknown Christ of Hinduism*, New York: Humanities, 1968, p. 54.
[9]W. Cantwell Smith, *The Faith of Other Men*, New York: New American Library, 1963, p. 124.

of continuity' which is 'confirmed in the experience of many who have become converts to Christianity from other religions. Even though this conversion involves a radical discontinuity, yet there is often the strong conviction afterwards that it was the living and true God who was dealing with them in the days of their pre-Christian wrestlings.'[10] This is naturally most clearly marked in Judaism, as in the case of the apostle Paul;[11] but I have also found that converts from Islam never regard the God whom they previously sought to worship as wholly false, but rather rejoice that they have now, in Jesus Christ, been brought to know, and have fellowship with, that God as he really is.

So, indeed, it is to Jesus Christ that we always, and inevitably, come back. 'A most sensitive, lonely man from Pakistan', John V. Taylor tells us, 'spoke at the New Delhi Assembly of the World Council of Churches about his conversion from Islam. All his longing was still for his own people, their language, their ancient culture; and in the factious and generally defeated church of that land he finds little consolation or fellowship. "I am a Christian," he confessed, "for one reason only—because of the absolute worship-ability of Jesus Christ. By that word I mean that I have found no other being in the universe who compels my adoration as he has done. And if ever some pundit or theologian should prove me wrong and show that, after all, the High God is not of the character which I see in Jesus, I, for one would have to blaspheme and turn my back on any such god."'[12]

The attitude of the Christian, then, is essentially that of positive, humble, but unashamed witness to Jesus. As Leslie Newbigin puts it, he

'points to the one Lord Jesus Christ as the Lord of all men... The Church does not apologise for the fact that it wants all men to know Jesus Christ and to follow him. Its very calling is to proclaim the Gospel to the ends of the earth. It cannot make any restrictions in this respect. Whether people have a high, a low or a primitive religion, whether they have sublime ideals or a defective morality makes no fundamental difference in this respect. All must hear the Gospel.'[13]

---

[10]L. Newbigin, *The Finality of Christ*, Richmond, VA: John Knox Press, 1969, p. 59.

[11]*Cf.* Acts 22:3f., 14f.; 24:14f.; Galatians 1:15f., *etc.*

[12]Taylor, *op. cit.*, p. 193

[13]Newbigin, *op. cit.*, p. 59.

Indexed Glossary

Arius of Alexandria—early fourth century church heretic who developed and popularized arguments using the Bible to deny the deity of Christ...............................46, 63

Arjuna—the warrior in conversation with Krishna (q.v.) in the Bhagavad Gita (q.v.), a Hindu (q.v.) scripture....286, 287, 294

Armstrong, Garner Ted—Son and former "heir-apparent" of Herbert W. Armstrong (q.v.), founder of Worldwide Church of God (q.v.) cult. Finally ex-communicated and disinherited for financial and moral problems. Started his own cult with same doctrinal aberrations. New cult called the Church of God International (q.v.), headquartered in Tyler, Texas...
114, 115, 121

Armstrong, Herbert W.—founder and leader of the Worldwide Church of God (q.v.) cult. Born in 1892. Denies biblical doctrines..............21, 24, 25, 114, 115, 116, 117, 118, 119, 120, 121, 122

ascendant—in astrology (q.v.), the astrological sign (q.v.) which is rising on the horizon at the time of the subject's birth.....160

Asmodeus—a fifteenth-century designation of Satan (q.v.)...230

Aspen Institute for Humanistic Studies—secular humanist (q.v.) organization....................................460, 461

Association of Research and Enlightenment—psychic (q.v.) organization founded by "sleeping prophet" Edgar Cayce (q.v.) in 1931. Devoted to publishing the psychic readings (q.v.) of Cayce and to winning adherents to its occultic (q.v.) tenets. Acronym is A.R.E.....................................169

astral-travel—the occultic (q.v.) practice described as one's spirit leaving one's body and traveling small or great distances. Some occultists claim this can be done at will.........156

astrology—the belief system asserting that human lives are controlled in some degree by the position of the stars and planets. There is fraudulent astrology, wherein astrological forecasts, or horoscopes (q.v.), are wholly invented, and occultic (q.v.) astrology, wherein horoscopes are determined by spiritistic (q.v.) means...154, 155, 160, 161, 162, 163, 164, 165, 166, 181, 192, 268, 269

ataraxia—Greek for the "state of unperturbedness."........418

atharva-veda—part of the Hindu (q.v.) wisdom literature...
285, 291, 292

atheism—belief in no god....413-433, 435, 436, 437, 438, 444, 445, 446, 447, 460, 463, 465, 481, 482, 490, 498, 500

Atlantean—in Theosophy (q.v.) cult, the second of three cycle levels thus far reached in human evolution..............88

atman—in Hinduism (q.v.), refers to the soul or spirit of a

C

Communism—(Marxian) political and philosophical system presupposing that creating the perfect society will perfect mankind morally, emotionally, and socially...435, 436, 439, 445, 446, 447, 448, 449, 450, 453, 454, 455, 459, 464

Communist Manifesto—early summary or "creed" of basic communist tenets, written by Karl Marx (q.v.) and Frederich Engels (q.v.)...................................438, 453

Comte, Auguste—(1798-1857) French philosopher and founder of positivism who believed God was an irrelevant superstition...................................420, 421

Concept of Dread and Philosophical Fragments, The—early book by existentialist (q.v.) philosopher Soren Kierkegaard (q.v.)...485

Concluding Unscientific Postscript—book by existentialist (q.v.) philosopher Soren Kierkegaard (q.v.)....................485

Confession of the Order—anonymous work extolling the occultic (q.v.) teachings and practices of the Rosicrucians (q.v.)...221

Confucianism—a religion of optimistic humanism (q.v.), founded on the teachings of Confucius (q.v.)...325-338, 341, 342, 346, 350, 355

Confucius—westernized form of Chinese K'ung Fu'tzu, Grand Master K'ung, the greatest sage of China. Born 551 B.C., died 479 B.C. Founder of Confucian (q.v.) movement......325-332, 335, 336, 337, 339, 340, 514

Conservative Judaism—one of the three main types of Judaism (q.v.), along with Orthodox (q.v.) and Reform (q.v.). Founded in the nineteenth century........................370, 371

coven—satanic (q.v.) or witchcraft (q.v.) term for an operating worship group of Satanists or witches. Analogous to a Christian church congregation...........167, 237, 263, 267

crystal ball—an occultic (q.v.) prop, self-descriptive, by which an occultic practitioner claims to be able to tell the future... 149, 181, 182, 183, 193

cult—from a Christian perspective, a religious group polarized around one central religious interpretation which denies, in one or more essential areas, biblical Christian doctrine. Cults usually claim to be the restoration of, or at least compatible with, biblical Christianity......9, 17, 18, 19, 20, 24, 88, 90, 97, 98, 99, 103, 104, 105, 106, 108, 111, 112, 113, 117, 121, 124, 126, 129, 133, 135, 171, 207, 253

Cumorah—Mormon (q.v.) cult designation for the hill near Rochester, New York, where founder Joseph Smith, Jr., (q.v.)

D

unknown or foretell the future. Uses a variety of methods...
158, 190, 191, 192, 193, 194, 195, 217, 256, 268, 269, 337

Divine Principle—book of doctrine by Unification Church (q.v.)
cult founder and leader Sun Myung Moon (q.v.). Gives the
impression that Moon is the second Messiah. Denies all
fundamental Christian doctrine............21, 87, 100, 101,
102, 103, 104

divining rod—a v-shaped instrument or branch used by dowsers
(q.v.) to find underground objects or water by psychic (q.v.)
means...186

Dixon, Jeane—well-known psychic (q.v.) and false prophetess
(q.v.). Born as Lydia Pinckert (q.v.).................181-185

doctrine—teaching, rule of faith........27, 37, 38, 39, 45, 46,
69, 71, 110, 112, 116, 118, 121, 123, 127, 129, 133,
223, 330, 332, 372, 387, 389, 401, 480, 486, 494

Doctrine and Covenants—one of the four standard and sacred
scriptures of the Church of Jesus Christ of Latter-day Saints
(q.v.) (Mormons). Contains "revelations" given to founder
Joseph Smith, Jr. (q.v.), second president Brigham Young (q.v.),
and two other Mormon presidents. First published as the
Book of Commandments (q.v.)..21, 66, 68, 70, 72, 73, 77, 78

dowsing—the occultic (q.v.) or fraudulent search for and
location of underground water or other objects with the use
of a divining rod (q.v.)..........................186, 187

Doyle, Sir Arthur Conan—author of Sherlock Holmes novels
and leading British spiritist (q.v.)....................242

Duke University—in Durham, North Carolina, the university
which first formed a department of parapsychology (q.v.) to
investigate and validate psychic (q.v.) phenomena........215

dukkha—in Buddhism (q.v.), the negation of suffering...
306, 309, 233

Dunninger, Joseph—with sleight-of-hand magician (q.v.) Harry
Houdini (q.v.), one of the foremost debunkers of fraudulent
spiritism (q.v.)...........................242, 243, 250

Durga—Hindu (q.v.) goddess of motherhood..............283

E

economic determinism—Marxist (q.v.) idea that, generally
speaking, economic forces control all of human social life.
One can only control society by acting dynamically in the
economic sector...............................450, 452

ectoplasm—in spiritism (q.v.), a protoplasmic substance which
streams forth from the body of a medium (q.v.) during a
seance (q.v.). Usually produced through trickery rather than

F

Frazer, Sir James George—(1854-1941) anthropologist and author of *The Golden Bough: A Study In Magic and Religion* (1890). Helped develop the evolutionary approach to religion....424

Freud, Sigmund—psychologist and proponent of the God-as-wish-fulfillment theory, founder of the psycho-analytic method of psychology........424

Fritz, Adolph—demon (q.v.) who communicated through psychic surgeon (q.v.) Arigo (q.v.). Arigo claimed Fritz was the spirit of a long-dead German doctor........218

G

gabras—the derisive name given Zoroastrians (q.v.) by Muslims (q.v.). Means "infidel."........362

Ganesa—in Hinduism (q.v.), the god of prudence and wisdom. Usually pictured as a short, red or yellow man with an elephant head........294

Gathas—five Zoroastrian (q.v.) sacred hymns........358

Geiger, Abraham—founder of Reform Judaism (q.v.)........371

Geller, Uri—Israeli psychic (q.v.) who claims power of telekinesis (q.v.), ESP (q.v.), etc........155, 214, 215

Gemarah—the Jewish commentary on the Mishnah (q.v.)...376

genetic fallacy—logical fallacy which is the error of assuming that a point has been proved simply because it has been traced to its source........428

geomancy—divination (q.v.) using a specially marked map or globe........195, 337

ghost—a spirit apparition. Occultists (q.v.) identify the spirits as the souls of persons who have died. Christians identify the spirits as demonic manifestations. Many accounts of ghosts are actually misidentifications of natural phenomena or outright fraud........196, 197, 198, 199, 259

ghuluw—Islamic (q.v.) term for "exaggeration."........383

Glanvill, Joseph—(1636-1680) philosopher and mitigated skeptic (q.v.)........419

gnosticism—claiming occult (q.v.) or mystical or secret religious knowledge. Refers to cults which say that Jesus was only a man who had the divine or Christ principle........132

gohonzon—in Nichiren Shoshu Buddhism (q.v.), a small black wooden box used as a shrine or altar........317, 322

Golden Plates—common designation for the supposed original form of *The Book of Mormon* (q.v.), one of the four sacred scriptures of the Mormons (q.v.)........65, 66

gospel—literally, the "good news." Defined biblically as the life, death, and resurrection of Jesus Christ for the atonement of mankind's sin (1 Corinthians 15:1-3ff)........17, 24, 37, 97, 106, 114, 115, 118, 151, 156, 185, 199, 235, 271, 272, 449, 460, 513, 514, 515, 516, 517, 518, 519

Granth Sahib—the sacred scriptures of Sikhism (q.v.).401, 402, 404

graphology—handwriting analysis.......................191

Great Learning—one of four written works attributed to Confucius (q.v.) dealing with the education and training of a gentleman.......................................329, 337

Guru Dev—Hindu (q.v.) spiritual leader who taught Transcendental Meditation (q.v.) founder Maharishi Mahesh Yogi (q.v.) and instructed him to develop TM (q.v.).................80, 81, 85

Guru Arjan—the compiler of the Granth Sahib (q.v.), the sacred scripture of Sikhism (q.v.).......................401, 404

H

Hadith—the Islamic (q.v.) traditions........382, 387, 391, 397

Hajj—Islamic (q.v.) pilgrimage to Mecca (q.v.).........391, 398

Halloween—originally the evening before All Saints' Day, when demons (q.v.) and spirits were "chased" away. Now refers to October 31, both a fun spoof of witchcraft (q.v.) and spiritism (q.v.), with children in costumes, etc.; and the most sacred day of the year for satanists (q.v.), witches (q.v.), and spiritists (q.v.)..........................261

Hanuman—the Hindu (q.v.) monkey god, lord of the winds....294

Hanukkah—Jewish holy day commemorating the Jewish rebellion led by Judas Maccabaeus against Syrian oppressors in 167 B.C.......................................370, 376

haoma—hallucinogenic drink used ritualistically in Zoroastrianism (q.v.)................................361

harakiri—ceremonial suicide performed by the Shinto (q.v.) Bushido warrior to atone for failure or bad judgment. Death was preferred to disgrace..........................354

Hare Krishnas—common name for members of the International Society for Krishna Consciousness (q.v.). Cult founded by His Divine Grace A. C. Bhaktivedanta Swami Praphupada (q.v.) in the 1960s. Hindu sect stressing monotheistic worship and strict ascetic practices. Denies exclusive claims of the Bible and Jesus Christ.....41, 42, 43

Harris, Martin—New York farmer who financed the first printing of the Mormon (q.v.) cult sacred scripture *The Book of Mormon* (q.v.).......................................66

Hegel, Georg W.—(1770-1831) idealist philosopher who

I

Islam—literally, "submission to the will of Allah." Religion
founded by Mohammed (q.v.) around A.D. 600....377-399, 400,
403, 404

Izanagi—in Shinto (q.v.), a celestial god...............351, 354

Izanami—in Shinto (q.v.), a celestial god.............351, 354

J

Jainism—Indian religion derived from Hinduism (q.v.). Founded
by Mahavira (q.v.) around 550 B.C. Rejects belief in a supreme
God..298-303

James, William—noted spiritist (q.v.)....................242

Jaspers, Karl—(1883-1969) atheistic (q.v.) existentialist (q.v.)
philosopher..420, 421, 479, 480, 481, 483, 493, 501, 502, 503

Jehovah's Witnesses—designation of followers and members of
the Watchtower Bible and Tract Society (q.v.) cult, founded in
1874. Deny the doctrine of the trinity, the deity of Christ,
the bodily resurrection, salvation by grace, etc....19, 22, 23,
24, 25, 44-63, 121

Jen—the Confucian (q.v.) doctrine of the golden rule.330, 331, 337

Jesus Christ Heals—book by Charles Fillmore (q.v.), founder of
Unity School of Christianity (q.v.) cult.................133

Jigai—the Shinto (q.v.) method of suicide by severing the jugular
vein. Committed by females in atonement for their sin..354

Jihad—Islamic (q.v.) for a holy war......................392

Jina—literally, "the conqueror." The designation given to
Mahavira (q.v.), founder of Jainism (q.v.). His religion achieves
victory over bodily desires.............................303

Jinn—Islamic (q.v.) designation for demon (q.v.)...380, 388, 390

jivanmukta—in Hinduism (q.v.), one who achieves moksha (q.v.)
before death..288

jnana—the path of knowledge, one of the three paths to achieve
moksha (q.v.) in Hinduism (q.v.)........................288

Jones, Jim—late founder and leader of the Peoples' Temple (q.v.)
cult in northern California. Taught he was more important
than Jesus Christ. Ridiculed the Bible and the Christian idea
of God. Taught his followers aggressive social reform.
Demanded absolute and unquestioning obedience from
followers. Led over 900 followers to commit suicide in
Guyana in 1978...24

Journal of Discourses—collection of teachings by second
Mormon (q.v.) president, Brigham Young (q.v.)..10, 70, 72, 78

K

nirvana—the Hindu (q.v.) concept of heaven or bliss, final
spiritual fulfillment. . . . 43, 88, 171, 283, 284, 296, 302, 305,
306, 309, 310, 311, 312, 313, 322

No Exit—existentialist (q.v.) novel by Jean-Paul Sartre (q.v.). . 496

nontheist—one who possesses no belief in God. 413, 423,
425, 459, 464

noumenal world—in philosophy to Kant (q.v.), the world as it
really is, without faulty perceptions. 423

numerology—closely related to astrology (q.v.). Uses numbers
associated with one's name and birthdate to determine one's
destiny, like a horoscope (q.v.). 165

O

occult—comes from the Latin word "occultus" and carries the
idea of things hidden, secret and mysterious. Under the
designation occult we would class at least the following:
witchcraft, magic, palm reading, fortune telling, Ouija
boards, tarot cards, Satanism, spiritism, demons and crystal
balls. 9, 149-160, 168, 169, 171, 172, 174, 180, 184,
186, 187, 188, 190, 191, 193, 194, 203, 205, 207, 210, 212,
215, 222, 237, 238, 240, 253, 267, 271, 273, 274, 275

O-Harai—literally, "the Great Purification." The most
important Shinto (q.v.) ceremony wherein the people purge
themselves of their sin. 355

Olcott, H. S. Colonel—one of the founding presidents of
Theosophy (q.v.). 311

Omar—according to Sunnite (q.v.) Moslems (q.v.), the second
Moslem caliph (q.v.) and principal advisor to the first caliph,
Abu Bakr (q.v.). 398

omen—a prophetic sign, associated with occultism (q.v.) or
spiritism (q.v.). 158, 192, 196, 256, 259, 268, 362

omnipotent—all-powerful. When designating an attribute of
God, it refers to God's ability to do anything possible of
being done. It does not mean that God can do what is
impossible logically (such as making two plus two equal
five) or actually (to cause His own demise). 32, 34, 388,
396, 424, 429, 430

omnipresent—present everywhere. When designating an
attribute of God, refers to the doctrine that everything is
immediately in the presence of God, not that God is
somehow part of everything. 32, 34, 135

omniscient—all-knowing. When designating an attribute of
God, it refers to God's complete and perfect knowledge. It

Q

sign—in astrology (q.v.), refers to the astrological or zodiac (q.v.) sign associated with a particular individual or event... 160, 161, 162, 163, 166

Sita—wife of Rama (q.v.). He is the Hindu (q.v.) incarnation of Vishnu (q.v.)..286

Siva—alternate spelling of Shiva (q.v.)................42, 283

skepticism—derived from Latin and Greek, indicates doubt, uncertainty, hesitation. In philosophy, refers to either (1) the theory of knowledge that says knowledge is unattainable; or (2) a specific school of philosophy, most notably as conducted by some early classical Greek philosophers..............413, 433

sleeping prophet—nickname for A.R.E. (q.v.) founder and psychic Edgar Cayce (q.v.)....................................169

sleight of hand—synonym for magic which is not supernatural but is based on trickery or dexterity, usually for entertainment purposes.....................152, 203, 215

Smith, Joseph, Sr.—father of Mormon (q.v.) cult founder Joseph Smith, Jr. (q.v.)..64

Smith, Joseph, Jr.—founder of the Mormon Church, the Church of Jesus Christ of Latter-day Saints (q.v.). Born 1805, died 1844. Claimed revelations from angels and God(s). Taught and practiced polygamy..............10, 20, 22, 64-79, 253

Smith, Lucy Mack—mother of Mormon (q.v.) cult founder Joseph Smith, Jr. (q.v.)................................64

Joseph Smith, Jr. (q.v.)................................64

smriti—Hindu (q.v.) writings which have a secondary authority below that of the sruti (q.v.).....................284, 285

Soka Gakkai—Japanese Value Creation Society, the lay organization of Nichiren Shoshu Buddhism (q.v.).......315, 317, 323

Soka Kyoiku Gakkai—original name of Soka Gakkai (q.v.)...
(See Soka Gakkai)

soma—in Hinduism (q.v.), either (1) one of the deities, or (2) the hallucinogenic plant or drink made therefrom which is ingested ritually as a part of Hindu worship...285, 294, 361

soothsayers—spiritists (q.v.) or mediums (q.v.).....195, 256, 268

sorcery—black magic (q.v.) or witchcraft (q.v.)...
158, 195, 213, 240, 256, 268, 269, 362

spell—a charm (q.v.) or incantation designed to influence someone or something psychically (q.v.) or occulticly (q.v.)...
76, 154, 192, 203, 256, 262, 268, 269, 285, 362, 429

spiritism—the worship of and communication with spirits alleged to be the spirits of people who have died but which are actually demonic (q.v.) manifestations.....240, 241, 242, 243, 251, 253, 254, 255, 256

T

transmigration—the belief that the soul or some life force passes after death into another body. Usually distinguished from reincarnation (q.v.), which restricts travel from one human body to another. Transmigration allows for transference of the soul from one life form to another (man to cow, etc.)....................42, 171, 172, 289, 301, 403

trinity—in biblical Christianity, the doctrine describing the tripersonal nature of God. Briefly stated, the doctrine teaches that within the nature of the one true God there are three eternally distinct persons: the Father, the Son, and the Holy Spirit. These three persons are the one God......27, 28, 45, 46, 96, 106, 107, 108, 109, 110, 111, 112, 116, 127, 174, 255, 393, 395, 396

Tripitaka—literally, the "three baskets." Refers in Theravada (q.v.) Buddhism (q.v.) to the three divisions of holy scripture. 306, 310, 322, 323

True Father and True Mother—Unification Church (q.v.) cult terms for founder Sun Myung Moon (q.v.) and his wife...104

trumpet speaking—in spiritism (q.v.) music or notes of music produced during a seance (q.v.) through a special trumpet, supposedly by the spirits...................243, 244, 245

Truth that Leads to Eternal Life—small book published by the Watchtower Bible and Tract Society (q.v.) cult and used to introduce prospective converts to Watchtower doctrines...62, 63

Tsunesaburo, Makiguchi—founder in 1930 of Soka Gakkai (q.v.)...315

Twelve Angas—the most sacred part of Jain (q.v.) scripture..303

Tylor, Sir Edward Burnett—(1832-1917) anthropologist, founder of cultural anthropology who helped develop the evolutionary theory of religion.................................424

U

Ummah—Islamic (q.v.) community of the faithful.........385

Ummaya—one of the Islamic (q.v.) dynasties.............383

Unification Church, The—cult founded by Sun Myung Moon (q.v.) and imported to the United States in 1971. Denies biblical doctrine. Promotes Moon as the "Lord of the Second Advent" (q.v.) (Messiah) 19, 20, 21, 23, 24, 99-104

unitarianism—in theology, the belief that God is only one person. Denies the deity of Christ and usually denies the personality as well as the deity of the Holy Spirit.......108

Unity School of Christianity—gnostic cult founded in 1889 by Charles and Myrtle Fillmore (q.v.). Headquarters in Unity Village (q.v.), Lee's Summit, Missouri. 131, 132, 133, 134, 135

Unity Village—headquarters of the Unity School of Christianity

Yasna—one of the division of Zoroastrian (q.v.) scripture..358, 359, 362

Yathrib—original name of town to which Mohammed (q.v.) fled when forced to leave Mecca (q.v.). Now known as Medina (q.v.) 380

Yin and Yang—symbols of Chinese thought, representing opposites. Popular in Chinese and Japanese religious thought and practice.......................101, 342, 343, 348

yoga—an exercise, whether spiritual, mental, physical, or some combination thereof by which one moves towards enlightenment......................85, 90, 283, 295

yogi—a devotee or teacher of yoga....................295

Yom Kippur—the most solemn and holy day in Judaism, the day of atonement................................369

Young, Brigham—second leader of the Mormon (q.v.) cult (q.v.). Moved the cult to Salt Lake City, Utah, in 1847. Practiced polytheism (q.v.) and polygamy (q.v.). Died in 1877...
66, 69, 70, 72, 77, 78, 79

Z

Zabur—in Islam (q.v.), refers to psalms of David which were considered scripture, but were not identical with the biblical psalms. Now lost................................387

zakat—Moslem (q.v.) practice of almsgiving..............391

Zarathushtra—variant spelling of Zoroaster (q.v.)..........356

zazen—in Zen Buddhism (q.v.), the method of meditation.318, 319

Zen Buddhism—quasi-religious form of Buddhism (q.v.) stressing meditation.90, 93, 316, 317, 318, 319, 320, 322, 323

Zend-avesta—a third-century A.D. commentary on the Zoroastrian (q.v.) scriptures, combined with those scriptures, the Avesta (q.v.)................................362

Zeno of Citium—founder of the Athenian philosophical school of the Stoics (q.v.) around 305 B.C....................417

Zion's Watchtower—early periodical published by Jehovah's Witnesses (q.v.) founder Charles Taze Russell (q.v.)........44

zodiac—in astrology (q.v.) the path and pattern of the major planets and stars through the sky. The zodiac is used to determine one's destiny and to predict the future...
160, 161, 162, 163, 164

Zoroastrianism—religion founded by Zoroaster (born c. 650 B.C.) stressing the eternal battle between good and evil...
356, 363, 514

Have You Heard of the

Four Spiritual Laws?

Just as there are physical laws that govern the physical universe, so are there spiritual laws which govern your relationship with God.

LAW ONE

GOD **LOVES** YOU, AND OFFERS A WONDERFUL **PLAN** FOR YOUR LIFE.

(References contained in this booklet should be read in context from the Bible wherever possible.)

Written by Bill Bright. Copyright © Campus Crusade for Christ, Inc., 1965. All rights reserved.

God's Love

"For God so loved the world, that He gave His only begotten Son, that whoever believes in Him should not perish, but have eternal life" (John 3:16).

God's Plan

(Christ speaking) "I came that they might have life, and might have it abundantly" (that it might be full and meaningful) (John 10:10).

Why is it that most people are not experiencing the abundant life? Because . . .

LAW TWO

MAN IS SINFUL AND SEPARATED FROM GOD. THEREFORE, HE CANNOT KNOW AND EXPERIENCE GOD'S LOVE AND PLAN FOR HIS LIFE.

Man Is Sinful

"For all have sinned and fall short of the glory of God" (Romans 3:23).

Man was created to have fellowship with God; but, because of his stubborn self-will, he chose to go his own independent way and fellowship with God was broken. This self-will, characterized by an attitude of active rebellion or passive indifference, is evidence of what the Bible calls sin.

Man Is Separated

"For the wages of sin is death" (spiritual separation from God) (Romans 6:23).

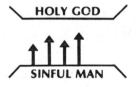

HOLY GOD

SINFUL MAN

This diagram illustrates that God is holy and man is sinful. A great gulf separates the two. The arrows illustrate that man is continually trying to reach God and the abundant life through his own efforts, such as a good life, philosophy or religion.

The third law explains the only way to bridge this gulf . . .

LAW THREE

JESUS CHRIST IS GOD'S ONLY PROVISION FOR MAN'S SIN. THROUGH HIM YOU CAN KNOW AND EXPERIENCE GOD'S LOVE AND PLAN FOR YOUR LIFE.

He Died in Our Place

"But God demonstrates His own love toward us, in that while we were yet sinners, Christ died for us" (Romans 5:8).

He Rose from the Dead

"Christ died for our sins . . . He was buried . . . He was raised on the third day, according to the Scriptures . . . He appeared to Peter, then to the twelve. After that He appeared to more than five hundred . . ." (I Corinthians 15:3-6).

He is the Only Way to God
"Jesus said to him, 'I am the way, and the truth, and the life; no one comes to the Father, but through Me' " (John 14:6).

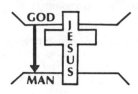

This diagram illustrates that God has bridged the gulf which separates us from Him by sending His Son, Jesus Christ, to die on the cross in our place to pay the penalty for our sins.

It is not enough just to know these three laws . . .

LAW FOUR

WE MUST INDIVIDUALLY **RECEIVE** JESUS CHRIST AS SAVIOR AND LORD; THEN WE CAN KNOW AND EXPERIENCE GOD'S LOVE AND PLAN FOR OUR LIVES.

We Must Receive Christ
"But as many as received Him, to them He gave the right to become children of God, even to those who believe in His name" (John 1:12).

We Receive Christ Through Faith
"For by grace you have been saved through faith; and that not of yourselves, it is the gift of God; not as a result of works, that no one should boast" (Ephesians 2:8,9).

When We Receive Christ, We Experience a New Birth.
(Read John 3:1-8.)

We Receive Christ by Personal Invitation
(Christ is speaking): "Behold, I stand at the door and knock; if any one hears My voice and opens the door, I will come in to him" (Revelation 3:20).

Receiving Christ involves turning to God from self (repentance) and trusting Christ to come into our lives to forgive our sins and to make us the kind of people He wants us to be. Just to agree intellectually that Jesus Christ is the Son of God and that He died on the cross for our sins is not enough. Nor is it enough to have an emotional experience. We receive Jesus Christ by faith, as an act of the will.

These two circles represent two kinds of lives:

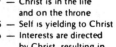

SELF-DIRECTED LIFE
S — Self is on the throne
† — Christ is outside the life
● — Interests are directed by self, often resulting in discord and frustration

CHRIST-DIRECTED LIFE
† — Christ is in the life and on the throne
S — Self is yielding to Christ
● — Interests are directed by Christ, resulting in harmony with God's plan

Which circle best represents your life?
Which circle would you like to have represent your life?
The following explains how you can receive Christ:

YOU CAN RECEIVE CHRIST RIGHT NOW BY FAITH THROUGH PRAYER

(Prayer is talking with God)

God knows your heart and is not so concerned with your words as He is with the attitude of your heart. The following is a suggested prayer:

"Lord Jesus, I need You. Thank You for dying on the cross for my sins. I open the door of my life and receive You as my Savior and Lord. Thank You for forgiving my sins and giving me eternal life. Take control of the throne of my life. Make me the kind of person You want me to be."

Does this prayer express the desire of your heart?

If it does, pray this prayer right now, and Christ will come into your life, as He promised.

How to Know That Christ Is in Your Life

Did you receive Christ into your life? According to His promise in Revelation 3:20, where is Christ right now in relation to you? Christ said that He would come into your life. Would He mislead you? On what authority do you know that God has answered your prayer? (The trustworthiness of God Himself and His Word.)

The Bible Promises Eternal Life to All Who Receive Christ

"And the witness is this, that God has given us eternal life, and this life is in His Son. He who has the Son has the life; he who does not have the Son of God does not have the life. These things I have written to you who believe in the name of the Son of God, in order that you may know that you have eternal life" (I John 5:11-13).

Thank God often that Christ is in your life and that He will never leave you (Hebrews 13:5). You can know on the basis of His promise that Christ lives in you and that you have eternal life, from the very moment you invite Him in. He will not deceive you.

An important reminder . . .

DO NOT DEPEND UPON FEELINGS

The promise of God's Word, the Bible — not our feelings — is our authority. The Christian lives by faith (trust) in the trustworthiness of God Himself and His Word. This train diagram illustrates the relationship between **fact** (God and His Word), **faith** (our trust in God and His Word), and **feeling** (the result of our faith and obedience) (John 14:21).

The train will run with or without the caboose. However, it would be useless to attempt to pull the train by the caboose. In the same way, we, as Christians, do not depend on feelings or emotions, but we place our faith (trust) in the trustworthiness of God and the promises of His Word.

NOW THAT YOU HAVE RECEIVED CHRIST

The moment that you received Christ by faith, as an act of the will, many things happened, including the following:

1. Christ came into your life (Revelation 3:20 and Colossians 1:27).
2. Your sins were forgiven (Colossians 1:14).
3. You became a child of God (John 1:12).
4. You received eternal life (John 5:24).
5. You began the great adventure for which God created you (John 10:10; II Corinthians 5:17 and I Thessalonians 5:18).

Can you think of anything more wonderful that could happen to you than receiving Christ? Would you like to thank God in prayer right now for what He has done for you? By thanking God, you demonstrate your faith.

To enjoy your new life
to the fullest . . .

SUGGESTIONS FOR CHRISTIAN GROWTH

Spiritual growth results from trusting Jesus Christ. "The righteous man shall live by faith" (Galatians 3:11). A life of faith will enable you to trust God increasingly with every detail of your life, and to practice the following:

G   Go to God in prayer daily (John 15:7).

R   Read God's Word daily (Acts 17:11)—begin with the Gospel of John.

O   Obey God moment by moment (John 14:21).

W   Witness for Christ by your life and words (Matthew 4:19; John 15:8).

T   Trust God for every detail of your life (I Peter 5:7).

H   Holy Spirit—allow Him to control and empower your daily life and witness (Galatians 5:16,17; Acts 1:8).

FELLOWSHIP IN A GOOD CHURCH

God's Word admonishes us not to forsake "the assembling of ourselves together. . ." (Hebrews 10:25). Several logs burn brightly together; but put one aside on the cold hearth and the fire goes out. So it is with your relationship to other Christians. If you do not belong to a church, do not wait to be invited. Take the initiative; call the pastor of a nearby church where Christ is honored and His Word is preached. Start this week, and make plans to attend regularly.

SPECIAL MATERIALS ARE AVAILABLE FOR CHRISTIAN GROWTH.

If you have come to know Christ personally through this presentation of the gospel, write for a free booklet especially written to assist you in your Christian growth.

A special Bible study series and an abundance of other helpful materials for Christian growth are also available. For additional information, please write Campus Crusade for Christ International, San Bernardino, CA 92414.

You will want to share this important discovery . . .